30

MARTYRS AND MARTYROLOGIES

Frontispiece St Agnes, panel of altar-piece (1450–70), formerly in the Lady Chapel of St John Maddermarket, Norwich, reproduced by courtesy of the Victoria and Albert Museum, London.

MARTYRS AND MARTYROLOGIES

PAPERS READ AT
THE 1992 SUMMER MEETING AND
THE 1993 WINTER MEETING OF
THE ECCLESIASTICAL HISTORY SOCIETY

EDITED BY

DIANA WOOD

PUBLISHED FOR
THE ECCLESIASTICAL HISTORY SOCIETY

BY

BLACKWELL PUBLISHERS

1993

© Ecclesiastical History Society 1993

First published 1993

Blackwell Publishers
108 Cowley Road, Oxford OX4 1 JF, UK

3 Cambridge Center,
Cambridge, Massachusetts 02142, USA

British Library Cataloguing in Publication Data
A CIP catalogue record for this book is available from the British Library

Library of Congress Cataloging in Publication Data
Ecclesiastical History Society. Summer Meeting (1992: University of
   Glasgow)
      Martyrs and martyrologies: papers read at the 1992 Summer Meeting
   and the 1993 Winter Meeting of the Ecclesiastical History Society/
   edited by Diana Wood.
         p.   cm.—(Studies in church history: 30)
      Includes bibliographical references.
      ISBN 0-631-18868-1
         1. Martyrdom (Christianity)—Congresses.   2. Christian martyrs—
   Congresses.   3. Martyrologies—History and criticism—Congresses.
   I. Wood, Diana, 1940-   .   II. Ecclesiastical History Society.
   Winter Meeting (1993: King's College, London)   III. Title.
   IV. Series.
   BR141.S85   vol. 30
   [BR1601.2]
   272—dc20   93-13278
                                                                                    CIP

Typeset in 11 on 12 pt Bembo
by Joshua Associates Limited, Oxford
Printed in Great Britain by
T. J. Press Ltd, Padstow, Cornwall

CONTENTS

CONTENTS

CONTENTS

PREFACE

The theme of 'Martyrs and Martyrologies', chosen by Professor David Loades, President of the Ecclesiastical History Society for 1992–3, proved to be extremely popular. It meant, inevitably, that more people than ever had to be left out when the selection of communications to be included in the volume was made. This was no reflection on the quality of the papers submitted, but in most cases the result of having to achieve a chronological balance in the volume. Rejecting communications is the least pleasant of the editor's duties, and she can only apologize to those who were disappointed. The papers included here therefore represent the main papers delivered at the summer conference of 1992 and that of January 1993, and a strictly limited selection of the communications offered in the summer.

The Society would like to express its gratitude to the University of Glasgow, and especially to the staff of Kelvin Hall, the warmth of whose hospitality in the summer did much to counteract the almost constant rain. We should also like to thank Dr Gavin White, of the Department of Theology and Church History, and Dr Michael Kennedy, of the Department of Medieval History, for all their hard work in connection with the conference and for organizing some very enjoyable outings. Our thanks, as always, are also due to King's College London for its hospitality in January.

The editor would once again like to thank Ann McCall of Blackwell Publishers for her unfailing help in the production of this volume.

Diana Wood

LIST OF CONTRIBUTORS

DAVID LOADES (*President*)
Professor of History, University of Wales, Bangor

DAVID BAGCHI
Lecturer in Theology, University of Hull

D. W. BEBBINGTON
Reader in History, University of Stirling

DOMINIC AIDAN BELLENGER
Headmaster of Downside School

STEWART J. BROWN
Professor of Ecclesiastical History, University of Edinburgh

EUAN CAMERON
Reader in Reformation History, University of Newcastle upon Tyne

CLAIRE CROSS
Professor of History, University of York

JANE E. A. DAWSON
John Laing Lecturer in the History and Theology of the Reformation, University of Edinburgh

SIMON DITCHFIELD
British Academy Post-doctoral fellow, University of York

SIMON DIXON
Lecturer in Modern History, University of Glasgow

RICHARD EALES
Lecturer in History, University of Kent

WILLIAM H. C. FREND
Emeritus Professor of Ecclesiastical History in the University of Glasgow

VICTORIA A. GUNN
Research Student, University of Glasgow

STUART G. HALL
Emeritus Professor of Ecclesiastical History, King's College London

PAUL A. HAYWARD
Research Student, St John's College, Cambridge

DAVID HILLIARD
Reader in History, The Flinders University of South Australia

CHRIS JONES
Research Student, Pembroke College, Oxford

DAVID KILLINGRAY
Reader in History, Goldsmiths' College, University of London

G. A. LOUD
Senior Lecturer in Medieval History, University of Leeds

JOHN ANTHONY McGUCKIN
Lecturer in Patristics and Byzantine Studies, University of Leeds

JAMES F. McMILLAN
Professor of History, University of Strathclyde

RACHEL MORIARTY
Tutor in Church History, Chichester Theological College

COLIN MORRIS
Emeritus Professor of Medieval History, University of Southampton

JANET L. NELSON
Reader in History, King's College London

R. M. PRICE
Lecturer in Church History, Heythrop College, University of London

PENNY ROBERTS
Lecturer in History, University of Warwick

MIRI RUBIN
Tutor in Medieval History, Pembroke College, Oxford

JOHN A. F. THOMSON
Reader in Medieval History, University of Glasgow

STEPHEN TURNBULL
Research Student, University of Leeds

LIST OF CONTRIBUTORS

SUSAN WABUDA

W. R. WARD
Emeritus Professor of Modern History, University of Durham

MARTIN WELLINGS
Minister on the Buckingham, Bicester, and Brackley Methodist Circuit

GAVIN WHITE
Lecturer in the Department of Theology and Church History, University of Glasgow

ABBREVIATIONS

Abbreviated titles are adopted within each paper after the first full citation. In addition the following abbreviations are used throughout the volume.

ActaSS	*Acta Sanctorum*, ed. J. Bolland and G. Henschen (Antwerp, etc. 1643ff.)
AHR	*American Historical Review* (New York, 1895ff.)
AnBoll	*Analecta Bollandiana* (Brussels, 1882ff.)
BIHR	*Bulletin of the Institute of Historical Research* (London, 1923–86)
BJRL	*Bulletin of the John Rylands Library* (Manchester 1903ff.)
BL	British Library, London
BN	Bibliothèque nationale, Paris
ChH	*Church History* (New York/Chicago, 1932ff.)
CSCO	*Corpus scriptorum Christianorum orientalium* (Paris, 1903ff.)
CSEL	*Corpus scriptorum ecclesiasticorum Latinorum* (Vienna, 1866ff.)
CYS	*Canterbury and York Society* (London, 1907ff.)
DNB	*Dictionary of National Biography* (London, 1885ff.)
EETS	*Early English Text Society* (London, 1864ff.)
EHR	*English Historical Review* (London, 1953ff.)
Foxe	*Acts and Monuments of John Foxe*, ed. G. Townsend and S. R. Cattley, 8 vols (London, 1837–41)
HBS	*Henry Bradshaw Society* (London/Canterbury, 1891ff.)
HR	*Historical Research* (London, 1986ff.)
JEH	*Journal of Ecclesiastical History* (Cambridge, 1950ff.)
JMedH	*Journal of Medieval History* (Amsterdam, 1975ff.)
LCL	*Loeb Classical Library*
MGH	*Monumenta Germaniae Historica inde ab a, c.500 usque ad a. 1500*, ed. G. H. Pertz et al. (Hanover, Berlin, etc., 1826ff.)
MGH.Const.	*Constitutiones et acta publica imperatorum et regnum* (1893ff.) = *MGH.L*, sectio 4
MGH.Ep	*Epistolae* (1887ff.)
MGH.ER	*Epistolae saeculi XIII e registris pontificum Romanorum selectae* (Berlin, 1883–94)
MGH.L	*Leges* (in folio) (1835–89)
	—1. Sectio: *MGH.LNG*
	—4. Sectio: *MGH.Const.*
MGH.LL	*Libelli de lite imperatorum et pontificum saeculis XI et XII conscripti* (1891–7)
MGH.LNG	*Leges nationum Germanicarum* (1886ff.) = *MGH.L* sectio 1
MGH.SRG	*Scriptores rerum Germanicarum in usum scholarum . . .* (1826–32), ns (1922ff.)
MGH.SRM	*Scriptores rerum Merovingicarum* (1884–1920)
MGH.SS	*Scriptores* (in folio) (1826–1934)
MidlHist	*Midland History* (Birmingham, 1971ff.)
n.d.	no date
n.p.	no place
ns	new series

ODCC	*Oxford Dictionary of the Christian Church*, ed. F. L. Cross (Oxford, 1957), 2nd edn with E. A. Livingstone (1974)
OMT	*Oxford Medieval Texts* (Oxford, 1969ff.)
os	old series
PaP	*Past and Present. A Journal of Scientific History* (London, 1952ff.)
PG	*Patrologia Graeca*, ed. J. P. Migne, 161 vols (Paris, 1857–66)
PL	*Patrologia Latina*, ed. J. P. Migne, 217 + 4 index vols (Paris, 1841–61)
PRO	Public Record Office, London
PS	*Parker Society* (Cambridge, 1841–55)
RHE	*Revue d'histoire ecclésiastique* (Louvain, 1900ff.)
RS	*Rerum Brittanicarum medii aevi scciptores*, 99 vols (London, 1858–1911) = Rolls Series
s.a.	*sub anno*
SC	*Sources chrétiennes*, ed. H. de Lubac, J. Danielou et al. (Paris, 1941ff.)
SCH	*Studies in Church History* (London/Oxford, 1964ff.)
ScHR	*Scottish Historical Review* (Edinburgh/Glasgow, 1904ff.)
SCH.S	*Studies in Church History. Subsidia* (Oxford, 1978ff.)
STC	*A Short-title Catalogue of Books Printed in England, Scotland, and Ireland, and of English Books Printed Abroad, 1475–1640*, ed. A. W. Pollard and G. R. Redgrave (London, 1926, repr. 1945, 1950)

INTRODUCTION

The concept of martyrdom has always presented problems to the Church. For a person to sacrifice his or her life for the faith is to practise the *imitatio Christi* in a very special sense. Moreover, the salvation of the martyr has always tended to be taken for granted; a thorny road to the narrow gate, but one of the most assured. However, the deliberate search for spiritual security by such drastic methods has usually been discouraged on the ground that true martyrdom must be in response to the will of God rather than man. For this reason the martyr's crown has often been a form of forbidden fruit, sin to seek but bliss to receive unsought. Consequently the standard method of justifying the persecution of one group of Christians by another has been to claim that the victims were not true martyrs but desperate fanatics who committed suicide by hurling themselves against the machinery of public authority, thereby provoking a just retribution for their crimes. The subjectivity of martyrdom can be illustrated from any period of the Church's history, but it emerges in a particularly acute form when the same people are both persecutors and victims within a short space of time, or when a church already 'under the Cross' seeks to justify the punishment of its own dissidents. Hugh Latimer, himself to die at the stake, denounced the Anabaptists whom his fellow Protestants were persecuting in Germany:

> And will ye argue that 'He goeth to his death boldly or cheerfully; ergo he dieth in a just cause?' Nay, that sequel followeth no more than this: A man seems to be afraid of death, ergo, he dieth evil. And yet our saviour Christ was afraid of death himself.[1]

The definition of martyrdom, in other words, depends not upon the fact or manner of death, but upon the cause died for. When the English Protestants began to go to the stake in 1555, they were swiftly denounced by their enemies as 'false, stinking martyrs', not because there was anything bogus about their sufferings, nor even because they were guilty of self-immolation, but simply on the grounds that the doctrine for which they died was false. They were contrasted with the true martrys who had died for the Catholic faith at the hands of pagans or infidels.

Any death which can be represented as sacrifice for a cause will consequently be a martyrdom in someone's eyes, and it is impossible to devise

---

[1] *Sermons of Bishop Latimer*, ed. G. E. Gorrie, *PS* (1844), p. 160.

an objective test. The conversion of a victim into a martyr is therefore the business of the apologist, and the success of the apologist depends ultimately upon the success of the cause. Catholic victims of the Arian persecution, for example, became saints and martyrs, while Arian victims of the Catholics remained victims, and usually obscure ones. Cranmer, Ridley, and Latimer were culture heroes within a generation of their deaths, while the memory of Thomas More or John Fisher was cherished only surreptitiously until a much later date. Thomas Becket, a saint and martyr for centuries, was suddenly demoted by the vagaries of Tudor politics into an obnoxious traitor. In assessing the historical significance of martyrdom, the martyrologist is therefore frequently more interesting than the principal actors in the drama. The blood of martyrs has been the seed of the Church because of the way in which that seed has been sown, watered, and tended by sympathetic propaganda. But what of martyrs who shed no blood? At what point does the use of the word cease to be literal and become metaphorical? The ramifications of these questions complicate the question of definition still further. Men and women have suffered exile or imprisonment for their convictions, and some have died in prison when there was no deliberate intention on anyone's part to kill them. Anabaptists migrated to Transylvania in the sixteenth century; Huguenots fled to England, and English Puritans to America in the seventeenth; Russian Christians escaped to America or Western Europe in the twentieth. Are such people martyrs? And if so, what of those who suffer civil disabilities or other deprivations, like English Catholics under the penal laws, or Greek Christians under the Ottoman Empire? At this point it becomes clear that the word can easily be devalued, as we do when we describe a sufferer as a 'martyr' to gout or to toothache. Properly speaking, martyrdom must involve death, although not necessarily violently inflicted, which can be directly attributed to the faith or cause which the victim has espoused. Execution by due process of law for an ordinary criminal offence, such as murder or armed insurrection, ought therefore to disqualify the candidate. But there have always been threads in the complex web of Christian thought which have sought to justify resistance to ungodly tyranny, and one man's criminal insurrection is another's heroic defiance.

One of the objectives in preparing this volume, and in setting up the conferences which it represents, has been to do justice in some measure to this rich and extremely controversial field of study. One limitation was not hard to make. This series is called *Studies in Church History*, and contributions have therefore been confined to Christian martyrs and martyrologies. There are, consequently, no papers on the psychology of the *mujahadeen*, nor upon the fate of political activists destroyed by the bombs which they intended for somebody else. The distinction between religion and politics is often a delicate one, however. Were the rebels who attempted to overthrow Mary Tudor in 1554 disgruntled Protestants opposed to her conservative reaction, or apprehensive nationalists who dreaded the prospect of a Spanish king? It is very unlikely that the Bolsheviks in 1917 and 1918 either knew or cared which of their opponents and victims were humble Christians, and which were (or could be represented as) class enemies. Some of the papers which follow skirmish warily along the frontiers of politics; others are entirely concerned with the spirituality of self-sacrifice. The further we look back into history, the more difficult it is to reconstruct the real human beings behind the stories. Martyrologists have not infrequently been more concerned to create treasure-houses of edifying *exempla* than to identify the nature of a spiritual crisis. In some cases it did not even matter whether the victims had a genuine historical reality or not. If martyrs did not exist, it might be necessary to invent them in order to give the Church in that particular place a boost to its morale or an intensified sense of identity. Scarcely any martyrology has been free from a didactic purpose, and in some cases this has involved arguing in a circle: only a true cause can produce true martyrs, *ergo*, a cause which produces martyrs must be true. To John Foxe the fiery purgation of his friends and colleagues not only testified to the truth of their own vision of God, it also justified a whole historiography of the Reformation. Not only was the Church of England a true church, it also occupied a specific place in Protestant eschatology. Foxe was perfectly well aware of Latimer's reservations, but he treated the Marian persecution as though it set the seal upon the Godliness of the policies of Henry VIII and Edward VI, to say nothing of the Elizabethan settlement, which it was one of his chief purposes to justify.

I make no apology for choosing this theme because of my own interest in John Foxe. He is, in many respects, the quintessential martyrologist. His history is more verifiable, and his mythology less obtrusive, than that of many others, but his purpose is basically the same. At the same time there was a human dimension to his writing which makes him more accessible to modern sympathies than many of his medieval predecessors.

> Why should God of his goodness suffer his children and servants so vehemently to be cruciated and afflicted ... why did the wicked so rage and flourish, and the godly so go to wrack?[2]

---

[2] John Foxe, *Acts and Monuments*, ed. Josiah Pratt, 8 vols (London, 1853–70), I, p. 289.

he cries in genuine bewilderment, when looking back upon the many traumas of the church in its long history. He knows the theologically correct answers, but they do not entirely assuage his grief and indignation. To say that God justifies those whom he loves by causing them suffering in the sight of the world speaks to the intellect rather than to the heart. Foxe was too close to his martyrs to give them the topoi of the ancient heroes, and in a sense bridges the gap between the classic age of martyrdom and the subtle and compelling human dramas which surround us in the present world. Because martyrdom, unhappily, is not a theme which can be consigned to history. As the papers in this collection make clear, it belongs both to the past and the present. No doubt it will belong to the future as well.

David Loades

WOMEN AMONG THE EARLY MARTYRS

by STUART G. HALL

T HE Pentecostal sermon attributed to Peter in Acts announces
Joel's prophecy fulfilled:

> It shall happen in the last days, says God, that I will pour some
> of my Spirit upon all flesh, and your sons and your daughters shall
> prophesy, your youths shall see visions and your elders shall dream
> dreams; yes, even on my slaves and slavegirls in those days I will pour
> some of my Spirit, and they shall prophesy.[1]

The gift thus overrides sex, rank, and social status; it is often overlooked
that the company on whom the Spirit falls in Acts 2 includes, beside the
restored Twelve, 'women and Mary the mother of Jesus and his brothers',[2]
and Acts in this respect agrees with Paul that in Christ 'there is no Jew nor
Greek, there is no slave nor free man, there is no male and female; you are
all one person in Christ Jesus.'[3]

This gift of the Spirit is primarily baptismal; it is a baptism of the Spirit
which washing in the name of Jesus Christ represents. Manifestations of
the Spirit include prophecy and divination, which soon in the Church are
seen as a special gift. Among those to whom that spiritual gift is accorded
are those who face public trial for the Name of Jesus, and who attest their
faith under that testing:

> When they turn you in, do not be anxious about how you are to speak
> or what to say; it will be given you at that time what you are to say. It
> is not you that speak, but the Spirit of your Father that speaks in you.[4]

There is no restriction to males in this process. The Spirit falls on women
in baptism, giving words of prophecy and visions, and so does martyrdom, and with it the opportunity to witness and speak with the voice of
the Spirit.

Dead martyrs no longer speak. But while they still live, they have
become vessels of that special gift, and must be listened to with appropriate care. Dionysius the Great, Bishop of Alexandria during the Decian

---

[1] Acts 2.17–18, adapting Joel 2.28–9.
[2] Acts 1.14.
[3] Galatians 3.28.
[4] Matthew 10.19–20, and parallels.

persecution of 249 to 251, deploys the authority of the martyrs to justify a moderate position in disciplining the lapsed. He stated his case to Fabius of Antioch, who favoured a rigorous policy, first listing the heroic acts of those who faced trial and died, and concluding:

> The divine martyrs themselves among us, who now are assessors of Christ, and share the fellowship of his kingdom, and take part in his decisions and judge along with him,[5] have espoused the cause of certain of the fallen brethren who became answerable for the charge of sacrificing; and seeing their conversion and repentance, they judged it had the power to prove acceptable to him who hath no pleasure in the death of the sinner, but rather his repentance; and so they received and admitted them to the worship of the Church as 'consistentes', and gave them fellowship in their prayers and feasts.[6]

Those concerned had probably been 'perfected' as martyrs by death before Dionysius wrote, though it is not certain. But clearly they are still alive when they make the judgement, and the possibility is open that they might somehow survive the persecution, and the special status of their words has to be recognized in the churches.

A clarification of terms is needed, commonplace in itself.[7] A martyr, μάρτυς, is simply a 'witness'. So living martyrs are quite possible. They have given their testimony, μαρτυρία. If they ratify it, confirming their testimony by dying, it becomes stronger, a present proof of Christ's Resurrection and the truth of the faith.[8] But essentially it is no different from 'confession', ὁμολογία, which can be 'unto death'. Confessors and martyrs are one and the same. We find living martyrs not only among the Montanists,[9] but at Rome, and even among the bishops around AD 200,

---

[5] Alluding to Matthew 19.28; I Corinthians 6.2–3; Revelation 20.4.

[6] Quoted by Eusebius, *Ecclesiastical History*, 6,42,5. I use *Eusebius Bishop of Caesarea. The Ecclesiastical History and The Martyrs of Palestine*, tr. with intro. and notes Hugh Jackson Lawlor and John Ernest Leonard Oulton (London, 1954, repr. 1927). The generally excellent Penguin Classics edition (*Eusebius, The History of the Church from Christ to Constantine* tr. G. A. Williams, rev. edn and intro. Andrew Louth, 2nd edn (Harmondsworth, 1989)), lacks complete marginal numeration, making its scholarly use very difficult.

[7] See, for instance, Michael Slusser, 'Martyrium III', *Theologische Realenzyklopädie*, 22 (1992), pp. 207–11, and bibliography; *A Patristic Greek Lexicon*, ed. G. W. H. Lampe (Oxford, 1961), under μάρτυς, ὁμολογέω and cognates. J. Ruyschart, 'Les "martyrs" et les "confesseurs" de la lettre des églises de Lyon et de Vienne', in *Les Martyrs de Lyon*, 177 = *Colloques Internationaux du Centre National de la Recherche Scientifique*, no. 575 (Paris, 1978), pp. 233–47, emphasizes the fluidity of the terms, and uses 'témoin' in preference to 'martyr' throughout.

[8] So Athanasius, *De Incarnatione*, 28–9 = *SC*, 199, pp. 362–70.

[9] Eusebius, *Ecclesiastical History*, 5,18,5–6.

Natalius[10] and Kallistos (= Calixtus I) as well as those imprisoned with Kallistos.[11] These confessors are an interesting reflection on the ecclesiastical status which their witness conveyed. They belong to the period when the formal orders of the Church are encroaching upon the traditional charismatic functions: apostles have been replaced in the succession of 'bishops and deacons',[12] and the duties and gifts of teachers and prophets are now associated with bishops and presbyters. Traditionally teachers ran their schools alongside, and sometimes in competition with, the episcopal congregations. Justin Martyr, Clement of Alexandria, and Perpetua's instructor Saturus are typical examples. Most of them end up labelled as heretics, like Valentinus and Ptolomaeus. Origen began independently, with a female patron, but in his time ordination to the presbyterate was coming to be needed.[13]

The Church at the end of the second century is in process of bringing order into its leadership and organization. It is no accident that the reconstructed *Apostolic Tradition* of Hippolytus of Rome gives us the classic account of the ecclesiastical status of the confessor. After describing the procedures for ordaining bishops, presbyters, and deacons he writes:

> But if a confessor has been in chains for the Name, hands are not laid on him for the diaconate or the presbyter's office. For he has the honour ($\tau\iota\mu\eta$) of the presbyterate by his confession. But if he be appointed bishop, hands shall be laid on him. And if he be a confessor who was not brought before a public authority nor punished with chains nor condemned to any penalty, but was only by chance derided for the name of our Lord and [perhaps = 'or'] was punished domestically, even though he confessed, hands shall be laid upon him for every order of which he is worthy.[14]

Thus the Church acknowledges the privilege granted to the confessor who has borne witness, seating him with the elders and awarding him

---

[10] Eusebius, *Ecclesiastical History*, 5,28,10.

[11] Hippolytus, *Refutation* 9,11,4, and 9,12,10–11, ed. Miroslav Marcovich, *Patristische Texte und Studien*, 25 (Berlin, 1986), 350, lines 25–30, and 352, lines 46–55.

[12] So first *I Clement*, 42–4, and *Didache*, 15 [conveniently in *The Apostolic Fathers*, I, Eng. tr. Kirsopp Lake = *LCL* (1912)].

[13] Full discussion in Ulrich Neymeyr, *Die christlichen Lehrer im zweiten Jahrhundert. Ihre Lehrtätigkeit, ihr Selbstverständnis und ihre Geschichte* = *Supplements to Vigiliae Christianae*, IV (Leiden, 1989).

[14] *Apostolic Tradition*, 10, 1–2, *The Treatise on the Apostolic Tradition of St Hippolytus of Rome*, ed. Gregory Dix (London, 1937), rev. edn Henry Chadwick (London, 1968), pp. 18–19; also in *Hippolyte de Rome, La Tradition apostolique*, intro. etc., Bernard Botte, 2nd edn (Paris, 1968) = *SC*, 11,2, ch. 9, p. 64, from which some of the wording above is derived.

allocation of the gifts by which the clergy lived (if $\tau\iota\mu\eta$, 'honour', be taken in the sense of clerical remuneration, as apparently in I Timothy 5. 17). But it protects itself from presumption to episcopal status, as in the case of Natalius at Rome,[15] and against aspiring confessors who had suffered only informal harassment, such as slaves, wives, and children beaten at home for their Christianity.

Hippolytus in the passage quoted refers to domestic violence. I need hardly say this was commonplace, and Roman society offered little protection against it. Even the Bible recommends it as a method of education (Proverbs 12. 7–11). Its extent and acceptability can perhaps be judged by canon 5 of the Council of Elvira, about 305.

> If any woman, impelled by furious anger, beat her maidservant with a lash so that she gives up the ghost within three days, and it be uncertain whether her death was intentional or accidental, she shall be admitted to communion after seven years if intentional, five years if accidental, after the performance of due penance.[16]

If a Christian lady can get away so lightly with murder, there were probably many slaves of both sexes who suffered or died for their faith almost unnoticed, unsung as martyrs and unrecognized as confessors. It also throws light on Hippolytus' insistence that slaves might not be baptized without the consent of a Christian owner, and not at all if their owner is pagan ($\dot{\epsilon}\theta\nu\iota\kappa\acute{o}s$).[17] Wives and children are also subject to domestic violence, of which we know little.

Whatever the situation over domestic violence, subordination is a powerful theme in respectable Christian circles, and is indeed a leitmotiv of the so-called *First Letter of Clement*. The Corinthians are there congratulated on their former godliness, honouring elders, moderating the young, and

> to the women you gave instruction that they should do all things with a blameless and seemly and pure conscience, yielding dutiful affection to their husbands. And you taught them to abide by the rule of subordination and to manage their households with seemliness, quite soberly.[18]

---

[15] See above, n. 10.

[16] Quoted from J. Stevenson, *A New Eusebius. Documents Illustrating the History of the Church to AD 337*, rev. edn W. H. C. Frend (London, 1987), p. 290, where further notes on cruelty to slaves are added.

[17] Hippolytus, *Apostolic Tradition*, 16, 4–5, Dix edn, pp. 23–4: 15 Botte edn, pp. 69–70.

[18] *I Clement*, 1,3 (tr. adapted from Lake's *LCL* edn).

The disorders current in Corinth are, says the author, due to envious ambition, and he lists its victims: first the biblical heroes, then the great Apostles Peter and Paul, and with them, in words echoed by Tacitus in his independent account of the persecution of Christians in Rome under Nero, 'a great multitude of the elect', who 'offered among us the fairest example in their endurance under many indignities and tortures'.[19] Finally, the women: 'Through jealous envy women were persecuted, Danaids and Dirkai, suffering terrible and unholy indignities: they steadfastly finished the course of faith and received a noble reward, weak in the body though they were.'[20] The terms 'Danaids' and 'Dirkai', which are certain in the oldest forms of the text, refer to classical myths. The fifty daughters of Danaus had suitors imported from Egypt, whom they slew in their marriage beds. Dirke, as a punishment for her atrocious cruelty to the helpless Antiope, was tied by her hair to the tail of a bull and dragged to death. Exegesis defeated commentators until a brilliant article by Hanns Christof Brennecke,[21] who took up a suggestion of A. W. Ziegler to show that the whole account of the apostolic and other martyrs in *I Clement*, 5–6, is expressed in athletic terms, and thus the point of comparison is that the women joined the men in the race, and won the same victory, crowned with martyrdom. In some forms of the myth[22] the Danaids were made prizes to be competed for by the suitors, which adds colour to the comparison: the women were not prizes, but prize-winners. The other comparison with Dirke similarly has only one point: her violent and horrible death. We thus find the author praising women among the martyrs. Their subordination is maintained, for they appear last; but their achievement is as noble as that of the male elect, despite their bodily infirmity.

Some of the later martyrological accounts find women in such a subordinate yet heroic role. In the various versions of *The Martyrdom of Justin and his Companions*,[23] Justin himself, the head of the school, is first questioned in some detail. Then the six members of the school are questioned more briefly. One is a woman named Charito, who in all

[19] *I Clement*, 6,1.

[20] Ibid., 6,2.

[21] Hanns Christof Brennecke, 'Danaiden und Dirken. Zu 1 Cl 6,2', *Zeitschrift für Kirchengeschichte*, 2 (1977), pp. 302–8. Brennecke gives full *Forschungsgeschichte* and documentation.

[22] Ibid., p. 305, n. 21.

[23] *Mart. Just.*, conveniently ed. in three Greek recensions and tr. Herbert Musurillo, *The Acts of the Christian Martyrs* (Oxford, 1972) = *Oxford Early Christian Texts*, pp. 42–61 [hereafter Musurillo]. Musurillo's translations, though useful, are at times sadly inaccurate.

recensions is the third to be questioned, following Justin and Chariton. In the earlier recensions the interrogation runs:

> To Chariton the prefect Rusticus said, 'Chariton, are you a Christian too?' 'I am a Christian,' said Chariton, 'by God's command.' Turning to Charito Rusticus the prefect said, 'And what do you say, Charito?' Charito said, 'I am a Christian by God's gift.'[24]

After the others are questioned, and Justin addressed again, all are led to flogging and execution with the phrase, 'They perfected their martyrdom in the confession of our Saviour.'[25] They are apparently free citizens, being beheaded for their crime.[26] In the group of pupils Chariton comes first, by chance or design. Charito is apparently dependent upon him, the similarity of names suggesting that she is not his wife, but his sister or daughter. She is the only female in the class, and is perhaps there as his dependant: a free-standing woman would be more remarkable. Her answer imitates Chariton's, only substituting 'gift' for 'command'. The expansive recension C piously suggests she is a dedicated virgin:

> 'I am not deceived,' said Charito to the magistrate. 'Rather I have become God's servant and a Christian, and by his power I keep myself pure and unstained by the taints of the flesh.'[27]

But this is not to be relied upon.

The proportions are different in two African martyrologies. Of the Scillitan Martyrs one, the spokesman and apparently teacher (he takes copies of 'books and letters of Paul, a just man' to court with him),[28] is accompanied by six other men and five women.[29] Since the women are listed separately, and the interrogations are not complete, we cannot detect whether there are married or otherwise related couples. In the case of *The Martyrdom of Saints Perpetua and Felicitas*,[30] the compiler lists the men first, beginning with the slaves 'Revocatus and his fellow-slave (*conserua*) Felicitas', where *conserua* plainly means that she is his matrimonial partner

---

[24] *Mart. Just.*, A,4,1–2; B,4,1–2. The longer question and Charito's answer in C,3,2–3, revealing an attitude of contempt for female judgement, are clearly secondary.

[25] Ibid., A,6; B,6; ἐτελείωσαν τὸ μαρτύριον ἐν τῇ τοῦ σωτῆρος ἡμῶν ὁμολογίᾳ, unhelpfully misrendered by Musurillo, 'fulfilled their testimony by their act of faith in our Saviour'.

[26] Ibid., A,5,1.6; B,5,1.8.

[27] Ibid., C,3,3.

[28] *Passio Sanctorum Scillitanorum*, Musurillo, 86–9, p. 12.

[29] Ibid., see especially the list at p. 15, where the name Speratus is misprinted as Sperata in the English.

[30] *Mart. Perp.*, Musurillo, pp. 106–31. See 2,1 and 4,5.

in so far as slaves may be such. After Saturninus and Secundulus, 'with them Vibia Perpetua'. The five are later joined by their instructor, Saturus. Here we have three men and two women in the class. Felicity is named after her partner; Perpetua as a single woman is named last, even though she is the leading figure.

In another martyrology the subordinate heroism of the woman is distinct. *The Martyrdom of Saints Carpus, Papylos and Agathonice*[31] records a trial at Pergamum, which Eusebius mentions in connection with the persecutions under Marcus Aurelius, but the Latin recension and some moderns prefer to place under Decius.[32] Carpus is apparently the leader, and is called 'Bishop of Gordos' in the opening of the Latin recension; he argues theologically in his own defence.[33] Papylos is in the Latin called Pamfilus and given the ecclesiastical rank of 'a deacon of Thyatira'. In fact, the joke he makes, asserting that he has 'many children', by which he means, 'children in the Lord in every province and city',[34] suggests that he is a travelling teacher; Carpus' apologetic argument might suggest he also is a teacher. The ecclesiastical ranks may well be secondary.

In the Greek recension, Agathonice is a spectator, and not on trial. Nailed to the stake for burning, Carpus declares that he has seen the glory of the Lord.[35] After the account of his death, the Greek continues:

> There was a woman named Agathonice standing there who had seen the glory of the Lord, which Carpus said he had seen; recognizing that this was a call from heaven, she raised her voice at once: 'Here is a meal that has been prepared for me. I must partake and eat of this glorious repast.' The mob shouted out: 'Have pity on your son.' And the blessed Agathonice said: 'He has God who can take pity on him; for he has providence over all. Let me do what I have come for.' And taking off her cloak, she threw herself joyfully upon the stake.[36]

Clearly she is a mother with a male child. In that she resembles Perpetua and Felicitas. Perpetua is finally relieved of her child by her father, and presumably by her Christian relatives, as we shall see. Felicitas' new-born daughter is entrusted to one of the sisters to bring up as her own.[37]

---

[31] *Mart. Carp.*; Musurillo, pp. 22–37, prints both recensions.
[32] Eusebius, *Ecclesiastical History*, 4,15,48; see Musurillo, p. xv and n. 8.
[33] *Mart. Carp.* A,5–20; B,2,1–4,6.
[34] Ibid., A.28–32; B,3,2–3.
[35] Ibid., A,38–9; εἶδον should be understood as, 'I have just seen.' This episode is attributed to Pamfilus in B,4,3, and is not related to Agathonice.
[36] Ibid., A,42–4.
[37] *Mart. Perp.*, 6,7–8; 15,7.

Whatever may be said of Agathonice's attitude to her son, it is not utterly improvident in committing him solely to God: the fellowship of the Church would do God's work for him. In the Roman Church about the year 250 there were 'above fifteen hundred widows and persons in distress, all of whom are supported by the grace and lovingkindness of the Master', that is, by the gifts of the faithful.[38]

Most striking is the voluntary suicidal martyrdom, resembling a death by suttee. In this she is not alone. During the local Egyptian persecution which anticipated the formal decrees of Decius in 248–9, one victim was an elderly virgin called Apollonia. They

> broke out all her teeth with blows on her jaws, and piling up a pyre before the city threatened to burn her alive, if she refused to recite along with them their blasphemous sayings. But she asked for a brief space, and, being released, without flinching she leaped into the fire and was consumed.[39]

This comes nearer the case of Agathonice than some other examples, such as the unnamed Roman matron who stabbed herself to death rather than be procured by Maxentius.[40] That matron is commended as a moral lesson, but not called a confessor or martyr. Valentina, who protested against the torture of another Christian woman, and was herself duly tried and killed, is similarly distant.[41] Much more germane is the case of Quintus:

> A certain Quintus, a Phrygian recently arrived from Phrygia, saw the beasts and turned coward. He it was who had made himself and some others come forward voluntarily. The governor used many persuasions on him, and got him to swear and to offer sacrifice. For this reason, brothers, we do not approve of those who come forward by themselves, since the Gospel does not so teach.[42]

This is probably an interpolation in the *Martyrdom of Polycarp*. The following chapter begins, 'At first the most admirable Polycarp when he heard this was not disturbed. ...' That plainly refers not to the incident of Quintus, but to the cries of the mob at the Smyrna games for Polycarp to be sought for, which precedes the account of Quintus. I therefore suppose

[38] Eusebius, *Ecclesiastical History*, 6,43,11.
[39] Ibid., 6,41,7.
[40] Ibid., 8,14,17.
[41] Eusebius, *Martyrs of Palestine*, 8,6–8.
[42] *Martyrdom of Polycarp*, 4, Musurillo, pp. 4–5.

the latter to be a polemical interpolation. Interpolated or not, it is distinctly polemical, and attacks the voluntary self-offering which it studiously attributes to the Phrygians. The incident takes place in Smyrna, another of the cities of Asia, like Pergamum, where Agathonice dies, and like Thyatira, from which her companion Papylos comes. We are thus in the prime area for the heresy we usually call 'Montanism', which the Greeks simply call the 'Phrygian heresy'. It is perhaps best to call it by its own members' name, the 'New Prophecy'.[43] Enemies of the New Prophecy certainly associate it with voluntary martyrdom, and perhaps rightly. Tertullian, the only disciple of the New Prophecy from whom we have any substantial writings, plainly adopts a rigorous and uncompromising view of persecution and martyrdom. Whereas in his earlier days he was prepared to permit the reconciliation of the lapsed and the avoidance of persecution, when he comes to write *On flight — De fuga* — any such evasion of God's good gift is apostasy, and there is no second penance. So significant is this that Frederick C. Klawiter has recently argued that voluntary martyrdom is the chief distinguishing point of the New Prophecy.[44]

I do not agree wholly with Klawiter. But the point remains that the New Prophecy boasts living martyrs, encourages voluntarism, and takes a hard line against the lapsed. This throws light on the two recensions of *The Martyrdom of Saints Carpus, Papylos and Agathonice*. The Latin is much tidier. Carpus has become a bishop, Pamfilus a deacon. Agathonice also is improved: she has more than one son (*miserere tibi et filiis tuis*),[45] her beauty when she removes her clothing is commented on by the crowd.[46] More importantly the lady is brought forward in regular order by the command of the proconsul, who demands that she sacrifice; and a formal sentence and execution by burning follow her refusal. One might too readily conclude that an account which gives no ecclesiastical rank to the men and which leaves the woman a voluntary martyr is original, and that it has been improved in an orthodox direction in the Latin version. But there are

[43] Recent accounts and documentation in W. H. C. Frend, 'Montanism. A movement of prophecy and regional identity in the early church', *BJRL*, 70 (1988), pp. 25–34; 'Montanismus': *Theologische Realenzyklopädie* (forthcoming); Ronald E. Heine, *The Montanist Oracles and Testimonia* = North American Patristic Society, Patristic Monograph Series 14 (Macon, GA, 1989), which supersedes earlier collections of documents.

[44] 'The role of martyrdom and persecution in developing the priestly authority of women in early Christianity. A case study of Montanism', *ChH*, 49 (1980), pp. 251–61.

[45] *Mart. Carp.* B, 6,2.

[46] Ibid., B, 6,4–5.

indications that the Latin is in some respects older than the Greek, and specifically in the proconsul's interrogation:

> 'What do you say? Offer sacrifice. Or would you follow the thinking of your teachers (*doctorum tuorum*)?' She replied, 'I am a Christian and have never sacrificed to the demons, but only to God. I desire gladly, if I am worthy, to follow the steps of the saints and of my teachers (*sanctorum doctorumque meorum*).'[47]

Both proconsul and martyr refer to Carpus and Papylos as Agathonice's teachers, *doctorum tuorum*, *doctorum meorum*. This tallies with the evidence of their own interrogations, as we have seen, in which Carpus discourses like an apologist, and Papylos confesses to having spiritual children in various places. We then have, as in other cases, the martyrdom of teachers and pupil together. Since this fits the position of teachers in the second century, and not so well with the ecclesiastical ranks of bishop and deacon, we may therefore be faced with two secondary versions of the martyrology: a Greek recension which has, by accident or design, been improved in a Phrygian direction, heightening the voluntary character of her death, and with a Latin one which has improved the status of her teachers with ecclesiastical office, but has preserved an original interrogation.

We turn to the martyrs of Lyons, probably to be dated to 177.[48] They include a large group of women, most of whose names are preserved in an ancient list. This list, divided into those beheaded, those given to the beasts, and those who died in prison, was already known to Eusebius,[49] and is presented by later sources, such as Gregory of Tours.[50] In the later sources it is stated that they numbered forty-eight in all; Gregory himself then gives the names of twenty-four men and twenty-one women. They were therefore in nearly equal numbers. There are three groups, the second and third explicitly naming those who were thrown to the beasts and those who died in prison. In each group the men are listed first, save for the final name of the bishop Photinus.

---

[47] Ibid., B, 6,1.

[48] Eusebius, *Ecclesiastical History*, 5, preface and 1–4, cites the martyrology at length (also in Musurillo, pp. 62–85).

[49] Eusebius, *Ecclesiastical History*, 5,4,3.

[50] *Glory of the martyrs*, 48; conveniently accessible in English in Raymond van Dam, ed. and tr. with intro., *Gregory of Tours. Glory of the Martyrs = Translated Texts for Historians. Latin Series* 3 (Liverpool, 1988), which has a useful note on p. 73.

We do not know the precise history of the martyrs of Lyons,[51] but some things are clear. One is that the allegations of monstrous practices of incest and (particularly) cannibalism are prominent. Christians prepared to deny their faith were not, as in other cases since Pliny, released, but continued to be held on a charge of murder, and suffered more in prison than those held as Christians.[52] The allegation of cannibalism was confirmed by non-Christian slaves belonging to the martyrs, who were terrified by the tortures; this turned formerly sympathetic members of the community against the Christians.[53] The ruling of the Emperor was finally sought, and at the second hearing the surviving apostates were given the opportunity to confirm their denial and go free.[54] The official position thus continued to sustain the line originally adopted by Pliny and confirmed by Trajan about 112, ignoring the alleged secret crimes, and punishing for mere Christianity.[55]

This provides a context for Biblis. Since her name appears in the first section of Gregory's list, she was apparently decapitated, and therefore a Roman citizen,[56] like half the total group. Confession of cannibalism by one who had been a Christian was anxiously sought.

> Biblis too, one of those who had denied, the devil supposed that he had already devoured; but wishing to use her slander as a further ground of condemnation, he brought her to punishment, that he might compel an already fragile and craven woman to state impieties against us. She however regained her senses under the torture and awoke, so to speak, from a deep sleep, when the passing retribution recalled to her mind the eternal punishment in hell; and she directly

---

[51] The celebration volume, *Les Martyrs de Lyon* (see above, n. 7), is essential reading but somewhat disappointing. For a judicious discussion of the problems generally, see W. H. C. Frend, *Martyrdom and Persecution in the Early Church* (Oxford, 1965), pp. 1–30, and for a comprehensive recent analysis, Winrich A. Löhr, 'Der Brief der Gemeinden von Lyon und Vienne (Eusebius, h.e. V,1–2[4])', *Oecumenica et Patristica. Festschrift für Wilhelm Schneemelcher* (Chambésy and Stuttgart, 1989), pp. 135–49. Some connection with the *senatusconsultum* of 175 seems probable (see J. H. Oliver and R. E. A. Palmer, 'Minutes of an Act of the Roman Senate', *Hesperia*, 24 (1955), pp. 320–49), though the Christian sources show no knowledge of the legal niceties or the price of gladiators, and most of the martyrs did not perform in the ring. For the polemical orientation against the New Prophecy, though not for the date, Pierre Nautin, *Lettres et écrivains chrétiens des iième et iiième siècles* (Paris, 1961), ch. 2, deserves more attention than it has received.
[52] Eusebius, *Ecclesiastical History*, 5,1,33.
[53] Ibid., 5,1,14–16.
[54] Ibid., 5,1,47–8.
[55] Pliny, *Epistulae*, 10,96,5–6, and esp. 97,2 (cited from Eng. version in Stevenson, *New Eusebius*, pp. 18–21).
[56] Eusebius, *Ecclesiastical History*, 5,1, 47 for the sentences.

contradicted the slanderers, saying: 'How could they eat their children, when they may not eat the blood even of irrational beasts?' And henceforth she confessed herself a Christian, and joined the inheritance of the martyrs.[57]

We must not delay on the identifying of the persecutors with the Devil, the motive of terror in Christian obedience, or the adherence to kosher food. First, we note that she is not the only one tortured for the same purpose of getting evidence of the atrocities: Sanctus, Maturus, Attalus, and Blandina are also singled out.[58] Biblis shares the experience of the two female deacons (*ministrae*) whom Pliny had tortured for the same information.[59] It was precisely their failure to confirm the horror stories which precipitated Pliny's enquiry to the Emperor as to whether it was the name of Christian, or the secret crimes connected with the name, that was punished; and it is plain that he is interested in what Christians ate.[60] The second thing about Biblis is that the martyrologist records the remembered words of confession, even though they are obscurely put in a rhetorical question: 'How could they eat their children, when they may not eat the blood even of irrational beasts?' This is her Spirit-given word, lovingly recorded. The third and most important is that she is a penitent apostate, and is added to the martyrs.

   The letter in which the account survives is a polemical document. It is addressed to the churches of Asia and Phrygia, which are precisely those torn by the New Prophecy dispute. A copy is apparently directed to Rome in the name of the martyrs themselves, if not actually written by them as Eusebius says.[61] The vital point is that the martyrs in prison won back most of the ten who denied at the first hearing, and reconciled them to the faith. Some presumably died in prison, where about eighteen perished altogether, and the conditions were worse for those held as murderers than for those held as Christians. At the second hearing, after the Emperor's ruling had been obtained, these penitents made a good confession and were executed with the rest.[62] The process of restoration is introduced thus: 'A mighty dispensation of God came to pass, and the measureless compassion of Jesus was displayed, in a manner rarely vouch-

[57] Ibid., 5,1,25–6.
[58] Ibid., 5,1,17–24.
[59] Pliny, *Epistulae*, 10,96,8.
[60] Ibid., 10,96,2 and 7.
[61] Eusebius, *Ecclesiastical History*, 5,4.
[62] Ibid., 5,1,11.32–5.45–8.

safed among the brethren, but not beyond the skill of Christ.'[63] This shows that it was not the rights of the confessor-martyrs that was in question, but the way they used it. So in the polemical passage of which extracts survive, the martyrs

> who also were such emulators and imitators of Christ . . . neither proclaimed themselves martyrs nor indeed did they permit us to address them by this name . . .. They loosed all and bound none . . .. They did not indulge in boasting against the fallen, but with a mother's compassion supplied the more needy with that wherein they themselves abounded; and pouring forth many tears on their behalf to the Father, they asked life, and he gave it them.[64]

Eusebius immediately emphasizes the relevance of this to the harsh treatment of the lapsed, and goes on to introduce his first account of the New Prophecy in Phrygia, before describing the letter in the name of the martyrs to Rome. It is not the authenticity of what is revealed to confessors that the document argues: their privileged judgement is presupposed. What is argued on the basis of their judgement is the rightness of reconciling the lapsed. Not only was it the judgement of the confessors: it was a special providence of Christ's mercy to keep the fallen Christians in prison where they could be brought to repentance and reconciled; and there is implicit appeal to the judgement of God in ratifying the reconciliation, when Biblis and the others made their confession good at the end.

Here a sharper line is needed than is sometimes drawn. W. H. C. Frend suggests that

> Montanism itself, and the *Acta Martyrum* from Lyon and Carthage [that is, of Perpetua and Felicity] all point to a movement within Christianity in the last quarter of the second century based on a profound conviction of the approaching end of the existing age and the glorification of the role of the confessor and martyr as vehicles of the Holy Spirit in bringing that about.[65]

Learnedly though this is argued, it misses the crucial point. The New Prophecy was not objectionable because it claimed rights for prophets and confessors, nor because it held to the imminence of the end of the world; these were widely-held views. It was objectionable because of the new

---

[63] Ibid., 5,1,32.
[64] Ibid., 5,2,2–6.
[65] *Les Martyrs de Lyon*, p. 174.

strictness which its prophets commended, tightening discipline over marriage, fasting, veiling, flight in persecution, and, above all, over the treatment of moral and religious lapse. This can be verified by simply comparing the early works of Tertullian with those he wrote after he accepted the New Prophecy. The martyrs of Lyons are thus champions of peace for the penitent lapsed, and their martyrology lies before us to argue that case against the New Prophets of Phrygia. Frederick C. Klawiter also misconstrues the position, when he argues that 'priestly power' was exercised by confessors like Perpetua among the Montanists, because unlike the Catholics they allowed confessors clerical authority even though they had not consummated their confession by martyrdom. This misplaces the issue, and obliges him incidentally to postulate that the founding women of the New Prophecy (Priscilla and Maximilla) were confessors, for which there is no evidence.[66]

At the head of the confessor-martyrs of Lyons stands another woman: Blandina. She is one of those singled out for pressure to confirm the allegations of monstrous behaviour. She is a slave, whose mistress, herself among the martyrs, fears that Blandina's physical weakness (or illness) will lead her to yield under torture. But she does not, and astonishes people by her vitality and endurance, repeatedly giving her testimony: 'I am a Christian, and with us no evil has any place.'[67] During this first phase of the interrogations, while Attalus, Maturus, and Sanctus suffer, Blandina is hung cruciform in the middle of the arena, exposed to the beasts, though they did not touch her.

> Even to look on her, as she hung cross-wise in earnest prayer, wrought great eagerness in those who were contending, for in their conflict they beheld with their outward eyes in the form of their sister him who was crucified for them, that he might persuade those who believe in him that all who suffer for the glory of Christ have unbroken fellowship with the living God.... she was taken down and reserved for another conflict ... she the small, the weak, the despised, who had put on Christ the great and invincible Champion, and who in many rounds vanquished the adversary and through conflict was crowned with the crown of incorruptibility.[68]

[66] 'The role of martyrdom and persecution in developing the priestly authority of women in early Christianity. A case study of Montanism', *ChH*, 49 (1980), pp. 251–61.
[67] Eusebius, *Ecclesiastical History*, 5,1,17–19.
[68] Ibid., 5,1,41–2.

The slave-girl among the confessors thus embodies the merciful Christ, and her judgement must be among those who reconciled the lapsed. It is difficult to see her as other than the leader, by divine appointment. Her final conflicts at the summer games are described in terms which confirm this. She encouraged especially the fifteen-year-old Ponticus, who is described as 'her brother', whether in the flesh her brother or not. Then,

> last of all, having like a highborn mother exhorted her children and sent them forth victorious to the King, travelled herself along the same path of conflicts as they did, and hastened to them ... And after the scourging, after the wild beasts, after the frying-pan, she was at last put in a basket and presented to a wild bull. For a time the animal tossed her, though by now she was unconscious ... Then she too was sacrificed [presumably her throat was cut], and even the heathen themselves acknowledged that never in their experience had a woman endured so many and terrible sufferings.[69]

The parallel with the Maccabean mother of martyrs[70] is obvious and has often been noticed. Less frequently, if ever, noticed is the paradoxical eminence of a woman and slave among the confessors. Dionysius of Alexandria included women in his tale of the Decian persecution, which concludes with the judgement of 'the divine martyrs among us' in favour of remitting sins to the lapsed.[71] But I know no discussion of the status of women as confessors, which is so pointed up by Blandina: she is the chosen embodiment of Christ's own death, the mother of all the martyrs. Their glory, and the judgement they give, must be hers. Suppose she had survived and turned up in Hippolytus' congregation in Rome as a confessor, would she have been seated with the presbyters? Presumably not, since the sexes were normally sharply separated. She could be given the same portion of the offerings, the same $\tau\iota\mu\acute{\eta}$. She might have sat with the official Widows. Clearly the charisma she is endowed with does not match the rising codes of ecclesial order, of which Hippolytus' is the best early example.

We turn finally to Vibia Perpetua and Felicitas.[72] Their martyrology is edited (by general consent) in the interest of the New Prophecy. The

---

[69] Ibid., 5,1,53–6.
[70] II Maccabees 7, esp. 20–41.
[71] Eusebius, *Ecclesiastical History*, 6,41,1–42,6.
[72] *Passio sanctarum Perpetuae et Felicitatis* [hereafter *Passio*]; Latin and English in Musurillo, pp. 106–31. See also W. H. C. Frend, 'Blandina and Perpetua. Two early Christian heroines', *Les Martyrs de Lyon*, pp. 167–77.

editor from the start challenges those who would restrict 'the one power
of the one Holy Spirit to particular periods, since the more recent are to be
considered greater' in view of the promise for the last times; that promise
is the prophecy of Joel with which this lecture began, quoted in rather
disorderly form from memory. He or she concludes, 'So we too recognize
and honour not only prophecies but visions equally promised, and reckon
the other powers of the Holy Spirit as for the service of the Church . . .'.[73]
Is the editor right in using the story in this way? I believe so. Almost half
the narrative (chapters 3–10) is written by Perpetua herself, a little less by
the editor (1–2 and 14–21), and the remainder (11–13) by another martyr,
Saturus. We should ask, why did Perpetua record her experiences? The
answer is not far to seek. She recognizes herself as a competent confessor,
and records her own sayings, visions, and spiritual experiences because
they are of value to the Church. After her first arrest, imprisonment, and
baptism, her brother urges her:

> 'Dear sister, you are now greatly privileged [*iam in magna dignatione es*;
> Musurillo fails to render the crucial *iam*], so that you might ask for a
> vision and it be shown you whether it is to be suffering or deferment
> (*an passio sit an commeatus*).' For my part, whatever I knew myself to
> speak about with the Lord, whose benefits I had experienced, I
> promised faithfully to report to him, and said, 'Tomorrow I will tell
> you.' And I asked, and this is what was shown me . . .[74]

This incident may be what determined Perpetua to write down all her
experiences, since the vision she received showed her passion to be
imminent. She recognized that she had a claim upon God, and exercised it.
She does the same in the matter of prayer. She wakes suddenly with the
name of her brother Dinocrates on her lips, and 'I knew at once that I was
worthy and ought to pray for him. I began to make earnest prayer for him
and to plead with the Lord.' Her first vision of Dinocrates, who had died
as a child of a facial cancer, shows him unable to reach a pool of water to
drink. He was presumably unbaptized, as were Perpetua and her other
brother or brothers when the story begins.[75] But she persists in prayer until
they are moved to the military prison ready for the games. Then another
vision is granted, in which Dinocrates can reach the water and is playing
happily. Thus her martyr-prayers can reach even the unbaptized dead.

---

[73] *Passio*, 1,3–5.
[74] Ibid., unfortunately Musurillo's English is very faulty.
[75] Against Augustine, *De origine animae* 1,12, *CSEL*, 60, p. 312, see Musurillo, n. 11.

Consideration of the other material confirms this. There is a clear message in the vision of Saturus, in which he visits heaven with Perpetua, interviews earlier martyrs, and returns with a strong moral message for 'the bishops Optatus and Aspasius the presbyter-teacher (*presbyterum doctorem*)' that they should settle their quarrel.[76] The other narrative material, which has apparently come to the editor by oral tradition, is similarly determined by the desire to record the confession. Poor Felicitas, eight months pregnant, fears she may have her execution deferred and not be allowed to suffer with the others. The others pray for her, and their prayer brings her an early delivery, with great pain. The climax comes in these words:

> One of the assistants to the prison guards said to her: 'You suffer much now—what will you do when you are tossed to the beasts? Little did you think of them when you refused to sacrifice.' 'Now what I suffer I suffer myself,' she replied. 'There, another will be in me to suffer for me, because I too will be suffering for him.'[77]

Even the gestures of the men going into the arena are interpreted as prophetic words of judgement upon the magistrates.[78] We should therefore see Perpetua's notes and the other material as a record of the words, graces, and visions accorded to the privileged confessors, written for the good of the Church. The confessors share the hopes and faith of their editor.

What else shall we say of Perpetua? She comes from a largely Christian home, despite her father's pleas to her to yield. After recording his most earnest plea to her not to bring disgrace on himself, her brothers, her mother, her aunt, and her child, she says, 'I was sorry for my father's plight, because he alone of all my kin was not going to rejoice at my passion.'[79] We know nothing of her husband, which is strange. No one in the story refers to him, though Perpetua is described as 'respectably married' (*matronaliter nupta*) by the editor. He might have been hostile. Justin's account of the martyrdom of Ptolomaeus and Lucius[80] includes an interesting female non-martyr. A well-connected Roman woman accepted the teachings of Christ, which alienated her from her husband's licentious ways. While he was away in Alexandria, he got involved in

---

[76] *Passio*, 11–13.
[77] Ibid., 15.
[78] Ibid., 18,7–8.
[79] Ibid., 5,1–5.
[80] Justin, *2 Apologia* 2, repr. with Eng. tr., Musurillo, pp. 38–41.

some other criminal practices, and she finally decided to divorce him. He then filed a suit against her and accused her of Christianity, but she obtained a ruling that her action for divorce be taken first. Frustrated in his prosecution of her, presumably because she had influential relatives and property, he took her teacher ($\delta\iota\delta\acute{\alpha}\sigma\kappa\alpha\lambda o\nu$) to court. The weight of Justin's argument falls on the fact that the teacher, Ptolomaeus, was convicted and executed solely on the confession of being a Christian, and without any reference to any crime. Lucius was there, and protested against this injustice, and was himself arrested and executed too, on similar grounds, and a third with them. But the woman appears to have escaped unpunished. Presumably the same could have happened for Perpetua, being of a propertied family, and her father's repeated persuasions were directed to modifying her attitude. Perhaps she also had a hostile husband. I incline to the view that he was actually dead, and that there was no cause to mention him in her notes of events; the editor had no information, and so wrote nothing about it. The editor is not too scrupulous about the family: his own summary fails to mention that her family were mostly Christian, noting only that one brother was a catechumen.[81] One reason for preferring this view is that the male child is finally left with Perpetua's father and family; another is that she is treated as a 'lady' (*dominam*) by her father,[82] as though she were of independent standing. Ignorance of her widowhood on the part of her editor is certainly possible. But none of this is compelling.

Secondly, there is Perpetua's teacher. She belonged to a class, a group which was arrested together: a slave couple, two men, and Perpetua. Of Saturus, Perpetua writes, when describing how she saw him in her dream about the ladder guarded by weapons and a fierce dragon, 'Saturus was the first to go up, he who had afterwards given himself up voluntarily on our account, because he had himself been our instructor (*ipse nos aedificauerat*), and when we were arrested he had not been present.'[83] Saturus would later fulfil the dream by leading the way to the scaffold. His position is comparable to that of Origen in Alexandria, who at the same period claims to have accompanied martyrs to their trial and execution, without being arrested himself. They included his own pupils, and some catechumens, including one named woman, Herais.[84] That Origen escaped arrest must

[81] *Passio*, 2,2.
[82] Ibid., 5,5.
[83] Ibid., 4,5.
[84] Eusebius, *Ecclesiastical History*, 6,3–4. That Origen's own apologetic letter is the source is apparent from his remark about Herais, quoted in 6,4,3.

be due to the influence of some of his admirers, or to the fact that he had been brought up a Christian and was not himself a convert: the Alexandrian martyrs of the period, like Perpetua's companions, were newly baptized or candidates for baptism. So, for what it is worth, was Alban, the British protomartyr, who perished at this period, if the oldest version of the martyrology is to be trusted, against Bede.[85] Frend tellingly argues that Severus did in 202 issue some edict against conversions to Judaism and Christianity, and is right to argue that the preponderance of converts among the martyrs of the period reflects it.[86]

Saturus, then, is a trainer of catechumens, who are baptized after their first arrest,[87] and he gives himself up in order to lead them through their trials. This is not regarded as improper or unusual, but reminds us of Quintus at Smyrna (who was perhaps the teacher of a group) and Agathonike at Pergamum. He is also a visionary, whose visions acknowledge Perpetua as his chief companion, as hers acknowledge him.

Perpetua herself, though said to be well educated (*liberaliter instituta*)[88] uses only conversational Latin, and could not have spoken or written as Tertullian or Cyprian do. She could never have become a teacher as the Early Church boasted teachers, sharing the difficulty of women generally. One or two teaching women can be named. Hermas was directed to give copies of his prophecy to Clement for the churches outside Rome, and to read one copy in the city in the presence of the presbyters who govern it, and to give one copy to Grapte—'and Grapte shall instruct the widows and orphans.'[89] The five women mentioned as teachers among Christian sects by Celsus (Helena, Marcellina, Salome, Mariamne, and Martha) are all doubtful starters except Marcellina, who appears to have promoted Carpocratianism in Rome.[90] The group of seven women who are tried in *The Martyrdom of Saints Agape, Irene and Chione*[91] appear to live a monastic life in flight from the persecution under Diocletian. Irene is accused of possessing 'so many tablets, books, parchments, codices and pages of writings of former Christians'. Being asked about their recent use, she

---

[85] So John Morris,'The date of St Alban', *Hertfordshire Archaeology*, I (1968), pp. 1–8.

[86] Frend, *Martyrdom and Persecution*, pp. 319–21. He underestimates the degree of Christianity in Perpetua's family.

[87] *Passio*, 3,5.

[88] Ibid., 2,2.

[89] Hermas, *The Shepherd*, Vis. II,4 = 8,3, ed. Molly Whittaker, *Die griechische christlichen Schriftsteller der ersten Jahrhunderte*, 48, 2 (Berlin, 1967), p. 7, 14–18.

[90] Origen, *Contra Celsum* 5,62; Irenaeus, *Adversus haereses* 1,25,6. Notes and further references in *Origène, Contre Celse III*, ed. with intro. Marcel Borret = *SC*, 147, pp. 168–9; *Origen, Contra Celsum*, ed. and tr., 2nd edn Henry Chadwick (Cambridge and New York, 1979), p. 312.

[91] Musurillo, pp. 280–93.

says, 'They were in our house and we did not dare to bring them out. In fact, it caused us much distress that we could not devote ourselves to them night and day as we had done from the beginning until that day last year when we hid them.'[92] These ladies were clearly students, and probably had a female leader. But such cases are rarely reported.

Among the followers of the New Prophecy, however, Perpetua, had she survived, could have taken the place of honour without difficulty. The early Tertullian could attack the disorderly and changeable ministries of the 'heretics', and he includes in sound subordinationist fashion: 'The very women ... how pert they are! They are bold enough to teach, to dispute, to enact exorcisms, to undertake cures—it may be even to baptize.'[93] Once he becomes a disciple of the New Prophecy, things are different. The movement itself is led by women. He calls it 'The Prophecies of Montanus and Prisca and Maximilla'.[94] When he attacks the decree encouraging moral laxity issued by the bishop of Carthage (or, as some suppose, Rome), he will not allow remission of adultery and fornication by bishops; even martyrs atone only for their own sin, and cannot acquit others. He can quote an oracle from the new prophecy, 'The Church has power to remit sin, but I will not do it, so that they may not commit other sins.'[95] One may suppose he was willing to allow prophets to determine individual cases. On one occasion he actually quotes the judgement of a prophet to clinch a metaphysical argument, a prophet who receives visions during the conduct of divine worship, and converses with angels and the Lord himself, discerning hearts and healing diseases. It is a woman he quotes.[96] In a church where the judgement of bishops is subordinate to the prophecies of assembled prophets of either sex, we may suppose that, if Perpetua had survived, she might have been found a place of honour.

But the New Prophecy was not to prevail, and neither could the rights of confessors. The show-down was to come when Cyprian, Bishop of Carthage, would clamp down on the leniency of confessors in Carthage, and oppose the rigour of Novatianist confessors in Rome, in the name of the exclusive judicial rights of bishops. But that is another story.[97]

[92] Martyrdom, 5.
[93] Tertullian, De praescriptione, 41; English from Stevenson, New Eusebius, p. 170.
[94] Tertullian, Adversus Praxean, 1.
[95] Tertullian, De pudicitia, 21,7.
[96] Tertullian, De anima, 9; conveniently in Stevenson, New Eusebius, pp. 175–6.
[97] E. R. Hardy, 'The decline and fall of the Confessor-Presbyter', Studia Patristica 15 (Berlin, 1984) = Texte und Untersuchungen, 128, pp. 221–5, provides a useful discussion, but the only woman he mentions is Julian of Norwich.

Women among the Early Martyrs

SOME CONCLUSIONS

In observing the women martyrs of the early period I have sailed into unexpected waters. It is not an area well worked. The views on women of the New Testament writers and the Gnostics have been well worked over. So have those of the classic monastic writers.[98] We find matters of order and authority prominent. Teachers play an unexpectedly large role, as against presbyters and bishops. So do the privileges of confessors and martyrs. While the customary second place of women may be expressed in their position in martyr-lists, their achievement is seen as bringing them level with their male counterparts, and by a remarkable inversion bringing the slave-girl Blandina to the very head. The social position of women may sometimes inhibit martyrdom, though in the case of Perpetua it makes her a natural leader, and she is literate enough to record her own martyr-confession for the use of the Church. Like male confessors, prophets, and teachers, the women were not to prevail. With the assimilation of bishops and presbyters to the cultic role of pagan and Israelite priesthoods, the primary functions of teaching, prophecy, and critical discernment were discontinued, or else engrossed by the same cultic officials. It is no accident that in recent times it is by putting all the weight on the purely cultic, irrational, and artificial factors, and rating as distinct, and ultimately subordinate, the doctrinal, diaconal, medical, and judicial work which women are patently competent to manage, that the strongest case can be made for excluding them from the Church's leading offices.[99] In the last resort I would rather be with the martyrs than with the priests.

King's College London

---

[98] For example, *Die Frau im Urchristentum*, ed. Gerhard Dautzenberger et al. (Freiburg, Basle, and Vienna, 1983); Elaine Pagels, *The Gnostic Gospels* (London and New York, 1979); Rosemary Radford Ruether, 'Misogyny and virginal feminism in the Fathers of the Church', in R. R. Ruether, ed., *Religion and Sexism. Images of Women in the Jewish and Christian Traditions* (New York, 1974), pp. 150–63; and on the Cappadocians, Graham Gould, 'Women in the writings of the Fathers. Language, belief and reality', in W. J. Sheils and Diana Wood, eds, *Women in the Church*, SCH, 27, pp. 1–13.

[99] Louis Bouyer, *Women in the Church* (San Francisco, 1984) [tr. from *Mystère et ministères de la femme dans l'église* (Paris, 1976)]; note esp. p. 88.

WOMEN, DEATH, AND THE LAW DURING
THE CHRISTIAN PERSECUTIONS

by CHRIS JONES

Blessed, too, are the women who are there with you as partners in your glorious confession . . . by displaying valour above their sex, by their steadfastness they have set an example to the rest of womankind as well (Cyprian, *Letter* 6.iii.1).

Indeed there are virgins to be found in this company: to their yield of sixtyfold the reward of a hundredfold has now been added, and they have gone forward to receive their crowns thanks to this twofold glory of theirs (Cyprian, *Letter* 76.vi.1).

SO wrote Cyprian in the mid-second century, highlighting the fact that women formed a significant proportion of those martyred in the persecutions in the centuries preceding the conversion of the Empire. Cyprian, like many other Christian authors, reserved the highest praise for female martyrs simply on account of their sex. It hardly needs to be pointed out that women were considered to be inferior to men in every conceivable fashion.[1] Hence, when they appeared in a male context, such as the brutal treatment meted out in the trials and subsequent executions for erroneous religious beliefs, they tended to attract attention and comment. Judging by the number of female martyrs who appear in the *Acta martyrum* and in such works as Eusebius' *Historia ecclesiastica*, the Roman authorities had few qualms over the use of judicial violence against the female sex. However, the Roman legal system was rife with exceptions, privileges, and distinctions, and taking into account the often surprised tone of writers on the persecutions, it would not be improbable to find that sex existed as a distinct category in Roman law. It is the intention of this paper to ascertain whether such a principle was in fact current in Roman legal texts, and then, drawing on the sources relating to the persecutions, it will attempt to discover if these theories were carried out in practice.

First of all a word must be said about Roman law itself and the working of privilege within it. The rank of an offender, and indeed of the offended, had an important bearing on the conduct and outcome of any

---

[1] See, for example, Jane F. Gardner, *Women in Roman Law and Society* (London, 1986).

case. Privilege determined whether a case went to court in the first place; once there it affected how the trial was conducted; and finally it would determine the type and severity of the sentence and punishment. At its most basic it can be seen as a system heavily favouring the strong over the weak. There were several categories of people who could expect to receive some measure of preferential treatment in the eyes of the law, but the most important division was that between those who were *honestiores*, on the one hand, and those who were *humiliores*, on the other. The former category included anyone of rank from senators down to *decuriones*, taking in equestrians and local aristocrats along the way, as well as veterans and soldiers (since military courts tended to benefit military offenders, against civilians at least).[2] The advantages of 'membership' of this group ranged from who exactly could be taken to court—it was, for example, illegal for a slave to accuse his own master[3]—to the punishment meted out after the trial. It was this latter aspect that was most crucial. *Honestiores* were not to be subjected to physical torture, which, like imprisonment, was not a punishment *per se* in Roman law.[4] Torture was merely a means of abstracting the truth during judicial inquiries and was carried out during the trial as part of the routine questioning of witnesses. During the fourth century the *honestiores* lost this privilege in certain cases involving treason and magical practices,[5] but during the persecutions they were still exempt. Equally, in capital punishment the system conferred exemptions on those of rank. Whilst a senator and a slave could both be convicted of the same crime under the same circumstances, the punishment would be different. For a senator, capital punishment did not mean death, but merely deportation or exile; effectively this meant the offender was dead to the law, but he escaped with his life. On the rare occasions when the *honestiores* did face execution they were entitled to the swiftest and most painless methods available, usually decapitation with a sword.[6] Slaves, on the other hand, received no such consideration and were generally subjected to crucifixion or burning at the very least.

Of other categories of exemption the most obvious is that of age. The *Digest* stated that malicious intent could not occur before the age of

[2] Peter Garnsey, *Social Status and Legal Privilege in the Roman Empire* (Oxford, 1970), p. 245.

[3] *Codex Theodosianus*, ed. and tr. Clyde Pharr, *The Theodosian Code and Novels and the Sirmondian Constitutions* (Princeton, 1952) [hereafter *CTheod*], IX, vi, 1 (376); IX. vi, 3 (397).

[4] *The Digest of Justinian*, ed. T. Mommsen and P. Krüger, tr. A. Watson (Philadelphia, 1985) [hereafter *Digest*], XLVIII, xviii, 7, and xix, 8, 3. See also Garnsey, *Social Status*, p. 149.

[5] Garnsey, *Social Status*, p. 141; *CTheod*. IX, xl, 1 and 10 (treason); IX, xv, 4–9 (magic).

[6] Ramsey MacMullen, 'Judicial savagery in the Roman Empire', *Chiron*, 16 (1986), pp. 147–66. See also Garnsey, *Social Status*, p. 152.

puberty.[7] Arcadius Charisius mentioned that persons under the age of fourteen are not to be tortured[8] (though he later added that all involved in cases concerning *maiestas* could be, leaving the reader to wonder which exemption cancels out which). Papinian recorded that Marcus Aurelius had quashed a case of incest brought against a certain Claudia on account of her age, adding that this, however, was no excuse for adultery.[9] Callistratus wrote that 'a person under fourteen should not be tortured in a capital case affecting another',[10] whilst Claudius Saturninus noted that where punishment was concerned 'regard must also be had to age'.[11] Outside legal circles 'a boy of fifteen called Dioscorus' was, according to Eusebius, tortured but was later released because 'in view of his youth he would [have] time to come to his senses'; and indeed he survived to Eusebius' own day (though without coming to his senses, as he had continued in the erroneous beliefs which had caused him the trouble in the first place).[12] Three companions of the martyrs Agape, Chione, and Irene were spared, and 'because of their youth [were] to be put in prison in the meanwhile.'[13] Indeed, Irene herself had received similar preferential treatment on account of her age, but, unlike the others, was soon after martyred anyway on account of her stubbornness.[14] Women, then, could receive preferential treatment at the hands of the authorities, but it now remains to be seen if this was for the same reasons as their male counterparts, their tender years, or whether, in fact, there was any distinction made because of their sex.

It is almost a truism to say that women were inferior at law in the later Roman Empire. They had few powers to bring their own suits, and were virtually hamstrung by the requirement that every legal action they undertook had to be approved by a guardian (*tutela*).[15] The Roman belief in *infirmitas sexus* sprang not from any opinion on their physical state, but rather from the idea that they had inferior critical faculties. Hence the legislation disadvantaging women at law was designed less as a conscious

---

[7] *Digest*, XLVIII, x, 22.

[8] Ibid., XLVIII, xviii, 10.1.

[9] Ibid., XLVIII, v, 39,4 (*Quaestiones*, bk 34).

[10] Ibid., XLVIII, xviii, 15.1.

[11] Ibid., XLVIII, xix, 16.3 (*de poenis paganorum*, sole bk).

[12] Eusebius, *Historia ecclesiastica*, tr. G. A. Williamson, Eusebius, *The History of the Church* (Harmondsworth, 1965), VI, xli, 19.

[13] *The Martyrdom of Saints Agape, Chione and Irene at Saloniki* [hereafter *Agape*], ed. and tr. Herbert Musurillo, *The Acts of the Christian Martyrs* (Oxford, 1972) [hereafter Musurillo], iv, 4, pp. 280–93.

[14] Ibid., vii, 2.

[15] Gardner, *Women in Roman Law*, pp. 5–31.

attempt at suppression and more as a defensive measure, protecting women from their own innate weakness.[16] In most of Roman law women were envisaged as the victims rather than as the protagonists of any crime. None the less there are several references in the *Digest* to the physical punishment of women. To begin with the most obvious and well-known passage which suggests some advantages we must turn to Ulpian. In *Sabinus* book 14 he stated that 'The punishment of a pregnant woman who has been condemned to death is to be deferred until she gives birth. Indeed I know it is the practice that she is not to be interrogated under torture so long as she is pregnant.'[17] This tradition survived well into the Middle Ages, but even before then the theory was adhered to in practice. The slave-girl Felicitas, a fellow martyr of Perpetua, was eight months pregnant when arrested. After much prayer, she duly gave birth and was thus able to join her fellow Christians in the arena, much to everyone's (including her own) delight.[18] In the *Martyrdom of Saints Agape, Chione, and Irene at Saloniki* the 'prefect' Dulcitius ordered that 'since Eutychia is pregnant, she shall be kept meanwhile in gaol.'[19] It is to be presumed that on this occasion prayers for divine intervention were in vain, as Eutychia is not subsequently mentioned amongst the martyrs. However, the eventual death of Felicitas does suggest that the legislators were concerned with the safety of the unborn child rather than making an exception on account of the victim's gender. Two further laws from the *Digest* would seem to confirm the view that it was the foetus and not the mother who was being protected. Again it was Ulpian (this time *Edicts*, book 33) who reported that 'if it is proved that a woman has done violence to her womb in order to bring about an abortion, the *praeses provinciae* should send her into exile.'[20] The second law suggests that Ulpian was not so much record-ing a ban on abortion, but rather upholding the father's right to determine the future of his lineage. According to Tryphonius, another woman was also exiled for causing herself to miscarry, but he added the reason; she did not want to bear a child for her recently divorced husband.[21] It seems that these laws were aimed at sorting out custody of children conceived before, but born after, divorce.

---

[16] Joëlle Beauchamp, 'Le Vocabulaire de la faiblesse féminine dans les textes juridiques de IIIe au VIe siècles', *Revue historique du droit français et étranger*, 54 (1976), pp. 485–508.

[17] *Digest*, XLVIII, xix, 3.

[18] *The Martyrdom of Saints Perpetua and Felicitas* [hereafter *Perpetua*], xv, 2–7, in Musurillo, pp. 280–93.

[19] *Agape*, iii, 7.

[20] *Digest*, XLVIII, viii, 8.

[21] Ibid., XLVIII, xix, 9.

There is a miscellany of other laws from the *Digest* and other sources
that hint at leniency for women. At 48.19.8, the *Digest* proceeds to give a
list of punishments available to provincial governors, beginning with the
remark that they 'do not have the right of killing by the axe' but only by
the sword. Amidst instructions on how to deal with enemies and deserters,
as well as miscellaneous advice on torture and who should be condemned
to the arena, there is the following passage:

> Women are customarily condemned to the service of convicts in the
> mines, either permanently or for a period; in a similar manner [they
> may be condemned to] the salt works. If, indeed, they are sentenced
> permanently, they are made as it were, *servae poenae*; but if they are
> sentenced for a fixed period, they retain their citizenship.[22]

On the face of it this passage suggests that women could not be executed.
It set out the laws regarding exile to the imperial mines in the same way
they are set out for men. It is impossible to believe, however, that it
excused women from capital punishment, even if only at the hands of
governors. The most likely explanation for it is that the whole section was
an anthology of clarifications compiled by the jurists, which cobbled
together replies to a number of independent queries on minor points of
law.[23] This passage was merely an assurance for one particular governor
that women condemned to the mines were to be treated in the same
fashion as men. Valerian's rescript of 258 to the senate, recorded in one of
Cyprian's last extant letters, can be explained in a similar way. In a list of
answers to several questions, it also gives the impression of differential
treatment for women:

> Bishops, presbyters and deacons are to be put to death at once ...
> senators, high-ranking officials and equestrians are to lose their status
> ... and if they should persist, they are then to suffer capital
> punishment as well. Furthermore the matrons are to be dispossessed
> of their property and dispatched into exile.[24]

It is to be assumed that should the *matronae* persist in their Christianity,
they too would undergo capital punishment. Initially they may appear to

[22] Ibid., XLVIII, xix, 8.8.
[23] It should be remembered that, unlike modern historians, the governors, lawyers, and judges
of fourth-century Roman courts did not have an edition of all the laws issued in the Empire,
as the *Theodosian Code* in the fifth century was the first attempt at collation on such an all-
embracing scale.
[24] Cyprian, *Ep.* LXXX, i, 2, in *The Letters of St Cyprian of Carthage*, ed. and tr. G. W. Clarke,
4 vols (New York, 1984–9).

be receiving more lenient treatment, but it should be remembered that they too would qualify as *homestiores*, but at the same time they were not covered by any of the previous categories in the rescript; either the senate had asked specially what was to be done with them, or Valerian's clerks were efficiently closing a legal loophole. Either way, women could expect the same punishment as their male counterparts.

The same cannot be said, however, in cases involving incest. Again women seem to be granted leeway on account of their sex alone:

> A woman, therefore, will suffer the same penalty as males only in that case where she has committed an act of incest forbidden by the *ius gentium*; for if it is only the observance of our own law that it is at issue, the woman will be excused the charge of incest [though not of adultery].[25]

The reasoning behind this statement is clarified later in the same title: 'Women who are mistaken in law are not liable to a charge of incest', and later still: 'Incest which is committed by way of an illicit marital union is customarily excused on the grounds of sex or age.'[26] Although ignorance of the law is usually held to be no excuse in court, it seems that this is the argument adopted in this case. Bearing in mind that women played little or no part in public life from the point of view of Roman law, this explanation becomes more credible and even logical. This exemption stemmed from the Roman perception of women explained above: it is a case of protecting women from their own inherent critical weakness. Overall, then, the *Digest* made few concessions to the sex of the recipients of judicial violence. However, as it made clear, governors and *iudices* had powers to vary the punishment according to the circumstances.[27] Hence this paper will now turn to the accounts of martyrdom and judicial violence in the persecutions to ascertain whether women were in fact treated differently, despite the lack of specific recommendations in law.

In Christian sources a basic narrative pattern emerges from all the accounts of martyrdom from the *Letter of the Churches of Lyons and Vienne* in 177, through the third and early fourth-century *acta martyrum*, and indeed continues further in, for example, the lives of Syrian saints in the sixth and seventh centuries. The story usually begins with the arrest of

---

[25] *Digest*, XLVIII, xix, 39.2.
[26] Ibid., 39.2 and 7.
[27] Ibid., XLVIII, xix, 11.

the protagonist,[28] frequently along with a group of other prospective martyrs,[29] either as a result of deliberate persecution[30] or on account of the disturbance they have caused in the local community.[31] They are then brought before the governor (a generic term for the official who happens to be presiding over the court)[32] for interrogation about their faith and are given their first opportunity to recant.[33] Under normal circumstances this offer is declined,[34] and often members of the crowd, recognizing the truth of God, also come forward spontaneously to confess their belief.[35] The offenders are then imprisoned for a period of time,[36] where they are visited by members of their family and of the local community and are further entreated to renounce their misguided views. At this stage the Roman authorities are still fairly indulgent, often believing that the Christians can be rationally dissuaded from their madness.[37] After a period of incarceration, the confessors (as they have now become) are once more led before the governor and are given a further chance of avoiding execution.[38] The interrogation becomes more thorough; the governors can be drawn into lengthy disputations on the existence of God and belief in Christ.[39] However, tempers and patience begin to wane on the part of both the authorities and of pagan on-lookers.[40] Torture is threatened and indeed is generally now applied,[41] to the evident delight of the majority of those present, though a distinct

---

[28] *The Martyrdom of Saints Carpus, Papylus, and Agathonice* [hereafter *Agathonice*], I, 1 (in Musurillo, pp. 22–37); Eusebius, *Hist. ecc.*, V, xxi, 1.

[29] Eusebius, *Hist. ecc.*, V, i, 5; *Agape*, ii, 1.

[30] *The Martyrdom of Pionius the Presbyter and his Companions* [hereafter *Pionius*], ii, 1 (in Musurillo, pp. 136–67); *The Martyrdom of Saints Montanus and Lucius*, ii, 1 (in Musurillo, pp. 214–39).

[31] *The Acts of Thecla*, ed. Ross Kraemer, *Maenads Martyrs Matrons Monastics* (Philadelphia, 1988), pp. 280–9 [hereafter *Thecla*] sect. 14.

[32] *The Acts of Saint Cyprian*, iii, 2–3 (in Musurillo, pp. 168–75); Jerome, *Ep.* I, 3, in Jerome, *Select Letters*, ed. and tr. F. A. Wright, *LCL* (1954).

[33] *The Martyrdom of Saint Conon*, iv, 3 (in Musurillo, pp. 186–93); *The Martyrdom of Bishop Fructuosus and his Deacons, Augurius and Eulogius*, ii, 3 (in Musurillo, pp. 176–85).

[34] *Agape*, iii, 1; Eusebius, *The Martyrs of Palestine* [hereafter *Mart. Pal.*], viii, 6–8, in Eusebius, *Ecclesiastical History*, ed. and tr. H. J. Lawlor and J. E. L. Oulton (London, 1927), pp. 327–402.

[35] *Thecla*, sect. 20; *The Martyrdom of Polycarp* [hereafter *Polycarp*], iv, 1 (in Musurillo, pp. 2–21).

[36] Eusebius, *Hist. ecc.*, V, i, 28; Cyprian, *Epp.* XXXIX, ii, 2; LXXVI, i, 2.

[37] *Perpetua*, iii, 1–9; *Pionius*, xii, 1–2.

[38] *Agape*, v, 1–2; *The Martyrdom of Saint Irenaeus Bishop of Sirmium*, iii, 4–5 (in Musurillo, pp. 294–301).

[39] Eusebius, *Hist. ecc.*, V, xxi; *Polycarp*, xi, 1–2.

[40] *Agape*, v, 8; *The Martyrdom of Saint Justin and Companions* [hereafter *Justin*], iv, 5–6 (in Musurillo, pp. 42–61); *The Martyrdom of Saint Crispina* [hereafter *Crispina*], iv, 1 (in Musurillo, pp. 302–9).

[41] *The Martyrdom of Saints Marian and James*, v, 4–7 (in Musurillo, pp. 194–213); *Agathonice*, iii, 2.

minority will express horror and admiration at the suffering and courage of the martyrs.[42] Finally, at the express desire of the crowd,[43] who play a major part in proceedings,[44] the governor will order the public execution of the stubborn and unrepentant Christians. This will happen either straight away,[45] or at the next convenient opportunity, if there is a suitable festival or public celebration at some point in the near future.[46] Like Peter, the martyrs were given three opportunities to betray the name of Christ, but, unlike him, they always persisted in their faith. The executions themselves are accompanied by some miraculous proof of the existence of God in the form of providential weather conditions or the survival of the martyr's body intact.[47] The method of execution often has symbolic overtones for both authorities and martyrs. Burning of offenders represents for the Christian a purification in the form of a baptism of fire,[48] whilst for the Romans it would also mean the complete eradication of the offender in the form of a human sacrifice.[49] Equally death in the amphitheatre was often depicted as a contest with the Devil, incarnate in the form of wild beasts.[50] (This allowed the Christians to win either way; if killed, the martyr was assured a place in heaven through Christ, whereas if the execution failed, it was a reminder of God's power on earth.) With a further exhortation for others to emulate the martyr, the account closes.

These accounts differed little according to whether the protagonists were male or female, though a woman would receive more praise for her suffering than a man, as it was less to be expected.[51] Women occupied a major part in narratives of martyrdoms, but it seems that generally they would undergo equally painful tortures: Agathonice was burnt along with

[42] Eusebius, *Hist. ecc.*, VI, xli, 19; Jerome, *Ep.* I, 6.

[43] *Pionius*, xviii, 3; *Thecla* sect. 20.

[44] On the role and effect of the crowd at executions in the later Roman Empire, see David Potter, 'Martyrdom as spectacle' (unpublished paper, Dept. of Classical Studies, University of Michigan). For a more general view of the interaction between authorities and crowds at executions, and the thin line between pity and enjoyment, see Michel Foucault, *Surveiller et punir: naissance de la prison* [tr. Alan Sheridan, *Discipline and Punish: the Birth of the Prison* (Harmondsworth, 1991)], esp. pt 1, pp. 3–69.

[45] *Agape*, vii, 1–2; *Crispina*, iv, 2.

[46] *Perpetua*, vi, 7–8; Eusebius, *Hist. ecc.*, V, iii, 37.

[47] *Thecla*, sect. 37.

[48] See Jacques le Goff, *La Naissance du purgatoire* (Paris, 1981), p. 67. Fire has three functions: punitive, purative, and as a reminder of the flames of hell and purgatory.

[49] The symbolism can be seen further in *CTheod*, IX, vi, 2, where the slave who has accused his master was to be burnt along with a copy of the written accusation.

[50] Eusebius, *Hist. ecc.*, V, i, 51.

[51] Ibid., VIII, xiv, 13; VI, v, 4; Cyprian, *Ep.* VI, iii, 1; *Mart. Pal.*, viii, 5.

Carpus and Pamphilus;[52] those martyred along with St Justin included a certain Charito,[53] but she was not mentioned as being singled out for any special treatment, merely being tortured and beheaded with the rest. Of the twelve Scillitan martyrs who were beheaded, five were women.[54] Potamiaena found herself the guinea pig in what seems to have been an experiment with a new kind of torture: 'Boiling pitch was slowly poured drop by drop over different parts of her body, from her toes to the top of her head',[55] before she was finally burnt with her mother. Likewise Agape, Irene, and Chione were burnt,[56] whilst Crispina was beheaded.[57] Perpetua and her slave Felicitas were first thrown to a heifer, which though injuring them did not actually kill them, the *coup de grâce* being administered by a rather nervous young gladiator.[58] There is little difference in the narrative in the case of Eusebius' *Historia ecclesiastica* or his *Martyrs of Palestine*. In the former, Apollonia, an old woman, 'was battered till they knocked out all her teeth',[59] Ammonarion, 'a most respectable young woman', underwent 'savage and prolonged torture',[60] whilst in the Thebaid, 'Women were tied by one foot and hoisted high in the air head downwards, their bodies completely naked without a morsel of clothing, presenting thus the most shameful, brutal and inhuman spectacles to everyone watching.'[61] A high proportion of the Martyrs of Palestine were women: Firmilian 'came to judge one, who, though in body a woman, was yet, in the strength of mind she possessed, a man.' After much torture, 'She was raised aloft on a gibbet and her sides lacerated.'[62] Jerome's account of a woman who survived seven blows of a sword in an attempt to behead her, recorded that she underwent extreme tortures before the attempted death sentence; her supposed lover had been dispatched by the first blow of the sword and had undergone the same ordeal as her beforehand.[63] For any examples of severity to men there are equal tales of the bravery of women. There are, however, two distinct differences where women were concerned.

---

[52] *Agathonice*, iv, 5.
[53] *Justin*, 1–2.
[54] *The Acts of the Scillitan Martyrs*, 16 (in Musurillo, pp. 86–9).
[55] Eusebius, *Hist. ecc.*, VI, v, 4–5.
[56] *Agape*, iv, 4; vii, 2.
[57] *Crispina*, iii, 1.
[58] *Perpetua*, xxi, 9.
[59] Eusebius, *Hist. ecc.*, VI, xli, 7.
[60] Ibid., VI, xli, 18–19.
[61] Ibid., VIII, ix, 1–2.
[62] *Mart. Pal.*, viii, 5–6.
[63] Jerome, *Ep.* I, 3–7.

The first of these comes in the form of the Roman authorities' penchant for threatening women with sexual violence. Though rarely, if ever, applied to men, rape was a common punishment used where Christian women were concerned. Potamiaena was first tortured, and then her judge 'threatened to hand her over to his gladiators to assault her physically'.[64] Likewise, Sabina, in *The Martyrdom of Pionius the Presbyter*, was warned, 'You will suffer something you do not like. Women who refuse to sacrifice are put in a brothel.'[65] Irene was first imprisoned rather than executed because of her age, but her continued insistence on reading Christian literature caused the governor to change his mind: 'I sentence you to be placed naked in the brothel', although no one would touch her there, and she was subsequently burnt.[66] Throughout the *Martyrs of Palestine* it seems that the threat of the brothel was a standard punishment for Christian virgins; the governor Hierocles 'was handing over God's holy virgins to brothel-keepers for wanton violence and bodily insult.'[67] Later on, about another governor, Eusebius recorded, 'Nor did the fury of his wickedness slake itself with men, but he threatened to torture women also, and delivered three virgins to licentious brothel-keepers.'[68] How close to the truth these examples are is open to debate, but they provide at least circumstantial evidence. The fact that they were reported suggests that they were acceptable propositions to their prospective audiences, and it seems that in the use of sexual violence, or at least the threat of it, the authorities treated women more, rather than less, severely than men.

In the Christian sources there is a different reaction to the torture and execution of women, both on the part of spectators and the authors themselves. The sight of women, and especially naked women, suffering evoked much sympathy from spectators, though the reaction was rarely enough to bring about a reprieve. Agathonice was stripped before being led out to the stake, 'but when the crowd saw how beautiful she was, they grieved in mourning for her.'[69] The governor who sentenced Thecla to the arena 'wept that such a beauty was going to be eaten by seals.'[70] When Perpetua and Felicitas were thrown, naked, into the arena, 'Even the crowd was horrified when they saw that one was a delicate young girl and

[64] Eusebius, *Hist. ecc.*, VI, v, 2.
[65] *Pionius*, vii, 6.
[66] *Agape*, iv, 4; vii, 2.
[67] *Mart. Pal.*, v, 3.
[68] Ibid., viii, 5–8.
[69] *Agathonice*, vi, 4–5.
[70] *Thecla*, sect. 34.

the other was a woman fresh from childbirth.'[71] The sight of women
suffering could evoke pity, but it did no more. It was still a problem of
which the authorities were aware and took measures to counter. Crispina
was sentenced to decapitation, but first had her head shaved 'that her
beauty might be first brought to shame.'[72] On occasion it was not
unknown for the crowd to intervene on the side of the victims; the
woman Jerome described as surviving seven strokes of the sword was
rescued by fellow Christians, who then substituted another body for hers
in the coffin, thus concealing the fact that she had survived.[73] Lactantius
recorded that prisoners were sometimes escorted to their place of
execution by soldiers, 'In case the women were seized from the hands of
their butchers by a popular riot.'[74] The reaction of the authors was one of
moral outrage; women are subjected to 'boundless sufferings', to 'tortures
terrible and horrifying', 'to every atrocity';[75] they display 'valour above
their sex'[76] that presents 'a bitter spectacle ... girt with suffering: a
grievous sight, carrying with it groans and lamentation'.[77] Although it was
obviously the case that women were expected to be, and indeed were,
treated in like manner to their male counterparts, this could not suppress a
feeling of surprise. Crowds could express indignation, but more often
than not they would be baying for blood equally fervently. Surprise came
from the fact that the women refused to break under what would be
considered severe pressure by male standards, rather than because of the
mere fact of their torture. The shame of defeat at the hands of a woman
weighed heavily on many governors. Torturers could be threatened with a
like fate unless they 'made the weaker sex confess a crime which manly
strength had not been able to conceal.'[78] In Eusebius there was a governor
who was 'ashamed to go on torturing without result and to be defeated by
women, so they [the women] died by the sword without being put to any
further test by torture.'[79] Christian authors could be outraged that
women, and especially virgins, were subjected to such treatment, but
much of this is rhetorical, aimed at even further scandalizing the pagan

[71] *Perpetua*, xx, 2.
[72] *Crispina*, iii, 1.
[73] Jerome, *Ep.* I, 12.
[74] Lactantius, *De mortibus persecutorum*, ed. and tr. J. L. Creed (Oxford, 1984), XL, 5.
[75] Eusebius, *Hist. ecc.*, V, i, 54; VI, v, 1.
[76] Cyprian, *Ep.* VI, iii, 1.
[77] *The Martyrdom of Tarbo*, ed. Sebastian Brock and Susan Ashbrock Harvey, *Holy Women of the Syrian Orient* (Berkeley, 1987), 259, p. 76.
[78] Jerome, *Ep.* I, 4.
[79] Eusebius, *Hist. ecc.*, VI, xli, 18–19.

persecutors in the same way that historians of the period would emphasize the barbarity of the Persian or Germanic invasions with tales of widespread rape and murder of women and children.[80] A look at similar accounts in pagan sources would only confirm that surprise and even admiration for women suffering came from the extremity of the situation rather than from the mere fact that it was taking place.[81]

It would seem, then, that in one respect at least women did achieve equality in the later Roman Empire. Their death and suffering, at the hands of the Roman judicial machinery, was no different from that endured by their male counterparts. In the Roman Empire, a criminal, no matter of which sex, would have received the same degree of pain and brutality, one as the other. The authorities had no qualms over the use of vicious torments, either as a punishment or as a means of arriving at the truth. Continued correct moral behaviour under the extreme test of physical pain would elicit praise and admiration for men and more so for women. It was not the fact that women were tortured and died so painfully that caused surprise, but the fact that they could show themselves the equals of men in their endurance. Ironically, in their access to the process of law they found themselves in an inferior position, but in punishment they could expect no such distinction. Under law in death alone were women the equals of men.

Pembroke College, Oxford

[80] For example, *Scriptores historiae Augustae Commodus*, tr. D. Magie, *LCL*, 3 vols (1922–32), xviii, 10ff.; Ammianus Marcellinus, *Res gestae*, tr. J. R. Rolfe, *LCL*, 3 vols (1971–2), XXIX, ix, 5; XXXI, vi, 7; Procopius, *Wars*, bk ii, tr. H. B. Dewing, *Procopius, Complete Works*, *LCL*, 7 vols, 1 (1961), viii, 35; ix, 9–10.
[81] For example, Pliny, *Ep.* IV, xi, tr. Betty Radice, *The Letters of the Younger Pliny* (Harmondsworth, 1963), on the execution of the Vestal Virgin Cornelia; or Ammianus Marcellinus, *Res gestae*, XXVIII, i, 28 and 45–56, on the conduct of women during the trials at Rome in 371.

MARTYR DEVOTION IN THE ALEXANDRIAN SCHOOL: ORIGEN TO ATHANASIUS

by JOHN ANTHONY MCGUCKIN

INTRODUCTION

THE Christian interpretation of fatal persecution was a complex one with distinct ecclesial themes merging with Jewish elements from apocalyptic and biblical literature, as well as Hellenistic motifs such as the constancy of the Socratic martyr. The New Testament understanding of the term 'martyr' is predominantly that of legal witness,[1] although some specific senses of blood-witness are emerging already in the first century[2] and have become common by the second.[3] Varying reactions can be traced in the literature of different parts of the Church: for example, in Rome, Alexandria, Asia, Africa, or Palestine.[4] This paper looks primarily at the Egyptian interpretation as a microcosm of the general development of the role of martyrs, and does so by reference to the writings of the theologians whose works cover the main phases of that process. It highlights the distinction that existed between the sophisticated literary interpretation of martyrdom, and the forms of popular devotion that flourished among the non-literate peasantry. The tension between the two approaches, witnessed in both Origen and Athanasius, is demonstrably resolved by the time of Cyril, who represents the harmonious synthesis of both traditions in the new conditions of Christian political ascendancy in fifth-century Byzantine Egypt. The peculiar circumstances of the Egyptian Church, in particular the unusually radical separation that existed there between town and country (and the class and cultural divisions reflected in that), as well as the specific challenge posed to Christianity by the enduring vitality of the old Egyptian religions in the countryside, both left their marks on the specific form of martyr devotion

---

[1] Cf. E. Gunther, *Martus: Die Geschichte eines Wortes* (Berlin, 1941); H. Strathmann, 'Martus', in G. Kittel and F. Friedrich, eds, *Theological Dictionary of the New Testament* (London, 1964), pp. 474–508.

[2] As, for example, in Rev. 2.13.

[3] *Martyrdom of Polycarp*, 2, PG 5, cols 1029–32: Irenaeus, *Adversus haereses*, 5.9.2, PG 7, col. 1144: Clement of Alexandria, *Stromateis*, 4,4–5, 21, PG 8, cols 1225f.

[4] For a general survey cf. R. Lane Fox, *Pagans and Christians* (London, 1986), pp. 419–92.

in Christian Egypt, but the most noteworthy aspect is arguably the sub-text of the theological encomia of martyrdom that seems to have the definite concern of subjugating the popular devotion to martyrs, con-fessors, and ascetics to the interests of the Church hierarchies.

ORIGEN c. 185–251

Eusebius tells us that in Origen's youth, the Emperor Severus (193–211) 'stirred up persecution in every place'.[5] This is, without doubt, a consider-able exaggeration, but there were episodes of local trouble for various churches, especially Alexandria. If the evidence of the *Historia Augusta* is taken,[6] the purpose of the Severan edict was to prevent proselytism, and was aimed at the leaders of the Christian movement, particularly those of higher rank.[7] At Carthage the famous passion of Perpetua and Felicitas dates from this time (202), as probably does Tertullian's treatise on martyrdom.[8] At Alexandria[9] Eusebius speaks, in a very odd phrase, of the martyrdom then of 'Leonides, said to be the Father of Origen'.[10]

Aline Roussell[11] has noticed that the manner of Leonides' death, by beheading, denotes his rank as a Roman citizen at a time before Caracalla's edict (212) extended that privilege widely, and places him in the upper of the three ranks of third-century Alexandrian society: Roman citizens, citizens of the *polis* of Alexandria, and native Egyptians. Eusebius tells us the famous story on this occasion of how Origen's mother prevented his bid for martyrdom by hiding his clothes. The story is largely part of Eusebius' pro-Origen apologetic, for in all probability even if he had run off to join his father no one would have wanted to arrest him anyway. The Severan persecution in 202 was entirely directed at the upper class of Roman citizens. Origen's name (the Son of Horus) denotes his native Egyptian birth, despite all his subsequent Hellenistic education, and

[5] Eusebius, *Historia ecclesiastica*, 6.1.1; 8.7, *PG* 20, cols 522, 756.

[6] *Vita Severi*, 17.1 (Aelii Lampridii), in H. Peter, ed., *Scriptores historiae Augustae*, 1 (Leipzig, 1884), pp. 247–99.

[7] Cf. W. H. C. Frend, 'A Severan Persecution? Evidence of the *Historia Augusta*', in *Forma Futuri: Studi in onore di Card. M. Pellegrino* (Turin, 1975), pp. 470–80; *Martyrdom and Persecution in the Early Church* (Garden City, 1964); T. D. Barnes, 'Legislation against the Christians', *Journal of Roman Studies*, 58 (1968), pp. 32–50.

[8] Tr. C. Dodgson, *Library of the Fathers*, 10 (Oxford, 1842), pp. 150–7.

[9] For a general treatment cf. P. Delehaye, 'Les Martyrs d'Égypte', *AnBoll*, 40 (1922), pp. 5–154.

[10] Eusebius, *Historia ecclesiastica*, 6.2.12.

[11] Aline Roussell, 'La Persecution des chrétiens dans Alexandrie au IIIe siècle', *Revue historique de droit français et étranger*, 2 (1974), pp. 222–51. Text discussed in H. Crouzel, *Origen* (Edinburgh, 1989), p. 6.

Roussell suggests he was the child of a mixed marriage between an impoverished citizen, who had taken to the profession of teacher of grammatics, and a native Egyptian woman. In such cases the children of the marriage always assumed the lower of the two ranks involved, and on these grounds Origen would not have qualified for capital punishment even if he had vigorously professed Christianity. This is borne out four years later (206), when Origen accompanied six of his pupils to their executions. On that occasion the Alexandrian crowd found the impunity of the teacher outrageous and nearly lynched him,[12] but there was no official move against him, despite his notoriety as a Christian and the fact that the prosecuting judge, Aquila, generally appears to have distinguished himself for his savagery.

Origen never himself refers to his father's death as a martyr, and is oddly taciturn and vague about the historical realities of the martyrdoms generally in his extant writings. It is clear, however, that Eusebius' account of the martyrdoms in Alexandria in 206[13] was based on what must have been Origen's own *Panegyric* on his executed disciples. In line with Origen's extant writings, we could presume from the outset that this lost text would have celebrated their philosophical constancy: martyrs, that is, in the Socratic tradition, as befitted their profession of the scholar's life.

In the main, Origen's attitude to martyrdom can be summed up as rather low key, despite the fact that in a treatise devoted to the theme, he describes it as the discipleship that received the 'promised hundredfold'. In the persecution of Maximin Thrax (235–8), two of Origen's colleagues were imprisoned, his patron Ambrose and the Caesarean priest Protoctetus. Origen disapproved of Christians volunteering themselves for arrest, and at this period he seems to have withdrawn into hiding, a practice he reminds his readers is sanctioned by the Gospels,[14] but having withdrawn he counsels his arrested friends not to be anxious in undergoing their present trials, which apparently involved their transfer to the court at Mainz.[15] This *Exhortation to Martyrdom* is his most extended treatment of the theme, and while it evidently presents itself as an encomium, its primary function as a philosophical protreptic scales down the enthusiasm until it is almost matter of fact. It is interesting, in this light, to

---

[12] Eusebius, *Historia ecclesiastica*, 6.4.1.
[13] Ibid., 6.4: 'As Origen himself expresses it, after receiving her baptism by fire Heraïs departed this life.'
[14] Mt. 10.23; cf. Origen, *Homilies on the Book of Judges*, hom. 9, *PG* 12, cols 987–8.
[15] Origen, *Exhortation to Martyrdom* [hereafter *ExM*], tr. J. J. O'Meara, *Ancient Christian Writers*, 19 (London, 1954); cf. *ExM*, 41, p. 185.

consider whether the literary sang-froid is part and parcel of the stock tradition of Socratic martyrdom or whether it marks a personal desire on the part of Origen to displace, in some degree, the growing Christian devotion to the martyr ideal. Nowhere in his text does he aver to his own flight. Nor does he apologize for it. His friends, rather, are to be consoled for the misfortune of their arrest, but having thus had their choice taken away from them, he urges them on to the inevitable test of fidelity they will have to undergo. In this way his whole argument is his justification for his flight. What he is suggesting as his sub-text is that the vocation of the wise man, the *didaskalos* who is initiated by the Logos, is no less elevated than that of the martyr. He has no apology to make for defending his own charism by prudent escape. Perhaps not for Origen was the response of the Roman Church which set the martyr above all other saints.

In a sense, Origen cannot quite set the balance between the Socratic virtue of scorning death for the truth's sake and the Christian encouragement of his friends to press on for the sake of the hundredfold reward and their identification with the crucified master. In Origen's text the idea that dominates is how the martyr must be constant, like a true wise man in control of all his fears and steadfast in his profession of the truth. He has some specifically Christian elements, of course, most notably his summaries on how the Church abhors and penalizes apostasy,[16] and his section on the necessity of the disciple to bear the cross.[17] But when he wishes to present a series of exemplary martyrs for their emulation it is to II Maccabees that he turns,[18] not to experiences closer to hand. Despite Eusebius' urgent desire[19] to endow Origen himself with the nimbus of the martyr,[20] it would seem that the latter saw the philosophical vocation which he was bent on pursuing as the highest of all callings, and in a discreet way he is even ready to reinterpret the sacrificial role of the martyr along philosophical lines to sustain his point.

The same kind of philosophical abstraction of martyrdom is witnessed in his *Contra Celsum*, written in about 246. Here he radically restricts the martyr tradition to a Socratic paradigm.[21] Once again the martyrs are the

---

[16] *ExM*, 6–10, pp. 146–50.

[17] *ExM*, 11–21, pp. 151–61.

[18] *ExM*, 22–7, pp. 162–7; cf. Origen, *Commentary on Romans*, 4.10, PG 14, col. 999.

[19] It was designed to offset the rising tide of anti-Origenism among the less educated by the strongest appeal Eusebius could make to popular sentiment in his day—that Origen ought to be venerated as a martyr.

[20] Yet, in the end he suffered heroically, in the Decian persecution, so that Eusebius' devotion was not ill judged.

[21] *Contra Celsum*, 3.8, PG 11, col. 929.

true wise men, undeterred from their profession of truth by the savagery of tyrants. What goes hand in hand with this approach, indeed characterizes it, is its presupposition of intellectual superiority, and social exclusivity. He is determined to dispel every hint of fanaticism or populism from the Church's tradition of martyrdom. So, he tells the reader of the *Contra Celsum*, the Church's martyrs are 'few and easily enumerable'. As in his *Exhortation to Martyrdom*, here the concept of martyr is severely restricted to the one who has died for the truth:[22] the loud implication being that the surviving confessor does not count. In advance he is heading off the kind of problem that Cyprian had to face with the confessors of his own church a few years later.[23] Origen might argue that the blood of the martyrs in heaven would intercede for sinners on earth, but his general doctrine of reconciliation restricts its gift to those whom the Logos has initiated, and he would be unlikely to grant that charism indiscriminately to confessors.[24]

This exclusive and philosophical approach, if this was all there was, would hardly prepare one for the very concrete and populist devotion to the martyrs that had emerged among the common people, and fixed on their physical remains as its focus of devotion even from the second century.[25] Clearly Origen's position is already somewhat disingenuous, and partly designed to suppress popular attitudes he knew to be prevalent. At other times in his writings, particularly when he is addressing the less educated directly, as, for example, in his weekday expositions of the Scriptures in the Caesarean Church, a slightly different attitude can be seen. Here he is more ready to develop on the one brief allusion in the *Exhortation*[26] where he admits the intercessory power of martyrs. In his *Second Homily on Leviticus*, Origen has a remarkable section on the seven remissions of sins.[27] While the first of these is baptism, he describes the

---

22 *ExM*, 50, p. 195; *Commentary on John's Gospel*, 2.28, *PG* 14, cols 176–7.
23 For the confessor as a significant power in the Church, cf. Eusebius, *Historia ecclesiastica*, 5.1.45; 5.2.5; 5.18.6 (Montanists), *PG* 20, cols 404f.; Cyprian, *Epistles*, 15–16; 17.2; 20–3; 27; 35–6, *PL* 4, cols 270f.; Eusebius, on Dionysius of Alexandria, *Historia ecclesiastica*, 6.42.5–6, *PG* 20, cols 614–15; Tertullian, *De pudicitia*, 22, *PL* 2, col. 1080; *Ad uxorem*, 2.4.1, *PL* 1, col. 1407; *Ad martyres*, 1.6, *PL* 1, col. 700; *De poenitentia*, 9.4, *PL* 1, col. 1354; *Scorpiace*, 10.8, *PL* 2, cols. 166–7.
24 Cf. J. McGuckin, 'Origen's doctrine of priesthood', *Clergy Review*, 70 (Aug. 1985), pp. 277–86; ibid., 70 (Sept. 1985), pp. 318–25.
25 The mid-second-century *Martyrdom of Polycarp* already has a motif of the quest for the ashes as relics, and the third-century *Acts of Thomas* has dust from the martyred Apostle's tomb curing a child.
26 *ExM*, 30, p. 171.
27 Origen, *Homilies on Leviticus*, 2, *PG* 12, col. 418.

second as the passion of the martyr. This is ostensibly high praise indeed, in the tradition of Tertullian, where martyrdom is the second baptism. But again there is a sub-text, for these two ways are unrepeatable events, and he immediately goes on to discuss other 'repeatable' ways, such as the third remission being almsgiving, and others such as converting sinners, forgiving the wrong-doer, and abundant charity. This would suggest, once again, that while giving martyrdom a place of high honour, he deliberately qualifies its significance in the ordinary life of the Church. In the Leviticus homily he suggests that the death of the martyr has redemptive value for others beyond its merely exemplarist force. Here, I think, he is touching upon some of the reasons the devotion of martyrs was so prevalent among ordinary Christians. In his *Commentary on Judges* he develops this theme and explains it on the basis of Revelation 6.10, which speaks of the souls of martyrs gathered under the heavenly altar. Origen describes the martyrs as currently assisting in the heavenly sacrifices, and admits that their merits intercede for the faithful on earth and also confound the psychic power of the aerial demons.[28] Both attributes featured largely in the popular, or non-philosophical, devotion to the martyrs, and both explained why it was desirable to be buried next to their mortal remains, so that one could avail of their guidance on the Day of Resurrection, a movement which contributed to centralizing the *martyrium*, and thus the cult of martyrs itself, in the ordinary liturgical experience of Christianity.[29] The stress on the physical, however, made it a movement that Origen did not wish to assist.

Yet even when Origen had completed his literary work, some of the Church's major persecutions lay still in the future.[30] The generation between Origen and Athanasius saw the elaboration of new aspects of the role of martyrs, not least the emergence of the desert hermit as the martyr for a new age when martyrdom was thought to lie definitively in the past. The writings of Athanasius give some interesting evidence on these changes and return us directly to Alexandria, revealing some aspects of the physical cult that relate specifically to the Egyptian way of death.

[28] *Commentary on the Book of Judges*, homily 7, PG 12, col. 981; also in the *Commentary on John's Gospel*, 6.36, PG 14, col. 293.

[29] Cf. H. Delehaye, *Les Origines du culte des martyrs = Subsidia hagiographica*, 20 (Brussels, 1912); A. Grabar, *Martyrium: Recherches sur le culte des reliques et l'art chrétien antique* (College de France, Fondation Schlumberger pour les études byzantines), 2 vols (Paris, 1946).

[30] Those of Decius (249–51), Valerian (257), Diocletian [The Great Persecution (303–11)], and Maximin Daia (311–13).

ATHANASIUS *c.* 300–373

In a large body of writings Athanasius' references to the martyrs are surprisingly few.[31] In a sense it is a theme that hardly figures for him except in a stock manner, for their appearance signifies only three or four things as far as he is concerned. In the first place, and it is his main usage, the martyrs are legal witnesses to the truth; that is, he applies the predominant New Testament sense of the word. In addition to this, he continues the high literary theme of the martyrs as being philosophically constant in their fidelity to their tradition. These are his normal approaches. In addition, two other aspects complete the picture, though neither of them is uniquely Athanasian; the first is that the martyrs' courage is one of the signs that the new age of Christ has arrived, and with it a transformation of the old human nature. His several references to women martyrs in particular, as something *contra naturam* being a sign of something *supra naturam*, is indicative of this approach. The last aspect is his habitual designations of the martyrs as a class alongside the 'choir' of prophets and patriarchs. The latter is an evident liturgical usage,[32] but it is largely a literary topos for him.

We gain far more interesting indications if we turn to his specific treatise on the *Life of Antony*. The shift from martyrdom to asceticism is already under way. Indeed, our first conclusion must be that it is Athanasius himself who is clearly encouraging that shift and ensuring its long-term endurance in the Christian tradition. Reading Athanasius we might even forget that the Alexandrian Church, under the soon-to-be-martyred Bishop Peter,[33] has expressed its canonical disapproval of those who eagerly sought physical martyrdom instead of being content to follow the prudent example of the Lord who fled from Herod and had taught his disciples to flee, for there, in Athanasius, this very characteristic is approvingly attributed to the eponymous hero of the narrative.[34] But although Athanasius attributes this as high praise to Antony, we have to

---

[31] He has only sixteen references *in toto*. Cf. G. Muller, who lists them in *Lexicon Athanasianum* (Berlin, 1952), p. 877.

[32] Cf. *De incarnatione*, *PG* 25, cols 144, 145, 181, 189.

[33] Peter was martyred in 311 after five years in hiding. His *Canonical Epistle* was published in 306 against the background of grave troubles in the internal order of the Church, and the complications of the Melitian schism. *St Dionysius of Alexandria: Letters and Treatises*, ed. and tr. C. L. Feltoe (London, 1918).

[34] *Life of Antony* [hereafter *LA*], tr. R. T. Meyer, *Ancient Christian Writers*, 10 (Westminster, Maryland, 1950); cf. ch. 46, p. 59.

remember how different were his own judgements on these matters, for despite being a man of considerable courage, like Origen, he was a great taker to flight, not one to stand his ground unnecessarily and risk arrest or death. For both littérateurs discretion was certainly the better part of valour, and this meant that for both, their doctrinal work took precedence, was simply more important than the quest for martyrdom. The monk as the new martyr inherited several of the characteristics that went along with the title. Even so, it is extremely odd to find Athanasius labouring to present the illiterate Egyptian Antony as a sophisticated neophilosopher, confounding the pagan professors who come out to consult him in the desert. It would seem that the theme was so firmly established in the martyr tradition that Athanasius could not part with it, however ill-fitting the garment had now become.

In the *Life of Antony* it is often difficult to distinguish Athanasius from his subject.[35] Some of the long discourses attributed to the father of monks are, quite obviously, Athanasian treatises on different themes.[36] Other concerns of the *Vita*, such as Antony's constant obedience to the hierarchy of Alexandria[37] and the perfect Nicene orthodoxy of his faith,[38] are clearly Athanasian ideological devices, regardless of their historical accuracy. None the less, the fact remains that Antony was not a philosopher, or a theologian, or a hierarch of the Church of Alexandria; he was a simple, illiterate man who had lived in the desert and fought demons, until in the eyes of all the rural Christians of Egypt he was a supreme exorcist, seer, healer, and man of God. Such was the locus of spiritual power here that neither Athanasius nor any of his successors in Greek Alexandria could afford the monastic movement to develop independently of them. So it was that Egyptian peasant Christianity, with its heavily phenomenal approach, was rearticulated and brought into line by the Christian urban and literary tradition.

The demonology and consciousness of the body and its mortality are so vivid in the desert literature as to be almost distinguishing marks of the Egyptian Church. Antony, after his initial period of asceticism near to the village, withdraws to a necropolis to begin his real spiritual struggle. There

---

[35] Cf. H. Dorries, 'Die Vita Antonii als Geschichtsquelle', *NachGott*, 14 (1949), pp. 17–29; T. D. Barnes, 'Angel of light or mystic initiate? The problem of the Life of Antony', *JTS*, 37 (1988), pp. 353–68.

[36] The discourse to the monks (*LA*, 16–43) ostensibly spoken by Antony is clearly Athanasius' theoretical excursus on demonology, attributed to one whose own praxis against them was one of his famed attributes while alive.

[37] *LA*, 67, tr. Meyer, p. 76; cf. Athanius, *Letter to Dracontius*, ch. 9, *PG* 25, cols 531–4.

[38] *LA*, 69–70, tr. Meyer, pp. 78–9.

he is almost killed by the physical beatings he receives from the demons.[39] Returning to the battle, he demonstrates his superiority over demonic powers, and his reputation is secured. The necropolis, with its hieroglyphic designs, was a very useful residence for the desert hermit, but a dangerous and frightful place too, for the demonic figures with jackal heads, which were depicted manipulating the souls of the dead, betrayed those places as the particular haunts of demons who were bent on harrowing their victims in Hell. Such was the instinctive Christian rereading of the Egyptian death legends.

The connection between the body and the spirit was graphic and vital in rural Egypt. In other parts of the *Life of Antony*, incubation healings are described at his cell, and even the pagans came to consult the holy man.[40] We are a long way from Origen's spirituality here, and for the next few centuries Coptic Christianity would be at the forefront of the anti-Origenist movement—frequently to such an extent that hierarchs such as Theophilus and Cyril,[41] themselves no lovers of Origen's memory, had to censure villages and monasteries for their anthropomorphism.

The necropoleis of Egypt obviously contained mummies, which being consecrated to the demons in Christian estimate were themselves seen as vehicles of demonic power. The *Lives of the Desert Fathers* contain stories of monks proving their fearlessness before the corpses, and even of one redoubtable monk pulling a mummy from its niche to use as his pillow during the night. When the demon inevitably began to whisper to him threateningly in the darkness, he pummelled the mummy until he drove it out, thus plumping up his pillow in the process.[42]

It is in this environment that the body of the ascetic who has conquered the demons in life is also endowed with immense power in death. The early signs of incubation ritual around Antony have grown in extent by the time of Cyril of Scythopolis,[43] where such phenomena are freely attributed to the ascetics, living and dead. This development, in turn, had a very close reciprocal relation to the increasing cult of the martyrs' remains. Athanasius in his *Life of Antony* gives us some revealing

---

[39] These are the famous trials of St. Antony, *LA*, 8–10, pp. 26–9.

[40] *LA*, 48, pp. 60–1.

[41] For Theophilus, cf. J. Quasten, *Patrology*, 3 (Utrecht, 1975), pp. 101, 103; for Cyril, cf. *Letter to Calosirius*, in L. Wickham, *Cyril of Alexandria, Select Letters* (Oxford, 1983), pp. xxx–xxxi, 214–21.

[42] Cf. H. Leclercq, 'Momie', in G. Cabrol, ed., *Dictionnaire d'archéologie chrétienne et de liturgie*, 15 vols (Paris, 1907–53); W. H. Mackean, *Christian Monasticism in Egypt* (London, 1920).

[43] Cyril of Scythopolis, *The Lives of the Monks of Palestine* [mid-sixth century], tr. R. M. Price (Kalamazoo, 1991).

information about the connection when he narrates Antony's death scene.[44] He is clearly interested here in suppressing a customary practice in his local church, and his need to invoke the popular authority of Antony to bolster his disapproval gives some indication that he knew he was up against a widespread Christian devotion. Here we witness the cultural gap between Hellenized Alexandria and the peasant Coptic churches of Middle and Upper Egypt:

> The Egyptians have the custom of honouring the bodies of holy men with funeral rites, and wrapping them in linen shrouds, especially the bodies of the holy martyrs. They do not bury them in the earth but lay them on couches, and keep them with them at home, thinking in this way to honour the departed.[45]

Antony tells his disciples to bury his body in secret:[46]

> 'Be diligent in this, and if you have any care for me at all, or any regard for me as a father, do not allow anyone to take my body to Egypt, lest they should keep it in their houses.'[47]

At this juncture the body of the martyr and the ascetic become almost synonymous in a physical *cultus* that focuses on aspects brought together from both traditions—of persecuted martyr and desert ascetic. It focuses on prayers for intercession for the forgiveness of sin, prayers for healing, protection, and release from demonic oppression, as well as petitions for guidance for the future and the benefit of the saint's second sight.

In the following generation the assimilation is not only complete and harmoniously synthesized, but even the patriarch of Alexandria himself has come round to it, and in the instance of Cyril we see the Bishop acting as hierophant and intermediary between the martyrs and the faithful. Cyril, like Ambrose before him, and the Empresses Pulcheria and Eudocia in his own day, have visions and dreams that lead them to discover the

[44] *LA*, 90–1, pp. 94–6.
[45] *LA*, 90, p. 94.
[46] The motif of disciples burying the master's body is a common one in the literature, not so the motive Athanasius ascribes to the command. He lays great stress on the secrecy attached to the place: 'To this day only those two disciples know the place of burial', but there were traditions of Hilarion venerating the tomb shortly after Antony's death. In 561 the site was 'acclaimed', and the relics were transferred to Alexandria, hence to Constantinople in 635 after the Islamic invasion, and thence to France after the Crusades. Since 1491 the relics have been kept in the church of St Julien, at Arles, and thence partially distributed to Rome and other European churches in smaller reliquaries, one of which is in the present author's possession.
[47] *LA*, 92, tr. Meyer, p. 96.

sacred remains of 'forgotten' martyrs from the earlier generations and to construct splendid shrines to house them.[48] By the fifth century, then, the cult of the martyrs' and ascetics' relics represented such a clear locus of power, alongside that of the palpable political power of the monks who led the celebration of the cult, that no Byzantine leader of any acumen could afford to be aloof from it.

CONCLUSION

In short, the Christian tradition never failed to honour its martyrs. The devotion to their heroic memory extended first of all to belief in their intercessory power for the forgiveness of sins, and subsequently to an enduring belief in the validity of their heavenly intercessions at the altar of God. The attitude of the literate hierarchy to the martyrs was, however, one that carried with it a degree of ambivalence. In the literary tradition of martyr encomia, we can discern an attempt to offer praises while simultaneously qualifying the power the martyrs (and, by implication, confessors) might be thought to exercise in the affairs of the Church on earth. In the case of Egyptian Christianity, we see the cultural gap between the educated and the rural Christians expressing itself in clearly distinct attitudes to martyr veneration. The writings of Origen and Athanasius witness to the way in which the Church leaders of the third and fourth centuries tried to assimilate and direct popular forms of devotion. By the fifth century the process had been completed, and in such a way that through the physical *cultus* of relics the gap between the Hellenistic philosophical tradition and the common people's quest for the phenomenal had been so narrowed that even hierarchs and members of the imperial household could be found at the forefront of the new forms of devotion.

University of Leeds

---

[48] For Cyril's discovery of the remains of Saints Cyrus and John, the 'healing martyrs' or 'holy unmercenaries', cf. J. McGuckin, 'The influence of the Isis cult on St. Cyril of Alexandria's Christology', *Studia Patristica*, 24 (1992), pp. 191–9; for Ambrose's discovery dream for Saints Gervase and Protasius, cf. Ambrose, Epistle 22, *PL* 16, cols 1019–26; for Pulcheria's dream and discovery of the relics of the forty martyrs of Sebaste, and Eudocia's triumphant *adventus* from Jerusalem with the relics of the protomartyr, cf. K. G. Holum, *Theodosian Empresses* (London, 1982).

MARTYRDOM IN EAST AND WEST: THE SAGA OF ST GEORGE OF NOBATIA AND ENGLAND

by WILLIAM H. C. FREND

MARTYRS were the heroes of the Early Church. For a long period after the reign of Constantine until Benedictine monasticism took over their mantle, their lives and exploits provided a focus for the idealism of Christians in Western Europe. They represented the victory of human steadfastness and loyalty in defence of the faith triumphing over irreligious tyranny and the powers of evil. In the East, however, where Constantine had emphasized as early as 324 his complete rejection of the persecutions of his pagan predecessors, it was not long before memories of the past were transformed to meet other pressing needs of the day. Threatened first by Germanic and Slav invaders and then by the armies of Islam, Byzantine cities sought the protection of martyrs and the heavenly hierarchy that led from them through the Archangel Michael to the Virgin herself. In Nobatia, the northernmost of the three Nubian kingdoms that straddled the Nile valley between Aswan and a point south of Khartoum, the military martyrs, George, Mercurius, Theodore, and Demetrius seconded the endeavours of Michael and the Virgin to preserve the kingdoms and their Christian religion.

Though since 312 the Church had not suffered persecution (if one leaves on one side the short-lived repression under Licinius, 320–3, and the scattered mob outbreaks in Julian's reign, 361–3), the aura surrounding those who had died as witnesses for their faith remained fresh. In both parts of the Greco-Roman world the late fourth, fifth, and sixth centuries witnessed the preservation of the martyr's heroic deeds in vivid epic accounts of their sufferings and miraculous deeds, recounted in homilies and sermons on the day reserved for their memory. In the West where the State could still be equated with Babylon and the Church with Jerusalem,[1] and the legacy of hostility between the two persisted, veneration of the martyrs and their relics varied in intensity and significance. Among the Donatist majority in North Africa in the fourth century the martyr remained the permanent symbol of the struggle between the saints and

---

[1] For this theme, see J. van Oort's study of the genesis of Augustine's *De civitate Dei*, *Jerusalem and Babylon* (Leiden, 1991), esp. ch. 4.

the secular powers, now abetted by the 'traditor' Church, that is, the African Catholics. In 401, nearly a century after the conversion of Constantine, Petilian, Bishop of Constantine, could write to his clergy telling them that Christ had ordained that, 'we should undergo death for the faith', that 'Christianity made progress by the deaths of its followers', that it was the sign of 'perfect faith', and that the texts from John 12.24–5 ('Except a corn of wheat shall die . . .') still applied.[2] He was saying what the great majority of his hearers believed. No church or chapel in the Numidian heartland of Donatism lacked its tomb of martyrs, whether genuine or not, beneath their altars, containing relics continually dedicated and rededicated with elaborate ceremonies. To be buried in or around a martyr's chapel was a sign of honour.[3]

The more orderly outlook of Augustine respected the established relations of harmony between Church and State and emphasized the moral worth of the martyrs' heroic deeds. He could paint the sufferings of Perpetua and Felicitas in lurid hues, but he would also warn his hearers against over-triumphant praise of their exploits that could cause the sin of pride.[4] Crispina (also a Donatist heroine) exemplified abnegation of worldly desires as well as fortitude in the face of death.[5] The martyr's courage came from God and not himself.[6]

With the martyr's death no longer a possibility in Christian times, however, hagiographers gave free rein to their imaginations by painting horrific and revolting tortures to which their heroes were subjected, all the time, however, surviving to taunt and try their tormentors. The epic accounts preserved by Prudentius, c. 400, in his *Peristephanon* (On the Crowns of Victory) record folk-memories of martyrs' deaths a century or more previously. He shows how at this period stereotypes were emerging. Magistrates were always cruel and stupid, foils to the heroism of the youthful and often high-born confessors. The miraculous was accepted as a matter of course. Thus, Romanus denounces idolatry long after his tongue is said to have been cut out,[7] and Quirinus damns the pagan crowd while floating even though weighed down with rocks, drowned in the river into which he had been thrown.[8] Christians found themselves

[2] Augustine, *Contra litteras Petiliani*, ii.89.196, *PL* 43, col. 321.
[3] For many examples, see A. Berthier et al., *Les Vestiges du Christianisme antique dans la Numidie centrale* (Algiers, 1942), esp. Pt iii, Le Culte.
[4] Augustine, *Sermo*, 280,281,282, *PL* 39, cols. 1280–6.
[5] Ibid., 284.3, and in particular, through God's grace, an argument, therefore, against Pelagius.
[6] *Enarratio in Ps.* 120.13, *PL* 37, cols 1616–17.
[7] Prudentius, *Peristephanon*, ed. I. Bergman, *CSEL* 61, x, lines 6–10, 121ff.
[8] Ibid., vii.

reminded of heroic sacrifices in the past, but introduced also to a world of fantasy that contributed in some cases towards accepting alienation from the world in favour of a life dedicated to Christ and his martyrs.[9] No wonder the arrival of martyrs' relics in a Christian city, such as Rouen in c. 396, aroused immense enthusiasm.[10] These relics would cleanse the dark folk-memory of some grievous injustice in the past,[11] as well as guarantee their healing properties to the individual in need, and protection of the community against calamity. The possession, too, of the relics of a celebrated martyr raised the prestige of a town, such as Saragossa, and contributed to that sense of civic pride which would prevail against temporary havoc caused by barbarian invaders.[12] The cult of relics, even if criticized by worldly-wise clergy, such as Vigilantius,[13] played its part in anchoring permanently the hearts of Western provincials to Christianity immediately before the great barbarian onset of 407.

In the East, the memory of the martyrs provoked a similar idealism, but with rather different emphases. The epic accounts of martyrs' sufferings in the eastern provinces of the Empire if anything outdo their western counterparts in horrific descriptions of tortures.[14] Being boiled in oil, having all one's bones broken, swallowing molten lead, and day-long scourging were commonplaces among the hagiographers. So, too, were the miracles of healing and conversion of pagans performed by the martyr, as well as his ability to survive all that his torturers could do and leave the pagan ruler baffled and impotent. The martyr thus becomes a supernatural being, endowed with invincible powers designed to protect individuals and communities against their enemies. No city in the East could afford to be without its heavenly protector.

One might perhaps have expected the martyr in the Byzantine Empire to become identified with anti-State forces, as he tended to be in Donatist North Africa. But this was not the case. Peter Brown has reminded us that despite the unifying influence asserted by the Mediterranean itself, there were differences in attitude towards the holy in East and West.[15] In the

---

[9] Thus Paulinus of Nola threw up his career in imperial service in 395 to dedicate his life to tending the shrine of Felix of Nola, a reputed martyr under the Emperor Decius in 250. He died c. 431.

[10] Victricius, *De laude sanctorum*, i, *PL* 20, col. 443.

[11] P. Brown, *Society and the Holy in Late Antiquity* (London, 1981), p. 16.

[12] Prudentius, *Peristephanon*, iv, lines 53–7.

[13] Jerome, *Contra Vigilantum*, *PL* 23, written in 406.

[14] Many examples quoted by H. Delehaye, *Les Passions des Martyrs et les genres littéraires* (Brussels, 1921), pp. 273–87.

[15] Brown, *Society and the Holy*, pp. 166–95, in a distinguished essay, 'Eastern and Western Christendom in Late Antiquity: the Parting of the Ways'.

East, even though the Great Persecution had continued longer than in the West and had been more severe, Constantine was able to repudiate convincingly the actions and beliefs of his pagan predecessors in the Tetrarchy,[16] and ostentatiously reach reconciliation with confessors. More important, however, was the strong element of continuity in the East between pagan and Christian culture, represented by the role of classical philosophy in Christian education and the formulation of doctrine, and during the reigns of Constantine and Constantius II the gradual but lasting integration of Church and Empire. Eusebius of Caesarea was only following contemporary opinion in claiming that Constantine was 'most dear to God', and 'earthly representation of the Divine Word'.[17] It is not surprising, therefore, to find that the tradition of divine protection for civic communities, exemplified by 'Diana/Artemis of the Ephesians' (compare Acts 19.27) being attributed in Christian times to martyrs, apostles, or to the Virgin herself. At Constantinople the Virgin took on the role of divine protector, and through the inspiration of this belief the Avars were repelled in July 626, their leader, the Khagan, admitting that no one could fight against her.[18] She alone 'knew how to conquer'.[19]

Lesser cities benefited from the patronage of similar divine protectors, most effectively from Michael the Archangel and his heavenly assistants, the military martyrs. These were Demetrius, George, Theodore, and Mercurius, military commanders in the Roman army who were believed to have died in the persecutions of Decius or Diocletian rather than forswear their faith. In 626 the people of Thessalonica believed that the martyr Demetrius, a native of the fortress-city of Sirmium and hence transformed into a soldier, had saved their city from the Slavs.[20] Military prowess combined with martyrdom was to have a similar role in preserving the Christian churches and communities of Byzantium's distant

---

[16] Eusebius, *Life of Constantine*, ed. I. A. Heikel, *Die grieschischen christlichen Schriftsteller*, *Eusebius*, I (Leipzig, 1902), ii.49: 'No sympathy with the former emperors'.

[17] Eusebius, *Historia ecclesiastica*, X.9.6, and *De laude Constantini*, ed. Heikel, 1.6, Constantine, 'administering this world's affairs in imitation of God himself, receiving as it were a transcript of the Divine sovereignty'.

[18] See N. H. Baynes, 'The Supernatural Defenders of Constantinople', *Byzantine Studies and other Essays*, ch. 17 (London, 1955).

[19] George of Pisidia, *Bell Avar*, ed. A. Pertusi (Ettal, 1959), lines 1–9: see A. Cameron, 'Corippus' Poem on Justin II; a terminus of Antique Art?' in *Continuity and Change in Sixth Century Byzantium* (London, 1981), vi, p. 165.

[20] See V. Saxer, 'Demetrius the Martyr' in Angelo di Berardino, ed. and Adrian Walford, tr., *The Encyclopaedia of the Early Church*, 2 vols (Cambridge, 1991), and for his share of the patronage of the city with the Virgin and Theodore, E. Pelikanidou, 'Thessalonica' in ibid.

daughter state of Nobatia, and adding to the social cohesion the Christian faith provided.

Though beyond the boundaries of the Empire, Nobatia and its associate kingdoms of Makuria and Alwah lay within Alexandria's ecclesiastical sphere of influence. In the first part of Justinian's reign the Monophysite patriarchate there was practically unchallenged. Thus, when in 542 the Empress Theodora organized the despatch of a mission under the monk Julianus to Nobatia, the kingdom embraced Monophysitism and the leadership of Alexandria.[21] It resisted Justinian's effort to persuade its ruler to reverse his decision and accept the Council of Chalcedon. Despite some attempts in later centuries by the Chalcedonians (or Melkites) to penetrate Nobatia, Monophysitism remained the predominant religion of the kingdom through the nine hundred years in which Christianity lasted.

The material remains of this civilization had attracted archaeologists since the creation of the Anglo-Egyptian condominium in the Sudan in 1898.[22] It was, however, the building of the High Dam at Aswan in 1965 that united twenty-three nations in a concerted effort to survey, explore, and save as much of ancient Nubian civilization as possible, before all traces were submerged under the waters of Lake Nasser that formed behind the High Dam.[23] Among many sites excavated by the international teams were Q'asr Ibrim, entrusted to a small British team under the auspices of the Egypt Exploration Society, and Faras, some fifty-five miles to the south, where the Poles under Professor Kazimierz Michalowski had carried out a sensationally successful excavation. Both Faras and Ibrim were important administrative and ecclesiastical centres in the kingdom of Nobatia. The discoveries made at these two sites complemented each other. The hoard of liturgical, patristic, and biblical documents found in and around the cathedral at Ibrim provided a literary background to the superb frescos that had once decorated the walls of the cathedral at Faras.[24] Together they revealed a great deal about the abundant religious life of the Nubian Christians.

On 3 January 1964, working with Professor J. M. Plumley, the writer found a group of three fragments of manuscript beneath a pillar that had fallen across the floor of the cathedral at Ibrim. One of the manuscripts

[21] The story is told by John of Ephesus, *Historia ecclesiastica*, pt iv.27, ed. E. W. Brooks, *CSCO*, *Scriptores Syri* (Paris and Louvain, 1935–6).
[22] See W. Y. Adams, *Nubia, Corridor to Africa* (London, 1977), 71ff.
[23] Ibid., 81ff.
[24] Published by K. Michalowski, *Faras, Die Kathedrale aus dem Wüstensand* (Einsiedeln, 1967).

was a liturgical piece in Old Nubian, the second, a finely illuminated fragment of manuscript, showing a bishop seated, holding a Bible, with arm outstretched as though delivering a homily. The third, however, was practically a full page of manuscript of the *Acta* of St George, written in Greek majuscules, but in a typical Nubian hand.[25] Further discoveries of manuscript containing fragments of the *Acta* followed, until six pages could be reconstructed, as well as a number of small but useful pieces. Long examination of the fragments has shown that the Nubian version of the *Acta* belongs to one of the earliest cycles of the legend, and indicates that the Nubians at Ibrim retained many of the liturgical traditions prevalent in Egypt and in the Byzantine Empire generally, before the Arab conquest of Egypt in the 640s.[26]

The surviving fragments of the *Acta* show that St George was in fact associated both with Cappadocia and Lydda, in Palestine. The legend bears all the marks of a typical epic account of a martyrdom compiled any time between about 350 and 500. The story is recounted by Nubian documents, completed by the Coptic *Acta*, and two early medieval Byzantine cycles, known as the Paris Version and Athens Version respectively.[27] It tells how Georgius, the son of Gerontius, a wealthy Cappadocian of senatorial rank, was born in the reign of the emperor Aurelian (270–5). His father was a pagan, but his mother, Polychronia, was a Christian and had him secretly baptized. All seems to have gone well, however, until one day Gerontius went to sacrifice to the gods and Georgius refused to accompany him. There was a quarrel, but that night Gerontius was struck with a fever. Georgius promised his recovery and remission of all his sins if he accepted the God of the Christians. Gerontius did so, was baptized, and died shortly afterwards.

Georgius leaves Cappadocia to join the Emperor's service. The Ibrim documents do not name the emperor, but other versions call him 'King Dadianus' and even 'Diocletianus'. He prospers and is determined to apply to the ruler for promotion to the rank of *comes*. Dadianus has his court at Diospolis (Lydda), but on entering the city Georgius is horrified at the sight of temples to the gods, especially Apollo and Herakles. Meantime, the King has been enraged by the progress of Christianity among his subjects. He has issued a decree to the effect that all who worshipped 'him whom Mary bore' in preference to the gods of his Empire should be put to

[25] See W. H. C. Frend, 'Fragments of a version of the *Acta S. Georgii* from Q'asr Ibrim', *Jahrbuch für Antike und Christentum*, 32 (1989), pp. 89–104.
[26] My conclusions derived from a study of the *Acta S. Georgii*, ibid., pp. 103–4.
[27] Ibid., pp. 89–90, where I have also outlined the legend of St George given below.

death. Georgius has now abandoned his idea of promotion, but is denounced to the ruler as a Christian and summoned to his presence. An altercation follows, with Georgius challenging the King to prove that Apollo really did shake the heavens and perform other acts worthy of his title as a god. The King loses patience, and George is haled off to prison. The next page of the Ibrim manuscript series describes the tortures to which Georgius was subjected. They include scourging with scourges made of the entrails of oxen, scraping the wounds with hair-cloth, stretching on a gibbet, being fitted with iron sandals with spikes, and finally having his brains crushed in an iron clamp called a 'crow'. These follow the pattern of horrific tortures beloved of Byzantine writers of epic accounts of martyrdom,[28] beginning with Eusebius' account of the Martyrs of Palestine, and the persecution in Upper Egypt of the Coptic Christians under Maximin in 311–12, when terrible punishments were visited on those who defied the authorities.[29]

Miraculously, Georgius survives and is freed from prison (according to the Coptic *Acta*) by the Archangel Michael, thus demonstrating the link between Michael, as commander of the angelic host, and a military martyr, such as Georgius. The cycle of renewed appearance before the King, torture, and release happens three times; during the interval between each Georgius succeeds in preaching and converting many of Dadianus' subjects. The King then changes his tactics. Georgius is invited to the royal palace. There, however, he meets and secretly converts the Queen, while appearing to promise the King that he would do his bidding and worship Apollo in the main temple of the city.[30] He has meantime converted a widow and healed partially her son, who has been born lame, deaf, and dumb.

Accompanied by the child, Georgius now enters the temple which contains the statues of Apollo and Herakles. Instead of worshipping these, however, Georgius curses them. The demon inside the statue of Apollo complains that he had been imprisoned unjustly because he had quarrelled with the Archangel Michael in paradise because he refused to venerate Adam. The Ibrim manuscript records Georgius' dismissal of this excuse and his condemnation of the demon to the abyss. Similar treatment is meted out to Herakles, whom Georgius drags from the base of his statute with his military belt. Enraged, the temple priests seize and bind

[28] See Delehaye, *Les Passions*, pp. 279ff.
[29] Eusebius, *Historia ecclesiastica*, viii.9.4–5.
[30] For discussion of this incident and parallels in other epic martyrdoms for a pretended concession by the martyr, see Delehaye, *Les Passions*, pp. 263–4.

Georgius. He is again brought before the King, who upbraids him for his deceit. This time there is no escape; Georgius is beheaded, along with the Queen and several thousands of the King's subjects. In the East his day was fixed as 23 April, and he was regarded as a 'great martyr'.

So much for the legend, parts of which have been preserved on the Ibrim manuscripts. The place, however, of Georgius in the hierarchy of protecting saints in Nubia is illustrated on frescos that decorated walls of the cathedral at Faras. Here we see him standing in military uniform, with his *cingulum* (belt) prominently displayed, wearing a cloak over his shoulder, and holding a decorated oval shield in his left hand. His right hand holds a long spear with which he is piercing a malevolent-looking but indistinct figure at his feet.[31] At Faras, however, the chief protectors were the Virgin and the Archangel Michael, who is shown standing, like Georgius, as a warrior in armour, with a dark violet cloak across his shoulders, but ornamented with a black net pattern, and embroidered with pearls to denote his higher rank. He holds in his right hand, across his body, a formidable broadsword, sheathed, but ready for instant use.[32] No less than twelve similar representations were found among the frescos at Faras.[33] Michael, in fact, took second place only to the Virgin, shown on the frescos as protector of the kingdom and its individual rulers.[34]

The cathedral at Ibrim was dedicated to the Virgin, and so, as at Constantinople itself and at Faras, she was the supreme protectress of the Church and people. At Ibrim and Faras she was associated also with military martyr-saints, and that included St George. How the cult of the saint spread from Diospolis, in Palestine, to Nubia is unknown, but of its popularity there can be no doubt.[35] In the Church of Abdullah Nirqi, north of Abu Simbel, about thirty miles south of Ibrim, the military saints, Mercurius, Theodore, George, and Demetrius share the available wall space with a representation of the Theophany.[36] Further south, at the

[31] Michalowski, *Faras* (Warsaw, 1974) (updated version of work referred to above, n. 24), p. 116, pl.14. The identification is very probable rather than absolutely sure, as the name below the word 'Hagios' on the fresco has been lost.
[32] Ibid., pl.41.
[33] Listed, ibid., p.324.
[34] Ibid., pl.34, and 66, and p. 273.
[35] For the spread of the cult of St George throughout the Byzantine East, see H. Delehaye, *Les Origines du culte des martyrs* (Brussels, 1933), pp. 86, 175, 184, 186, 213, 237.
[36] Paul van Moorsel, Jean Jacquet, and Hans Schneider, *The Central Church of Abdullah Nirqi* (Leiden, 1975), pp. 109–11.

monastry of el Ghazali, in the Sudan, a monk scratched an invocation to Georgius and the prophets on a vessel he was using.[37]

Where does the dragon slain by the mounted figure fit in? George is usually shown standing, though he is mounted on a fresco from Abd el Qadir, north of Faras.[38] There is a possibility, however, that in course of time his exploits became conflated with those of another military martyr, Mercurius, with whom he was sometimes associated. At Ibrim, fragments of the *Acta Mercurii* were also discovered on the same level and not far from those of the *Acta S. Georgii*.[39] Mercurius was believed to have been a general in the time of the Emperor Decius (249–51) and martyred on his refusal to sacrifice to the gods. In legend, recorded on the pages of the *Acta* discovered at Ibrim, he appears in a vision to the monastic leader Pachomius, who is stated to be entertaining Athanasius. The incident is placed during Athanasius' exile by the Emperor Julian in 361 (though Pachomius had died in 346). In the vision, which is hidden from Athanasius, Mercurius described to Pachomius how he had been sent by God to mete out justice to the apostate Emperor, and how he had killed him with his long spear, on which the apostate's blood still ran. The frescos at Faras show vividly how the Nubians imagined the scene. Mercurius is seated on a magnificently caparisoned steed, transfixing with a long spear a crouching figure at the horse's feet.[40] If one were to alter 'Mercurius' to 'George' one would have the well-known representation of the saint, mounted, and spearing or riding down the dragon of paganism, which the apostate Emperor represented.

The Nubian kingdom, like the Byzantine Empire itself, was protected by a hierarchy of heavenly beings, starting with Christ himself and the Virgin, and descending through the Archangel Michael to the military martrys believed to have suffered for their faith at the hands of persecuting emperors. They not only assured protection for the weak, but resistance to all attacks against the Christian state whencesoever these might come, whether from pagans or Muslims. It was in this guise that the cult flourished in medieval Nubia, increasingly threatened by Muslim tribes

[37] P. L. Shinnie and H. N. Chittick, *Ghazali, a Monastery in the Northern Sudan* = Sudan Antiquities Service, Occasional Papers, no. 5 (Khartoum, 1961), p. 98.

[38] See U. Monneret de Villard, *Nubia Mediaevale*, 4, plate clxxv (Cairo 1935–53), and for a possible second example, from Abdullah Nirqi, P. van Moorsel, 'Gli scavi olandesi in Nubia' = *Acta of the Seventh International Congress of Christian Archaeology* (Barcelona, 1972), p. 594, plates 7 and 8.

[39] W. H. C. Frend, 'Fragments of an *Acta Martyrum* from Q'asr Ibrim', *Jahrbuch für Antike und Christentum*, 29 (1986), pp. 66–70.

[40] Described and illustrated in Michalowski, *Faras*, pp. 200–3, and plates 42 and 43.

from across the desert to the west. The cult also flourished in Palestine during the crusading era, and the Crusades seem to have ensured its popularity finally in England.

George had not been wholly unknown in England before that time. A version of his *Acta* had been translated into Anglo-Saxon, and a church at Doncaster dedicated to him in 1061.[41] But it was the returning crusaders, particularly, it would appear, from the Third Crusade, in which Richard I shared the leadership, that established his cult firmly in England, along with that of St Margaret of Antioch and other Byzantine saints. The process, however, was gradual. At that time Edward the Confessor was England's patron saint, and in 1222, St George's Day was only declared a minor holiday at the Synod of Oxford. In the Hundred Years War, however, the red cross on a white background associated with St George became a sort of uniform worn by English soldiers. Edward III founded the Order of the Garter in 1347 under the patronage of St George. Finally, in 1415, while Henry V was away fighting in Normandy, Archbishop Chichele declared that St George's Day, 23 April, should become one of the chief holy days in the year. 'St George for England' replaced 'St Edward the Confessor' as the national patron. Though sometimes challenged,[42] the symbol of steadfastness, endurance, and loyalty to a right cause, returning to the original martyr-tradition current in Western Europe, would seem not unreasonable qualities to demand of a major nation in the world today embodied in its patron saint.

University of Glasgow

---

[41] See *ODCC*, 'George St. Patron Saint of England and Martyr', from which the information in this paragraph is taken.

[42] Thus, the somewhat desultory correspondence in *The Times*, 24 April–10 May 1992. Interestingly, while the claims of King Edward the Martyr, murdered at Corfe Castle in 978, and even St Radegund, were pressed as substitutes, no attempt was made to restore Edward the Confessor, while the record of the discovery of the actual MSS of the *Acta S. Georgii* at Q'asr Ibrim was refused publication.

BEDE AND THE MARTYRDOM OF
ST OSWALD

by VICTORIA A. GUNN

IN recent years there has been a definite growth of interest in the royal
saints of the early medieval period. Specifically from France,
academics such as Robert Folz, and from Britain, historians such as
David Rollason and Susan Ridyard, have turned their erudition and their
pens to elucidate this topic.[1] The scope of this paper will be to examine
one of the saints who has been of interest to these authors: St Oswald of
Northumbria. That Oswald was considered a saint from early after his
death is not in any doubt: Bede's *Historia ecclesiastica* makes this quite clear.
Rather, this paper turns its attention to the nature of that sanctity in order
to decide whether or not Bede actually perceived Oswald as a martyr. To
look at this question this study will firstly compare Oswald with other
Anglo-Saxon martyr-kings. Secondly, it will observe what comments
Bede actually makes concerning Oswald's sanctity. And, finally, it will see
how he is categorized and discussed in other contemporary and near-
contemporary texts.

Predominantly, Oswald has been regarded as a martyr-king—an
individual whose sanctity was attained through dying for the Christian
faith. In Folz's categorization Oswald is *Le Roi martyr de la foi.*[2] Ridyard,
too, has accepted Oswald's classification as a martyr, stressing that sanctity
was attained at the moment of death.[3] To illustrate this she has compared
Bede's depiction of Oswald to Abbo's portrayal of St Edmund, emphasizing that in both cases sanctity was achieved through death at the hands of a
pagan.[4] Indeed, Colgrave also emphasized the importance of death,
stating that Oswald had perished fighting against his foes, as Edwin had,
and the enemy in each case was the heathen Penda, 'so that each was in a
sense a martyr who died fighting for the Faith.'[5]

---

[1] Robert Folz, *Les Saints Rois du moyen âge en occident vi*^e*–xiii*^e *siècles*) = *Société des Bollandistes,
Subsidia Hagiographica*, 68 (Brussels, 1984); D. W. Rollason, 'The cults of murdered royal saints
in Anglo-Saxon England', *Anglo-Saxon England*, 11 (1983), pp. 1–22; Susan J. Ridyard, *The
Royal Saints of Anglo-Saxon England* (Cambridge, 1988).

[2] Folz, *Les Saints Rois*, p. 46.

[3] Ridyard, *Royal Saints*, p. 240.

[4] Ibid., p. 93.

[5] Anonymous of Whitby, *Vita sancti Gregorii Magni*, ed. and tr. B. Colgrave, *The Earliest Life of
Gregory the Great* (Cambridge, 1985), p. 43.

However, there appear to be problems with these theories. Firstly, Ridyard's comparison of Oswald and Edmund does not accentuate the different circumstances which prevailed at the death of each of these saints. Edmund, according to Abbo, had been defeated and was required to submit to the pagan leader Hinguar. Oswald's position, however, appears to be less defensive. The geographical location of Maserfelth, that is Oswestry, if correct, would suggest that Oswald did not fall at the hands of an invading pagan, but was, in fact, the aggressor.[6] Moreover, the location of Oswestry may suggest that Oswald was attempting to prevent a coalition between the Welsh and the Mercians—a coalition that was perhaps more a direct threat to his own power than to the faith of his 'nation'. Seen in these terms, Ridyard's comparison of Oswald with Edmund and the consequent concentration on the act of death seems too simplistic.

Secondly, Colgrave's argument implies that the deaths of both Edwin and Oswald were directly attributable to Penda. However, in Edwin's case, Bede makes it quite clear that Penda was merely Cædwalla's assistant.[7] This is crucial for it meant that ultimately Edwin died at the hands of a Christian not a pagan, for Bede states that Cædwalla professed to be a Christian.[8] (It also means that Folz's categorization of Edwin is, in fact, wrong, for Edwin is not *Le Roi martyr de la foi*, rather he is more like *Le Roi massacre*!)[9] The basic argument of Colgrave, like that of Ridyard, is insufficiently nuanced.

The apparent lack of acknowledgement of the complexities surrounding the deaths of Oswald and Edwin, found in both Ridyard and Colgrave's assumptions, perhaps relates to the inherent inconsistencies in Bede's own narration of these events. For example, when discussing Edwin's death, as has been shown, Bede's emphasis is placed on the Christian Cædwalla. Yet, when noting Oswald's death, Bede appears adamant that he was killed by 'the same heathen people and the same heathen Mercian king as his predecessor Edwin'.[10] These two statements essentially contradict each other. The latter allows for an interpretation such as that of Colgrave, centred on the idea that both died for a Christian

[6] J. M. Wallace-Hadrill, *Bede's Ecclesiastical History of the English People: a Historical Commentary* (Oxford, 1988), p. 102.
[7] Bede, *Historia ecclesiastica* [hereafter *HE*], ed. B. Colgrave and R. A. B. Mynors, *Bede's Ecclesiastical History of the English People*, OMT (1969), ii, 20, p. 202.
[8] Ibid.
[9] Folz, *Les Saints Rois*, p. 45.
[10] Bede, *HE*, iii, 9, p. 242.

cause at the hands of pagans. The former one, however, suggests that at least in Edwin's case this was not so.

With regard to this, and in direct relation to Ridyard's comments, there is another point to note concerning the location of Maserfelth. If the historian's assumptions are correct, and Oswald was essentially the aggressor rather than the defender at this battle, it is interesting that Bede clearly avoids giving his audience this impression. In fact, by centring his discussion on the fact that it was heathen people that killed Oswald, he gives the impression that they were the attackers, not Oswald. Indeed, this is further emphasized by Bede in book iv, chapter 14, where he indicates once again that Oswald was slain in battle by the heathen. One could easily infer from this that Oswald was martyred, and yet Bede stops short at explicitly saying this. Nowhere in the *Historia ecclesiastica* does Bede specifically designate Oswald as a martyr. In essence, it would seem that Bede is attempting to generate the image of martyrdom whilst failing to bring it to its full conclusion. The inconsistencies of Bede's text, and the modern historian's reception of these complexities, may well lie behind the problem of over-simplification.

In actuality, a closer comparison with Abbo's Edmund reveals the distinct difference of emphasis in the two texts. In general, Bede's reference centres on what Oswald achieved during his life and then the power he had following his death. Abbo's text, on the other hand, concentrates on the immediate events which led to Edmund's martyrdom.[11] Accordingly, though he gives a brief characterization of Edmund's kingship, the text moves on quickly to discuss the slayers of Edmund,[12] Edmund's consultation with his bishop as to how he should respond to Hinguar's demands, and his decision to ignore the bishop's advice to submit—a decision which would ultimately lead to Edmund's martyrdom.[13] And in chapter 10 the martyrdom itself is concluded with an exact statement concerning Edmund's passion and entry into the heavenly court.[14] Essentially Edmund's sanctity was, as Ridyard noted, attained at the moment of death.

Bede, however, offers far less information on the events which led to Oswald's death. Indeed, the passage directly referring to this reads more like an obituary notice than a portrayal of martyrdom. Bede merely notes

---

[11] Abbo, *Passio sancti Eadmundi regis et martyris*, ed. M. Winterbottom, *Three Lives of English Saints* (Toronto, 1972), pp. 67–87.
[12] Ibid., for characterization, see pp. 70–1; for the slayers, p. 71.
[13] Ibid., p. 74.
[14] Ibid., p. 79.

that at the end of his nine-year reign, Oswald was killed by the heathens at a great battle at Maserfelth on 5 August, in the thirty-eighth year of his life.[15] One could argue that the martyrdom is implied by the repetition of the word 'paganus' in this notice. However, as has already been noted, no explicit reference to martyrdom is made here or elsewhere in the text in relation to Oswald.

If one compares this with texts which relate to the martyrdom of other kings one can see just how unusual this is. Thus Abbo's Edmund is consistently referred to as a martyr: for example, in the preface he is introduced as 'Eadmundus rex et martyr', and his entry into heaven is likewise as 'rex et martyr'.[16] Following his death his body is referred to as 'sacratissimum corpus martyris'.[17] In chapter 12 he is referred to as 'beatissimum regem et martyrem ⟨Eadmundum⟩'.[18]

In fact, if one compares Oswald with other Anglo-Saxon martyr-kings the omission of 'martyr' terminology relating to him becomes even more unconventional. For example, in Byrhtferth of Ramsey's *Vita Oswaldi* it is specifically noted that King Edward was predestined and foreordained by Christ to share a martyr's dignity.[19] Following his death he was called 'martyr of God'.[20] Moreover, the concentration in this text again directly relates to the immediate events which led to Edward's death and a description of this death. In this sense it is more like Abbo's Edmund than Bede's Oswald. As one would expect, the vocabulary of martyrdom is also found in Edward's *Passio*.[21] Essentially the death of a king by martyrdom was too important an event to go unmentioned without the rhetoric of martyrdom accompanying it.

The same emphasis on the phraseology of martyrdom can be seen in the opening paragraphs of Simeon of Durham's *Historia Regum*. Even though this text is twelfth century in date, it has been shown that this passage may derive from an eighth-century text.[22] In other words, a text which was contemporary with that of Bede. Here Simeon is concerned with recording the martyrdom of the royal saints Æthelberht and

[15] Bede, *HE*, iii, 9, p. 242.

[16] *Passio Eadmundi*, pp. 67, 79.

[17] Ibid., p. 80.

[18] Ibid., p. 81.

[19] Byrthferth of Ramsey, *Vita Oswaldi*, ed. D. Whitelock, *EHD*, 1, 2nd edn (London, 1979), pp. 911–17, p. 914.

[20] Ibid., p. 915.

[21] *Passio et miracula sancti Eadwardi regis et martyris*, ed. C. E. Fell, *Edward King and Martyr* = Leeds Texts and Monographs, ns 3 (Leeds, 1971), see, for example, p. 11.

[22] Rollason, 'Cults of murdered royal saints', p. 5.

Æthelred. Accordingly, he notes from the outset that it is fitting to commence his history with their lives and triumph of martyrdom, demonstrating the glory of their holiness.[23] This alone perhaps emphasizes the status of such royal martyrdom. Simeon then continues to describe their lives in two main sections. The first centres on their lives and emphasizes the type of characteristic associated with 'spiritual martyrdom' which is found described in such works as Gregory the Great's *Dialogues*.[24] Thus they strove to live as virgins, had the distinction of unconquerable patience, and were adorned with the grace of unwearying prayer. Nevertheless, Simeon makes it clear that these virtues are offered merely to give a foretaste of those 'plants of virtue rooted within them'.[25] The second, longer section of the text concentrates in detail on the immediate events which led to their martyrdom.[26] Once Simeon has introduced this, the terminology of martyrdom abounds in relation to these two individuals.

One could, of course, argue that these texts bear little relationship to Bede's *Historia ecclesiastica*, for they are not necessarily contemporary with his text. Nevertheless, the critical point pertains to the status of the martyr. From his reading of Eusebius, Augustine, and Gregory the Great, Bede could not have failed to see the importance of the martyr in the hierarchy of the saints. Indeed, in Gregory's *Dialogues* one is shown a martyr-king in the case of Hermangild.[27] This chapter offered Bede a model of a king who died for his faith. Interestingly, however, it was a model Bede did not use. In fact, like the Edmund and Edward texts, Gregory's emphasis is on the immediate events which led to Hermangild's death. Thus Gregory narrates Hermangild's resolution not to abandon his Christian faith to Arianism, his consequent deposition as king by his Arian father, and finally details concerning his torture and death. Hermangild, too, is called 'king and martyr'.[28] The above evidence, hopefully, shows that, firstly, Bede's omission of rhetoric relating to a martyrdom of Oswald was very unusual if he was considered a martyr. And, secondly, that the status of martyrdom was such that even a highly

---

[23] Simeon of Durham, *Historia regum*, ed. T. Arnold, *Symeonis Monachi opera omnia*, RS, 75, 2 (1885), p. 4.

[24] Cf. Carole Straw, *Gregory the Great: Perfection in Imperfection* (London, 1988), p. 98; Gregory the Great, *Dialogues*, tr. O. J. Zimmerman, *The Dialogues of Gregory the Great* (New York, 1959), p. 160.

[25] Simeon, *Historia regum*, p. 5.

[26] Ibid.

[27] Gregory the Great, *Dialogues*, pp. 166–8.

[28] Ibid., p. 167.

selective author such as Bede would have been unlikely to leave out the designation of martyrdom.

This is, in fact, shown clearly if one compares Bede's description of Oswald with that of the cases of three martyrs which he describes in his *Historia*. Thus in book i, chapter 7, Bede discusses the 'blessed martyr' St Alban. St Alban is consistently and specifically referred to as a martyr and, like the stories of Hermangild, Edmund, and Edward, Bede concentrates on offering details both of the martyrdom and the immediate events which led to it. Of the execution, Bede noted that at the place where the valiant martyr was beheaded he received the crown of life which God has promised to those who love him.[29]

Again in book v, chapter 10, in describing Hewald the White and Hewald the Black, Bede speaks definitely of their martyrdom. He concentrates on the events which led to it and emphasizes the torture of Hewald the Black before his death. Bede then goes on to show how 'Heavenly miracles were not lacking at their martyrdom.'[30] As in the other cases of martyrdom relevant to this paper, Bede follows the typical pattern in his depiction of these martyrs—so why is this not evident in his portrayal of Oswald?

Ultimately the historian is perhaps wrong to look at Oswald's sanctity solely in the terms of martyrdom. Indeed, it is time to question whether or not Bede actually considered Oswald to be a martyr. Folz has queried whether the omission of the topoi and title of the martyr was merely a personal preference on Bede's part.[31] In fact, it may be possible to go further on this point and argue that at the time Bede wrote his *Historia* even the sources of information from which he drew were reserved about designating Oswald a martyr. It was predominantly from Hexham that Bede gathered most of his information on Oswald.[32] Monks at Hexham were crucial to the development of the cult, and this is especially true of one man who had connections with Hexham: Willibrord. Yet, although his calendar mentions Oswald, the martyrology which appears to be closely connected with it does not. This is important for, as Wilson has indicated, the *Martyrologium Hieronymianum*'s contents were probably related to the area from which Willibrord came.[33] If Hexham designated

[29] Bede, *HE*, i, 7, p. 32.

[30] Ibid., v, 10, p. 482.

[31] R. Folz, 'Saint Oswald roi de Northumbrie: étude d'hagiographie royale', *AnBoll*, 98 (1980), pp. 49–74, at p. 59.

[32] D. P. Kirby, 'Bede's native sources for the *Historia Ecclesiastica*', *BJRL*, 48 (1965), pp. 341–71, at p. 350.

[33] *The Calendar of St Willibrord*, ed. H. A. Wilson, *HBS*, 55 (1918), p. xiv.

Oswald a martyr, surely it would be fair to assume that either Willibrord or one of his assistants would have added him to this martyrology.

The miracle stories relating to Oswald also appear carefully to avoid offering the idea that Oswald was a martyr. This is most startlingly clear in relation to the miracles which occur at the site at Denisesburn, where Oswald erected his pre-battle cross. The point here is that this site and event had nothing to do with Oswald's death. Indeed, Bede notes that, 'Innumerable miracles of healing are known to have been wrought in the place where they prayed, doubtless as a token and memorial of the king's faith.'[34] The implication is clear—these miracles were as a direct result of Oswald's faith during his life, not because of a sanctity achieved through death. This is further emphasized in Bede's description of the miracle cure of the boy at Bardney, who suffered with recurrent fevers. This boy was advised to sit by Oswald's tomb, where his fever was miraculously kept at bay. The important point for this paper is that Bede concludes:

> It is not to be wondered at that the prayers of the king who is now reigning with the Lord should greatly prevail, for while he was ruling over his temporal kingdom, he was always accustomed to work and pray most diligently for the kindgom which is eternal.[35]

Once again the implication is clear. This miracle occurred because of what Oswald did whilst he was alive.

Such an emphasis is also visible in Bede's discussion of those miracle stories which actually related to Oswald's death. Thus the miracles at the place where he died occur not because of his death at the hands of a pagan, but because 'while he was *alive* he never ceased to care for the sick and the poor.'[36] Moreover, when discussing the miracle of the Briton's horse at Maserfelth, Bede notes that this 'intelligent man' conjectured that the patch which was greener and more beautiful than the rest of the field was where 'some man holier than the rest of the army had perished'—that is to say that Oswald's sanctity was already established during his life.[37]

However, the *Historia ecclesiastica* is not the only text which avoids introducing an idea of Oswald as a martyr. Both Wormald and Folz have commented on the fact that Oswald is absent from Bede's martyrology.[38]

[34] Bede, *HE*, iii, 2, p. 214.
[35] Ibid., iii, 12, p. 250.
[36] Ibid., iii, 9, p. 242.
[37] Ibid., iii, 10, p. 244.
[38] P. Wormald, 'Bede and Benedict Biscop', in G. Bonner ed., *Famulus Christi: Essays in Commemoration of the Thirteenth Centenary of the Birth of the Venerable Bede* (London, 1976), pp. 141–69, at p. 151; Folz, 'Saint Oswald roi', p. 59.

Indeed, in his autobiographical note at the end of the *Historia*, Bede stresses that he has written a martyrology of the feast-days of the holy martyrs. A martyrology in which he carefully tried to record everything he could learn 'not only on what date, but also by what kind of combat and under what judge they overcame the world.'[39] If one observes this statement, the absence of Oswald, if Bede thought he was a martyr, seems unusual. This is made all the more poignant when one realizes that Bede does discuss the martyrdom of St Alban, the two Saints Hewald and St Æthelthryth in his martyrology.[40] That is to say that even though the text is primarily concerned with martyrs and saints of the Persecution and Late Antique period, Bede did include those martyrs he had commented specifically on in his *Historia ecclesiastica*.

Nevertheless, one ninth-century manuscript of this martyrology does have certain later additions, including, under August, an entry for the 'holy king Oswald'.[41] The interesting point here is that Oswald is not accorded the title 'martyr', whereas other martyrs, in general, are named and then classified by this title. This lack of categorization becomes more significant when one looks at other near-contemporary martyrologies and calendars. For example, the second-earliest prose calendar from England after that of Willibrord, number 63 in the Digby Collection (a ninth-century text assigned to the north of England), also classifies Oswald only as 'Saint Oswald—king'.[42] A similar entry is recorded in the early-ninth-century Irish *Martyrology of Tallaght*.[43] Again Oswald is witnessed but not categorized.

The lack of classification is most stark, however, in three other texts. The first is the Irish *Martyrology of Oengus*. This martyrology, which is contemporary with that of Tallaght, makes the following ambiguous comment on Oswald's death date: '... with holy Oswald whom we implore, the noble overking of the Saxons.'[44] Clearly there is no inference of martyrdom to be drawn from this. The second and third of these texts are, in fact, related, as in the case of Oswald one appears to draw on the

---

[39] Bede, *HE*, v, 24, p. 570.

[40] H. Quentin, *Les Martyrologes historiques du moyen âge. Etude sur la formation du martyrologe romain* (Paris, 1908), pp. 105–6.

[41] Vatican City, Biblioteca Apostolica Vaticana, MS Vat. Pal. 833; Quentin, *Les Martyrologes*, pp. 20–1.

[42] *English Kalendars before A.D. 1100*, ed. F. Wormald, *HBS*, 72 (1934), pp. 1–13, at p. 9; cf. David Rollason, *Saints and Relics in Anglo-Saxon England* (Oxford, 1989), p. 73.

[43] *The Martyrology of Tallaght*, ed. R. I. Best and H. J. Lawlor, *HBS*, 68 (1931), p. 60.

[44] *Felire Oengusso celi de: The Martyrology of Oengus, the Culdee*, ed. W. Stokes, *HBS*, 29 (1905), p. 174.

other.[45] The *Martyrology of Usuard*, the source for which was the *Martyrology of Wandelbert*, mentions Oswald on 5 August, stating that he was 'saint Oswald, king of the English, whose acts are commemorated by the venerable priest Bede in his history of his people.'[46] In fact, the *Martyrology of Wandelbert* is even less specific in its statement, and focuses merely on mentioning Oswald as pious king of the English, whose merit and virtue are remembered.[47] The point is that, on the whole, all three of these martyrologies stressed the individual's suffering and martyrdom for Christ, where it had occurred, but such a notice is missing for Oswald. He is remembered for his acts, his miracles, and his virtue—not for martyrdom. Essentially, the knowledge concerning Oswald of the authors of these texts gave them no reason to portray him as a martyr.

Further to this, it is important to note that other near-contemporary sources which discuss Oswald (and are often drawing on Bede's description) also underplay the idea of martyrdom, if they imply it all. Accordingly, in his York Poem, Alcuin emphasizes the merits and sanctity of Oswald during his life and his outstanding virtue.[48] Indeed, Alcuin, like Bede, stresses that 'The greatness of Oswald's faith and the power of his merits gained added lustre after his death through his miracles.'[49] Fundamentally, his sanctity increased after his death, but existed during his life, and did not relate to the manner of his death. A similar emphasis can be seen in Aelfric's depiction of Oswald in his *Lives of the Saints*.[50] These writers had been influenced by their reading of Bede's work, from which they did not find reason to conclude that Oswald was a martyr.

In essence, the title of this paper, 'Bede and the martyrdom of St Oswald', is a misnomer. It is clear from a comparison of Bede's text with other sources relating to the martyrdom of kings that there is little reason to think that Bede (and possibly those developing the cult in its early stages) perceived Oswald as a martyr. Although the evidence of martyrologies and calendars may be inconclusive, the silence of the *Historia ecclesiastica* in terms of the terminology and topoi normally associated with martyrdom is stark and more than likely deliberate. Bede

---

[45] J. Dubois, 'Le Martyrologe metrique de Wandelbert', *AnBoll*, 79 (1961), pp. 257–93, at pp. 281–92; J. Dubois, *Le Martyrologe d'Usuard: Texte et commentaire*, Société des Bollandistes (Brussels, 1965), p. 279.

[46] Dubois, *Le Martyrologe d'Usuard*, p. 278.

[47] Ibid., p. 279.

[48] Alcuin, *Versus de patribus regibus et sanctis eboricensis ecclesiae*, ed. Peter Godman, *Alcuin: the Bishops, Kings, and Saints of York = OMT* (1982), pp. 26, 28.

[49] Ibid., p. 30.

[50] Aelfric, *Lives of the Saints*, ed. W. W. Skeat, 2 (London, 1900), see, for example, p. 129.

did not consider Oswald to be a martyr. It appears that in his portrayal of Oswald, Bede, in fact, was offering a unique picture of sanctity—a sanctity based on the intensity of Oswald's faith during his life. And, as is seen in the sources which deal with Oswald after Bede's death, it was a sanctity that could not easily be placed in the existing categories of martyr, confessor, or virgin.

University of Glasgow

THE FRANKS, THE MARTYROLOGY OF USUARD, AND THE MARTYRS OF CORDOBA

by JANET L. NELSON

The bodies of holy martyrs, which the Romans buried with fire, and mutilated by the sword, and tore apart by throwing them to wild beasts: these bodies the Franks have found, and enclosed in gold and precious stones.

FOR the author of the longer prologue to *Lex Salica*, writing in 763–4, in the reign of Pippin I, the first king of the Carolingian dynasty, the Franks' devotion to the martyrs was the secret of their success. It proved the strength of their Christian faith; it was at once the manifestation and the explanation of special divine favour. *Vivit qui Francos diligit Christus....*[1]

The Franks had some justification for priding themselves on their special devotion to the cults of martyrs. Gregory of Tours, whom the Franks by the Carolingian period had come to see as the narrator of their history, also wrote in praise of martyrs.[2] That early, the feats of martyr saints were marked in Gaul by readings of *passiones* recounting their sufferings and deaths. Gregory somewhat disingenuously says that this was done to encourage the devotion of rustics.[3] But bishops, including Gregory himself, were enthusiastic devotees of martyr cults, especially of martyred bishops (since *passiones* continued a thriving genre in the seventh century not least because the activities of Frankish kings and nobles ensured a supply of new episcopal victims, it was not, in fact, only the

---

[1] 'Christ lives who loves the Franks...', *Lex Salica, 100-Titel Text*, prologue, *MGH.LNG*, IV, 2, ed. K. A. Eckhardt (Hanover, 1969), pp. 6–8.

[2] *In gloria martyrum* [and other hagiographical works], ed. B. Krusch, *MGH.SRM*, I, ii (Hanover, 1885), Eng. tr. R. van Dam (Liverpool, 1988), with an excellent introduction, esp. pp. 11–15, on Gregory's placing of martyrdom 'in the context of the ecclesiastical community'. For Gregory and his work in general, see G. de Nie, *Views from a Many-windowed Tower* (Amsterdam, 1987), and W. Goffart, *Narrators of Barbarian History* (Princeton, 1988), ch. 3.

[3] *In gloria martyrum*, c.63, p. 81, tr. van Dam, p. 87, '... mos namque erat hominum rusticorum ut sanctos dei quorum agones relegunt attentius venerentur.' On ways of hearing such stories and making spiritual use of them, see P. Brown, *The Cult of the Saints* (London, 1981), pp. 79–84.

Romans who made martyrs[4]) and of martyrs whose relics were housed in episcopal churches.[5] Frankish kings and nobles, as well as bishops, 'made' martyr cults in the other sense too: their acquisitiveness for relics was one aspect of a more general acquisitiveness. In his *Histories*, Gregory records how the Merovingian King Childebert I in 542 attacked Zaragoza and brought back the robe (*stola*) of St Vincent in triumph to Francia, founded the monastery of Saint-Germain-des-Prés and endowed it with relics, including Vincent's robe.[6] Monasteries patronized by the Frankish elite thus were natural centres for the production of martyrologies: it was probably between 615 and 629, the heyday of Merovingian power, that an expanded version of the so-called *Martyrologium Hieronymianum* was produced at Luxeuil, in Burgundy.[7]

Between about 838 and 855, no fewer than four substantial martyro-logies—by Florus, Hrabanus, Wandalbert, and Ado—were produced, respectively, at Lyons, Mainz, Prüm, and Lyons again.[8] Neither the timing—the reigns of Louis the Pious and Lothar I—nor the locations were coincidental; any more than the production of the two great universal histories of the later Carolingian period in the same area was coin-cidental.[9] In the Frankish heartlands, called after 843 the Middle King-dom, lay the religious foundations where a sense of Frankish identity was most strongly cultivated, and with it a sense that the Frankish realm was now the cultic centre of the Christian world. Thanks to massive transfers of relics into Francia in the reigns of Charlemagne and Louis the Pious, the Franks could now see themselves as the special custodians of the martyrs—and the martyrs as the special custodians of the Franks.[10] The

---

[4] For seventh-century *passiones* and their context, see P. J. Fouracre, 'Merovingian history and Merovingian hagiography', *PaP*, 127 (1990), pp. 3–38.

[5] See P. Brown, 'Relics and social status in the age of Gregory of Tours', in his collected essays, *Society and the Holy in Late Antiquity* (London, 1982), pp. 222–50.

[6] *Libri Historiarum X*, ed. B. Krusch and W. Levison, *MGH.SRM*, 1, 2nd edn (Hanover, 1937–51), III, c.29, pp. 125–6.

[7] Ed. G. Rossi and L. Duchesne, *Acta Sanctorum Bollandiana*, Nov. 2, 1 (Paris, 1894). Against Duchesne's attribution to Auxerre and the late sixth century, see B. Krusch, 'Nochmals die Afralegende und das Martyrologium Hieronymianum', *Mittheilungen des Instituts für oester-reichische Geschichtsforschung*, 21 (1900), pp. 1–27, at pp. 9–27. J. Dubois, *Les Martyrologes du Moyen Age latin* (Turnhout, 1978), p. 33, holds to Duchesne's views, but without mentioning the arguments of Krusch.

[8] On these, see W. Wattenbach, rev. W. Levison, *Deutschlands Geschichtsquellen im Mittelalter* [hereafter Wattenbach-Levison], 1 (Weimar, 1952), pp. 60–1; Dubois, *Les Martyrologes*, pp. 37–45; J. M. McCulloh, 'Historical Martyrologies in the Benedictine Cultural Tradition', in W. Lourdaux and D. Verhelst, eds, *Benedictine Culture 750–1050* (Louvain, 1983), pp. 114–31.

[9] H. Löwe in Wattenbach-Levison, 3 (Weimar, 1957), pp. 328–9.

[10] P. J. Geary, *Furta Sacra. Thefts of Relics in the Central Middle Ages* (Princeton, 1978, rev. edn, 1990). Cf. also M. Heinzelmann, *Translationsberichte und andere Quellen des Reliquienkultes*

political dimension was implicit in the imperial relic collection presided over by Charlemagne's sister at Chelles, with its carefully itemized pieces of martyrs from Italy, from southern and western Gaul, from Bavaria, Saxony, and Northumbria.[11] Imperial control was explicit in the decree of the Council of Mainz in 813 that no relics be authenticated without the say-so of the *princeps*;[12] and the propagandistic function of relic acquisition was especially clear in the years from 824 to 830, as Louis the Pious, Lothar, and the clerics who served (and sometimes tactfully admonished) them sought to reaffirm the special bond between the Franks and Rome.[13]

Usuard, monk of Saint-Germain-des-Prés, drew on all the martyrologies I have already mentioned (and also that of Bede) to produce one of his own—which was destined to become the most widely-diffused and influential martyrology of Western Christendom for the rest of the Middle Ages and beyond. Not all who drew on it acknowledged, or perhaps knew, that they were doing so. If all the later martyrologies derived the whole or in part from Usuard's were added up, they would, according to Usuard's editor, run to 'hundreds, even thousands of manuscripts'.[14] By cutting down on the wording of previous martyrologists, Usuard saved some space, so that, while still producing a relatively compact book, he could provide martyrs for every single day of the year, and brief biographical details for many of them. His field of vision spanned the universal Church, from Asia to Ireland and Scotland: though Usuard's sources had included Patrick and Bridget, his was the first continental martyrology (thanks probably to oral information from Irish monks) to contain entries for Fintan, Ciaran, Cainnach, and—last but certainly not least—Columba.[15]

(Turnhout, 1979), pp. 31–42, 94–9; and the useful list of no fewer than 74 items assembled by H. Fros, 'Liste des translations et inventions de l'époque carolingienne', *AnBoll*, 104 (1986), pp. 427–9.

[11] See J. Laporte, 'Reliques du Haut Moyen Age à Chelles', *Revue d'art et d'histoire de la Brie et du pays de Meaux*, 37 (1986), pp. 45–58.

[12] *MGH.L*, 3, *Concilia*, II, p. 272.

[13] See J. Fried, 'Ludwig der Fromme, das Papsttum und die fränkische Kirche', in P. Godman and R. Collins, eds, *Charlemagne's Heir. New Perspectives on the Reign of Louis the Pious* (Oxford, 1990), pp. 231–73, at p. 263.

[14] J. Dubois, *Le Martyrologe d'Usuard* (Brussels, 1965), p. 14; cf. ibid., p. 5, where Dubois stresses that Usuard's work was the 'essential link in the chain of martyrologies' leading from the Early Church to modern times. The Roman Martyrology produced in 1583, declared official by the pope in 1584, and (after successive revisions) still in use, was based on Usuard's Martyrology. See also for a concise account of Usuard's work, Dubois, *Les Martyrologes*, pp. 45–56.

[15] See Dubois, *Martyrologe*, p. 101; and for Usuard as abbreviator, pp. 105–10.

Clearly no further justification is needed for talking at this conference about the Martyrology of Usuard. But what about the immediate historical context of its production? It carries a preface, addressed to Charles the Bald, *dominus regum piissimus*, and *sapientissimus rex*: 'It should be understood [says Usuard] that I undertook this work through no *jeu d'esprit*, but rather, as was right, I obeyed your commands which as ever were directed to the welfare of the Catholic faithful.'[16] The work was dedicated to the King, because he had commissioned it. Should we take that literally? No, says Dom Dubois. 'Ce que nous savons du personnage de Charles le Chauve interdit de supposer qu'ait eu le moindre compétence pour apprécier le valeur et l'intérêt des martyrologes. . . .'[17] So the dedicatory preface reveals merely a *bon courtisan* making his pitch for patronage? Nevertheless, Dubois is clear that a copy of the work was presented to Charles—and that royal approval helps explain its exceptionally wide diffusion.[18] In what follows, I want to argue that Charles did indeed solicit the Martyrology of Usuard and that the commission makes sense in terms both of the work's general context, by reference to contemporary Frankish piety and political ideas (the two were of course inseparable), and of the work's specific context, by reference to Charles's, and Usuard's, interest in Spain and in the martyrs of Cordoba.

First, then, Charles was a plausible connoisseur of martyrologies. There was nothing perfunctory about his cultivation of martyr saints. Among earlier medieval rulers, Charles was exceptional in the intensity and range of his devotion and his grasp of its political uses. He had learned some lessons at his father's court, where Einhard glossed the significance of the arrival from Rome of the bones of SS Petrus and Marcellinus, and where Hilduin, in the 830s, explained the special potency of St Denis, 'the outstanding martyr'. As king, Charles would endow the monastery of Saint-Denis on an unprecedentedly lavish scale, instituting commemorative feasts for himself and his close kin.[19] His consecration as King of the

---

[16] Dubois, *Martyrologe*, p. 144, '. . . ut sciretur non me in hoc usum levitatis conamine, sed potius vestris, ut erat dignum, paruisse imperiis catholicorum fidelium solito consultentibus utilitati.'

[17] Dubois, *Martyrologe*, p. 38. Cf. the characteristically measured response of P. Riché, *Instruction et vie religieuse dans le Haut Moyen Age* (London, 1981), ch. 12, p. 41: 'ce jugement me paraît sévère.'

[18] Dubois, *Martyrologe*, pp. 17–18.

[19] I do not share Dubois' view, *Martyrologe*, pp. 118–19, that Usuard's treatment of St Denis, namely, the provision of two distinct feasts for the bishop of Athens (3 Oct.) and the bishop of Paris (9 Oct.), thus flouting the identification between the two made by Hilduin, argues against Charles as primary sponsor of the Martyrology's production and diffusion. As Dubois acknowledges, Saint-Germian and Saint-Denis were rival establishments (hence Usuard's

Franks took place in the Church of St Stephen the Protomartyr, at Metz. Hincmar, drawing this to the King's attention, and reminding him of his father's tribulations, struck a resonant chord: for Charles's personal piety, as reflected in his private prayer-book, centred on the likening of his own 'wounds' to Christ's, and on self-identification with the suffering David whose humiliation was a necessary route to salvation.[20] Over eighty per cent (122 out of 149) of the saints whose names appear in Charles's charters, because their churches were beneficiaries of his generosity, were martyrs listed in Usuard's Martyrology.[21] As for the personal acquaintance with the tradition of Frankish devotion to the martyrs, Charles very probably knew Gregory's work and (like his father) possessed a copy of *Lex Salica* (including the longer prologue), as, certainly, did leading members of the Frankish aristocracy.[22] If Charles wanted a martyrology, that was in line with his perception of the protective power of the martyrs and of the way martyr cults consolidated the bond between the Franks and their kings. Charles's concern had a further dimension. Previous martyrologies had been produced in the Middle Kingdom of his brother Lothar, and notably at the great centre of Lyons. Lothar died in 855. In commissioning Usuard not long after that date, Charles was staking his own claim to Lothar's inheritance as patron and as imperial head of the Carolingian house.

Even before the 850s, however, Charles had taken a keen interest in the politics of the Ebro valley region. It was dominated in the ninth century by a local *muwallad* (Muslim convert) family, the Banu Kasi, over whose successive leaders the Umayyad regime in Cordoba rarely managed to assert its control. As the long reign of the amir Abd al-Rahman II (822–52) drew to a close, the Banu Kasi were more often than not in rebellion. In

---

implicit rejection of new claims for St Denis). Charles successfully sought the benefits, and the services, of both—and celebrated Denis's feast on 9 October. Dubois' research on the manuscripts of the Martyrology shows that, in addition to the copy (plus dedication) presented to Charles, Usuard's 'original', Paris, BN, MS. lat. 13745 (without dedication), was kept at Saint-Germain, where revisions were entered (probably by Usuard himself) through-out the 860s. Dubois' argument that Usuard was already interested in martyrologies (and necrologies), and had been preparing materials for years before the late 850s seems very plausible, but strengthens, in my view, rather than weakens, the case for a royal commission to complete the work.

20 For further references on Charles's piety, see J. L. Nelson, *Charles the Bald* (London, 1992), pp. 15, 85.
21 Dubois, *Martyrologe*, pp. 139–40.
22 See R. McKitterick, 'Charles the Bald and his library: the patronage of learning', *EHR*, 95 (1980), pp. 28–47; *The Carolingians and the Written Word* (Cambridge, 1989), pp. 60, 239–40, 246–9. Also Riché, *Instruction*, chs 7 and 8.

the 840s, the head of the family, Musa ibn Musa, lord of Tudela, sought an alliance with Charles: that is the probable explanation of the arrival of a Cordoban embassy at Rheims in 847 'to seek a peace with Charles'.[23] The next year, there was Cordoban backing for a rebellion in the Frankish-ruled Spanish March, which resulted in the expulsion from Barcelona of the governor whom Charles had appointed there. More serious still, the rebels included the count of Gascony, and, it seems, supported Charles's nephew and rival, Pippin, who until 849 had been a serious contender for the kingdom of Aquitaine. Only in 850 did Charles's men recover control of Barcelona.[24] It was at this point that the martyr movement began in Cordoba.

This movement certainly arose, in part, from the religious concerns of a small group of Cordoban Christians, whose activities were recorded by a local priest named Eulogius.[25] The growing appeal of Arab culture to members of the Christian elite, and the growing number of converts to Islam, seemed to require a drastic, and dramatic, response. Eulogius' friends involved themselves in public debate with Muslims, denounced the Prophet, and thus sought, and achieved, martyrdom. Between 850 and 857 there were forty-four Cordoban martyrs.

It has been suggested that 'the beginnings of the movement were largely accidental',[26] and previous commentators have dwelled (some more sensitively than others) on the religious aspects of the martyr movement.[27] It is, of course, written up by Eulogius almost entirely in

[23] *Annales de St Bertin*, ed. F. Grat, J. Vielliard, and S. Clémencet (Paris, 1964), p. 53, tr. J. L. Nelson, *The Annals of St-Bertin* (Manchester, 1991), p. 64. For the Banu Kasi, see R. J. H. Collins, *Early Medieval Spain, Unity in Diversity* (London, 1983), pp. 190–2, 233–4. On Musa ibn Musa, the essential study is C. Sanchez Albornoz, 'El tercer rey de España', *Cuadernos de Historia de España*, 49–50 (1969), pp. 5–49.

[24] See Nelson, *Charles the Bald*, p. 161. A key source on these events is a letter written by the Cordoban priest Eulogius to the bishop of Pamplona, ed. in J. Gil, *Corpus Scriptorum Muzarabicorum* [hereafter *CSM*], 2 vols (Madrid, 1973), 2, *Ep.* iii, pp. 497–503.

[25] Eulogius, *Memoriale Sanctorum*, ed. Gil, *CSM*, 2, pp. 366–459: Book i includes theological justification (aimed probably against local sceptics) for the cult of confessors and martyrs who 'were not dragged violently to martyrdom but came of their own accord' in protest at, for instance, the harsh treatment of church property; books ii and iii consist largely of the martyr acts proper. In the *Liber apologeticus martyrum*, ed. Gil, *CSM*, 2, pp. 475–95, written near the end of his life, Eulogius returned to the problem of voluntary martyrdom. For his *Documentum Martyriale*, see below, n. 28. E. P. Colbert, *The Martyrs of Cordoba* (Washington, 1962), offers an excellent discussion of the texts. See now also the remarkable study of R. B. Wolf, *Christian Martyrs in Muslim Spain* (Cambridge, 1988).

[26] Collins, *Early Medieval Spain*, p. 213.

[27] A. Cutler, 'The ninth-century Spanish Martyrs' Movement and the origins of Western Christian missions to the Muslims', *Muslim World*, 55 (1965), pp. 321–39, interestingly brings out eschatological aspects, and draws parallels with thirteenth-century Franciscans' ideas of

religious terms, as *acta martyrum*, with the characteristic traits of the genre: plenty of direct speech, circumstantial detail, military imagery, family drama, women.[28] At the same time, Eulogius addressed himself very seriously to the theological problem of voluntary martyrdom, and conscientiously explained away the absence of miracles associated with the martyrs' deaths.[29] But there are signs that the movement had a political context, and that that context involved the Franks. In 848, as the Cordoban embassy was returning (or had just returned) from Francia, Eulogius set off from Cordoba for Francia in search of his brothers. In a long letter recording his abortive journey (he could get no further than Zaragoza), Eulogius explained that his brothers had been exiled, apparently a short while before, and had fetched up in the East Frankish kingdom of Charles's brother and at that time close ally, Louis the German.[30] Exile smells of politics. From 850 to 852 Charles was involved in further intrigues with Musa ibn Musa. The alliance seems finally to have paid off when, thanks to Musa's pressure, the count of Gascony yielded to Charles and handed over Pippin of Aquitaine into captivity in Francia.[31] The next evidence for Frankish interest in Spain comes some five years later with the sending of a pair of monks from Saint-Germain-des-Prés to seek the body of St Vincent at Valencia.[32] On the way, they

---

mission. For a survey of the historiography and reflections on the martyrs' religious motives, see Wolf, *Christian Martyrs*, chs 3 and 9.

[28] Eulogius' *Documentum Martyriale*, ed. Gil, *CSM*, 2, pp. 459–75, was a treatise of encouragement specifically written for two women who sought martyrdom. It needs further study for what it suggests of the gender dimension to martyrdom and martyrology. Wolf, *Christian Martyrs*, pp. 65–7, cites relevant material, but neglects the dimension. It is not neglected, in the case of the rich later medieval evidence, by Miri Rubin, below, pp. 153–83.

[29] In the *Vita* written by his friend Paul Alvar soon after Eulogius' own martyrdom in 859, he is called *fauctor* [*sic*] *anelantissimus martirum*, c. 13, ed. Gil, *CSM*, 1, p. 338. Wolf, *Christian Martyrs*, pp. 77–104, rightly stresses the differences between the situation of the martyrs of Cordoba and those of the Early Church, and convincingly explains these in terms of divisions within the Cordoban Christian community: there was no collective sense of persecution to generate a receptive Christian 'audience'. (Cf. below, p. 76, and n. 44.) Wolf's concluding argument (pp. 107–19) that the Cordoban martyrdoms were provoked by profound anxieties about the preservation of Christian religious identity within Muslim society, is interestingly developed but at bottom less radical than he seems to claim. Less convincing (and unnecessary to that argument) is his contention that Eulogius, and the martyrs whose literary memorial he produced, had very different concerns. The *Documentum* is relevant here: see above, n. 28.

[30] *Ep.* iii, cc. 1, 6, ed. Gil, *CSM*, 2, pp. 497, 499–500. See also Paul Alvar, *Vita Eulogii*, c. 9, ed. Gil, *CSM*, 1, p. 335.

[31] Nelson, *Charles the Bald*, p. 162.

[32] Aimoin, *Translatio SS. Georgii, Aurelii et Nathaliae*, PL 115, cols 939–60. Aimoin, a monk of Saint-Germain-des-Prés, was Usuard's former teacher; Löwe, in Wattenbach-Levison, 4 (Weimar, 1974), p. 579.

learned that the body was no longer at Valencia (it had already been forcibly removed by the bishop of Zaragoza, who was keeping Vincent under an assumed name to deter other interested parties[33]). Instead, they were told, relics of new martyrs could be obtained in Cordoba.

One of those relic-seekers from Saint-Germain was Usuard; and the story of his Cordoban journey was recorded from his own account by his fellow monk Aimoin.[34] What it clearly shows (though this emerges less clearly from the retellings of twentieth-century hagiographers[35]) is the intimate involvement in the mission, from start to finish, of Charles the Bald. His *auctoritas* sent the two monks off,[36] and it surely lay behind their first destination—going to Spain from Paris by way of Beaune, in Burgundy, would otherwise have been a bit like heading for John o'Groats by way of Beachy Head. It happened that at Argilly, near Beaune, was the residence (*villa*) of Hunfrid, recently invested by Charles with lands and office in Burgundy and on the Spanish March;[37] also that Hunfrid had already been in contact with, indeed entered into a treaty (*foedus*) with, 'Abdiluvar', the leading man in Zaragoza, and equipped Usuard with a letter of recommendation to him. When the monks reached Zaragoza (having received more help *en route* at Barcelona from the local count, an appointee of Charles), an interpreter was available to translate Hunfrid's letter, and the local ruler 'although a barbarian faithfully obeyed his ally's command' and found the monks a group of travelling companions setting out for Cordoba—where they duly arrived on 17 March 858. Thanks to the help of the local bishop, they acquired the relics of three martyrs, George, Aurelius, and Natalie,[38] then they asked the bishop to parcel the relics and close them with his own seal 'and address them to King Charles'.[39] Returning via Zaragoza, where they were given letters for Hunfrid, and a safe-conduct, they again made for Hunfrid's *villa* in Burgundy, where they were joyfully received. Thence

---

[33] According to the slightly different version of this story by the same author, Aimoin, in the *Translatio Beati Vincentii*, PL 126, cols 1014–26, an Aquitanian monk's vision ensured that Vincent's relics were identified: they ended up in Aquitaine, at Castres (dep. Tarn): see Geary, *Furta Sacra*, pp. 61–2.

[34] See above, n. 30.

[35] B. de Gaiffier, 'Les Notices hispaniques dans le Martyrologe d'Usuard', *AnBoll*, 55 (1937), pp. 268–83; Dubois, *Martyrologe*, pp. 93–6, 128–32.

[36] *Translatio*, c. 1, PL 115, col. 941, and for the rest of the journey, see cc. 2–15, cols. 941–8.

[37] On Hunfrid's career, see further below, p. 79.

[38] Eulogius, *Memoriale Sanctorum*, II, c. x, ed. Gil, CSM, 2, pp. 416–30, describes these martyrdoms at length (Natalie, Aurelius' stalwart wife, is here called Sabigotho).

[39] PL 115, c. 11, col. 946, '. . . sub assignatione Karoli regis'.

they made it back to Francia,[40] where in due course they were received by the King:

> It is impossible for us to express how delighted the glorious King Charles was at the martyrs' arrival, when he had read over to himself the accounts of their passions. He was happy because Gaul had proved worthy during the period of his reign to receive such flowers . . . But he did not neglect to choose Mancio to go to Cordoba and search out on the spot the truth of what had happened. When Mancio came back, the king learned what had been omitted from the martyrs' deeds before and what was worth recording by memory or in writing.[41]

Given the genre of our information, it's not surprising that the religious aspect of these transactions takes centre stage. But the name Mancio hints at another kind of significance: this man can probably be identified with the Mancio who in the 860s was at Charles's court, along with other young nobles (they included several future bishops), and from 867 to 877 served as a royal notary.[42] The use of such a man as an emissary suggests a mission of some political importance, and that had surely been true of Usuard's mission too.

What were Charles's motives? He had had little choice over involvement in and across the Pyrenees. Once Pippin of Aquitaine had found support in that region, Charles was bound to look for counter-allies there. But the policy had a history. As a boy, Charles would have learned of successful Frankish interventions in Spain in Merovingian times; and he had his head stuffed full of his grandfather's exploits—including the story of the Roncesvalles campaign. No reader of Einhard (and Charles *was* a reader of Einhard) could fail to see the benefits to the Franks of plunder and tribute. After 843 Charles had only one frontier that seemed to offer any prospects of that sort—a Pyrenean frontier. What is only intermittently recorded by contemporary writers who aren't primarily interested

---

[40] Usuard's return is noted as a final entry under 858 in the *Annales de St Bertin*, ed. Grat, p. 79, tr. Nelson, p. 89.

[41] *Miracula* (book iii of the *Translatio*), c. xxviii, *PL* 115, col. 957. Mancio witnessed two fresh martyrdoms in Cordoba.

[42] I accept the identification with the Mancio who was one of the comrades of Radbod, future bishop of Utrecht, *Vita Radbodi Traiectensis episcopi*, *MGH.SS*, XV, p. 569. Here Mancio is said to have been the future bishop of Châlons-sur-Marne (893–908): see R. McKitterick, 'The palace school of Charles the Bald', in M. T. Gibson and J. L. Nelson, eds, *Charles the Bald. Court and Kingdom*, 2nd edn rev. (London, 1990), pp. 326–39, at p. 329. For Mancio as notary, see G. Tessier, *Receuil des actes de Charles II, le Chauve*, 3 vols (Paris, 1943–55), 3, pp. 78–9.

in these areas remote from Francia, can, in fact, be traced as a thread running through Charles's reign. He knew enough about the Umayyad regime in Cordoba to exploit its weaknesses, notably its lack of control in the Ebro valley. Conversely, the amir knew enough about Charles's tactics to be anxious to forestall his interventions—hence the rich gifts sent to Charles in 863 and 865.[43]

Now I am certainly not claiming that the Cordoban martyrs were some kind of fifth column. I do think, however, that the problems of the Umayyad regime were such that at least a faction of Spanish Christians saw sense in a resistance movement, and that the timing of their action was not fortuitous. In fact, Eulogius himself at one point suggests that political circumstances were part of the picture. He writes of 'rebellion in the provinces', of hostility against the amir Mohammed (852–86) on the part of his own people, because of his 'avarice and the tributes imposed on the Christians'.[44] Clearly Mohammed's regime in its early years looked distinctly shaky.[45] In his letter to Bishop Wiliesind of Pamplona, written c. 852, Eulogius compared his own sufferings 'under the wicked empire of the Arabs' to Wiliesind's enjoyment of 'the lordship of a Christian prince'.[46] Was the implicit aspiration here more than a pious hope? Still further north, in the land of the Franks, there may have been what seemed to Eulogius quite promising possibilities. After 849 Charles the Bald had sufficient authority in Aquitaine, and on the Spanish March, and sufficiently powerful agents in those areas, to intervene repeatedly across the Pyrenees, encouraging rebellion against Cordoba. In the longer term, Charles might have hoped to extract regular gifts from Cordoba or, at least, from the lords of the Ebro valley—a kind of *paria* system *avant la lettre*. No frontier offered better prospects. If Charles had such dreams, he was in good company: his father Louis the Pious had written to the

---

[43] *Annales de St Bertin*, 863, 865, ed. Grat, pp. 102, 124, tr. Nelson, pp. 110, 129: 'camels carrying couches and canopies'.

[44] Eulogius, *Memoriale Sanctorum*, III, cc. iv, v, pp. 441–3: 'Even the amir's concubines, so they say, hate him. . . . He also cut the soldiers' pay.' Eulogius saves his fiercest denunciations, though, for the Christian tax-farmers recruited by the amir: a significant comment on the prevalence of collaborationist attitudes among the local Christian elite. For Christians in the Cordoban bureaucracy, see Wolf, *Christian Martyrs*, pp. 11–14.

[45] The instability of the Cordoban regime in the ninth century is now penetratingly discussed by Wolf, *Christian Martyrs*, pp. 15–20, and by R. Fletcher, *Moorish Spain* (London, 1992), ch. 3. Though Wolf, p. 18, discusses the implications of an alliance between Toledans (perhaps including Christians and muwallads) and the Christian king of Asturias, Ordoño I, against Cordoba in 852–4, Frankish contacts are unmentioned in this context.

[46] *Ep.* iii, c. 9, ed. Gil, *CSM*, 2, p. 501. for the kingdom of Pamplona in the ninth century, see Collins, *Early Medieval Spain*, pp. 249–51.

leading men and the people of Merida in 826 in very similar circumstances: he sympathized with their subjection to unjust taxes—and
encouraged them to resist. Further, Louis had seen the possibility of co-
ordinating a Meridan rebellion with his own military efforts to quell
unrest in the Spanish March: 'We shall send an army next summer to our
March', he told the Meridans, 'and it will wait for you to tell it the right
time to move forward.'[47] Only with hindsight can we dismiss all this as a
chimera.

Usuard's mission represented, at one level, Charles's political response
to the martyr movement: the encouragement of dissidents, the
strengthening of a chain of command between the King's Frankish
power-base and Frankish magnates down in the Languedoc and the
south-west—who, in turn, had their own networks of intrigue and
influence straddling the Pyrenean frontier. But Charles set his sights
wider still: he would take responsibility for the *utilitas catholicorum
fidelium*[48]—that is, of Latin Christians at large. Such concerns had already
led Charles to commission a range of expert opinions on the burning
theological issue of the 840s and 850s: Predestination. Uniquely among
Carolingian rulers, Charles could appreciate both the doctrinal problem
and its political implications—the threat to social order, to *princeps* as well
as to *episcopus*.[49] His theologians believed him capable of understanding
the 'mysteries of divine wisdom' (*divinae sapientiae mysteria*).[50] They
expected him to act as arbiter.

In the 840s and 850s the *utilitas catholicorum fidelium* was also under
threat beyond—but tantalizingly *just* beyond—the frontiers of Charles's
share of the Frankish realm, in Spain.[51] In 847, according to the *Annals of
St-Bertin*, 'all the Christians in that realm', threatened by persecution, sent
Charles a tearful petition requesting his protection.[52] The author of the
Annals at this point, Prudentius, Bishop of Troyes, was himself of Spanish

---

[47] Louis' letter, curiously neglected in recent historiography, was preserved among Einhard's
letters in a unique manuscript, ed. K. Hampe, *MGH.Ep*, V, i (Berlin, 1898), pp. 115–16.
Though the editor dates it '830 *in*?' Colbert, *Martyrs*, p. 134, more plausibly dates it to 826, and
also notes that while Hampe rightly accepted the manuscript's 'Merida', earlier editors, in-
credulous at the idea of Frankish intervention in south-western Spain, emended to 'Zaragoza'.

[48] See above, n. 16.

[49] Hincmar, *Third Treatise on Predestination*, *PL* 125, col. 386.

[50] Ratramnus, *On Predestination*, *PL* 121, col. 13. The key study is D. Ganz, 'The Debate on
Predestination', in Gibson and Nelson, eds, *Charles the Bald*, pp. 283–302.

[51] Cf. *Annales de St Bertin*, 843, ed. Grat, p. 45, tr. Nelson, p. 56: Charles's kingdom extended
'usque ad Hispaniam'.

[52] *Annales de St Bertin*, 847, ed. Grat, p. 54, tr. Nelson, p. 64, with n. 1 (where, however, it is
wrongly suggested that the Cordoban martyr movement was already under way at this date).

parentage, and well-informed on Spanish affairs. We should take this information seriously (and perhaps no less seriously Prudentius' attribution of a role in the threatened persecution to a Frankish convert to Judaism, the former palatine clerk Bodo, who in 839 had established himself in Zaragoza[53]). Whether the activities of Eulogius and his friends were quite what Charles had had in mind is another question: living martyrs have minds of their own, which makes them hard for authorities (including those on their side) to control. By the late 850s it was a matter of naming and claiming.[54] If sponsoring Usuard's expedition promised political as well as spiritual benefits for Charles, so, too, did the commissioning of Usuard's Martyrology. Dom Dubois has been able to show that Usuard wrote the core of the work not long after his return from Spain,[55] and before he received news of Eulogius's martyrdom, which happened on 11 March 859,[56] while various scrapings-out and writings-in in Usuard's manuscript show successive additions through the 860s. The Martyrology's production can be set still more firmly in its historical frame. In 858 Charles faced the stiffest tests of his reign: he was campaigning against Northmen ensconced near Paris when, at the beginning of September, his realm was invaded by his brother Louis the German. At the turn of the year Charles overcame his enemies and achieved a kind of restoration, which he himself attributed to the intercession of martyr saints. His commission to Usuard, and his reception of the work, would fit well in the winter of 858–9 and the spring of 859 respectively. From now onwards Charles began very seriously to contem-

---

[53] *Annales de St Bertin*, 839, ed. Grat, pp. 27–8, tr. Nelson, p. 42. Bodo's ability to influence Cordoba is taken seriously by H. Löwe, 'Die Apostasie des Pfalzdiakons Bodo (838) und das Judentum der Chasaren', in G. Althoff et al., eds, *Person und Gemeinschaft im Mittelalter. Karl Schmid zum fünfundsechzigsten Geburtstag* (Sigmaringen, 1988), pp. 157–69, who points, illuminatingly, to a wider universe of relations between Jews, Muslims, and Christians, spanning the Black Sea (the Jewish kingdom of the Chasars) and the Mediterranean, within which Bodo's influence at Cordoba could become credible.

[54] The process whereby martyrs are recognized and appropriated is illuminatingly discussed in the contribution of Miri Rubin to the present volume, below, pp. 153–83, while Stuart Hall, above, pp. 2–3, points out the Early Church's difficulty in controlling living martyrs (but cf. Eulogius' *Documentum*, above, n. 28—were women easier, or less easy, than men for (male) 'namers' to control?).

[55] Usuard left Cordoba on 11 May 858, and finally arrived back to Esmans (where the community of Saint-Germain was in temporary residence) on 20 October 858; Aimoin, *Translatio*, c. 11, *Miracula*, III, c. 28, PL 115, cols 947, 957. See also above, n. 40.

[56] The date is given by Paul Alvar, *Vita Eulogii*, c. 15, ed. Gil, *CSM*, I, p. 340. Oddly, Eulogius' name is entered 'sur grattage' in Usuard's manuscript at 20 September: Dubois, *Martyrologe*, p. 306. Dubois, p. 96, discusses this discrepancy without finding any explanation. Could 20 September have been the date on which Usuard received the news?

plate the revival of a Frankish Empire which incorporated, and trans-cended, that of Rome.[57]

Usuard's Martyrology, like its predecessors, reflected the concerns of the Church universal. The persecutions of the early Christian past had, after all, affected every province of the Roman Empire. They had taken their toll in Italy: and it looks as if Hunfrid, who had kin in north-eastern Italy, gave Usuard the names of a group of Italian martyrs from that region by way of supplement to his Martyrology.[58] But of all those provinces, there was one whose saints found in Usuard's work *une place de choix*: that was Spain.[59] Usuard added in some cases to the information in earlier martyrologies; more significant, he added thirteen new entries on Spanish saints, such as Julian of Toledo and Isidore of Seville, on whom he had probably gained information during his visit in 858. Most striking of all, and quite certainly the result of Usuard's personal mission, were the commemorations of no fewer than thirty of the martyrs of Cordoba, on whose deaths Eulogius had been Usuard's key informant, and who finally included Eulogius himself, martyred only months after Usuard's visit to Spain.[60] I will give a single example of these new Spanish martyrs—I like to think Charles the Bald took a personal interest in this one, for the martyr's heavenly birthday was the king's earthly birthday:

> 13 June—the priest Fandila was beheaded and achieved martyrdom at Cordoba.[61]

---

[57] On the events of 858–9, see Nelson, *Charles the Bald*, pp. 185–93; and for Charles's political ideas, see Nelson, 'Translating images of authority: the Christian Roman emperors in the Carolingian world', in M. M. Mackenzie and C. Roueché, eds, *Images of Authority. Papers presented to Joyce Reynolds on the Occasion of her 70th Birthday* (Cambridge, 1989), pp. 194–205.

[58] As suggested by Dubois, *Martyrologe*, pp. 97–8, 121; and 'Le Martyrologe d'Usuard et le manuscrit de Fécamp', *AnBoll*, 985 (1977), pp. 43–71, at pp. 48–9, 57. This suggestion is strengthened by evidence recently signalled by U. Ludwig and K. Schmid, 'Hunfrid, Witagowo und Heimo in einem neuentdeckten Eintrag des Evangeliars von Cividale', in R. Härtel, ed., *Geschichte und ihre Quellen. Festschrift für F. Hausmann* (Munich, 1987), pp. 85–92, at pp. 90–2. (I am very grateful to Stuart Airlie for this reference.) Ludwig and Schmid follow Dubois in dating Hunfrid's 'contribution' to Usuard after 864, when Hunfrid, who had joined a rebellion against Charles, was expelled from the Spanish March and went to Italy (*Annales de Saint Bertin*, 864, ed. Grat, p. 112, tr. Nelson, p. 118). It seems to me more likely that Hunfrid supplied Usuard with the list of Italian martyrs in the early 860s as a gesture of devotion to Charles, thus as an expression of political ties through liturgical ones, *before* falling from favour. Hunfrid's Italian connections clearly pre-existed 864 and explain his flight to Italy rather than (or as well as) vice versa.

[59] Dubois, *Martyrologe*, p. 93.

[60] See above, n. 56.

[61] Dubois, *Martyrologe*, p. 246. The date was 853. Cf. Eulogius, *Memoriale Sanctorum*, ed. Gil, *CSM*, 2, pp. 444–5. See Wolf, *Christian Martyrs*, pp. 30, 115.

Charles the Bald had commanded Usuard to go through existing martyrologies and collect the feasts of the saints *in quandam unitatem*. That unity, in the minds of Charles and his Frankish contemporaries, embraced the Christians of Spain. A century after Pippin's prologue to *Lex Salica*, Charles, his sights set on an imperial title, could hope to reawaken and refocus the Franks' sense of mission through their special devotion to martyred saints. The interest of a Frankish king and would-be emperor, as well as the enterprise of a Frankish monk, ensured that the Cordoban martyrs found their place in the permanent liturgical memory of Latin Christendom. Those martyrs' fates probably helped to establish prejudices of lasting significance—to foreshadow the ending of attitudes that favoured *convivencia* in Spain; and to shape the new and distinctively bloody-minded vengefulness of the Christian West thereafter. In the eleventh and twelfth centuries there would be new *gesta Dei*, through *Franci* of a new kind who nevertheless thought of themselves as the lineal descendants of the Franks of old.[62] Oral literature had preserved the memory of Charlemagne and his paladins. Roland and Oliver and Turpin, recalled from the heroic age of martyr cultivators, were themselves recast as martyrs, and in Spain.[63] If the latter-day *Franci* who named and claimed them had Zaragoza and Cordoba ringing in their heads, *those* names also echoed through another lively medium of social memory: the Martyrology of Usuard.

King's College London

---

[62] For *gesta Dei per Francos*, and for Urban II at Clermont allegedly appealing to his audience to emulate Charlemagne and Louis the Pious and the Franks, see J. Riley-Smith, *The First Crusade and the Idea of Crusading* (London, 1986), p. 25.

[63] For tales of Charlemagne and his paladins in the age of the Crusades and long after, see now J. Fentress and C. Wickham, *Social Memory* (Oxford, 1992), pp. 154–62, with the thought-provoking observation (among many), at p. 160, n. 11, that Ademar of Chabannes, writing in early eleventh-century south-western France, claimed that Charlemagne 'ruled Spain as far as Cordoba, which has a Rolandian ring to it'. The origins of the ideas of Crusade and *Reconquista* remain fruitful areas of research, not least because of their continuing resonance: see C. Morris's fine paper in the present volume, below, pp. 93–104, and F. Fernández-Armesto, 'The survival of the notion of *Reconquista* in late tenth- and eleventh-century León', in T. Reuter, ed., *Warriors and Churchmen in the High Middle Ages. Essays Presented to Kral Leyster* (London, 1992), pp. 123–44.

THE IDEA OF INNOCENT MARTYRDOM IN LATE TENTH- AND ELEVENTH-CENTURY ENGLISH HAGIOLOGY

by PAUL A. HAYWARD

K INGS and princes who were classed as 'innocent martyrs' or 'passion-sufferers' because they were thought to have been murdered in Christlike circumstances were known in many parts of Europe in the Middle Ages.[1] This paper is about six Anglo-Saxon saints of this type, who are also distinguished by their youth. All of them were thought to have been boys or teenage males when they were martyred. To date, work on these saints has concentrated on questions concerning the origins of their cults, and their relationship to the institution of kingship.[2] The purpose of this paper, however, is to draw attention to the ways in which certain religious communities redefined their sanctity in the late tenth and eleventh century, and to make some tentative suggestions about the possible uses to which these cults were put in this milieu.

The six martyrs in question are Saints Æthelberht and Æthelred of Ramsey, Æthelberht of Hereford, Edward the Martyr, Kenelm, and Wigstan; and the primary evidence for the way in which their cults were used in the tenth and eleventh century comprises some seven *passiones*.[3]

---

[1] This type of sanctity (variously labelled as 'innocent martyrdom', *souffre-passion*, and *strastoterptsi*) was known in Bohemia, England, France, Kievan Russia, and in Scandinavia. See now R. Folz, *Les Saints rois du moyen âge en occident (VIe–XIIIe siècles)* = *Subsidia Hagiographica*, 68 (Brussels, 1984), esp. pp. 23–45, 57–9; 'Trois Saints rois "Souffre-passion" en Angleterre: Osvin de Deira, Ethelbert d'Est Anglie, Édouard le Martyr', *Académie des Inscriptions et Belles-Lettres: Comptes rendus des séances de l'année 1980*, pp. 36–49; N. W. Ingham, 'The sovereign as martyr, East and West', *Slavic and East European Journal*, 17 (1973), esp. pp. 1–2; 'The Martyred Prince and the Question of Slavic Cultural Continuity in the Early Middle Ages', in H. Birnbaum and M. S. Flier, eds, *Medieval Russian Culture* = *California Slavic Studies*, 12 (Berkeley and Los Angeles, 1984), pp. 31–53.

[2] See, for example, D. W. Rollason, 'The cults of murdered royal saints in Anglo-Saxon England', *Anglo-Saxon England*, 11 (1983), pp. 1–22; A. T. Thacker, 'Kings, saints and monasteries in pre-Viking Mercia', *MidlHist*, 10 (1985), pp. 1–25. There is also an extensive literature devoted to the origins of the cult of Edward the Martyr and the question of its political significance. See now S. J. Ridyard, *The Royal Saints of Anglo-Saxon England: a Study of West Saxon and East Anglian Cults* (Cambridge, 1988), pp. 154–71, 243–51.

[3] The seven Lives are: (1) Byrhtferth, *Passio SS. Ethelberti atque Ethelredi regiae stirpis puerorum* (*Bibliotheca Hagiographica Latina, Antiquae et Mediae Aetatis* = *Subsidia Hagiographica*, 6, 2 vols (Brussels, 1898–1901), with *Novum Supplementum*, ed. H. Fros = *Subsidia Hagiographica*, 70

The dating of these Lives is fraught with difficulty,[4] but most of them seem to have been composed between 1050 and 1130,[5] at a time when the authority of many monastic saints' cults required stabilization.[6] But the

---

(Brussels, 1986) [hereafter *BHL*], no. 2643), in T. Arnold, ed., *Symeonis Monachi opera omnia*, *RS*, 2 vols (London, 1885), 2, pp. 1–13, as sections i–ix of Symeon of Durham's *Historia Regum*; (2) *Passio et translatio beatorum martyrum Ethelredi atque Ethelbricti* (*BHL* 2641-2), ed. D. W. Rollason, *The Mildreth Legend: a Study in Early Medieval Hagiography in England* (Leicester, 1982), pp. 90–104; (3) *Passio S. Æthelberti, regis et martyris* (*BHL* 2627), ed. M. R. James, 'Two Lives of St. Ethelbert, King and Martyr', *EHR*, 32 (1917), pp. 236–44; (4) *Passio S. Eadwardi, regis et martyris* (*BHL* 2418), ed. C. Fell, *Edward King and Martyr* = *Leeds Texts and Monographs*, ns 3 (Leeds, 1971), pp. 1–16; (5) *Vita S. Kenelmi, regis et martiris* (*BHL* 4641n), transcribed from Oxford, Bodleian Library, MS Douce 368, fols 80r–83v, in R. von Antropoff, 'Die Entwicklung der Kenelm-Legende' (unpubl. inaugural dissertation, Bonn, 1965), pp. IV–XXIV; (6) *Lectiones S. Kenelmi* (*BHL* 2641m), transcribed from Cambridge, Corpus Christi College, MS 367, pt 2, fols 45r–48r, in von Antropoff, 'Die Entwicklung', pp. XXXIII–XXXVI; (7) *Vita S. Wistani, Regis et Martyris* (*BHL* 8975), preserved in three diverse thirteenth- and fourteenth-century recensions found in Oxford, Bodleian Library, MS Rawlinson A.287, fols 121–3v (ed. W. D. Macray, *Chronicon Abbatiae de Evesham ad Annum 1418*, *RS* (London, 1863), pp. 325–32 [hereafter *Vita S. Wistani*]), in Gotha, Landesbibliothek, MS I.81, fols. 44r–v, and in London, BL, MS Harley 2253, fol. 140v (see N. R. Ker, ed., *Facsimile of British Museum MS. Harley 2253*, *EETS*, os 255 (Oxford, 1965), fol. 140v).

4 The least certain is that of the *Vita S. Wistani*. None of three extant recensions is earlier than the thirteenth century, but textual parallels suggest that they all derive from a common source written at Evesham, possibly by Prior Dominic (*fl. c.*1100–30). J. C. Jennings, 'The writings of Prior Dominic of Evesham', *EHR*, 77 (1962), pp. 298, 304. D. W. Rollason, *The Search for St. Wigstan, Prince Martyr of the Kingdom of Mercia*, Vaughan Papers in Adult Education, 27 (Leicester, 1981), p. 9, argues that the Gotha and Harley texts date from the ninth century, but the textual parallels, their form, and their manuscript context (Gotha I.81 is a legendary of abbreviated *vitae*, while the other Lives in Harley 2253 are both abbreviated texts) suggest that they are condensed versions of the Life written at Evesham.

5 The *Vita S. Kenelmi*, for example, appears to have been composed between 1054 and *c.*1075. The *terminus a quo* is established by the preface, which declares an intention to append some modern miracles to its account of the Saint's life (fol. 80r), and the first of these miracles is said to have happened in the time of Godwine, 'who was abbot then' (fol. 82r), implying that the text was composed after his death in 1053 (*Anglo-Saxon Chronicle*, tr. D. Whitelock, D. C. Douglas, and S. I. Tucker (London, 1961) (C, D), *s.a.* 1053). The text also appends miracles (fols 82v–83r) said to have occurred under Abbot Godric (1054–1066×68) and the first Norman abbot, Galanus (*c.*1070–5), but these may be later additions to the text.

The exception to the pattern is the *Passio SS. Ethelredi et Ethelberti*, which seems to have been written up in the late tenth or early eleventh century, for the text is imbued with the language and style of Byrhtferth. See further, M. Lapidge, 'Byrhtferth of Ramsey and the early sections of the *Historia regum* attributed to Symeon of Durham', *Anglo-Saxon England*, 10 (1982), pp. 100–18. Rollason, *Mildreth Legend*, pp. 15–18, argues for dependence on an earlier text now lost, but the words introducing the text need not imply a written source. Judging by the context, Byrhtferth is more likely to have been writing up a set of received oral legends.

6 The best explanation of the sudden flood of hagiography which appeared after the Conquest remains that it was a response to Norman doubts about the authority of certain cults. See R. W. Southern, *Saint Anselm: a Portrait in a Landscape* (Cambridge, 1990), pp. 312–20; M. Brett, 'The Use of Universal Chronicle at Worcester', in *L'Historiographie médiévale en Europe*, Paris, 29 mars–1er avril 1989 (Paris, 1991), pp. 280–1.

function of these texts is a separate issue outside the scope of this paper. For present purposes, it is sufficient to note that these Lives do not appear to have been instrumental in creating the images of sanctity found in them. Rather, they would seem to have been designed to preserve certain received versions of their subjects' legends which had been devised by oral means in the communities for whom the Lives were written.[7]

More to the point, these saints' Lives present their subjects in essentially the same way. The saints are all boys or adolescent males of outstanding royal pedigree, who either become kings or are potential heirs to the throne. They are all murdered through no fault of their own by powerful rivals who wish to gain the kingship for themselves, and in the case of three saints the murderer is a jealous queen. Often explicitly forewarned of their impending deaths, they go to meet their ends with a simple faith in God, and die without offering any resistance. St Wigstan, for example, is a mere *filiolus*, 'not yet come of age', and descended from two collateral lines of the Mercian royal house. He is offered the kingship by the universal assent of the prelates, magnates, clergy, and people upon the death of his father, King Wigmund. Yet he refuses the crown, entrusting the reins of power to his mother and the leading magnates, and adopting the religious life. Brihtferth, a rival inflamed with lust and the desire to rule (*cupiditate . . . regnandi succensus*), asks the Saint's mother for her hand, but the Saint advises her to turn down the offer on the grounds that the marriage would violate canon law. Enraged, Brihtferth plots Wigstan's death, and eventually hacks his head open with a sword in the act of offering him the kiss of peace.[8]

The other Lives have similar stories, but the significant thing about all of them is the way in which they interpret their subject's death and manner of living. Much is made of the saints' youth (Kenelm, for example, is an outstandingly beautiful seven-year-old boy),[9] and this is associated with a singular emphasis on the saints' physical and mental purity. Moreover, the central virtue put forward in these Lives is the *preservation* of purity through celibacy. Byrhtferth would have us believe, for example, that Æthelberht and Æthelred 'strove to live as virgins, carefully preserving a chaste body', even though they were still in 'the

---

[7] The preface to the *Vita S. Kenelmi* fol. 80r, for example, mentions a number of earlier sources, but these seem to have comprised mainly songs and verse in the vernacular. See also *Passio S. Æthelberti*, vii (p. 241). The way in which the Lives were composed is explained in my forthcoming study of these legends, *The Idea of Innocent Martyrdom in Earlier Medieval England*, pt 5.

[8] *Vita S. Wistani*, pp. 326–31; 'De Sancto Wistano', Harley 2253, fol. 140v; 'De Sancto Wistano', Gotha I.81, fol. 44r–v.

[9] *Vita S. Kenelmi*, fols 80v, 81r (the text twice states his age!).

helplessness of childhood'.[10] Edward the Martyr is said to have refused to allow his mind to fall under the influence of the charms of the flesh, always striving to appear as one who would please God with 'integrity of mind and body'.[11] The saints' simplicity and purity is often in direct contrast to the inner turmoil of those who would destroy them. Byrht-ferth says of Thunor (the thegn who murders the Kentish princes), for example, that his mind was vexed by demons and disfigured by the lascivious itching of impure thoughts.[12]

Furthermore, the saints' martyrdom is interpreted not as the means by which they attained sanctity, but as though it were a sign of their innocence and the reward of their celibacy. Edward's death is the 'pro-clamation' (*praeconium*) of his innocence, the thing which leads to his virtues and merits being discussed everywhere;[13] Thunor's plots against the Kentish princes are an assault upon innocence itself;[14] and Kenelm's *innocentia* is a personal quality which will be 'tested' by his murderer's desire to rule, purified by mortal suffering, and received into the bosom of Christ.[15] Kenelm is said to have been so pure that God arranged his martyrdom in order to save his innocence from the corrupting influences of royal culture and secular rule.[16] In the argument of the Lives, these saints are not 'innocent martyrs' because they died blameless deaths,[17] but because their guiltless deaths, miracles, and youth prove that they were pure and innocent.

That the Lives were meant to be understood in this way is demon-strated by William of Malmesbury's reading of the *Life of Wigstan*, according to which the Saint was killed because his nobility had irritated his murderer. Moreover, God sent down a column of light from heaven which exposed the murder and honoured the Saint, because 'there was

---

[10] *Passio SS. Ethelberti atque Ethelredi*, section ii (p. 5).

[11] *Passio S. Eadwardi*, p. 2, lines 1–5.

[12] *Passio SS. Ethelberti atque Ethelredi*, section 3 (p. 6). See also, *Lectiones S. Kenelmi*, fol. 46r–v (the inner anguish of Cwenthryth, Kenelm's murderer), and *Vita S. Wistani*, p. 328 (Brihtfirth's lust for Queen Ælflæd).

[13] *Passio S. Eadwardi*, p. 8.12–14. See also p. 7.7–12 (Edward's uncorrupt corpse is a sign of his *innocentia*).

[14] Byrhtferth, *Passio SS. Ethelberti atque Ethelredi*, section 3 (p. 7). See also sections 5 and 6 (p. 9).

[15] *Lectiones S. Kenelmi*, fol. 45v. See also *Vita S. Kenelmi*, fol. 8or.

[16] *Lectiones S. Kenelmi*, fol. 45r, quoting Wisd. 4.11: 'Raptus est ne malicia mutaret intellectum illius, aut ne fictio deciperet animam illius.' Kenelm's Lives are notable for their scrupulous adherence to an orthodox Augustinian line on grace and free will: the Lives stress the Saint's almost pre-lapsarian purity, but God's grace is the crucial ingredient in his sanctity. See also ibid., fols 45r, 47r; *Vita S. Kenelmi*, fol. 8or.

[17] Æthelberht has *innocentia cordis* and is a *rex innocens et simplex* well before his death. See *Passio S. Ethelberti*, vii (p. 240), iii (p. 238).

nothing more pure in God than Wigstan's *innocentia*.' Wigstan's sanctity derives not from his death, but from his purity and the divine grace which it inspired.[18]

There are scarcely any earlier records of the legends of these saints to compare with these versions of their legends,[19] but it is likely that they represent substantial reinterpretations of the martyrs' sanctity. Most of the cults seems to have arisen soon after the saints' deaths at various dates between 650 and 1000, and to have been centred upon their tombs, which were housed in minster churches affiliated to their families.[20] Nothing much is known about how these cults were created, but their utility was probably related to the functions of these minsters. In general, such churches were set up and maintained by royal patronage to serve the private religious needs of the king's family, to help in the administration of their kingdoms, and to provide bases from which the clergy could convert the surrounding region.[21] The cults may have been set up,

[18] *De gestis regum Anglorum libri quinque*, ed. W. Stubbs, 2 vols, *RS* 90 (London, 1887–9), 1, pp. 263–4.

[19] There is for Edward the Martyr (d.978) the *Vita S. Oswaldi* (ed. J. Raine, *Historians of the Church at York and its Archbishops*, *RS*, 3 vols (London, 1879–94), 1, pp. 399–475), an early account written by Byrhtferth of Ramsey between 995 and 1005, within 27 years of the murder (see M. Lapidge, 'The hermeneutic style in tenth-century Anglo-Latin literature', *Anglo-Saxon England*, 4 (1975), pp. 91–3). But this was produced for an audience of reformed monks (see also S. Millinger, 'Liturgical Devotion in the Vita Oswaldi', in M. H. King and W. M. Stevens, eds, *Saints, Scholars and Heroes: Studies in Medieval Culture in Honour of Charles W. Jones*, 2 vols (Collegeville, Minnesota, 1979), 1, pp. 239–64), and already shows signs of moving towards the interpretation found in Edward's *Passio*. For the rest, all of whose cults originated between 650 and 873/4, there are no records of their legends which seem to have been written before 975. The account of the murder of the Kentish princes in the Parker manuscript of the *Anglo-Saxon Chronicle* (*s.a.* 640) is a marginal addition which dates from about 1100. J. M. Bately, ed., *The Anglo-Saxon Chronicle: a Collaborative Edition*, vol. 3, *MS A* (Cambridge, 1986), pp. xl–xli, 29, n. 3.

[20] The cult of St Wigstan, for example, seems to have been focused upon his tomb in the mausoleum his grandfather, King Wiglaf (827–40), had built at Repton, and archaeology has shown that it was converted into a pilgrimage church, at great expense, soon after his death in about 850 and before 873/4, when the place was devastated by Vikings. See now, H. M. Taylor, 'St. Wystan's Church, Repton, Derbyshire: a reconstruction essay', *Archaeological Journal*, 144 (1987), pp. 205–45; M. Biddle, 'Archaeology, Architecture, and the Cult of Saints in Anglo-Saxon England', in L. A. S. Butler and R. K. Morris, eds, *The Anglo-Saxon Church: Papers in History, Architecture, and Archaeology in Honour of Dr H. M. Taylor* = *Council for British Archaeology, Research Report*, 60 (London, 1986), pp. 16, 18, 22. The only anomaly is the cult of St Æthelberht, whose principal centre from the eleventh century, when it is first well attested, was not in his native East Anglia, but at Hereford Cathedral: see Thacker, 'Kings, saints and monasteries', pp. 16–18.

[21] The centre of Kenelm's cult, Winchcombe Abbey, for example, seems to have been set up by King Cenwulf of Mercia (796–821) as a family mausoleum, a royal archive, and as the administrative hub of his family's own sub-kingdom centred on Winchcombe. See W. Levison, *England and the Continent in the Eighth Century* (Oxford, 1946), pp. 252–8; S. R.

therefore, in order to enhance the status and authority of royal families,[22] but they were probably first and foremost an expression of the private religious devotion of the families from which the saints came.[23] Moreover, the minster clergy may have used these cults to help convert the countryside, for when they emerge into the historical record in the eleventh century the cults are all associated with sacred wells and trees.[24] But whatever the precise motives involved, it seems likely that these cults emerged in a fairly secular context, where the form of the saints' legends would have been shaped to a large extent by the needs and enthusiasms of various lay sections of the Church.

More to the point, the invention of the Lives' interpretation of the martyrs' sanctity is almost certainly to be associated with the monasteries of Ramsey, Winchcombe, and Evesham, who took over the relic cults of Saints Æthelred and Æthelberht, Kenelm and Wigstan in the late tenth and early eleventh century.[25] These monasteries were communities of

---

Bassett, 'A probable Mercian royal mausoluem at Winchcombe, Gloucestershire', *Antiquaries Journal*, 65 (1985), pp. 83–5. Note that Shaftesbury Abbey should also be seen as a West Saxon royal *Eigenkloster* when Edward the Martyr's cult emerged around 1000, even though this event post-dates the monastic reform. See further, *Asser's Life of King Alfred*, ed. W. H. Stevenson and D. Whitelock (Oxford, 1959), section 98; M. A. Meyer, 'Women and the tenth-century English monastic reform', *Revue Bénédictine*, 86 (1977), pp. 341–2, 350.

[22] The prevailing view is that these cults were instruments in the forward march of royal authority. See esp. Rollason, 'Murdered royal saints', pp. 15–20; *Mildreth Legend*, pp. 41–51; Ridyard, *Royal Saints*, esp. pp. 169, 244–8.

[23] On the culture and significance of royal sanctity in Germanic kingdoms, see now P. Corbet, *Les Saints ottoniens. Sainteté dynastique, sainteté royale et sainteté féminine autour de l'an Mil = Beihefte der Francia*, 15 (Sigmaringen, 1986). For Corbet, Ottonian royal sanctity was not primarily a tool for the promotion of particular causes or for the legitimation of the royal line, but a manifestation of the royal family's religious prestige. It depended ultimately on the personal virtue of the saints themselves and, in most cases, on the devotion of the friends and relatives who initiated their cults. Moreover, it had virtually no discernible political impact.

[24] See, for example, *Vita S. Kenelmi*, fol. 81r–v (a tree and two wells); *Passio S. Eadwardi*, pp. 8.7–11 (a well). These shrines seem to have been of long standing when the lives were written, and sacred landmarks of this type seem to have been focal points for popular participation in the cults (see J. M. H. Smith, 'Oral and written: saints, miracles, and relics in Brittany, c.850–1250', *Speculum*, 65 (1990), esp. pp. 326, 338). For the currently unfashionable view that these cults were manifestations of a popular yearning for royal saints arising from Germanic paganism, see W. A. Chaney, *The Cult of Kingship in Anglo-Saxon England: the Transition from Paganism to Christianity* (Manchester, 1970), pp. 77–84; E. Hoffmann, *Die heiligen Könige bei den Angelsachsen und den skandinavischen Völkern, Königheiliger und Könighaus = Quellen und Forschungen zur Geschichte Schleswig-Holsteins*, 69 (Neumünster, 1975), pp. 16–58.

[25] Kenelm's cult fell into the hands of the reformed monks when Winchcombe Abbey was refounded by Benedictine monks from Ramsey Abbey in about 970 (see Byrhtferth, *Vita S. Oswaldi*, p. 435). The relics of Wigstan were translated to Evesham in the reign of Cnut (1017–35) (see *Vita S. Wistani*, pp. 325–6, 331–2), and those of Æthelberht and Æthelred to Ramsey in 978×992. See *Translatio Martyrum Ethelredi atque Ethelbricti* (BHL 2642), in

reformed monks who enjoyed greater freedom from unwanted aristo-
cratic and royal interference and improved endowments, which enabled
them to devote greater energy to the pursuit of the monastic life, and the
Lives' versions of the martyrs' legends contain much that would seem to
relate to this milieu. The *Lives of St Kenelm*, for example, cast the Saint's
sister, Cwenthryth, in the role of his murderer and antitype. Now this
Cwenthryth is almost certainly the historical figure of that name who
appears in several authentic ninth-century documents as the daughter of
Cenwulf, Kenelm's father.[26] She was the abbess of a strategic minster in
Kent, and a Canterbury document from the 820s describes her as the heir
to Cenwulf's *hereditas*; there is here no sign that she was responsible for
any scandal involving the murder of her brother.[27] The Lives' version of
events appears to be a misogynist reading arising out of a monastic
propensity for attributing evil deeds to uncooperative and usurping
queens. The same tendency would seem to have been at work in the *Life of
Edward* even though this was composed for a community of nuns. In the
earliest account, written within twenty-seven years of the Saint's death,
the murderers are identified as 'zealous thegns of Æthelred',[28] but the
Passio, written eighty-odd years later, casts Edward's stepmother,
Ælfthryth, in the role of chief plotter.[29]

The Lives also define the sanctity of their subjects by their rejection of
the royal state, a familiar topos in monastic hagiography.[30] The saints'
martyrdom is defined as the means by which they exchanged the
ephemeral kingship of this world for an everlasting *hereditas* and *regnum* in

---

Rollason, *Mildreth Legend*, pp. 102–4. For the dating of this event, see Rollason, 'Murdered
royal saints', p. 18, n. 90.

[26] See P. H. Sawyer, *Anglo-Saxon Charters: an Annotated Handlist and Bibliography* (London, 1968),
nos 165, 1434, 1436. See further P. Sims-Williams, *Religion and Literature in Western England,
600–800* (Cambridge, 1990), p. 166, n. 107; Levison, *England and the Continent*, p. 252.

[27] Sawyer, *Anglo-Saxon Charters*, no. 1436. This document is part of a series concerned with a
dispute between Archbishop Wulfred of Canterbury (805–32) and Cwenthryth as abbess of
Minster-in-Thanet. See further, N. Brooks, *The Early History of the Church at Canterbury, Christ
Church from 597 to 1066* (Leicester, 1984), pp. 132–42, 176–206.

[28] Byrhtferth, *Vita S. Oswaldi*, p. 449.

[29] *Passio S. Eadwardi*, pp. 4–5. Other texts of this date make the same accusation. See, for
example, Osbern, *Vita S. Dunstani*, ed. W. Stubbs, *Memorials of St. Dunstan, Archbishop of
Canterbury*, RS, 63 (London, 1874), p. 115. Moreover, in the mid-twelfth-century *Liber
Eliensis*, ii.56 (pp. 127–8) the killing of Abbot Brihtnoth of Ely by a secret method is added to
her misdeeds. See further, K. Sisam, 'A secret murder', *Medium Aevum*, 22 (1953), p. 24.

[30] For this topos in the hagiography of Saints Edith and Wulfthryth, see Ridyard, *Royal Saints*,
pp. 83–9; S. Millinger, 'Humility and Power: Anglo-Saxon Nuns in Anglo-Norman Hagiography', in J. A. Nichols and L. T. Shank, eds, *Medieval Religious Women = Cistercian Studies*,
71, 2 vols (Kalamazoo, 1984), 1, pp. 117–19.

heaven.[31] Their sanctity is defined in opposition to the ethos of the warrior court. Æthelberht and Æthelred, for example, are said to have been

> enriched with the offices of self-abasing humility, thrice blessed with the titles of unconquerable patience, devoting the full extent of their capacity for exertion to the giving of alms, vested with the privileges of indefatigable hearts for prayer, and drunk with the many reflections of the goodness of the father of spirits.[32]

Riches, office, honour, privilege, ambition, strenuousness, and drinking are all inverted in the sanctity of these princes.

The Lives' interpretation of the saints' martyrdom, with its emphasis on their youth and purity, would seem to owe much to monastic thinking about virginity, childhood, and salvation.[33] Children were thought to possess an almost angelic and pre-lapsarian purity in both body and mind by virtue of their virginity,[34] and the monastic life was frequently conceived as a means of preserving this condition or of returning to it. Honorius Augustodunensis, for example, explains the monastic custom of shaving as a salvific ritual which returns monks to a childlike state: 'We shave ... in order to look like boys; by imitating their humility and innocence we shall dine with the Lord and enter into the kingdom of heaven, and we shall be equal with the angels, who forever flourish in a youthful age.'[35]

Yet the monks were also conscious of the moral frailty of children, of how easily this state of innocence was lost.[36] Moreover, they were particularly concerned to ensure that the children who were entrusted to their

---

[31] See, for example, *Vita S. Wistani*, p. 328; *Lectiones S. Kenelmi*, fols 45v, 46r.

[32] Byrhtferth, *Passio SS. Ethelberti atque Ethelredi*, section 2 (pp. 4–5).

[33] The emphasis on youth is also likely to have been influenced by the biblical legend of the Holy Innocents but textual allusions to the biblical story or to the principal Latin homilies for their feast are entirely lacking in the Lives. The question of the insular legends' debt to earlier boy-martyr legends (especially the Legend of St Just) and medieval ideas about infant *innocentia* is discussed in detail in my forthcoming study, *The Idea of Innocent Martyrdom in Earlier Medieval England*.

[34] For early medieval monastic notions of virginity and their allegiance to concepts of pre-lapsarian and childlike innocence and *simplicitas*, see further J. Bugge, *Virginitas: an Essay in the History of a Medieval Ideal = International Archives of the History of Ideas*, ser. minor, 17 (The Hague, 1975), pp. 35–41.

[35] Honorius Augustodunensis, *Gemma animae*, i.195 (quoting Matt. 18.3) (*PL* 172, col. 603CD).

[36] M. de Jong, 'Growing up in a Carolingian monastery: Magister Hildemar and his oblates', *JMedH*, 9 (1983), esp. pp. 105–6; P. Riché, *Education et culture dans l'occident barbare, VIe–VIIIe siècles* (Paris, 1962), pp. 499–508; 'L'enfant dans le société monastique au XIIe siècle', in R. Louis, et al., eds, *Pierre Abélard—Pierre le Vénérable* (Paris, 1975), pp. 689–701.

care as oblates and pupils did not lose this primal simplicity.[37] The *Constitutions of Lanfranc*, for example, have numerous provisions designed to limit opportunities for sexual acts amongst the oblates and with older monks, and to prevent the acquisition of sexual habits. They provide for strict supervision of conversations, sleeping, and even trips to the lavatory.[38] Moreover, most eleventh-century monks are likely to have entered monasteries as oblates. A unique list from New Minster, Winchester, indicates that of the forty-one new monks between about 1030 and 1070, thirty-five entered as oblates.[39] This institutional situation created audiences with special moral needs: a younger audience, embarking on its sexual development and needing to be taught the value of preserving its purity and innocence; and an older one, sometimes tempted to homosexual acts, and needing to be taught to respect the boys' virginity.[40]

The Lives' interpretation of the martyrs' sanctity would seem to fit into this context extremely well, for the moral of these legends is that God saves those who preserve their physical and mental purity by refusing to engage in sexual acts and lecherous thoughts. Moreover, one of the Lives, a set of Lections on St Kenelm, survives in a Worcester manuscript of the third quarter of the eleventh century.[41] William of Malmesbury's *Life of Wulfstan*, a bishop of Worcester in this period (1062–95), describes how he taught the sons of the rich who had been put in his care to preserve their virginity: 'Sedulously, he poured on them wholesome advice: not to be arrogant, but to assume humility, and above all not to injure the purity

---

[37] P. A. Quinn, *Better than the Sons of Kings: Boys and Monks in the Early Middle Ages* (New York, 1989), pp. 156–74; De Jong, 'Magister Hildemar and his oblates', esp. pp. 111–12.

[38] D. Knowles, ed., *The Constitutions of Lanfranc* (London, 1951), pp. 3, 5, 7, 21, 28, 31, 73, 112, 115–16, and esp. 117–18. See also T. Symons, ed., *Regularis Concordia* (London, 1953), pp. xli, 7–8.

[39] London, BL, MS Stowe 944, fols 21–2. See C. N. L. Brooke, *The Monastic World 1000–1300* (New York, 1974), p. 88.

[40] Homosexual practices seem to have been a significant problem in eleventh-century English monasteries. Witness, for example, the alarm which broke out at Christ Church, Canterbury, when a monk threatened to expose widespread homosexual practices in the monastery and to name one of Archbishop Lanfranc's favourites. Osbern, 'Miracula S. Dunstani', in *Memorials of St. Dunstan*, pp. 144–53. See also Herbert de Losinga's letter to Norman the Ostiary (ed. R. Anstruther, *Epistolae Herberti de Losinga, Osberti de Clara, et Elmeri Prioris Cantuarensis* (Brussels, 1846), no. 6, pp. 7–13).

[41] Not only is the manuscript from Worcester (M. R. James, *Descriptive Catalogue of the Manuscripts in the Library of Corpus Christi College, Cambridge*, 2 vols (Cambridge, 1911–12), 2, pp. 199–204; N. R. Ker, *Catalogue of Manuscripts Containing Anglo-Saxon* (Oxford, 1957), pp. 108–10), but its version of Kenelm's life was the one used by John of Worcester (B. Thorpe, ed., *Florentii Wigorniensis Monachi Chronicon ex Chronicis*, 2 vols (London, 1848–9), 1, p. 65).

of the flesh (*mundicia carnis*) lest, impelled by the deceit of youth, they should assuage their bodies in the slough of pleasure.'[42] It is easy to see how this *Life of Kenelm* could have fitted into this context. The story was sufficiently appealing to provide the oblates with an attractive child-hero, whose values they could put into practice in their own lives,[43] while satisfying the monks in the audience by catering to a desire for 'serious entertainments', didactic stories about Christian heroes and kings. In short, the Lives' interpretation of the sanctity of the martyrs agrees so well with the milieu of the reformed monasteries that the conclusion that it evolved for use in this context seems inescapable.

There is no problem in seeing the cult of Edward being used in this way at Shaftesbury, even though it was a community of *nuns*, for the use of saints as gender specific role-models seems to have been a rediscovery of the twelfth and thirteenth centuries.[44] In general, eleventh-century saints demanded pleasing rather than strict imitation.[45] The legend and cult of St Æthelberht, however, require some additional explanation. For the cult was centred upon Hereford Cathedral, and his earliest Life was written there during a period when its clergy were remarkably secular and hardly at all monastic. Bishop Leofgar, for example, died in battle fighting the Welsh in 1056,[46] and there seem to have been married and hereditary clergy within the cathedral chapter until well into the twelfth century.[47]

[42] R. R. Darlington, ed., *The Vita Wulfstani of William of Malmesbury*, Camden 3rd ser., 40 (London, 1928), iii.8 (p. 50). Note also the passages describing Wulfstan's special attention to books which commended chastity. See, for example, ibid., i.5, iii.6, iii.12.

[43] The youth of the martyrs seems to have been deliberately emphasized. Æthelberht, for example, is said to have been a fourteen-year-old (*Passio S. Æthelberti*, vii (p. 239)), and Kenelm a seven-year-old (*Vita S. Kenelmi*, fols 80v, 81r). Both of these ages were derived from the popular scheme widely known through Isidore of Seville, *Etymologiarum sive Originum Libri XX*, ed. W. M. Lindsay (Oxford, 1911), ix.19 and v.38. In this scheme, seven is the entry point into *pueritia*, a period of purity when one cannot yet have offspring; while fourteen is the entry point into *adolescentia*, the age at which men become old enough to get married and engage in sexual intercourse. See further, J. A. Burrow, *The Ages of Man: a Study in Medieval Writing and Thought* (Oxford, 1988), pp. 82–3.

[44] See C. W. Bynum, *Jesus as Mother: Studies in the Spirituality of the High Middle Ages* (Berkeley, 1982), pp. 95–102; D. Robertson, 'The inimitable saints', *Romance Philology*, 42 (1988–9), pp. 435–6.

[45] See, for example, Abbo of Fleury, *Passio S. Eadmundi*, ed. M. Winterbottom, *Three Lives of English Saints* (Toronto, 1972), xvii.16–28 (p. 87).

[46] *Anglo-Saxon Chronicle* (D), s.a. 1055. There is no evidence for the use of a rule (such as those associated with Chrodegang of Metz), or for a 'reform' of the chapter in the eleventh or twelfth century. See further, F. Barrow, *The English Church 1000–1066: a History of the Later Anglo-Saxon Church*, 2nd edn (London and New York, 1979), pp. 217–18, against A. T. Bannister, *The Cathedral Church of Hereford: its History and Constitution* (London, 1924), pp. 22–5.

[47] See J. Barrow, 'Hereford bishops and married clergy, c.1120–1240', *HR*, 60 (1987), pp. 2–4; A. Morey and C. N. L. Brooke, *Gilbert Foliot and his Letters* (Cambridge, 1965), 191–9, 269–70.

Nevertheless, this context may yet provide an explanation for the redefinition of Æthelberht's sanctity in monastic terms.

From the late eleventh century the bishops of Hereford were learned career clergymen,[48] who were engaged in a campaign to suppress clerical marriage and hereditary benefices in their diocese.[49] It may be that they were responsible for introducing the interpretation of Æthelberht's sanctity found in his earliest-known Life as a way of persuading the clergy of St Æthelberht to give up their wives. For the Life shows a marked concern with marriage. Æthelberht is martyred after having been compelled to seek the hand of Offa's daughter in marriage, almost as though divine providence wished to rescue him from the loss of his virginity;[50] and the martyrdom inspires Offa's daughter to offer herself as a bride of God.[51] Moreover, the anti-marriage theme is even more marked in the version of the legend which Gerald of Wales wrote for the cathedral at the end of the twelfth century,[52] suggesting that the cult had a continuing importance at Hereford as a means of suppressing clerical marriage.

In short, the cults of these innocent martyrs would appear to have been used by the religious communities which inherited them in the late tenth and eleventh century to meet their own moral needs. These communities seem to have adapted amenable royal cults of long-standing and unquestioned authority to fulfil internal disciplinary and pedagogical functions. This involved reinterpreting the saints' martyrdom as a sign of virginal purity, but the attitudes involved were essentially conservative. The hagiologers were attempting to maintain moral standards which were threatened by a constant turnover of new, and often young, members and the human frality of both monks and abbots. On the evidence of the Lives, it would seem that the cults of these saints were not simply tools for the promotion of the custodian communities' wider social and political causes. Moreover, the hagiological and religious content of their legends, all too often dismissed as mere literary padding, would seem to have held

---

[48] See, for example, the Lotharingian Bishop Robert (1079–95). His learning in the quadrivium and the abacus is well attested. See William of Malmesbury, *De gestis pontificum Anglorum libri quinque*, ed. N. E. S. A. Hamilton, *RS*, 52 (London, 1870), pp. 300–3.

[49] See Barrow, 'Hereford bishops and married clergy', pp. 1–8.

[50] *Passio S. Ethelberti*, iii (pp. 237–8).

[51] *Passio S. Ethelberti*, viii (p. 240). According to the *Passio*, she became an anchorite in the Fens.

[52] *Vita regis et martyris Æthelberti* (BHL 2628), ed. James, 'Two Lives', pp. 222–36. See further, R. Bartlett, 'Rewriting Saints' Lives: the case of Gerald of Wales', *Speculum*, 58 (1983), esp. pp. 602–3. Gerald was using the expansion of the *Passio S. Æthelberti* (BHL 2627) which Obsert of Clare wrote in the mid-twelfth century.

high importance and meaning for their religious audiences, if not for wider secular audiences as well. These cults were, in part at least, significant means whereby religious communities maintained their internal cohesion and controlled their social formation.[53]

St John's College, Cambridge

[53] On saints' cults, especially cults of monastic founders, as instruments of communal continuity, see esp. P. Rousseau, *Pachomius: The Making of a Community in Fourth Century Egypt* (Berkeley, 1985), ch. 9.

MARTYRS ON THE FIELD OF BATTLE BEFORE AND DURING THE FIRST CRUSADE

by COLIN MORRIS

THE First Crusade was an important episode in the history of martyrdom. While some of the crusaders were martyrs in the old style, giving up their lives rather than renounce Christ, the expedition established in the consciousness of Western Europeans the idea of a new route to the status of martyr, which could be earned by those who fell in battle against the unbeliever, fighting for Christ and for his people. From this time onwards crusading preachers regularly offered the stole of martyrdom to those who served in Palestine, Spain, and elsewhere, in the war against the Muslims. It is not surprising that recent historians, in particular Jonathan Riley-Smith, John Cowdrey, and Jean Flori, have given close attention to the establishment of this new model of martyr in the closing years of the eleventh century.[1] It may seem that there is little more to add on the subject, but the development is so significant in the context of our present conference that it may be worth while to return to this well-trodden battlefield. What I want to do in this paper is to examine the foundation of this new style of martyrdom in the thinking of earlier centuries, and then to look once more at its impact upon the early stages of the Crusade itself.

Before the middle of the eleventh century there are very few instances of the description of those who fell in battle against pagans as martyrs. This treatment was given to St Oswald of Northumbria (who died in 642 in battle with the heathen Penda of Mercia) and St Edmund (killed in 869 or 870 by the heathen Danes). In 799 Duke Gerold of Bavaria was killed fighting against the pagan Avars, and some twenty years later a monk of Reichenau had a vision which assured him that Gerold was among the ranks of the martyrs, because he had died in defence of the Church. He is

---

[1] J. Riley-Smith, 'Death on the First Crusade', in D. Loades, ed., *The End of Strife* (Edinburgh, 1984), pp. 14–31; H. E. J. Cowdrey, 'Martyrdom and the First Crusade', in P. W. Edbury, ed., *Crusade and Settlement* (Cardiff, 1985), pp. 45–65; J. Flori, 'Mort et martyre des guerriers vers 1100: l'exemple de la première croisade', *Cahiers de Civilisation Médiévale*, 34 (1991) [hereafter *CCM*], pp. 121–39. Riley-Smith gives examples of 'conventional martyrdom' on p. 20 and n. See also J. Riley-Smith, *The First Crusade and the Idea of Crusading* (London, 1986), esp. pp. 114–19 and 150–5.

sometimes counted as the first warrior-martyr, although he more probably belongs to the tradition of Oswald and Edmund, leaders who were reverenced by their local churches without (as Albrecht Noth has suggested) any award of official recognition at a higher level.[2] They provide only a few, remote precedents for the conviction which arose that crusaders at their death in warfare might hope for the reward of martyrdom, and to understand the upsurge of the new spiritual ambition we have to turn not to these cases, but to the thought of the Carolingian and post-Carolingian age.

The writers of the court were familiar with the idea of wars fought in the name of Christ, for the defence of Christendom or even (more hesitantly) for its extension. Warfare, in their thought, was the function of the anointed ruler, sustained by the prayers of the Church. A classic text is the letter written by Alcuin on Charlemagne's behalf to Pope Leo III in 796:

> It is our part, with the help of the divine mercy, outwardly to defend with arms the holy church of Christ on all sides from the incursion of the pagans and devastation of the unbelievers . . . It is your part, most holy father, to assist our army with your hands lifted to God like Moses.[3]

Here we are a long way from the First Crusade, when (to the wonder of contemporaries) there was no king or emperor, and when the expedition was authorized and preached by the pope. It is, however, noticeable that the warrior king may be described in terms more suited to hagiography, and he may be seen as the leader of a sanctified army. In the German poem, *Ludwigslied*, written in 881, the Franks are presented as God's faithful, *alle godes holden*. Louis is summoned to help by God himself, and the treatment of the poem is similar to that of a saint's life; the pagan invasion is even presented as a test of his sanctity:

> *Sô thaz uuarth al gendiôt, korôn uuolda sîn god,*
> *ob her arbeidi   so iung tholôn mahtî*
> *Leitz her heidine man Ober sêo lîdan.*

[2] See A. Noth, 'Die Anfänge des Kriegermartyriums', in his *Heiliger Krieg und heiliger Kampf in Islam und Christentum* (Bonn, 1966), pp. 95–109. The classic discussion of the historical basis of the cult of St Edmund is the article by D. Whitelock, 'Fact and fiction in the legend of St Edmund', *Proceedings of the Suffolk Institute of Archaeology*, 31 (1970), pp. 217–33; see also C. Hahn, '*Peregrinatio et natio*: the illustrated life of Edmund, king and martyr', *Gesta*, 30 (1991), pp. 119–39.
[3] E. Duemmler, ed., *MGH.Ep*, 4 = *Karolini Aevi*, II (Hanover, 1985), *ep.* 93, p. 137.

When that was ended, God wished to test him,
If he could suffer   trials so young,
Letting the heathen   cross the sea to him.[4]

This is a saintly king who could easily have become a martyr king.

While official propaganda concentrated on the anointed emperor, other literature was concerned with the standing of the warriors who fell in battle. In 878 the Frankish bishops wrote a letter of enquiry to Pope John VIII about the status of those who had been killed in recent fighting against the unbeliever. The Pope's answer was emphatic:

> Because your reverend brotherhood has modestly asked me whether those who, for the defence of the holy church of God and for the state of the Christian religion and of the public good, have recently fallen in battle, or shall fall in future for the same cause, can obtain forgiveness (*indulgentiam*) for offences, we answer boldly in the mercy of Christ our God that the repose of eternal life will receive those who in the piety of the Christian religion have fallen in battle fighting against pagans and unbelievers.

For further assurance the Pope absolved them and commended them to God by his prayers.[5]

It would be hazardous to say too much about the nature of the promises which were being given, because relatively little material of this sort survives. There is, however, no sign that in the ninth century they were being shaped either by language about martyrdom or by the issue of dispensations from penance. In all probability popes did not consider themselves authorized to bestow the rank of martyr, which God alone could give; and thought about the penitential system, and the place of the papacy within it, was still not very advanced. It is in the eleventh century that we find the general promise of salvation to faithful warriors being 'earthed' (so to speak) in the status of martyrdom or in the grant of indulgences, that is, remission of due penance. One might hazard a guess that the reason was the weakening position of the lay power and the tendency for other authorities, and in particular the popes, to authorize war. The armies were thus no longer performing their normal duties to their secular lord, and the soldiers needed a definition of their standing

---

[4] Text in P. Piper, ed., *Die älteste deutsche Literatur* (Berlin, 1884), p. 259.
[5] E. Caspar, ed., *Registrum Iohannis VIII Papae*, MGH.Ep, 7 = *Karolini Aevi*, V (Hanover, 1912–28), *ep.* 150, pp. 126–7. See also the statement of Leo IV in 853, which later became a text of canon law, *Ep*, 5 = *Karolini Aevi*, III (Hanover, 1898), *ep.* 28, p. 601.

and a promise of spiritual reward. In this paper we are concerned with the evolution of martyr-language, rather than with the remission of penance, although the two concepts developed side by side.

It is tempting to discern a connection between the new ideal of the warrior-martyr and the respect for men who faithfully serve their lord. If we had more early vernacular poetry, we might overhear more appeals to fighting men to engage in battle in the service of Christ, their Lord. The Old Saxon poem *Heliand*, lines 3995–4004, proclaims that

> We should remain with him; should suffer with our Lord. That is the duty of a thane (*Degen*), that he together with his prince should stand fast, to die with him in glory.

There is no doubt that the old Germanic expectation was that heroes die with a glorious *dom* or reputation. This passage goes much further: it implies that there was a special status accorded to those who died with their lord on the field of battle, and that this status naturally extended to warriors for Christ. On this theory, martyrdom in battle would be a theological idea rooted in primitive German militarism: yet another instance of the takeover of medieval spirituality by the warrior class or (alternatively, to put it the other way round) the Christianization of the cult of the warrior. It is, however, more difficult than one would think to trace throughout the centuries any special reverence paid to death with one's lord in battle. Its existence can be demonstrated most conclusively in the century before the Crusades. The classic statement of the ideal was in the late Anglo-Saxon poem *The Battle of Maldon*, and current views are tending to view this poem as a powerful expression of a new ideal. It is difficult to parallel in earlier Germanic literature, but it is echoed in material of the early eleventh century, such as the laws of Cnut in England: 'God will be loyal to the man loyal to his lord.' The truth may well be that the more personalized social structures which developed in the late Carolingian period led to a more intense personal relationship between man and lord. We may be discerning a shift, in the years around 1000, towards a lay ethic which could be transmuted, by a short route, into loyalty to Christ on the field of battle.[6]

---

[6] For the whole controversy, with a survey of previous literature and references, see R. Frank, 'The Ideal of Men dying with their Lord in Battle in *The Battle of Maldon*', in I. Wood and H. Lund, eds, *People and Places in Northern Europe 500–1600: Essays in Honour of P. H. Sawyer* (Woodbridge, 1991), pp. 95–106. Frank notes that death for one's lord is expressly treated as martyrdom in the French epic poem, *Garin le Loherain*, but in its present form this certainly should be dated after 1100.

However this may be, we begin to find in the course of the eleventh century the use of martyr-language for those who die in warfare in the service of Christ. The principle applies both to warfare against unbelievers and to the struggle against false Christians. An early and curious instance can be found in Ralph Glaber, who tells of a certain Wulferius, a monk of an abbey in central France, who saw in a vision a church full of men dressed in white robes and wearing purple stoles, the mark of martyrdom. They explained that 'We are all men of Christian profession, but while we were fighting for the defence of our country and the catholic people against the Saracens the sword severed us from the earthly flesh.' This belief that Spanish monks, who died fighting against the Moors, were to be counted as martyrs seems to be unique, at least until the emergence of the Templars codified the idea of the killer monk.[7] Another example, with a much more specific historical reference, was provided by Pope Leo IX, who led an army against the Normans (an example of papal military initiative which was not universally popular, even among his supporters) and was distressed that he had taken men to their deaths in the disaster at Civitate in 1053. He was reassured by visions of the slain in glory among the ranks of the martyrs:

> Since they had voluntarily suffered death for the faith of Christ and the deliverance of his people in distress, he proved by many revelations that by divine grace they had everlasting joy in the heavenly kingdom. For they appeared in various ways to these same faithful of Christ, saying that they were not to be mourned by funerals and ceremonies, but were joined with the holy martyrs in glory on high.[8]

Some years later the militant Erlembald, the knight who led the *Patarini* at Milan, was treated as a martyr by Gregory VII after he was killed there in 1075. The bronze memorial tomb to Rudolf of Swabia, who died fighting for Gregory VII against Henry IV in 1080, did not quite describe him as a martyr, but it came close to it: 'For him, death was life. He died for the Church.' In the late 1080s the Pisan *Carmen* greeted Viscount Ugo, who

---

[7] J. France, ed., *Rodulfi Glabri Historiarum Libri Quinque*, ii.19, pp. 84–5. The preceding chapter makes it quite clear that Ralph thought that the vision referred to monks killed fighting the Moors in Spain.

[8] Wibert (?), *Vita Leonis Papae*, ii. 11, J. M. Watterich, ed., *Pontificum Romanorum Vitae* (Leipzig, 1862), p. 166. This account was written well before the Crusade. The later life by Bruno of Segni, contained in his *Libellus de simonaicis*, vi, specifically attributes these visions to Leo himself: *MGH.LL*, II (Hanover, 1892), p. 551.

had fallen in battle against the Muslims of North Africa, as 'a martyr, who will grow red and glorious in the judgement to come.'[9]

Before 1095, therefore, there are signs that it was becoming more acceptable to use martyr-language for those slain on the field of battle, although the number of cases is still limited. The idea of martyrdom in battle, however, does not seem to have been prominent in the original promise of salvation by Urban II. He saw this as rooted in the remission of penance, and he does not appear to have said that those who fell on the expedition would have the status of martyr. The mentions of martyrdom in the later versions of his address are not substantiated by his letters or the canons of Clermont, and in themselves are somewhat vague. This reticence is not surprising, for while Urban had power to remit penance, it was not for him to say whether God would grant the rewards of martyrdom to a given person.[10] There is little doubt that those on the expedition were taught to place their trust in such promises of the Gospel as 'Every one who has left houses or brothers or sisters or father or mother or children or lands for my name's sake, will receive a hundredfold, and inherit eternal life'; or 'If any man will come after me, let him deny himself, and take up his cross, and follow me.'[11] By itself, this way of thinking went no further than the assurances which we have already encountered in the Carolingian period. When we ask how these promises were made effective in detail, we encounter a paradox: with only a little over-simplification, the position seems to be that Urban promised remission of penance and never mentioned martyrdom, and the crusading chroniclers wrote about martyrdom and never, or almost never, the indulgence for penance.

Accordingly, it has been suggested by Jonathan Riley-Smith that the idea of martyrdom was slow to enter the awareness of the crusaders, and

---

[9] *Carmen in victoriam Pisanorum*, ed. H. E. J. Cowdrey, 'The Mahdia campaign of 1087', *EHR*, 92 (1977), pp. 1–29, stanzas 46–8.

[10] On the ambiguities of the preaching ascribed to Urban II, see Riley-Smith, 'Death on the First Crusade', pp. 22–3. Jean Flori, on the other hand, has argued that the idea of martyrdom by death in battle was by 1095 already sufficiently established for it to be understood that Urban was promising this reward: see his articles, 'Guerre sainte et rétributions spirituelles dans la deuxième moitié du XIe siècle', *RHE*, 85 (1991), pp. 617–49; and *CCM*, 34 (1991), pp. 121–39. Flori understands the earlier, general promises of heavenly reward as conferring the status of martyr, and on this assumption is able to point to a strong battlefield-martyr tradition before the First Crusade; but the stress on visions would seem to indicate that contemporaries were not so sure, and required what they regarded as reliable evidence.

[11] Matt. 19.29 and 16.24. The first is quoted at the beginning of Albert of Aachen's *Historia Hierosolymitana*, *Recueil des Historiens des Croisades, Historiens Occidentaux* (Paris, 1879), IV, pp. 265–713; the second forms the first words of the *Gesta Francorum*, ed. R. Hill, *Gesta Francorum et aliorum Hierosolimitanorum* (Edinburgh, 1962) [hereafter *GF*].

only occupied their minds when Antioch had been reached in autumn 1097, after more than a year's travel and campaigning. This is an interesting idea, although it runs into the difficulty that there is so little material of which we can say with confidence that it was written before Antioch. Partly for that reason, partly because they regarded the idea of martyrdom in battle as generally accepted before 1095, John Cowdrey and Jean Flori have argued that it was in the consciousness of the crusaders before they set off, and would naturally and rapidly have been applied by them to their condition. What I want to do now is to look at what evidence we have of the thought about martyrdom at the beginning of the Crusade. I shall do this in the light of the possibility, for which I have already argued, that the promise of salvation for death in battle had for centuries been founded on general considerations of the mercy of God or the assurances in the Gospels, but that it was only recently, and to a limited extent, that these assurances had come to be rooted in the concepts of indulgence or martyrdom. Since martyrdom is our theme here, can we find any missing links in the form of passages in which crusading literature was struggling with an understanding of it, not yet fully formed?

The first step can be seen even before the expedition departed, in the recruiting-song *Jerusalem mirabilis*:

Illuc quicumque tenderit	Whoever marches to that place,
Mortuus ibi fuerit,	If there he shall his death embrace,
Caeli bona receperit	The goods of heaven he will gain,
Et cum sanctis permanserit.	and with the saints he will remain.[12]

The words are important because of their presence here in pre-crusade propaganda, although, of course, we have no idea how widespread the use of this song was. They have no obvious connection with the so-called indulgence, or remission of penance. They may be a reference to an old idea that those who die at Jerusalem will receive a heavenly reward, but they certainly bring close to the new recruits the idea that death on the expedition will enrol them in the ranks of the saints. The term 'martyr' is not used, but the promise of ranking with the saints bring us close to it.

On the expedition itself, the only material we have which can be said, with complete confidence, to have been written before the fall of Antioch are a few letters which were sent back to the West. They offer some

<hr>

[12] C. Blume and G. M. Dreves, eds, *Analecta Hymnica Medii Aevi*, 45b (Leipzig, 1904), no. 96, p. 78.

material of interest for our subject. The devout layman Anselm of
Ribemont wrote an account of the expedition for the use of Archbishop
Manasses of Reims, apparently just after the arrival at Antioch. In it he
included a list of those who died in battle at Nicaea, and another of those
who died in peace there (*in pace quieuerunt*). He accompanied it with a
request to readers to 'pray God for us and for our dead', remarking that
they had 'acquired for themselves so glorious a name'. He did not actually
say that they are martyrs, although those last words might well imply it.
After the splendid victory of 28 June 1098 he wrote again, once more
asking readers to pray to God 'for us and for our dead'. This time there is
no list: one suspects that there were now too many. From our knowledge
of later theology, we might suppose that the request for prayers indicates
that Anselm was not thinking in terms of martyrdom; indeed, Leo IX had
already said that martyrs need no mourning or funeral ceremonies. Yet
that would be a rash conclusion. After the fall of Jerusalem, Archbishop
Manasses wrote to Bishop Lambert of Arras with the request, 'Pray for the
bishop of Le Puy, for the bishop of Orange, and for all the others who,
crowned by so glorious a martyrdom, died in peace.' It must be remembered that *martirium* was commonly used for suffering, did not have as
specific a meaning as it was soon to acquire, and does not seem to have
conferred a guaranteed status which rendered further prayer unnecessary.
The picture here is of the glorious dead honoured for their suffering, on
the brink of their recognition as martyrs.[13]

At about the time of the arrival at Antioch, another letter was being
written to the West by Bishop Adhemar of Le Puy and Patriarch Simeon
of Jerusalem, about October 1097, and here the distinguished writers
reported a vision of the Patriarch himself which extended the reward
universally:

> Hear too, brethen, the miracle which the same most holy Patriarch
> sends to all Christians: how the Lord himself appeared to him in a
> vision, and promised to those labouring in this expedition that each
> will come before him on that awful and final day of judgement
> wearing a crown.[14]

[13] H. Hagenmeyer, ed., *Epistulae et chartae ad historiam primi belli sacri spectantes* (Innsbruck, 1901)
[hereafter Hagenmeyer], *epp.* VIII.11–12, pp. 145–6; XV.21, p. 160; and XX.5, p. 176.
[14] Hagenmeyer, *ep.* VI.4, p. 142. For an assessment of the story of Peter's vision, see E. O. Blake
and C. Morris, 'A hermit goes to war: Peter and the origins of the First Crusade', *SCH*, 22
(1985), pp. 79–107.

It is tempting to wonder whether this is a reference to an original vision which inaugurated the appeal to the West from the Church of Jerusalem, since it is clearly being given great prominence. It must be said, however, that the reports of Peter the Hermit at Jerusalem ascribe a vision to Peter, but not to the Patriarch. Again, the actual word 'martyr' was not used: it *never* occurs in the letters written during the Crusade, except in reference to the martyr-saints of the past; but the crown which was promised reminds us strongly of accepted language about the crown of martyrdom.

In all probability, the *Gesta Francorum* was the earliest narrative of the Crusade to be written, but as evidence of thinking during the first few months it must be used with caution, since the probability is (at least in my own view) that the first nine books were written after the successful completion of the siege of Antioch. It does, however, contain one or two specific references to martyrdom which can be thought with some confidence to reflect pre-Antioch ideas. Its first mention of martyrs refers to the destruction by the Turks of the forces of Peter the Hermit and Walter the Penniless in October 1096. Here the word has its traditional meaning, for it refers to those who refused to deny the faith when they were captured, and to the 'priest celebrating mass, whom they promptly martyred upon the altar.' By the time he was writing, the author clearly thought that martyrdom was a recurrent theme of the expedition, for he recorded that 'these men were the first to receive blessed martyrdom for the sake of the Lord Jesus.' The next reference, at the siege of Nicaea in May 1097, seems to involve a vision in authentication of martyrdoms. If that is right, it dates the episode as a definite recollection from the early campaigns, not merely a later reflection upon them:

> Many of our men received martyrdom there and gave up their happy souls to God with joy and gladness, and many of the poor died of hunger for the name of Christ. Triumphing in heaven, they wore the stole of the martyrdom they had received, saying with one voice: 'Lord, avenge our blood, which was shed for you'.[15]

The passage is an important one, because it also shows the crusaders struggling with another of the uncertainties of martyrdom, and receiving reassurance that it was not only those who died in battle, but the poor also who died of need, who received the heavenly reward. This is not the only sign of a sharp distinction between death in battle and death from misfortune or accident. When the erroneous report of the destruction of

---

[15] *GF*, p. 17. For the earlier martyrs, see *GF*, p. 4.

the Crusade arrived at the imperial camp in Asia Minor, Bohemond's half-brother Guy launched into a speech of mourning for him:

> Why did I not die at once, when I came out of my mother's womb? Why have I come to this miserable day? Why was I not drowned in the sea? Why did I not fall off a horse and break my neck, so that I died at once? Would that I had received blessed martyrdom with you, that I might see that you had received a glorious end![16]

It is interesting to notice, too, that in a letter to Monte Cassino written from Constantinople in June 1098, when the crusaders were engaged in a critical struggle outside Antioch, the Emperor Alexius expressed his confidence in their heavenly reward:

> A multitude of knights and footsoldiers have gone to the eternal tabernacles. Some of them were killed, some died; they are indeed blessed, since they met their end with a good intention. For this reason we should not consider them as dead, but as alive and translated to life eternal and incorruptible.[17]

There may be some hints here that the Basileus's Latin advisers were, as we would expect, in touch with thinking among the crusaders, not only in the confident assertion of the heavenly reward, but also in the careful inclusion of those who died a natural death, as well as those who were killed, in the ranks of the saints.

By this time we have gone beyond material which can, with any sort of confidence, be seen as reflecting the thought of the earliest days. There are, however, just two additional points about other chronicles which were close to the experience of the First Crusade itself, and in which we also find this 'missing link' approach to martyrdom, characteristic of people who are in varying degrees thinking about it, but not with total confidence. Albert of Aachen was certainly conservative on the subject. He had no doubt about the granting of a heavenly reward to warriors who died in the service of Christ, but when we look to see whether he thought of them as martyrs we find that the specific references are very few indeed, especially when we remember the large size of the chronicle; and these few instances tend to occur in speeches or sermons ascribed to

---

[16] *GF*, pp. 64–5. With little doubt, we have here a speech composed by the anonymous author at Antioch, but he was a member of Bohemond's circle, and it can be regarded as evidence of the Norman concern with martyrdom and the distinction which was being drawn between death in battle by misadventure.

[17] Hagenmeyer, *ep.* XI.5, p. 153.

others. On the death of particularly important men he likes to record the solemnity of their burial ceremonies and the distribution of alms made in their memory; and for him *martirium* (a word of which he is quite fond) is normally used for 'suffering' in general, with no implication of heavenly reward. Albert was on the whole a conservative thinker, and he seems to have been only marginally influenced by ideas of martyrdom on the field of battle.[18]

There is one other important feature of the early material which has already emerged, and which we need to note. The status of martyr was guaranteed by visions. This has already been apparent in the vision of Leo IX about the dead at Civitate, in the vision (if that is what it was) recorded in *Gesta Francorum* about fallen comrades at Nicaea, and in the general promise of salvation given to Patriarch Simeon of Antioch. The importance of visions as establishing immediate enrolment in the ranks of the martyrs runs through the literature of the First Crusade, as, for instance, in the vision which Anselm of Ribemont had of Enguerrand of St Pol, a knight who had recently been killed and was able to show Anselm the very beautiful house in which he was now living, with a prophecy that for Anselm himself an even more beautiful one was being prepared.[19] This prominence of visions is important for our purpose. It establishes that you do not become a battlefield martyr by papal grant, or even on the basis of the general tradition of the Church. Martyrdom was a very special privilege, and the only way, at first, that one could be absolutely sure was by what we may call visionary insurance.

The idea that a Christian who died in battle against the unbeliever would receive a heavenly reward had a substantial history before the First Crusade, but (with the exception of a very few early instances) such heroes had not been described as martyrs. After 1050 we encounter more use of such language, but it seems to have been the First Crusade which inserted the idea into the common stock of Western thought, and we can see the chroniclers and letter-writers beginning to formulate and digest it. The Crusade had the same effect on other parts of the self-image of Catholic

---

[18] For Albert's views on martyrdom, see C. Morris, 'The aims and spirituality of the First Crusade as seen through the eyes of Albert of Aachen', in *Saints and Saints' Lives: Essays in Honour of D. H. Farmer* = *Reading Medieval Studies*, 16 (Reading, 1990), esp. pp. 107–8. The vexed question of Albert's relationship to his original material would demand much more space than is appropriate here. In the text I have assumed that he does indeed reflect the thought of the Lorraine contingent of 1096–9, either because (as has often been argued) he was using an early 'Lorraine chronicle' or because (as Susan Edgington has forcefully suggested) the first six books were written immediately after the expedition itself.

[19] J. H. and L. L. Hill, eds, *Le Liber de Raymond d'Aguilers* (Paris, 1969), pp. 108–9.

warriors, who came to be envisaged as knights of Christ (*milites Christi*), as Westerners (*occidentales*), as defenders of a society defined as Christendom (*christianitas*), and (in the event of their death) as martyrs. The early stages, which I have been exploring in this paper, still had elements of hesitation. There was no clear papal promise of the status of martyr. It still seemed appropriate to ask for prayers for those who had undergone martyrdom, and there was uncertainty about the position of those who died of want, disease, or accident while marching with the army. Above all, martyr status needed authentication by vision, which to the men of the time gave certain and secure knowledge. Logically at least, the vision of Patriarch Simeon of Jerusalem provided assurance that all who died on the expedition would be crowned in the Lord's presence, although there are no clear references to this promise outside Simeon's own letter. Already, however, in the early days of the Crusade its members were struggling with this question of martyrdom and its meaning for them, and it was to become a consistent element thereafter in the conduct of the holy war against the unbeliever.

University of Southampton

BORIS AND GLEB: PRINCELY MARTYRS AND MARTYROLOGY IN KIEVAN RUSSIA

by R. M. PRICE

THE first canonized Russian saints were the princes Boris and Gleb (d. 1015), and the early accounts of their martyrdom, dating to the late eleventh or early twelfth century, are among the most important works of early Russian hagiography. It is the aim of this paper to locate these texts in the history of European martyrology, and to identify where they exhibit originality.[1]

I

The texts tell the following story. Prince Vladimir of Kiev, the first Russian prince to become a Christian, had numerous sons by a number of wives; Boris and Gleb, who had the same mother, were the youngest of these. On their father's death, on 15 July 1015, their eldest half-brother, Svyatopolk, who happened conveniently to be in Kiev, determined to secure for himself all or most of the paternal inheritance. Boris, who had been sent by his father on an expedition against the nomads only shortly before, was in a good position to march on Kiev; but he refused to do so, and instead disbanded his army, insisting that it would be wrong to contend against his elder brother. Svyatopolk promptly sent a band of his henchmen, who murdered Boris (on 24 July). Reflecting that a path of crime is easier to pursue than abandon, he then proceeded against the younger brother Gleb, who was murdered in a boat on the Volga (on 5 September). At this, another brother, Yaroslav, took up arms to avenge his brothers, and fought a fierce and bloody war, which concluded in 1019, with Svyatopolk in exile, where he was soon to die, and Yaroslav reigning in Kiev.

This tale is recounted in three early texts. Immensely popular in medieval times was the *Tale* (or *Legend*) *and Passion and Eulogy of the Holy Martyrs Boris and Gleb* (the *Tale*, for short). This text is closely related to a second, briefer, text—the entry under 1015 in the so-called *Primary*

---

[1] Good introductions to the cult and associated literature are Andrzej Poppe, 'La Naissance du culte de Boris et Gleb', Essay 6 in *The Rise of Christian Russia* (London, 1982), and Vladimir Vodoff, *Naissance de la chrétienté russe* (Fayard, 1988), pp. 242–8, 275–85.

Chronicle which has survived in two very similar recensions, the *Novgorod First Chronicle* and the so-called *Tale of Bygone Years*. Thirdly, there is the *Lesson* (or *Reading*) *about the Life and Murder of the Blessed Passion-sufferers Boris and Gleb* (the *Lesson*, for short), written by Nestor, a monk of the Kievan Caves Monastery.[2] There is general, though not universal, agreement that these three texts belong to the period between 1070 and 1120, but the precise dates of the three texts, and the relationship between them, are among the most disputed problems of Old Russian scholarship.[3] The *Lesson* and the *Tale* tell a similar story in very different styles: the *Lesson* follows strictly the conventions of contemporary Byzantine hagiography, while the *Tale*, though scarcely less stylized, is much more distinctive and hard to categorize. For our purposes it is enough to note the different character of the two texts, without attempting to determine their relationship. But the dispute for priority between the *Tale* and the Chronicle entry affects our picture of the development of early Russian martyrology. The two texts are closely related: they tell not only the same story, but in very similar wording. The difference between them is that the *Tale* is substantially longer than the Chronicle entry, adding little in the way of facts, but rich in inserted speeches and other rhetorical embellishments. This suggests that either the *Tale* is an expanded version of the Chronicle entry, or the Chronicle entry is an abridgement of the *Tale*.[4] Although both works contain more hagiographical features than are normal in chronicles and more historical information than is normal in hagiography, this question evokes the most important and imponderable of the historico-critical problems: was the tale of Boris and Gleb first developed in a secular narrative, a primitive chronicle or perhaps a saga, or in the context of hagiographical eulogy? These related questions have

---

[2] 'Passion-sufferer' translates *strastoterpets*. The oft-repeated claim that this word was not simply a synonym of *muchenik* (martyr), but was applied to those who died not for the faith, but in imitation of the Passion of Christ, is questioned by Vodoff, *Naissance*, pp. 257–8.

[3] For the *Tale* and *Lesson* I use the edition by D. I Abramovich (Petrograd, 1916), reprinted with an introduction by Ludolf Müller as *Die altrussischen hagiographischen Erzählungen und liturgischen Dichtungen über die heiligen Boris und Gleb* (Munich, 1967) [hereafter Abramovich], pp. 1–51. For the Chronicle entry, I use D. S. Likhachev, ed., *Povest' vremennykh let*, 2 vols (Moscow and Leningrad, 1950), 1, pp. 89–96 [hereafter *Povest'*], while comparing it to *Novgorodskaya pervaya letopis'* (Moscow and Leningrad, 1950), pp. 168–74. See now Paul Hollingsworth, *The Hagiography of Kievan Rus'* (Harvard, 1992), which contains translations of the *Tale* and *Lesson*, and much useful bibliography.

[4] For these two positions contrast Fairy von Lilienfeld, 'Die ältesten russischen Heiligenlegenden', in *Aus der Byzantinischen Arbeit der DDR*, 1, Berliner Byzantinische Arbeiten, 5 (1957), pp. 237–71, and N. N. Il'in, *Letopisnaya stat'ya 6523 goda i ego istochnik* (Moscow, 1957), pp. 189–209.

been much debated, and no common or even dominant view has emerged.

As a small contribution to the debate, I would like to draw attention to two biblical citations that occur, in identical contexts, in both texts. Both the *Tale* and the Chronicle cite Proverbs 1. 16–19, but while the first attributes it vaguely and inaccurately to the 'prophet', the latter rightly attributes it to Solomon.[5] This suggests that the *Tale* is prior, and the chronicler is making a pedantic correction. But a further biblical citation points in the opposite direction. After describing the miserable death of Svyatopolk, both texts proceed to compare him to Lamech, who, according to Genesis 4. 24, was punished seventy-sevenfold. Both texts alter this to seventyfold, with only the Chronicle quoting the Genesis passage in full.[6] The natural explanation is that the inaccuracy arose from the chronicler's loose citation of the passage and the *Tale*'s dependence on the Chronicle. I would claim no decisive weight for my analysis of these passages, but at least they illustrate the fact that good arguments can be advanced in favour of the priority of either text. The obvious deduction is that neither of them is directly dependent on the other, but both on a common source, most accurately transmitted now in one text and now in the other.

If the common source contained biblical citations, it must have been a work of hagiography. But there are pointers to the existence of an ultimate source of a very different character. For instance, both texts give the curious detail that on Vladimir's death the flooring where he lay was taken apart, and his body lowered by ropes on to a sledge, and so conveyed away.[7] This is explained in both texts as an attempt to conceal his death: this is nonsense, since modern scholars have recognized these details as standard funerary procedure in pre-Christian Russia, and since both texts go on to relate that the body was immediately laid out in public in the Church of the Mother of God, in Kiev.[8] But the obvious deduction has not been made: surely, the explanation of secrecy must have arisen from a misunderstanding by Christian writers of a pagan burial custom that by their time had been replaced by a fully Christian ritual. If this is so, they had before them a written text that gave the details of Vladimir's funeral. Neither a hagiographical work nor a chronicle entry would have included such details off their own bat. This points to the existence of a primitive

[5] Abramovich, p. 32, line 17. *Povest'*, p. 90.
[6] Abramovich, p. 47, lines 18–20. *Povest'*, p. 98.
[7] Abramovich, p. 29, lines 3–6. *Povest'*, p. 89.
[8] Il'in, *Letopisnaya stat'ya*, p. 202.

secular narrative, or saga, of the deaths of Boris and Gleb as the ultimate source of the texts that have come down to us.[9] One implication of this suggestion is that the story of Boris and Gleb is likely to contain many more genuine historical elements (hard though these are to distinguish from fictional ones) than in the theory, for instance, that, in everything beyond the bare essentials, the story is a free invention, based on motifs culled from earlier hagiography.[10]

II

Whatever the original form of the tale of Boris and Gleb, the extant texts, even the Chronicle, offer a hagiographical presentation that needs to be seen in the broader context of developments in hagiography in other parts of Europe. Of particular relevance is the family of texts and cults devoted to martyred princes.[11] The extension of the notion of martyrdom to include princely victims of war or political rivalry rather than religious persecution was a widespread phenomenon, alien to the Byzantine world (in other respects the dominant influence on early Russian culture), but common to a number of north European countries. Interestingly, some of the earliest examples are English ones—Oswald (d. 642), Æthelberht of Hereford (d. 794), Edmund of East Anglia (d. 870). Several of them, of the eleventh and twelfth centuries, are Scandinavian, which is significant in view of the Norse origins of the Russian princely family and the continuing links between the two cultures.

Closest to the story of Boris and Gleb are the martyrdoms of St Wenceslas of Bohemia (d. 932) and St Magnus of Orkney (d. 1116). St Wenceslas deserves particular attention, since he is mentioned in the *Tale*,[12] and since two Slavonic versions of his *Life*, the so-called *Vostokov* and *Nikolsky* legends, had achieved circulation in Russia by the time the

---

[9] The existence both of an *Urlegende* used by both the Chronicle and the *Tale* and of a saga as the ultimate source was deduced in the 1950s with a different and much longer array of arguments by Ludolf Müller, in a series of studies summed up in 'Neue Forschungen über das Leben und die kultische Verehrung der heiligen Boris und Gleb', *Opera Slavica*, 4 (Göttingen, 1963), pp. 295–317. His theory did not win general acceptance, but holds the field in the sense that the debate then ground to a halt.

[10] Specifically, the *Life of Wenceslas*. This is the theory of Il'in, *Letopisnaya stat'ya*, p. 209 and *passim*.

[11] See N. W. Ingham, 'The sovereign as martyr, East and West', *Slavic and East European Journal*, 17 (1973), pp. 1–17.

[12] Abramovich, p. 33, line 11.

extant accounts of Boris and Gleb were written.[13] After describing the Saint's exemplary piety and his desire for martyrdom, though not, the text hastens to add, at the hands of his brother, the *Life* narrates how his younger brother Boleslav invites him to his castle. Wenceslas suspects his brother's treachery, but goes nevertheless. After a night of prayer, he goes to church to hear Matins. On the steps of the church he is attacked by his brother, who drops his sword. Wenceslas returns it, suggesting that it would, however, be more proper for Boleslav to get his henchmen to commit the murder than perform it himself; Boleslav takes this good advice. Many elements of this memorable narrative recur in the account of the martyrdom of Boris—the guilt of evil advisers, the murderer's pretence of friendship, the victim's lengthy prayers and hearing of Matins immediately before the murder, above all, the theme of self-sacrifice brought out by the refusal either to escape or resist. These common features arise from the common ideology behind both accounts, but suggest too some influence of the Czech story on the Russian one. The martyrdom of Gleb is more closely paralleled in the Magnus Sagas.[14] In both, the martyr (in contrast to Boris and Wenceslas) tries to persuade his murderers to spare him; in both, the sanctity of the martyr is assured by the appearance of a miraculous light above his place of burial. It is significant that no such signs are claimed in the case of Boris: that he died as a martyr was proved by his Christlike acceptance of death, and did not need the same miraculous proof.

The development of the cult of princely martyrs in Slavic and Scandinavian cultures during these centuries—a development that arguably distorted the very notion of martyrdom—invites a common explanation. It has been suggested that these cults derive from elements in Norse paganism, notably the human sacrifice of priest-kings on behalf of their people, linked to the myth of Odin's self-oblation to himself.[15] This intriguing theory helps to explain the prominence of these cults in northern Europe, but does not contribute to the interpretation of the actual texts, which describe political murders in terms of Christian

[13] These texts are in Josef Vajs, ed., *Sborník staroslovanských literárních památek o sv. Václavu a sv. Lidmile* (Prague, 1929). They should be compared to the early Latin literature, in Josef Pekař, *Die Wenzels- und Ludmila-Legenden und die Echtheit Christians* (Prague, 1906).

[14] G. Vigfusson, ed., *Icelandic Sagas*, 3 (London, 1893), contains translations of the *Long* and *Short Magnus Sagas*; the *Long Saga* incorporates (in translation) a Latin eulogy. That in the martyrdoms of both Gleb and Magnus the martyr's own cook is forced to commit the murder is an oddly precise similarity, which may point to a wide oral dissemination of the Gleb story.

[15] Edward S. Reisman, 'The cult of Boris and Gleb: remnant of a Varangian tradition?' *Russian Review*, 37 (1978), pp. 141–57.

martyrdom. The ideology remains in large part conventional. The Lives of Wenceslas and Magnus, and the early eulogies in their honour, do not develop themes that distinguish their cult from that of other saints: there is the same stress on the saint as edifying example of Christlike virtue and heavenly intercessor able to help the individual in need. But it needs no interpretative finesse to detect that these cults served the special purpose of being a glorification of outlying local churches, a stimulus and focus for a new sense of national loyalty, and a validation of the authority of princely dynasties. There is even a hint in these stories that the death of the prince is a sort of blood sacrifice, which simultaneously expresses the cost of nationhood and sanctifies it.

It is a mark of originality in the Boris and Gleb texts that they develop these themes explicitly and eloquently. All these texts, *Tale*, *Lesson*, and Chronicle entry, close with a eulogy (different and independent in each case) that brings out the significance of the cult—even though eulogies are alien to the traditional genre of martyrology. The Chronicle describes the martyrs as 'intercessors for the Russian land, radiant luminaries praying at all times to the Lord for their people' and their own relations; they are entreated to 'subdue the pagans under the feet of our princes . . . freeing them from intestine wars and the machinations of the devil.' Russia is described as blessed by their blood.[16] The *Tale* addresses a similar apostrophe to the martyrs: 'In truth you are kings of kings and princes of princes, for it is through your aid and protection that our princes are victorious over those who rise up against them.' The text compares them favourably with St Demetrius of Thessalonica: he defends only a single city, while they protect the whole Russian land (which brings out, incidentally, the influence of the Byzantine cults of military saints). The martyrs are again entreated to intercede at the throne of heaven that Russia be protected from both external attack and civil strife.[17]

The danger of civil strife relates to the main and most distinctive aspect of the political *Tendenz* of these texts, which has been explored with particular thoroughness by Soviet scholars.[18] The Russian lands were

---

[16] *Povest'*, pp. 93–4. Since this eulogy is not contained in the *Novgorod First Chronicle*, it must be an addition to the *Primary Chronicle* (of *c.* 1095) and date to the time of the compilation of the *Povest'* itself (*c.* 1113). Other evidence points to this date as the time when the cult became a truly national one: see Vodoff, *Naissance*, p. 281, and N. N. Voronin, 'Anonimoe skazanie o Borise i Glebe, ego vremya, stil' i avtor', *Trudy otdela drevnerusskoy literatury* [*TODRL*], 13 (1957), pp. 11–56.

[17] Abramovich, pp. 49–51.

[18] Especially D. S. Likhachev, 'Nekotory voprosy ideologii feodalov v literature XI–XIII vekov', *TODRL*, 10 (1954), pp. 77–91. See, too, Martin Dimnik, 'The "Testament" of Iaroslav "the Wise": a re-examination', *Canadian Slavonic Papers*, 29 (1987), pp. 369–86.

divided into a number of principalities, all ruled by members of the Riurikid dynasty, who addressed one other as 'brothers'. There was an agreed hierarchy, where a senior prince was addressed by his juniors as 'elder brother' or 'father and brother' (terms used by Boris of Svyatopolk in the texts before us). A constant concern of responsible Russians, right down till the Mongol conquest, was the need for effective co-operation between the various princes, both to avert civil strife and to achieve effective joint action against the hostile nomads to the south and east. The basis for this co-operation could only be acknowledgement of the leadership of the senior prince or princes, which had, of course, to be balanced by senior princes' respecting the rights of junior ones. It is obvious that the story of Boris and Gleb is propaganda for this political programme. All the texts stress that Boris in particular chose not to defend himself against Svyatopolk out of respect for his authority as the elder brother, while the dismal fate of Svyatopolk was a lesson that senior princes could not afford to trample on their juniors. This theme is developed with particular energy in the eulogy at the end of the *Lesson* which draws an explicit moral:

> Observe, brethren, how great was the submission which the saints showed their elder brother. If they had opposed him, they would scarcely have been deemed worthy of such a gift from God to work miracles. Nowadays there are many young princes who do not submit to their elders but oppose them, and are killed. These are not deemed worthy of such a grace as these saints were.[19]

It is this development of national and political themes, this stress on the cult as uniting the nation around a specific political programme, that constitutes the most obvious original theme in the accounts of the martyrdom of Boris and Gleb.

III

If the according to Boris and Gleb of Christ's title 'King of kings' gave them a share in his regal authority, as martyrs they partook in his Passion, and this duality is an echo of the Christological paradox. It is accentuated in the texts before us, especially in one of them, by a further feature that may also strike us as particularly distinctive, and that is the strong pathetic note, alien to the style of traditional hagiography, and particularly

[19] Abramovich, p. 25, lines 5–9.

unexpected in the context of saints represented as heavenly warriors.
Pathos is absent from the *Lesson*, which follows faithfully the prescrip-
tions of Byzantine hagiography; it is present, however, in the Chronicle
entry and highly developed in the *Tale*. There we read how Boris, when
he first suspects Svyatopolk's evil intent, is overwhelmed with self-pity:

> [He] reflected on the beauty and grace of his body, and was all soaked
> in tears. He wished to control himself, but could not. All who saw
> him wept likewise over his youth, both his graceful body and his
> honourable character. Everyone lamented in his soul with heartfelt
> sorrow, and all were stunned by grief. For who would not break into
> sobs on beholding before the eyes of his heart this terrible death?[20]

Both Boris and Gleb, while accepting death on the one hand, utter on
the other lengthy and rhetorical laments, partly over each other or the
decease of their father, but also over themselves:

> [Gleb:] Woe is me, woe is me! Hear, O heaven, and hearken, earth.
> And you, Boris my brother, hear my voice. I have called to Basil my
> father and he has not listened to me: do you too not wish to listen to
> me? Witness the grief of my heart and the wound of my soul; witness
> my tears, flowing like a river![21]

The contrast between this language and the stiff upper lip of the traditional martyr has led scholars of Russian birth to claim the influence of
popular dirges. Others point to the gift of tears, which is doubtfully
relevant, since, in the words of an anonymous Syriac text, 'Tears of
anguish out of sorrow or over the dead are certainly not rewarded, for
they are merely a natural phenomenon.'[22] Neither suggestion is plausible.
Anyone, however, with a knowledge of Greek literature, classical or
Byzantine, will recognize the true origin of this genre of rhetoric, which
goes back ultimately to the threnodies of Attic tragedy. It is not entirely
absent even from Byzantine hagiography. Take, for example, an episode
in the *Life of St Eustace* (of which there was an Old Russian translation that
is actually cited in the *Lesson*).[23] Eustace flees to Egypt, where his two
infant sons are carried off simultaneously by wild animals (they are

[20] Abramovich, p. 31, lines 3–8.
[21] Abramovich, p. 42, lines 5–9.
[22] In A. J. Wensinck, 'Über das Weinen in den monotheistischen Religionen Vorderasiens', in
Gotthold Weil, ed., *Festschrift Eduard Sachau* (Berlin, 1915), p. 27.
[23] *Pamyatniki literatury drevney Rusi, XII vek* (Moscow, 1980), pp. 226–44. Cited at Abramovich,
p. 4, lines 10–17.

subsequently rescued independently and brought up in the same village without recognizing each other—until a final recognition scene when the whole family is reunited). At this regrettable mishap he loses his *sang froid*, and exclaims:

> Woe is me, once flourishing, but now stripped bare! Woe is me, once rich, but now like a prisoner! Woe is me, once served by a host of people, but now left alone, deprived even of my own children! But do not forsake me, O Lord, for ever, and do not despise my tears![24]

The shift from lamentation to prayer is also a feature of the laments in the *Tale*, and goes back, of course, to the Psalms, but the actual language is that of Greek rhetoric. But it does not follow that the *Tale* is keeping to the norms of hagiography, for the *Life of Eustace* is not a typical hagiographical text. It is evident that this passage, in both narrative content and style, derives from the Greek novel of the imperial period, whose heroes and heroines are constantly finding themselves in improbable scrapes and breaking into floods of tears and stylized lamentation. The language and the sentiment remain alien to martyrology proper. The one context where the lament was fully integrated into Byzantine religious writing is that of the sorrows of the Virgin Mary at the foot of the Cross. A hymn in the Greek liturgy for Good Friday develops the theme as follows:

> Striking her breast, she cried out in anguish: Alas, divine child! Alas, light of the world! Why, Lamb of God, have you departed from my eyes? ... My son, where has the beauty of your form departed? I cannot bear to see you unjustly crucified.[25]

The pathetic note so strong in the *Tale* is not, therefore, original in itself. But what *is* original and, as far as I am aware, unprecedented in hagiography is the placing of laments in the mouths of martyrs. This undermines the very purpose of martyrology, which is to represent their death as not defeat but victory, not tragedy but triumph. Although the reader is not meant to become tearful, it does not offend against the rules of the genre for the occasional martyr to be lamented by the members (especially female ones) of his own family.[26] These cannot regularly be

[24] I follow the Old Russian translation (pp. 232–4), which is very close to the Greek (*PG* 105, col. 393D).

[25] *Synekdemos orthodoxou* (Athens, 1912), pp. 286–7. For the gradual expansion of this theme from the seventh till the fourteenth century in the Byzantine Holy Week liturgy, see Demetrios I. Pallas, *Die Passion und Bestattung Christi in Byzanz* (Munich, 1965), pp. 30–66.

[26] E.g., the lament of the mother of St Hiero (*PG* 116, cols 117D–120A). The laments of the parents of Alexis (though not a martyr) in the *Life of Alexis* are particularly relevant, since this

expected to show the manly spirit of the mother of the Maccabean martyrs, especially when the sorrows of the Virgin Mary provide an honourable precedent. But for the martyr himself to break into the laments of the unhappy heroes and heroines of sentimental fiction is contrary to the very nature of the genre.

Admittedly, the tearfulness of Boris poses less of a problem, since his free choice of the path of non-resistance and sacrificial death stamps him as a genuine martyr, but the martyrdom of Gleb is more seriously aberrant. When he hears of his brother's murder, he expresses a wish to die, but purely in order to rejoin his brother, not out of desire for a martyr's crown. When his murderers descend on him, he breaks down in tears and pleads at great length for mercy. That in his last breath he quotes the biblical verse, 'Through your endurance you will gain your lives', scarcely alters the fact that what makes him a martyr is not acceptance of death in imitation of Christ, but simply the fact that he is an innocent victim.[27] The story of Boris and Gleb implies that veneration for a Christ-like death is due not only to heroic martyrs for the faith, but also to the murder victim, who is merely innocent and pitiable. It would, however, be an anachronism to see in this an anticipation of the tender compassion of St Francis or St Bonaventure. It was not in suffering *tout court*, but in the paradox of princely humiliation that Kievan Russia saw an image of the Passion of Christ. The figure of the princely martyr was a novel variation in the early medieval ideal of kingship, not a harbinger of the dolorism of late medieval piety.[28]

As original elements in the accounts of the martyrdom of Boris and Gleb I have singled out the political themes and the note of pathos. But it is not these or any individual themes that most intrigue, but rather the wide range of sources and analogues exhibited by the texts as a whole. On a first reading they seem straightforward enough, but under examination they reveal a masterly blend of disparate elements. Biblical archetypes of righteous suffering, the alternation of anguish and assurance in the Psalms, themes and motifs from traditional martyrology, the rhetorical

---

text was one of the most celebrated works of all medieval hagiography and was translated into Russian in the eleventh or twelfth centuries.

[27] Abramovich, pp. 40–2. It is part of this emphasis that the Gleb of hagiography is an adolescent, although the historical Gleb was a grown man.

[28] For these and other Russian princely martyrs, in the tradition of Boris and Gleb, see G. P. Fedotov, *The Russian Religious Mind: Kievan Christianity* (Cambridge, MA, 1946), pp. 104–10, and Michael Cherniavsky, *Tsar and People: Studies in Russian Myth* (New Haven and London, 1961), pp. 5–43.

expression of emotion in Greek narrative, the north European model of the princely martyr, Russian dynastic politics and nascent national feeling: all these elements feed into a synthesis that illustrates the breadth and virtuosity of the culture of Kievan Russia and its position within, not outside, the European mainstream.

Heythrop College, University of London

ST EILUNED OF BRECON
AND HER CULT*

by JOHN A. F. THOMSON

T HE cult of St Eiluned is much more fully documented than the
Saint herself, being described in two sources, of the twelfth and
fifteenth centuries. These must therefore be the starting-point for
an investigation both into the Saint's historicity, which is at best dubious,
and into the significance of the cult, which throws light on religious
practices over a very lengthy period. Aspects of these practices, and com-
parisons with other cults elsewhere, may well point to an early origin for
this one.

As it is preferable to work from more secure evidence through the
sketchier sources to more hypothetical ideas, the two sources with which
we must start are the *Itinerarium Cambriae* of Gerald of Wales, written
about 1190, in which he gives an elaborate description of a hilltop festival
near Brecon, and the *Itineraries* of William Worcestre, of 1478, which
show that the cult still persisted there, although possibly in a less
elaborate form. These accounts may be supplemented by some additional
information on folk practices in the manuscript of Hugh Thomas, from
the early eighteenth century—although this derives largely from Gerald, it
may add some additional information about the cult. Gerald and
Worcestre both describe the Saint by the name 'Elevetha'. Thomas calls
her 'St Lhud', and suggests that Gerald had called her 'Almedha'.
Obviously the 'v' in 'Elevetha' could be read as 'n', and the 'm' in
'Almedha' as 'in'. The name of 'Eiluned' must have been preserved locally,
because on a map of Breconshire (NGR, SO 058286) a site is designated as
St Elyned's Chapel.

Gerald's account refers to the twenty-four daughters of Brechan, from
whom the land derived its name, Brecheniauc, and states that with them
all living their lives in an odour of sanctity, many churches throughout
Wales bore their names.

> One of these is in the province of Brecheniauc, not far from the chief
> castle of Aberhotheni,[1] situated on the peak of a certain hill, and is

* I am grateful to my colleague Dr S. R. Airlie for reading an earlier draft of this paper and for
  making various suggestions to improve it.
[1] Aberhonddu or Brecon.

called the church of St. Elevetha: for this is the name of the holy
virgin, who, scorning marriage with an earthly king, triumphed in
wedding the eternal king in blessed martyrdom.

Now her solemn feast is celebrated in the same place each year on
the first day of August, where on that day many of the people
assemble from distant parts; and those who are sick with various
diseases are accustomed to receive the health they desire through the
merits of the holy virgin. It is worth my while saying what normally
happens at almost every feast of this virgin here. You would see men
and girls, sometimes in the church, sometimes in the cemetery, and
sometimes in a dance which takes its course around the cemetery
with singing, suddenly fall to the ground, at first quiet as if fallen into
a trance, and then immediately leaping up as if seized by a frenzy,
miming publicly with hands and feet those tasks which they
normally did unlawfully on feast days. You would see one man
setting his hand to the plough, another rousing oxen as with a goad,
and both, as if to ease their toil, lifting up their voices in their usual
kind of barbarous songs. You would see one imitating the art of the
cobbler, another that of the skinner. You would see one woman
pretending to carry a distaff, drawing out the thread to its length with
her hands and arms, and then combing the drawn-out thread as if
coiling it on a spindle, and another walking to and fro with the
threads as if laying out a web; you would be amazed at a third sitting
weaving as if the web were already set up, casting her shuttle back and
forth, and alternately striking the cloth at close quarters with her
reed. Finally, you would be astonished at them being brought into
church with their offerings to the altar, as if they had been awakened,
and returning home.[2]

This account gives the impression of some barely Christianized cult,
intended to bring prosperity to the community in both its agricultural and
its craft works. The mention of 'tasks which they normally did unlawfully
on feast days' may, however, suggest that the ritual also had some kind of
expiatory role and was perhaps even an attempt to obtain healing for
injuries sustained for such unlawful works, although Gerald makes no
reference to such cures taking place. This would parallel some of the
healings recorded in the *Miracula* of Gregory of Tours.[3] The practices

[2] Giraldus Cambrensis, *Opera*, ed. J. F. Dimock, *RS* (London, 1868), 6, pp. 31–3.
[3] I. N. Wood, 'Early Merovingian devotion in town and country', in D. Baker, ed., *The Church in
Town and Countryside*, *SCH*, 16 (1979), pp. 62–3.

followed, however, give more of an impression of folk customs than of recognized ecclesiastical rites.

William Worcestre does not allude to this collective cult, but describes a more individual form of recourse to the alleged site of the Saint's martyrdom:

> St. Elevetha, virgin and martyr, one of the twenty-four daughters of the petty king of Brecknock in Wales, twenty-four miles from Hereford;[4] she lies in the church of the virgin nuns of the town of Usk and was martyred on a hill one mile from Brecon where a spring of water welled forth, and the stone on which she was beheaded remains there, and as often as someone in honour of God and the said saint shall say the Lord's Prayer or drink of the water of the spring, he shall find a hair of the said holy woman upon the stone: a great miracle.[5]

This account shows the persistence of the legends of the Saint, which, indeed, were still preserved in popular traditions at an even later date. Hugh Thomas probably compiled his account in the first decade of the eighteenth century—he states in his record of the legends of St Kynauc that he had visited the site in 1702.[6] Both there and in his description of the sufferings and martyrdom of 'St Lhud', he claimed to draw on popular traditions, 'of the poor Ignorant Country People', or 'of the Inocent [*sic*] Country People',[7] as well as from earlier sources. He inserts into the passage from Gerald's *Itinerarium* the story of her flight in disguise to avoid marriage to a young prince, her ill-treatment by the inhabitants of various villages, whom she subsequently cursed, and who suffered unpleasant fates as a result, her establishment in a hermitage by 'the Lord of the Manor', and her ultimate martyrdom, when her frustrated lover discovered her, pursued her, and struck off her head. When the head came to rest, a spring of water welled forth, and a chapel was later built on the site of her hermitage.[8] This chapel survived until the time of the

---

[4] *Recte*, 36 miles.
[5] William Worcestre, *Itineraries*, ed. J. H. Harvey (Oxford, 1969), pp. 154–5. I have made one or two slight modifications to Harvey's translation. Worcestre also refers, pp. 62–3, to the twenty-four children of Brychan. Eiluned is here called 'Adwenhelye'.
[6] London, BL, MS Harley 4181, fol. 70r.
[7] Ibid., fol. 76r.
[8] Ibid., fols 76r–v. The account was printed, with some modifications to avoid offending the susceptibilities of the readers—for example, the transcript omits the fact that in one village the Saint was suspected of being a harlot—by G. E. F. Morgan, 'Forgotten sanctuaries', *Archaeologia Cambrensis*, ser. 6, 3 (1903), pp. 215–18.

Reformation. The writer claimed to have heard this account of the Saint's sufferings from the present lord of the land, who also told about continuing popular devotion to the site:

> To this place the young People of the towne did use to come every Mayday and have many sports and Devertions from an abuse of the Devout custom of Visiting the Church in former times but this is now quite laid aside.[9]

These passages pose questions for the historian, both about the background of the saint and about the nature of her cult. Other references to her by name are few, brief, and problematical. She is mentioned in the two so-called Brychan texts, the *De situ Brecheniauc*, in the London, British Library, Manuscript Cotton Vespasian A.xiv, and the *Cognacio Brychan* in Cotton Domitian I.[10] The references are very brief, in a list of the twenty-four daughters of Brychan. The Vespasian manuscript dates from about 1200, roughly contemporary with Gerald, but may originate in the collection at Gloucester, around 1130 or later, of hagiographical material from Llandbadarn Fawr, in West Wales, and possibly from Llandaff.[11] The *De situ Brecheniauc* was probably copied from an earlier manuscript, at least as old as the eleventh century,[12] and the reference reads: 'Eiliveth. filia Brachan. ygrugc gors anail', with a Latin gloss above, 'i. Jn agere lacus caltionis'.[13] The *Cognacio Brychan* manuscript is much later, dating from the sixteenth century, but probably derives from one of the thirteenth. It reads: 'Elyvet in Monte Gorsauael, que pro amore castitatis martirazata est.'[14] There is clearly a parallelism between the Welsh text in the *De situ* and the Latin of the *Cognacio*: 'ygrugc' is evidently 'In Crug.', meaning 'on the hill', and it is easy to see possible palaeographical confusion between 'gors anail' and 'Gorsauael'. The Latin gloss in the *De situ* is far from clear,

[9] BL, MS Harley 4181, fol. 77r.

[10] Both were edited by A. W. Wade-Evans, *Vitae sanctorum Britanniae et genealogiae* = Board of Celtic Studies, University of Wales, History and Law Series, 9 (Cardiff, 1944). The same author studied the texts in 'The Brychan documents', *Y Cymmrodor*, 19 (1906), pp. 18–50. The only reference to the Saint in the Bollandist *Acta sanctorum augusti*, 1 (Paris and Rome, 1867), derives from Gerald.

[11] K. Hughes, 'British Museum MS. Cotton Vespasian A. XIV ('Vitae Sanctorum Wallensium'): its purpose and provenance', in N. K. Chadwick et al., *Studies in the Early British Church* (Cambridge, 1958), p. 197. There was a slightly earlier parallel interest in early saints in Brittany in the eleventh century. Julia M. H. Smith, 'Oral and written: saints, miracles and relics in Brittany, c.850–1250', *Speculum*, 65 (1990), p. 313.

[12] E. G. B. Phillimore, 'A fragment from Hengwrt MS. 202', *Y Cymmrodor*, 7 (1886), pp. 105–6.

[13] Wade-Evans, *Vitae*, ix, xiii, p. 315.

[14] Ibid., xix, p. 318.

and Wade-Evans's translation of it as 'the mound of the holding's mere'[15] is at best conjectural and is certainly far from illuminating, as 'caltionis' has no discernible meaning, unless it is the genitive of either a personal or a place name.[16] It may be wiser to disregard the gloss as a late addition which may be misleading—Wade-Evans suggests that the Vespasian manuscript was copied by someone who did not understand Welsh, and that the gloss may therefore misrepresent the original meaning.[17] A more plausible interpretation of the readings in this case would be to take 'Gors anail/Gorsauael' as meaning 'Gorsaf haul', 'the station of the sun' or 'solstice', thereby connecting the site and the Saint with some traditional solar cult.[18]

Before examining the practices recorded by Gerald, it is necessary to note one further piece of twelfth-century evidence. Bishop Bernard of St David's (1116–49) granted the 'Chapel of Saint Haellid' to the prior and convent of Brecon, and his successor confirmed the grant.[19] This probably is a reference to the same Saint and suggests that her cult went back at least half a century before Gerald's account, perhaps contemporary with the collection of material later incorporated in the Vespasian manuscript. It is, however, at this point that a great gap emerges between the earliest records and the alleged date of the Saint.[20] If one follows the Brychan documents, one sees that they not only contain the genealogy of the eponymous chieftain from whom Brycheiniog was allegedly named, but also assign him a fifth-century Irish origin.[21]

The natural reaction to the Brychan documents is to dismiss them with total scepticism, but one fact must give one pause, namely, that archaeological evidence supports Irish connections with Brycheiniog—Brecknock has a higher proportion of Ogam inscribed early Christian stones than any other Welsh shire except Pembroke. The frequency of stones with Irish characteristics in the latter shire is hardly surprising geographically, but their occurrence in Brecknock is. Although none of the stones of the earliest type occurs in the immediate vicinity of Brecon town, and the

---

[15] Wade-Evans, 'The Brychan documents', p. 34.

[16] I owe this suggestion to Professor Derick S. Thomson.

[17] Wade-Evans, *Vitae*, xiii.

[18] I owe this suggestion to Mr Donald G. Howells, to whom I am deeply indebted for help with this paper, particularly on linguistic problems.

[19] Morgan, 'Forgotten sanctuaries', p. 219.

[20] D. N. Dumville, 'Sub-Roman Britain: history and legend', *History*, 62 (1977), p. 175, warns justifiably against overreliance on medieval sources for the Dark Age period.

[21] Wade-Evans, *Vitae*, pp. 313–18. 'The Brychan documents', p. 7.

centre of the Eiluned cult,[22] it is not unreasonable to assume that the higher proportion of early Christian stones in this shire than in neighbouring Glamorgan and Monmouth reflects the prominence of this area in early Christian Wales. This may indicate some substratum of truth behind the alleged Irish origin of Brychan. A further noteworthy characteristic of these early Welsh stones is the stress laid on filiation in the inscriptions, because although this was natural in Celtic tribal society, it was uncharacteristic of contemporary Christianity.[23] It possibly reflects a fusion of the social values of Celtic tradition with the new religion.

It is not only the stones which suggests that early Brecknock Christianity absorbed some customary pagan traditions, because aspects of the cult also hint at the adaptation of pagan customs to a Christian milieu. Gerald's description of rituals depicting the routines of ploughing, spinning, and weaving may point to some form of sympathetic magic, and it is also noteworthy that 1 August, or Lammas, the date of the Saint's festival, and 1 May, the date mentioned by Hugh Thomas as that on which the young people of Brecon visited the site, were two of the calendar feasts of the Celtic year. The coincidence may point to some pre-Christian cult which was taken over by the Church. If the references in the Brychan texts to 'Gors anail/Gorsauael' do refer, as suggested, to a possible solar cult, this too would indicate a possible attempt to Christianize some earlier practice, although not one associated with the major feasts of Celtic tradition.

A similar pagan background may be reflected in the stories of the Saint's martyrdom. Gerald does not mention this, but the story recorded by Worcestre, and elaborated in the folk traditions noted by Thomas, states that she died by beheading, and that a spring of water gushed forth at the point where the Saint's head came to rest. A parallel case to this from North Wales is that of St Winifred, in Flintshire, who was also beheaded while trying to escape a frustrated lover, and at the place of whose decapitation a spring gushed out. This spring, rather than any collection of corporal relics, remained the centre of Winifred's cult. A variant story is told of St Kynauc, Eiluned's brother—when he was martyred by beheading, his head dropped into a well, which then dried up.[24] These

---

[22] I. Ll. Foster, 'The Emergence of Wales', in I. Ll. Foster and G. Daniel, eds, *Prehistoric and Early Wales* (London, 1965), p. 218. V. E. Nash-Williams, *The Early Christian Monuments of Wales* (Cardiff, 1950), pp. 69–82.

[23] L. Alcock, 'Wales in the Fifth to the Seventh Centuries AD: archaeological evidence', in Foster and Daniel, *Prehistoric and Early Wales*, pp. 204–5, 207.

[24] Wade-Evans, *Vitae*, pp. 292–3; BL, MS Harley 4181, fol. 71r; Smith, 'Oral and written', p. 341.

stories have obvious common origins, the importance of springs and
rivers as focal points of ritual in pagan Celtic religion, and the cult of the
severed head, which was frequently connected with venerated waters.
Welsh and Irish literature contain allusions to severed heads possessing
magical qualities, and the head and neck of a woman have been found
behind the wicker lining of a well on a British site in Buckinghamshire. In
a well at Caerwent an image of a mother goddess has been preserved, and
in a pagan shrine from the same area, probably contemporary with the
late Roman period, a head image has been found.[25] Although nothing
visible remains of St Eiluned's chapel itself on Slwch Hill, there is a well
there, with a megalith nearby, which may possibly have been the stone
mentioned by Worcestre.[26] The combination of these factors may well
mark out the site of the later chapel as a pre-Christian cult centre.

If the site, and the cult observed there, reflect a Christianizing of an
existing holy place, an early date for its origins appears probable. It was a
matter for debate in Dark Age Christianity how such pagan sites should be
approached, and a story told by Gregory of Tours provides a possible
Merovingian parallel to the development of the Eiluned cult. A newly
appointed bishop came to a place where the local rural population were
accustomed to make offerings in a lake, and built a church of St Hilary on
the shore of the marsh, telling his people not to stain their souls with vain
rites, but rather to adore the relics of the Saint there, as he could act as
their intercessor with God. There was no religion, he said, in a swamp.[27]
The establishment of a Christian cult on an earlier pagan site sounds very
similar to what probably happened in Wales. At a later date, Gregory the
Great gave similar advice to Mellitus for transmission to Augustine of
Canterbury, laying down that pagan temples should be converted to
Christian use, and that Christian solemnities should be kept in place of
pagan sacrifices.[28] The rituals recorded by Gerald may contain elements of
such an adapted cult.

Not all Dark Age Christian leaders were so willing to compromise with
the pagan world—certainly Martin of Tours took active measures to

[25] Anne Ross, *Pagan Celtic Britain* (London, 1967), pp. 20, 104–5; Miranda J. Green, *The Gods of the Celts* (Gloucester, 1986), pp. 31–2, 131, 155, 218. Smith, 'Oral and written', pp. 323, 329, 335, notes similar well cults in other parts of the Celtic world.

[26] Morgan, 'Forgotten sanctuaries', pp. 222–3; F. Jones, *The Holy Wells of Wales* (Cardiff, 1954), pp. 96, n. 37, 146.

[27] Gregory of Tours, *Liber in gloria confessorum*, ed. W. Arndt and B. Krusch, *MGH.SRM*, I (Hanover, 1885), pp. 749–50. P. Brown, *The Cult of the Saints* (Chicago, 1981), pp. 125–6, attributes this story to the *Vitae Patrum*, but the reference appears to be incorrect.

[28] Bede, *Ecclesiastical History*, ed. B. Colgrave and R. A. B. Mynors, *OMT* (1969), i, 20, pp. 106–9.

destroy altars erected to individuals who were shown not to be saints, and pagan temples. He is also recorded as cutting down a tree to which pagan rites were attached.[29] Similar attacks on holy places in nature, including springs, were made by some of his successors. Among the pagan practices which were denounced in Gallic councils of the sixth and seventh centuries were the worship of holy trees and holy springs.[30] The Church did not pursue any single strategy, and it may well be that the geography of the holy in Italy, Gaul, Spain, and Africa, where Christian cult sites were new ones,[31] reflected greater success for the more hard-line party there. But even in Gaul there was, as we have seen, some scope for conversion by infiltration, and this may well have been the pattern which operated in Wales.

The allusions to the cult suggest that it probably had an early origin, but do not give much assistance in resolving the questions of the Saint's historicity and the nature of her alleged martyrdom, which must remain not proven. Whether or not she was a historical figure, however, the belief in her martyrdom was at any rate a historical fact. It was the lesson which this taught which was the basic function of the cult, and as the story associated with it emphasized that she died to save her virginity, it must clearly be seen as a hagiographer's device to stress the importance of that particular virtue. The similar fate of St Winifred was related in order to point the same moral. One must, I think, take the idea of a martyr in the original sense of the Greek word meaning 'a witness'. The story was intended to give testimony to a particular truth which was being taught. The fact that she was described as being of noble family (as so many Dark Age saints were) again mirrors early hagiographical tradition, which tended to pick its saints from the ranks of the powerful.

The other striking feature of the cult is its long survival, because it demonstrates that although the Church had come to terms with pagan society in the conversion period, by adaptation rather than by confrontation, pagan elements still survived in popular religion. The survival of another well cult in the fifteenth century is recorded in 1410, at no great distance, on the English side of the border. In that year, Bishop Mascall of Hereford forbade recourse to a well at Turnaston, on the river Dore, some

---

[29] Sulpicius Severus, *Life of St. Martin*, tr. B. M. Peebles, in *The Fathers of the Church*, 7 (New York, 1949), pp. 118–21.

[30] Brown, *Cult of the Saints*, p. 125; A. H. M. Jones, 'The Western Church in the Fifth and Sixth Centuries', in M. W. Barley and R. P. C. Hanson, eds, *Christianity in Britain, 300–700* (Leicester, 1968), p. 15.

[31] Brown, *Cult of the Saints*, p. 91.

ten miles from his episcopal city and six miles upstream from Pontrilas.[32] The episcopal mandate related that many subjects of the diocese had recourse to the well, even carrying mud away from it as a relic. The Bishop's ban on such actions does not state if the practice was regarded as purely pagan or if, as at Brecon, there may have been some unmentioned veneer of Christianity over it. The removal of the mud from the well may, however, in its desire for preserving something tangible, parallel Worcestre's story of the miraculous appearance of the so-called relic of a hair at St Eiluned's well.[33]

One of the most striking features of the Eiluned cult was its persistence to the end of the Middle Ages, and it may indeed have spread out from its original site at Brecon. Worcestre states that the Saint's body was preserved at Usk, where a house of Benedictine nuns was founded in 1236.[34] Although this indicates that the church authorities were still giving their blessing to the cult at this date, there is little sign that it acquired the same degree of popularity there as it had at Brecon. Worcestre himself laid more stress on the practices at the spring than on any of the relics at Usk, Leland did not mention the Saint in his description of the house at Usk in his *Itinerary*, and among the offerings recorded there in the *Valor Ecclesiasticus* there is no mention of any shrine.[35] A reference to a 1520 agreement between the prior and the vicar of Brecon suggests that the former had a right to offerings at the chapel, but again these are not mentioned in the *Valor Ecclesiasticus*.[36] This would suggest that the level of appeal which the cult had at Usk cannot have been great, however much it survived at Brecon, either in the religious terms described by Worcestre or in Hugh Thomas's description of folk customs. By this time, of course, the original function of the 'martyrdom' and the moral and spiritual teaching to be drawn from it had been forgotten.

University of Glasgow

[32] *Register of Robert Mascall*, CYS, 21 (1917), pp. 74–5.
[33] Hair is not a common feature in connection with Welsh wells: Jones, *Holy Wells of Wales*, p. 96. One wonders if there is a link with the association of Medusa-type heads and healing springs in the pagan period: Ross, *Pagan Celtic Britain*, pp. 90–1.
[34] W. Dugdale, *Monasticon Anglicanum* (London, 1823), 4, p. 591.
[35] T. Hearne, ed., *Leland's Itinerary* (Oxford, 1744), 5, p. 12. *Valor Ecclesiasticus*, 4 (London, 1822), pp. 365–6.
[36] Morgan, 'Forgotten sanctuaries', p. 219. *Valor Ecclesiasticus*, 4, p. 401.

THE POLITICAL SETTING OF THE BECKET
TRANSLATION OF 1220

by RICHARD EALES

BETWEEN 1170 and 1220 the cult of Thomas Becket had spread widely within Christendom, bearing with it the primary message that the Archbishop was a martyr who had died for the liberties of the Church, and in opposition to royal oppression.[1] But no well-documented medieval cult, and certainly no major cult, is adequately characterized in such as simple and straightforward way. If 'the *causa beati Thome* became the symbol of the rights of the church throughout the thirteenth century' and beyond,[2] this did not prevent it embracing other ideas and aspirations, some of them in apparent tension with each other, from the 1170s onwards. Over much of Europe the image of the Martyr's fortitude confronting the King's tyranny, already to some extent pre-sold in the propaganda of the exile years 1164 to 1170, required no qualification. In England, as Beryl Smalley has pointed out, 'Writers had the more difficult task of combining loyalty to their king with defence of ecclesiastical freedom',[3] especially after Henry II had achieved a *rapprochement* with the Church. One way of handling this problem was to universalize the cult, by emphasizing that it ultimately transcended issues of royal-clerical relations, however important. Becket was portrayed as the martyr of the age, whose death had benefited the whole of Christendom. Such beliefs, made more plausible by the extraordinary miracle-working achievements of the tomb at Canterbury, led at their extreme to the systematic comparison of Becket's death with that of Christ. In the long-running debate over martyrdom and asceticism as rival models of sainthood, Thomas could be portrayed, with varying degrees of plausibility, as an ideal type, whose life and death embodied both. However universal, the cult also put down strong local roots; apart from Canterbury, most obviously at London, where he was born, and in the province of Rouen, the Seine valley, from where his family

---

[1] No attempt has been made here to give full references to the enormous literature on Thomas Becket's life and cult. The starting point for the former is now Frank Barlow, *Thomas Becket* (London, 1986); for the latter the works of Foreville and Duggan cited below.

[2] Anne Duggan, 'The Cult of St Thomas Becket in the thirteenth century', in Meryl Jancey, ed., *St Thomas Cantilupe Bishop of Hereford: Essays in his Honour* (Hereford, 1982), p. 30.

[3] Beryl Smalley, *The Becket Conflict and the Schools* (Oxford, 1973), p. 193.

originated.[4] But a local dedication, or patron, or association with an existing cult, could give St Thomas a special role almost anywhere in Europe. Aspects of his cult were also imitated, sometimes implicitly, sometimes with almost embarrassing opportunism, as in the local canonization of William of Perth at Rochester, after he was murdered there in 1201.[5] The fame of St Thomas was diffused through almost every means known to the age: personal networks of family and locality; organizations within the Church, especially the Cistercian Order; liturgy, letters, lives and miracle collections, sermons, Latin and vernacular poetry; music; painting, sculpture, and stained glass; cult objects, ranging from elaborately decorated *châsses* to badges and vials of water.[6]

Those who organized or reported the translation of 1220 could therefore draw on an exceptionally wide range of popular and learned traditions. The ceremony of 7 July at Canterbury had the effect of bringing many of them together into a new synthesis, as well as extending the practice of the cult by furnishing it with a major new feast day and by importing the concept of the fifty-year jubilee, whose origins have been investigated by Raymonde Foreville.[7] In the words of another French historian, the translation 'contributed to giving the cult of St. Thomas the character which it retained until the end of the fifteenth century.'[8] Specialist studies of liturgy, music, and preaching have all done something to confirm this view, despite gaps and uncertainties in the evidence. Art historians have also been concerned with the events of 1220, as marking the culmination of the influential early-Gothic rebuilding programme at

---

[4] Raymonde Foreville's crucial articles on the diffusion of the cult in France are reprinted in *Thomas Becket dans la tradition historique et hagiographique* (London, 1981). Two of them (one in a revised form) are in Foreville, ed., *Thomas Becket: Actes du Colloque International de Sédières* (Paris, 1975) [hereafter *Becket, Colloque*], pp. 135–52, 163–87. See also Foreville, 'Thomas Becket et la France Capétienne', in Christopher Harper-Bill et al., eds, *Studies in Medieval History presented to R. Allen Brown* (Woodbridge, 1989), pp. 117–28.

[5] On the general process of diffusion, see many of the contributions in *Becket, Colloque*; Duggan, 'Cult', pp. 22–9; A. Duggan, *Thomas Becket: a Textual History of his Letters* (Oxford, 1980). On St William of Rochester, see refs in D. H. Farmer, *The Oxford Dictionary of Saints*, 2nd edn (Oxford, 1987), pp. 438–9.

[6] E. Walberg, *La Tradition hagiographique de S. Thomas Becket avant la fin du XIIe siècle* (Paris, 1929), and Tancred Borenius, *St. Thomas Becket in Art* (London, 1932) are the key works on the literary and artistic expressions of the cult. See also *Becket, Colloque*; Denis Stevens, 'Music in Honor of St Thomas of Canterbury', *Musical Quarterly*, 56 (1970), pp. 312–48; Phyllis B. Roberts, *Thomas Becket in the Medieval Latin Preaching Tradition* (The Hague, 1992).

[7] Raymonde Foreville, 'L'idée de Jubilé chez les theologiens et les canonistes', *RHE*, 56 (1961), pp. 401–23, reprinted in Foreville, *Becket*; Raymonde Foreville, *Le Jubilé de Saint Thomas Becket* (Paris, 1958), esp. pp. 1–11, 21–45.

[8] Amaury d'Esneval, 'La survivance de Saint Thomas Becket à travers sons quatrième successeur, Etienne Langton', in *Becket, Colloque*, pp. 111–14, quotation at p. 114.

Canterbury. Though the building itself had been substantially complete since 1184, glazing and wall painting, as well as the fitting up of the shrine itself, seem to have been under way between 1218 and 1220. In a letter of January 1219, one of a series authorizing the translation, Pope Honorius III allowed Stephen Langton to devote part of the offerings at the cathedral to the *renovatio* of its east end.[9]

More generally, ecclesiastical historians have not neglected the importance of the various interests involved in the events of 1220. For the Canterbury monks it represented the apparent culmination of long-standing attempts to keep their church at the centre of ecclesiastical affairs in England, an objective kept firmly in mind through the various events which had conspired to delay the translation of the martyr's body into his shrine since 1174. Most recently, they had returned from interdict and exile, only to find Kent a leading theatre of civil war between 1215 and 1217.[10] In 1220 it appeared that the monks had at last won through and secured their position, though this was in some ways illusory. A further attempt to advance their claims after Langton's death in 1228, by forging an elaborate charter of St Thomas himself confirming all their privileges, came to ignominious failure by 1238 with the detection of the forgery and resignation of the prior.[11] For Archbishop Stephen Langton, the ceremony of 1220, in the presence of the King, the papal legate, and almost all the English episcopate, marked the success of his attempts to reimpose order and arbitrate between conflicting parties in the kingdom, wiping away the memory of his suspension by Innocent III in 1215–16, and justifying the faith which the new Pope, Honorius III, had in him. Langton's self-identification with Becket during the years of his own exile down to 1213, largely at Pontigny, made the symbolism of the translation especially apposite. In the autumn of 1220 he was able to go on to Rome and secure the withdrawal of the legate Pandulf, together with an undertaking that no more legates would be sent to England in his lifetime. All

<hr/>

[9] Foreville, *Jubilé*, p. 165. The scale of building work just before 1220 remains uncertain; see the suggestions in Madeleine H. Caviness, 'A lost cycle of Canterbury paintings of 1220', *Antiquaries Journal*, 54 (1974), pp. 65–74; Madeleine H. Caviness, 'Canterbury Cathedral Clerestory: the glazing programme in relation to the campaigns of construction', *Medieval Art and Architecture at Canterbury before 1220* = *British Archaeological Association Conference Transactions*, 5 (1982) [hereafter *Canterbury before 1220*], pp. 46–55.

[10] R. W. Southern, *The Monks of Canterbury and the Murder of Archbishop Becket* (Urry Memorial Lecture, Canterbury, 1985), and Christopher R. Cheney, *Pope Innocent III and England* (Stuttgart, 1976), pp. 208–20, are useful surveys of a complex subject, documented in the Canterbury letter collections and the chronicles of Gervase of Canterbury.

[11] C. R. Cheney, '*Magna Carta Beati Thomae*: another Canterbury Forgery', *BIHR*, 36 (1963), pp. 1–26, repr. in Cheney, *Medieval Texts and Studies* (Oxford, 1973), pp. 78–110.

these points have been brought out in modern studies of Langton and papal policy.[12]

In the light of this, it might reasonably be asked what remains to be said about the translation of 1220 and the role of the martyr's cult in early thirteenth-century England. An answer emerges if the emphasis is shifted further towards the political setting of the event. Though historians of the cult have remarked that it 'could be used to weld together the political and religious settlement', or that 'for the monarchy, it marked the establishment of its authority under the protection of the papal legate; and, for the generality of the people, it marked the restoration of peace and order',[13] they have not pursued these issues very far. Political historians have generally glossed over the translation, despite the attention given to it in contemporary chronicle sources. David Carpenter, in his recent reassessment of the minority of Henry III, placed the event in a precise narrative context, but he also called it 'England's latest tourist attraction', and focused attention almost exclusively on the diplomatic business being transacted among the leading figures present in Canterbury.[14] The argument that great church or court ceremonies, or later medieval parliaments, were important because they brought many important people together, almost regardless of their substantive business, has some validity. But an excessive emphasis on the audience risks devaluing the occasion itself. The translation ceremony was clearly planned, and carefully timed, well in advance, as the papal letters of January 1219 testify. Probably Langton had such an event in mind before he returned to England in May 1218. It took place in unique circumstances: the minority of an English king who had acknowledged that he held his kingdom as a papal fief. Several features of this situation, in themselves quite well known, may yield new conclusions if looked at in relation to the Becket translation.

First, there is the fact that the pacification process in England between 1217 and 1224 was a gradual and cautious one, whose outcome at several stages appeared uncertain.[15] The Regent William Marshal, until his death

[12] F. M. Powicke, *Stephen Langton* (Oxford, 1928); Kathleen Major, ed., *Acta Stephani Langton Cantuariensis Archiepiscopi*, CYS,50 (1950); Cheney, *Innocent III*; Jane E. Sayers, *Papal Government and England during the Pontificate of Honorius III, 1216–1227* (Cambridge, 1984), pp. 162–94. See above, n. 8.
[13] Sayers, *Honorius III*, p. 190; Duggan, 'Cult', p. 38.
[14] D. A. Carpenter, *The Minority of Henry III* (London, 1990), pp. 193, 200–3, quotation at p. 193.
[15] Besides Carpenter, *Minority*, the major recent studies are Robert C. Stacey, *Politics, Policy and Finance under Henry III 1216–1245* (Oxford, 1987), pp. 1–44; J. C. Holt, *Magna Carta*, 2nd edn (Cambridge, 1992), pp. 378–405.

in May 1219, the Justiciar Hubert de Burgh, and the Bishop of Winchester, acting with the papal legates, Guala from May 1216 to September 1218 and Pandulf from then until July 1221, had first to agree among themselves and then to persuade powerful magnates to accept their decisions. The royal government might in theory be restoring order and enforcing obedience; in practice it could sometimes do no more than preside over compromises and agreements. In these circumstances, the additional weapons of the Church were valuable, if not indispensable. Pope Innocent III had already excommunicated Prince Louis of France and his baronial allies just before his death in July 1216. Guala then had the task of enforcing this papal policy on the English Church. Pandulf found himself even more directly involved in such matters than his predecessor, especially after William Marshal bequeathed the regency to him in 1219, in name at least.[16] Already in May 1219 he was seeking to discover the terms on which the custody of castles had been granted earlier in the minority, and in May 1220 the Pope wrote several letters to England, presumably in reply to the legate's suggestions, urging amongst other things that no one should hold more than two royal castles.[17]

Second, the practical concerns of the legates, the bishops, and other church leaders in England to support programmes of pacification, while quite explicable in terms of immediate needs, were also underpinned by theological influences emanating from Paris, of which Stephen Langton, whose teaching career there lasted twenty-five years, until 1206, was a leading exponent.[18] In his study of Peter the Chanter, who exercised a considerable and perhaps defining influence on the future prelate, J. W. Baldwin pointed to parallels between 'Langton's conception of the church as the congregation of the faithful, both clerics and laymen' and 'the baronial notion of the community of the realm'. Baldwin accepted, though, that the Archbishop's partisanship and involvement in the drawing up of Magna Carta were exaggerated by some chroniclers, and concluded only that 'no definite correlations can be drawn, but the possible connection is too tantalizing to be excluded.' It is possible to go

---

[16] Cheney, *Innocent III*, pp. 391–400; Sayers, *Honorius III*, pp. 162–94; Fred A. Cazel, 'The Legates Guala and Pandulf', in P. R. Coss and S. D. Lloyd, eds, *Thirteenth Century England II* (Woodbridge, 1988), pp. 15–21.

[17] Carpenter, *Minority*, pp. 142, 189–90; text of one 1220 letter in W. W. Shirley, ed., *Royal and other Historical Letters illustrative of the Reign of Henry III*, 2 vols, RS (1862, 1866), I, pp. 535–6. See also Richard Eales, 'Castles and Politics in England, 1215–1224', *Thirteenth Century England II*, pp. 23–43.

[18] See above, n. 12; Smalley, *Becket Conflict*, especially pp. 204–5, 214–15; Duggan, 'Cult', pp. 36–8.

much beyond this in estimating the influence of theological ideas on English politics and the criticism of some aspects of royal power, though such theories must be balanced by an awareness of the many ways in which Magna Carta and subsequent documents emerged from the evolution of secular law and custom.[19] Less speculatively, it is clear that Peter and his followers strongly supported Becket's cause, and his status as a martyr.[20] They were much preoccupied with the many smaller issues of practical justice and administration which concerned the post-Becket generation of educated churchmen, as it became obvious that great debates over church freedom had not done away with the older need to compromise and co-operate with royal power, only somewhat changed its terms. The requirement of social justice in order to secure an effective peace was all too obviously a concern in the minority of Henry III.

Third, an important contemporary issue which overlapped heavily with questions of practical politics and religious ideals was that of the crusade. Peace within Christendom, desirable in itself, was also from the papal point of view the essential prelude to a successful crusade. For the individual the status of *crucesignatus*, however seriously assumed, could also be a means of dealing with political problems at home. John took the cross in March 1215, largely to strengthen his relations with Rome in the face of the impending crisis in England. His nine-year-old son Henry did the same at the time of his first coronation in October 1216, so effectively taking over his father's unfulfilled vow.[21] Pope Innocent III's violent condemnation of Prince Louis' English expedition in 1216 was largely a reaction to the fact that it threatened to direct resources away from the crusade. There is considerable evidence that either Innocent or his successor Honorius III had explicitly licensed English crusaders to divert their energies into fighting against Louis and his allies, whom Innocent called worse than Saracens, if not in full discharge of an expedition to the Holy Land, at least as a necessary preparation for it. Contemporary chronicles and royal records describe the civil war in terms of a crusade. The royalists at the battle of Lincoln in 1217, according to the Dunstable

---

[19] John W. Baldwin, *Masters, Princes and Merchants: the Social Views of Peter the Chanter and his Circle*, 2 vols (Princeton, 1970), quotation at 1, p. 166. Other assessments of clerical influence in Cheney, *Innocent III*, pp. 375–86; Holt, *Magna Carta*, pp. 216–31, 281–2.

[20] Baldwin, *Masters*, 1, pp. 145–7, 256–7; Smalley, *Becket Conflict*, pp. 201–5.

[21] On English crusading in this period, see Christopher Tyerman, *England and the Crusades 1095–1588* (Chicago, 1988), pp. 86–99; Simon Lloyd, *English Society and the Crusade 1216–1307* (Oxford, 1988), pp. 198–209; Cheney, *Innocent III*, pp. 239–70.

Annals, advanced wearing white crosses.[22] Crusading ideals were also by this time strongly linked with the cult of St Thomas. Henry II's penance for his part in the murder, agreed in 1172, included the promise to go on crusade as soon as practicable, and meantime to provide enough money to sustain 200 Templar knights for a year. Henry's subsequent ambivalence about keeping his vow aroused widespread criticism in England, most famously from Gerald of Wales, but he did remit large sums to Jerusalem. A copy of his will of 1182, in which he made arrangements for further substantial payments, was deposited at Canterbury Cathedral, perhaps in acknowledgement of the 1172 terms.[23] There was also the hospital of St Thomas of Acre, set up in Acre around the time of the Third Crusade, and soon associated with Richard I, who was later regarded as its founder. Later, in the 1220s, the Order acquired a London house on land which had once belonged to Thomas Becket's father, and also in 1227-8 the Order in the East was reformed by Peter des Roches, the Bishop of Winchester, who had played a leading role in the tutelage of the young Henry III.[24] It is important that at the time of the Becket translation in 1220 successful crusading in the Holy Land appeared a more realizable goal than at any time since 1193. This was the mid-point of the Fifth Crusade, between the capture of Damietta in 1219 and the disastrous advance up the Nile in 1221 which led to total defeat. For a year or more it might have seemed that a new crusading conquest had begun, and required only to be followed up.

Fourth, in considering the links between Becket's exceptional status as English saint and martyr, and the exceptional political circumstances which surrounded the translation of his relics in 1220, it is useful to look also at the ways in which other English cults were employed at the same time. Hugh of Avalon, Bishop of Lincoln, who died in 1200, had already acquired an extraordinary reputation as a holy man, and as a figure in national affairs, despite his foreign origin.[25] At his funeral in Lincoln both

---

22 Simon Lloyd, 'Political Crusades in England, c.1215–17 and c.1263–5', in P. W. Edbury, ed., *Crusade and Settlement* (Cardiff, 1985), pp. 113–20; Tyerman, *England and the Crusades*, pp. 133–44. Dunstable Annals, in H. R. Luard, ed., *Annales Monastici*, 5 vols, RS (1864–9) [hereafter *Ann. Mon.*], 3, p. 49.

23 Tyerman, *England and the Crusades*, pp. 36–56; H. E. Mayer, 'Henry II of England and the Holy Land', *EHR*, 97 (1982), pp. 721–39; W. Stubbs, ed., *The Historical Works of Gervase of Canterbury*, 2 vols, RS (1879–80), 1, pp. 298–300.

24 A. J. Forey, 'The military order of St Thomas of Acre', *EHR*, 92 (1977), pp. 481–503. Many other accounts are less critical in separating contemporary evidence from later traditions.

25 Henry Mayr-Harting, ed., *St. Hugh of Lincoln* (Oxford, 1987). See also the documents transcribed in D. H. Farmer, 'The Canonisation of St Hugh of Lincoln', *Lincs. Arch. Reports and Papers*, 6, pt 2 (1956), pp. 86–117; and the Lives: Decima L. Douie and Hugh Farmer, eds.,

King John and King William of Scotland had helped to carry his coffin. But the petition for canonization reached the Pope only in 1219, and was then remitted to a small English commission headed by Stephen Langton, who pushed the process through efficiently, though with full attention to the evidence, much of which survives. The bull of canonization was issued on 16 February 1220; his first feast day was celebrated at Lincoln on the following 17 November. Though St Hugh's cult was always strongest in the large diocese of Lincoln, there is considerable evidence, including the reaction of contemporary chroniclers to the canonization,[26] that he was regarded as a notable addition to the calendar of English saints, a figure who had shown the ability to infuse religious principle into politics. Even more intriguing is the contemporary role of Wulfstan, Bishop of Worcester, who died in 1095, but was formally canonized in 1203, this time following the report of a commission overseen by Archbishop Hubert Walter.[27] The canonization was brought about almost entirely on the initiative of the bishop and chapter of Worcester, but at some subsequent point King John, whose itinerary brought him to Worcester in most years of his reign, seems to have taken an interest in the cult. In 1211, if the Burton annals can be believed, John attempted unsuccessfully to make political capital out of the legend of Wulfstan refusing to surrender his staff of office to William the Conqueror on the grounds that it had been conferred on him by Edward the Confessor.[28] Whether or not John was attracted to St Wulfstan because he saw him as a witness to rightful royal power over the Church, he chose in 1216 to be buried at Worcester near to the body of the Saint. Only after that did there follow, in 1218, an elaborate translation of Wulfstan's relics in the presence of a large gathering, including the young King Henry. In effect, John himself was being laid to rest, and a symbolic statement made of his reconciliation, and that of his house, with the Church. Recent work on John's tomb, a strikingly personalized marble effigy, which shows him, unusually, holding a naked sword, has suggested that it constituted a novel portrayal of kingship. The

---

Magna Vita Sancti Hugonis, 2 vols (London, 1961); Richard M. Loomis, ed., *Gerald of Wales, the Life of St Hugh of Avalon* (New York, 1985).

[26] Most notably the Barnwell Annals, in W. Stubbs, ed., *The Historical Collections of Walter of Coventry*, 2 vols, RS (1872–3), 2, p. 243.

[27] Emma Mason, *St Wulfstan of Worcester c.1008–1095* (Oxford, 1990), pp. 254–79, on the growth of his cult, pp. 279–85, on the canonization.

[28] Burton Annals, in *Ann. Mon.*, 1, p. 211. See Emma Mason, 'St. Wulfstan's staff: a legend and its uses', *Medium Aevum*, 53 (1984), pp. 157–79; Peter Draper, 'King John and St. Wulfstan', *JMedH*, 10 (1984), pp. 41–50.

traditional dating of the effigy to 1232, from the Tewkesbury Annals, may not be conclusive, and it is possibly earlier.[29] In any case, it most probably was designed to symbolize the fact that John at least died a loyal son of the Church, *crucesignatus*, wielding the sword against its enemies. The cult of Edward the Confessor also carried special political implications in these years. Edward's canonization had been achieved in 1160–1, after a failed attempt in 1138–40, largely because the efforts of the Westminster monks were then effectively backed by Henry II, capitalizing on the favour he enjoyed through his recent recognition of Alexander III against his schismatic opponent.[30] But Henry's successors showed little concern to extend the royal cult or accord it special treatment. The relationship, in contrast with that of St Denis and the Capetians, was an interrupted one. In John's reign it was opponents of the King who exploited the name of St Edward, drawing on secular as well as religious traditions to demand the restoration of his good laws and customs in 1215.[31] Henry III's quite new and single-minded devotion to the Westminster cult manifested from 1220 onwards can be seen as a reflection of his personal piety, but also as a response to political events.

It may now be possible to suggest how some of the surrounding circumstances conditioned the translation ceremony at Canterbury. On 17 May 1220 Archbishop Stephen Langton crowned the young King in Westminster Abbey.[32] This second coronation, for which papal authorization had been sought the previous October, was a calculated attempt to boost Henry's prestige, and so to face down the defiance of some magnates and officials who were ignoring the instructions of the minority government. With this in mind, it was a lavish symbolic event. David Carpenter calculated that 'at least £760 was spent on the ceremony and the celebrations, thus exhausting a good proportion of the revenues from the exchequer's Easter term', but also suggested that it represented a good investment on the part of the King's advisers.[33] King and Archbishop each took advantage of the occasion: Henry to lay the foundation-stone for his

---

[29] Jane Martindale, 'The Sword on the Stone: resonances of a medieval symbol of power', *Anglo-Norman Studies*, 15 (1993) (forthcoming); Tewkesbury Annals, in *Ann. Mon.*, 1, p. 84. See also Barrie Singleton, 'The remodelling of the East End of Worcester Cathedral in the earlier part of the thirteenth century', *Medieval Art and Architecture at Worcester Cathedral = British Archaeological Association Conference Transactions*, 1 (1978), pp. 105–15.

[30] Bernhard W. Scholz, 'The canonization of Edward the Confessor', *Speculum*, 36 (1961), pp. 38–60.

[31] As in the supposed reply of the papal nuncio to John in 1211, Burton Annals, in *Ann. Mon.*, 1, pp. 209–14, and above, n. 28. See also Holt, *Magna Carta*, pp. 113–14.

[32] Carpenter, *Minority*, pp. 187–221 is a full narrative of events in the summer of 1220.

[33] Carpenter, *Minority*, pp. 162, 187–91, quotation at p. 188.

projected rebuilding of Westminster Abbey, Langton to promulgate the recent canonization of Hugh of Lincoln. On the day after the coronation, according to the Dunstable Annals, all the barons present swore that they would resign any royal castle or offices in their possession at the King's request, a programme which Pope Honorius and the legate Pandulf were ready to back up with ecclesiastical sanctions.[34] The King and his advisers almost at once departed on a journey to York, where a settlement was concluded with King Alexander of Scotland. This first appearance of the young Henry in the north of England enabled his advisers to hear and determine several major disputes and to recover several castles; above all, on the return journey south in late June, Rockingham and Sauvey, which had been retained by the Earl of Aumâle in open defiance of earlier orders. Carpenter suggested that this was something of a windfall, the product of an on-the-spot decision by royal commanders that 'the castle was there for the taking' rather than a planned operation. But contemporary chroniclers generally represented the royal progress to the north, sandwiched between the great ecclesiastical events of May and July 1220, as an important advance in the assertion of royal power.[35]

The court had certainly to be back in the south of England for the translation ceremony on 7 July, which was evidently long planned. The martyr's body was removed from its tomb in the crypt of Canterbury Cathedral only on the night of 4 July, if the variant date of 27 June in one early source is regarded as a misreading,[36] by Langton, Richard, Bishop of Salisbury, and some of the Christ Church monks. Objections to the division of relics were often expressed by contemporary writers, especially those with local loyalties, but Langton, who had apparently secured an arm of St Wulfstan in 1218, is known to have removed some fragments of bone, one of which he presented to the Pope later in the year. The subsequent induction of the Saint into his new shrine took place in the presence of the King, the legate, the Archbishop of Canterbury, the Archbishop of Reims, who presided at the service, an unnamed Hungarian archbishop, and seventeen bishops. Almost every English chronicle, no matter how local, mentions the event; a number give quite

---

[34] Dunstable Annals, in *Ann. Mon.*, 3, p. 57; and on sanctions for recovery of castles, above, n. 17.

[35] Carpenter, *Minority*, pp. 194–9, quotation at p. 199. Barnwell Annals, 2, pp. 244–5, may exaggerate Henry's triumph, but almost every chronicler mentions the fall of Rockingham.

[36] 5 Kalends July for 5 July, appendix to the Quadrilogus Life of Becket, in J. C. Robertson, ed., *Materials for the History of Thomas Becket*, 7 vols, RS (1875–85), 4, p. 426; Foreville, *Jubilé*, p. 8. The translation date of 7 July was elaborately computed to coincide with the Old Testament period of jubilee (Lev. 25); Duggan, 'Cult', pp. 38–9.

detailed descriptions of it.[37] The Barnwell annalist carefully notes the 540-day indulgence offered to those who were at Canterbury within fifteen days of the ceremony: 40 for the Pope, the legate, and each of the archbishops present, 20 for each of the bishops. These, as Foreville remarks, were exceptionally generous benefits for the papacy to authorize at this date, comparable only with crusade indulgences.[38] The liturgy of the ceremony, so far as it can be reconstructed, appears to have emanated from Langton or his circle and to have echoed the language of the papal letters in 1219 and a sermon which Langton himself may have delivered at the translation, or perhaps its anniversary in 1221.[39] One element emphasized in all of these was Becket's special status as *the* English martyr and saint. A second Langton sermon, delivered in Rome on 29 December 1220, suggested that England might be called a thorn, since it had produced such sharp persecutions of the Church, yet it had also produced roses, which represent glorious martyrs: St Alphege, St Edmund, and most recently St Thomas. For this reason, more good might be hoped for from the English thorn. Langton in this text also drew on the theme of the banqueting-house for a succession of images, in one of which the wine-jars at the feast stand for martyrs of the Church, and the wine their blood.[40] The real banquet which took place in Canterbury in July 1220 was closely described in some sources, and clearly intended to be seen as the counterpart to the coronation feast two months earlier. It was held in the great hall of the Archbishop's palace, which a recent reconstruction has confirmed was second in size only to Westminster Hall in medieval England. Begun by Hubert Walter, the building was probably finished by Langton in time for the translation.[41] An extraordinarily detailed account of the feast survives in a Latin poem attributed since the 1920s to Henry of Avranches. Clearly this is more than a literal description, not just in

[37] See especially Dunstable Annals, in *Ann. Mon.*, 3, p. 58; Waverley Annals, in *Ann. Mon.*, 2, pp. 293–4; F. Madden, ed., *Matthaei Parisiensis Historia Anglorum*, 3 vols, RS (1866–9), 2, pp. 241–2; Barnwell Annals, 2, pp. 245–6. On the setting, see also William Urry, 'Some notes on the two resting places of St. Thomas at Canterbury', *Becket, Colloque*, pp. 195–208.

[38] Barnwell Annals, 2, p. 246; Foreville, *Jubilé*, pp. 37–45, 165–6.

[39] Foreville, *Jubilé*, pp. 89–95, compares the surviving texts; see also Duggan, 'Cult', pp. 39–40. The sermon text is in Phyllis B. Roberts, *Selected Sermons of Stephen Langton* (Toronto, 1980), pp. 65–94. At p. 10 Roberts suggests the text 'may well represent a latter amalgam of two stages of Langton's preaching on Becket in 1220 and 1221'.

[40] This text, recovered only recently, is in Roberts, *Selected Sermons*, pp. 53–64. For the attribution of the sermon to Langton, see Phyllis B. Roberts, *Stephanus de Lingua-Tonante: Studies in the Sermons of Stephen Langton* (Toronto, 1968).

[41] Tim Tatton-Brown, 'The Great Hall of the Archbishop's Palace', in *Canterbury before 1220*, pp. 112–19.

alleging that 33,000 diners were accommodated in the hall, but also in the carefully symbolic picture it gives of two tables, one of secular magnates, headed by the King, and the other of ecclesiastics, headed by the legate, along with a detailed account of the food and drink. Although the attribution of the poem to Henry of Avranches has recently been queried, it is still accepted as a contemporary source.[42] The literal truth of the hospitality behind the poetic account is borne out by some of the chroniclers, and also by the Christ Church Treasurers' Accounts, partially published by C. E. Woodruff in 1932. The jubilee year of 1220 showed, as might be expected, an exceptionally high figure for offerings in the cathedral: £1,142, as against an average of less than £400 later in the 1220s, but also exceptionally heavy expenses, the cellarer alone being allowed £1,154 in 1220, compared with £442 in 1219. Much more of the cost must have been borne by the Archbishop himself.[43]

All the evidence, though, suggests that the translation of 1220 served more than just Canterbury, or even archiepiscopal, purposes. It was intended as a symbol, and effectively as a means to help bring about the renewal, of peace and right order in the English Church and Kingdom. Becket's cult, not surprisingly for such a major movement, had already assumed a whole range of political meanings, in addition to, or growing out of, its thaumaturgic, penitential, and other functions. St Thomas stood as a model for the rights and duties of the clergy, an ideal life and death of the good pastor, which had obvious implications for the place of the clergy within society as a whole and in relation to royal power. Just as Edward the Confessor could be a means to criticize later kings as well as a royal saint who glorified monarchy, so Becket's posthumous fame could stand not just for resistance to royal tyranny, but also reconciliation with rightful royal power. Henry II's penance of 1174 had been proclaimed, with whatever degree of truth, as crucial to his success in preserving his authority against revolt, shown by the almost simultaneous capture of the King of Scots. This cycle had effectively run through again between 1206 and 1220, with the Becket example being used by ecclesiastical writers from Innocent III downwards to argue that John was simply repeating the worst excesses of his father in his treatment of Stephen Langton. Langton

[42] Text in Josiah C. Russell and John P. Heironimus, *The Shorter Latin Poems of Henry of Avranches* (Cambridge, Mass., 1935), pp. 64–78; attribution discussed in David Townsend and A. G. Rigg, 'Matthew Paris' Anthology of Henry of Avranches', *Mediaeval Studies*, 49 (1987), pp. 353–90, esp. pp. 360–1, 372–3.

[43] C. E. Woodruff, 'The financial aspect of the cult of St. Thomas of Canterbury', *Archaeologia Cantiana*, 49 (1932), pp. 13–32.

did not become a martyr, but John's volte-face in 1213 was seen, with some wishful thinking, as analogous to 1174, with hopes for future co-operation both in England and in the crusade. Those hopes and aims were just as important in 1220. The Becket cult cannot therefore be categorized as 'anti-royal', but as one which had the potential to be used against royal power in some circumstances. This issue was distorted by J. C. Russell in his much-quoted article 'The canonization of opposition to the King in Angevin England', in which he made Becket the foundation and model of a whole series of supposedly anti-royal cults in thirteenth-century England.[44] Such ideas could emerge under pressure of circumstances, as in the 1260s, but were not necessarily fixed or continuous, nor did they constitute the only meanings of the cults in question, as Russell seems to imply. They could be used for a variety of purposes and the context is always crucial.

One of the clearer features of the period was though a growing sense of pride in the Englishness of English saints, and the evidence suggests that in Henry III's minority the English saints, St Wulfstan, St Hugh, and others, as well as St Thomas, were thought to be active in healing the ills of the Kingdom of England. Political historians as well as ecclesiastical historians need to take this seriously, because prestige and loyalty were as important in consolidating the young King's precarious authority as sieges and administration. Recent writing on the minority has tended, quite reasonably, to emphasize the role of faction and political self-interest in the process of pacification. But it was also conditioned by a wide range of political and religious ideas and values. Among these a prominent part was played by the cults of saints, and above all by the cult of the martyred Thomas Becket, intentionally brought into a new focus in the translation of 7 July 1220.

University of Kent

---

[44] J. C. Russell, 'The canonization of opposition to the King in Angevin England', in C. H. Taylor, ed., *Anniversary Essays in Mediaeval History, by Students of Charles Homer Haskins* (New York, 1929), pp. 279–90. By contrast, Duggan, 'Cult', pp. 41–4, underplays the significance of the Becket cult for *secular* politics.

THE CASE OF THE MISSING MARTYRS:
FREDERICK II'S WAR WITH THE CHURCH
1239-1250*

by G. A. LOUD

T HE Emperor Frederick II was excommunicated by Pope
Gregory IX on Palm Sunday (20 March) 1239.[1] Over the next six
years a number of peace negotiations and offers took place, all of
which ultimately failed, despite a belief at the imperial court in the spring
of 1244 that success had been achieved.[2] Finally, at the Council of Lyons,
on 17 July 1245, Frederick was declared deposed and 'deprived of all
honour and dignity' by Pope Innocent IV, and his subjects' oaths of fealty
made null and void.[3]

Modern historians would almost all agree that the causes of the dispute
were fundamentally political rather than religious, and the reluctance of
successive popes to come to terms owed more to a determination to destroy the political power of the Staufen, to protect papal authority and
independence from the Empire, and to vindicate the hierocratic claims of
the see of Peter, than to any real anti-ecclesiastical bias or action on the
part of the Emperor.[4] Hence while, at least for public consumption,
Innocent IV did not absolutely rule out the prospect of a peace agreement
after 1245, he stressed to his supporters that there was no possibility of
either Frederick or any of his sons being restored to the imperial dignity or
the royal thrones of Sicily or Germany which he had forfeited.[5] None the

---

I am grateful to Peter Herde, Bernard and Janet Hamilton, and John Cowdrey for discussion
and advice concerning this paper.
[1] Rolandino of Padua, *Chronica Marchie Trivixane*, ed. A. Bonardi, *Rerum Italicarum scriptores*, 2nd
edn (Città di Castello, 1933–9), p. 64.
[2] Frederick wrote to his son Conrad to this effect just after Easter: J. A. Huillard-Breholles,
Historia Diplomatica Friderici Secundi, 6 vols in 12 (Paris, 1852–61) [hereafter HB], 6(i),
pp. 176–7.
[3] The bull of deposition is printed in *MGH.ER*, ed. C. Rodenburg, 2, pp. 88–94, no. 124, and
also *MGH.Const*, 2, pp. 508–12, no. 400. It can also be found in a number of contemporary
chronicles, notably the *Annales Placentini Gibillini*, *MGH.SRG*, 23, pp. 490–1, and Matthew
Paris, *Chronica Majora*, ed. H. R. Luard, 7 vols, *RS* (1872–84), 4, pp. 445–55.
[4] E.g., Thomas Curtis van Cleve, *The Emperor Frederick II of Hohenstaufen. Immutator Mundi*
(Oxford, 1972), esp. pp. 418–19, 482–3, 489–90; David Abulafia, *Frederick II* (London, 1988),
esp. pp. 308–20. Gregory was already making preparations for an invasion of Sicily by the
autumn of 1239, HB, 5(i), pp. 390–4, *MGH.ER*, 1, pp. 733–7, nos 833–4.
[5] *MGH.ER*, 2, p. 208, no. 277 (Jan. 1247); p. 251, no. 336 (May 1247); 3, p. 162, no. 195 (March
1253).

G. A. LOUD

less, the justification for Frederick's excommunication and eventual deposition was on religious grounds. Vague and indeed dubious as many of the charges against him in 1239 were, they included not merely general accusations concerning oppression of his kingdom (Sicily), but that he had attacked the Church, deliberately kept a large number of Sicilian bishoprics vacant, confiscated ecclesiastical lands and imprisoned clerics. Indeed, Gregory IX had made such complaints to Frederick long before his excommunication.[6]

As the dispute grew longer, so it became more bitter, and papal propaganda portrayed Frederick unequivocally as the enemy of the Church. The capture of two cardinals and a number of other senior clerics at sea in May 1241, as they journeyed to a papal council at Rome, and their subsequent detention in the *regno* provided obvious proof, to papalist eyes at least, of the Emperor's persecution of the Church.[7] From 1245 onwards the condemnation of Frederick was relentless. He had been deposed 'for the innumerable excesses of his impiety'.[8] He was 'the tyrant who openly and continually uses the arms of persecution against God and the Church ... he has scourged not only the Church but indeed almost all Christian people and for a long time poured the poison of his ferocity onto churchmen.'[9] The nobles from the kingdom of Sicily, whose plot against him had been discovered in the spring of 1246, and who had succeeded in escaping to Rome, were told by Innocent that 'we give thanks to divine clemency which has snatched you from the hands of Pharoah', and a manifesto at the same time to the clergy and people of Sicily compared Frederick, 'the despiser of the Christian faith and the persecutor of the Church', to the Emperor Nero.[10]

---

[6] HB, 5(i), pp. 286–9, esp. p. 287, and cf. *MGH.ER*, 1, pp. 637–9, no. 741 (Apr. 1239) to the Archbishop of Rouen in justification of the excommunication, and ibid., pp. 573–6, no. 676 (Feb. 1236).

[7] The best contemporary account of this is in *Annali Genovesi di Caffaro e de' suoi continuatori*, 3, ed. C. Imperiale di Sant'Angelo, *Fonti per la storia d'Italia* (Rome, 1923), pp. 104–6, 111–13. Cf. also Richard of S. Germano, *Chronicon*, ed. C. A. Garufi, *Rerum Italicarum scriptores*, 2nd edn (Bologna, 1935) [hereafter RSG], pp. 208–9, and *MGH.ER*, 1, pp. 713–17, nos 812–13, 815.

[8] *MGH.ER*, 2, pp. 134–5, no. 177 (Apr. 1246), 'pro innumeris sue impietatis excessibus ab imperii caderet dignitate.'

[9] *MGH.ER*, 2, pp. 150–1, no. 199 (June 1246) to Archbishop Siegfried of Mainz, 'tyrampnus F. quondam Romanorum imperator contra Deum et dictam ecclesiam persecutionis arma incessanter et patenter exercet ... idem F. non solum ecclesiam set etiam totum fere Christianorum populum flagellarit, et quamdiu in viros ecclesiasticos virus sue feritatis effunderit.' These phrases are in part repeated in ibid., 2, pp. 184–5, no. 247 (Oct. 1246), and pp. 234–5, no. 309 (March 1247).

[10] *MGH.ER*, 2, p. 125, no. 166, 'Gratias agimus divine clementis, quod vos de manu Pharaonis aripui.' Cf. ibid., pp. 126–7, no. 168, 'fidei Christiani contemptor, persecutor ecclesie' (both Apr. 1246).

Furthermore, the bull of excommunication, after reciting numerous other crimes, real and imagined, went on to suggest that he was 'strongly suspected' of heresy, and adduced as proof of his contempt for orthodox Christianity his use of Muslim servants and his friendly relations with the Sultan of Egypt.[11] His 'heresy', as well as disobedience to papal authority and persecution of the Church, increasingly became a theme of papal polemics. For example, in a letter of November 1247, in which he ordered renewed preaching of the crusade against the Emperor in Germany, Innocent alleged that he was 'a limb of the Devil and a minister of Satan, the wretched precursor of antichrist [who] conspires towards the destruction of the orthodox faith'.[12] Such apocalyptic claims were especially emphasized in the circle of propagandists around Cardinal Rainier of Viterbo, who was among the most active and embittered opponents of the Emperor in the College of Cardinals.[13] The charge of heresy was also levied against Frederick's son-in-law, and major ally in north-eastern Italy, Ezzolino da Romano, and by association, therefore, this too reflected on Frederick himself.[14] From soon after his original excommunication, and long before his deposition at Lyons, the war against Frederick was preached as a crusade, which as one papal letter in support of the German anti-king William of Holland said, 'is not his [William's] own cause but a common one which belongs to all Christians'. Those who took part in this crusade would receive remission of their sins just as did those who fought in aid of the Holy Land.[15]

To the pope, Frederick's supporters were *ipso facto* excommunicate, as he was. If clerics, they were to be deprived of their benefices. If laymen,

---

[11] See above, n. 3, esp. *MGH.ER*, 2, p. 92, and *MGH.Const*, 2, p. 511 for the passage in question.

[12] *MGH.ER*, 2, p. 328, no. 456, 'quod cum F. quondam imperator, membrum diaboli, sathane minister et infelix prenuntius Antichristi, ad destructionem orthodoxe fidei ... aspiret.' Among other references to Frederick as a precursor of the Antichrist is that in Innocent's statutes for ecclesiastical liberties in the kingdom of Sicily of December 1248, ibid., 2, p. 434–7, no. 613, at p. 434.

[13] See, in particular, Ernst Kantorowicz, *Frederick II* (London, 1931), pp. 591–5; van Cleve, *The Emperor Frederick II*, pp. 481–3, 515; Peter Herde, 'Ein Pamphlet der päpstlichen Kurie gegen Kaiser Frederick II. von 1245/8 (Eger cui lenia')', *Deutsches Archiv für Erforschung des Mittelalters*, 23 (1967), pp. 468–538. Matthew Paris, *Chronica Majora*, 5, p. 146, said on Rainier's death in 1250, 'indeffesus fuerat Fretherici persecutor et diffamator.'

[14] *MGH.ER*, 2, p. 40, no. 52 (March 1244), p. 381, no. 542 (Apr. 1248), ibid., 3, pp. 93–5, no. 113 (June 1251).

[15] Ibid., 2, p. 356, no. 504 (Feb. 1248), to the Bishop of Chur, 'causa ista non est propria sed communis et ad omnes pertinet Christianos.' The crusade against Frederick was being preached in Genoa in 1240, *Annali Genovesi*, 3, p. 98; and in February 1241 a papal chaplain was given authority to commute the vows of crusaders to the Holy Land in Hungary so that they could defend the Church against Frederick, *MGH.ER*, 1, pp. 706–7, no. 801.

they were to lose their fiefs and other properties. Marriage contracts and dowry arrangements they entered into were invalid, and on their deaths they were to be denied burial.[16] But to the Emperor the papal supporters were equally, *ipso facto*, traitors, and to be treated as such. Those who fought against him were to forfeit their lives, and their descendants all claim to their property.[17] This meant that the imperial campaigns of the 1240s were conducted with what was, even by medieval standards, extraordinary brutality. Rebellious towns were on occasion entirely destroyed, and their surviving inhabitants dispersed elsewhere.[18] The execution of prisoners, especially during sieges, became the norm. According to the chronicler Rolandino of Padua, all captured noblemen were executed on principle.[19] Salimbene alleged that men of the Church were sometimes hanged without the chance to make confession, and he saw the Emperor's defeat at Parma in 1248 as divine punishment for his cruelty during the siege. A contemporary annalist from Parma itself suggested that the execution of prisoners, women as well as men, was only brought to a halt during the siege because of the pleas of the Emperor's allies from Pavia.[20]

Nor were the clergy exempt from such treatment. General measures were taken to ensure the loyalty of churchmen to the Emperor, especially in the kingdom of Sicily. A number of bishops considered unreliable were exiled from the *regno* soon after his excommunication in 1239, and central

[16] Excommunication, *MGH.ER*, 1, p. 640, no. 742 (Apr. 1239); ibid., 2, p. 14, no. 16 (Aug. 1243); deprivation of benefices, ibid., 2, pp. 280–1, nos 381–2 (June 1247), p. 313, no. 431 (Sept. 1247), pp. 452–3, no. 635 (Jan. 1249), p. 468, no. 654 (Feb. 1249); loss of property, ibid., 2, p. 171, no. 231 (July 1246), and fiefs, ibid., p. 358, no. 508 (March 1248); marriage and dowry, ibid., 2, pp. 357–8, no. 507 (March 1248); burials, ibid., p. 253, no. 339 (May 1247), pp. 358–9, no. 509 (March 1248).
[17] 'Edictum contra infideles imperii italicos', (Feb. 1239), *MGH.Const*, 2, pp. 286–9, no. 213, esp. cl. 4.
[18] E.g., Monte Sant'Angelo, HB, 5(i), p. 565 (Dec. 1239); Benevento (1250), F. Ughelli, *Italia Sacra*, 2nd edn., 10 vols (Venice, 1717–21), 8, p. 137.
[19] *Chronica Marchie Trivixane*, pp. 73–4, 'quod talis est mos imperii, cum capitur aliquis, dum sit nobilis, si pugnando capitur imperio contradicens—est autem ultimo supplicio datus est et, sicut visum decet nobilem, pena capitis est punitus.' Numerous other instances of such atrocities can be cited, e.g., at the sieges of Faenza and Benevento in 1240, *Chronica Regia Colonienis*, ed. G. Waitz, MGH.SRG, 18, p. 277; Benevento, Biblioteca Capitolare, Cartella 376, no. 15; the execution of the son of the Doge in response to Venetian raids in the Adriatic, also in 1240, RSG, p. 208; and the mutilation of Genoese prisoners 1245, *Annali Genovesi*, 3, p. 165.
[20] Salimbene de Adam, *Chronica*, ed. O. Holder-Egger, *MGH.SS*, 32, pp. 197, 330; *Annales Parmenses maiores*, *MGH.SS*, 18, pp. 672–3. Cf. Matthew Paris, *Chronica Majora*, 4, p. 648 on the siege, 'decretum est ... ut nullus hostium captorum caperetur incarcerandus et redimendus, sed statim decapitaretur.'

and north Italian bishops loyal to the Pope were also driven from their sees.[21] Other churchmen considered suspect, and their relatives, were arrested and imprisoned.[22] Those who obeyed the papal interdict on the *regno* and refused to celebrate Mass were driven from their homes and had their property confiscated.[23] Some clergy suffered more. The 1245 bull of deposition spoke of clerics who 'are forced to submit to [judicial] duels, are imprisoned, killed and made to suffer on the gallows'.[24] The problem, of course, is to estimate how far such claims had any reality, or were greatly exaggerated in the interests of papal propaganda. Even the bull of deposition prefaced these charges with the cautionary phrase *ut asseritur*. That many of the other claims about the maltreatment of the clergy come from chroniclers as gossipy and unreliable, in their different ways, as Salimbene and Matthew Paris, does not make sober analysis any easier.

Yet enough evidence survives to suggest that such charges rested on a subtratum of fact. Given the determined campaign waged by the papacy to undermine the loyalty of his subjects, it is not surprising that the Emperor was prepared to mete out draconian treatment to papal agents. Immediately after his excommunication, Frederick promulgated a series of regulations for the kingdom of Sicily, taxing the clergy, depriving those who were not natives of the *regno* of their benefices, and expelling all non-native friars, and controlling, and largely preventing, contact with the papal court. Those who entered the *regno* with papal letters directed against the Emperor, cleric or lay, men or women, were ordered to be hanged.[25] Matthew Paris recorded the hanging of two Franciscans carrying papal letters intended to suborn various nobles in 1243, and the Parma annalist wrote that men became afraid to carry such letters for fear of mutilation.[26] Towards the end of his life the Emperor resorted to even more drastic measures. In 1249 he ordered that those carrying papal letters proclaiming his excommunication and the interdict on his lands, or friars trying to undermine his rule in Sicily, were to be burned alive.[27]

---

[21] RSG, p. 200, recorded the expulsion of the bishops of Teano, Carinola, Venafro, and Aquino in 1239; for that of the bishop of Fondi in October of that year, HB, 5(i), pp. 462–3. For the exiled bishops of Fermo and Cesena, *MGH.ER*, 2, pp. 167–8, no. 275 (July 1246), and pp. 206–7, no. 274 (Jan. 1247).

[22] The arrest of the archpriest of S. Germano and his brother, RSG, p. 205; that of a nephew of the bishop of Carinola, HB, 5(i), pp. 554–5.

[23] HB, 6(ii), pp. 580–1 (late 1247) = *MGH.Const*, 2, pp. 376–7, no. 269.

[24] *MGH.ER*, 2, pp. 91–2, 'cogunter subire duella, incarcerantur, occiduntur et patibulis cruciantur.'

[25] RSG, pp. 200–1.

[26] *Chronica Majora*, 4, p. 256, *Annales Parmenses maiores*, p. 671.

[27] HB, 6(ii), pp. 699–703.

That friars were singled out, both by imperial mandates and in the narrative accounts, is hardly surprising, given that they filled as important a role in the papal campaign against Frederick as they did in the thirteenth-century fight against heresy. Members of the mendicant orders played a large part in drafting the anti-imperial manifestos of the papal chancery and of the circle around Cardinal Rainier of Viterbo.[28] They also acted as preachers of the crusade against him, as fund-raisers for the campaign, and were crucial in the efforts to undermine his authority, especially in his power-base in the kingdom of Sicily.[29] All except a handful of those in whom the Emperor thought he could trust were expelled from the *regno* in the autumn of 1240 (as indeed they had also been at the time of Frederick's first dispute with the papacy in 1229), although there is some evidence that, at least in the case of the Dominicans, the ban may have been later rescinded.[30] The Emperor alleged that a group of friars had encouraged the treasonous rebellion of the citizens of Viterbo in 1243, and that other friars had been involved in the conspiracy to murder him in 1246.[31] When, in 1247, Innocent freed the citizens of Benevento from the excommuncation they had incurred for supporting Frederick, since their support was the result of coercion (a move which should probably be interpreted as an attempt to foment rebellion there, which indeed broke out two years later), his agent was a Franciscan.[32] Frederick actually wrote to the General Chapter of the Dominicans about 1246 to complain of the activities of brothers who exploited the credulity of common people to stir up dissent against him (he tactfully did not ascribe this to the policy of the Order as a whole).[33]

The number of medicants who suffered as the consequence of such actions cannot be determined, particularly given how vague and general

[28] Herde, 'Eine Pamphlet der päpstlichen Kurie', p. 494.
[29] As preachers of the crusade, *MGH.ER*, 2, p. 123, no. 162 (Apr. 1246), p. 302, no. 416 (July 1247), pp. 448–9, no. 630 (Jan. 1249), pp. 532–3, no. 720 (May 1249), ibid., 3, pp. 35–6, no. 48 (Feb. 1251), and for a later period cf. Norman Housley, *The Italian Crusades. The Papal-Angevin Alliance and the Crusades Against Christian Lay Powers, 1254–1343* (Oxford, 1982), pp. 116–18. As messengers, *Annali Genovesi*, 3, p. 151. As fund-raisers, Matthew Paris, *Chronica Majora*, 4, p. 654. Note also that in 1249 the Piacenzans captured Pontremoli 'ex operatione plurium fratrum Predicatorum', *Annales Placentini Gibellini*, p. 498.
[30] RSG, pp. 156, 207. Giulia Barone, 'Federico II di Svevia e gli ordini mendicanti', *Mélanges de l'école française de Rome. Moyen Age*, 90 (1978), pp. 615–16.
[31] HB, 6(i), pp. 143, 405. Matthew Paris, *Chronica Majora*, 5, p. 573. Cf. E. Winkelmann, *Acta imperii inedita saeculi XIII et XIV*, 2 vols (Innsbruck, 1880–5), 1, p. 318, no. 359, there dated to 1240, but more probably to be connected with the conspiracy of 1246.
[32] *MGH.ER*, 2, p. 302, no. 416.
[33] HB, 6(i), pp. 479–80.

the contemporary accounts of persecution were. But suffer some of them did. Allusion has already been made to the savage punishments threatened for those acting as papal messengers. Salimbene wrote that friars become afraid to come near imperial-held cities in northern Italy in case they were accused of carrying papal letters, and those who entered such cities in all innocence were maltreated, tortured, and sometimes killed.[34] The arrest and (sometimes) execution of friars spreading news of the Emperor's deposition was also mentioned by the Franciscan chronicle of Jordan of Saxony.[35] More specific evidence is rarely if ever available, with one exception. Salimbene reported the torture and execution of an important fellow Franciscan and friend of his, Simon of Montesarchio, who was or had been the Order's procurator at the papal court, in 1248. There can be no doubt that from the point of view of the imperial authorities Simon was a traitor. He was, to judge by his name and indeed Salimbene's express testimony, a native of the *regno* (Montesarchio is in the Valle Caudine to the west of Benevento), and he had been sent there specifically to foment rebellion.

With the case of Simon of Montesarchio we come to the crux of this paper, for in his chapter-heading Salimbene referred to him as a man 'who was crowned as a martyr' (*qui fuit martyrio coronatus*). If one thinks of him as one who died bearing witness to the Christian faith, as Salimbene clearly did, 'subjected to eighteen different tortures (*martyria*), all of which he bore patiently; nor could his torturers extract anything from him except divine praise', then the attribution was clearly just.[36] And yet this raises the question of all the others, whether friars or other clerics, or laymen, who died fighting or were executed in support of the papacy against Frederick II. Were they not, too, martyrs, who died fighting for the Church in a holy war against a manifest enemy of God and agent of the Devil?

To judge by the papal documentation, the answer to this question was resoundingly 'no'. We have only one other case in which a victim of Frederick II was hailed as a martyr, and that reference comes not in any letter of Innocent IV himself but in a pamphlet of Rainier of Viterbo, preserved only in the Chronicle of Matthew Paris. This described, in great and lurid detail, the hanging of Bishop Marcellinus of Arezzo, the papal

---

[34] Salimbene, *Chronica*, p. 330.
[35] Quoted by Barone, 'Federico II di Svevia e gli ordini mendicanti', p. 620.
[36] Salimbene, *Chronica*, pp. 315, 317–18; esp. p. 318, 'Tandem imperator fecit eum capi et decem et octo martyria intulit sibi, que omnia sustinuit patienter; nec aliquid potuerunt carnifices extorquere ab eo nisi laudem divinam.'

Rector of the March of Ancona, at Vittoria, the Emperor's camp outside
Parma, on 21 February 1248; and then proceeded to enumerate a series of
other alleged crimes by Frederick and his accomplices, including the
murders of the two other bishops, and the blasphemous profanation of
the Cross and Christian images by his Saracen troops. The Bishop's death,
at the hands of 'this impious leader, having like his father the devil great
anger against the Church of God', was expressly portrayed as martyrdom,
and his journey to the scaffold, exposed to the mockery and ill-treatment
of the Saracen executioners, compared with that of Christ to the Cross.
After his death his body was left hanging for three days, cut down and
buried by some Franciscans, then exhumed by the executioners, and after
further indignities 'once again suspended, not to be cut down without
special permission of the new Pilate'. But though 'the body of the martyr'
was left on show for ten more days, it still miracuously remained
unputrified. This appalling treatment of a bishop, by a man who so
despised the Christian faith that he allowed heresies to be preached in his
dominions, was contrasted with the Sultan of Egypt, who, though an
unbeliever, had allowed the crusading army to withdraw unharmed in
1221, and with the courteous behaviour of the Greeks to a captive
cardinal.[37]

According to Matthew Paris, this pamphlet roused great indignation
against Frederick, yet (a characteristic addition) the vices of the papal side
were such that its effect was largely nullified. (The implication, of course,
is that its impact was very limited, but Matthew is so tendentious that one
is left in doubt as to its reception.) But what is certain is that the portrayal
of Marcellinus as a martyr in this tract by Cardinal Rainier, apparently
written very soon after his death, was not followed by Innocent IV,
despite the fact that the dead Bishop had been an active and trusted papal
agent since the very early stages of the conflict.[38] Admittedly, in a letter to
the Bishop of Fano in June 1248 the Pope described Marcellinus as one
who 'had such purity and fervour of faith that, persisting in the defence of

---

[37] *Chronica Majora*, 5, pp. 61–7. Marcellinus was named as Rector in two letters of March 1247,
MGH.ER, 2, p. 268, no. 363, p. 275, no. 373. Cardinal Rainier had been his predecessor in
that office, ibid., 2, p. 561, no. 758 (June 1244).

[38] Innocent granted Marcellinus the revenues of the see of Ancona (which was his native town)
in November 1240, and in December of that year wrote to the prelates of 'Sclavonia' (Croatia
and Bosnia?) to secure financial support for him, since he was forced to remain at Ancona
'pro ecclesie Romane negotiis', *MGH.ER*, 1, pp. 695–6, no. 788, pp. 702–3, no. 795. This
backs up what Rainald said about his long exile in Ancona 'in penury'. For his activities there,
see also ibid., 1, pp. 705–6, no. 799 (Jan. 1241), 2, p. 14, no. 16 (Aug. 1243), and p. 294, no. 403
(June 1247).

ecclesiastical liberty, he suffered great losses [or in the context perhaps 'he made great expenditure'] and finally was not afraid to undergo danger of death on its behalf.' Yet this fulsome, and one might think in the circumstances deserved, tribute, was not written in justification of, or to encourage, the holy war against Frederick II. It was, in fact, part of a letter arranging for payment of money owed to the dead Bishop's brother, to be repaid from the property of his see.[39] The Bishop's sacrifice was not otherwise noted by the papal chancery, and no effort was made to exploit his 'martyrdom'.

Indeed, despite the general accusations about his persecution of the Church, the papacy did not utilize those slain by Frederick II as martyrs whose deaths sanctified its cause. In the twelfth century those who had died on crusades to the East had been considered as martyrs, at least by contemporary chroniclers.[40] And in 1268, on the eve of his battle of Tagliacozzo against Frederick's grandson Conradin, Charles of Anjou allegedly claimed that those who died would receive divine reward.[41] Yet although the war against Frederick II after 1239 was a holy war against the 'precursor of Antichrist', in which the spiritual rewards were the same as those given to men who fought in the Holy Land (and by the late 1240s those who had already vowed to go to the Holy Land were being encouraged to fight against Frederick instead),[42] the theme of martyrdom had no place in papal propaganda. Not even clerics executed while fulfilling papal instructions were seen as martyrs. The only reference to martyrs in this context are the two, quite unofficial, ones which have been discussed above. Why should this have been the case?

The reasons were probably twofold. First of all, there was the general question of martyrdom and sanctity, and the papal attitude to this. Secondly, there was the 'genuineness' of the crusade against the Emperor Frederick, or, at least, how convincingly this could be portrayed, and the degree of popular support manifested for it.

---

[39] *MGH.ER*, 2, pp. 407–8, no. 577, 'illam fidei puritatem et fervorem habuit, quod defensioni ecclesiastice libertatis insistens, dispendia multa substinuit, et tandem pro ipsa mortis subire periculum non expavit.' The debt was also acknowledged in a letter to Marcellinus's brother on the same day, *Les Registres d'Innocent IV*, ed. E. Berger, 3 vols (Paris, 1884–1921), no. 3992.

[40] Thus the *Gesta Francorum*, ed. Rosalind Hill (London, 1956), p. 17, on those who died at the siege of Nicea, 'multi ex nostris illic receperunt martyrium'; and on the Second Crusade, Odo of Deuil, *De profectione Ludovici VII ad Orientem*, ed. Virginia Gingerick Berry (New York, 1948), p. 118, 'finis . . . martyrio meruit coronari.'

[41] *Annales Sanctae Iustinae Patavini*, *MGH.SS*, 19, p. 191. Housley, *The Italian Crusades*, p. 166.

[42] *MGH.ER*, 2, pp. 326, 329, 332, nos 453, 459, 465 (all Nov. 1247), pp. 373–4, no. 534 (Apr. 1248).

It was perfectly possible for a martyr not to be a saint. This statement would seem axiomatic if those who died on crusade were to be considered as martyrs. But the same also applied to churchmen who died for the faith. When the papal legate in Languedoc, Pierre de Castelnau, was murdered in 1208, Innocent III announced him to be a martyr, but there was never any question of canonization, not least because there were no miracles attributed to him (and, given his unpopularity in Languedoc, the chances of a local cult were hardly very high).[43] Martyrdom might indeed be seen as one of the possible *criteria* for canonization, but it was neither (obviously) a *sine qua non* nor, indeed, sufficient without other qualifications. Nevertheless, murdered churchmen could attract popular and unofficial cults. But though from the later twelfth century onwards there were a number of flourishing local cults of martyred 'saints' in Western Christendom, the papacy's attitude to these was generally unenthusiastic. The popes were anxious to stress their own monopoly over canonization, one which had only been clearly established a very few years before the final break with Frederick II, and did not look with favour on local and unauthorized cults. While thirteenth-century popes did canonize, very swiftly, a number of recently deceased saints, those tended to be ones either known personally to the popes or whose promotion to the ranks of sainthood would be of very clear and obvious value to the Church—the prime example of which was the canonization of the murdered inquisitor Peter of Verona (Peter Martyr) in 1253, seen as a standard-bearer of the Church in the fight against heresy.[44]

But the case of Peter Martyr is an interesting one, precisely because it was fairly unusual. Peter filled the criteria of sanctity not just because of the manner of his death, but because of clear evidence for holy life, and abundant and immediate miracles, one of which, according to his biographer Thomas of Lentini, occurred on the very day of his death. It is also clear that there developed an immediate and very strong local cult.[45] But after his canonization, and that of St Stanislau of Cracow in the same year, there were to be no further martyrs canonized for more than two centuries. The papacy was generally very wary about martyr cults.[46] While

[43] André Vauchez, *La Sainteté en Occident aux derniers siècles du Moyen Age d'après les procès de canonisation et les documents hagiographiques* (Rome, 1981), pp. 43–4.

[44] Ibid., pp. 126–7, 173–83. Cf. for the papal monopoly of canonization Eric Waldram Kemp, *Canonization and Authority in the Western Church* (Oxford, 1948), pp. 82–106.

[45] *Acta sanctorum April*, 3 (Paris, 1866), pp. 694–727, esp. p. 706. (The bull of canonization, 24 March 1253, is contained therein, pp. 708–10.)

[46] Vauchez, *Sainteté*, pp. 480–2. Salimbene, *Chronica*, p. 175 wrongly ascribed the death of St Stanislaus to Frederick II—in fact, he died in 1079!

Peter of Verona became enshrined as St Peter Martyr, it is notable that another very prominent murdered inquisitor, Conrad of Marburg (d. 1233), was never expressly referred to as a martyr in papal letters, even though in the immediate aftermath of his death Gregory IX did describe him as 'a man of consummate virtue and a beacon of the Christian faith'; and a later Dominican attempt to have him canonized failed.[47] Conrad's reputation as a man who condemned the innocent along with the guilty cannot have helped him to have been considered as a genuine martyr.[48] But the papacy was not, in general, keen on martyr cults, and was unlikely therefore to encourage them by widespread use of the term.

Furthermore, such cults, and especially those of murdered bishops (such as Marcellinus of Arezzo, and the bishops of Gerace and Cefalù, whose deaths Cardinal Rainald also ascribed to Frederick II)[49] were far more a north European phenomenon than an Italian one—and the main theatre of war between Frederick II and the papacy was Italy. In addition, given that the majority of churchmen who died at the hands of the imperialists were probably friars, it is significant that the early Franciscans showed no great interest in the cult of saints from their own ranks, except for that of Francis himself.[50] One should therefore perhaps not be so surprised at the lack of emphasis on the Church's martyrs in the anti-Frederician propaganda.

Secondly, there is the question of the papal crusade and its credibility. Recent historiography has stressed how much the crusades against Christians, far from being an aberration, were part of the mainstream of the Christian holy war and Christian thought.[51] But how far did the anti-imperial crusade find recruits outside those Lombard communes which had good political reason to oppose authoritarian imperial control? How

---

[47] *MGH.ER*, 1, pp. 453–5, no. 560, 'virum consumate virtutis et preconem fidei Christiani'; cf. ibid., pp. 455–6, no. 561 (both Oct. 1233). The attempt at canonization is mentioned by the early fourteenth-century *Chronica Ordinis Fratrum* of Galvano Fiamma, ed. G. Odetto, *Archivum Fratrum Praedicatorum*, 10 (1940), pp. 352–3.

[48] *Chronica Regia Coloniensis*, pp. 264–5. *MGH.ER*, 1, pp. 544–7, no. 647 (July 1235), esp. p. 544.

[49] Matthew Paris, *Chronica Majora*, 5, pp. 64–5. Nothing at all is known about the bishop of Gerace, allegedly drowned 'in aquis vehementibus' (a hot spring?) two years earlier, but Aldoynus of Cefalu, who according to Rainier was murdered by a hired assassin in Rome after 'having been driven from his see for fifteen years', is known to have been in exile from 1234, and also earlier, in 1222-3. See Norbert Kamp, *Kirche und Monarchie im Staufischen Königreich Siziliens*, 4 vols (Munich, 1973–82), 2, p. 970; 3, pp. 1055–63.

[50] Vauchez, *Sainteté*, pp. 134–5, 182–3, 197–9.

[51] Norman Housley, 'Crusades against Christians; their origins and early development, c. 1000–1216', in P. W. Edbury, ed., *Crusade and Settlement. Essays Presented to R. C. Small* (Cardiff, 1985), pp. 17–36, and Housley, *The Italian Crusades*, *passim*, but esp. pp. 252–7. E. Siberry, *Criticism of Crusading 1095–1274* (Oxford, 1985), pp. 175–89.

convincing was much of the papal propaganda? Were accusations of heresy really very effective against an emperor well known as an active persecutor of heretics?[52] Would churchmen executed as traitors by the imperialists have generally been considered as martyrs? Salimbene wrote of Simon of Montesarchio that 'God made many miracles through him', and Cardinal Rainald alleged that because the Bishop's body remained for ten days unputrified this was therefore miraculous.[53] But this is all very vague, and there is no evidence that either of these two 'martyrs' ever attracted any cult. Had they done so, then surely there would have been some trace of papal investigation, as there was in other cases.[54] If one reads the Italian chroniclers of the time, even those from Guelf cities, one is struck by the matter-of-fact way in which they described the papal–imperial struggle. The Emperor might be at war with the Church, but, Salimbene apart, one finds no trace of the rhetoric of papal propaganda, of the holy war against the precursor of the Antichrist and limb of the Devil. The Genoese annals, for example, while careful not to use his imperial title after the deposition of 1245, and even quoting a bull in which the Pope condemned the 'persecutor of the Church', still called their city's enemy 'the lord Frederick'.[55]

One might feel that by not emphasizing the martyrdom of those clergy killed by Frederick II the Church missed a trick, failing to utilize a potential weapon in its polemical campaign. But the papacy distrusted martyr cults, and it may be that such seed would anyway have fallen on stony ground. One might also wonder whether the Pope and his advisers really believed their own rhetoric, or did they know in their heart of hearts that their claim to be fighting a holy war was a hollow one, and that those who died did so rather for the political advantage of the Roman Curia than for the good of the Christian Church as a whole? That, too, would explain the missing martyrs.

University of Leeds

---

[52] E.g., *MGH.Const*, 2, pp. 126–7, no. 100 (1224), pp. 195–7, no. 158 (1232), pp. 280–5, nos 209–11 (1238/9). See generally, Kurt-Victor Selge, 'Die Ketzerpolitik Friedrichs II.', in J. Fleckenstein, ed., *Probleme um Fredrich II.* (Sigmaringen, 1974), pp. 309–43.

[53] Salimbene, *Chronica*, p. 318; Matthew Paris, *Chronica Majora*, 5, p. 63.

[54] As, for example, in that of Simon of Collezzone (d. 1250), for which *Les Registres d'Innocent IV*, no. 5769 (Apr. 1252).

[55] *Annali Genovesi*, 3, pp. 181–2.

CHOOSING DEATH? EXPERIENCES OF MARTYRDOM IN LATE MEDIEVAL EUROPE*

by MIRI RUBIN

PROBABLY one of the most emotive words in our ethical and religious languages, 'martyrdom' poses the historian with a complex array of powerful images and awesome actions. Its very naturalness, as a grounding moment through which religions and radical movements are substantiated and made public, raises serious problems of perspective, empathy, judgement: studying martyrdom brings us in touch with some of the most admirable and some of the most repugnant and saddening aspects in human behaviour. Religions, parties, and nations claim martyrs as unambiguous signs of virtue, truth, and moral justification, and thus render martyrdom seemingly obvious. Painful, yes, but admirable; chilling, but satisfying, since in it men and women turn into gods, become myth-makers, and lend legitimation to whoever may claim them. So martyrdom—its discussion, definition, the claim to its virtue and beauty—is always open to appropriation, to competition, to contestation.

Although martyrdom is presented as an absolute, it is intrinsically amenable to historical change. As I researched and reflected on it over the last year in response to your kind invitation, I found myself wrestling with a variety of impressions which grew into observations on the relative nature of experiences of pain and death claimed as martyrdom. It soon became clear that the act of martyrdom is twofold: it is a choice taken in testing circumstances by an individual, or a group; but it is also a social-collective act, that of martyr-making, of martyr-naming. Thus a double-edged perspective is necessary in order to contain the variety of contexts in which martyrdom is practised: in the intention of the martyr/victim, and in the interpretations of those who will declare a given demise to be the crowned death of a martyr. As we enter the area of interpretation we must perforce step into fields of authority and dissent, of perspective and subjectivity; of meaning, as one man's cult of a martyr is another woman's superstition.

During the central and later medieval centuries acts of martyrdom had

* I wish to thank Helen Phillips, Jean-Claude Schmitt, Shulamit Shahar, André Vauchez, and Jocelyn Wogan-Browne for some stimulating conversations while I was thinking about this paper.

lost their spectacular presence as Christianity was being disseminated into a largely pagan world north-west and east of the Mediterranean basin. Even after the first rush of epoch-making martyrdoms in the Roman Empire, the frontiers of mission and the political frontiers of Christianity and Islam were producing a trickle of martyrdom encounters, and figures who were integrated into the world of liturgy, prayer, and popular example. The early martyrs, with whose blood Christianity had become established in the Roman world, were joined by a sprinkling of missionary monks, victims of Muslim conquest, or of the ravages of the Norsemen. But as Europe came to be a Christian community, occasions for persecution and execution by tyrants and hostile pagan rulers declined. There was a definite sense in which martyrdom was receding—that martyrs were few and precious; that their remains were treasures which could not be matched.[1] The dilemma now faced was to shape the meaning of the tradition of martyrdom: how should this world come to terms with this end of martyrdom? What should the appropriate location and use of memories of martyrs be? What authority might those who had not suffered an equal sacrifice claim in a Christian world? To martyrdom could be added the growing sustained notion of sainthood; and the legacy of martyrdom interacted with popular notions of justice and virtue which were to produce impulses towards martyr-naming increasingly divergent from official ecclesiastical choices.[2]

But let us first think of the mundane use, through metaphor and metonymy, by which the notion of martyrdom was deployed in daily life. A patient would complain of his martyrdom at the hands of a physician.[3] When Froissart described the terrible carnage after the siege of Limoges, in 1370, he wrote, 'May the Lord receive their souls for they were true martyrs.'[4] The engaging Brother Giles, one of the early Franciscans, used to say as he retired to his cell after dinner, and having been tormented by the Devil in the past, 'Expecto martyrium.'[5] Martyrdom was incorporated

[1] P. Geary, *Furta sacra* (Princeton, 1978), pp. 33–4, 45, 93.
[2] See A. Vauchez, *La Sainteté en Occident aux derniers siècles du moyen-âge d'après les procès de canonisation et les documents hagiographiques* = *Bibliothèque des études françaises d'Athènes et de Rome*, 241 (Rome, 1981); D. Weinstein and R. M. Bell, *Saints and Society: the Two Worlds of Western Christendom, 1100–1700* (Chicago, 1982).
[3] N. G. Siraisi, *Medieval and Early Renaissance Medicine: an Introduction to Knowledge and Practice* (Chicago, 1990), p. 167.
[4] S. Luce, ed., *Chroniques de J. Froissart* (Paris, 1878), 7, c.666, p. 250: 'car plus de trois mil personnes, hommes, femmes et enfans, y furent deviiet et decolet celle journée. Diex en ait les ames, car il furent bien martir!'
[5] *Vita beati fratris Egidii*, in *Scripta Leonis, Rufini et Angeli sociorum S. Francisci*, ed. R. Brooke (Oxford, 1970), pp. 318–49; at c.16, p. 344.

into the routines of self-mortification, into lifestyles of difference, of self-conscious testing and torment. It also induced the study and contemplation, the writing, reading, and representation of martyrs of old, and narratives of martyrdom, the *passiones*, came to be seen as veritable holy relics. *The Early South-English Legendary*, of *c.*1280, conveys such a sense view in its *vita* of St Kenelm, a Mercian prince who was allegedly killed by his sister's order in 821. There the account of the martyrdom is conveyed to Rome by a divine missive:

þat writ was puyr on Englisch i-write:
ase men it radden pere;
And for-to tellen with-oute ryme:
þeos wordes it were:
'In klent covbache kenelm, kyngues sone, lijth onder ane þorne, is
heued him bi-reued'
þis writ was wel nobleliche:
i-wust and up i-do,
And i-holde for gret relike:
and 3eot it is also;
The nobleste relike it is on þar-of:
þat is in þe churche of rome.[6]

The narrative of martyrdom thus became a deposit of truth and tradition, which could be read, or treated as a magical link with the past. It came to find its place in the elaborate liturgical incorporation of martyr-lore in the readings and the litanies of feast days and into the office of the Mass. Martyrdom lore was also absorbed into new literary forms by the eleventh century, as authors of heroic deeds blended the epic and the narrative of martyrdom.[7] Think of the great *Chansons de geste*, whose heroes could rival the *milites Christi* soon to receive endorsement and recognition by Gregory VII and his successors; was their effort not a witness of faith? were their strivings and ultimate deaths not in the service of the faith? In the *Chanson de Roland*, Archbishop Turpin exhorted the fighting men before Ronscevaux to confess and pray, but assured them that those who died would be martyrs and reach paradise before the Day of Judgement. The Church of St Romanus, at Blaye, claimed to possess the remains of

[6] *The Early South-English Legendary or Lives of Saints*, 1, ed. C. Horstmann, *EETS*, 87 (1887), p. 352, lines 259–64. T. J. Heffernan, *Sacred Biography: and Their Hagiographers in the Middle Ages* (Oxford, 1988), p. 35.
[7] A. G. Elliott, *Roads to Paradise: Reading the Lives of the Early Saints* (Hanover, NH, 1987), pp. 182–4.

Roland, Oliver, Turpin, and others, and a twelfth-century pilgrim's guidebook to the route to Compostella mentions the site, and the body of 'beati Rotolandi martyris'.[8] Thus notions and values of martyrdom intersected with the literature of warriors' deeds to provide a whole new layer of meaning for the lives of those who fought for Christianity and died for it.

So the telling of martyrdoms contained powerful messages which could be embellished for new generations. But the cessation of martyrdom also led to the development of new options for perfection in other types of death. Already Gregory the Great could write of spiritual martyrdom, and in the eleventh and twelfth centuries robust notions of an exemplary and painful life as a *passio* were taking root. The author of the *Hali Meiðhad* in the mid-twelfth century claimed that virginity could be the equal of any ancient martyr's death, signalling one of the most persistent themes in female spirituality.[9] A death to sexual reproductive life was inverted into a life in Christ as his special bride, and the late medieval authors likened the choice of a life of virginity to a death and rebirth as Christ's bride. The Middle English *Life of Seinte Juliana* of *c.* 1230 describes her being stripped by her father for whipping by her tormentors, when she exclaimed:

> Swa muche quoð ha ich iwurde him þe leouere: So ich derure þing
> for his luue drehe.[10]

St Agnes's death is described in Osbern Bokenham's *Life* of *c.* 1445:

> And þus þis holy mayde, þis innocent,
> Cruelly martyrd for crystys sake,
> To hym as hys spouse he dede take.[11]

And this purity preserved for the ultimate lover was dramatically mocked by tormenters, who attempted to violate it, like those of Lucy, who sent her to a brothel. So the martyrdoms of old were being rewritten and translated to provide examples for lives of perfection. The lives of female virgin martyrs were the staple of monastic and lay reading and spectator-

---

[8] Ibid., p. 142. See Professor Morris's article, above, p. 104, for a discussion of the development of the idea of martyrdom in Holy War.

[9] *Hali Meiðhad*, ed. B. Millett, EETS, 284 (1982), pp. 22–3.

[10] *Þe liflade of St. Juliana*, ed. O. Cockayne and E. Brock, EETS, 51 (1872), p. 16.

[11] Osbern Bokenham, *Legendys of Hooly Wummen*, ed. M. S. Serjeantson, EETS, 206 (1938), p. 126, lines 4600–2.

ship in plays and sermons and iconography. Martyrdom was preserved as a tradition which provided some guide-lines for perfect lives.

*   *   *

But could any contemporary form of perfection rival or displace the authority of ancient martyrdom? In the world of late medieval Christianity—varied, localized, multifarious, full of flavour and accent, questions and dissent—the Church recognized very few martyrs. Christian martyrs may, in fact, have been fewer, but what is striking is the steering away from naming and recommending as martyrs people who had suffered death in the recent past. Becket in the twelfth century and Peter Martyr in the next are notable exceptions. This tension is reflected in the attitudes which were developing within the Franciscan Order itself, towards the legacy of perfection and mission left by St Francis. Although Francis did not die for his faith, despite his many attempts to imperil his life in mission, he was none the less marked with the most powerful mark of confirmation and authorization, he had lived the *imitatio Christi* through the *stigmata* given to him and marked on his body (see plate 1). In his *Vita prima*, written in 1228, Thomas of Celano links *stigmata* and Francis's earlier attempts to seek martyrdom in mission, to Syria, Morocco, and Spain:

> Sed bonus Deus ... cum iam ivisset usque in Hispaniam, *in faciem ei restitit*, et ne ultra procederet, aegritudine intentata, eum a coepto itinere revocavit ...
>
> In omnibus his Dominus ipsius *desiderium* non *implevit*, praerogativam illi reservans gratiae singularis.[12]

The *Vita secunda* written by him twenty years later gives a much more diffuse notion of the event; it is described as very private, the witnessing brethren, Rufinus and Elias, are no longer mentioned (Elias was excommunicated in 1232 for support of Frederick II). The *stigmata* here possessed an insufficiently clear message, and so in 1263 Bonaventure wrote the third Life, the *Legenda maior*, and ordered the destruction by fire of all the copies of Thomas of Celano's second Life.[13] In

---

[12] Thomas of Celano, *Vita prima*, in *Analecta franciscana*, 10, pt i, c.20, pp. 43–4. See also J. Moorman, *A History of the Franciscan Order from its Origins to the Year 1517* (Oxford, 1968), pp. 60–1.

[13] On the attitudes of Franciscans to sanctity see Vauchez, *La Sainteté*, pp. 131–8. On the hagiography of Francis's life see J. Moorman, *The Sources for the Life of S. Francis of Assisi* (Manchester, 1940).

Plate 1   Stefano di Giovanni Sassetta, *The Stigmatization of St Francis* (Panel from altar-piece), wood, trefoiled top, painted area 87.6 × 52.7 cms, reproduced by courtesy of the Trustees, the National Gallery, London.

Bonaventure's hand, Minister General since 1256, a sure line of succession and authority was attached to the *stigmata*, linking it to Francis's rule and to papal patronage:

> Ad cuius observantiam fratres ferventer inducens, dicebat, se nihil ibi posuisse secundum industriam propriam, sed omnia sic scribi fecisse, sicut sibi fuerant divinitus revelata. Quod ut certius constaret testimonio Dei, paucis admodum, diebus evolutis impressa sunt ei stigmata Domini Iesu digito *Dei vivi* tanquam bulla summi Pontificis Christi ad confirmationem omnimodam regulae et commenda- tionem auctoris, sicut post suarum ennarationem virtutum suo loco inferius describetur.[14]

Bonaventure himself imitated the great imitator of Christ, as he ascended Mount Alverna to contemplate and pray and hope for illumina- tion, and to receive the same burning mark of love on his body.[15] So a whole world of Franciscan writing interpreted that singular experience in the literature of perfection which followed. Most notably, Bonaventure in his commentary on the *Regula bullata* claimed Francis's legacy to the Order as one of martyrdom, the highest level of love of Christ, and mission as the highest context for the realization of that love in conjunc- tion with the love for one's neighbour, whom Christ had come to redeem, through attempts at conversion. Martyrdom, and the martyrdom suffered in mission, was the highest level of union with God, through the physical living of Christ's Passion, juxtaposed with the imitation of his poverty. As the Franciscan Order suffered its fatal split in the debate about Poverty, a tragic twist was to create a new type of Franciscan martyr, as the followers of Peter John Olivi, the Beguines of Narbonne and Beziers, were per- secuted, and hundreds were burnt around the year 1300. They were imitating Christ through the inspiration of a new prophet, Olivi, whose word was to them as holy as Scripture. These followers of Olivi turned his tomb into a shrine, and then offered themselves as martyrs as the inquisi- torial fires burnt. We encounter here then the richness of martyrdom language, split and turned against itself within the Order. It is this density of meaning, and the possible inversions and relapses inherent in martyrdom language, which explain the papacy's wariness of going so far as endorsing forms of contemporary perfection as martyrdom, or indeed as sanctifying.

[14] St Bonaventure, *Legenda maior*, in *Analecta franciscana*, 10, c.4, at p. 577.
[15] E. R. Daniel, 'The desire for martyrdom: a *leitmotiv* of St. Bonaventure', *Franciscan Studies*, 32 (1975), pp. 74–87, at p. 75.

These tensions are manifest in the differing experiences of mission unto death which Franciscans came to experience as time passed. The earliest Franciscan martyrs are the group of seven who arrived in Morocco in the late summer of 1227, and of whose fate we are informed by a letter of Brother Mariano of Genoa to Elias. In the flush of enthusiasm, and still under the spell of Francis's own example, this group of Franciscans sailed to Ceuta and Morocco to begin their mission. Their story is anything but spectacular. Upon arrival they were thrown into gaol, where they laboured for eight days, and then, in mid-October, they were beheaded. Their journey verged on what thinkers later in the century would see as suicidal, as complicit with the tyrant's desires, and not qualifying for martyrdom, but these were heroes within the Order.[16] The Order became more uneasy, uncomfortable with the uncontrolled and unplanned throwing of lives away in gestures which showed neither preparation nor introspection nor grave intention. The experience of two late fourteenth-century Spanish Franciscans, Juan de Cetina and Pedro de Dueñas, who were executed in the Alhambra in 1397 is instructive. Fitting with the model of personal development recommended by Bonaventure, these men joined the Order, spent years in study, spent time in spiritual retreat in Franciscan hermitages, then resolved to go on mission to the Muslims in the Holy Land, and sought permission, as required, from the Provincial of Castile. They never reached Jerusalem, because travelling south they passed through the Nazari kingdom, which they could have done quite safely had they behaved. But the missionary fervour was strong, and they began preaching against Islam in Grenada, and were arrested. The *Vita* claims that they were interrogated by the Sultan himself, and one version claims that he beheaded them with his own sword. Their bodies were recovered by the Mercedarian Brethren (an order founded by a Dominican in 1218, dedicated to the ransoming of Christians), and passed on to Cordova, where they began to work miracles, and enjoyed a martyr cult among the Spanish Franciscans. We encounter again mission/martyrdom, but more explicitly controlled within the Order, and consciously integrated into forms of personal exploration, learning, and contemplation espoused by the Order.[17]

A tension is revealed here between the unwillingness of the central

[16] F. Russo, 'Le fonti della passione dei SS. martiri di Ceuta', *Miscellanea franciscana*, 34 (1934), pp. 350–6. Clare wished to go on mission to Morocco too, but was refused; on this and the early missions see Moorman, *History of the Franciscan Order*, pp. 228–32.
[17] D. Cabanelas, 'Dos mártires franciuscanos en la Granada nazarí: Juan de Cetina y Pedro de Dueñas', *Estudios de Historia y de Arqueología medievales*, 5–6 (1985–6), pp. 159–75.

160

institutions of the Church to recognize living, contemporary martyrdom, and the active seeking of martyrdom within some of its most forceful milieus, that of evangelical perfection. Francis's life was an ongoing attempt to achieve a perfect imitation of Christ through the quest for martyrdom, but it ultimately endorsed a life of perfection in the world, as his own body came to be approved by the red-hot marks on his stig-matized limbs. And this marking of the body, the burning of the human flesh, was appropriated into a practice which could inspire the many. Religious women, some of whom ended their days as shunned and degraded heretics, carried the sign: like Guilelma, the woman who appeared in Milan in the 1260s bearing a child in her arms, and who bore *stigmata* and was claimed to be the incarnation of the Holy Spirit. She was encouraged and protected by the Cistercians of Chiaravalle, outside the city, where she was buried after her death in 1271, only to be exhumed by papal decree in 1300, her body burnt, and her ashes strewn to the four corners of the earth, leaving nothing tangible from which a cult could be sustained.[18] Or her contemporary Elizabeth of Spalbeek of Herkenrode Abbey, in the diocese of Liège, who claimed to have had *stigmata*.[19] She drew venom from the pen of the Franciscan Gilbert of Tournai, who was outraged by her and by other Beguines, and described their lives in his collection of problematic practices prepared for the discussion of the Council of Lyons in 1274, the *Collectio de scandalis ecclesiae*:

> Sunt apud nos mulieres, quae Beghinae vocantur, et quaedam eorum subtilitatibus vigent et novitatibus gaudent … Inter huiusmodi mulierculas una est et fama surrexit iam quasi publica, quod ipsa est Christi stigmatibus insignita. Quod si verum est, non foveat latebras sed apertius hoc sciatur; si vero non est, hypocrisis et simulatio confundatur.[20]

Female mysticism, and the type of imitations which could culminate in the claim of *stigmata*, were seen as subversive and lacking in credibility.[21] They threatened the sort of balanced edifices of reason and faith, of love

---

[18] M. Goodich, *Vita perfecta: the Ideal of Sainthood in the Thirteenth Century* = Monographien zur Geschichte des Mittelalters, 25 (Stuttgart, 1982), pp. 203–4.

[19] On her see W. Simons and J. E. Ziegler, 'Phenomenal religion in the thirteenth century and its image: Elisabeth of Spalbeek and the Passion cult', *SCH*, 27 (1990), pp. 117–26.

[20] A. Stroick, '*Collectio de scandalis ecclesiae* nova editio', *Archivum franciscanum historiae*, 24 (1931), pp. 33–62, c.25, pp. 61–2; A. Vauchez, *Les Laïcs au moyen-âge: pratiques et expériences religieuses* (Paris, 1987), pp. 246–7.

[21] See A. Vauchez, 'Les Stigmates de saint François et leurs détracteurs dans les derniers siècles du moyen-âge', *Mélanges d'archéologie et d'histoire*, 80 (1968), pp. 595–625.

and intellectual knowledge which were being carefully wrought and exemplified in figures such as Anselm, Francis, and Aquinas. It also threatened the authority of parochial sacramental practice. These signs of gentle and non-violent imitation, the *stigmata*, conceded a form of perfection which could be taken up, claimed, appropriated, and integrated into private worlds which eschewed order and authority. We witness, then, that in the generations which immediately followed Francis's example an engagement with the meaning of his message of perfection, with the tension between the ordinary and the charismatic, the routines of life and the disruption which is martyrdom, the tension between the poles Seamus Heaney has called 'penance and gush'.

Accustomed as we are to seek the models of martyrdom and perfection in groups of rigorous religious dedication, a whole new world of martyr-naming in late medieval society is revealed to us once we look beyond, at lay communities, as they honoured even some of their humblest members. Here is a sort of popular understanding of martyrdom, one which identified that supreme sacrifice in the suffering of the virtuous, of the pure, of the good, in sufferings undeserved, unmerited, and wantonly inflicted. A *mentalité*, a deep and engrained understanding, a sort of morality is here revealed. Innocence sullied, purity misunderstood, created not only sympathy, but a drive to remedy this breach of the cosmic order in acts of expiation through veneration and posthumous loving and tender care for the 'martyr'.

One of the most striking examples of such communal martyr-naming, which has reached us, thanks to the disapproval of that active Dominican inquisitor Stephen of Bourbon, was the making of a martyr's cult around that most famous of greyhounds, Guinefort. In his *De septem donis Spiritus Sancti* written between 1254 and 1261, in the last of sixteen sections, that on Pride, Stephen deals with the forms of disobedience resulting from pride, among them *superstitio*. In his usual method he discusses the term and uses *exempla* to illustrate its workings:

> Sic faciebant nuper in diocesi Lugdunensi, ubi, cum ego predicarem contra sortilegia et confessiones audirem, multe mulieres confitebantur portasse se pueros suos apud sanctum Guinefortem. Et cum crederem esse sanctum aliquem, inquisivi, et audivi ad ultimum quod esset canis quidam leporarius, occisus per hunc modum.[22]

[22] J.-C. Schmitt, *The Holy Greyhound: Guinefort, Healer of Children since the Thirteenth Century* (Cambridge, 1983), p. 2.

It happened on the estate of the Lord of Villars, in the region of the Dombes, north of the city of Lyons. While the lord and lady had been away from the house, and the nurse left the child alone for a moment, a huge serpent entered the house and approached the cradle. Seeing this the greyhound chased the serpent, fought with it, bit it, was bitten by it, and finally overpowered it. The scene was a bloody one. When the nurse discovered it, she called the mother and then the father, who 'drew his sword and killed the dog'. They soon discovered the mistake, and buried the dog in a well, covered with stones, but the manor was destroyed and was eventually abandoned. Stephen continues:

> Homines autem rusticani, audientes nobile factum canis, et quomodo innocenter mortuus est pro eo de quo debuit reportare bonum, locum visitaverunt, et canem tanquam martyrem honora- verunt et pro suis infirmitatibus et necessitatibus rogaverunt, seducti a diabolo et ludifacti ibi pluries, ut per hoc homines in errorem adduceret.[23]

Stephen is hardly a sympathetic observer of this local martyr cult. Inquisitors rarely are. And yet this collective impulse to mark and remedy the evil done, rectify the cosmic order by venerating the dog unjustly killed, reflects a desire to re-establish justice for fear of retribution (the lord's estate had been devastated); but also a wish to partake in the virtue which flows from the sacrifice implicit in martyrdom. And here we find a fundamental structure of martyrdom cult: once recognized as a martyr's death, that death is made into a significant marker: of one group as opposed to another, we and they, Christians and pagans, or, as in this case, righteous villagers and misguided lord. It is also a source of benefit, of grace. Proximity to it can bring health and protection. And here the popular cult of Guinefort differs little from the structure of the cult of the martyrs in early Christianity, where they too were such markers, and where commemoration of martyrs served not only to animate and sustain the family and then the community of Christians, but to be used as the most powerful relics of early medieval society.[24]

The contexts in which such popular recognition could be earned were varied, and they all bespoke an unjust violent death. There were women like the Danish Marguerite of Roeskilde, killed in 1176 by her husband; or Panacea, a young woman killed by her mother-in-law in the village of

---

[23] Ibid., p. 3.
[24] P. Brown, *The Cult of Saints: its Rise and Function in Latin Christianity* (Chicago, 1981), ch. 2, esp. pp. 30–3.

Valsena, in northern Italy, in 1383; or the simple Marguerite of Louvain, a servant girl who was killed by robbers and attempted rapists in woods near the town of Villers, in Brabant, in 1225 while travelling with her employers, who were killed too. The cult developed under the patronage of the Duke of Brabant (whose responsibility it was to ensure safety on highways), and the Cistercian monastery of Villers.[25]

Innocent men could earn the veneration of popular cult, like Honorius of Buzançais in the thirteenth century, a livestock merchant who was killed near Poitiers by some servants he had chastised; or Buonmercato de Ferrare, a clerk who was lynched to death in 1383 on suspicion of having killed the rector of a Ferrarese church. William of Rochester was a simple pilgrim when he was killed in 1201 by an ungrateful foundling to whom he had given protection; Gerald of Cologne was a German pilgrim, killed by brigands near Cremona in 1241. Similarly, the German Nantuin was on the pilgrimage route to Rome when he was apprehended by some priests at Wolfratshausen, near Munich, accused of pederasty, and burnt alive.[26] These pilgrims could have stayed at home, but they went on route, on a quest, evoking the widespread convergence of the meaning of *peregrinatio* and *martyrium*.[27] Thus the anxieties related to travel abroad, distance from friends and protectors, and the age-old frustrations of young *vis-à-vis* old (like the case of bride and mother-in-law), or of wife with violent husband (like Marguerite of Roeskilde) were constructed through the language of popular piety into rituals of reassuring vengeance of the unjust death through the loving and aggrandising recognition of a martyr's cult and martyrological retelling. Indeed, the *Ancrene wisse* likened all martyrs to children, to spoilt children of rich parents, who deliberately tore their clothes to shreds so that they might be given new ones. Theirs is an indulgent father, who would give them a garment brighter than the sun ('schenre þen þe sunne').[28] The most powerful area of affective anxiety involves children, and the most adamant popular demand for recognition of martyrdom, one which the medieval papacy refused, was that of child-killing, in the deaths of those new medieval child-martyrs, allegedly victims of Jewish violence, the victims of ritual murder.

From Norwich comes the first known story of the killing of a Christian

---

[25] Vauchez, *La Sainteté*, pp. 174–5; Goodich, *Vita perfecta*, p. 196.

[26] Vauchez, *La Sainteté*, pp. 175–6.

[27] See the discussion in the context of Old Irish usage, T. Charles-Edwards, 'The social background to Irish *peregrinatio*', *Celtica*, 11 (1976), pp. 43–59.

[28] *Ancrene wisse* (*parts six and seven*), ed. G. Shepherd, *Exeter Medieval English Texts* (Exter, 1985), p. 9.

pre-pubescent boy for the purposes of Jewish ritual or as re-enactment of the Crucifixion, elaborated by Thomas of Monmouth, and so penetratingly studied by Gavin Langmuir.[29] The story struck a chord, as it combined the loss of that which is most precious, a child, with the otherwise suspect Jewish rituals and Jewish guilt. We need not claim that a strong hatred towards Jews existed in Norwich in 1144, but rather that a clever rendering of this type of tale of martyrdom, with Jews as executioners, was achieved by the spinner of the yarn. From that moment on, not only was little William visited in Norwich to the enjoyment of the cathedral, but a powerful narrative was constructed, one which derived much of its power from existing notions of Holy Innocence and of the merits which a martyr showered upon the community which produced or witnessed the drama (see plate 2).[30] This is popular martyr-making at its very best: like so many martyrs of old, the boy martyr was a virgin, beset by cruel and scheming enemies. This topos elicited strong responses in the popular religiosity of the later Middle Ages,[31] indeed, from its very inception it depended on a particular, a not unlettered, rendering of preexisting stories about Jews, and on popular notions of martyrdom to create its potent fascination, which led communities of Jews in Lincoln, Blois, Bury, Trent—and in many other places—to death.

A fifteenth-century addition to an illuminated manuscript of the twelfth century of a 'Life of Christ and the Virgin' includes a prayer to St Robert, the martyred boy of Bury St Edmunds, a case of 1190:

> Ave dulcis puer beate Roberte qui infancie tempore floruisti martirii palma, ora pro nobis . . .

The prayer then addresses God:

> Deus qui beato Roberto talem fortitudinem tribuisti ut in puerili corpusculo gloriosum pro nomine tuo subiret martirium, concede propicius ut ipsius intercendentibus meritis ab omnibus nos absolvas peccatis.[32]

[29] G. I. Langmuir, 'Thomas of Monmouth: Detector of ritual murder', *Speculum*, 59 (1984), pp. 820–46. See also *idem*, 'The Knight's Tale of young Hugh of Lincoln', *Speculum* 47 (1972), pp. 459–82.

[30] See the interesting case of martyr-naming in early medieval Georgia, B. Martin-Hisard, 'Martyre et baptême en Géorgie (IXe–Xe siècles)', in H. Dubois, J.-C. Hacquet, and A. Vauchez, eds, *Horizons marins, horizons spirituels (Ve–XVIIIe siècles)* (Paris, 1987), 1, pp. 95–104.

[31] Vauchez, *La Sainteté*, pp. 176–7.

[32] H. Copinger Hill, 'S. Robert of Bury St. Edmunds', *Proceedings of the Suffolk Institute of Archaeology and Natural History*, 21 (1931–3), pp. 98–107; facing p. 104.

Plate 2   *William of Norwich*, panel of altar-piece formerly in the Lady Chapel of St John Maddermarket, Norwich, reproduced by courtesy of the Victoria and Albert Museum, London.

This child martyr thus became assimilated not only into private prayer, but also into the aspirations of the monastery itself, the beneficiaries of his shrine and its merits. John Lydgate, monk of Bury, wrote a prayer, and the last stanza invokes all the merits of the martyr:

> Haue upon Bury þi gracious remembraunce
> That hast among hem a chapel and a shryne,
> With helpe of Edmund, preserve hem fro grevaunce,
> King of Estynglond, martir and virgyne,
> With whos briht sonne lat thy sterre shyne,
> Strecchyng your stremys thoruh al þis regioun,
> Pray for alle tho, and kepe hem fro ruyne,
> That do reverence to both your passioun.[33]

The martyrdom trope is thus alive, as a younger martyr re-enforces the merits bequeathed by the old. Henry III had in his chapel in Nottingham Castle an altar-frontal of St William of Norwich, and an altar-frontal depicting William of Norwich which accompanied an altar-piece with St Edmund, King and Martyr.[34] Edward I was interested in the cult of little Hugh of Lincoln, and provided his newly-built shrine at Lincoln with alms in 1299 and 1300, a decade after the expulsion of the Jews.[35] Liturgically, literarily, in terms of its religious sentiment, here we have a martyrdom *par excellence*, and yet it is the type of martyrdom which the Church refused to recognize, despite the abiding strength of its appeal and the quasi-formal location of its influence and cult. The Church felt very uncomfortable with new martyrs, and with child martyrs above all. Child martyrs just were—they had no history of saintliness, no life of growing merit, no biography of conscious religiosity; they were born and soon died, and were thus hard to evaluate, to grasp.

The story had soon reached Germany; by the mid-thirteenth century similar tales were told there. An interesting case is that of the Rhenish boy martyr Werner of Oberwesel. A number of southern German chronicles relate under the year 1287 that a boy, Werner, had been killed by the Jews. The boy was found dead, washed up on the bank of the Rhine at Bacharach—the body of a boy who had worked for some Jews at

[33] *The Minor Poems of John Lydgate*, ed. H. N. MacCracken, *EETS*, extra series, 107 (1911), p. 139, lines 33–40.
[34] P. Binski, D. Park, and C. Norris, *Dominican Painting in East Anglia: the Thornham Parva Retable and the Musée de Cluny Frontal* (Woodbridge, 1987), p. 445.
[35] D. Stocker, 'The shrine of Little St Hugh', in *Medieval Art and Architecture at Lincoln Cathedral* (London, 1986), pp. 109–17, at p. 109.

167

Oberwesel. He was identified by a serving-girl and was proclaimed to be the victim of the Jews for whom he had worked. His body began to work miracles, and as the pieces of the ritual murder accusation came together, a regional massacre flared up in which many Jews perished. Ultimately Emperor Rudolf exacted a heavy fine from the towns of Oberwesel and Boppard. Equally unambiguously the Archbishop of Mainz delivered a sermon in which he recommended that Werner's body be exhumed and burnt and that his ashes be dispersed. But in Bacarach, within a few months, the chapel of St Cunibert, where the body lay, was being extended, and in 1289 a dozen bishops from the papal entourage provided it with indulgences to encourage devotion and pilgrimages. Against the archiepiscopal disapproval and imperial ire stood popular devotion, and the support of the Count Palatine. A number of vernacular works in Flemish and in German were composed in the fourteenth century, and by 1400 a Latin work, *Passio antiqui sancti Werneri*, was in circulation, together with an office of nine lessons. There was a continuous interest in the shrine from multiple quarters, so that by 1426 Cardinal Giordano Orsini sanctioned an investigation, with the intention of achieving canonization for little Werner, during his tour of the region as papal emissary. We have the inquest's findings of 1428–9, supported by the Count Palatine, Louis III, but no further formal preoccupation with it. By this time Werner was said to have been a virgin, to have emanated from peasant stock, and to have carried with him at his death a *putatorium*, an instrument for digging vines, so he was adopted as the patron saint of wine-growers and of vintners. Werner came close to transcending the boundary between popular and official martyr, closer than most. It is interesting to note that such transcendence was most possible within the Empire, where rife political particularism could nurture a local cult of a martyr, quite apart from the intervention of State, Church, bishop, or inquisitor.[36]

So the Jews provided a nexus of enmity and violence within which latter-day martyrdoms could be imagined and narrated. They were, after all, actors at the original martyrdom, Christ's Passion. It is in a world alive with pogroms, in Franconia of the fourteenth century, that one of the most breath-taking acts of popular martyr-naming took place. In April 1338, in the wake of a Host-desecration accusation in the town of Röttingen, Arnold of Uissinghiem, a young member of a local gentry family, led a crowd of knights, artisans, and riff-raff in an orgy of

[36] Vauchez, *Les Laïcs au moyen-âge*, pp. 157–68.

destruction of Jewish communities in Franconia, a wave of violence known as the Armleder uprising, which also destroyed clergy and raided religious houses on its trail. By late summer, imperial forces caught up with the mob and arrested Arnold, who was then tried in Kitzingen and sentenced to death by decapitation. His remains were carried to his village church of Uissingheim, where he was buried in a magnificent tomb. The inscription on the tomb told of Arnold, a martyr who was cruelly killed by the Jews and their friends. His body was said to work miracles, and a cult developed around him, in the church where his remains rest until this very day.[37]

So a strong impulse towards the recognition of merit and its application to the common good moved people to recognize the victims of unmerited violence as martyrs, and to elaborate cultic practices in their honour. This was a far cry from the highly reflective turn which definitions of martyrdom were taking in scholarly discussion, and the rather stringent reserve with which the papacy and church hierarchy observed popular attempts to name contemporaries as martyrs comparable with those of the age of persecution. The merits of the early martyrs were, after all, embodied in the very fabric of the Church; they made the Church. Missionaries brought Christianity to pagan peoples, female martyrs kept the faith alive until it was formally recognized and allowed to flourish. The merits of the Apostles were grounded in the great cathedrals of Europe and the Near East, Christ's own blood and the relics of his Passion lay in Jerusalem and in choice deposits of his blood on European soil, and devotional works such as the *Legenda aurea* created a constant link with that source of early virtue and example.

Theological discussion insisted on the element of choice in martyrdom, and explored the reaches of intention. Once a martyr was willing to die, death itself was no longer important, it merely sealed the perfection already achieved. The emphasis in such discussion is not on pain, but on knowing choice—little surprise, then, to find that so many martyrs were described in late medieval martyrologies as undergoing terrible and hideous torture, but never feeling a pain, nor suffering bodily injury. When Cecilia was scalded in a bath for a day and a night, she did not even sweat; when Juliana was bound and thrown into the fire, she prayed for deliverance for the sake of the bystanders, so angels descended and put out every spark. When she was put into a vessel of boiling pitch, it became

[37] K. Arnold, 'Die Armledererhebung in Franken 1336', *Mainfränkische Jahrbuch für Geschichte und Kunst*, 26 (1974), pp. 35–62, at pp. 51–3.

cool and pleasant to the touch.[38] In these vernacular accounts the martyr is very much in control of her ordeal, with the help of her God. The moment of death is chosen, and the *mise-en-scène* controlled. The martyrological account moves between the need to fascinate, shock, and terrorize in order to convey the sense of extraordinary ordeal, and a keenness to maintain the sense of God's omnipotent control and the dignity and power of the martyr, the free will in the act.

* * *

Having explored this apparent divergence in modes of using the concept of martyrdom and the collective interpretations given to it in the later Middle Ages, having looked at the new types of martyrs who were animating piety, pilgrimage, and the fiercest identification, at a popular level, often unrecognized by official naming, let us now examine those who were recognized. Here again, a tradition of martyrdom had been created for every people: not only the Apostles, but the national heroes—a Boniface, a Denis. To these were added at distinct moments in the eleventh and twelfth centuries the crowns of martyred kings and princes who fought iniquity and toed a line of happy coexistence with the Church in the fragile Christian kingdoms of Europe: Edmund of East Anglia, martyred in 870; Olaf of Norway, killed in 1030; Boris and Gleb, killed in 1015, virgin sons of St Vladimir, first Christian Duke of Kiev.[39] The achievement of martyrdom would live on as the finest accolade for a king: Joinville's *Life of St Louis* attempts, after all, to represent the King as a quasi-martyr. And most proudly the Church's martyred bishops, standing fast against the other type of ruler, who threatened or at least challenged the new vista of a Christian society under papal leadership: St Stanislas, Bishop of Cracow, torn limb from limb at the altar in 1079 by King Boleslaus the Cruel (who had been excommunicated by the Bishop) who was canonized in 1253, and that dazzling martyr Thomas Becket, killed in 1172.[40] But by the mid-thirteenth century there seems to be a retrenchment in thinking about the recognition of contemporary lived experience

---

[38] For Cecilia see James of Voragine, *Legenda aurea*, ed. T. Graesse (Leipzig, 1850), c.169, p. 776: 'Tunc iratus Almachius jussit eam ad domum suam reduci ubique tota nocte et die jussit eam in bulliente balneo concremari. Quae quasi in loco frigido mansit nec modicum saltem sudoris persensit'; *The Early South English Legendary*, p. 495. On Juliana see *Pe liflade of St. Juliana*, pp. 66, 68.

[39] Vauchez, *La Sainteté*, pp. 187–97. On Boris and Gleb see Dr Price's interesting article in this volume, above, pp. 105–15.

[40] Vauchez, *La Sainteté*, pp. 197–9.

as martyrdom; facing the varieties of religious enthusiasm which were sweeping Europe from the eleventh century, and with consideration of whole new arenas of possible death far away from the network of scrutiny and observation: the Holy Land, Armenia, Southern Spain. But most of all, it was the fear of enthusiasm which culminated in the drastic and persecuting measures against the exponents of poverty, against those who dared to redraw the contours of Christian perfection. And this institutional impulse interacted strongly with a variety of other ideas: the greater attention in ethical thinking to intention as the determinant of value in human action, the emphasis on internal and spiritual contemplation as necessary for spiritual growth, and, above all, parochial practice for the unlearned, the unsophisticated. So when James of Voragine (d.1298) came to assemble his encyclopaedia of Christian example, the *Legenda aurea*, 91 of 153 chapters narrated the lives of martyrs, introducing 131 figures and followers who suffered such death, mostly Apostles and virgin martyrs.[41] James chose few more recent figures, but when he did he created narrative contexts which rendered their deaths as classic martyrdoms. Peter of Verona, canonized only a decade before the composition of the *Legenda aurea*, met the criteria of conscious choice of death, in his case at the hands of Cathars:

> Pro hac quo que mortem subire cupiens hic principaliter a domino attentis et crebris postulationibus supplicasse probatur, quod non sineret eum ex hac luce migrare, nisi sumto pro illo calice passionis: nec fraudatus est tandem a desiderio suo.[42]

The choice was consciously made:

> non divertentem ab hoste, sed exhibentem se protinus hostiam et caesoris sustinentem in patientia truces ictus dimisit spiritu petente superna in ipso loco passionis occisum ... In ipsa die sui martirii confessor, martir, propheta et doctor quodammodo esse promeruit.[43]

Martyrdom came to be linked to service and conformity, to deaths suffered not in enthusiasm and devotion, but in fulfilling duty; it became an essential act of obedience. In his reply to an objection in article 2 of the question on martyrdom in the *Summa theologiae*, Thomas Aquinas argued:

> martyrium complectitur id quod summum in obedientia esse potest, ut scilicet aliquis sit obediens usque ad mortem: sicut de Christo

---

[41] A. Boureau, *La Légende Dorée: le système narratif de Jacques de Voragine (d. 1298)* (Paris, 1984), pp. 111–13; on martyrdom and martyrology in general see the whole section, pp. 111–33.

[42] James of Voragine, *Legenda aurea*, p. 279.

[43] Ibid., p. 281.

legitur ... quod *factus est obediens usque ad mortem*. Unde patet quod martyrium secundum se est perfectius quam obedientia absoluta dicta.[44]

Anticipating the relativizing possibility inherent in his words, Aquinas examines a variety of virtuous deaths, such as that of a woman who dies to preserve her chastity, but concludes that the martyr must indeed be dying for faith, not for any other worldly truth, otherwise there may well be martyrs for geometry!

> Alioquin si quis moreretur pro confessione veritatis geometriae, vel alterius scientiae speculativae, esset martyr: quod videtur ridiculum. Ergo sola fides est martyrii causa.[45]

*   *   *

But if we are truly to appreciate the context of belief, death, and witness in the later Middle Ages, then this is not ridiculous, and we *must* relativize the notion of faith, because issues of truth and faith were contested in these centuries as never before. Not only the question of authority, but the whole thrust of Christian history was being increasingly questioned as apocalyptic interpretations of the course of world events took root from the late twelfth century. Such views came to engulf not only sections of the Franciscan Order, but attracted an eminent physician, diplomat, astrologer, and theologian such as Arnald of Villanova, and tertiaries and lay people all over northern Italy, southern France, the Rhineland, the Low Countries, and Catalonia. Additionally, forms of perfection through poverty and through retiring contemplation were creating a series of alternatives to parochial practice, to family life, to the ordered acceptance of scholarly written authority, evading the ever-longer arms of Church and State. With the spread of the written vernacular, such challenges could become especially threatening, and the attempts to extirpate adherence often ended in the creation of what I would call martyrs, the knowing sufferers of death for the sake of a transcendental truth and the true love of Christ. Martyrs were made in late medieval Europe, bodies burnt. Let us meet some of these martyrs.

*   *   *

[44] Thomas Aquinas, *Summa theologiae*, Blackfriars edition (London, 1966), II, IIae, qu. 124, art. 3, ad 2; 42, p. 50.
[45] Thomas Aquinas, *Summa theologiae*, qu. 124, a. 5, 2, p. 54. See Albert Camus' reflection, 'Je n'ai jamais vu personne mourir pour l'argument ontologique', in 'Un Raisonnement absurde', in *Le Mythe de sysiphe* (Paris, 1942), pp. 13–90, at p. 15.

On the first day of June 1310 such a fire burnt in the Place de Grève, in Paris. There Marguerite Porète, a Beguine of Hainaut, was executed for her teachings. Already around 1295 she had been brought to the episcopal court of the Valenciennes, in front of Bishop Guy II of Cambrai, to answer accusations of heresy related to the teachings of a book which she had written and had circulated. This book was the *Mirouer des simples ames anienties et qui seulment demourent en vouloir et desir d'amour*.[46] The book was written in vernacular French of a decided Picard, northern dialect. The work was condemned by the Bishop, and Marguerite was warned not to disseminate it any more, or risk being 'relaxed' to the secular arm. But Marguerite persisted, and acted not only in her natal Hainaut, but sent a copy of her book to Bishop Jean of Châlons-sur-Marne and spread her teachings to simple people, Beguines and Beghards. She was called in front of the new Bishop of Cambrai, Philip of Marigny, and the Inquisitor of Hainaut, and was sent south to Paris for more searching examination. There she entered the custody of the Dominican Inquisitor William Humbert, who had his hands full with the trial of the Templars just then, so they saw little of each other—not only because William was so engaged, but because Marguerite refused to take the preliminary oath which began the process of examination. She preferred to linger in prison for some eighteen months, until the spring of 1310. Then, having no inquisitorial material to go by, since Marguerite had never undergone examination, William decided to use another strategy which could lead to condemnation. He had extracted from Marguerite's little book a list of articles and citations, which were to be examined by twenty-one regents—theologians of the University of Paris. By 11 April these were unanimously declared heretical, and by 30 May Marguerite could be declared a relapsed heretic, and sent to the fire on the morrow.[47] Contemporaries commented on her bearing, as we hear from the monastic chronicler of St-Denis, who was in a good position to know, since another monk from the monastery, Peter, had been one of the twenty-one condemning scholars:

> Multa tamen in suo exitu poenitentiae signa ostendit nobilia pariter ac devota, per quae multorum viscera ad compatiendum ei pie ac etiam lacrymabiliter fuisse commota testati sunt oculi qui viderunt.[48]

[46] *Le Mirouer des simples âmes*, ed. R. Guarnieri, *Corpus Christianorum, continuatio mediaevalis*, 69 (Turnholt, 1986).

[47] R. E. Lerner, *The Heresy of the Free Spirit in the later Middle Ages* (Berkeley, 1972), pp. 68–78.

[48] 'Continuatio Chronici Guillelmi de Nangiaco', *Recueil des historiens des Gaules et de la France*, 20, p. 601.

Marguerite cut a formidable figure, and a moving one. This account of Marguerite's death uses the trope characteristic of martyrological accounts: the fine death which moves spectators to tears or even to conversion.

Now what was so disturbing about this book, what so subversive, that it required swift condemnation and destruction? The *Mirouer* is structured as a dialogue of 60,000 words between Love and Reason about the conduct of Soul, a dialogue into which various other figures interject and participate and then disappear, figures such as Truth, Temptation, Virtue. The hostile entry in the court chronicle of the kings of France describes her work:

> Et le lundi ensivant, fu arse ou lieu devant dit, une beguine clergesse qui estoit appellée Marguerite Porée qui avoit trespassée et trans-cendée l'escripture devine et es articles de la foy avoit erré, et du sacrement de l'autel avoit dit paroles contraires et prejudiciables. Et pour ce, des maistres expers en theologie avoit esté condampnée.[49]

The thread which runs through the work is an affirmation of the striving of a soul burning with love, propelled by the energy of that love into an orbit where ordinary earthly forces of law, convention, and custom can no longer exercise the slightest influence.[50] This is the spirit free; and an important opposition in Marguerite's language is between *franchise* and *servage*.[51] In the journey, which is divided into six stages of ascent, a conventionally pious Christian, bound by rules of the Church, practising the virtues of Christianity, could progressively move from being bound by reason, by the law of social organization, by roles, expectations, and considerations within the finite, human sphere,[52] into the seventh stage, stranger than all, becoming God, indeed a return to God, deification:

> RAISON. Et qui estes vous, Amour? dit Raison. N'estes vous pas une des Vertuz avec nous, pouse que vous soiez dessus nous?
>
> AMOUR. Je suis Dieu, dit Amour, car Amour est Dieu, et Dieu est amour, et ceste Ame est Dieu par condicion d'amour, et je suis

---

[49] *Grandes chroniques deFrance*, ed. J. Viard (Paris, 1934), 8, c.65, p. 273.

[50] On Marguerite's work, see K. Ruh, '"Le miroir des simples âmes" der Marguerite Porète', in H. Fromm, W. Harms, and U. Ruberg, eds, *Verbum et signum*, (Munich, 1973), 2, pp. 365–87; M. G. Sargent, '"Le mirouer des simples âmes" and the English mystical tradition', in K. Ruh, ed., *Abendländische Mystik im Mittelalter* (Stuttgart, 1986), pp. 443–65.

[51] E. Zum Brunn, 'Non willing in Marguerite Porète's "Mirror of annihilated souls"', *Bulletin de l'Institut historique belge de Rome*, 58 (1988), pp. 11–22.

[52] On ladder as image of perfection see A. Boureau, 'L'Eglise médiévale comme preuve animée de la croyance chrétienne', *Terrain*, 14 (1990), pp. 113–18, at p. 118.

Dieu par nature divine, et ceste Ame l'est par droicture d'amour. Si que ceste precieuse amye de moy est aprinse et menee de moy sans elle, car elle est muee en moy, et telle fin, dit Amour, prent ma norriture.[53]

This process of ongoing *rapprochement* with God which is earned at the cost of losing human attributes, is the problematical dilemma posed by Marguerite. For in her formulations she has no space and no time for those mundane virtues which keep human society in place. Early in the work Soul proclaims:

> L'AME. Je le vous confesse, dit ceste Ame, dame Amour; ung temps fut que je y estoie, mais ores en est il ung aultre; voustre courtoisie m'a mise hors de leur servage. Et pource leur puis je maintenant bien dire et chanter:
> > Vertuz, je prens congé de vous a tousjours,
> > Je en auray le cueur plus franc et plus gay;
> > Voustre service est troup coustant, bien le sçay.[54]

It was such exultant declarations which were to draw the attention of inquisitors and examiners throughout the later Middle Ages, when dealing with those religious sects which they saw as libertine, and lawless. Marguerite was, of course, neither. Indeed, as opposed to those accusations levelled at other religious women, and very frequently at the Beguines, not a single accusation of unruliness or incontinence in living was levelled against her.

Marguerite's challenge was not only a plan for individual spiritual progression which anticipated a stage in which it broke off from the gravitational forces of human social and religious organization, it was also an explicit engagement with the very utility of the remedies, sacraments, channels of mediation offered by the church. Her imagining of a stage in which a human needed no longer the help of these procedures offered by the Church came close to challenging the basic tenet of salvation through ecclesiastical adherence and practice alone. Because her soul needed none of these any longer to secure unity with God:

> Ceste, qui telle est, ne quiert plus Dieu par penitance ne par sacrement nul de Saincte Eglise, ne par pensees ne par paroles ne par oeuvres, ne par creature d'ycy bas ne par creature de lassus . . .[55]

---

[53] *Le Mirouer*, c.21, lines 41–9, p. 82.
[54] *Le Mirouer*, c.6, lines 6–12, p. 24.
[55] Ibid., c.85, p. 242, lines 20–3.

MIRI RUBIN

Marguerite also deploys the language of romantic longing powerfully, drawing on a language which Beguine writers had made their own, in describing her love of God. She uses the expectation of jealousy implicit in passionate love, and also that of bliss. When questioned whether she would ever prefer another lover, the Soul answers:

> Je me amoye tant 'avec' luy, que pource je ne povoye de liger respondre; et se je n'eusse amé estre avec luy, ma response eust esté breve et ligere. Et toutesfoiz m'esconvint il respondre, se je ne vouloie perdre et moy et luy, por laquelle chose mon cueur suffroit grant destresse . . .[56]

The union of Soul and God is so complete that Soul has, in fact, suffered a death, or in Marguerite's words—a martyrdom:

> Et ainsi, sire, ma voulenté prent sa fin en ce dire; et pource est mon vouloir martir, et mon amour martire: vous les avez a martire amenez; leur cuider est bien a declin alez.[57]

Marguerite uncannily raises, indeed embraces, the fate that was to be her own only a few years later.

In her love, Marguerite even cuts herself off from the Beguines, the milieu in which she received her religious initiation, and which was frequently suspected of Free Spirit tendencies which Marguerite's words so powerfully express. And she takes on Beguines, friars, and priests:

> Beguines dient que je erre,
> prestres, clers, et prescheurs,
> Augustins, et carmes,
> Et les freres mineurs,
> Pource que j'escri de l'estre
> de l'affinee Amour.[58]

Unlike Hildegard of Bingen, who claimed she was merely an unlearned woman ordered by God to write down her visions, the 'infilling of her reason',[59] or Bridget of Sweden, who claimed that God had said to her 'I am your God . . . you will be my canal',[60] Marguerite does not tediously

---

[56] Ibid., c.131, p. 386, lines 103–8. On the language of romance used by Mechtild of Magdeburg see F. Beer, *Women and Mystical Experience in the Middle Ages* (Woodbridge, 1992), pp. 78–108.
[57] Ibid., c.131, p. 388, lines 129–32.
[58] Ibid., c.122, p. 344, lines 98–103.
[59] S. Flanagan, *Hildegard of Bingen: a Visionary Life* (London, 1989), pp. 53–6; and a quote from her hagiographer, p. 57.
[60] Vauchez, *Les laïcs au moyen-âge*, p. 240.

insist on her unworthiness, or her vessel-like function in conveying divine words of wisdom. Marguerite speaks what she knows to be true—the only truth. She did not write in Latin in the intimacy of a religious house; Marguerite wrote to be read, or rather read out, and heard and followed. She was suffused with literature and possessed eloquence which she deployed without apology—she took on the world.

A male adherent followed Marguerite, one Guiard of Cressonsacq (of the Beauvaisis), who claimed to be the Angel of Philadelphia of the Apocalypse, in an idiom of millenarianism which had become aligned with that of religious poverty. As the guardian angel of the Church of Philadelphia, a church of the elect before the coming of the third and final age, he espoused Marguerite, yet it is not clear when they met, whether already in the north, or only in Paris. In the very collection which contains the transcripts of Marguerite's trial proceedings we also find accounts of Guiard's examination on the very same days. For defending Marguerite's view he was also tried (unlike Marguerite, he was interrogated), condemned, and relaxed to the secular authorities for execution. At the eleventh hour Guiard chose to save his skin, and exchanged the chance of becoming a 'martyr' for a life in the royal prison, and Marguerite was burnt without him.[61]

*   *   *

So there were certain beliefs which could win one a martyr's death quite predictably, if they were frequently voiced and steadfastly held. In the fifteenth century eucharistic error and its concomitant implications as a critique of sacerdotal efficacy was one such belief. It was thought to have been pronounced by John Hus, together with positions that offended the whole sacerdotal edifice, many of them taken to be Wycliffite error. Hus was condemned to the flames by the Council of Constance, a body he had come to meet with hopes of compromise and reconciliation (plate 3). Five years earlier such error spoken, in a far more direct and startling form, led to the burning of the craftsman John Badby at Smithfield, in the presence of the great prelates and magnates of England. Now John Badby had argued consistently, first in 1409 to Thomas Peveril, Bishop of Worcester, and then, in 1410, at Blackfriars, in London, a simple but consistent

---

[61] On Guiard, see R. E. Lerner, 'The "Angel of Philadelphia" in the reign of Philip the Fair: the case of Guiard of Cressonessart', in W. C. Jordan, B. McNab, and T. F. Ruiz, eds, *Order and Innovation in the Middle Ages: Essays in Honor of Joseph R. Strayer* (Princeton, NJ, 1972), pp. 343–64; on Guiard's death see pp. 346–7.

MIRI RUBIN

position concerning the Eucharist: that material bread remained on the
altar after the words of consecration, that he would not believe that
Christ's Body was present until he saw it in the hands of a priest, and that
Christ could not have given his own Body to his disciples while still
present at the Last Supper. He also claimed that any person had as much
authority as a priest to perform the eucharistic miracle; echoing an even
stronger Lollard claim, that any good man is better than a bad priest.
Arguing so simply, with no *subtilitas*, he left no room for compromise or
evasive formulation. So, facing both archbishops, many bishops, the
Chancellor of the realm, Edward, Duke of York, he repeated his opinions
at another session, at St Paul's on 1 March 1410; the chroniclers describe a
horrible spider coming out of his mouth as he spoke. Once his sentence
was announced a royal writ for his burning was very quickly issued. The
mood was ripe for the execution of a Lollard, for the making of an
example to deter and instil fear, and one of the few English Lollard
martyrs was made.[62]

But in a bizarre improvization on the narrative moment in a *passio*,
when offers are made to the martyr in an attempt to persuade him or her
to recant and be saved, the Prince of Wales, faggots already burning under
Badby, had him removed from the barrel which encased him, and
approached him with an offer of a royal pension (3*d.* a day) if he were to
give up the foolishness of his error. But even though he had already smelt
the smoke, heard the crackling of twigs, and felt the terrifying heat rising
all around him, Badby refused. He was to be executed, as the assembled
grandees wished him to be, but also as he wished to be; he must have been
sure of his place in heaven, in the company of martyrs of old.[63]

* * *

In the very same fire that burnt Marguerite in Paris on that spring day of
1310 another person was put to death, a relapsed convert from Judaism.
We know little of this man, except that he had begun to blaspheme
against the Virgin in public, begging the attentions of neighbours and
authorities, and ultimately the fire: 'Eodem die [cum], quidam de
Judaïsmo dudum ad fidem conversus, iterum sicut canis as vomitum conversus... ibidem incendio crematur.'[64] Suicidal? lunatic? irresponsible

---

[62] See P. McNiven, *Heresy and Politics in the Reign of Henry IV: the Burning of John Badby* (Woodbridge, 1987), esp. pp. 199–219.
[63] Ibid., pp. 209–18.
[64] 'Continuatio Chronici Guillelmi de Nangiaco', p. 601.

178

Plate 3   Stefano di Giovanni Sassetta (1392–1450), Italian, *Burning of the Bohemian Heretic Jan Hus*, 1415, tempera and gold leaf on panel, 24.6 × 38.7 cms, purchased 1976, reproduced by kind permission of the National Gallery of Victoria, Melbourne.

seeker of notoriety? We cannot know. But this Jew was an heir to a robust tradition of active martyrdom which moved and inspired medieval Jews, and sometimes drew admiration as well as horror from their Christian beholders. Fed on the ancient traditions of Jewish martyrdom at the hand of the Romans, and on even earlier myths, like those of the death of the Maccabees, and Hanna and her seven sons during the period of Seleucid rule, Jewish martyrdom drew immediacy and a host of new models from the events which took shape in the Rhineland in and around 1096, and which recurred throughout the later Middle Ages.[65] The ideal was to sanctify God's name, and never to deny or shame it by accepting baptism. Whereas an earlier halachic tradition recommended only a lenient duty of martyrdom, one which was to be confined to public confrontations, and which exempted women and children, the new Ashkenazi, Franco-German communities, those who bore the crusading massacres and the brunt of ritual murder pogroms, were more radical and defiant in their

---

[65] R. Chazan, *European Jewry and the First Crusade* (Berkeley, CA, 1987).

notion of martyrdom.[66] Theirs was vibrant and collective action; it stressed the reward awaiting the martyr, and interacted with the enthusiasm of crusading itself and with the fervour of Christian religious practices and polemic encounters. Jewish communities first tried to avert an approaching catastrophe, they pleaded with rulers, tried to bribe leaders of mobs, prayed and fasted, but when it became clear that destruction was nigh, this was faced by many in a frenzy of delight: as fathers killed their children, husbands their wives. This is the terrible martyrdom which gives identity, which marks one group clearly apart from the other, one which turns adversity to hilarity, suffering to the promise of infinite reward. Some Jews pretended to accept baptism only to gain access to a crucifix or baptismal water and shout profanities before their death. These actions were recounted by amazed Christian observers and writers like Albert of Aachen a decade after the crusade pogroms,[67] but was also enshrined in the genre of Jewish lament, a sadly abundant literary product of medieval Jewish experience.[68] Martyrdom was meant not only to sustain the identity of individual and community in refusal of conversion, even at the moment of death, and nurture future generations, it was a belligerent act against the enemy, the Christians, who would no longer be able to torment a person who had turned into a martyr.

If martyrdom came to embody the ultimate sanction of love and truth, then we need not be surprised to find it affirming and sustaining such persecuted groups and individuals of late medieval society. Not even those groups whose critique of the Church was grounded in an abhorrence of material practices such as pilgrimage and the cult of saints' relics, not even the dualist Cathars and the anti-clerical Waldensians, failed to develop a nurturing cult of their own martyrs. Depositions collected by the inquisition of Bologna, which dealt with northern Italian Apostolics between 1295 and 1307, mention beliefs such as 'Dolcino was saved, and a saint in heaven'; 'Ugolina ... who was burnt and dead for the same heresy, was a good and holy woman', 'Rolandinus de Ois, condemned for heresy, was in paradise and prayed for her.' These martyrs were even believed to work miracles for the surviving *credentes*:

> dicebat quod heretici faciebant virtutes et miracula, et ... dixit quod
> audiverat quod Mantue fuerunt combusti quidam heretici et

[66] J. Katz, *Exclusiveness and Tolerance: Studies in Jewish–Gentile relations in Medieval and Modern Times* = *Scripta Judaica*, 3 (Oxford, 1961), pp. 82–91.
[67] *Recueil des historiens des Croisades. Historiens occidentaux*, 4, pp. 292–3.
[68] See, for example, the elegies which followed the massacre in Troyes in 1288, A. Darmsteter, 'Deux élégies du Vatican', *Romania*, 3 (1874), pp. 443–86.

apparuerunt magna luminaria super eis et fecerant miracula et virtutes.[69]

Their remains were collected and venerated, as by Beatrice Bocadiferro, who admitted in a trial of 1307 that she had relics: bones, hair, body parts solidified in the fire, which she kept in silken and precious cloths and covered with glass, relics which she honoured, 'flessis genibus, habens spem et fiduciam in eis . . .'[70] When confronted by their inquisitors, some *sorores* improvised on a phrase from the Sermon on the Mount, asserting that *credentes* and apostolic martyrs 'will inherit the earth . . .'.[71]

So the persecuted sects of the Alps, of northern Italy and southern France, Cathars, Apostolics, and Waldensians, were sustained by practices and aspirations whose use by orthodox Christians drew criticism and ridicule.[72] But *theirs* were, of course, the *true* martyrs. The contestation over the honour of the name is reflected in the inquisitorial investigation of some Piemontese Waldensians. Among the erroneous opinions attributed to a smith of Caramagnola in 1397:

> de glorioso beato Petro martire dixisti quod fuit malus et peccator et non sanctus, et est damnatus in inferno, quia persequebatur servos Christi, dicendo hereticos et Valdenses, a quibus fuit interfectus dictus sanctus Petrus, esse servos Christi; et quod mors fratris Iacobi Bechi fuit preciosior coram Deo quam mors beati Petri martiris.[73]

The making of martyrs, and the degrading of the martyrs of others, sustained identities; and it was a war of worlds, of cosmic pictures, unbridgeable, leading to the ongoing desire and need for new martyrs.

* * *

All this forces us to appreciate the variety of adherences and affinities for which people could live and die in the later Middle Ages, and the ways in

---

[69] R. Orioli, *"Venit perfidus heresiarcha": il movimento apostolico-dulciniano dal 1260 al 1307* (Rome, 1988), n.99, p. 166.

[70] Ibid., p. 167.

[71] Ibid., pp. 168–9.

[72] On Cathar notions of the persecutions awaiting them and the example of martyrdom given by Christ and the Apostles, see the tract of *c.* 1240–50, the *Book of Two Principles: Un Traité néomanichéen du XIIIe siècle: le Liber de duobus principiis, suivi d'un fragment de rituel cathare*, ed. A. Dondaine (Rome, 1939), pp. 143–7.

[73] G. G. Merlo, 'Pietro di Verona–S. Pietro and L. Sebastiano: Difficoltà e proposte per lo studio di un inquisitore beatificato', in S. Boesch-Gajano martire, eds, *Culto dei santi: istituzioni e classi sociali in età preindustriale* (L'Aquila and Rome, 1984), pp. 471–88, at pp. 473–4.

which value is so often earned at the cost of life. The mark of martyrdom, so great a privilege, so binding an act, left to its beholders and lovers so great a store of memory, so strong a sense of cohesion, so inspiring an example; it was a gift of love, and with love martyrs were remembered in the medieval Jewish communities, in the readings on feast days in churches, in the collective memory of Waldensian families, in the moving verses of Jewish poets. Their love and their laments draw us into the terrible logic of martyrdom, the aestheticization of death and torment, the belief that some deaths are celebrations. In this, the raw convergence of Love and Death—Eros and Thanatos—is the terrible claim that death is the utmost exploration of pleasure, and the truest token of love.

William Blake, that extraordinary Christian, tested the necessary bond between death and love in the words he put into Jesus' mouth in the *Via Crucis* section of *Jerusalem*:

> Jesus said: 'wouldest thou love one who never died
> For thee, or ever die for one who had not died for thee?
> And if God dieth not for Man and giveth not himself
> Eternally for Man, Man could not exist; for Man is Love
> As God is Love; every kindness to another is a little Death
> In the Divine Image, nor can Man exist but by Brotherhood.'[74]

In the Christian tale it was by his death that God had earned Man's love for him, the willingness to be martyred in turn for him; and here is encapsulated the logic of martyrdom, as lived and understood by so many in the late medieval centuries, as it is in the throes of ethnic and nationalist strife in today's Europe. That death creates a debt, and social relations are fed by such debts and sacrifices at all levels. Every giving is a taking away, a dispossession, which awaits a return, and these exchanges are love, not disinterested, but very interested, and thus densely binding. Because every martyr beckons another in death.

Those who did die for their faith, those who burned, and often with their infamous books, with the dignity extolled of old, the dignity and calm of the martyr-to-be, transcending the fear and the pain in the knowledge of truth and the expectation of divine recognition and recompense, were in the later medieval centuries not Christians tested for their faith, but those exactly who criticized, questioned, or indeed rejected that faith: mystics, Jews, heretics. The fires of religious indignation, as

---

[74] William Blake, *Jerusalem*, in *Blake, Complete Writings*, ed. Geoffrey Keynes (Oxford, 1966), ch. 4, pl. 96, p. 743, lines 23–8.

opposed to those of mere judicial disapproval, burnt for Marguerite Porète, for Jews who refused baptism or preferred to cut the throats of their children, and then their own, with knives ritually blessed, for the Cathars of Mont Segur; they burnt for Jan Hus, and for those who still insisted that the sacramental structure which worked spirit in matter, matter conceived by dualist critique as essentially corrupt and evil, could not hold. These are the late medieval martyrs, who provoked, cajoled, discussed, disputed, and then—when no accommodation could be found—burnt for their beliefs. It was this context of criticism and dissent which produced late medieval martyrs—not only the dissenting voices silenced by the flames, but sometimes bound up into the drama, death was also experienced by those who went out to argue with them, correct them.

Pembroke College, Oxford

MEDIEVAL HERETICS AS PROTESTANT MARTYRS

by EUAN CAMERON

TWO themes which figure repeatedly in the history of the Western Church are the contrasting ones of tradition and renewal. To emphasize tradition, or continuity, is to stress the divine element in the continuous collective teaching and witness of the Church. To call periodically for renewal and reform is to acknowledge that any institution composed of people will, with time, lose its pristine vigour or deviate from its original purpose. At certain periods in church history the tension between these two themes has broken out into open conflict, as happened with such dramatic results in the Reformation of the sixteenth century. The Protestant Reformers seem to present one of the most extreme cases where the desire for renewal triumphed over the instinct to preserve continuity of witness. A fundamentally novel analysis of the process by which human souls were saved was formulated by Martin Luther in the course of debate, and soon adopted or reinvented by others. This analysis was then used as a touchstone against which to test and to attack the most prominent features of contemporary teaching, worship, and church polity.[1] In so far as any appeal was made to Christian antiquity, it was to the scriptural texts and to the early Fathers; though even the latter could be selected and criticized if they deviated from the primary articles of faith.[2] There was, then, no reason why any of the Reformers should have sought to justify their actions by reference to any forbears or 'forerunners' in the Middle Ages, whether real or spurious. On the contrary, Martin Luther's instinctive response towards those condemned by the medieval Church as heretics was to echo the conventional and prejudiced hostility felt by the religious intelligentsia towards those outside their pale. As Peter Wesenbec (1546–1603) put it in his *Oration on the Christian Waldenses and Albigenses* of 1585:

> Luther, surely an undoubted servant of God, in the preface and introduction with which he splendidly adorned the confession of

---

[1] See the analysis in E. Cameron, *The European Reformation* (Oxford, 1991), esp. pp. 135, 191–3.
[2] See, for instance, the critiques of Augustine by Luther and Calvin, in O. Scheel, ed., *Dokumente zu Luthers Entwicklung (bis 1519)*, 2nd edn. (Tübingen, 1929), p. 192; Calvin, *Institutes*, III. xi. 15; and discussion in Cameron, *European Reformation*, p. 123.

faith of the Bohemian brethren and their followers, and defended it against the suspicions of the ill-disposed, frankly admits, that just as at first he did not cease to persecute with real hatred these Waldensian and Pikart brethren with whom we are concerned, as though they were damned people; so, after he had learned of their confessions and devout writings, he recognized that the utmost injustice had been done to the best of men, and that those whom the popes condemned as heretics, ought rather to be praised as saints and martyrs . . .[3]

Luther was, of course, quite accustomed to finding support in unexpected quarters for his beliefs—after they had been formed! He is better known for his discovery, in late 1519, that he had in ignorance taught the doctrines of Hus; or that, in 1522, he would have seemed to have been a follower of Wessel Gansfort, if only he had read his books a little earlier.[4] There is no reason, I suggest, to imagine that any other Reformer would have looked with any greater initial favour than Luther on the teachings of a medieval heretic. Few of the reformers, brought up as they were in the milieux of the urban and university-based clergy, would have had either motive or opportunity to meet any survivors of the popular heretical movements, before they themselves became missionaries of dissent. Guillaume Farel, the proto-Reformer of the Vaud and Geneva, was a rare exception who had probably met some in his native Dauphiné. His grandfather, François Farel, the notary of Gap, had employed some Alpine Waldenses as servants about 1500. François later spoke in their

---

[3] P. Wesenbecius, *Oratio pro Waldensibus et Albigensibus Christianis*, as ed. in J. Camerarius, *Historica narratio de fratrum orthodoxorum ecclesiis* (Heidelberg, 1605), p. 413. Luther's original preface reads: 'Ipse inquam cum essem Papista, vere et ex animo istos Pighardos Fratres odiebam magno zelo Dei et Religionis . . . Denique cum aliquando in aliquot libros Johannis Huss imprudens incidissem, et scripturas tam potenter et pure tractatas vidissem, ut stupere inciperam, cur talem et tantum virum exussissent Papa et Concilium: mox territus, clausi codicem, suspicatus venenum sub melle latere. . . . Ibi coepit gaudium cordis mei; et circumspectis omnibus, quos Papa pro haereticis damnaverat et perdiderat, pro sanctis et martyribus laudabam, praesertim quorum pia scripta vel confessiones potui reperire.' See [Unity of Brethren], *Confessio fidei ac religionis, baronum et nobilium regni Bohoemiae, serenissimo ac invictissimo Romanorum, Bohoemiae, etc. Regi . . . 1535 oblata* (n.p., 1558), sigs A4r–v. See also J. Gonnet and A. Molnár, *Les Vaudois au moyen âge* (Turin, 1974), p. 290. Other evidence of Luther's early attitudes to the Bohemians is found in the early lectures on *Psalms* and *Romans*; see references in Gonnet and Molnár, *Les Vaudois au moyen âge*, pp. 286–7; also M. Lambert, *Medieval Heresy: Popular Movements from the Gregorian Reform to the Reformation*, 2nd edn. (Oxford, 1992), p. 381 and n.

[4] For discussion see, e.g., A. G. Dickens, *The German Nation and Martin Luther* (London, 1974), pp. 93–6 and nn.

defence, but did so on the grounds that not just their morality, but also their Catholic orthodoxy was impeccable.[5]

On the contrary, those religious writers who linked the Reformation with earlier heresies before about 1550 did so in the cause of reactionary, pro-Catholic polemic. They adopted this tactic for reasons steeped in the assumptions of tradition and continuity on which late scholasticism relied. Since the orthodox witness of the Church was ancient and true, all opinions contrary to that orthodoxy must already have been condemned, implicitly or (more likely) explicitly. Thus, in the 1370s Johannes Brevicoxa (Jean Courtecuisse) stipulated that 'since the entire Catholic faith has already been approved ... every heresy has been damned and excommunicated by a General Council', and argued, against Gratian, that it was not strictly possible to frame a 'new' heresy, that is, something not already condemned.[6]

The mentality behind this approach was perfectly exemplified by some of the *summae* on heresy published on the very eve of the Reformation, like those of Guy of Perpignan or Bernard of Lützenburg. In such works the heresies of the past were catalogued and listed in alphabetical order, as a closed and defined syllabus of possible errors.[7] One task, therefore, for the anti-Protestant polemic was to identify in the teachings of the Reformation those elements which fell within some previously-condemned heretical system, and proclaim the heresy thus discerned. Both legally and theologically this approach was simple and (apparently) sufficient. The most startling and famous use of this tactic was made by Johannes Eck during the Leipzig disputation of 1519, when he threw the accusation of Hussite errors against Luther. Slightly later, Luther wrote to Ambrogio Catharino in 1521 of how 'I shall be condemned by the very holy satellites [of Antichrist] and called a Waldensian and a Wycliffite.'[8]

Moreover, such accusations continued to be made. Johannes Eck would once again, in his *Enchiridion*, or *Handbook of Common Places*, accuse

[5] E. Cameron, *The Reformation of the Heretics: the Waldenses of the Alps, 1480–1580* (Oxford, 1984), pp. 17, 111, based on Paris, BN, MS latin 3375, vol. 1, fols 449v–52r.
[6] See J. Brevicoxa, 'A Treatise on Faith, the Church, the Roman Pontiff, and the General Council', in H. A. Oberman, *Forerunners of the Reformation: the Shape of Late Medieval Thought Illustrated by Key Documents* (Philadelphia, 1981), pp. 76–84.
[7] Guido [Terreni] de Perpiniano, *Summa de haeresibus et earum confutationibus* (Paris, 1528); Bernhardus de Lutzenburgo, *Catalogus haereticorum omnium pene, qui a scriptoribus passim literis proditi sunt ... iv libris conscriptis. Quorum quartus Lutheri negotium nonnihil attingit* (Cologne, 1522).
[8] For Leipzig, see, e.g., B. J. Kidd, ed., *Documents Illustrative of the Continental Reformation* (Oxford, 1911), pp. 47, 49–50; for Luther's reply to Ambrogio Catharino, see Gonnet and Molnár, *Vaudois au moyen âge*, p. 289, n. 21.

Luther of simply resuscitating old heresies.[9] Alfonso de Castro of Zamora, a Spanish Franciscan, published at Cologne in 1534 a work entitled *Against all Heresies*, which simply presented all the heresies which had risen up against the Church in an alphabetically arranged digest according to subject. Under 'food', for instance, it was noted that the error of eating all foods at all times was held by Jovinian, the Waldenses, and the Lutherans. Later the denial of the need for auricular confession was attributed to the Waldenses, Jacobites, and Luther. Under 'pope', de Castro claimed that denial of papal supremacy was passed down from the Waldenses to Wyclif, thence to Hus, and thence to Luther.[10] Ortuinus Gratius, or Hardouin de Graetz, is mostly remembered nowadays as the supposed 'recipient' of the *Letters of Obscure Men* and as the author, according to Rabelais, of a work entitled *The Art of Breaking Wind decently in Company*.[11] In his own time he was better known for his *Fasciculus*, otherwise *A Bundle of Things to Seek for and to Avoid*, a collection of theological texts, published in 1535. In the dedication to this work he referred to the confession submitted by one of the factions in the Czech Unity of Brethren (usually called the 'Waldensian brethren') to the King of Bohemia in 1508. There Gratius noted that 'at some points it does not differ much from those things which are commonly handed out by "certain people" [that is, the Lutherans], such that they may be seen to have received it from them.'[12]

Catholic theologians who used this tactic made two assumptions. First, they hoped, naïvely as it turned out, that associating the new Reformers with the old heretics would blacken them sufficiently to deter further converts: that belief in the 'wrongness' of ancient heresies and the integrity of the ancient Church was widespread and strong enough to withstand Lutheran attacks. Secondly, it was generally easier, and certainly more clear-cut, to attack the consequences of the Reformers' teachings, such as the denial of auricular confession, of ritual fasting, of priestly immunity, or of papal primacy, than it was to trace their beliefs to their theological sources and identify where they had 'gone wrong'. That

[9] Johannes [Maier von] Eck, *Enchiridion locorum communium* (Ingolstadt, 1541), fol 5v: 'Sic Lutherani relinquentes verum et vivum fontem ecclesiae, fodiunt cisternas dissipatas haereticorum, Wikleff, Husz, Albigentium etc.' Cf. fols 11v, 162v. The original edition appeared in 1535.

[10] A. de Castro, *Adversus omnes hereses*, in *Opera* (Paris, 1578), arts 'cibus', col. 254, 'confessio', col. 303, and 'papa', cols 785–7.

[11] F. Griffin Stokes, *Epistolae obscurorum virorum: the Latin Text with an English Rendering* (London, 1909), *passim*; François Rabelais, *Pantagruel*, ch. 7.

[12] O. Gratius, *Fasciculus rerum expetendarum ac fugiendarum* (Cologne, 1535), epistola dedicatoria to Johannes Helmannus, sig. Aiv verso.

the consequences were heretical was beyond doubt; where the well-spring of the error lay was a matter of intense debate.[13] Heresies which had already been explicitly condemned did not need or deserve to be analysed minutely from within, or challenged by an orthodoxy whose precise stance, for instance on justification, was not yet by any means clear.[14]

The most startling evidence of this attitude appeared rather later in the sixteenth century. It was the resurrection, against the Protestants, of accusations of amoral libertinism which had been levelled against heretics in the Middle Ages. Not only the more extreme and sometimes near-hysterical 'free spirits',[15] but also the relatively sober and puritanical Waldenses had been accused of holding nocturnal meetings at which orgiastic excesses were routinely committed.[16] In line with such accusations, one finds Salmeron claiming that the Lutherans did not regard fornication as a sin.[17] Similarly, the French Catholics during the Wars of Religion would attempt to 'de-humanize' the Huguenots by stigmatizing them with the same accusations of ritual sexual excess as their Waldensian antecedents.[18]

*   *   *

The stratagem of blackening the new Reformers with the old heresies did not just fail: it backfired against the old Church to a quite remarkable degree. Catholics had hoped that prospective converts to the Reformation would fear, or be appalled by, the opprobrium and contempt traditionally

---

[13] Some theologians did, of course, attempt the latter course, e.g. Jakob von Hochstraten or John Fisher: see S. E. Ozment, 'Homo viator: Luther and late medieval theology', in his *The Reformation in Medieval Perspective* (Chicago, 1971), pp. 148–52; S. Ickert, 'Defending the Ordo salutis', *Archiv für Reformationsgeschichte*, 78 (1987), pp. 81–97; R. Rex, *The Theology of John Fisher* (Cambridge, 1991), pp. 110–28.

[14] For the dilemmas facing the Catholic Church in the 1530s over justification, see, e.g., D. Fenlon, *Heresy and Obedience in Tridentine Italy: Cardinal Pole and the Counter Reformation* (Cambridge, 1972); P. Matheson, *Cardinal Contarini at Regensburg* (Oxford, 1972); B. Collett, *Italian Benedictine Scholars and the Reformation* (Oxford, 1985), and a summary in E. Cameron, 'Italy', in A. Pettegree, ed., *The Early Reformation in Europe* (Cambridge, 1992), pp. 188–214.

[15] R. E. Lerner, *The Heresy of the Free Spirit in the Later Middle Ages* (Berkeley, 1972), pp. 20ff., 65, 78–80, 117ff.

[16] Cameron, *Reformation of the Heretics*, pp. 108ff.

[17] A. Salmeron, *Commentarii in evangelicam historiam et in acta apostolorum* (Cologne, 1602–4), 5, treatise 38, as cited by J. Ussher, *Gravissimae quaestionis, de Christianarum ecclesiarum in occidentis praesertim partibus, ab apostolicis temporibus ad nostram usque aetatem continua successione et statu, historica explicatio* (London, 1613), p. 160. Cf. Cameron, *Reformation of the Heretics*, p. 108, n. 31, for similar accusations against Waldenses.

[18] References in Cameron, *Reformation of the Heretics*, p. 111, nn. 49–50. Discussed in Ussher, *Gravissimae quaestionis . . . explicatio*, pp. 159f.

felt for earlier heretics by 'good Christian' society. Instead, the Protestants looked again at the older heretics and saw in them, with progressively greater certainty, a foreshadowing of their own mission. Thus the 'heretics' did not drag the Reformers down; the Reformers dragged the heretics up. This process did not happen immediately or as a single development. Rather, the Protestant analysis of medieval heresies evolved in a process of dialectical exchange with Catholic antagonists. First of all, the heretics excited sympathy and sorrow because of the persecutions and punishments which they had endured; they became 'martyrs' in the conventional sense of the word, those who suffered for their faith. Secondly, however, they came to be cited as evidence of a continuing undercurrent of anti-Roman dissent running throughout the Middle Ages, when 'Satan was let loose' within the Church. Thirdly, and finally, their records and remains were examined with ever more meticulous care to establish that they were indeed the true Christians which Protestant apologetic claimed them to be. Eventually this re-examination of the antecedents of the Reformation would teach the mainstream Protestant churches to place their Reformation, and the earlier dissenting movements, in the context of the cosmic warfare of the Apocalypse. Incorporating heretics into church history in this way served to redress the imbalance referred to at the start of this paper: it imbued the Reformation with a sense of its continuity and tradition no less potent than its sense of renewal.

The first step in this process was to claim the heretics as martyrs for their opposition to the Roman Church. Medieval heretics figured in the great Protestant martyrologies, like those of Jean Crespin, Ludwig Rabus, or John Foxe, as adjuncts to a much larger corpus of edifying stories of the sufferings of early Protestants themselves. Many early Protestants had responded to their persecutors with defiance and conviction, ensuring for themselves, as 'pertinacious heretics', martyrdom on a greater scale than their medieval forbears.[19] At best, the medieval heretics celebrated as martyrs had to be relatively recent victims of persecution, for whom sufficient records or even eyewitness accounts were available. This excluded the Hussites, except for Hus and Jerome of Prague, leaving, of 'martyrs' against the Roman Church before the Reformation, essentially the Lollards of England and the Waldenses of the Alps and Provence. John Foxe was unusual, if not actually unique, in the meticulous thoroughness with which he sought out and copied records of English heresy trials from

[19] See Cameron, *European Reformation*, pp. 356–8.

the fifteenth and early sixteenth centuries. Extracts and summaries of Lollard material form the largest single body of evidence of pre-Reformation dissent in the first half of the *Acts and Monuments*.[20] While recent scholarship has, of course, superseded Foxe's extracts as an archival source for popular Lollardy, there seems to be general assent that he handled those records which he did publish honestly, and did not significantly deform or misrepresent his material.[21]

The Waldenses were treated in a slightly different fashion. Although extensive trial materials survived for these people, like Peter Zwicker's dossier from north-eastern Germany in the 1390s,[22] or an even larger corpus from the Dauphiné in the 1480s and 1490s,[23] these records of individual victims were generally not available to the first generation of Protestant martyrologists. The first of the Dauphiné records, for example, were only released from the archiepiscopal palace at Embrun when it was besieged in 1585 during the Wars of Religion, and were not fully exploited until they reached Cambridge in the 1650s.[24] What the Waldenses lacked in terms of accessible cases of individual martyrdom, they more than made up for in the spectacular collective punishments and sufferings which they endured. In 1545, after five years of threats preceded by ten years of lesser harassment, the Waldensian communities of the Massif du Luberon, in Provence, suffered the execution of an appalling edict issued by the *Parlement* of Aix-en-Provence. By this edict several entire villages, settled by Vaudois colonists chiefly from the south-western Alps, were ordered to be razed and their inhabitants massacred.[25]

---

[20] See John Foxe, *The Acts and Monuments*, ed. J. Pratt, 4th edn, 8 vols (London, n.d.), 3, pp. 107ff., 531ff., 581ff., 702ff.; 4, 123ff., 173ff., 205ff., 221ff., 557ff.

[21] For the case for Foxe's veracity, see A. G. Dickens, *The English Reformation* (London, 1964), pp. 46ff. In some cases Foxe may have misled by omission, or by alleging falsehood on the part of the inquisitors. See a striking example discussed in S. Brigden, *London and the Reformation* (Oxford, 1989), p. 92, based on Foxe, *Acts and Monuments*, ed. Pratt, 4, p. 175.

[22] Wolfenbüttel, Herzog-August-Bibliothek, Cod. Helmst. 403, as discussed and calendared by D. Kurze, *Quellen zur Ketzergeschichte Brandenburgs und Pommerns* = *Veröffentlichungen der historischen Kommission zu Berlin*, 45 (Berlin and New York, 1975), pp. 18–31, 77–261.

[23] These materials are now chiefly contained in Cambridge, University Library, MSS Dd. 3. 25–6; Trinity College, Dublin, MSS 265–6; Archives Départmentales de l'Isère, Grenoble, MSS B 4350–1, and Paris, BN, MS latin 3375, vols 1–2, as described in Cameron, *Reformation of the Heretics*, pp. 268–9.

[24] See the account in Cameron, *Reformation of the Heretics*, pp. 234, 242, for the Embrun records now at Cambridge. The Grenoble dossier, originally from the Chambre des Comptes of the Dauphiné, was not fully exploited until J. Chevalier, *Mémoire historique sur les hérésies en Dauphiné* (Valence, 1890); the Paris dossier was first analysed extensively in J. Marx, *L'Inquisition en Dauphiné* (Paris, 1914).

[25] The fullest recent treatment of this episode is that in G. Audisio, *Les Vaudois du Luberon: une minorité en Provence (1460–1560)* (Mérindol, 1984), pp. 296–407.

Ten years later the Waldenses living in the Duchy of Savoy began to be persecuted, first by the occupying French regime and then by the restored Duke Emanuele Filiberto. This campaign culminated in an ultimatum from the Duke to his heretic subjects, followed by an armed invasion. Most unusually for a 'martyrology', the sufferings of these Waldenses culminated in partial, conditional, success: their sovereign failed to subdue them by force, and gave them strictly limited terms under which they could practise their religion.[26] Meanwhile the Waldensian emigré communities living in Calabria suffered another series of atrocious massacres in 1560–1.[27] These three persecutions, in 1540–5, and 1555–61, and 1560–1 respectively, took place well within the era of the Reformation, and were probably provoked, at least in part, by the presence of Reformed preachers in each case. However, the Vaudois thus attacked owed their social identity and cohesiveness, as well as their name, to their medieval tradition of dissent; it is nowadays generally accepted that they were not quite yet fully integrated into the Reformed churches at the time in question. They were, therefore, 'heretic' martyrs rather than just rural Protestants.[28]

Two important points need to be noted about the exploitation of medieval dissenters and their sufferings by the martyrologists. First, it was accepted by the early martyrologies that, for understandable reasons, the victims of persecution need not have been absolutely perfect (that is, Protestant) Christians. Their beliefs might have been tainted by continuous pressure from their Catholic neighbours. Thus Crespin could remark on how the Vaudois realized by the 1530s that 'their churches were badly managed in several respects, as it were enveloped in the ignorance and darkness of the preceding age.'[29] Of the people of Provence, it was said that 'God always reserved some little seed of piety' in them; and also 'that little light of true knowledge which God had given them, they laboured by all means to kindle and increase'; but that contact with the Reformers had revealed 'how many and great errors they were in, into which their old ministers, whom they called Barbes . . . had brought

---

[26] See sources cited in Cameron, *Reformation of the Heretics*, pp. 162–4, and nn.

[27] For the Calabrians, see Foxe, *Acts and Monuments*, ed. Pratt, 4, pp. 472–3, based on H. Pantaleon, *Martyrum Historia* (Basle, 1563), p. 337; a modern account is in A. Armand-Hugon, *Storia dei valdesi II: dall'adesione alla Riforma all'Emancipazione (1532–1848)* (Turin, 1974), pp. 35–42.

[28] For the revision according to which the final integration of the Vaudois into the Reformed churches is dated to the 1560s, see the agreement between Cameron, *Reformation of the Heretics*, pp. 155–66, 191–9, 213–15, and Audisio, *Vaudois du Luberon*, pp. 409–29.

[29] From the account of Martin Gonin in J. Crespin, *Actes des Martyrs* (n. p., 1565), p. 138.

them, leading them from the right way of true religion.'[30] Likewise, 'ministers [of the Waldenses of Piedmont] instructed them secretly, to avoid the fury of their enemies who could not abide the light; albeit they did not instruct them with such purity as was requisite.'[31] This same reserve about the doctrinal errors of the Waldenses persisted in later martyrological writings: Theodore Beza could say at one point that 'little by little purity of doctrine had died out amongst them', or elsewhere that the passage of time had caused piety and true doctrine to 'decline' or 'be corrupted'.[32]

One should not overstate this first observation: the martyrologists were quite clear that the 'heretics' were successful in abstaining from most of the cultic rituals of popular Catholicism, and that they knew a great deal more of the truths of the faith than their Catholic neighbours, and more indeed than most clerics.[33] These two characteristics, avoidance of traditional 'superstitions' and self-taught scriptural knowledge, supplied the reasons for John Foxe's praises of the later Lollards. Such practical consequences deduced from Lollard teaching (though not their under-lying theology) do go some considerable way to justify the claims by Foxe, and by recent scholarship, that the Lollard programme anticipated that of the Reformation.[34] Nevertheless, in the *Acts and Monuments* Foxe was as aware as Crespin or Beza had been that not all the old heretics had been perfect: not, at least, beyond all possible doubt. On those who might truly have lapsed into real error he wrote: 'But in this point I do not plee as the advocate of heretics, if there be any who are heretics indeed . . . heresy is altogether to be suppressed truly . . . [but] I require doctrine which should rather bridle the heresies, than the heretics.'[35] At the other extreme, he recognized the possibility that an accused Lollard might not have been entirely detached from Catholicism: Joan John, tried for heresy in London in 1511, had allegedly replied to those who asked for alms for Our Lady of Walsingham, 'Take this in worship of our Lady in heaven,

[30] Foxe, *Acts and Monuments*, ed. Pratt, 4, pp. 474–5, translating Crespin. Cf. paraphrase of this by Peter Wesenbec in Camerarius, *Historica narratio*, p. 420.

[31] Foxe, *Acts and Monuments*, ed. Pratt, 4, p. 508.

[32] T. de Bèze, *Icones, id est, verae imagines* . . . (n. p., 1580), sig. Cc. i; *Histoire ecclésiastique des églises réformées au royaume de France* ('Anvers' [i.e. Geneva], 1580), 1, pp. 23, 35f.

[33] See Foxe, *Acts and Monuments*, ed. Pratt, 4, pp. 490, 494.

[34] Ibid., pp. 205, 218. For modern arguments to similar effect, see Anne Hudson, *The Premature Reformation: Wycliffite Texts and Lollard History* (Oxford, 1988), pp. 508ff.; A. G. Dickens, 'Heresy and the Origins of the English Reformation', in his *Reformation Studies* (London, 1983), pp. 363–82; J. F. Davis, *Heresy and Reformation in the South East of England, 1520–1559* (London, 1983); Brigden, *London and the Reformation*, pp. 122ff.

[35] Foxe, *Acts and Monuments*, ed. Pratt, 3, pp. 102, 104.

and let the other go.' This, Foxe remarked, 'declareth, that for lack of better instruction and knowledge, she yet ignorantly attributed too much honour to the true saints of God departed, though otherwise she did abhor the idolatrous worshipping of the dead images.'[36] Others on the fringes of the Lollard movement had quickly defected, or confessed and abjured more eccentric beliefs, whose 'fearful falls and dangerous defections' Foxe said he had no intention to 'excuse or condemn'.[37]

The second major point to note is this: the martyrologists, in this particular tradition, could allow the possibility of doctrinal error, because doctrinal purity was not, strictly speaking, the point at issue. The point was not to urge that the heretics had necessarily been perfect in all respects: but rather that they were better Christians than those who persecuted and punished them, and that their persecutors had acted with barbarous and antichristian cruelty. To quote Foxe again, they had 'nothing mitigated their envious rage, no, not against the very simple idiots; and that sometimes in most frivolous and irreligious cases.' Even if there had been errors taught in the Church aplenty, the fault lay in the persecutors who too readily punished rather than trying to convert.[38] This emphasis, on the sufferings of the victims and the inhuman barbarity of the persecutors, explains why the martyrologies could deal in such detail with the circumstances of the execution of heretics, their patient reponse to the cruelties which they endured, and (often) signs of divine displeasure against their tormentors. One example will illustrate this point. Estienne or Estève Brun, from Réotier, near Embrun, had taught himself to read and write, and studied the New Testament, even learning the Latin equivalents to certain passages in the French. He was compelled to abjure heresy in 1538; in 1540 he was captured and condemned by a Franciscan named Domicelli. The account of his martyrdom went on to describe how he

> suffered death with an unconquerable constancy, since having been for such a long time tied to the stake, without the flames turning towards him, as though turned away by the gusty wind, eventually the executioner struck him a blow on the head with a hook; he said to him 'since I am condemned to be burned alive, why do you want to beat me to death?' At this he was run through and struck down with several blows, very cruelly, then thrown dead into the fire and con-

[36] Ibid., 4, p. 176.
[37] Ibid., p. 179.
[38] Ibid., pp. 179–80; also 3, pp. 99, 172–3.

sumed, while it was publicly proclaimed that no-one was to speak of his death, on pain of similar punishment.[39]

This preoccupation of the martyrologies with the wrongness of the persecutor, rather than the complete rightness of the victim, explains a final otherwise perplexing point. The narratives of the sufferings of the Waldenses were published almost as fully, sometimes in the same words, by moderate Catholic commentators as by Protestant martyrologists. Hence Thomas Cormier of Alençon reported the massacres in Provence fully, in a history of the reign of Henri II, published in 1584. The *politique* historian of Henri IV's reign, Jacques-Auguste de Thou, incorporated in his *History of his Times* the Crespin material on the sufferings of the Vaudois of Provence and the Piedmontese war of 1560–1.[40] Finally, the legal submission made by Jacques Aubéry, the lawyer who in 1550–1 unsuccessfully prosecuted the leaders of the Provençal massacres, was published in Latin in 1619 and in French in 1645. This concentrated on the errors and legal improprieties of the original prosecution of the heretics, while acknowledging that there was good reason to suspect them of being 'meschant garçons et sacrementaires'.[41]

* * *

So far this paper has dwelt on the Protestant martyrologists' first response to the heretics of earlier ages: that they were fellow sufferers of Roman cruelty and persecution. It was soon recognized that the usefulness and importance of previous critics of the Roman Church extended far beyond mere companionship in misfortune. The Reformation faced a further polemical challenge from its Romanist detractors, in some respects the reverse of that discussed earlier: the charge of novelty. The argument set out by such critics was summarized in logical form by John Foxe thus:

> That forasmuch as an ordinary and a known church visible
> must here be known continually on earth, during from the
> time of the apostles, to which church all other churches
> must have recourse:

---

[39] *Histoire ecclésiastique* (1580), I, p. 26. Brun's martyrdom is also reported in Crespin, *Actes des Martyrs*, pp. 154f., but without the details cited.

[40] T. Cormerius, *Rerum gestarum Henrici II regis Galliae* (Paris, 1584), fols 48r–53r; J. A. Thuanus, *Historiarum sui temporis* (Paris, 1604–8), 1, pp. 455–73; 3, pp. 19–50. See Cameron, *Reformation of the Heretics*, pp. 240–1.

[41] J. Aubéry, *Pro Merindoliis ac Caprariensibus actio*, ed. D. Heinsius (Leiden, 1619); idem, *Histoire de l'exécution de Cabrières et de Mérindol* (Paris, 1645).

And seeing there is no other church visible, orderly known
to have endured from the apostles' time, but only the
church of Rome:
They conclude, therefore, that the church of Rome is that
church whereunto all other churches must have recourse.[42]

The corollary of this was, of course, that the Reformed churches could
not in any sense claim to be the 'true' Christian Church, since their teachings were of such recent date and contrary to the continuous and
undoubted witness of the Roman tradition. Catholics were, as Foxe put it,
'so far beguiled in [their] opinion as to think the doctrine of the Church of
Rome, as it now standeth, to be of such antiquity, and that the same was
never impugned before the time of Luther and Zuinglius now of late.'[43]
Foxe attributed this argument to the first generation of Catholic
controversialists, Johannes Eck, Albert Pighius, and Stanislaus Hosius.[44] It
continued to be made by numerous others. As James Ussher summarized
it in 1613,

> Those crafty people accuse the restorers of the old religion of novelty:
> and they affirm that they do not know of a single town, village, or
> household which for the whole of fifteen centuries was not imbued
> with their teaching. As though the matter were beyond any con-
> troversy, they assert it as manifest fact, that no mortal person in the
> whole earth before the time of Martin Luther (that is before the year
> 1517) existed, who held to the same faith which the disciples of
> Luther, Calvin, or other heresiarchs (as they call them) profess.
> Rather those people (says Bristow) must confess, that their church
> never existed in the world—never, I say, at any time—before this age
> of ours.[45]

---

[42] Foxe, *Acts and Monuments*, ed. Pratt, 1, p. 8.
[43] Ibid., p. xxiii.
[44] Ibid., pp. 7–8. Cf. also preface, ibid., p. xxxiv. Cf. A. Pighius, *Controversiarum praecipuarum in
comitiis Ratisponensibus tractatarum, et quibus nunc potissimum exagitatur Christi fides et religio,
diligens et luculenta explicatio* (Paris, 1549), fols 175r–190r, esp. fol. 177r: 'conabimur . . . tantum
meminisse et revocare ad memoriam, ecclesiae filios, in praedictis teneri vivere, ab antiquo,
imo ab initio observatis in Ecclesiastica domo ritibus, consuetudinibus, et legibus'; also
S. Hosius, *Confutatio Prolegomenων Brentii* (Cologne, 1560), esp. pp. 1–2: 'Ante quadraginta
hos annos is fuit orbis universi status . . . Erat terra labii unius et sermonum eorundem . . .
Multitudinis credentium erat cor unum, et anima una. Sicut unus Deus ab omnibus
colebatur, ita fides una retinebatur.'
[45] Ussher, *Gravissimae quaestionis . . . explicatio*, epistola dedicatoria, referring to R. Bristow, *A
Brief Treatise of Diverse Plain and Sure Wayes . . .* (Antwerp, 1574).

The argument had a number of branches, explored in the late sixteenth and early seventeenth centuries by such indefatigable controversialists as the Jesuits Robert Bellarmine and Jakob Gretser. Gretser, for example, in his curiously entitled *Murices of Catholic and German Antiquity* cited numerous examples of German popular linguistic usage to show how Catholic ritual had sunk long and deep into the consciousness of the people, proving that their past was Catholic, not proto-Protestant.[46]

The Protestant response was to invoke not just those condemned by the old Church as heretics, but all sorts of critics and opponents of the Roman hierarchy and its teachings and practices to demolish this argument. The argument was something like the following. The true Christian Church existed from the apostolic age through the persecutions and late empire, more or less within the Roman communion; although some 'errors' crept into it in the early Middle Ages, it still remained basically pure. The real divorce of the 'true' from the Roman Church took place round about the time between the Gregorian 'reforms', in the late eleventh century, and the pontificate of Innocent III, in the early thirteenth. In this period new orders of monks, canon law, scholastic theology, and priestly rituals extinguished the true faith. From that point until the advent of the Reformation

> the true church of Christ, although it durst not openly appear in the face of the world, oppressed by tyranny; yet neither was it so invisible or unknown, but, by the providence of the Lord, some remnant always remained from time to time, which not only showed secret good affection to sincere doctrine, but also stood in open defence of truth against the disordered church of Rome.[47]

This 'remnant' could be identified in part, with learned and spiritual critics of the Church from within, but to a much greater degree, with those whom the Roman hierarchy denounced as heretics. Indeed, the evolution of the post-Hildebrandine Church helped the argument along. That very same movement of disciplinary and doctrinal clarification in the high Middle Ages first encouraged criticism of clerical faults, and then defined the irregular or extreme versions of such criticism as 'heresy'. The concept, the legal definition, and the procedures for repressing

---

[46] J. Gretser, *Murices Catholicae et Germanicae antiquitatis, sectariorum praedicantium pedibus positi et sparsi* (Ingolstadt, 1608), *passim*. A *murex* or *tribulus* was an iron contraption in the form of a tetrahedron which would impale or unhorse anyone who stepped on it, whichever way it was thrown on the ground.

[47] Foxe, *Acts and Monuments*, ed. Pratt, 1, p. xxi.

'heresy', and thus heresy itself, rose alongside the medieval papacy; if not for precisely the reasons identified by the Protestants.[48]

Elements of this argument were to be found in some martyrologies, not least that of Foxe quoted above. However, the classic exponent of this argument was the second-generation ultra-Lutheran controversialist Matthias Flacius Illyricus. His *Catalogue of Witnesses to the Truth, who have cried out against the Pope before our Time*, first published in 1556, provided in its prefaces, and indeed in its title, the classic statement of this interpretation of medieval church history. Through the publication of an edition by Simon Goulart at Geneva in 1608, it was incorporated into Calvinist as well as Lutheran literature.[49] It then established a pattern for Protestant analyses of medieval heresy, which lasted until the nineteenth century. For present purposes, this paper will focus only on a handful of points about the 'true Church' argument developed by Flacius Illyricus and his successors. These points made the argument into a coherent response to the accusation of novelty, and thus caused the Reformed churches' ideas of their own history and identity to be elaborated further.

First, 'martyrdom' in the common sense of suffering dreadful punishment for the sake of truth, became much less important than the original meaning of the word *martyrion*, that is, 'witness' or 'testimony'. It was more important that the opponents of the Roman Church had lived and spoken out than that they had died; the manner of their deaths became relatively less significant. The emphasis shifted decisively, and permanently, to the substance of what the 'heretics' had said, taught, and done: because that substance was now essential to prove that those accused of heresy had really conserved the 'true Church'. Individual details of persecution, normally found only for the later Middle Ages, gave way to general summaries of belief, which could be discovered for all heretics of all periods. Secondly, the multifarious groups of 'heretics' of the high and late Middle Ages tended to be homogenized and assimilated into a single movement, albeit one known by various names. Because this entailed most of the distortions which crept into the Protestant analysis of their alleged 'forbears', it is worth charting it in a little detail.

A remarkable assimilation occurred between the portrayals of the Waldenses and that of the later Hussites, especially the Czech Unity of Brethren. In the later fifteenth and early sixteenth century the term

---

[48] See Lambert, *Medieval Heresy*, pp. xii, 35ff.

[49] M. Flacius Illyricus, *Catalogus Testium Veritatis qui ante nostram aetatem reclamarunt papae* (Basle, 1556, and Geneva, 1608); see the theory of church history contained in the prefaces, esp. in the 1608 edn., sigs **, fols 3v–4r.

'Waldensian Brethren' had already been used to describe the later Hussites, especially the Taborites and their heirs, whether by hostile commentators like Aeneas Sylvius Piccolomini (Pius II) or even members of the Unity itself, like Luke of Prague.[50] Luther referred to the Bohemian Brethren as 'Pikarts' and 'Waldenses', as noted earlier. As the sixteenth century progressed, the Unity seem to have regarded the title of 'Waldensian Brethren' as less and less a term of opprobrium: it was used in the edition of one of their confessions, published by Flacius Illyricus in 1568, and in the texts of the *Consensus* of Sandomierz in 1570.[51] However, the assimilation of Waldenses and Hussites did not stop at this comparatively simple confusion or transference of names. Protestant writers, following on from Ortuinus Gratius' *Fasciculus*, used statements of the beliefs of the Unity of Brethren to characterize all Waldenses, at every era since their first appearance in the late twelfth century. Flacius Illyricus' main entry on the Waldenses drew on Pius II's articles on the Bohemians to document the beliefs of Valdes and his followers at Lyons.[52] The views of the Bohemian 'Waldenses' could then be cited to challenge or disprove some claims made about the thirteenth-century Waldenses in the text of the so-called 'Passauer Anonymous', also known as the 'Pseudo-Reinerius treatise', a version of which Flacius also incorporated into his article.[53] This fusion of Bohemian and Waldensian material was copied by John Foxe, and even by a resident pastor in the Waldensian valleys of Piedmont, Scipione Lentolo.[54] Marquard Freher, in his *Some Distinguished*

---

[50] Aeneas Sylvius Piccolomineus, *Historia Bohemica*, in his *Opera* (Basle, 1551), pp. 102ff.; for the Brethren and Luke of Prague, see Gonnet and Molnár, *Vaudois au moyen âge*, pp. 249ff., 276ff., 348ff.; also Lambert, *Medieval Heresy*, pp. 355, 384ff.

[51] *Confessio Waldensium de plerisque nunc controversiis dogmatibus ante 134 annos contra claudicantes Hussitas scripta, nostrisque temporibus statui, ac rebus pulchre correspondens*, ed. M. Flacius Illyricus (Basle, 1568); on the *Consensus Sendomirensis*, see, e.g., B. J. Kidd, *Documents Illustrative of the Continental Reformation* (Oxford, 1911), pp. 658f.; cf. also B. Lydius, *Waldensia*, 2 vols (Rotterdam and Dordrecht, 1616–17), which is entirely composed of material from the Hussites, the Taborites, or the Unity of Brethren. Amedeo Molnár long claimed that there was a real and close association between all the later Waldenses and Hussites: see Gonnet and Molnár, *Vaudois au moyen âge*, pp. 211–82. Neither Audisio or myself have found any evidence to support this in the behaviour of the Vaudois of the Alps or Provence, as, e.g., in G. Audisio, *Les "Vaudois": Naissance, vie et mort d'une dissidence (xiie–xvie siècles)* (Turin, 1989), pp. 82ff. However, some Taborite treatises were translated into Provençal, possibly in the early sixteenth century, for reasons which remain to be fully elucidated: see the MSS listed by Gonnet and Molnár, *Vaudois au moyen âge*, pp. 348ff.

[52] Flacius Illyricus, *Catalogus* (1556 edn.), pp. 704–12, 760–1.

[53] Ibid., pp. 723–57.

[54] Foxe, *Acts and Monuments*, ed. Pratt, 2, pp. 264–71; for Lentolo's use of Flacius Illyricus, see S. Lentolo, *Historia delle grande e crudeli persecutioni fatti ai tempi nostri ... contro il popolo che chiamano valdese*, ed. T. Gay (Torre Pèllice, 1906), pp. 19–22. This edition is a partial

Ancient Writers on Bohemian Matters, published in 1602, likewise juxtaposed the Pseudo-Reinerius treatise on authentic thirteenth-century Waldenses with the material dating from Luke of Prague and the Major Unity's correspondence with Wladislaw of Hungary in the 1500s.[55] Freher's texts on the Waldenses were then extensively quoted by James Ussher in his own massively complex treatise, *A Historical Explanation of the Most Weighty Question of the Unbroken Succession and State of the Christian Churches, especially in the West, from the Apostolic Times up to our Own Age*, which appeared in 1613.[56]

Much more problematical, to our eyes, was the attempt to run together the Waldenses and the Albigenses or Cathars. The Cathars were, after all, almost certainly dualist heretics, albeit varying between moderate and extreme dualism, whose theology diverged on a whole range of fundamental themes from orthodox Christianity.[57] The early Waldenses had been so close to orthodoxy that in their most primitive stage it has been claimed their only deviation was the insistence on preaching without sanction from the hierarchy. One of their few early surviving writings is Durand of Osca's *Liber antiheresis*, largely written against the Cathars.[58] These problems which, for us, make the idea of equating the Waldenses and Cathars absurd, did not bulk nearly so large for late sixteenth-century writers, whose access to sources was limited, and whose perspective was dominated by confessional concerns. Peter Wesenbec of Jena (1546–1603), whose *Oration on the Christian Waldenses and Albigenses* was first published in 1585, regarded the diversity of names by which the heretic groups were known as unimportant: they were called Waldenses from Waldo, Poor of Lyons from Lyons, 'Picardi' either from Picardy or from a corruption of 'Beghard', Albigenses from Albi, and 'Tholosani heretici' from Toulouse.[59] The accusation of Manichean dualism was bracketed along with the accusation of outrageous libertine vice, as the product of

---

transcription of the original in Bern, Stadtsbibliothek, MS 716; copy in Oxford, Bodleian Library, MS Barlow 8.

[55] M. Freher, ed., *Rerum Bohemicarum antiqui scriptores* (Hanover, 1602), includes on pp. 222ff. the Pseudo-Reinerius Treatise, on pp. 238ff. the *Confessio fidei fratrum Waldensium* sent to Wladislaw II, on pp. 245ff. the *Oratio excusatoria*, and on pp. 249–68 the *Excusatio fratrum Waldensium . . . contra binas literas D. Augustini*; the last three were all written by the Unity of Brethren *c.* 1508.

[56] Ussher, *Gravissimae quaestionis . . . explicatio*, esp., e.g., pp. 234–5, 296–9.

[57] For a recent survey see Lambert, *Medieval Heresy*, pp. 105ff.

[58] Ibid., pp. 62ff.; on Durand of Osca or Huesca (there is debate about the name), see pp. 74ff.

[59] Wesenbec, *Oratio*, in Camerarius, *Historica Narratio*, pp. 411–12.

priestly invective and prejudice.[60] Jean Chassanion's *Histoire des Albigeois*, published in 1595, claimed that the medieval darkness had been pierced 'here and there by some rays of the light of [the] Gospel, by which several people in various places were enlightened in the knowledge of the truth', like the Vaudois, the followers of Peter of Bruis, and the Albigenses.[61] With judicious selection of ecclesiastical source-texts, Chassanion portrayed the Albigenses as preaching against the intercession of saints and purgatory, and in favour of Christ as the sole sufficient mediator; it was also alleged that they rejected a corporal presence in the Eucharist, on the basis of a text originating from the Bohemian Brethren. Finally, they avoided taking part in 'Roman superstitions'.[62] The allegations that they rejected the Resurrection, the Old Testament, or marriage, or were Manichaeans were again denounced as slanders.[63]

Philippe de Marnix's *Tableau of the Differences in Religion*, first published in 1599, made similar points, noting how the Albigenses were compelled by persecutions to retire to the Savoyard Alps, to the Dauphiné, Piedmont, Calabria, and Bohemia.[64] Rather startlingly, he concluded that their teachings appeared 'nothing more nor less than as if they had extracted them, word for word, from the books of John Calvin or Martin Luther.'[65] This running together of the various heretics was copied by Nicholas Vignier, in his *Theatre of the Antichrist* of 1610. The persecuting Antichrist had, among his other evils, habitually misrepresented the victims of his persecution: so, to refute the accusation made by Henry of Clairvaux that the Cathars held dualist beliefs, Vignier cited the Unity of Brethren's defensive pieces written to Wladislaw of Hungary, and the confession of the Vaudois of Mérindol, in Provence, in 1541.[66] The complete elision of Waldensianism and Albigensianism was most fully demonstrated in the Histories of the Vaudois and the Albigenses commissioned by the Huguenot churches of the Dauphiné from Jean-Paul

---

[60] Ibid., pp. 414ff.
[61] J. Chassanion, *Histoire des Albigeois: touchant leur doctrine et religion, contre les faux bruits qui ont esté semés contre eux, et les écrits dont on les a à tort diffamés*... ('Monistrol en Velay' [= Geneva], 1595), pp. 24–9.
[62] Ibid., pp. 37–48.
[63] Ibid., pp. 51–5.
[64] P. de Marnix, Sr. de Ste-Aldegonde, *Le Tableau des differens de la religion, traictant de l'église*..., 2 vols (Leiden, 1603–5), I, fol. 151v; for the full entry, see I, fols 149r–153r.
[65] Ibid., I, fol. 154r.
[66] N. Vignier, *Théatre de l'antechrist, auquel est respondu au Cardinal Bellarmin* (n.p., 1610), pp. 235ff. For further instances of the elision of Albigenses and Waldenses, see the works of Agrippa d'Aubigné, Forbes of Corse, Basnage, and Allix referred to in Cameron, *Reformation of the Heretics*, pp. 235, 249–51; Allix also amalgamated the Albigenses and the Lollards.

Perrin, which appeared in 1618–19.[67] The work was translated into English by Samson Lennard and published at London in 1624: Lennard's preface noted how 'the truth of which religion and visibilitie of this our Church of England, is made manifest in this history for the last foure hundred and forty yeares: which confutes that common and triviall objection of the common adversarie, that our religion began with Luther.'[68] To compound these amalgamations of heresies, Lennard's first part was entitled 'the Historie of the Waldenses, commonly called in English Lollards'.[69]

A third major consequence followed from the elision of these various dissenting movements in Protestant church history. Since the beliefs of the various movements were assumed to be, at least in their general drift, identical both with each other and with the broader consequences of the Reformation itself, it was possible to pick and choose the most acceptable testimonies, those alleged beliefs and practices which conformed most closely to modern Protestant practice, and then proclaim these as the 'true' teaching and behaviour of *all* medieval heretics. The resulting image of medieval heresy was not just homogenized, but also, so to speak, purified and sanitized.

* * *

At this point one should perhaps pause to consider the mentality behind the writing of this highly charged, controversial church history. In the earlier martyrological writings, Protestant publicists had good reason to claim that the Lollards and Waldenses, like the Protestants, had rejected large parts of the sacramental, ritualistic system of late medieval Catholicism—at least in theory. However, this analysis was soon extended to all medieval heretics: it was claimed that they had all been roughly similar

---

[67] J.-P. Perrin, *Histoire des Chrestiens Albigeois* (Geneva, 1618); and *Histoire des Vaudois* (Geneva, 1619); for details on the origins of these works see Cameron, *Reformation of the Heretics*, pp. 234–5.

[68] [J.-P. Perrin], *The Bloudy Rage of that Great Antichrist of Rome, and his superstitious adherents, against the true Church of Christ, and the faithful professors of his Gospell. Declared at large in the Historie of the Waldenses and Albigenses, apparently manifesting unto the world the visibilitie of our Church of England, and of all the reformed Churches throughout Christendome, for above foure hundred and fiftie years last past* (some copies variously entitled *Luther's Fore-runners, or, a Cloud of Witnesses, deposing for the Protestant Faith*), tr. S. Lennard (London, 1624), preface to William Earl of Pembroke. There was also a partial German translation by J. J. Grassern, *Waldenser Chronick, von den Verfolgungen, so die Waldenser, Albigenser, Picarder und Hussiten, etc. Fünffthalb hundert Jahr lang durch ganz Europam uber dem H. Evangelio haben aussgestanden . . .* (Basle, 1623).

[69] [Perrin], *Bloudy Rage*, tr. Lennard, pp. 1–66 (first page-sequence).

anti-papal evangelicals, distinguished only by an unimportant diversity of names. In this enterprise, Reformed church historians bound themselves to argue against the sources to a prodigious extent, as their Catholic antagonists lost no time in pointing out.[70] For much of this century, church historians have tended to disparage their theologically motivated predecessors: our task has been to rise above confessional antagonisms, rather than to sympathize with them. In this topic, however, we have a dilemma which cannot be answered simply by being either patronizing or Whiggish. Either the Protestant historians of medieval heresy believed their analysis was correct, or they did not. If they were insincere, then the Reformed churches' perception of their past was based on a widely-disseminated piece of conscious falsification. Given the Reformers' general integrity, and especially their humanist heritage of faithfulness to the sources, this conclusion seems impossible to accept.[71] If, on the contrary, the Protestants genuinely believed that all, or nearly all, the medieval heretics were truly the 'godly remnant', then they were allowing theological certainty to get the better of their critical faculties, and indeed of common sense. In short, the increasing stridency with which Protestant apologists claimed all earlier dissenters as the 'missing links' between themselves and an earlier, uncorrupt Church needs some serious explaining.

Part of the answer may lie in the continuing challenge which they faced from Catholic antagonists, and which forced the debate along with a momentum of its own. Flacius Illyricus, John Foxe, and the others had claimed that the old heretics were the missing 'true church' which anticipated the Reformation. In the last decades of the sixteenth century and throughout the seventeenth a sequence of highly scholarly Catholic polemics replied that the heretics were nothing of the sort. They then deployed and published a quite formidable array of medieval texts to prove that they were not (in this respect, of course, they were precisely reversing the original Catholic stance described earlier). English Jesuits like Nicholas Sanders, in his *On the Visible Monarchy of the Church*, or Robert Parsons, in *Of the Three Conversions of England*, had pointed out, for instance, that earlier authorities for popular heresy, such as Guy of Perpignan, Gabriel du Préau, or Bernhard of Lützenburg, had attributed practices and beliefs to the heretics quite at variance with Protestantism. These had included sexual libertinism; the forbidding of all oaths in all

[70] See, e.g., cases of the English Jesuits, and Bellarmine as discussed below, n. 73.
[71] Compare the Reformers' attitudes to Scripture as a source-text, e.g., in Cameron, *European Reformation*, pp. 136ff.

circumstances; the abhorrence of capital punishment for any crime; contempt for the Apostles' Creed and the *Ave Maria*; refusal to use any prayer but the Lord's Prayer; attributing the power to hear confessions and consecrate the Host to laymen; a neo-Donatist refusal to believe in the power of a sinful priest validly to consecrate the Eucharist; insisting that priests should live only on alms; and saying the Lord's Prayer seven times to bless their bread at mealtimes.[72] This line of argument portrayed the heretics as at best eccentric, at worst subversive of Christian society and morals, and in any case far removed from the Reformation. Its greatest seventeenth-century exponent was J.-B. Bossuet: at one point in his *History of the Variations of the Protestant Churches* he deployed a detailed Waldensian trial record dating from 1495 to show that the Vaudois held three sorts of beliefs: those rejected by Catholic and Protestant alike, such as Donatist attitudes to the sacraments, and the rejection of oaths or judicial homicide; some (unspecified) held by Vaudois and Protestants but not Catholics; and finally beliefs held by Vaudois and Catholics but not Protestants, such as the seven sacraments and the Real Presence.[73]

There is evidence that some Protestant writers were troubled, at least by the allegedly dualist views attributed to the Cathars. James Ussher's *Succession and State of the Christian Churches* embarked on a highly tortuous argument surrounding the Albigenses. He accepted that there must have been some dualist heretics in Lombardy and southern France, but alleged that the Waldenses had been wrongly tarred with the 'Manichaean' brush. Hence the Waldenses were sometimes accused falsely, Ussher said, of rejecting the Old Testament. Ultimately he decided that the Albigenses and Waldenses were one thing, the 'Manichaeans' another: one might admit that dualist errors were held by 'Manichaeans staying in the lands of the Albigenses', but the accusations were false when applied to 'the whole race of the Albigenses', which also included the Waldenses.[74]

On the whole, though, even James Ussher, one of the most meticulous and thorough of all these early scholars of the records of heresy, remained

---

72 N. Sanderus, *De visibili monarchia ecclesiae libri VIII* (Würzburg, 1592), pp. 469–81; also 'N. D.' [= Robert Parsons, S.J.], *A Treatise of Three Conversions of England*, 3 vols (n. p., 1603), 1, pp. 513–46. See discussion of these in Ussher, *Gravissimae quaestionis . . . explicatio*, pp. 158–74, which also cites Jodocus Coccius, *Thesaurus Catholicus, in quo controversiae fidei . . . explicantur*, 2 vols (Cologne, 1600–1), 1, bk 8, art. 3.
73 J.-B. Bossuet, *Histoire des variations des églises protestantes*, in *Oeuvres*, 20 (Versailles, 1817), pp. 160–9. The original MS version of the trial is in Paris, BN, MS latin 3375, I, fols 215r–276v.
74 Ussher, *Gravissimae quaestionis . . . explicatio*, pp. 224–36. A further long discussion of the Albigenses, where they are regarded as sharing beliefs and identity with other groups such as the Waldenses and Humiliati, occupies ibid., pp. 291–372.

untroubled by any apparent differences between the various groups of heretics who were not dualists. The reason was that the Catholic scholars had, so to speak, succeeded too well. So many heretic groups had been unearthed, so many diverse doctrines described in the inquisitorial texts, that they could not all be correct, given that, as every good Protestant realized, all these 'heretics' had been Godly Christians of the same stamp. The diversity of allegations proved their falsity; the conflict between Catholic witnesses discredited them all. The only reliable sources, then, were testimonies from the heretics themselves: which inexorably drew attention back to the safely proto-Reforming statements of the Bohemian Brethren of the 1500s and the Provençal Vaudois of the 1540s.[75]

So strong, then, was the Protestant certainty that the medieval heretical movements were all Godly, evangelical rejections of papal 'superstition' and tyranny that it could ride out almost any accusations of eccentricity or vice on the part of the heretics. The more Catholic propagandists produced evidence to malign or tease apart the heretical groups, the more convinced the Protestants became of their essential unity and godliness. Nothing less, I suggest, than an argument drawn from exegesis of Scripture itself could have imparted this level of certainty. That argument located the history of heresy within the prophecies of the Apocalypse, and emerged very early in the development of the Protestant church history. The key was found in Revelation 20:

> Then I saw an angel coming down from heaven with the key of the abyss and a great chain in his hands. He seized the dragon, that serpent of old, the Devil or Satan, and chained him up for a thousand years ... so that he might seduce the nations no more till the thousand years were over. After that he must be let loose for a short while ... When the thousand years are over, Satan will be let loose from his dungeon; and he will come out to seduce the nations ...[76]

This apocalyptic was incorporated by Foxe into his chronology of the churches. The chaining of the Devil lasted a thousand years, within which the Church went through some three centuries of suffering, about three centuries of flourishing, and a further three centuries or so of decline, while still 'tolerable, and [having] some face of a Church'. Around AD 1000 came the time of Antichrist and the loosing of Satan, which

[75] This is the argument used repeatedly by Ussher, *Gravissimae quaestionis ... explicatio*, e.g., pp. 173, 301–3.
[76] Revelation 20.1–3, 7–8 (NEB).

lasted some four hundred years, until the time of Wyclif and Hus. Finally, there came the 'reformation and purging', up to Foxe's own time.[77] A very similar chronology was followed by James Ussher's *Succession and State of the Christian Churches*.[78] This apocalyptic understanding of church history turned the rule of 'Antichrist' in the medieval Church, and therefore the place of the heretics as the torch-bearers of the truth, into a matter of revelation and belief rather than one of mere critical opinion.

* * *

As I suggested earlier, it does not seem possible that the Protestant polemics were actually unscrupulous or cynical in their manipulation of the evidence for religious dissent in the Middle Ages. By and large, they did not try to insert doctrines into the sources for heresy which were never there in the first place: one does not find justification by faith attributed to the Waldenses, for example. Rather, the Protestants made the heretics acceptable by a number of tactics. First, they selected and criticized their sources, in the overwhelming conviction that they were rescuing their subjects from centuries of inquisitorial misrepresentation. There was some justification for doing this: not all inquisitors had been equally scrupulous in drawing up their lists of heretic dogmas and practices, and some had a decided taste for the radical or the sensational.[79] In the age which produced the *Malleus maleficarum*, not every ecclesiastical source was immaculately critical and cautious. However, the second Protestant tactic was to amalgamate all the heresies more or less into a single movement, allowing the 'approved' dogmas to be selected according to ever more rigorous confessional criteria. Thirdly, the Protestants, like their Catholic predecessors, concentrated on those aspects of heretic belief which challenged Rome and its practices.[80] Finally, those popular heretics who survived were made acceptable in a different sense, in that they were evangelized, converted, and supplied with 'correct' Protestant preachers. The Waldenses of the Dauphiné and the Lollards of England simply disappeared, as they were swallowed up in the Protestant churches of those regions. The Waldenses of the Duchy of Piedmont-Savoy retained their separate name and identity, which was transferred to the Calvinist Church of Savoy, and ultimately of all Italy. They were, however, no less

[77] Foxe, *Acts and Monuments*, ed. Pratt, 1, pp. 4–5.
[78] Ussher, *Gravissimae quaestionis . . . explicatio*, sigs A2v–A3r.
[79] For inquisitorial texts, see Cameron, *Reformation of the Heretics*, pp. 39, 120ff.
[80] Cf. ibid., pp. 76ff., for this preoccupation of inquisitors.

thoroughly 'Calvinized' than their neighbours west of the Alps.[81] Only in the case of the Hussites was there a period of real mutual negotiation and exchange of views before the erstwhile heretics drifted into reform or back to Rome.[82]

It is not easy to say just why the Protestant leaders bothered so much with heresy. One hesitates to think that any real conversions were made by such arguments, though the possibility should not be excluded entirely. The primary role of the analysis of heresy was that it gave the Reformation a past, a continuity, a sense of tradition with which to counter Rome's strongest card, its evident (or apparent) antiquity. No attempt was made to claim any group of heretics as forbears of any one specific confession, Lutheran or Calvinist, as opposed to the Protestant Reformation in general. The heretic martyrs gave the Reformed churches a history which brought them together, even when their theology seemed determined to prise them apart.

University of Newcastle upon Tyne

---

[81] For Lollards, see Lambert, *Medieval Heresy*, pp. 372–81; for Waldenses, ibid., pp. 362–7; Cameron, *Reformation of the Heretics*, pp. 155ff., 171ff., 213ff.; Audisio, *Les "Vaudois"*, pp. 233–6.
[82] Lambert, *Medieval Heresy*, pp. 381–9.

LUTHER AND THE PROBLEM OF MARTYRDOM

by DAVID BAGCHI

KINGSLEY AMIS once had great fun imagining how the modern world might have turned out if Luther had successfully been bribed with the offer of a cardinalate.[1] A much more likely *mise-en-scène* is that suggested by Kierkegaard, who preferred to think how much better the world, or at least Danish Protestantism, would have been had Luther become a martyr.[2] What makes the martyr's crown a more plausible item of ecclesiastical headgear for Luther than a cardinal's hat is that the idea of martyrdom was so important to him. Its importance was by no means restricted to the four years or so during which he daily expected to have to witness to the Gospel with his own blood: from his earliest lectures on the Psalms to his last lectures on Genesis, martyrdom and its implications for the Christian life were a central theme. In between Luther became not the first martyr of the Reformation, as he (no less than Kierkegaard) would have preferred, but its first martyrologist. In spite of this, Luther's attitude to martyrdom has never, to my knowledge, been the subject of a full-scale study.[3] In this paper I want to highlight some of the issues which would have to be explored further in any such study, and also to indicate the sense in which martyrdom became a problem for Luther.

Martyrdom was important to Luther above all because it epitomized his idea of the Church as a suffering community, an idea integral to his theology of the Cross. In 1539, in his only sustained treatise on the nature of the Church, he explicitly identified suffering and persecution as a mark, indeed a sacrament, of the Church.[4] Admittedly, this treatise dates

---

[1] Kingsley Amis, *The Alteration* (London, 1976).

[2] *The Journals of Søren Kierkegaard*, ed. Alexander Dru (Oxford, 1938), no. 1304, pp. 497f.

[3] The first chapter of Robert Kolb's *For All The Saints: Changing Perceptions of Martyrdom and Saint-hood in the Lutheran Reformation* (Macon, 1987) is the fullest treatment of this issue, and I shall return to it at the end of the paper. The focus of Kolb's study is, however, on developments in second- and third-generation Lutheranism, not on Luther himself. Heiko Oberman gave due weight to the importance of martyrdom to Luther's ecclesiology in his *Luther: Mensch zwischen Gott und Teufel* (Berlin, 1982), esp. pp. 269–85 (Eng. tr. *Luther: Man between God and the Devil* (New Haven and London, 1989), esp. pp. 254–71). Lennart Pinomaa, in *Die Heiligen bei Luther* (Helsinki, 1977), includes a useful discussion on the saints as imitators of Christ's Passion: see pp. 134–7.

[4] *Von den Konziliis und Kirchen* (1539), *D. Martin Luthers Werke. Kritische Gesamtausgabe*, ed. J. C. F. Knaake et al., 64 vols (Weimar, 1883–) [*Weimarer Ausgabe*—hereafter *WA*], 50, p. 641, lines

---

from a time when the German Lutheran principalities were politically and militarily isolated, and the siege mentality it betrays should not surprise us. But Luther was saying much the same thing well before even his own life was in danger, as we can see from his first major theological work. In the course of his lectures on the Psalms of 1513–15, Luther broke off to give a 'sermo de martyribus', taking as his text one of the least promising verses in the entire Bible for such purposes, 'Moab is my wash pot; upon Edom I cast my shoe' (Psalm 60. 8)—or, as it was known to Luther in the Vulgate, 'Moab is the pot of my hope' (Psalm 59). Luther explains, rather enterprisingly, that the pot represents this troublous life, in which the faithful are thoroughly cooked and turned into angelic food fit for heaven. Jesus Christ is the good cook, who boils his saints vigorously, but spares the ungodly because they are to be discarded. The moral is clear: do not avoid temptations and tribulations, because the way of suffering, the way of the Cross, is the only sure way to heaven. This was the basis on which the martyrs hoped to be worthy of their crowns, and all Christians are called to martyrdom in this sense.[5] As St Augustine warned: 'Whoever is not willing to imitate the holy martyrs may not enter their fellowship.'[6]

'Whoever is not willing to imitate the holy martyrs . . .'. These words took on a greater poignancy between 1518 and 1522, when Luther's public protests against indulgences and papal power began wonderfully to concentrate his mind on the prospect of his own martyrdom. When Luther claimed John Hus (burned at the Council of Constance a century before) as a forerunner, he saw him as providing not only an intellectual pedigree, but also a dramatic *memento mori*, an example of what could be expected from continued opposition to the papacy.[7] Even after 1522, Hus remained an important sign of how God works with his saints. Hus's sufferings confirmed him as a true Christian, for Christians are, as St Paul says, 'the

---

35ff. Eng. tr. in *Luther's Works*, ed. J. Pelikan and H. T. Lehmann, 56 vols (Philadelphia and St Louis, 1955–86) [hereafter *LW*], 41, p. 164).

[5] *Dictata super Psalterium* (1516), *WA* 3:342–5 = *LW* 10:286–9.

[6] Ibid., *WA* 3:345, lines 1–3 = *LW* 10:289.

[7] It is a significant if easily overlooked point that Luther's famous confession 'We are all Hussites' was prompted by the thought of martyrdom. See Luther's letter to Spalatin of *c.*14 February 1520, *D. Martin Luthers Werke. Kritische Gesamtausgabe: Briefwechsel*, 18 vols (Weimar, 1930–85) [hereafter *WABr*], 2, p. 42, lines 22f.: 'Bellum Domini est, qui non venit pacem mittere. Tu ergo cave, ne speres Christum in terra promoveri cum pace et suavitate, quem vides proprio sanguine pugnasse, et post eum omnes martyres. Ego imprudens hucusque omnia Iohannis Huss et docui et tenui. Docuit eadem imprudentia et Iohannes Staupitz. Breviter: sumus omnes Hussitae ignorantes.'

refuse of the world, the offscouring of all things' (I Corinthians 4. 13), who are ever despised by the world.[8] They also illustrated God's characteristic way of dealing with his children, bringing them low before raising them up. In this case, God has vindicated Hus by keeping his memory alive and by renewing his cause in recent times.[9] The papacy achieved nothing by his murder except to make the light of the Gospel shine more brightly in the hearts of the godly,[10] in the same way as the Jews gained nothing from persecuting the Apostles except their own dispersion.[11]

As the flames of Constance had proved that God was on Hus's side, so the rightness of Luther's cause was confirmed by the first martyrdoms of the Reformation proper. When, in July 1523, two Augustinian friars, Johann van Esschen and Heinrich Voes, were burned in the market square in Brussels, Luther saw it as a guarantee that theirs was the true Church which, in a sort of bloody apostolic succession, had always been persecuted and which would be persecuted to the end of the world.[12] Hus remained a potent symbol of evangelical martyrdom, but to his name could now be added those of contemporary martyrs of the Reformation. Little wonder, then, that Luther seized so eagerly the role of martyrologist, composing both an open letter of consolation for the compatriots of the Brussels martyrs, and a hymn, his first ever, 'Eyn newes lyed wyr heben an'.[13] Over the next four years, Luther wrote memorials for Heinrich of Zütphen, the preacher of Bremen who was lynched on his way to trial in December 1524; for Georg Winkler, the pastor of Halle, murdered on the open road in April 1527; and for Leonhard Kayser, burned in Bavaria in August of the same year.[14]

[8] See, for example, *Praelectiones in prophetas minores* (1524), on Zeph. 13, *WA* 13:509.25–33. Also *In Esaiam enarrationes* (1527–30), on Isa. 49, *WA* 31.II:399.22.
[9] Ibid., on Isa. 26, with scholia of 1532–4, *WA* 25:174.39–41. Also *Praelectiones in prophetas minores* (1524), on Zeph. 13, *WA* 13:509.27–33.
[10] *In primum librum Mose enarrationes* (1544, delivered between 1535 and 1540), on Gen. 49, *WA* 44:744.21–25 = *LW* 8:226.
[11] Sermon for Epiphany (6 Jan. 1524), *WA* 14:326.3–9.
[12] *Festpostille* (1527) on John 3, *WA* 17.II:425.15–21.
[13] See *Ein Brief an die Christen im Niederland* (1523), *WA* 12:(73), 77–80, and, for the hymn, *Erfurter Enchiridion* (1524), *WA* 35:411–15 = *LW* 53:211–16. For a recent treatment of the hymn, see Martin Rössler, 'Ein neues Lied wir heben an. Ein Protestsong Martin Luthers', in Hans-Martin Müller and Dietrich Rössler, eds, *Reformation und Praktische Theologie. Festschrift für Werner Jetter zum 70. Geburtstag* (Göttingen, 1983), pp. 216–32. For details of memorials for the Brussels martyrs by other Lutheran propagandists, see Hildegard Hebenstreit-Wilfert, 'Martyrerflugschriften der Reformationszeit', in Hans-Joachim Köhler, ed., *Flugschriften als Massenmedium der Reformationszeit* = *Spätmittelalter und Frühe Neuzeit*, 13 (Stuttgart, 1981), pp. 397–9.
[14] See *Von Bruder Henrico in Ditmar verbrannt* (1525), *WA* 18:(215), 224–40 = *LW* 32:(261), 265– 86; *Von Herrn Lenhard Keiser zu Baiern um des Evangelii willen verbrannt* (1527), *WA* 23:(443),

So far, all was going according to the plan laid down by the Psalmist and St Paul: the ungodly were prospering, while the righteous were being accounted as sheep for the slaughter. Luther greeted the news of these martyrdoms with relief and gratitude.[15] But already a serious difficulty had emerged, the first of two challenges to Luther's belief that suffering was a mark of the true Church. Why had Luther himself been deemed unworthy of martyrdom?[16] During the 1520s this thought troubled him more rather than less, particularly as close friends began to fall victim to Catholic persecution. By July 1527 it had all become too much. He suffered what we would today call a nervous breakdown, precipitated by the death of his friend Winkler. For several weeks Luther was unable to work, and suffered deep depressions and even fainting spells. The cause was a belief that God had abandoned him, had made him a second Job, by not accounting him worthy of martyrdom.[17] Two of the martyrologies (or passions, strictly speaking) date from this time, and it is possible that Luther was trying to make sense of God's plan by writing about them. Certainly his own anxieties frequently come to the surface. In his memorial for Kayser, the Bavarian martyr, he wrote:

> How it shames me when I read this story that I had not long ago been found worthy to suffer the same. After all, I was ten times more deserving of it in the world's eyes. Very well, my God. If that is how it is to be, then so be it. Thy will be done.[18]

Eventually, in the first weeks of 1528, the depression lifted; but Luther never overcame his regret that he was not martyred. As much as ten years later, he could still lament it as 'the thorn in the flesh of which Paul speaks'.[19]

452–76; and *Tröstung an die Christen zu Halle über Herrn Georgen* [*Winkler*], *ihres Predigers Tod* (1527), *WA* 23:(390), 402–31 = *LW* 43:(141), 145–77. Although it is not explicitly concerned with any particular martyrdom, the brief letter of consolation to the evangelicals of Worms of 24 Aug. 1524, *WABr* 3:138–40 = *LW* 43:(71), 77–9, also falls into this category.

[15] See, for example, his letter to Jacob Montanus, 26 July 1523, *WABr* 3:117.9–11: 'Ex Flandria bona accepimus nuncia, esse duos ex nostris fratribus pro verbo dei exustos Brusselle in foro publico spectaculo, deo gratia per Christum.'

[16] See the brief extract from Johann Kessler's *Sabbata* reported in *WABr* 3:239, n. 3.

[17] For his identification with Job, see his letter to Agricola, 21 Aug. 1527, *WABr* 4:235.10. For a fuller description of Luther's breakdown, see Heinrich Bornkamm, *Luther in Mid-Career, 1521–1530* (London, 1983), pp. 554–61.

[18] *Von Herrn Lenhard Keiser*, *WA* 23:474.16–19.

[19] *In primum librum Mose enarrationes* (1544, delivered between 1535 and 1540), on Gen. 27, *WA* 43:519.1 = *LW* 5:131. See also the introduction to *Deuteronomion Mose cum annotationibus* (1525), *WA* 14:498.22–4 = *LW* 9:5, and *An der Kurfürsten zu Sachsen und Landgrafen zu Hessen*

It was not, however, the only thorn of this sort which the 1520s had in store for Luther. These years saw not only the Godly (or at least one of them) prospering, but also the ungodly slaughtered like sheep. In May 1525 a peasant army under the leadership of Thomas Müntzer was crushed at the battle of Frankenhausen, and in 1527 the first Anabaptists were executed for their beliefs. What did this mean for Luther's conviction that the presence of suffering and persecution demonstrated the presence of the true Church? The question was complicated by the fact that Müntzer also had a 'theology of the Cross',[20] and in his opinion it was a more consistent one than that maintained by 'Doctor Liar' and 'Brother Easy-living'—the splendid names Müntzer reserved for Luther. The phenomenon of 'false' martyrdom made it vital that Luther reassess his simple but perhaps simplistic test for the true Church.

Luther's first instinct was a characteristic one. He firmly believed that Müntzer and other radicals were inspired by the Devil, and seems to have expected that their diabolic inspiration would reveal itself at the point of death. That is the only explanation I have for his rather tasteless desire for detailed reports of Müntzer's behaviour under torture, on the grounds that it would be 'useful to know how that haughty spirit behaved itself'.[21] Luther was clearly not pleased by the reports: Müntzer stood up well to interrogation and made a reasoned defence of his actions based on the Old Testament.[22] Then he must have been asked the wrong questions, came Luther's reply.[23] Luther's reaction was to provide the next best thing to a diabolic confession, and republish Müntzer's own words with a commentary designed to reveal the true origin of this murderous spirit.[24]

The equanimity with which Müntzer and, later, Anabaptists faced

---

von dem gefangenen Herzog zu Braunschweig (1545), *WA* 54:402.21–8 = *LW* 43:276n. It may be significant that in these references to the martyrdom he never achieved Luther distances himself, in the first instance, by using a generalized, Pauline 'I', in the others, by using 'we'.

[20] See Tom Scott, *Thomas Müntzer: Theology and Revolution in the German Reformation* (Basingstoke, 1989), pp. 19, 61–5, and 83. Luther acknowledged this in *Eyn Brieff an die Fürsten zu Sachsen von dem auffrurischen geyst* (1524), *WA* 15:211.18–21: 'Darumb er auch grewlich schreyet und klagt, Er müsse viel leyden, So doch sie bisher niemand widder mit faust noch mund noch fedder hat angetast, und trewmen yhn selbs eyn gros kretz, das sie leyden. So gar leychtfertig und on ursach mus der Satan liegen, er kan doch da sich nicht bergen.'

[21] See Mark U. Edwards, Jr., *Luther and the False Brethren* (Stanford, 1975), pp. 67–9.

[22] See Johann Rühel's letter to Luther of 26 May 1525, *WABr* 3:511.58–66.

[23] See Luther's reply to Rühel of 30 May 1525, *WABr* 3:515.28–516.3.

[24] *Eine schreckliche Geschichte und ein Gericht Gottes über Thomas Müntzer* (1525), *WA* 18:(362), 367–74.

execution was clearly a problem. But the phenomenon was new neither to Luther nor to the Church. In 1528 Luther wrote:

> I judge the constancy of the Anabaptists in death to be similar to that of the Donatists whom Augustine describes, and of the Jews in the ruins of Jerusalem of whom Josephus wrote, and many others like them. There can be no doubt that their fanaticism [furor] stems from Satan, especially when they die blaspheming the sacrament.

This behaviour is then contrasted with that of a Lutheran martyr.

> Holy martyrs, such as our Leonhard Keyser, die with fear and humility, and with a leniency towards their enemies born of magnanimity; but [the Anabaptists] compound their obstinacy with loathing and indignation towards their enemies, and that is how we see them die.[25]

Zwingli's death on the battlefield, and his supporters' attempts to make a martyr of him, were just as much evidence of fanaticism for Luther.[26] It is perhaps worth noting that in first desperately looking for evidence of a last-minute recantation and in then attributing constancy in the face of a gruesome end to diabolical rather than divine strength, Luther employed precisely the same tactics against martyrs for the radical cause as Catholic polemicists used against Protestant martyrs.[27]

Luther's trump card against Anabaptist martyrdom was, however, the one Augustine had used against the Circumcellions. What made someone a martyr was not the degree of their suffering but the truth of their cause: 'non poena sed causa facit martyrem.'[28] This was to become a stock argument of the sixteenth century, by which, for instance, Foxe would deprive Thomas Becket of his martyr's crown, and Harpsfield, all Foxe's

---

[25] See Luther's letter to Wenceslaus Linck of 12 May 1528, WABr 4:457.9–15.
[26] See Luther's letter to Bernhard Rothmann of 23 Dec. 1532, WABr 6:403.13–17: 'Vides enim Zwinglium cum tot symmystis suis poenas dedisse sui dogmatis horribili satis exemplo, si illi possent commoveri. Sic periit et Munzer, Hetzer et alii plures, manifeste Deo monstrante istis monstris irae suae, quam oderit istos impios spiritus, licet indurati, ceu Judaei et Philistaei, talia contemnant, et nescio quos martyres celebrent.' See also his letter to Martin Görlitz, 3 Jan. 1532, WABr 6:243.9–11 and Kurtzes Bekenntnis vom heiligen Sakrament (1544), WA 54:143.13f. = LW 38:289. On Luther's reaction to his former colleague Carlstadt, another radical who claimed to have been 'martyred' by Luther's rejection of him, see Luther's letters to Amsdorf, 27 Oct. 1524, WA 3:361.14, and to Crusius, 30 Oct. 1524, WABr 3:366.14.
[27] See Hebenstreit-Wilfert, 'Martyrerflugschriften der Reformationszeit', p. 426.
[28] See the lectures on I John 2 (20 Aug. 1527), WA 20:644.1–4 = LW 30:239; the sermon for 13 July 1539, WA 47:851.9–11, 15, 29f.; the sermon for Estomihi Sunday (8 Feb. 1540), WA 49:25–9; and Kurtzes Bekenntnis (1544), WA 54:141–67 = LW 38:303f.

martyrs of theirs.[29] Perhaps because it was capable of falling into the wrong hands, Luther refined Augustine's test with a more objective one of his own, the fundamental principle of his theology of the Cross that sufferings which are self-inflicted cannot be considered a legitimate imitation of Christ's Passion.[30] True martyrs are those whose suffering is inflicted by God who, like a loving parent, uses his rod only because he loves us—as Luther reminded his own mother (whose liberal use of the rod he still remembered in adult life!) during her final illness at about this time.[31] Those who affect spectacular renunciations of their own choosing, whether Anabaptist separatists or papistical monks and nuns, are martyrs not of Christ, but of the Devil.[32]

In the late 1520s, then, we see that both Luther's personal crisis, prompted by the thought that he was not worthy to be a martyr, and the equally pressing problem of false martyrs, presented a serious challenge to his earlier, naïvely positive, evaluation of martyrdom. The next step, then, is to look at his utterances on the subject in the period from the 1530s onwards, to see if these difficulties modified his view of martyrdom. There is some evidence to suggest that they did. This period of Luther's life is, of course, dominated theologically by his great lecture series on Genesis (1535–40). Again and again in these lectures we find him applauding the prolonged trials of the patriarchs at the expense of the sharper but shorter pains of the martyrs.

---

[29] See A. G. Dickens and John Tonkin, *The Reformation in Historical Thought* (Cambridge, Mass., 1985), p. 48. Luther himself cast doubt on Thomas Becket's martyr status as early as 1520, when he dated a letter 'in die S. Thomae Martyris (ut creditur a multis)'. See the letter to Spalatin of 29 Dec. 1520, *WABr* 2:243.49.

[30] See, for example, *Die sieben Bußpsalmen* (1525), *WA* 18:489.25ff. = *LW* 14:152. On the subject of legitimate imitation of Christ's Passion, see esp. Walther von Loewenich, *Luther's Theology of the Cross* (Belfast, 1976), pp. 118–22 and 127f., and Pinomaa, *Die Heiligen bei Luther*, pp. 134–7.

[31] See his letter to his mother Margarethe of 20 May 1531, *WABr* 6:103.14–104.1.

[32] At the back of Luther's mind was a popular German proverb. A 'Devil's martyr' was one who worked hard to little effect, and Luther used the phrase to describe religious and others who put their trust in works and self-inflicted sufferings—including the 'new monastics', the radicals. In this way he was able to link (in his own mind, at least) the religious orders, Anabaptists, sacramentarians, and the Devil. For examples of this proverb employed against religious, see: *Auslegung deutsch des Vaterunsers* (1519), *WA* 2:90.11–13 = *LW* 42:31; sermon on John 8 (7 Oct. 1531), *WA* 33:525.11–21 = *LW* 23:327; on John 8 (28 Oct. 1531), *WA* 33:580.41–581.5 = *LW* 23:359; *In epistolam S. Pauli ad Galatas commentarius* (1531, publ. 1535), on Gal. 5, *WA* 40.II:8f. = *LW* 27:8; *Enarratio Psalmi XC* (late 1534/early 1535), *WA* 40.III:563.19f. = *LW* 13:123. For its use against Zwingli, see e.g. *Kurtzes Bekenntnis* (1544), *WA* 54:155.15–17 = *LW* 38:303f.

The situation of our so-called [*quos sic appellamus*] martyrs is most fortunate; for, strengthened by the Holy Spirit, they overcome death in one hour and surmount all perils and temptations. Noah, however, lived among the ungodly a full six hundred years, amid many serious temptations and dangers.[33]

If they are compared with Abraham their sanctity and virtues become altogether vile and filthy. ... There was never an apostle, patriarch or martyr who could have shown such unswerving obedience [as Abraham].[34]

The examples of the patriarchs show that life can be a greater and truer martyrdom than any death, no matter how spectacular. This idea, repeated frequently throughout the Genesis lectures,[35] looks suspiciously like a self-serving attempt to explain why Luther, the patriarch of Wittenberg, had been spared the stake when others were not. But if this is the case, it goes much further than a simple assertion that God had even greater trials in store for him.[36] The Genesis lectures represent a desacralizing of actual martyrdom: the sanctity of the 'so-called martyrs' is contemptuously dismissed as 'vile and filthy'. And when, in a sermon from 1540, Luther hails the Devil as the greatest martyr of all, the process of desacralizing seems complete.[37] The hymn for the Brussels martyrs and the moving memorial for Heinrich of Zütphen seem a world away. It is as if the challenges to Luther's concept of martyrdom of the mid-1520s, his own unexpected survival, and the false martyrs, had completely reversed his earlier, positive evaluation.

The picture is, however, more complicated; because as well as debunking martyrs in the Genesis lectures, Luther can also laud them in a quite unexpectedly sentimental way.

[33] *In primum librum Mose enarrationes* (1544), on Gen. 6 (*WA* 42:267.14–20 = *LW* 2:7f.).

[34] Ibid., on Gen. 22, *WA* 43:209.19–27 = *LW* 4:103.

[35] Ibid., on Gen. 5, *WA* 42:246.18 = *LW* 1:335; ibid., on Gen. 11, *WA* 42:414.26–33 = *LW* 2:216f.; ibid., on Gen. 11, *WA* 42:424.25–8 = *LW* 2:230; ibid., on Gen. 21, *WA* 43:165.8f. = *LW* 4:41; ibid., on Gen. 26, *WA* 43:491.29–39 = *LW* 5:90; ibid., on Gen. 31, *WA* 44:51.28–32 = *LW* 6:70; ibid., on Gen. 36, *WA* 44:210 = *LW* 6:282; ibid., on Gen. 37, *WA* 44:271.22–6 = *LW* 6:363; ibid., on Gen. 37, *WA* 44:292.9f. = *LW* 6:390.

[36] Luther already suspected in the midst of his breakdown that his martyrdom was meant to be spiritual rather than physical. See his letter to Agricola of 21 Aug. 1527, *WABr* 4:235.16–19: 'Ita fit, ut a tyrannis mundi nihil patiar quidem, dum alii occiduntur, exuruntur et pereunt pro Christo, verum eo plus a principe ipso mundi patior in spiritu.'

[37] See the sermon for Estomihi Sunday (8 Feb. 1540), *WA* 49:27.16f.: 'Sic Diabolus maximus martyr, sed damit sucht er, ut totum mundum seducat.'

When St Agnes was being carried off to prison and torture, she said that she felt just as if she were being led to a dance.[38]

Thus the holy virgin martyrs Agatha, Lucy, and many others ... regarded death as a game and sin and hell as nothing. They were completely certain of the forgiveness of sins, eternal life, and the best intention of the Father. Even in the midst of death they were joyful and fearless. Thus they say concerning the exceptionally distinguished martyr Vincentius that when, after first being struck with clubs and later tortured with the rack, he was compelled to go on bare feet through live coals, he said he was walking on roses. In this way he made fun of the savage tortures and laughed at the burning coals and the glowing iron as though it were a game and a joke.[39]

These little hymns to the Church's traditional martyrs, especially to the young virgins Agnes, Agatha, Lucy, and Anastasia, in some cases straight out of James of Voragine's *Legenda aurea*, are not restricted to the Genesis lectures, but occur frequently in his other writings of the time too.[40] The same years provide further evidence of a positive attitude towards martyrdom. Luther continued to appeal to the memory of the Reformation martyrs (who by now, of course, included the English martyr Robert Barnes, another close acquaintance)[41] and to Hus's martyrdom,[42] just as he did in less complicated times. Indeed, he continues to cite the superhuman

[38] *In primum librum Mose enarrationes* (1544), on Gen. 48, *WA* 44:718.40–719.5 = *LW* 8:191.

[39] Ibid., on Gen. 49, *WA* 44:766 = *LW* 8:255f.

[40] See the sermon on Psalm 110 of 1535, *WA* 41:211.38–212.30 = *LW* 13:333; *In primum librum Mose enarrationes* (1544), on Gen. 49, *WA* 44:766 = *LW* 8:255f.; ibid., on Gen. 35, *WA* 44:189 = *LW* 6:255; *Der XXIII Psalm, auff ein abend uber Tisch ausgelegt* (1536), *WA* 51:293.32–294.1 = *LW* 12:177; sermon on John 14 (1537), *WA* 45:568:27–569.11 = *LW* 24:118; ibid., on John 14, *WA* 45:587.15–18 = *LW* 24:138; ibid., on John 14 and 15, *WA* 45:639.22–640.5 = *LW* 24:196f.; ibid., on John 15, *WA* 45:713 = *LW* 24:277; ibid., on John 16, *WA* 46:109.10–34 = *LW* 24:420; ibid., on John 15, *WA* 45:639.22–640.5 = *LW* 24:196f. For a much earlier appeal to the young women martyrs, see *Epistel S. Petri gepredigt und ausgelegt* (1523), *WA* 12:382.18–21 = *LW* 30:127.

[41] See the introduction to *Deuteronomion Mose cum annotationibus* (1525), *WA* 14:498.22–4 = *LW* 9:5; *In primum librum Mose enarrationes* (1544, delivered between 1535 and 1540), on Gen. 4, *WA* 42:212.35–213.7 = *LW* 1:288; ibid., on Gen. 25, *WA* 43:393.15–18 = *LW* 4:41; *Wider das Bapstum zu Rom vom Teuffel gestifft* (1545), *WA* 54:281.3–16 = *LW* 41:354. See also the preface to *Bekantnus des Glaubens die Robertus Barns gethan hat* (1540), *WA* 51:449–51.

[42] See *De servo arbitrio* (1525), *WA* 18:651.5; *Der CXII Psalm Davids gepredigt* (1526), *WA* 19:336.3; *In Esaiam enarrationes* (1527–30), on Isa. 26, and scholia of 1532–4, *WA* 25:174.22, 40; ibid., scholia on Isa. 41, *WA* 25:263.33–9; ibid., scholia on Isa. 60, *WA* 25:369.20–4; *Sprüche, mit denen sich Luther getröstet hat* (1530), *WA* 30.II:706.20–6 = *LW* 43:174; *In primum librum Mose enarrationes* (1544), on Gen. 6, *WA* 42:276.38–277.2 = *LW* 2:21; ibid., on Gen. 49, *WA* 44:744.21–5 = *LW* 8:226.

strength and constancy of martyrs as a proof of faith and an indication of God's presence, just as if the Anabaptists had never been.[43]

Luther's attitude to martyrdom in the last ten to fifteen years of his life is therefore rather puzzling. He seems to entertain at the same time a positive evaluation of the heroics of St Agnes and her companions, ancient and modern, stemming from the 1510s and early 1520s, and a negative evaluation of these same heroics as vile and diabolical, prompted by his crises of the mid-1520s. My own view is that this tension is more apparent than real. Luther's presentation of the daily sufferings of the patriarchs as genuine martyrdoms is entirely consistent with a theology of the Cross which goes back to the Psalms lectures of 1513: all Christians are called to be martyrs, as they are called also to be saints and priests; and the lifelong sufferings of patriarchs (who, of course, also represent ordinary Christians with more humdrum domestic arrangements) are joined with the passing agonies of the virgin martyrs in a common 'martyrdom of all believers'.[44] But even if the tension in Luther's later thought on martyrdom is only apparent, it is apparent none the less, and it would surely have puzzled the hearers of the Genesis lectures and those many readers who turned to these lectures as the definitive statement of his theology. If I may be allowed to conclude this paper by broadening its scope, I would suggest that the puzzling legacy which Luther left on the subject of martyrdom might well hold the key (or at least a key) to a wider problem of Protestant martyrology.

Although Luther was the first martyrologist of the Reformation, his followers were the least successful of all Protestants at the art of martyrology. Anglicans had their Foxe, and Calvinists their Crespin; but Lutherans had only the splendidly obscure Ludwig Rabus, whose *Histories of God's Chosen Martyrs* (1552) is as little known as the *Acts and Monuments* is famous. The reasons for the relative failure of Rabus's book have recently been studied by Robert Kolb. Not the least significant reason, in Kolb's view, was Luther's own implacable opposition to the cult of the saints, which helped to divert the martyrological impulses of Lutherans

---

[43] See the sermon on John 6 (1531), *WA* 33:226.25–41 = *LW* 23:145; *In primum librum Mose enarrationes* (1544), on Gen. 45, *WA* 44:584.25–30 = *LW* 8:7; ibid., on Gen. 45, *WA* 44:617.35–8 = *LW* 8:52; *Der XXIII Psalm, auff ein abend uber Tisch ausgelegt* (1536), *WA* 51:291.21–6 = *LW* 12:174; sermon on John 14 (1537), *WA* 45:572.21–8 = *LW* 24:122; ibid., on John 15, *WA* 45:639.9–640.5 = *LW* 24:196f.

[44] See the sermon on Ps. 110 (1535), *WA* 41:211.38–212.30 = *LW* 13:333, where, in the context of an exposition of the universal priesthood, St Agnes and the other martyrs are hailed as 'rechte, heilige Pfaffen und Pfeffin' for offering up the sacrifice of their own bodies and providing examples by which to encourage and console others.

into more historical directions, such as the compilation of the *Magdeburg Centuries*.[45] Kolb's case for Luther's influence on later Lutheran martyrology is worth considering. But I think this paper has shown that the Reformer's aversion to saint-worship is not the only factor involved. Luther left to posterity in his last years an extremely ambivalent evaluation of martyrdom, and it is likely that this legacy played its part in preventing Lutheranism from making a greater contribution than it did to the Protestant martyrological tradition.

University of Hull

[45] Kolb, *For All The Saints*, pp. 11–27.

MARTYROLOGIES AND MARTYRS IN THE FRENCH REFORMATION: HERETICS TO SUBVERSIVES IN TROYES*

by PENNY ROBERTS

THE chief martyrology of the French Protestants or Huguenots, the *Histoire des martyrs*, was the work of a Walloon refugee in Geneva, Jean Crespin.[1] The *Histoire* focuses on the martyrs of the French Reformation, but also describes the ordeals of those in Scotland, England, and Flanders, as well as of medieval precursors of Protestant ideas, such as Hus and Wyclif. Later versions of the text include the martyrs of the Early Church, whose faith the Huguenots claimed to be reviving and in whose sufferings they believed themselves to be sharing. The *Histoire* quickly became popular in the fledgeling Reformed churches of France, avidly read from the pulpit and in the home. The accounts of the courage of the martyrs no doubt reinforced the resolution of a group destined to remain a minority, and who became increasingly resigned to their fate. During the civil strife known as the French Wars of Religion, religious tensions were exacerbated by political and military conflict. However, the incident which provoked the outbreak of the wars in 1562 was the massacre of a Huguenot congregation at Vassy, in Champagne, and, indeed, the wars were to be particularly noted for their brutal sectarian violence.

Another work from the Genevan press which recorded the events of the religious conflict was the *Histoire ecclésiastique des églises réformées*, compiled by Theodore Beza from contributions sent to him by churches throughout France.[2] The *Histoire ecclésiastique* reveals that the Reform movement, and thus the sectarian violence of the wars, was largely an urban phenomenon. Although in this paper the persecution of Huguenots will be discussed in general terms, specific examples will be drawn from the city of Troyes, in Champagne, where the congregation was fortunate to have its own chronicler and martyrologist, Nicolas Pithou, a lawyer and

---

* All translations are the author's own.
[1] Jean Crespin, *Histoire des martyrs persecutez et mis à mort pour la verité de l'évangile, depuis le temps des apostres jusques à présent*, ed. D. Benoît, 3 vols (Toulouse, 1885–9) [hereafter Crespin], is the 1619 edition. The first edition appeared in 1554; after Crespin died in 1572 his work was continued by Simon Goulart.
[2] *Histoire ecclésiastique des églises réformées au royaume de France*, ed. G. Baum, E. Cunitz, and R. Reuss, 3 vols (Paris, 1883–9) [hereafter *Hist.ecc.*], first published in 1580.

notable, and a leading member of the Reformed Church at Troyes. His memoir was written as one of the contributions to Beza's compilation, and constitutes an invaluable mine of information for the relations between the faiths and the fate of Pithou's co-religionists in his native city.[3]

The forms of martyrdom witnessed during the French Reformation may be roughly divided into four categories. Firstly, what might be termed the traditional, that is, burning at the stake (as heretics); secondly, public execution by hanging (as traitors); thirdly, random massacres by Catholic soldiers or mobs (as undesirables); and, finally, systematic murder by order of the authorities (as trouble-makers).

Burning at the stake was characteristic of the early years of the Reformation prior to the civil wars, and was accompanied by elaborate ritual, incorporating humiliation and mutilation of the 'heretic', in accordance with the customary punishment for deviants, such as homo-sexuals and witches.[4] The burning was a public spectacle, designed to purge the community of undesirable elements and to discourage others from committing the same errors. In 1543 Jean du Bec, a former priest from Sézanne, in Brie, was sentenced by the Paris Parlement to be degraded and burned alive in Troyes as a native of the diocese.[5] Macé Moreau, a book-pedlar, arrested as he passed through Troyes on his way from Geneva to Paris, was similarly sentenced, and having been tortured, and having refuted those friars who tried to make him recant, was burned along with his books.[6] Furthermore, Moreau was said to have gone to the stake joyfully, singing a psalm on the theme of his salvation to come. Such high spirits and constancy in the face of death probably served Protestant propaganda better than it did the authorities' hope that the spectacle would act as a deterrent to those attracted to the new religion.

Huguenots were also sentenced and burned in effigy in their absence. A royal official, Pierre Girardin, was accused of hosting a clandestine assembly in 1555, but he was forewarned and managed to leave Troyes before the justices caught up with him. However, insufficient evidence

---

[3] Paris, BN, MS Dupuy 698, Nicolas Pithou, 'Histoire ecclésiastique de l'église réformée de la ville de Troyes', 515 fols [hereafter Pithou].

[4] For a detailed and informative discussion of Protestant martyrdom and its development in France, see David Nicholls, 'The Theatre of Martyrdom in the French Reformation', *PaP*, 121 (1988), pp. 49–73.

[5] Crespin, 1, p. 381; Pithou, fols 36r–37r.

[6] There is some confusion over the date of Moreau's execution: Crespin, 1, pp. 547–8, states that it took place in 1550, and Pithou, fols 42–4, in 1549; whilst the trial record of the Paris Parlement, in the Bibliothèque municipale de Troyes, MS 1291, fol. 126, is dated 5 Oct. 1546.

was forthcoming, and Girardin returned, his name cleared, and having acquired the sobriquet 'Maubruslé', or 'Misburned'.[7] In August 1562 the dramatic escape of the Huguenot minister Jacques Sorel was followed by the burning of a sour herring (a *hareng soret*, from a play on his name) and a French Bible in the pulpit from which he had previously conducted services.[8] This was a graphic illustration and warning, if one were needed, of the fate which awaited the minister who was captured.

From about 1562, with the beginning of the wars, judicial execution became the preferred method, so that Huguenots were hanged as traitors rather than burned as heretics, thus, it was hoped, reducing the effectiveness of the martyrs' message. In September 1562 two lawyers, Pierre Clément and Nicolas Beau, were sentenced for bearing arms against the king.[9] After interrogation and torture to reveal their accomplices, they were to be hanged in the market-place, their bodies left for twenty-four hours and then displayed. Despite the secularization of the process, the Catholic Church still attempted, unsuccessfully, to extract an abjuration from the condemned men.

The tension of the first decade of the French civil wars often degenerated into mob violence of the most brutal sort, the psychology of which has been explored in some depth, notably by Natalie Zemon Davis and Denis Crouzet.[10] Dissatisfied with the restrained nature of the punishment meted out by the magistrates, a crowd could take the law into its own hands; sometimes involving the official executioner, however reluctantly, to lend legitimacy to their actions.[11] Thus, when Clément declared on the scaffold 'Lord, you know that it is not for some murder or other crime which I have committed, that I am here, but for supporting your quarrel', the Catholics were angered and demanded vengeance.[12] After Clément was hanged, the crowd cut him down, burned the soles of his feet, cut off his nose and genitals, and gouged out his eyes. Eventually, when it had been disfigured beyond recognition, the corpse was dragged through the streets to Clément's house and the porches of other

---

[7] Pithou, fols 80r–85r.

[8] Ibid., fol. 232v; *Hist.ecc.*, 2, p. 469.

[9] Crespin, 3, p. 279; *Hist.ecc.*, 2, pp. 470–1; Pithou, fols 248v–250r.

[10] Natalie Zemon Davis, 'The rites of violence: religious riot in sixteenth-century France', *PaP*, 59 (1973), pp. 51–91. Denis Crouzet, *Les Guerriers de Dieu: la violence au temps des troubles de religion (c.1525–c.1610)*, 2 vols (Paris, 1990). Also see Janine Estèbe, *Tocsin pour un massacre: la saison des Saint-Barthélemy* (Paris, 1968).

[11] On the reluctance of the official executioner in Troyes to become involved, Pithou, fols 268v, 379r.

[12] Ibid., fol. 250r.

Huguenots, and finally thrown into the river. A similar fate awaited Beau. Thus Catholics re-enacted the ritual humiliation and mutilation formerly exercised by justice on heretics, but in a more unrestrained, unpredictable, and, therefore, frightening manner.

Dissatisfaction with official proceedings also created the circumstances for the nomination of the only Catholic martyr in Troyes. A youth was sentenced to be hanged in 1561 for instigating the pillage of a Huguenot pharmacist, who was said to have scorned Catholic devotions. The crowd attacked and chased off the executioner, and a priest took the body down and carried it to a nearby abbey, where it was placed on an altar, and attempts were made to revive it; successfully, according to the Catholics (although the youth died soon afterwards), faked, according to Pithou.[13] The dead man was declared a martyr and named St Innocent, and pieces of the gallows were taken as relics. However, this was consistent with mob intervention at public executions and the crowd's determination to ensure that their sense of justice was satisfied, whether or not religion was a factor. Whilst, on this occasion, Catholics rescued from the gallows one of their co-religionists, they equally showed their displeasure when the executioner of a Huguenot noble failed to make a clean job of it, in 1558.[14] Yet, as religious conflict intensified, Catholics showed themselves much less sympathetic to the suffering of Huguenot martyrs and content to participate in prolonging their agony.

It was not only on the occasion of official executions that Catholics directed their anger against their Protestant fellow citizens. In what was essentially an oral culture, the cry of 'Heretic' or 'Lutheran' was sufficient to spark off a riot, and displays of irreverence towards churches, statues, or a local cult were particularly provocative.[15] In 1558 Claude Portesain, a poor goldsmith, was assaulted and imprisoned for refusing to doff his hat before a church in Troyes which, when challenged, he referred to as 'a pile of stones'; he was later beaten to death by Catholic prisoners for refusing to go to Mass.[16] Sometimes the crowd became so carried away that mistakes were made. The cathedral at Troyes housed the relics of a local

---

[13] Ibid., fols 174v–177r. 'Poncelet Meusnier et Jacques de Brienne; premiers chroniqueurs Troyens', *Revue de Champagne et de Brie*, 13 (1882), p. 439, and 14 (1883), p. 58 [hereafter 'Meusnier et Brienne'], for the Catholic view.

[14] Pithou, fols 99v–101r; the executioner claimed that there had been a devil on the condemned man's neck, which had deflected his blows with its horns. 'Meusnier et Brienne', 14 (1883), p. 57.

[15] J. R. Farr, *Hands of Honor: Artisans and Their World in Dijon, 1550–1650* (Ithaca and London, 1988), pp. 160–4, discusses oral culture in the sixteenth-century French city.

[16] Pithou, fols 107r–108r.

virgin, Sainte-Mathie, on whose feast day pilgrims gathered to visit the shrine. On this day, in 1559, a shearer's joke to the woman next to him provoked her to incite the mob to 'Get the Lutheran who is mocking the blessed Saint Mathie!'[17] The shearer was set upon and killed, although he was universally held to have been a devout Catholic.

In the cities of France, Huguenot citizens were murdered in their homes or dragged into public view, assaulted in the streets or in nearby fields, as they returned from services, temporary exile, or imprisonment. Their attackers were their neighbours and fellow workers, those who bore a grudge, or those who were angered by their refusal to conform. A rash word, a defiant gesture, the publication of an edict of toleration, or a development in the civil war, could all provoke anti-Huguenot violence. At Bar-sur-Seine, a Protestant refuge just to the south of Troyes, a massacre of more than 140 Huguenots occurred in August 1562.[18] Numerous brutal stories were circulated: that one victim's heart was removed and passed round to be bitten by each of the soldiers; of pregnant women being disembowelled and babies run through whilst suckling at the breast. The ritualistic violence perpetrated against the Huguenots often culminated in the victim's body being thrown into a river, preferably in areas where refuse was usually dumped. This practice was common throughout France, and was designed to degrade both the victim and their faith.[19]

The catalogue of mutilations performed on Huguenots during the wars is as gruesome as it is long. Although many of the stories may be apocryphal, their repetition by different reporters in widely scattered locations, as revealed in the *Histoire ecclésiastique*, suggests conformity at least in what was expected, if not in what occurred in practice. If we accept the truth, at least in part, of the phenomenon of brutal sectarian violence in France, how are we to explain it? The association with the traditional forms of punishment for heresy have already been discussed. Davis argues that the violence was part of a ritual purification of society and dehumanization of the victims. Crouzet also points to a Catholic psychology of violence, but rather driven by eschatological fervour and concerned with acting as God's avengers against Huguenot 'devils'.[20]

---

[17] Ibid., fols 123v–124r. For other cases of mistaken identity in this context, see Barbara Diefendorf, *Beneath the Cross: Catholics and Huguenots in Sixteenth-Century Paris* (Oxford, 1991), pp. 53, 69, and Davis, 'The rites of violence', p. 73, n. 68.

[18] Pithou, fols 237v–242r; *Hist.ecc.*, 2, pp. 476–8; Crespin, 3, p. 280.

[19] Here I agree with the view of Crouzet, *Les Guerriers de Dieu*, 1, pp. 246, 329–30.

[20] Davis, 'The rites of violence', pp. 81–3, 85; and Crouzet, *Les Guerriers de Dieu*, *passim*.

It is misleading, however, to suggest that all French Catholics were involved to a greater or lesser degree in the martyrdom of Huguenots. Some, because of personal ties or family loyalties, were prepared to offer protection to their Protestant neighbours, whilst others objected to the bloodshed and division within the community created by the troubles. There is evidence to suggest that the murders were often the work of the same individuals, who also seem to have been operating under direction from the authorities. Official sanction lay behind the systematic, secretive, and cold-blooded killing of Huguenot prisoners in Troyes. In 1563 several prisoners were hunted out and murdered, and their bodies thrown on a dung-heap.[21] In 1572, following the Saint Bartholomew's Day massacre in Paris on 24 August, about thirty-five Huguenots were rounded up and imprisoned. On 4 September they were called forward and dispatched one by one, and their bodies slung into a ditch.[22] The victims were carefully selected, either as prominent members of the Reformed Church in the city or as individuals who had antagonized the authorities in the past. As a number of those targeted had previously held municipal or royal office, there may also have been an element of political rivalry in the decision.

The murders of prisoners in Troyes seem, then, to have resulted from specific commands from local officials; other isolated incidents may also have formed part of a more general directive to get rid of the Huguenots. The lack of convictions or punishment for such activities suggests at least tacit approval by the authorities. Certainly members of the administration appear to have turned a blind eye to the persecution suffered by Huguenot citizens. This situation was exacerbated when, as in the case of Troyes, the provincial governor was an arch-Catholic who was unlikely to intervene on behalf of Protestant appeals for justice. From 1563 the governor of Champagne was the leader of the Catholic faction, the Duke of Guise. In addition, vacillating royal policy, to the frustration of both faiths, may have encouraged local elements to seize the initiative in dealing with the Huguenots in their midst. Thus much of the responsibility for the massacres must be attributed to the various layers of authority: national, provincial, and municipal.

Who were the martyrs of the French Reformation? As in the movement as a whole, artisans predominate in the lists of victims, although the particular occupations they pursued vary between towns: in Troyes,

---

[21] Pithou, fols 273r–275r.
[22] Paris, BN, MS Dupuy 333, fols 66r–75r; Pithou, fols 371–82.

joiners, painters, goldsmiths, and drapers are most conspicuous. Those prominent in the local Reformed church might be particularly targeted; the elders and representatives of the congregation were usually drawn from the ranks of merchants, lawyers, and doctors, that is, those groups who also predominated in the membership of the municipal administration.[23] The Huguenot martyrs were also overwhelmingly male. This is not to say that the few women involved reveals less female zeal for the faith, but rather a customary immunity from persecution by the authorities, as a man was often summoned before the courts to answer for the religious misconduct of a wife or daughter.[24] Nevertheless, women were subject to taunts insinuating that Protestant services were an excuse for orgies in which they gave themselves freely.[25] An outspoken or defiant gesture, such as refusing to kneel before a statue of the Virgin or to attend Mass, could cause the mob to massacre women, and such a pretext was not always necessary. In 1572 an embroiderer's wife enraged her Catholic assailants by declaring that, 'You enact the Passion, but God will exact vengeance', and was consequently subject to ritual abuse, and her body finally thrown into the Seine.[26]

Children, like women, sometimes immune from prosecution as the responsibility of their parents, could and did figure among the victims of violence. The participation of 'innocents' was employed by both religions as a source for propaganda. The murder of young Huguenots was portrayed as a measure of Catholic barbarity; whilst the involvement of children in the ritual of dragging Protestant corpses through the streets, as they were said to have done with Clément and Beau in 1562, elevated the Catholic cause in rooting our heresy.[27] Priests were sometimes said to have supplied youngsters with stones and other ammunition in order to provoke a confrontation between the faiths, as did the

---

[23] H. Heller, *The Conquest of Poverty: the Calvinist Revolt in Sixteenth-Century France* (Leiden, 1986), p. 143, on the leadership of the Reformed churches in the towns being drawn from among the urban notables. Also see J. M. Davies, 'Persecution and Protestantism: Toulouse 1562–75', *HistJ*, 22 (1979), p. 50.

[24] On women treated less harshly, see Davies, 'Persecution and Protestantism', pp. 48–9; Pithou, fol. 235r.

[25] Pithou, fols 228v, 242r; *Mémoires de Claude Haton: le récit des événements accomplis de 1553 à 1582, principalement dans la Champagne et la Brie*, ed. Felix Bourquelot, 2 vols (Paris, 1857), 1, p. 48, discusses Protestant wife-swapping, which he refers to as 'charité fraternelle'. Crouzet, *Les Guerriers de Dieu*, 1, pp. 244–6.

[26] Pithou, fol. 382r; Paris, BN, MS Dupuy 333, fol. 72r.

[27] 'Meusnier et Brienne', 14 (1883), p. 49. Pithou, Crespin and the *Hist.ecc.* make no mention of the participation of children on this occasion. Cf. Crouzet, *Les Guerriers de Dieu*, 1, pp. 76–91; Davis, 'The Rites of Violence', pp. 87–8.

clergy of Saint-Jean, in Troyes, in 1560.[28] The killing of Huguenot children was also associated with putting a check on the next generation, as has been argued for the symbolic castration of male corpses and assaults on pregnant women.[29]

All of the martyrs, whether men, women, or children, are accredited with the strength of their convictions, allowing them to approach their fate with fortitude. Yet our sources are hardly disinterested parties, and we ought to be circumspect about some of the reported declarations and brave actions of the victims, particularly in circumstances when probably the only surviving witnesses were the murderers themselves, as in 1572. The resilience and eloquence of Huguenots in the face of death is part of the convention of martyrologies. The Protestant depiction of unwavering faith, a mixture of joyful resignation and defiance, leaving many spectators impressed and edified, may be matched by the contradictory version by Catholic writers of the same event, describing recantation and recognition of the evils of Protestantism. However, embracing death for one's faith is the prerogative of those who are on their way to the stake or the scaffold, or in prison without hope of release. The martyrologists are frank about the survival instinct of some of the victims in their descriptions of scrambles to reach the haven of a Catholic friend's house, a roof, a hospital, or outside the city gates; this is as true of ministers as of their congregations.[30] Pithou recounts numerous such stories, and of Huguenots disguising themselves or attempting to bribe their assailants. Once captured, then was the time for commitment to the cause, unless another opportunity presented itself for evasion. This more practical side certainly provides for most of us a more empathetic view of the path to martyrdom.

The progression from the traditional burning for religious dissent to the calculated disposal of trouble-makers and possible political rivals, demonstrates that, by 1572, the murder and martyrdom of Huguenots had become decided by local politics rather than purely religious issues. This is the other story which the martyrologists of the French Reformation have to tell. Catholic officials were no longer interested in persuading errant believers to return to the fold, but rather in the removal of potential subversives among the citizenry. It was the role of the martyrol-

---

[28] Pithou, fols 160–1.

[29] Estèbe, *Tocsin pour un massacre*, p. 197; Crouzet, *Les Guerriers de Dieu*, 1, pp. 244–8.

[30] The minister Sorel made a dramatic escape on horseback in 1562, Pithou, fol. 230; *Hist.ecc.*, 2, p. 469.

ogists to lend dignity to the last moments of their co-religionists, deprived of the opportunity of a public platform on which to bear witness to the faith for which they would lose their lives.

University of Leeds

JOHN FOXE AND THE TRAITORS:
THE POLITICS OF THE MARIAN
PERSECUTION (*PRESIDENTIAL ADDRESS*)

by DAVID LOADES

... not long after this he was sent to the Tower, and soon after condemned of treason. Notwithstanding the queen, when she could not honestly deny him his pardon, seeing all the rest were discharged, and especially seeing he last of all others subscribed to king Edward's request, and that against his own will, released to him his action of treason and accused him only of heresy; which liked the archbishop right well, and came to pass as he wished, because the cause was not now his own, but Christ's; not the queen's but the church's.[1]

CRANMER'S condemnation for treason was almost as great an embarrassment to John Foxe as it had been to the Archbishop himself. Obedience to lawful authority was axiomatic to both, as to all the orthodox reformers of the first generation. Against Catholic accusations that all Protestants were natural subverters of established order, they argued that the good Christian would be least a traitor to his Prince.[2] Preaching upon the text 'Render unto Caesar' in November 1550, Hugh Latimer had declared,

... it is thy bounden duty to pay him truly that which is granted; for it is a due debt, and upon peril of thy soul thou art bound to obey it. Yea, I will say more; if the king should require of thee an unjust request, yet art thou bound to pay it, and not to rebel and resist against the King.[3]

It is not, therefore, surprising, that according to his own apologetic account, Cranmer should have allowed himself to be persuaded, in spite of all the scruples which he later alleged, that King Edward was acting lawfully in altering his father's succession settlement. So convinced was he

[1] Foxe, 8, p. 38.
[2] William Tyndale made one of the earliest and most forceful statements of this position in *The Obedience of a Christian Man* (Hesse, 1528), p. 32: 'He that judgeth the king judgeth God; and he that resisteth the king resisteth God and damneth God's law and ordinance...'.
[3] Sermon at Stamford, 9 Nov. 1550: *Sermons of Bishop Latimer*, ed. G. E. Gorrie, PS (1844), p. 300.

that it could not be treason to obey the monarch's personal command that he pleaded 'not guilty' when he was arraigned in the Guildhall on 13 November 1553. However, in so doing he missed the point, just as Foxe did when he sought to excuse him on the grounds that he had only followed the best expert advice. It was not, of course, treason to obey King Edward while he was alive, even if his commands were unlawful. Cranmer's treason, like that of his co-defendants, lay in maintaining that position after Edward's death. The indictments are quite specific upon that point. No treasonable action is alleged before 6 July 1553.[4] Given the outcome of the power struggle in that month, it was pointless to argue that the councillors now sitting in judgement had been equally guilty in their response to the King's pressure, and simply untrue to claim that 'all the rest' had been discharged. Cranmer was properly convicted, and there was no particular reason why the Queen should pardon him. Nor did she, in fact, do so. Foxe was correct in claiming that Mary decided not to carry out the sentence for treason, reserving Cranmer for what she considered to be the higher jurisdiction of the Church, but wrong to imply that any specific pardon was issued. The Archbishop later, and correctly, described himself as a 'dead man before the law'.

The problem, however, lay deeper than the particular circumstances of Cranmer's reaction to the proclamation of Queen Jane, in the nature of the Anglican Church as it was conceived by its founding fathers. Richard Hooker summed up that nature most comprehensively in *The Laws of Ecclesiastical Polity*, but the views which he expressed were shared equally by John Jewel, Cranmer, Foxe, and Stephen Gardiner.

> ... there is not any man of the Church of England but the same man is also a member of the commonwealth; nor any man a member of the commonwealth which is not also of the Church of England ... so albeit properties and actions of one kind do cause the name of a commonwealth, qualities and functions of another sort the name of a Church to be given unto a multitude, yet one and the self-same multitude may in such sort be both ...[5]

To Hooker, and to all the others, including Stephen Gardiner when he wrote *De vera obedientia oratio*, that nature also involved a double

---

[4] PRO, Baga de Secretis, K.B. 8/23. Calendared in the *Fourth Report of the Deputy Keeper of the Public Records*, App. 2, pp. 237–8.
[5] Richard Hooker, *Of the Laws of Ecclesiastical Polity*, ed. Isaac Walton (Oxford, 1885), viii, 1, p. 2.

allegiance to the monarch as Supreme Head.[6] An Englishman, therefore, who was born the king's subject, was as bound by the ecclesiastical law as he was by the temporal law. Henry VIII had been perfectly willing to define continued allegiance to the papacy as High Treason, although it could be just as much a matter of religious conscience as adherence to transubstantiation. Naturally the Protestants had had no problem with this type of treason, but when Mary reversed the process she impaled them on the horns of a dilemma. Most English Catholics had accepted the changes introduced by Henry and Edward, much as they may have disliked them, because they accepted the lawfulness of the king's authority.[7] It now remained to be seen whether the Protestants, deeply imbued with convictions about the royal supremacy, would follow suit. Stephen Gardiner, who had no respect for Protestant convictions, clearly believed that they would. Hence his irritated remark to Sir James Hales, that he should 'rather look to the Queen's proceedings' over the celebration of the Mass than concern himself with the letter of the law. Hence, also, his willingness to chivvy potentially awkward consciences into exile, rather than allow them to set an example of defiance at home. Even Cranmer might have been left alone, treason or no treason, if he had not deliberately drawn attention to himself by denouncing the Mass in a public document.[8]

Although some of the more ardent spirits undoubtedly welcomed the prospect of persecution, most Protestants were as reluctant to be forced into a choice between conscience and allegiance as the Catholic recusants were later to be under Elizabeth. During the early months of Mary's reign many, including Foxe, kept a low profile and hoped, against all the evidence, that Mary would be contented with a partial and formal restoration. Foxe even addressed a petition to the Parliament of April 1554 against the restoration of the Act of Six Articles:

> You are the fathers of the land; treat us as sons; remember what you owe to yourselves, to your own noble blood; let clemency be seen. You have a queen who, as she is most noble, is a princess willing to hearken to all sober and wholesome counsels. You have a chancellor

---

[6] Pierre Janelle, *Obedience in Church and State; Three Political Tracts by Stephen Gardiner* (Cambridge, 1930); G. Redworth, *In Defence of the Church Catholic; a Life of Stephen Gardiner* (Oxford, 1990), pp. 66–7.

[7] The best recent exposition of this view is R. Whiting, *The Blind Devotion of the People; Popular Religion and the English Reformation* (Cambridge, 1989).

[8] Foxe, 6, p. 539; 8, pp. 37–8; D. M. Loades, *The Oxford Martyrs* (London, 1970), p. 118.

eminent in learning, and not evil by nature, if the influence of certain men are absent . . .[9]

He was clutching at straws, but it is significant how far he was prepared to go to avoid any imputation of sedition or disloyalty. Even more remarkable is the autobiographical note of Thomas Mountain who, along with others, was imprisoned in the Marshalsea for religious reasons at the beginning of February 1554.

When Mr. Wyatt was up in Kent, and so coming to London and lying in Southwark, he sent one of his chaplains . . . to know whether we would be delivered out of prison or no . . . Then we all agreed and sent him this answer, 'Sir, we give you most hearty thanks for this your gentle offer; but forasmuch as we came in for our conscience, and sent hither by the council, we think it good here still to remain till it please God to work our deliverance as shall seem best to his glory and our lawful discharge . . .'[10]

In this delicate and somewhat ambiguous situation the Lord Chancellor was tempted to regard all treason as religious in inspiration, but he was not yet entitled to regard religious dissent in itself as treasonable. Although the Protestant Prayer Book had been withdrawn, and the Queen as Supreme Head was bent on restoring the traditional order, the heresy laws had not yet been restored to the statute book. Before the end of 1554, although there were Protestants who were also traitors, there was nothing treasonable about Protestantism itself. After the second Act of Repeal, however, the situation changed. It never became treason to reject the papal authority, but it did involve defiance both of the law and of the Queen's wishes. When Cranmer was finally tried for heresy in September 1556, he was totally disconcerted to find that it was again the shadow of treason with which his conscience had to struggle. He appeared in St Mary's Church, in Oxford, prepared to defend the orthodoxy of his views on the eucharistic presence and the nature of the Church, only to find himself confronted not only with his defiance of the canon law since 1533, but also with his present defiance of an authority which he persisted in regarding as lawful.

'If I have transgressed the laws of the land', he protested, 'their majesties have sufficient authority and power, both from God and by

[9] BL, MS Harleian 417, fol. 123; J. F. Mozley, *John Foxe and his Book* (London, 1940), pp. 39–40.
[10] 'The troubles of Thomas Mowntayne . . .' in J. G. Nichols, ed., *Narratives of the Days of the Reformation*, Camden Society, 77 (1859), p. 185.

the ordinance of the realm, to punish me; whereunto I both have been, and at all times shall be, content to submit myself.'[11]

If the Queen was offended with him, she should subject him to her own jurisdiction, not invoke that of a foreign power. In recognizing the alien authority of Rome, Mary was being a traitor to her own estate. However, neither Cranmer nor Foxe was willing to draw from that premise a logical conclusion of lawful resistance, and neither had any real answer to the proposition with which Dr Story confronted the Archbishop.

> ... the same laws, being put away by a parliament, are now received again by a parliament, and have as full authority now as they had then; and they will now that ye answer to the Pope's Holiness; therefore by the laws of this realm ye are bound to answer him.[12]

There is no doubt that it was Cranmer's inability to resolve this problem which led to his recantations. His conscience was just as uneasy as it had been in November 1553, as is demonstrated by the opening of his first submission.

> Forasmuch as the King and Queen's majesties, by consent of their parliament, have received the Pope's authority within this realm, I am content to submit myself to their laws herein, and to take the Pope for the chief head of this church of England ...[13]

Only a robust assertion that the prince had no power over a Christian conscience could lead to any other conclusion, and twenty years of declaring that obedience was due to the monarch for conscience' sake had undermined his ability to reach any such conclusion. Nicholas Ridley showed a clearer vision, although he had been no less strenuous as a defender of the royal supremacy.[14] By defining the Church primarily as the congregation of the faithful, he deliberately weakened its bonding with any particular community, and reintroduced in a different form that concept of a double allegiance from which the Church of England had been endeavouring to escape. Although Ridley was not called upon to

---

[11] Foxe, 8, p. 63.

[12] Ibid., p. 54.

[13] *The Works of Thomas Cranmer*, ed. J. E. Cox, *PS* (1844–6), 2, App. p. 43.

[14] Foxe, 7, p. 524, 'I acknowledge an unspotted church of Christ ... that is the congregation of the faithful; neither do I allegiate or bind the same to any one place, as you said, but confess the same to be spread throughout the world; and where Christ's sacraments are duly ministered, his gospel truly preached and followed, there doth Christ's church shine as a city upon a hill.'

tread that path, such thinking inevitably led to the fully-developed resistance theory of a John Knox or a Christopher Goodman, to whom the profession of a true faith was the first test of political legitimacy.[15] No Protestant had embraced such doctrine willingly, because in the early days of the Reformation the principal enemy had been the papacy, and princes had usually been the reformers' allies. Only the Lutherans, faced with the crisis of the Schmalkaldic war, had to justify their decision to confront the Emperor in arms. However, when princes turned against the Reformation, first in France and then in Scotland and England, the question which John Knox addressed to Heinrich Bullinger in 1554 could not be evaded, 'Whether obedience is to be rendered to a magistrate who enforces idolatry and condemns true religion?'[16]

Bullinger was unable, or at least unwilling, to answer, but a solution lay ready to hand in some later Lutheran writings, notably the Magdeburg *Bekenntnis* of 1550, wherein it was argued that superior powers are ordained of God not as an end in themselves, but in order to do justice.[17] Since the princes no less than the Emperor are powers ordained of God, the princes have a duty to uphold justice if the Emperor fails, or refuses, to do so. In 1556 Knox returned to Scotland on a preaching tour, and although he escaped the clutches of the Scottish hierarchy, he was nevertheless condemned to death in his absence as a heretic. This prompted him two years later to publish an *Appellation* against his sentence, in which he adapted the German theory to his immediate needs. Nobles, no less than kings, have the powers of their offices assigned by God. Both alike are 'ordained for the profit and utility of others', and if kings become tyrants, then the duty to defend the common weal devolves upon the nobles.[18] As Quentin Skinner has pointed out, this is not really a political theory, since the obligations of the aristocracy are drafted in purely religious terms;[19] but when such obligations are taken up, as they were shortly after by the Lords of the Congregation, it would be hard to describe the outcome as anything other than political. By the time that the *Appellation* appeared, two Englishmen had responded to the challenge presented by Queen

[15] Quentin Skinner, *The Foundations of Modern Political Thought* (Cambridge, 1978), 2, pp. 234–5.
[16] Ibid., p. 189.
[17] E. F. M. Hildebrandt, 'The Magdeburg Bekenntnis as a possible link between German and English resistance theory in the sixteenth century', *Archiv für Reformationsgeschichte*, 71 (1980), pp. 227–53; Skinner, *Foundations*, 2, pp. 207–10.
[18] J. R. Gray, 'The political theory of John Knox', *ChH*, 8 (1939), pp. 132–47.
[19] Skinner, *Foundations*, 2, p. 211; J. E. A. Dawson, 'Resistance and Revolution in sixteenth century thought: the case of Christopher Goodman', in J. van den Berg and P. J. Hoftijzer, eds, *Church, Change and Revolution* (Leiden, 1991).

Mary in a slightly different way. Both John Ponet in 1556 and Christopher Goodman in 1558 argued that a prince who commits crimes such as murder or robbery should be brought to justice as a private citizen. Goodman, in particular, made a clear distinction between the office and the person of the ruler. If rulers become tyrants, or

> ... transgress God's laws themselves, and command others to do the like, then have they lost that honour and obedience which otherwise their subjects did owe to them, and ought no more to be taken for magistrates ...[20]

Consequently, to maintain the law of God against a ruler who was endeavouring to subvert it could not by any stretch of the imagination be described as treasonable.

Unfortunately, although these arguments were addressed to the English situation, they did not meet the case. Even if Cranmer had been willing to regard his allegiance to Mary as having been dissolved by her idolatry, that did not get him round Story's argument that the papal authority, and all that that implied, had been recognized by Parliament and was therefore a part of the law of England. It was no use John Ponet claiming that the duty to defend the law of God devolved upon the nobility, when that same nobility had been a partner in subversion. Neither Ponet's constitutionalism, nor Knox's view of the responsibility of the nobility as 'inferior magistrates' in the German sense could provide a remedy for the persecuted Protestants of Marian England; which may be why there was no religious rising, at least after the laws were changed in January 1555. That same respect for due process which prevented Catholics from rebelling against Edward VI protected Mary a few years later. At the same time it was perfectly reasonable for the Council to regard religious dissent and political subversion as two sides of the same coin. Logically, a positive law which was contrary to the law of God was no true law, and not binding upon the conscience. Sir Thomas More had so argued, and so had Mary herself when confronted with the Protestant legislation of 1549.[21] To her, the consent of Parliament was no more binding than any other expression of political will, but the majority of her subjects did not share her scepticism. Had they done so, her bid for the

---

[20] Christopher Goodman, *How Superior Powers Ought to be Obeyed of their Subjects* (Geneva, 1558), pp. 187–8.

[21] 'I have offended no law, unless it be a late law of your own making for the altering of matters in religion, which, in my conscience, is not worthy to have the name of law.' Mary to the Council, 22 June 1549; Foxe, 6, p. 7. D. M. Loades, *Mary Tudor; a Life* (Oxford, 1992), p. 146.

throne in July 1553 might well have been unsuccessful. Consequently the radicalism of Knox or Goodman would have had to break down Englishmen's respect for the temporal law as well as their religious conservatism before the Queen's authority could be seriously endangered. That could have happened, but it did not in the relatively short time during which the situation appertained. In the meanwhile English Protestants who regarded her as an idolater, and the Pope as Antichrist, continued unhappily to accept her as their legitimate ruler, and her laws as valid. At no time was the Pope given the protection of the treason laws, so it remained technically heresy rather than treason to reject his authority, a consideration which may have been of some comfort to Cranmer, but did not alter the substantial fact that the Catholic Church from 1554 to 1559 was the Church by Law Established.

There was a possible way round this, which was logical, but again depended upon old-fashioned views about the authority of Parliament. Theoretically the royal supremacy had never been created by Parliament. The Acts of 1533–6 had merely recognized and enforced a situation which was deemed to have been willed by God in the remote past.[22] By the same token, therefore, the Acts of Repeal had only signalled a change of attitude, not a change in the underlying situation. A Protestant could continue to recognize the Queen as Supreme Head without being in breach of the law. In one sense this made little difference, since it was clearly Mary's intention to use whatever authority she possessed in defence of the papal jurisdiction and the traditional faith. However, it also made it possible to argue that, in so doing, the Queen was seeking to alienate an intrinsic aspect of the office of monarch—to give away her own power and with it a part of the inheritance which was due to her successor. 'By the scripture the king is chief', Cranmer declared at his trial, 'and no foreign person in his realm above him . . .'.[23] No incumbent for the time being was entitled to diminish an office which he held in trust, and Mary's action was therefore unlawful, not in respect of statute, but of a much older and more fundamental law, at once natural and Divine. In this way it was possible to argue that a king might be defied in order to protect some fundamental aspect of kingship; so had generations of rebels argued from the days of King John to the Pilgrimage of Grace. Sometimes they succeeded, and subsequent generations honoured them as the defenders of English liberty; sometimes they failed, and were stigmatized

---

[22] 26 Henry VIII c.1: *Statutes of the Realm*, 3, p. 492: 'Albeit the King's Majesty justly and rightfully is and oweth to be the Supreme Head of the Church of England . . .'
[23] Foxe, 8, p. 51.

as traitors on the Harringtonian principle that when treason prospers, it ceases to be treason.

In writing the *Acts and Monuments*, John Foxe was well aware of the sensitivity of this issue, and of how little the resistance theories of Goodman and Knox commended themselves to Queen Elizabeth. However much the new queen might wish to distance herself from her sister's policies, it was not safe to assume that those who had opposed the previous regime could look for the favour of the new. He had therefore to face not only the central problem of Cranmer's treason, but also the ambiguous position of those other Protestants who had died at the hands of the executioner instead of having been relaxed to the secular arm by the minions of Antichrist. He was, of course, spared what could easily have been the most difficult case of all by the recantation of John Dudley, Duke of Northumberland, after his condemnation in August 1553. Dudley, for reasons which are still obscure, but which may well have been connected with a fatalistic streak in his nature, consented

> ... to hear mass ... and denied in word that true religion which before time, as well in king Henry the Eighth's days as in king Edwards, he had oft evidently declared himself both to favour and further—exhorting also the people to return to the catholic faith as he termed it...[24]

At the time the English Protestants were angry and devastated by his defection. 'Woe worth him', Lady Jane is reported to have said, 'who would have thought that he would do so?'[25] However, his standing with the Protestant leadership had not been high in the last year of his life, and Cranmer, in particular, had had good cause to resent his high-handed interference in ecclesiastical matters. So it is a little surprising that Foxe, writing with the benefit of ten years hindsight, did not seize the opportunity to denounce him as a 'carnal gospeller', thus both explaining his defection and distancing genuine believers from his notoriously unpopular regime. Perhaps it was not politic to write in such a manner of Lord Robert Dudley's father, and his fate was handled with brief and low-key disapproval.[26] Sir John Gates, who had followed the same course, he

[24] Foxe, 6, p. 388.
[25] *A Chronicle of Queen Jane, and of the first two years of Queen Mary*, ed. J. G. Nicholas, *Camden Society*, 48 (1850), pp. 18–19.
[26] In 1559, in the *Rerum in Ecclesia Gestarum*, Foxe had included such an uncomplimentary description of John Dudley, but it was cut out of the English edition in 1563. I am indebted to Mr Tom Freeman for drawing my attention to this fact.

passed over without comment, while of Sir Thomas Palmer, the third victim of the July coup, he observed laconically that he 'confessed his faith that he learned in the gospel.' This would seem to put Palmer into a different category, and makes the lack of elaboration surprising. However, another account of his last words represents him as having said that he had been a great reader of the Bible, and a very poor follower of its precepts, which is not quite the same thing. Palmer had been no more a martyr than Northumberland.

A more difficult case was presented by Henry Grey, Duke of Suffolk. Suffolk was executed on 23 February 1554 for the undoubted treason of having attempted to take up arms against the Queen in Leicestershire in the previous month. In so doing he had also shamefully abused the pardon which he had been given only a month earlier for his prominent involvement in the usurpation of his daughter. Foxe, however, accorded him the accolade of a 'Godly End', which might perhaps be described as a 'one-star' martyrdom, putting into his mouth a last speech which went as close as possible to reconciling the contradictions of his position.

> Masters, I have offended the Queen and her laws, and am thereby justly condemned to die, and am willing to die, desiring all men to be obedient. And I pray God that this my death may be an ensample to all men, beseeching you also to bear me witness that I die in the faith of Christ, trusting to be saved by his blood only, and by no other trumpery, the which died for me and for all them that truly repent and steadfastly trust in him . . . [27]

Whether or not these were the Duke's exact words is immaterial. They must have represented his sense fairly enough, because there were plenty of people still alive nine years later who would have heard them. Moreover, Sir Thomas Wyatt, who could have been a more suitable example, and was certainly a martyr in the eyes of many Londoners, was accorded no such treatment. Foxe reported his exoneration of Elizabeth and the Earl of Devon upon the scaffold, but otherwise recorded his execution without comment. The same was true of the great majority of the others who died as a result of the rebellion of January 1554, including the innocuous Guildford Dudley, of whom he merely observed that he was '. . . an innocent by comparison of them that sat upon him'—which did not amount to a denial of his guilt. The only exceptions were one Walter Mantell, and Lady Jane Grey herself. Mantell was a Kentish gentleman

[27] Foxe, 6, p. 545.

who had been condemned for appearing with Wyatt in arms, and who was sent down to Kent for execution on 27 February. He was a known Protestant who, upon the scaffold, was offered a pardon in return for his submission to the Catholic Church. He refused the offer, and died the traitor's death to which he had been sentenced. Foxe described him as 'a worthy gentleman ... who chose rather to die than to have his life for dishonouring God.'[28] Mantell left behind him an Apology, which Foxe printed, in which he refuted claims which were apparently made before his death that he had been reconciled to the Catholic Church. This document is dated 2 March, and was probably written the day before his execution. Foxe carefully avoided any statement to the effect that Mantell died for his faith, while clearly implying that he died because of it. Although his case was very similar to Suffolk's, there was a subtle but important difference in the manner of its presentation.

Jane Grey was different again. She was technically guilty of treason, because although a minor, she was well above the age of criminal responsibility as that was then defined. On the other hand, it was very easy to represent her as an innocent dupe, and her famous learning and piety marked her out for special consideration. The *Acts and Monuments* contain three of Jane's letters of pious exhortation, and a verbatim report of her conversation with John Feckenham, which is in substance a brief and lucid account of Protestant teaching on justification and the Eucharist.[29] Jane is represented as welcoming her fate, not only as a purgation of her temporal guilt, but also of those sins against God which nobody else seems to have noticed, but which were presumably an *a priori* assumption for the faithful. Her performance on the scaffold was remarkably similar to her father's ten days later, for which it may have provided a model.

> Good people, I am come hither to die, and by a law I am condemned to the same. The fact against the Queen's highness was unlawful, and the consenting thereunto by me; but touching the procurement and desire thereof by me or on my behalf, I do wash my hands thereof in innocency before God, and the face of you, good Christian people, this day ... I pray you all to bear me witness that I die a true Christian woman, and that I do look to be saved by no other means, but only by the mercy of God, in the blood of his only son Jesus Christ.[30]

[28] Ibid., pp. 546–8.
[29] Ibid., pp. 415–25.
[30] Ibid., p. 424.

Jane's treason was a matter of form rather than substance, and her depart-
ing from the world was a model of propriety. In that sense she could be
described as a 'three-star' martyr; one who had testified repeatedly and
publicly to her faith, and who accepted death as the justice of God rather
than man. That was clearly how Foxe wished to portray her, in spite of the
fact that her Protestantism was really an irrelevance. Like her father, she
was not, properly speaking, a martyr at all unless resistance to an ungodly
ruler constituted defence of the faith, and that, as we have seen, Foxe was
a long way from admitting.

All the cases which we have examined so far were those of traitors
under the original law of 1352. But Mary also created new treasons, and
one of these, by the statute 1 and 2 Philip and Mary, c.10, was to pray that
the Queen's heart might be turned or her days shortened, and it was under
the terms of this Act that George Eagles was condemned in 1557.[31] Eagles,
familiarly known as 'Trudge over the world' because of his restless
wanderings, was a hedge preacher, a man of little learning, but one who
'... manfully served and fought under the banner of Christ's church'.
Eagles's preaching attracted large numbers, particularly in the Chelms-
ford area, which brought him within the scope of the Act against
Seditious Assemblies, and a proclamation was issued, offering a reward of
£20 for his capture. Once taken, he was considered to be of sufficient
importance to merit interrogation by the Bishop, and it was presumably
Bonner who decided that he should be tried at the assizes rather than by an
ecclesiastical court. Foxe's comment on this decision is instructive,

> ... albeit it was well known, that poor Eagles never did anything
> seditiously against the Queen, yet to cloak an honest matter withal,
> and to cause him to be more hated of the people, they turned religion
> into a civil crime and offence ...[32]

In 1553 Cranmer had been reprieved from a traitor's death to face the
more heinous charge of heresy, but in 1557 the relatively obscure Eagles
was steered in the opposite direction, because heresy did not attract
sufficient opprobrium! Eagles admitted at his trial that he had prayed for
the Queen's heart to be turned, but denied the treasonable rider. Being
condemned, he consistently refused to admit that he had offended, and
although he went to his end with becoming piety, no scaffold speech was
recorded of him, nor did he leave any written testimony behind, unlike
the others whose cases we have examined. Foxe headed his account of

[31] Foxe, 8, pp. 393–7.
[32] Ibid., p. 395.

Eagles's sufferings 'A most painful traveller in Christ's gospel, who for the same gospel, most cruelly was martyred by the cruel papists.'[33] If Jane Grey had been an innocent traitor, George Eagles was no traitor at all, because the whole substance of his crime was his Protestant faith. Foxe did not attempt to argue that it was actually a Protestant's duty to ask God to shorten the days of an idolatrous ruler, or even that Parliament had acted wrongfully in declaring such an action to be treason, but merely that Eagles was not guilty of the crime for which he was condemned. In so far as Parliament made Protestantism a statutory offence, it was through the heresy Acts, not through the treason Acts, and it was Eagles's persecutors in Essex, not the legislators, who met with the assorted grisly ends ordained for those who seek innocent blood.

One of the reasons why Foxe emphasized so strongly the judgemental aspect of Mary's reign was that he simply did not know what to do about an idolatrous ruler, much less about a Parliament which concurred in such perversity. Moreover, writing in the reign of Elizabeth, it was much safer not to address such issues which could, for the time being at least, be set on one side in the wake of the settlement of 1559. It was not difficult in 1563, when the danger appeared to be passed, to excuse the failure of the Godly to defend either themselves or their principles between 1553 and 1558.

> ... it shall not be unprofitable, but rather necessary and to our great comfort to consider and examine in the scriptures, with what prophecies the Holy Spirit of the Lord hath premonished and fore-warned us before, of these heavy persecutions to come upon his people by this horrible Antichrist. For as the government and con-stitution of times, and states of monarchies and policies, fall not to us by blind chance, but be administered and alloted unto us from above; so it is not to be supposed that so great alteration and mutation of kingdoms, such a general and terrible persecution of God's people ... cometh without knowledge, sufferance and determination of the Lord ...[34]

In such circumstances, not only was there no particular merit in resist-ance, it could also be seen as a near-blasphemous attempt to frustrate the purposes of God. Treason against an idolatrous queen remained treason, and could not be condoned by the cause in which it was carried out, how-ever Godly. The traitor, on the other hand, was an individual human

[33] Ibid., p. 393.
[34] Foxe, I, p. 289.

being who had his, or her, own account to make with God. Each case was different. Cranmer could eventually be a 'five-star' martyr, because his treason was a separate issue, and he died for his faith, in accordance with his own wishes, but by the Queen's command. George Eagles could be a martyr because he had been unjustly condemned and because his real offence had been religious. Rebels and conspirators might make a Godly end, and feature in the *Acts and Monuments*, but Foxe never explicitly used the word 'martyr' to describe them—the 'star' rating, of course, is my own gloss. Jane Grey might be regarded as a sacrificial lamb; but neither her father nor Walter Mantell could be presented in that light. Foxe, like Cranmer, had a double vision of the Church. On the one hand, it was the community of the faithful, identified by doctrine and usage; but, at the same time, it was the commonwealth of England in its ecclesiastical aspect. Logically there was no connection between the two visions, and that is one of the reasons why there has been scholarly debate about the concept of an 'Elect Nation'.[35] Foxe was too familiar with the whole reformed tradition to regard England as a New Jerusalem, yet at the same time the Tudors were agents of divine providence in a special sense. The fortunes of the Marian traitors therefore became an important part of his historiography of the Reformation. His message was not always intellectually consistent, but that did not diminish its impact. He was not prepared to denounce Mary as 'another Athalia', or to praise those who had sought to deprive her of her throne, yet the images which he created—of Cranmer stretching out his hand to the flame, or of a blindfolded Jane Grey groping for the block—influenced generations of men and women who had no need or desire to trace the intellectual roots of their prejudices.

University of Wales, Bangor

---

[35] William Haller, *Foxe's Book of Martyrs and the Elect Nation* (London, 1963); V. Norskov Olsen, *John Foxe and the Elizabethan Church* (Berkeley, California, 1973).

HENRY BULL, MILES COVERDALE, AND THE MAKING OF FOXE'S *BOOK OF MARTYRS*

by SUSAN WABUDA

I N a preface to his *Acts and Monuments*, John Foxe explained why his ecclesiastical history was so deeply concerned with martyrs.

> I see no cause why the Martyrs of our time deserue not as great commendation as the other in the primitiue church, which assuredly are inferiour vnto them in no point of praise, whether we looke vpon the nomber of them that suffered, or the greatnes of their tormentes, or their constancy in dieng [*sic*], or also consider the fruite that they brought to the amendement of mens liues, and the encrease of the gospel.

Foxe 'thought it not to be neglected, that the precious monumentes of so manye matters, and men moste meete to be recorded and registred in bookes, should lye buried by my fault in the pit of obliuion.'[1]

For Foxe and other sixteenth-century martyrologists, like Miles Coverdale, the monuments of the martyrs were not only their beliefs and heroic actions, but the documents which recorded their achievements. Letters and other papers written by the martyrs served as relics. Coverdale's preface to his last book, *Certain most godly, fruitful, and comfortable letters of ... true Saintes and holy Martyrs of God*, compared the writings of the Marian martyrs with those of 'the old auncient Saincts & chosen children of god', those men and women 'whose conuersation in old time was beautifyed with syngular giftes of the holy ghost.' The recent martyrs 'were moste desirous by their pen and writing, to edify their brethren, [who were] other poor lambes of Christ, and one to comfort an other in

---

[1] I wish to express my thanks to Dr Frank Stubbings and the staff of Emmanuel College, Cambridge, for their generous assistance in allowing me to consult the manuscripts in their care, and also the staff of the British Library. Thanks are also due to Professor Patrick Collinson for reading this paper. John Foxe, *Actes and Monuments . . .* (London: John Day, 1563) [*STC*, 11222], sigs B6r–B6v [hereafter Foxe (1563)]. The second volume of the second English edition, John Foxe, *The First ([and] Second) Volume of the Ecclesiasticall history contaynyng the Actes and Monumentes* (London: John Day, 1570) [*STC*, 11223], will be cited hereafter as Foxe (1570). I have silently expanded most common sixteenth-century abbreviations in quotations, and have modernized punctuation.

him.' Coverdale also referred to his desire to publish their 'most notable monuments', for which 'great cause haue we to praise god.'[2]

In the past twenty years historians have begun to take a new look at Foxe and his sources.[3] Leslie P. Fairfield has traced the influence that the hagiographer and manuscript collector John Bale had upon Foxe.[4] Also, Professor Patrick Collinson has written about Foxe's veracity as a historian, his techniques and use of material, and what information from the records he included and excluded. Collinson has demonstrated that Foxe was only one member of a large, co-operative effort designed to collect manuscripts and bring them to publication, starting in exile during the Marian persecution. Edmund Grindal, based in Strasbourg, was responsible for organizing the flow of manuscripts, and he sent them to Foxe in Basle. Grindal originally envisioned that the manuscripts would be shared out between many exiles, including Coverdale, for editing. There would be a 'division of labour'. Grindal felt that the various documents which were 'in the possession of our friends', should be 'polished a little', and printed separately.[5]

Eventually Foxe began to pull the documents into the compendious history which has become completely identified with him. This paper will argue, however, that Grindal's original strategy, to give the monuments to the world in separate works, was never completely superseded. I will bring forth new information on the manner in which Foxe was assisted and influenced by friends, including Coverdale, and especially by Henry Bull. We will explore how they used the manuscripts that came into their possession, and their reasons for printing the documents. We will be particularly concerned with the manner in which they edited material. I will show that they altered the original sense of some manuscripts.

The best-known of Foxe's surviving manuscripts are a dozen volumes in the Harleian collection of the British Library,[6] and scholars have made

---

[2] Miles Coverdale, comp., *Certain most godly, fruitful, and comfortable letters of such true Saintes and holy Martyrs of God* ... (London: John Day, 1564) [*STC*, 5886], sigs A2r–A4r.

[3] J. A. F. Thomson, 'John Foxe and some sources for Lollard history: notes for a critical appraisal', *SCH*, 2 (1965), pp. 251–7; John Fines, 'Heresy trials in the Diocese of Coventry and Lichfield, 1511–12', *JEH*, 14 (1963), pp. 160–74.

[4] Leslie P. Fairfield, *John Bale: Mythmaker for the English Reformation* (West Lafayette, Indiana, 1976), pp. 135–6, 152.

[5] *The Remains of Edmund Grindal, D.D.*, ed. William Nicholson, PS (1843), pp. 219–38; Patrick Collinson, *Archbishop Grindal 1519–1583: the Struggle for a Reformed Church* (London, 1979), pp. 79–82, and 'Truth and Legend: the veracity of John Foxe's Book of Martyrs' in A. C. Duke and C. A. Tamse, eds., *Clio's mirror: Historiography in Britain and the Netherlands* (Zutphen, 1985), pp. 31–54. Also, London, BL, Additional MS 19400, fol. 97r.

[6] BL, MSS Harley 416–426 and 590; and also MSS Lansdowne 335, 388, 389, 819, 1045.

much use of them. However, very few historians have recently consulted two important, related sets of manuscripts that belong to the Foxe corpus. Since the editing of the Parker Society volumes nearly 150 years ago, three manuscripts belonging to Emmanuel College, Cambridge, have been almost completely ignored.[7]

The Emmanuel manuscripts have been owned by the college since its earliest years of existence, if not its foundation in 1584. In a 1597 inventory, we find that '6. bookes of monumentes of Martyrs' were kept with the library's furnishings, and seem to have been given a place of special prominence, almost as relics.[8] Since then, the manuscripts have been rebound into three volumes,[9] and are now known as Manuscripts 260, 261, and 262. Each is more than 150 folios in length, and they are made up of more than 200 miscellaneous documents in total. The majority of items are autograph letters, or contemporary copies, by the martyrs themselves, including John Hooper (the Edwardine Bishop of Gloucester and Worcester), Nicholas Ridley (former Bishop of London), John Bradford, and John Philpot. A sizeable number of letters are from the Coventry weaver John Careless, who died in prison in 1556. Not all of the letters were reproduced by the Parker Society in the mid-nineteenth century, and the collection also includes other material, including prayers, sermons, and even Robert Wisdom's repudiation of a recantation he made in 1543, some of which has never been printed at all.[10]

---

[7] The working notes of the Parker Society's editors can be found in Cambridge, Emmanuel College Library [hereafter ECL], BOX LIB.10.5. The contents of ECL, MSS 260, 261, and 262 were listed by Montague Rhodes James in *The Western Manuscripts in the Library of Emmanuel College* (Cambridge, 1904), pp. 159–66. Scholars who have been most aware of them recently include Dr John Fines, who consulted them for his *Biographical Register of Early English Protestants and Others Opposed to the Roman Catholic Church 1525–1558*, A–C, temp. edn (Abingdon, 1981); D–Z, typescript. He has also brought the manuscripts to the attention of others, including J. W. Martin, in 'Sidelights on Foxe's account of the Marian martyrs', in *Religious Radicals in Tudor England* (London, 1989), pp. 171–8.

[8] ECL, MS BUR 8. 1, pp. 14 (rebinding of the manuscripts for 16d. in October 1598), 191 (library inventory of 1597); Sargent Bush, Jr and Carl J. Rasmussen, *The Library of Emmanuel College, Cambridge, 1584–1637* (Cambridge, 1986), pp. 15, 76, and the same authors', 'Emmanuel College Library's first inventory', *Transactions of the Cambridge Bibliographical Society*, 8 (1985), pp. 514–56, esp. p. 554.

[9] Two of the original bindings are kept in ECL, BOX LIB.10.5. They are marked 'LETTERS OF HOLY MIRTYRS' and 'LETTERS. AND PRAYERS. WITH OTHER WORKES OF HOLYE MARTYRES'.

[10] Sermons and sermon notes include: ECL, MS 261, fols 52r–53v, Wisdom on the creed and decalogue, fols 57r–60v, Wisdom's translation of a German sermon, 1559, fols 69r–87v; MS 262, fols 27r–39r, 54r–57v, Curtop's 1552 Paul's Cross sermon, fols 261r–267r. Wisdom's 'revocacyon' of his recantation, which has never been published in its entirety, is the longest document in the collection. ECL, MS 261, fols 88r–130v.

There can be no question that the Emmanuel manuscripts were the actual monuments used by Foxe and Coverdale. Their pages bear copious signs that they were edited for sixteenth-century publications. Scrawled upon the letters themselves are directions to the printers, pointing hands, marks which refer to pagination in several printed works, and crossed-out lines. In 1852, Aubrey Townsend, editor of the Parker Society's volumes of Bradford's work, discovered a fragment from a proof sheet of the *Certain most godly letters* in the binding of Manuscript 260. He noted that both the fragment and many of the manuscripts were marked by the same coarse hand.[11] Indeed, we find identical markings on the margins of some of the leaves of British Library, Additional Manuscript 19400, leading me to conclude that some of the documents in it once belonged with the Emmanuel material.[12]

Moreover, we find written on some of the letters, in a different hand: 'Restore this to mr fox.'[13] On Wisdom's translation of a German sermon, which may have been used once to bind other documents, we find the note: 'Mr Dayes wrytings wherein are letters of Careles & other.'[14] Fortunately the writer of these emendations, unlike those of the coarse hand, has left his signature: 'perused by me henry Bull: & I will further see to the correction herof at the prynters handes.'[15] Due to this fortuitous notation, we can identify Bull's characteristic brisk handwriting on many documents in the Emmanuel collection, and we will return to consider his connection with Foxe and Coverdale once we discuss why some of this material was written in the first place, and why it was collected together.

In this paper we will mainly concentrate upon the letters in the Emmanuel collection. Many of them were written by those who were incarcerated for their reformed religious beliefs, who refused to accept the re-establishment of the papal supremacy in England under the rule of Queen Mary Tudor. Some of the prisoners were condemned and executed with comparative swiftness. Others, like Careless, languished for years. They were held in various prisons, often in appalling conditions of privation and squalor, sometimes 'lying in fetters and chaynes'.[16]

Despite such obstacles, many of the prisoners contrived to have ink, pens, and paper. Under the guise of food, a bladder of ink-powder was

---

[11] The fragment is from p. 357 of *Certain most godly letters*. It, and a descriptive note from Townsend, can be found in ECL, BOX LIB.10.5.

[12] BL, Additional MS 19400, including fols 25r–26v, 30v, 56r–56v, 71v.

[13] ECL, MS 260, fols 44r–44v; BL, Additional MS 19400, fol. 102v.

[14] ECL, MS 261, fol. 87v.

[15] ECL, MS 261, fol. 14r. Also, BL, Additional MS 19400, fol. 30v: 'Restore this agayne to Bull.'

[16] *Certain most godly letters*, sig. A3v.

smuggled to Philpot. When the keeper of the Bishop of London's Coal House confiscated a pen-case and ink-horn from him, Philpot managed to find replacements.[17] To judge from the extreme length of their letters and accounts of their examinations, some prisoners whiled away many hours by writing.

The letters that the prisoners wrote to relatives, friends, supporters, and others in the world outside (or in other prisons) were not meant to express only private sentiments. Rather, each missive was an opportunity for the prisoners to instruct their associates and all with whom their friends shared the letters. Most letters were written with a wider readership in mind. The prisoners wanted others to take heed of their example, and to profit spiritually from their willingness to suffer all for their beliefs, even loss, imprisonment, torture, and death at the stake. The prisoners encouraged their friends to be steadfast in their faith, and heartened each other to sacrifice their lives with gladness. Careless wrote to several condemned prisoners in Newgate: 'O happy and blessed are you that ever you were born, that the Lord will vouch you worthy of this great dignity, to die for his sake.'[18] The writers admonished their readers to turn away from popish practices, and they served as spiritual advisers.[19] Coverdale summarized the prisoners' motives for writing when he declared that they wished to 'edify their brethren',[20] to build up the Protestant Church by comforting their friends, and to spread their beliefs as widely as possible.

The prisoners' advice was almost invariably couched in scriptural terms. Indeed, a fundamental stylistic feature of many of their letters was a profound biblicism, their vigorous application of Scripture's verses and topoi to their own circumstances, in order to rise above their troubles, to justify and propagate their views. Thus John Bradford comforted Joyce Hales with texts and images from Matthew's Gospel and Romans. He intended to lift her from a deep spiritual crisis, and yet find words which would be applicable to his own, or any Protestant's, plight. '"If God be with us, who can be against us?" The Lord is with you; your Father cannot forget you; your spouse loveth you. If the waves and surges arise, cry with

---

[17] Foxe, 7, pp. 647–8, 680–1.

[18] ECL, MS 260, fols 229r–230r; *Certain most godly letters*, pp. 565–8, Foxe, 8, pp. 179–80.

[19] For background, see Maria Dowling and Joy Shakespeare, 'Religion and politics in mid-Tudor England through the eyes of an English Protestant woman: the recollections of Rose Hickman', *BIHR*, 55 (1982), pp. 94–102, esp. p. 100; Patrick Collinson, 'The role of women in the English Reformation: illustrated by the life and friendships of Anne Locke', *SCH*, 2 (1965), pp. 258–72.

[20] *Certain most godly letters*, sigs A2r–A4r.

SUSAN WABUDA

Peter, "Lord, I perish;" and he will put out his hand and help you.'[21] We find this style of writing already well established by Mary's reign, and it was not limited to clergymen, like Bradford. The writings of Anne Askew and John Lascelles, who were burnt in 1546, also made similar use of the Bible's imagery. John Bale, who edited Askew's writings for publication, felt that she and her companions went to the stake with 'a bundle of the sacred scriptures inclosed in their hearts'.[22] The Emmanuel manuscripts show us that, even earlier, one Matthew Greston wrote comforting words in a scriptural vein to a man who was imprisoned in London in the late 1520s or 1530s.[23] The prisoners' scriptural style many have sprung both from responses to persecution and from the increasing availability of the Bible in English.

Although the main purpose of the letters was to edify, many prisoners did include some short references to friends or news about mutual acquaintances. Such personal information usually seemed secondary to the main burden of the letter. If it appeared, it was generally placed at the end of a missive, almost as an afterthought. Perhaps the prisoners would have given greater space to private information, if they had not feared that their letters might be intercepted by authorities who would use their letters against them. In two letters Careless seems to have written the names of friends and then partially crossed them out, so that his correspondents would be able to decipher them, but an intrusive official might not. While in the keeping of Bishop Edmund Bonner in 1555, Philpot, before he was searched, 'cast away many a sweet letter and friendly' which he had received, so that his associates would not be implicated.[24]

The prisoners had an additional obstacle to the dissemination of their ideas. Although their tracts were meant to be circulated as widely as possible, the Marian press was strictly controlled, and very few Protestant

---

[21] Rom. 8.31; Matt. 8.25; ECL, MS 260, fols 34r–37r; *Certain most godly letters*, pp. 322–30, esp. p. 326; Foxe, 7, pp. 230–4; *The Writings of John Bradford . . . containing letters, treatises, remains*, ed. Aubrey Townsend, *PS* (1853), pp. 108–17.
[22] *Select works of John Bale, D.D.*, ed. Henry Christmas, *PS* (1849), esp. p. 190. Askew's and Lascelles's writings were reprinted in Foxe, 5, esp. pp. 545–9, 551–2.
[23] ECL, MS 260, fols 91r–91v. This is a later copy of a letter which was supposed to have been sent to one imprisoned 'for the testimonie of christ' in 'busshopp Stokleys tyme. About Anno Domini 1527'. John Stokesley became Bishop of London in 1530. For matters of style, see Collinson, 'Veracity', pp. 49–50.
[24] Careless also sometimes used initials instead of names. BL, Additional MS 19400, fols 64r–65v, 69r–70r, and fol. 72r. Philpot: Foxe, 7, pp. 647–8, 680–2. In 1546 Anne Askew and William Playne were arrested due to intercepted letters. Edward Ayscu, *A Historie . . .* (London: G. Eld, 1607) [*STC*, 1014], pp. 306–9; Foxe, 8, p. 700.

works were printed covertly in England.[25] In order to spread their opinions, the prisoners and their friends copied out documents by hand and circulated their manuscripts. Multiple manuscript copies of some of the letters still survive,[26] and we are given unique glimpses in the Emmanuel collection of the manner in which copying was done. Moreover, we are told about the men and women who brought the letters out of prison to the wider world.

John Careless occupied much of his time in prison by copying, sometimes for payment. In a letter to Robert Harrington, Philpot recorded that he left a copy of St Ambrose, 'which I have translated against the Arrians' with 'Careles to be copied out'. Philpot also prepared a vast account of his numerous examinations by authorities, and Careless copied it as well. Philpot sent a copy of his examinations to a member of Lord de la Warre's household at Whitefriars, in London, and eventually Harrington had a copy 'with hym over the sea'.[27] Once Careless became involved in a controversy about free will, he kept extra copies of his own letters,[28] and a woman, one of his benefactors, whose name he did not reveal, conveyed one of his letters from the King's Bench, possibly all the way to Warwickshire.[29]

To gain the widest possible readership, the prisoners had to send their writings to continental presses, and their books had to be smuggled back to England.[30] A precedent had been established during Henry VIII's reign, when Askew's examinations and letters were brought over the sea by German merchants, who delivered them to Bale (then in his first period of exile) for publication in Wesel.[31] Philpot's examinations, and a polemic

[25] Philippa Tudor, 'Protestant books in London in Mary Tudor's reign', *London Journal*, 15 (1990), pp. 19–28.

[26] For example, Ridley's letter 'ad fratres qui christum cum cruce amplectuntur'. BL, Additional MS 19400, fols 52r–53r (not in Ridley's hand, but initialed by him); ECL, MS 260, fols 111r–111v (copy); *Certain most godly letters*, pp. 32–8 (with translation); Foxe, 7, pp. 430–1 (English).

[27] Thomas Whittle offered to pay Careless for a copy of Philpot's examinations, which he wanted for a friend. Foxe, 7, pp. 723–4. Philpot to Harrington, ECL, MS 260, fols 65r–65v. Also, Careless of Augustine Bernher, ECL, MS 260, fols 242r–243r (not printed in *Certain most godly letters*); ECL, MS 262, fols 115r–126v. Christina Hallowell Garrett, *The Marian Exiles* (repr. Cambridge, 1966), pp. 177–8.

[28] BL, Additional MS 19400, fols 62r–63r, 73r–74r.

[29] Careless to Bernher, BL, Additional MS 19400, fols 72r–72v.

[30] For William Punt's activities as an illicit book agent, see Tudor, 'Protestant books', pp. 22–3; ECL, MS 260, fols 276r–276v; *The Works of Nicholas Ridley, D.D.*, ed. Henry Christmas, PS (1843), pp. 363–6, 376–7; Bradford, *Letters*, pp. 58–9, 179, 213; Foxe, 7, pp. 426–7, 8, p. 384; Garrett, *Marian Exiles*, pp. 263–4.

[31] By May 1547 Askew's printed works were distributed in England. *The first examinacyon of Anne Askewe . . . with the Elucydacyon of Johan Bale* ([Wesel: D. van der Straten], 1546) [*STC*, 848]; *The lattre examinacyon of Anne Askewe . . .* ([Wesel: D. van der Straten], 1547) [*STC*, 850]; both

against Arians, were among the works that reached presses overseas.[32] We must credit John Careless's copying, and perhaps Robert Harrington's smuggling, for helping Philpot's writings to reach publication.

John Foxe made use of Philpot's examinations in the second Latin edition of his history of the Church, which he began in exile.[33] As we have already seen, Foxe amassed not only printed works by the martyrs,[34] but the manuscripts channelled to him by Grindal. Once they returned to England after Mary's death, Foxe and his friends continued to collect manuscripts for new, expanded English editions, because many letters and tracts which had been concealed from authorities could be released for public consumption.

Until now Henry Bull has received almost no recognition as a friend of Foxe, nor as a collector and editor of manuscripts. For the first time, the Emmanuel collection, and Additional Manuscript 19400, enable us to identify Bull as the real editor of Coverdale's *Certain most godly letters*, and, as such, an important contributor to the *Acts and Monuments*. John Foxe and Henry Bull were fellows together at Magdalen College, Oxford, in the 1540s. By 1550 Bull had developed friendships with continental reformers. He was expelled from his fellowship soon after Mary's accession, as the result of a protest he and Thomas Bentham made—when they snatched the censer out of the hand of the officiating priest in the college choir during Mass, because they wanted to prevent the offering of incense to an idol.[35]

Mutual friends made valuable references to Bull in their letters to Foxe. William Wyntropp acknowledged Bull as among those who 'have not bowed theyr knees to baall', and this may indicate that Bull also fled

---

reprinted in Bale's *Select Works*. See esp. pp. 196, 243–4. Also, *The Letters of Stephen Gardiner*, ed. James Arthur Muller (Cambridge, 1933), pp. 277–8, 293.

[32] *The examinacion of the constaunt Martir of Christ, John Philpot*, printed with *An Apologie of Johan Philpot written for spitting vpon an Arrian* [Emden: E. van der Erve, 1556?] [*STC*, 19892]; *The Examinations and writings of John Philpot, B.C.L.*, ed. Robert Eden, *PS* (1842), pp. 293–318.

[33] John Foxe, *Rervm in Ecclesia Gestarum* . . . 2 vols (Basle: Nicolavm Brylingervm et Joannem Oporinum, [1559]–1563), pp. 543–631.

[34] Other printed works which eventually made their way into the *Acts and Monuments* include Askew's writings, and Lascelles's letter. *The first examinacyon of Anne Askewe*, and *The lattre examinacyon*: Foxe, 5, pp. 538–49; *Uvicklieffes Wicket . . . With the protestacion of Jhon Lassels late burned in Smythfelde*, overseen by M[iles] C[overdale (London: John Day? 1548?)] [*STC*, 25591]; Foxe, 5, pp. 551–2.

[35] A. B. Emden, ed., *A Biographical Register of the University of Oxford A.D. 1501 to 1540* (Oxford, 1974), pp. 82, 212–14; *DNB*, 3, p. 239, 7, pp. 581–90; *Original Letters Relative to the English Reformation*, tr. and ed. Hastings Robinson, *PS* (1846–7), 2, pp. 418–21; John Strype, *Ecclesiastical Memorials* (Oxford, 1822), 3 (1), p. 82.

abroad during Mary's reign.[36] In 1560, after Foxe's return, Bull was again in his company. Indeed, Bull frequently visited Foxe at John Day's house.[37]

Four books were issued under Bull's name and editorship, including the popular *Christian prayers and holy meditations*, which contained prayers by Bradford.[38] Bull's first book was an essay by John Hooper, with related correspondence, comprising four documents in total. It appeared in 1562, a year before the first English edition of the *Acts and Monuments*. The manuscripts survive together in the Emmanuel collection, and are those which Bull marked that he 'perused' for the printer. The title of the tract was supplied by Hooper himself: *An apologye . . . againste the vntrue and sclaunderous report* that he should encourage those who had treasonably cursed Queen Mary in January 1555. Three letters were appended: a letter informing Hooper of the arrests made in Bow Churchyard, his reply, and his letter to those who were taken to the Bread Street Counter. The letters were reprinted by Foxe in 1563.

Hooper ended his tract with an appeal to circulate his manuscript: 'I praye thee (gentle reader) as soone as thou readest this treatise, kepe it not close, but make it open and spare not.' His plea was one of the factors that motivated Bull to put the tract into print, probably soon after it was found. Grindal, now Bishop of London, may have had a hand in the discovery of the documents and approved of Bull's edition.

Bull viewed the discovery of Hooper's *Apologye* as a sign from heaven. In his preface Bull exclaimed: 'Beholde the prouidence of god, who hath now brought this worke to lighte, which otherwise by the negligence of some was like to pearishe.' Bull used the tract to castigate the papists, whose 'wicked dealinge' had defamed Hooper. Bull argued that in 'this pithye, learned, and worthy little pece of worke', Hooper had helped to advance God's glory 'in the innocente sufferinge of his saintes, thus torne and rente by tiranny, tormentes, lyes, and sclaunders for his names sake.'

Bull urged his readers to give any similar works in their possession to

---

[36] Wyntropp to Foxe, BL, MS Harley 416, fol. 106r; John Strype, *Annals of the Reformation* (Oxford, 1824), 1(1), pp. 309–10. Also, ECL, MS 260, fol. 82v, MS 262, fol. 175r. *Athenae Oxonienses* (London, 1691), 1, col. 146, says that Bull was an exile, but he is not mentioned in Garrett's *Marian Exiles*.

[37] In addition to Wyntropp, William Playfere was a friend to Foxe and Bull. BL, MS Harley 416, fols 106r, 113r–113v, 118r–118v. Also, MS Harley 417, fols 108r–108v (I owe many of these references to Mr Thomas Freeman).

[38] *Christian praiers and holy meditations*, comp. H[enry] B[ull] (London: Henry Middleton, 1570) [*STC*, 4029], including pp. 28–44, 171–201, 213–19, 324–32. It appeared in seven editions, 1568–90.

the world. He argued that any who knew of writings by the martyrs, but failed to reveal them, would 'defraude' the congregation of Protestant believers of 'worthye monuments'. Hooper and others had written many fruitful works 'in prison, in bands, in fetters, but fewe are come to lighte.' Would his readers, like 'ingratfull people', allow 'these Godly laboures, these painful trauales, thus to pearishe?' Hooper and his fellows had been eager to have their works disseminated, 'to wytnesse to the worlde that whiche they taughte and sealed with theyr bloud, and to profyt their bretheren.' In the name of Hooper and the other victims, and 'in behalfe of the churche of God', Bull pleaded 'for the rest of their workes', so that they could be 'set abroad in printe to the commodity of many.'[39]

Many documents were assembled as a result of Bull's search, with Foxe and Coverdale, for the monuments of the martyrs during Elizabeth's reign. In the foreword to the *Certain most godly letters*, Coverdale made yet another plea for manuscripts, 'which shall God willing, be published hereafter, if they in whose handes they remaine, wil bring them to light.'[40] The *Certain most godly letters* were printed by Day, and issued in 1564 under Coverdale's name, with his preface. However, close inspection of the manuscripts, and in particular of the emendations, shows that the alterations are in Bull's handwriting. As he was nearing eighty, Coverdale may have required assistance for the demanding task of preparing the many documents for publication. Although Bull's name does not appear in the printed work, we cannot doubt that he was the real editor. Indeed, a letter to Bull from Thomas Upcher confirms Bull's role as manuscript collector and editor. When Upcher heard that 'my beloved Mr Bulle' intended to print the letters of that 'sayncte of God John Careles', Upcher sent Bull as many of Careless's letters as he could find, and also a letter by Bradford.[41]

---

[39] Hooper's manuscripts: ECL, MS 261, fols 1r–14r. The texts are all in what is probably Hooper's hand, including the letter addressed to him, which he copied over. Bull, in addition to his notation that he had 'perused' the documents (fol. 14r), also jotted on the manuscript: 'The copie of Mr Hopers answer to the former letter' (fol. 12r), and a few other short comments. Fols 13r–14r are marked in a third, anonymous hand, with the signatures of the printed *Apologye*'s pagination. On fol. 14r we also find 'approbatur Edm. London'. The printed version: *An apologye made by the reuerende father and constante Martyr of Christe John Hooper late Bishop of Gloceter and Worceter againste the vntrue and sclaunderous report that he should be a maintainer and encorager of suche as cursed the Quenes highnes that then was, Quene Marye*, ed. Henry Bull (London: John Tisdale and Thomas Hacket, 1562) [*STC*, 13742], esp. sigs B3r, B4r–B4v, C1r, C5v, C6r–D3v. Foxe reprinted all three letters, but not Hooper's tract, in his 1563 edition, pp. 1020–2. Hooper's two letters only appeared in *Certain most godly letters*, pp. 120–3. The material was reprinted in Hooper's *Later Writings*, ed. Charles Nevinson, *PS* (1852), pp. 549–67 (apology), 612–17 (letters).
[40] *Certain most godly letters*, sig. A4r, margin.
[41] BL, Additional MS 19400, fol. 71v, written upside down on the verso of Careless's letter to

In addition, if we compare the *Certain most godly letters* with the first two English editions of the *Acts and Monuments*, of 1563 and 1570, we discover that Foxe and Bull shared the documents, discussed what they intended to print, and relied upon each other's printed versions of the prisoners' letters. Professor Collinson has advised us that in attempting to understand how Foxe composed his history of the Church, we must be concerned with 'the exercise of paring, shaping, and discarding' his sources.[42] The Emmanuel documents can expand our understanding of how Foxe and his friends went about their paring, shaping, and discarding, as they created their interpretations of the years of persecution of the mid 1550s.

On a document written by the martyr Thomas Whittle, Bull wrote: 'Thes ij letters of whittelles wold be reade advysedly & the superfluous thinges lefte out, as in other letters it shalbe necessitye to do the like.'[43] As he prepared the prisoners' letters for publication, Bull deleted lines, added his own material, and rewrote whole sections. Moreover, some of his changes made their way into the *Acts and Monuments*. Among the things which Bull deemed superfluous and omitted were the items of personal information with which some of the letters concluded. He did not print Careless's comments to Augustine Bernher about the movement and exile of their friends: 'Mr Levinge is gone over the sea with Rose and crowleye but his wyffe is still in london and hathe all youre thinges saffelye but she dwelled not there as shee dydd.'[44] Bull also rewrote the paragraph in Philpot's letter to Harrington which referred to Careless and the copying he did for him.[45]

It may be possible that by eliminating the prisoners' private remarks Bull wished to shield from publicity the survivors of persecution. Upcher did not want his name to be printed, but authorized Bull to use his initials.[46] But by doing so Bull concentrated the readers' attention upon

---

Margery Cooke. Upcher gave Bull at least ten letters, and wanted them returned to him. Bull marked each of them: 'Restore this to vpcher.' BL, Additional MS 19400, fols 66r, 71r, ECL, MS 260, fols 131r–132v, 213r, 236r, 238r, 240r, 241r–242v. See also ECL, MS 262, fols 127r–135r. Upcher was ordained by Grindal in 1560. Collinson, *Grindal*, pp. 114, 172; BL, MS Harley 416, fol. 106r. One Hopkins also shared a letter by Careless with Bull. ECL, MS 260, fol. 217r.

[42] Collinson, 'Veracity', p. 36.

[43] ECL, MS 260, fol. 33r, crossed out.

[44] ECL, MS 260, fols 215r–216v, these lines crossed out, and deleted in Foxe (1570), pp. 2109–10. Crowley and Rose are not mentioned in Garrett, *Marian Exiles*. For Thomas Lever, see pp. 219–21.

[45] ECL, MS 260, fols 65r–65v, *Certain most godly letters*, pp. 239–41.

[46] BL, Additional MS 19400, fol. 71v. Bull and Foxe printed Careless's two letters to Upcher as from 'T. V.' *Certain most godly letters*, pp. 580–5, Foxe (1570), pp. 2109, 2112; Foxe, 8,

those who had been martyred, and away from any who had been exiled, even though those who had gone abroad had also endured much.[47] Bull's editing enhanced the scriptural style of the letters, and their universal application, by removing personal or mundane details which otherwise might have distracted the readers. Bull also withheld original information that showed that the prisoners were involved in the free will controversy. That he heartily disliked the free will men is clear from a comment he wrote on one manuscript, and printed in a marginal gloss, that their spirit was 'arronyous, froward, & vnquiet'.[48]

Like Bull, Foxe also suppressed evidence that the prisoners, including Careless, were well acquainted with the free will men,[49] and he emphasized the heroism of the martyrs at the expense of recognizing others who had suffered. From marginal comments in the *Certain most godly letters*, we know that in 1564 Foxe was discussing with Bull (or Coverdale) what he planned to put in the next edition of the *Acts and Monuments*.[50]

To see how they shared the documents, and relied upon each other's versions of them, let us discuss briefly one set of letters, those of John Philpot, who was burnt in December 1555. In his 1563 edition Foxe printed only two of Philpot's letters, one to Careless, and one to women who were about to go into exile. Perhaps no more were available then, or, more probably, Foxe was working in too much haste to reproduce any others. Twelve letters appeared a year later in the *Certain most godly letters*, including two Foxe had already printed. Of the twelve, Foxe reprinted only six in the 1570 *Acts and Monuments*, plus seven new ones, most of which had been given to him by Philpot's correspondent Lady Elizabeth Vane. For at least one of the letters Foxe reprinted in his second edition he depended not upon the manuscript copy, but upon the version printed by Bull. In the manuscript of Philpot's letter to his sister we read the request at the end: 'And haue me commended to my brother Thomas, desiringe him to satisfie my sureties desier.' These lines were crossed out, and although Bull jotted in the margin, 'put in this', they do not appear in the

---

pp. 183–5, 189–91. For Foxe, Collinson, 'Veracity', pp. 33–4. Compare Martin, 'Foxe's account', p. 177.

[47] See my forthcoming article, 'Equivocation and recantation during the English Reformation: the "Subtle Shadows" of Dr Edward Crome', 44 (1993).

[48] ECL, MS 262, fol. 27r (written upside down). 'Arronyous' was printed as 'arrogant', perhaps because Bull's scrawl was hard to read here. *Certain most godly letters*, p. 245, margin.

[49] Collinson, 'Veracity', pp. 44–5; Martin, 'Foxe's account', pp. 171–8. My thanks to Dr Fines for sharing his information on Careless and the free will men.

[50] *Certain most godly letters*, sig. A4r, margin, fol. 46 margin; Wabuda, 'Crome'.

Certain most godly letters. In 1570 Foxe printed this letter almost exactly as Bull had, and also suppressed Thomas's name.[51]

Close inquiry also reveals why Foxe did not publish in his second edition some of the six letters that Bull deemed fit to print. Foxe did not reproduce Philpot's letter to Careless on the free will men, which Bull had already criticized in his gloss. Nor did Fox reprint Philpot's letter to Anne Hartipole, which urged her to rejoin the reformers after she had faltered and attended Catholic Mass, or, as Philpot expressed it, after she had been bitten by 'the old serpente our auncient enemy'.[52] Such material was excluded by Foxe, because it did not corroborate his fundamental position that the beleaguered Protestants had been not only heroic, but unified in opinion during the years of persecution.

*　　*　　*

Henry Bull spent the last years of his life as a physician in London, and he died in the first half of 1577. Presumably many of his papers stayed with his friends, though his will mentions that those books which were not to be put aside for the use of his sons or his wife, Margaret, were to be sold.[53] Among his last works was a translation of Luther's *Commentarie Vpon the Fiftene Psalmes.* Foxe recommended it for publication and wrote the preface. He rejoiced that Bull lived long enough to complete it, and that he received from his labour the greatest 'spirituall consolation' of his life.[54]

Three years after Bull's death, a person we know only by the initials 'A. F.' issued and wrote a preface to his last posthumous work, a collection of Hooper's expositions upon several psalms. Although we cannot be certain, it is possible that A. F. was actually Foxe's wife, Agnes, who was

---

[51] Foxe first mistook a letter by Careless to be one of Philpot's. Philpot's letters appear with one of Careless's in the section Foxe devoted to Careless. Foxe (1563), pp. 1449–50, 1535–8. The same letter of reply to Careless, and the same letters by Philpot, in the same order as printed by Foxe (1563), were printed in the *Certain most godly letters* in Philpot's section, pp. 216–50, esp. pp. 226–39. Also, Foxe (1570), pp. 2002–24, esp. p. 2006. The manuscript letter is a copy not in Philpot's own handwriting, ECL, MS 260, fols 162r–163v. For Lady Vane, Foxe, 7, p. 234.

[52] *Certain most godly letters*, pp. 247–9.

[53] Bull's will was made 13 March 1577 and proved on 4 July. London, PRO, PROB 11/59, fols 218v–220r.

[54] Martin Luther, *A Commentarie Vpon the Fiftene Psalmes, Called Psalmi Graduum*, tr. Henry Bull (London: Thomas Vautroullier, 1577) [*STC*, 16975], Foxe to the reader. Foxe's recommendation: BL, MS Harley 417, fol. 130v (I owe this reference to Mr Thomas Freeman).

literate and well acquainted with Bull. If Agnes Foxe was A. F., then this may mark the only instance that she ventured into print.[55]

Foxe must have kept many of the manuscripts Bull had used. Gilbert Burnet tells us that the founder of Emmanuel College, Sir Walter Mildmay, procured our documents from Foxe and put them in the library.[56] Even so, a few sheets which were part of the same group eventually came into the possession of Sir Henry Spelman, and thus to the British Library as Additional Manuscript 19400.

In a letter to the reader at the beginning of Hooper's *Certeine comfortable Expositions*, A. F. exulted, 'Manie are the monuments . . . and volumes of the faithfull left as legacies to the Church of Christ.' They were 'true riches' and 'the treasure of the Church', and A. F. also acknowledged Bull's gathering of documents.[57] Foxe, Coverdale, and Bull seized the opportunity to preserve the martyrs' writings, and did indeed rescue them from the 'pit of oblivion'. However, they did not reproduce them exactly as the Marian prisoners had written them. The image of the martyrs that they advanced was one of extreme heroism. Foxe and Bull did not have to invent that quality, because those who had suffered were, in a large measure, courageous men and women. But they were not so far removed from earthly matters as Bull and Foxe would have us believe, that they were no longer concerned with the mundane, including the fate of a friend's belongings.

In addition to providing us with the original manuscripts of the martyrs, the Emmanuel collection allows us to place Foxe among those friends and collaborators who also wished to preserve the monuments of the martyrs as a testament to the tenacity and righteousness of the Protestant Church.

Shelton, Connecticut

---

[55] Bull gathered together the papers for the last three of the four psalms printed. John Hooper, *Certeine comfortable Expositions . . . vpon the XXIII. LXII, LXXIII. and LXXVII. Psalmes*. ed. Henry Bull and A. F. (London: H. Middleton, 1580) [*STC*, 13743], preface; reprinted in Hooper, *Later writings*, pp. 177–373. I am grateful to Professor David Loades for suggesting that 'A. F.' could have been Agnes Foxe. See BL, MS Harley 416, fols 106r–118v; *DNB*, 20, pp. 142–7.

[56] Gilbert Burnet, *The History of the Reformation of the Church of England*, ed. Nicholas Pocock (Oxford, 1865), 2, p. 457. My thanks are due to Mr Thomas Freeman for this reference.

[57] Hooper, *Certeine comfortable Expositions*, preface.

THE SCOTTISH REFORMATION AND THE
THEATRE OF MARTYRDOM*

by JANE E. A. DAWSON

POOR John Knox felt a distinct sense of inferiority when he sat down to write the first book of his *History of the Reformation in Scotland*.[1] Unlike his English friend John Foxe, he could not draw upon the stories of hundreds of martyrs and fit them into the complete history of the persecuted Church from its beginning until the present day. To make matters worse, Foxe would duplicate Knox's labours by incorporating the stories of most of the Scottish martyrs into his 1570 edition of the *Acts and Monuments*.[2] In his ambition to be both the historian and the martyrologist of the Scottish Reformation, Knox thought he faced an immediate and apparently overwhelming problem: that of a distinct shortage of martyrs. Yet he was quickly reassured once he began assembling the details of those who had vigorously opposed the 'manifest abuses, superstition and idolatry', which characterized the Catholic Church in Scotland before the Reformation. Martyrs soon began to appear before his eyes, and Knox consoled himself, 'Albeit there be no great number, yet are they more than the Collector would have looked for at the beginning.'[3]

Although Knox had no equivalent of the fires of Smithfield to illuminate his tale, he found sufficient evidence to fill book i of his *History*. It provided a fitting introduction to the gripping story he was so anxious to relate of the years 1558 to 1561, when he himself had played a starring role in the great contemporary struggle between Christ and Antichrist. By its location at the very beginning of his *History*, Knox ensured that, for Scotland, the theatre of martyrdom became the prologue for the great Reformation drama itself. With obvious allowances for the different denominational perspectives, that is how it has been viewed ever since.

If we assume, however, that the triumph of Protestantism was not as inevitable as it appeared to John Knox, then it is worth looking at the

* I am most grateful to Dr John Durkan for his helpful comments upon an earlier draft of this article.

[1] W. C. Dickinson, ed., *John Knox's History of the Reformation in Scotland*, 2 vols (Edinburgh, 1949) [hereafter Knox, *Hist.*].
[2] Scottish material in vols 4 and 5 of Foxe. I am grateful to Thomas Freeman for this information.
[3] Knox, *Hist.*, 1, p. 6.

theatre of martyrdom in Scotland for its own sake.[4] The point which had struck Knox so forcibly was how few martyrs Scotland could boast. There were only about twenty between 1528 and 1558, fewer than in contemporary England, France, the Netherlands, or the Holy Roman Empire.[5] The reason for the relatively small number was the Catholic Church of Scotland's policy of minimal execution. It wanted to prevent the spread of heresy by executing certain individuals, but it did not, and probably could not, mount a sustained persecution of all those who might hold heretical beliefs. For a short period the ecclesiastical authorities had the full backing of the King, James V, for a more comprehensive campaign. This led to an increase in executions between 1533 and 1539, peaking in 1539, when eight heretics were put to death. After James V's own death, in 1542, both the unstable political conditions caused by the minority of Mary, Queen of Scots, and the divisions within the Church, made it impossible to follow a consistent policy of repression. Although the religious authorities remained anxious to execute some individuals, they were equally willing

---

[4] D. Nicholls, 'The theatre of martyrdom in the French Reformation', *PaP*, 121 (1988), pp. 49–73. The English evidence is discussed in S. Byman, 'Ritualistic acts and compulsive behavior: the pattern of Tudor martyrdom', *AHR*, 83 (1978), pp. 625–43.

[5] The small overall population of Scotland made a simple comparison of numbers of martyrs throughout Europe a very rough guide indeed. The near complete loss of Scottish episcopal records undoubtedly reduced the total of martyrs, but the names of the known Scottish martyrs and their dates and places of execution were as follows:

1528	Patrick Hamilton (St Andrews)
c. 1533	Henry Forrest (St Andrews)
1534	Norman Gourlay (Greenside, Edinburgh)
	David Stratoun (ditto)
c. 1538	Andrew Alexanderson(?)
1539	William Keillour (Castle Hill, Edinburgh)
	John Beveridge (ditto)
	Duncan Simpson (dito)
	Robert Forster (ditto)
	Thomas Forret (ditto)
1539	Jerome Russell (Glasgow)
	N. Kennedy (ditto)
1539	Anonymous man (Cupar)
1544	James Hunter (Perth)
	James Ronaldson (ditto)
	Helen Stirk (ditto)
	Robert Lamb (ditto)
	William Anderson (ditto)
1546	George Wishart (St Andrews)
1550	Adam Wallace (Castle Hill, Edinburgh)
1558	Walter Miln (St Andrews)

to see most of those who had been suspected or convicted of heresy recant quietly or leave the country instead of facing death.[6]

The policy of minimal execution meant that the theatre of death in Scotland was performed on a national stage. The heresy trials became a form of entertainment and were turned into major events in the court calendar. James V liked to attend the trials, and some were conveniently staged in his palace at Holyrood, in Edinburgh. The King was also prepared to participate in the drama himself. In 1534 he came to the abbey church in Holyrood dressed all in red. At the end of the disputation over the articles, he laughed at some of the replies of one of the defendants, Katherine Hamilton, and called her over to him. The King, who was a kinsman of Katherine, was able to persuade her to make enough of a recantation to save her from the fire. He had previously saved her brother, James, who had also been summoned for heresy, by ordering him to leave the country. These two Hamiltons avoided the fate of their brother Patrick, who, six years earlier, had been the first Protestant executed in Scotland. The King also tried to talk Norman Gourlay and David Stratoun, two more of the accused, into a recantation, but he failed, and they were duly burned.[7]

Five years later, in 1539, at the peak of the trials, the King was accompanied by so many court dignitaries that a grandstand had to be constructed in Holyrood to accommodate them.[8] The national dimension of the trials was enhanced by the efforts made to assemble nobles and bishops from all over the country to lend their presence and authority to those occasions. The serried ranks of notables were meant to overawe the defendant. The scaffolding stage, erected against the chancel wall in the Edinburgh Blackfriars church in 1550, provided seats for the secular and ecclesiastical lords, away from the press of common people in the body of the church. Such seating arrangements were also intended to intimidate those on trial. In this instance, it failed to upset the accused, Adam Wallace, from Kyle, who was quite prepared to bandy words with the Earl of Huntly over the competence of his judges.[9]

St Andrews, the ecclesiastical capital of Scotland, was the second

<hr/>

[6] A useful history of early Protestants (to 1546) and their respective fates is provided in M. Sanderson, *Cardinal of Scotland* (Edinburgh, 1986), app. 3, pp. 270–84 [hereafter Sanderson]. Their beliefs are discussed in J. Kirk, 'The religion of early Scottish Protestants', *SCH.S*, 8 (1991), pp. 361–411 [hereafter Kirk].

[7] Knox, *Hist.*, 1, pp. 24–5; Foxe, 4, pp. 579–80.

[8] Knox, *Hist.*, 1, p. 26, n. 3; R. K. Hannay, ed., *Rentale Sancti Andree*, Scottish History Society, ser. 2, 4 (Edinburgh, 1913), pp. 64, 93.

[9] Knox, *Hist.*, 1, pp. 114–16; Foxe, 5, pp. 636–41.

principal location, alongside Edinburgh, for the staging of heresy trials and executions. The metropolitan cathedral provided a suitably awe-inspiring setting for the major disputations over heretical doctrines which were part of the trials of Patrick Hamilton, George Wishart, and Walter Miln. The largest roofed space in Scotland, with its excellent acoustics, gave ample room for big audiences to come to hear the proceedings.[10] By contrast, the people in Glasgow were only provided with one spectacle when, in 1539, Jerome Russell and N. Kennedy were tried and executed.[11]

The central location of the trial and the importance of making a national example of a prominent heretic had to be balanced against the need to impress upon his local community the serious consequences of espousing heresy. In an attempt to incorporate this local dimension, the precise execution site was sometimes specially chosen so that the burning could be seen from afar by the particular local community. Henry Forrest was tried and executed in St Andrews, but his fire was placed at the north church stile, near the cathedral, so that it might be visible across the Tay estuary by the people of Forfar.[12] Only once did the overwhelming local significance of the event dictate the place of trial and execution. As part of a major campaign against heresy in 1544 within Perth, four men and a woman were executed inside the burgh. The theatrical element of burning out heresy was also abandoned as the condemned men were hanged like common criminals and the woman drowned in the River Tay, even though she carried a babe-in-arms.[13]

The general policy of putting on a grand, national performance for the heresy trials and executions suited the defendants as much as their accusers. The heretical leaders themselves were equally willing to exploit the theatre of death and, if they could, transform it into a theatre of martyrdom. They positively welcomed the trials as a battle of wits and a platform to express their views. They had no intention of recanting, for they viewed the whole process as a test of, and witness to, their faith. As death was an opportunity for glorious martyrdom, they did not want to change the ending of the play.

In this sense, the ecclesiastical authorities and the martyrs co-operated

[10] D. McRoberts, ed., *The Medieval Church of St Andrews* (Glasgow, 1976), pp. 108–9.
[11] Knox, *Hist.*, 1, pp. 27–8.
[12] Ibid., pp. 21–2; Foxe, 4, pp. 578–9. To see the fire, the people of Forfar would have had to go to the coast or climb the Sidlaw Hills.
[13] Knox, *Hist.*, 1, p. 55; Foxe, 5, pp. 623–5. All the Perth victims were craftspeople and their executions were possibly as much a punishment for a previous insurrection as for heresy: see M. Verschuur, 'Merchants and craftsmen in sixteenth-century Perth', in M. Lynch, ed., *The Early Modern Town in Scotland* (London, 1987), p. 42.

to ensure that the whole drama was performed, culminating in a public execution. There was a grey area before roles had been fixed when this tacit collusion did not operate. It was therefore acceptable in 1534 for George Gilbert, a chaplain in Brechin, to escape by being rescued by his Angus supporters from episcopal custody, because the play had not really started.[14] Once that grand performance had begun, both sides wanted the drama carried through to the bitter end. This meant that the elaborate precautions taken in 1546 at the execution of George Wishart, the most important Protestant leader to be burned, were probably unnecessary. Hearing strong rumours of a rescue attempt, Cardinal David Beaton ordered a hundred extra troops to guard the prisoner, and even placed primed cannons on the castle walls to cover the stake throughout the execution. Beaton had badly miscalculated the nature of the threat. He was the one in need of protection, but not until the execution was completed. A few months later, at the end of May 1546, he was murdered, allegedly in revenge for Wishart's death.[15]

If the main actors were all agreed that once it started, the show must go on, they were diametrically opposed over the content of the script and the characterization of the players. During the trial, the two sides used the weapons of language and argument to win the battle of words and ideas. The execution drama concentrated more upon non-verbal communication, when gestures, demeanour, and symbolic action conveyed the meaning of what was being done. In both parts of the production the two sides strove to present their own version of the proceedings and to win the battle of characterization. The religious authorities wanted to demonstrate that they were condemning a heretic, whilst the accused portrayed himself as a persecuted martyr.

The policy of example pursued by the Scottish Church increased the emphasis upon the central character in the trial by placing him under an even brighter spotlight than normal. This brought with it considerable dangers for the ecclesiastical authorities in the fight over characterization. The heretics were usually articulate, determined people, who were capable of stealing the show. By a virtuoso solo performance, they could change the theatre of death into the theatre of martyrdom. To combat this threat, the authorities employed two different forms of expertise. At the trials, they used sharp-witted lawyers like John Spens to act as prosecutors and retain the intellectual initiative. Despite the occasional histrionic

[14] Kirk, p. 381.
[15] Foxe, 5, pp. 627, 634–5. For Beaton's murder, Knox, *Hist.*, 1, pp. 76–8; Sanderson, pp. 214–30.

performance from an accuser such as John Lauder in Wishart's trial, who allegedly frothed at the mouth and spat in the face of the defendant,[16] the judicial dramas were relatively well organized. The same level of expertise was not forthcoming in the stage management of the executions. When the message depended upon the visual impact of symbolic action rather than words, precise, careful management was essential. All the lowly members of the cast had to perform their parts correctly, and the whole production must proceed without a hitch. Simple technical incompetence could ruin the whole effect.

The death of Patrick Hamilton proved how a rushed and bungled job could lead to disaster. The authorities had handled the lively trial well, but made the mistake of proceeding straightaway to the execution after dinner on the same day as the condemnation. The speed of the preparations lulled some observers into thinking that Hamilton was simply being taken to see the stake as a ploy to make him recant. The fire was set outside St Salvator's College, in St Andrews, where Hamilton had taught. The symbolic significance was considerable, but it was not a very practical placement, particularly with an east wind blowing straight off the sea. The fire was both difficult to start and to keep burning. The gunpowder was so badly placed that it scorched Hamilton's left hand, but failed to get the blaze going. Men were sent to the Castle to fetch more powder and wood, and Myreton, a local baker, brought armfuls of straw in a vain attempt to speed up the execution.[17] The strong wind created further problems by blowing the fire over Friar Alexander Campbell, knocking him to the ground and burning the front of his cowl. Knox, who recounted this incident in his *History*, added that these burns drove the friar mad and he later died in a frenzy.[18] In a less colourful account, John Foxe cited eye-witnesses who recalled that at the stake Patrick Hamilton had prophesied that his accuser, Friar Campbell, would appear before God in judgement by a particular day the following month. The Prior of the St Andrews Dominicans duly died by the stated time, and the Protestants were able to interpret this as a divine sign confirming the truth of Hamilton's doctrine.[19]

In the midst of the incompetence and disarray of his executioners,

---

[16] Knox, *Hist.*, 2, p. 234; Foxe, 5, pp. 628–9. These Protestant accounts obviously gave very biased descriptions of the trials and especially of Lauder's alleged behaviour.

[17] A. Mackay, ed., *R. Lindsay of Pitscottie Historie and Chronicles of Scotland*, 2 vols, *Scottish Text Society* (1899–1911), 1, p. 308 [hereafter Pitscottie].

[18] Knox, *Hist.*, 1, p. 14.

[19] Foxe, 4, p. 563.

Patrick Hamilton was able to play his own part as protomartyr of the Scottish Reformation to perfection. He seized the initiative and, using the occasion of giving his outer garments to his servant, made a speech explaining the purpose of his death to everyone present. His calm control during the execution left the bystanders with the impression that they had witnessed a martyrdom and not the death of a heretic.[20]

An international audience interpreted Hamilton's execution in a different way. The University of Louvain congratulated the Archbishop of St Andrews upon his firm stance against Lutheran heresy and his willingness to make an example of Hamilton.[21] But Archbishop James Beaton would have done better to pay heed to his own servant's advice. Having witnessed the execution himself, John Lindsay told his master: 'My Lord, if ye burn any more, except ye follow my counsel, ye will utterly destroy yourselves. If ye will burn them, let them be burnt in low cellars; for the reek of Master Patrick Hamilton has infected as many as it blew upon.'[22] The last part of Lindsay's comment has become so familiar a quotation that the preceding advice has been overlooked. Nearly thirty years later Simon Renard, the imperial ambassador in England, wrote in very similar terms to Philip II after he had witnessed the death of John Rogers, the protomartyr of the Marian persecution.[23] Neither man objected to executing heretics, but they wanted to dispense with the theatrical drama of a public burning. By suggesting that heretics should be killed in deep cellars, Lindsay was also reminding Archbishop James Beaton of a peculiarly Scottish problem. The Scots did not necessarily oppose the death penalty for heresy, but they did not understand the ceremonies of the execution. A Scottish audience was simply not familiar with the theatre of death in any form.

The absence of formalized and ritualized executions by the Scottish State created a major problem for the Church when it wanted to stage a dignified burning for heresy. Although treason was a capital crime in Scotland, few actually paid that penalty, and even when there were executions they lacked the overt didactic messages conveyed by the full theatre of death staged in other European capitals.[24] The Stewart monarchy had not yet turned executions for treason into a major State

---

[20] Knox, *Hist.*, 1, pp. 13–14, 15, 23; Kirk, pp. 371–2.
[21] Foxe, 4, pp. 561–2.
[22] Knox, *Hist.*, 1, p. 18.
[23] Simon Renard to Philip II, 5 Feb. 1555, R. Tyler et al., eds, *Calendar of State Papers, Spanish* (London, 1862–1954), 13, p. 138.
[24] P. Spierenburg, *The Spectacle of Suffering* (Cambridge, 1984).

performance asserting the power and majesty of royalty. Local Scottish courts frequently utilized the death penalty, and many lesser crimes incurred such a sentence. But they employed little ceremonial in either their trials or executions. Sentence was usually followed swiftly by execution, carried out on the local gallows hill, close to the meeting-place of the court. Unlike the elaborate and professional performances which were staged in other parts of Europe, the theatre of death in Scotland was an amateur affair. Scottish society certainly ritualized violence, but within the context of the blood-feud. Victims were sometimes tortured or mutilated as an act of vengeance, but this was not done before a public audience. The public rituals of the blood-feud were those of peace-making and settlement. In Scottish justice, solemn display was kept for reconciliation, not for execution.[25]

This left the Scottish Church without the wider context of the theatre of death to educate its audience for the execution of heretics. With no native tradition of heresy, there had been few precedents of heretics being publicly burned. The people of Scotland had not been taught what to expect from the whole process of trial and execution. It is not surprising that the message the audience received was not always the same as the one which the religious authorities sought to convey.

Indeed, the established traditions of the Scottish system of private justice could easily be exploited by the martyrs for their own advantage. They could destroy the Church's presentation of an impersonal condemnation of heretical doctrine by emphasizing the personal element. Feuds between kin-groups, and inter-personal disputes, were such a common feature of Scottish life in this period that it was simple to present heresy proceedings in those terms. By personalizing the drama of the trial and execution, the accused changed his image in the eyes of the audience. This was achieved in two very different ways by Sandie Furrour and George Wishart.

While he was in prison on heresy charges, Sandie Furrour's wife had had an affair with their local parish priest. At his trial, Furrour (Furbour or Turnour) used his personal grievance against the priest to suggest that the clerical estate had fabricated the heresy charge to silence his legitimate criticisms of clerical morality and behaviour. He proceeded to turn the trial into a farce. He merrily leapt up on to the platform and gambolled about demanding in a loud voice where the rest of the players were. After abusing the prosecutor throughout the trial, he refused to recant and burn his bill of heretical articles. He decided to 'drown' it instead by chewing up

[25] K. Brown, *Bloodfeud in Scotland 1573–1625* (Edinburgh, 1986).

the parchment and spitting it out into the face of his accuser. The use of slapstick comedy to disrupt normal procedures would have been readily understood by his audience. Each year they experienced the ceremonies of the Boy Bishop and the Abbot of Misrule, when the techniques of inversion were used to belittle the clergy and in so doing defuse resentments against them. Furrour, with his ridicule and his personal plight as a cuckold, exploited the anti-clerical resentments of his audience. His tactics were so successful that the court let him go.[26]

A more common method of personalizing the heresy proceedings was that employed by George Wishart, who turned his trial into a personal duel with Cardinal David Beaton. The subsequent murder of the Cardinal fixed this image even more firmly in people's minds. At his execution, Wishart was reported to have foretold Beaton's death. The murderers explicitly justified their action as revenge for Wishart's execution at Beaton's hands.[27] This peculiar mixture of intellectual duel, martyrdom, and blood-feud was enough to demolish the image of calm and impersonal justice in dealing with heresy which the ecclesiastical authorities had tried to present.

As well as losing its impersonal façade, the Church's presentation of the threatre of death was undermined by the use of the trials as a means of internal discipline. The execution of heretical leaders, many of whom were in holy orders, warned all Scots not to follow a similar path, but it provided a specific reminder to those clerics who were pressing hard for church reforms. Throughout this period, the Scottish Church was divided over the nature and extent of the reforms which it needed to undertake and its attitude towards Protestant heresy. Those clerics who favoured coercion used the trials and executions as a test of the loyalty of the advocates of far-reaching reform. Any suggestion of leniency towards heretics was treated with deep suspicion, as the Archbishop of Glasgow discovered in 1539, when he wanted to spare Kennedy and Russell rather than send them to the stake. The three ecclesiastical advisers sent from St Andrews to assist in the trial vehemently opposed the move. They played upon the long-standing rivalry between the two archdioceses to suggest that the Archbishop of Glasgow could not be seen to be less fervent in the pursuit of heresy than his counterpart in St Andrews. They added, for good measure, some veiled threats about Cardinal Beaton's likely reaction to any hint of softness.[28]

[26] Knox, *Hist.*, 1, pp. 18–19.
[27] Ibid., pp. 74, 77–8; Pitscottie, 2, p. 81.
[28] Knox, *Hist.*, 1, pp. 27–8.

The use of a heresy trial to force a member of the ecclesiastical hierarchy to define his position can be seen at Wishart's trial in 1546. Both Cardinal David Beaton and George Wishart seemed to have tried to make Dr John Winram, subprior of St Andrews and an active reformer, declare himself one way or another. Beaton chose Winram to preach the sermon at Wishart's trial. He took as his text Matthew 13, giving what in the circumstances was a most ambiguous interpretation of the parable of the wheat and the tares, and saying that heresy should be judged by the touchstone of Scripture.[29] After his condemnation, Wishart refused to talk to anyone but Winram. Despite this double pressure, Winram managed to keep his balance on his personal tightrope. But to do so he was forced to side with the ecclesiastical authorities in their persecution of heresy in this and all the later trials held in St Andrews. Winram only openly espoused the Protestant cause in 1559.

The divisions within the Scottish Church weakened the unity which was so important to the successful production of the theatre of death. If a heretic were to be portrayed as an outcast, rejected by all, it was essential that the Church was united and in harmony with the rest of society. The absence of a single, agreed ecclesiastical position ensured that the policy of repression itself remained a matter of dispute, and it was inevitably caught up in the wider political battles within the Scottish Church and Government which raged after James V's death in 1542. In these circumstances, it was impossible for the persecution of heresy to be pursued with any consistency. The policy of minimal execution increased the danger that the selection process would appear arbitrary and unjust. Some clerics who held unorthodox views did not seem to be troubled by the ecclesiastical authorities or were encouraged to retire into the safety of exile, whilst others, such as the vicar of Dollar, Thomas Forret, were designated heresiarchs and singled out for immediate death.[30] At the royal court Sir David Lindsay could, with impunity, write plays highly critical of the ecclesiastical hierarchy, but William Keillour, a Dominican friar, was executed in 1539 after his play on Christ's Passion depicted the bishops and regular clergy as Pharisees, blinding the people to the truth.[31]

The inequality and inconsistent nature of the policy of selective persecution brought it into disrepute. The last execution before the Reformation provided the most notorious example of its misuse and demonstrated that by 1558 the entire policy was unworkable. The

[29] Knox, *Hist.*, 2, pp. 233–4; Foxe, 5, pp. 627–8.
[30] Foxe, 5, p. 623; Sanderson, app. 3.
[31] Knox, *Hist.*, 1, p. 26; Kirk, p. 386.

Scottish Church had been deeply embarrassed by the preaching-tour which John Knox had made in the winter of 1555 to 1556. They had proved unable, or unwilling, to make a serious attempt to arrest him, but immediately after Knox left the country the authorities summoned him on heresy charges and carried through a shadow trial. They then had the dubious satisfaction of burning Knox's effigy at the Market Cross in Edinburgh.[32] During the next two years Archbishop John Hamilton of St Andrews struggled to contain the growing problem of heresy by private persuasion and his own programme of reform. But after the First Band had been signed by the Protestant Lords in December 1557, and the open preaching which followed, the primate needed more than words. He sought a dramatic gesture to demonstrate that he could be firm over heresy. He decided to reactivate the policy of execution, and chose Walter Miln as his victim.

Miln was a priest who had been converted to Protestantism in Germany and on his return to Scotland had married. In April 1558 two of Hamilton's agents came to Dysart, on the south Fife coast, to find evidence of Miln's heresy. According to Pitscottie, they caught Miln in a poor woman's house, warming himself by the fire and teaching the Ten Commandments.[33] They arrested Miln and took him for trial in St Andrews. Miln was over eighty years old, and so weak that he had to be helped into the pulpit in St Andrews Cathedral to stand trial. Thanks to the good acoustics and his own determination to give a vigorous defence of his opinions, Miln's voice was heard by all who had packed into the cathedral.[34] Whether it was the persuasiveness of his views or sympathy for an infirm old man who was being manipulated by the primate, the people of St Andrews refused to co-operate in the execution. Neither the Provost of the burgh nor the Archbishop's Chamberlain would act as temporal judges. Sir Patrick Learmonth, the Provost, promptly left town to avoid any association with the affair at all. To make matters worse, the Archbishop's servants suddenly found that there was no tar or rope or other necessaries for the burning to be had in the whole burgh. In desperation they cut the guy-ropes from the Archbishop's tented pavilion to provide cord to tie Miln to the stake. Despite the posse of armed men guarding the prisoner, a crowed of angry youths forced the executioners to permit Miln

[32] Knox, *Hist.*, 1, pp. 122 n. 2, 124, 181. Knox appealed against his sentence in his tract the 'Appellation', ed. D. Laing, *The Works of John Knox*, 6 vols (Edinburgh, 1846–64), 4, pp. 465–520.
[33] Pitscottie, 2, p. 130.
[34] Foxe, 5, p. 645.

to speak before the fire was kindled.[35] The disruption did not end with Miln's death. A cairn of stones kept appearing on the execution spot overnight, although the ecclesiastical authorities dismantled it each morning and threatened with excommunication anyone caught placing a stone.[36] All the symbolism of an orderly trial and execution demonstrating the perils of heresy had been subverted by the hostile reaction of the St Andrews audience. It was their interpretation of the drama that Miln had died a martyr which prevailed. That view was carried to its own ritual conclusion a year later when St Andrews had its 'Day of Reformation'. Having removed the statues from all the churches in the city, they were brought to the exact spot of Miln's execution and ceremonially burned as idols.[37] The audience had successfully hijacked the theatre of death at a heretic's execution and through their own actions turned it into the theatre of martyrdom.

When faced with the threat of Protestant heresy, the Scottish Church had adopted the risky policy of minimal executions to serve as national examples. This could work only if the Church and the whole community were united in their opposition to heretical doctrines and determined to cleanse society by fire from the contagion of heresy. It was essential that the ritual of the theatre of death was both clearly understood and seen to be completely justified. Unfortunately, the Scottish Church failed to convince its audience on either count. Their own divisions, technical incompetence, and the lack of adequate explanation of their aims undermined the Church's production of the theatre of death. The failure of the ecclesiastical authorities provided a golden opportunity for the accused to attempt to steal the show. They were able to present their own script and characterization and to claim that they were martyrs, not heretics. For most of the productions of the theatre of death, the Scottish audiences were faced with two rival characterizations. However, by 1558, the audience had ceased to be the passive recipient of the different messages of the drama and had decided to take control of the production. The theatre of death was only fully transformed into the theatre of martyrdom of the Scottish Reformation when the audience itself became an active participant.

New College, University of Edinburgh

[35] Ibid., p. 646.
[36] Knox, Hist., 1, p. 153.
[37] Foxe, 5, p. 647; for the 'Day of Reformation', see J. Dawson, '"The face of Ane Perfyt Reformed Kirk": St Andrews and the early Scottish Reformation', SCH.S, 8 (1991), pp. 415–18.

AN ELIZABETHAN MARTYROLOGIST AND HIS MARTYR: JOHN MUSH AND MARGARET CLITHEROW

by CLAIRE CROSS

O N 25 March 1586 for refusing to plead on a charge of harbouring Catholic priests Margaret Clitherow was pressed to death in York.

She was in dying one quarter of an hour, a sharp stone as much as a man's fist put under her back; upon her was laid to the quantity of seven or eight hundreth weight, at the least, which, breaking her ribs, caused them to burst forth of the skin. Thus most victoriously this gracious martyr overcame all her enemies, passing [from] this mortal life with marvellous triumph into the peaceable city of God, there to receive a worthy crown of endless immortality and joy.[1]

This quotation forms the climax of *A True Report of the Life and Martyrdom of Mrs Margaret Clitherow*, written by the seminary priest John Mush within three months of her death. Mush produced his work with a quite explicit didactic purpose.

It hath been a laudable custom in all ages from the beginning of Christ his church [he wrote on the first page] to publish and truly set forth the singular virtues of such her children as either in their lives by rare godliness did shine above the rest, or by their patient deaths most stoutly overcame all barbarous cruelty, and both by their lives and deaths glorified God, encouraged to like victory their faithful brethren, and with invincible fortitude confounded the persecuting tyrants . . .

This communication will explore the ways in which intentionally or unintentionally the martyrologist created his martyr.[2]

In a literal sense the question can be answered very simply. Without the

---

[1] John Mush, 'A True Report of the Life and Martyrdom of Mrs. Margaret Clitherow', late sixteenth-century manuscript in York Minster Library, T. D. 1 [hereafter YML, T.D. 1], fol. 67r.; printed in J. Morris, ed., *The Troubles of Our Catholic Forefathers related by themselves*, ser. 3 (London, 1877), p. 432. Apart from book-titles, spelling has been modernized throughout.
[2] YML T.D. 1, fol. 1r, damaged, missing part supplied from York Bar Convent, V 69, p. 1; Morris, *Troubles*, p. 360.

True Report only the barest facts of Margaret Clitherow's life would still be current. She was born about 1553, the daughter of Thomas Middleton, a York wax chandler and one-time sheriff of the city, and his second wife, Jane Turner, herself the child of a substantial York inn holder. In July 1571, when she would have been about eighteen years old, the register of St Martin's, Coney Street, recorded the marriage of Margaret Middleton to a wealthy York butcher, John Clitherow, a widower some years her senior. She, but not her husband, who always conformed, first emerged in the civic records in June 1576 for refusing to attend her parish church, now Holy Trinity, King's Court. On account of her advanced pregnancy she was excused from appearing before the Lord Mayor and Alderman to give her reasons for failing to go to church, but there can be little doubt that she shared the opinions of other women in her parish who believed their presence at Protestant services would damn their souls, 'because there is neither altar, sacrifice or true priest.' After the birth of her child she was imprisoned for recusancy in York Castle in 1577, not being released for almost a year. In 1578 the High Commission fined her husband 30s. for her refusal to go to church, and in April 1579 proceeded to order him to pay 12d. weekly for every one of her absences from Holy Trinity, King's Court. In October 1580 the High Commission again required her attendance, and, since she 'denied to take an oath to reform herself in religion now publicly received', committed her for six months a close prisoner to the Castle, from which she was released the next April because of the approaching birth of another child. Twice convicted of recusancy at the Quarter Sessions, she was again sent to the Castle in March 1583, but set free on bond in May 1584. She then remained at liberty until her final arrest and sentence in March 1586. Because of the loss of both the Assize records and the records of the Council in the North, no official account survives of her trial, condemnation, and execution.[3]

Consequently, but for John Mush's *True Report*, nothing apart from this skeletal outline would now be known of Margaret Clitherow's life, and virtually nothing at all about the manner of her death. Around 30,000 words in length, Mush's martyrology is very traditional in form. After an introduction in which he mentioned that 'they have martyred of late

---

[3] York City Archives Housebook, 26 fols, 68v, 97v–98v; Quarter Sessions Minute Book, F 3, fols 667r, 739r; E 22, fol. 192r; Borthwick Institute, York, PRY/MCS 1, fol. 57r; H C AB, 9 fols, 94v, 160r, 165r, 183r, 212v; H C AB 10, fols 51v, 101r; H C bonds 101; M. Claridge [K. Longley], *Margaret Clitherow* (London, 1966), p. 188; K. Longley, *St Margaret Clitherow* (Wheathampstead, 1986), pp. 1–2.

divers good Catholic priests and lay persons, among whom suffered the last day at York [26 November 1585] one priest and one layman [Hugh Taylor and Marmaduke Bowes] and a little after one woman' (which places the writing of the *True Report* between 25 March and June 1586, when a further two priests died at the Knavesmire), Mush devoted the next sixteen short chapters not to any sort of chronological account of her life, but rather to her spiritual development which laid the foundation for her martyrdom. In 'the virtuous education of Mrs Margaret Clitherow' he described her conversion two or three years after her marriage,

> when she heard first of the Catholic faith and church, for before she frequented the heretical service, not suspecting there had been any other true way to serve God . . . Even at the first, fully resolving rather to forsake husband, life, and all, than to return again to her damnable estate . . .'

He followed this with short disquisitions upon 'her humility, the foundation of all her virtues', 'her perfect charity and love of God', 'her obedience to her ghostly father', 'her charity to her neighbours', 'her zeal and fervour in the catholic religion', 'her alacrity and joy in mind and body', before turning to reports 'of her devotion and spiritual exercise', 'of her abstinence', and 'of her pilgrimage'. Next he recounted 'her marvellous desire to suffer for Christ and his truth', 'her contempt of the world, and all pleasures thereof', 'her discretion and prudence in all her businesses', 'the love she had amongst her neighbours', 'the persecutions she suffered among the good' (that is, amongst her fellow Catholics, few of whom were so fervent or as heedless of the implications of their actions as she), and 'her diligence in observing other folk's virtues'.[4]

Then, but only then, Mush reached Margaret Clitherow's 'apprehension', 'arraignment', and 'martyrdom'. At this point he abandoned his analysis of her spiritual virtues to concentrate upon a narrative, the details of which he could only have obtained at second hand. He related how officers from the Council in the North searched Margaret Clitherow's house in the Shambles. They discovered Mass vessels and vestments, and frightened one of the young boys into confessing that Mass had indeed been said in the house. 'A rumour was spread in the town, that the boy had accused her for harbouring and maintaining divers priests, but especially two by name, that was Mr Francis Ingleby of Rheims, and Mr John Mush

---

[4] YML T.D. 1, fols 5r, 8r–v, 11v, 16r, 20r, 24r, 25v, 27r, 30v, 31v, 34v, 36v, 40r, 41v, 45r; Morris, *Troubles*, pp. 358, 368–9, 395.

of Rome.' Imprisoned first in the Castle on 14 March 1586, Margaret
Clitherow subsequently appeared before two assize judges and several of
the Council in the North in the Guildhall. Having indicted her under the
law of 1585, which prohibited the harbouring of Jesuit and seminary
priests, Judge Clinch asked whether she would plead guilty or not guilty.
Margaret Clitherow, denying that she had ever maintained any who were
enemies of the Queen, answered merely, 'Having made no offence, I need
no trial.' Neither that day nor the next could the judge prevail upon her to
enter a plea. 'All the people about her condemned her of great obstinacy
and folly, that she would not yield; and on every hand persuaded her to
refer her trial to the country, which could not find her guilty, as they said,
upon such slender evidence.' At this juncture the judge had no alternative
but to explain to her the penalty reserved at law for those who would not
plead:

> You must return from whence you came, and there in the lowest part
> of the prison, be stripped naked, laid down, your back upon the
> ground, and as much weight laid upon you as you are able to bear,
> and so to continue three days [with]out meat or drink, except a little
> barley bread and puddle water, and the third day to be pressed to
> death, your hands and feet tied to posts, and a sharp stone under your
> back.

Once she had fully understood her position at law, the authorities hoped
she would allow her trial to proceed.[5]

First members of the Council in the North came to her in her cell with
assurances that if she would hear just one Protestant sermon she would be
reprieved. Then her friends and kinsfolk tried to persuade her to claim
benefit of her condition, for if she were pregnant she would not be put to
death before the baby's birth, but she refused to confirm that she was with
child. With nothing resolved, the assize judges left the city, giving order
that the penalty should not be implemented before 25 March at the
earliest. In the interim friends and officials alike made further attempts to
get her to yield. Protestant ministers visited her in her cell to try to
persuade her to plead, or to claim benefit of her pregnancy, but once more
she refused either course, though she admitted she thought it was more
probable that she was with child than not. Giles Wigginton in particular
took great pains to try to get her to relent. 'Good Mistress Clitherow, take
pity on yourself. Christ himself fled his persecutors, so did his apostles;

[5] YML T.D. 1, fols 46r, 49v, 64v, 48v, 50r, 52v, 53r–v; Morris, *Troubles*, pp. 411, 413, 416, 417.

and why should not you then favour your own life?' Neither Henry May, her stepfather, Lord Mayor for that year, nor other Protestant preachers had any more success. The impasse could not be broken, so on 23 March the sheriffs informed her that the law would be allowed to take its course in two days time, and she employed her last hours sewing a linen habit to wear at her martyrdom. She passed her final night in spiritual preparation, and on the morning of Lady Day 1586, 'having trimmed up her head with new inkle' [ribbons or tape], she 'went cheerfully to her marriage'. After his description of Margaret Clitherow's barbarous death, Mush added a very lengthy and vituperative 'conclusion, wherein is partly showed the unjust dealings of the heretics with this martyr'.[6]

This impassioned account of a York butcher's wife, whom God had so beautified with such 'plentiful graces' and adorned 'with so rare gifts' as to enable her to go 'as thy loving spouse to so gracious a marriage day, that she might so virtuously enter thy triumphant city in her bloody scarlet robe', brilliantly succeeded in preserving the memory of Margaret Clitherow. From the beginning it seems to have circulated freely in whole or in part in manuscript among the English recusant community. The most dramatic three chapters on her apprehension, trial, and death were early detached from the main text, and it was this section which first appeared, much abbreviated, in print at Mechelen in 1619 as *An Abstracte of the Life and Martirdome of Mistres Margaret Clitherowe* . . . , dedicated to her daughter, Anne, then an Augustinian canoness at St Ursula's, Louvain. *The True Report* must indeed have provided the main contemporary source of evidence for the process which resulted first in 1929 in her beatification, and then in her canonization in 1970. In this sense there can be no doubt at all that Mush through his literary activities created, as he desired, a permanent memorial to his martyr. A further question, though, remains to be asked: had he and his fellow priests consciously or unconsciously inspired in Margaret Clitherow this yearning for martyrdom?[7]

An almost exact contemporary of Margaret Clitherow (he was born in 1552), and like her a native of Yorkshire, John Mush as a very young man may have been a servant of Thomas Vavasour, a Cambridge disciple of John Fisher who had given over the study of theology on the accession of

[6] YML T.D. 1, fols 58v, 65v, 68r; Morris, *Troubles*, pp. 422, 430, 433.
[7] YML Add. MS 151; [John Mush], *An Abstracte of the Life and Martirdome of Mistres Margaret Clitherowe* . . . (Mackline, 1619, repr. Scolar Press, 1979); for scholarly discussion of the manuscript versions of *The True Report* see Claridge, *Margaret Clitherow*, pp. 182–3 and Longley, *Saint Margaret Clitherow*, p. 192; YML T.D. 1, fol. 29v; Morris, *Troubles*, pp. 392–3.

the Protestant Edward VI to pursue medicine on the Continent. Early in Elizabeth's reign, having by this time married, Vavasour established a medical practice in York, from the first refusing to conform to the new religious settlement. A marked man after the Rebellion of the Earls, throughout the 1570s Vavasour underwent periods of imprisonment in the Hull Block Houses, where he eventually died in 1585. On his forcible removal from the York scene, his wife, Dorothy, assumed the leadership of York Catholics and set up house in the parish of Holy Trinity, King's Court, and it may well be that she was one of the chief means of Margaret Clitherow's conversion. In 1576 her eldest son, Thomas Vavasour, and John Mush set out together for the newly founded English seminary at Douai to train for the priesthood.[8]

Originally meant to provide university courses in arts and theology for English students reluctant for religious reasons to study at Oxford or Cambridge, by the time Mush entered Douai the college had been transformed into a seminary to prepare young men for the English mission. Under William Allen's oversight the students received instruction in preaching, dialectic, and, for propaganda purposes, in the principle tenets of Protestantism. In ecclesiastical history they concentrated on the Catholic history of England. Pastoral theology formed a central part of their course, and they gave over much of their time to devotional exercises. Because of the political situation, in 1578 Allen transferred the college from Douai to Reims. More students were arriving at the seminary than he could accommodate, and in 1579 he dispatched Mush to finish the arts course and to begin his study of theology at the newly reorganized English College at Rome.[9]

The religious atmosphere at the English College, recently assigned by the Pope to Jesuit directors, seems to have been even more charged than that at Douai. With remorseless insistence the lecturers fortified the students for the deaths they might well die once they returned to England. Reminders of martyrdom faced them on every hand. Paintings of the torture chamber and the scaffold adorned the main rooms of the college. St Philip Neri reputedly greeted the students with the salutation 'Salvete flores martyrum!' Every autumn they undertook the *Spiritual Exercises* of Ignatius Loyola, contemplating the suffering of Christ, for whom they

---

[8] H. Aveling, *The Catholic Recusants of the West Riding of Yorkshire 1558–1790* = *Proceedings of the Leeds Philosophical and Literary Society*, 10, pt 6 (1963), p. 218; R. Rex, 'Thomas Vavasour, M.D.', *Recusant History*, 20 (1991), pp. 436–54; J. Wadham, 'Saint Margaret Clitherow her "Trial" on trial', *Ampleforth Journal*, 76 (1971), p. 21; Claridge, *Margaret Clitherow*, pp. 54–5.
[9] A. O. Meyer, *England and the Catholic Church under Queen Elizabeth* (London, 1915), p. 97.

might soon be about to give up their lives. God had called them by their teaching and example to save their country from heresy. Religion and patriotism combined to demand the martyr's sacrifice.[10]

This ardent desire to win England back to the Catholic faith shines through every sentence of the declaration made by the Jesuit Edmund Campion when he came into England with Robert Parsons in 1580.

> Be it known to you that we have made a league . . . cheerfully to carry the cross you shall lay upon us, and never to despair of your recovery, while we have a man left to enjoy your Tyburn, or to be racked with your torments, or consumed with your prisons. The expense is reckoned, the enterprise is begun: it is of God, it cannot be withstood. So the faith was planted, so it must be restored . . .[11]

Within a year, on 1 December 1581, Campion suffered a traitor's death under the treason law of Edward III, inspiring an immediate literary response.

> God knows it is not force nor might,
> Nor war nor warlike band,
> Nor shield and spear, nor dint of sword
> That must convert the land.
> It is the blood of martyrs shed,
> It is that noble train,
> That fight with word and not with sword
> And Christ their captain.[12]

John Mush shared to the full this cult of martyrdom. Time and again in his *True Report* he referred to 'the blood of martyrs which is the plenteous seed of Christ his church', and in his opening chapter dwelt on the fructifying power of this blood.

> In the primitive church they persecuted her that she should remain barren and bring forth no increase; now they labour also to the same effect, but principally to subvert and destroy her already born children. And as she then cast her seed of blood to the generation of many, so now she fighteth with blood to save those that she hath borne, that the lily roots being watered with the fruitful liquor of blood, may keep still and yield new branches hereafter with so much

---

[10] Meyer, *England and the Catholic Church*, pp. 109–10.
[11] Quoted in P. McGrath, *Papists and Puritans under Elizabeth I* (London, 1967), pp. 168–9.
[12] Quoted in Meyer, *England and the Catholic Church*, p. 244.

more plentiful increase by how much more abundantly such sacred steams flow among them.[13]

With this intense mental preparation for martyrdom behind him, Mush returned as a priest to England in the autumn of 1583 and embarked upon his ministry in the north. At this particular time Margaret Clitherow was serving her third period of imprisonment in York Castle, and so it may not have been until her release on bond in the spring of 1584 that Mush encountered, or re-encountered, her and became her spiritual director; he can only have known her intimately for the last two years of her life. In his *True Report* he conceded that other priests had influenced his spiritual daughter. Indeed, Margaret Clitherow's virtue enabled her to gain benefit from all the priests with whom she came into contact, old priests as well as the seminarists;

> although some ghostly father might have been thought, worthily, not of that sufficiency which was requisite for her direction in every point ... yet her confidence was so strong in God that she never doubted but he would endue and furnish every his priest, for the time of her need, with sufficient wisdom and discretion to direct her actions as should be most to his honour and her own spiritual good.

Nevertheless, it was to Mush principally, and to his seminary trained colleagues, that 'this golden woman' committed herself and 'did utterly forsake her own judgement and will in all her actions, to submit herself to the judgement, will and direction of her ghostly father.'[14]

Fresh from Rome, Mush passed on to Margaret Clitherow some of the spiritual practices he had experienced at the English College. In the service of God 'she utterly forsook herself, and would not in any wise follow her own fantasy, but committed all wholly to the guiding and direction of her ghostly father.' He approved the form of her private prayer and her public devotions, when in York shriving her twice a week and regulating the occasions when she might communicate at Mass. Her spiritual reading consisted of the Reims translation of the New Testament, Thomas à Kempis, *Of the Imitation of Christ*, and William Perin's *Spiritual Exercises*, based on the *Exercises* of Ignatius Loyola. He certainly more than once discussed martyrdom with her. When she raised with him as a matter of conscience whether she might still continue to entertain priests without her husband's knowledge and in defiance of the law of 1585, Mush con-

---

[13] YML T.D. 1, fols 2r, 3r; Morris, *Troubles*, p. 362.
[14] YML T.D. 1, fols 16r, 16v–17r; Morris, *Troubles*, pp. 378, 379.

firmed that she did well to persist in her meritorious actions, but warned her what the outcome might be. ' "Then", quoth he merrily, but yet always he thought it would happen to her reward, "You must prepare your neck for the rope." "God's will be done," said she, "but I am far unworthy that honour." '[15]

At another time in his talks with her he mentioned martyrdom even more directly.

> When they had been talking of these dangerous times, wherein, as appeareth, heretics are sorry to spare any cruelty, and it hath been told her that it could not be but the devil would storm at the daily serving of God, which was brought to pass by her means, and stir his ministers to hinder so great a good, and that certainly their malice would be deadly against her; that if she escaped their bloody hands, yet she should be cast into perpetual prison, she would with a smiling countenance wag her head and say, 'I pray God his will may be done, and I have that which he seeth most fit for me. But I see not in myself any worthiness of martyrdom; yet, if it be his will, I pray him that I may be constant and persevere to the end.'[16]

Between July 1582 and November 1585 six seminary priests, William Lacey, Richard Kirkman, James Thompson, William Hart, Richard Thirkeld, and Hugh Taylor, died for their alleged treason at the Knavesmire. For Margaret Clitherow this then became her place of pilgrimage.

> Her desire was greatly often to go thither, where so many her ghostly fathers had shed their blood in witness of the catholic faith, where they had triumphed over the world, the flesh and the devil, from whence they had ascended into heaven, where she earnestly wished, if it were God's will, for the same catholic cause to end her life, and where she hoped one day God should be glorified in the memory of his martyrs.[17]

Although many York lay people, including Margaret Clitherow, had undergone lengthy periods of imprisonment for recusancy, until 1585 only priests had been called upon to sacrifice their lives. Then, in the autumn of 1585, a layman, Marmaduke Bowes, was put to death for harbouring a priest. It is understandable, therefore, that when arrested in

[15] YML T.D. 1, fols 19v, 27r, 30r; Morris, *Troubles*, pp. 382, 390, 393; A. Stacpoole, 'York Martyrs', in A. Stacpoole, ed., *The Noble City of York* (York, 1972), p. 694.
[16] YML T.D. 1, fol. 35r; Morris, *Troubles*, pp. 397–8.
[17] Stacpoole, *The Noble City*, p. 715; YML T.D. 1, fols 31v–32r; Morris, *Troubles*, p. 395.

the spring of 1586 on an identical charge, Margaret Clitherow should have assumed that her own time had come, when it seems all that the authorities had intended to do was to curb her nonconformity. Before her first examination, when about to be taken from the Castle to appear before her judges, she devised a gesture of defiance to encourage her fellow Catholics. Remarking to Anne Teshe, another recusant with whom she shared her cell, ' "Before I go, I will make all my brethren and sisters on the other side [of] the hall merry", . . . she made a pair of gallows on her fingers, and pleasantly laughed at them.'[18]

Even after Judge Clinch had unwillingly condemned her to death, Margaret Clitherow still did not feel confident that the penalty would be carried out. This was apparently the only time during her incarceration that she attempted to contact Mush, 'desiring him to pray earnestly for her, for it was the heaviest cross that ever came to her, that she feared she should escape death.' She never seems to have sought spiritual guidance on the matter of refusing to plead. When Protestant ministers urged her not to hazard her life, arguing that Christ himself and his Apostles had fled their persecutors, she spurned their advice, not least because it came from Protestants. 'God defend I should favour my life in this point. As for my martyrdom, I am not yet assured of it, for that I am yet living; but if I persevere to the end, I verily believe I shall be saved.'[19]

Confronted with her decision, Mush subsequently had no choice but to defend it. She would not allow her trial to proceed, he maintained, for two reasons; firstly, to spare her children and servants from giving evidence against her, and, secondly, to exonerate the jury, which would have had to pronounce upon her guilt, from any responsibility for her death.

> These were her own reasons [he declared] which sufficiently defend and clear her from all her slanderers of obstinacy, desperation, or other crime at all; nay, they convince a rare and marvellous charity in her at that time. And though in all her speeches and doings she showed great wisdom, yet surely in none appeared more than in this refusal to be tried by the country.[20]

The choice of her death seems to have been Margaret Clitherow's alone. Mush can in no way be held responsible for consciously encouraging her to seek this fate. Nevertheless, he and other seminary priests

18 K. M. Longley, 'The "Trial" of Margaret Clitherow', *Ampleforth Journal*, 75 (1960), pp. 335–64; YML T.D. 1, fol. 49r; Morris, *Troubles*, p. 412.
19 YML T.D. 1, fols 56v, 58r; Morris, *Troubles*, pp. 420, 422.
20 YML T.D. 1, fol. 75r–v; Morris, *Troubles*, p. 436.

seem to have been the chief means of mediating to her the cult of martyrdom propagated in their colleges on the Continent. In this respect, Mush can be seen at the very least as an accessory to her death. In the prayer he addressed to 'the sacred martyr' at the close of his work he may have sensed this; he certainly recognized the paradox whereby his spiritual daughter through martyrdom had become his mother, and he, in life her ghostly father, was now her son.

> Remember me, I humbly beseech thy perfect charity, whom thou hast left miserable behind thee ... I was not so able to help thee as thou art now to procure mercy and grace for me; for thou art now all washed in thy sacred blood from all spots of frailty, securely possessing God himself; whereas I yet a woeful wretch, and clothed with impiety ... Be not wanting, therefore, my glorious mother ... to obtain mercy and procure the plenties of such graces for me, thy miserable son, as thou knowest to be most needful for me, and acceptable in the sight of our Lord, which hath thus glorified thee; that I may honour him by imitation of thy happy life, and by my death, which he will give me, to be partaker with thee and all holy saints of his kingdom, to whom be all glory and honour, now and for ever. Amen.[21]

Mush, in fact, survived the persecution of the last two decades of Elizabeth's reign to serve on the northern mission for over thirty years. By writing the *True Report*, and perhaps even more by his priestly ministry to Margaret Clitherow, he helped create a martyr. Despite his reverence for martyrdom, he himself never attained a martyr's crown. In the words of Bishop Challoner, 'After having suffered prisons and chains, and received even the sentence of death for his faith, he died at length in his bed, in a good old age, in the year 1617.'[22]

University of York

---

[21] YML T.D. 1, fol. 87v, damaged, missing part supplied from York Bar Convent, V 69, pp. 137–8; Morris, *Troubles*, p. 440.
[22] Quoted in Morris, *Troubles*, p. 359.

MARTYRS ON THE MOVE: RELICS AS VINDICATORS OF LOCAL DIVERSITY IN THE TRIDENTINE CHURCH[1]

by SIMON DITCHFIELD

ROBERT BELLARMINE put it with his customary clarity and forcefulness when he wrote:

> There is nothing that they [the Protestants] shudder at and abhor more than the invocation of saints, the cult of relics and the veneration of images. For they consider that these things constitute manifest impiety and idolatry.[2]

It was in recognition of this pressing reality that Rome—principally via the agency of the Sacred Congregation of Rites and Ceremonies—sought to put its house in order. It did so in two main ways: on the one hand, it relaunched official saint-making—the year of the congregation's foundation (1588) saw the first official canonization after a hiatus of over half a century.[3] Hand in hand with this went the tightening up of canonization procedure which was to culminate in a papal bull of 1634 that remained the final word on the subject until well into this century.[4] On the other hand, regional churches were required to submit their local saints' offices to Rome for approval. In addition, the authentication, translation, and display of relics became subject to unprecedented regulation.[5] Against

---

[1] I would like to thank warmly my colleague Dr Amanda Lillie for the trouble she has taken to look over this text. Her eagle eye and unfailing sense of the grammatically possible have done much to chasten my prose.

[2] *De controversiis christianae fidei* (Ingolstadt, 1601), 2, p. 826.

[3] The saint in question was the Spanish Franciscan missionary Diego of Alcalá (d. 1464). The previous ceremony, involving the canonizations of Saints Benno and Antonino of Florence, had taken place in 1523. For a convenient handlist of saints canonized from 1588 to 1767, see the appendix to P. Burke, 'How to be a Counter-Reformation saint', in the same author's *The Historical Anthropology of Early Modern Italy* (Cambridge, 1987), p. 60.

[4] *Coelestis Hierusalem cives* was issued on 5 July 1634. For the text see *Bullarium Romanum*, 14 (Turin, 1868), pp. 436–40.

[5] E.g. *Copias de authenticas de cuerpos santos que se han sacado del Reyno, y otras varias escrituras pertocantes a la invencion de los mismos cuerpos santos que por duplicadas se juntan en este legajo*, Cagliari, Archivio Arcivescovile, MS no. 14 (1614–50), doc. no. 12, dated 9 Sept. 1640, which reveals that before a relic could be transported, it had to be furnished with two copies of the necessary document—one sealed inside the reliquary and the other attached to its exterior. Cf. *Constitutiones et decreta condita in synodo diocesana Placentina* (Piacenza, 1610), pp. 23–5, for more general regulations concerning the translation of relics and their display in churches.

such a background, the case under study here might seem at first to contradict the spirit of the times, since it involved the arrival of an unprecedented number of martyrs' relics from a source whose historical credentials had yet to be fully recognized. It will be the contention of this paper that not only was this traffic in relics substantially in accord with the ethos of the Tridentine Church, but that where it did conflict with the latter, this served to enrich considerably perhaps the greatest (if indirect and in some respects unwitting) long-term intellectual contribution of the Tridentine Reformation: its laying of the foundations of modern historical method.

On 15 January 1648 the hagiographer and ecclesiastical historian Pietro Maria Campi interrupted the long-delayed printing of his life's work: *Dell'historia ecclesiastica di Piacenza* to incorporate a detailed account of the arrival in Piacenza, between 1643 and 1647, of some twenty bodies of Early Christian martyrs, together with the relics of a further eighty-eight. Their provenance was the catacombs under and around the churches of S. Saturno, S. Lucifero and SS Mauro and Lello, just outside the walls of Cagliari, in Sardinia, which had only begun to be excavated in 1614. Their most notorious champion and publicist, the canon lawyer and antiquarian Dionigio Bonfant—whom Campi, in an inspired misreading, always referred to as Buonsanti—had claimed in a book of over 600 pages, published in 1635, the status of martyr for almost all the 300-plus bodies which had been found.[6] For Bonfant, the recurrent initials 'B. M.' in the uncovered inscriptions could have no other meaning than *beatus martyr*. He simply ignored other, less rewarding interpretations such as *bonae memoriae*, *bene meritus* or *bene moriens*.[7]

The exclusive supplier of the relics to Piacenza was the Capuchin preacher Bonaventura de'Baccarini, a Piacentine then resident in Cagliari. The first three bodies arrived in 1643; five more in 1646; and a further twelve in 1647, 'all save one most glorious martyrs of Christ'. Over the same period, relics from a further eighty-eight named saints, 'all of them invincible martyrs of the Lord', also arrived.[8]

---

[6] Dionigio Bonfant, *Triumpho de los santos del reyno de Cerdenna* (Cagliari, 1635).

[7] The fullest available account for what follows is Campi's own: P. M. Campi, *Dell'historia ecclesiastica di Piacenza*, 3 vols (Piacenza, 1651–62), I, pp. 181, col. 2–183, col. 1; 3, pp. 208, col. 1–214, col. 1. But see also C. Poggiali, *Memorie storiche di Piacenza*, 11 (Piacenza, 1763), pp. 349–53. Contemporary reference to events of 1648 relating to the relics which arrived the year before may be found in the unpublished diary of Benedetto Boselli (d. 1670), Piacenza, Biblioteca comunale [hereafter BCPc], MS Pallastrelli 126, pp. 183–6.

[8] Campi, *Dell'historia ecclesiastica*, I, p. 182, col. 1. The names of the twenty martyrs whose complete bodies Piacenza received are given on the same page. For the list of the other eighty-eight whose relics were sent to Piacenza, see pp. 182, col. 2–183, col. 1.

All this abundant sacred treasure was carefully distributed throughout the community at the behest of the donor, de'Baccarini; Campi himself receiving no less than three martyrs' bodies in return for his prominent role as publicist and official historian of the whole affair, though one of these, S. Domenica, had been sent in direct response to Campi's request for an appropriate relic to give to the Convent of the Annunziata, in Piacenza, for their recently rebuilt church—a senior member of whom had been his aunt, Maura Campi. Indeed, de'Baccarini appears to have acted on Campi's request in a particularly concrete fashion; as he put it in a letter of 15 April 1646:

> I am writing to give you the news that our most benevolent God through the intercession of that glorious father Saint Augustine [the Convent belonged to the Augustinian Order] has heard the prayers of these virgins of the Santissima Annunziata, because the body of a holy martyr is now ready as you requested. Four days ago I saw it with my own eyes together with others in its underground burial place and with my own hands I helped the labourers to dig and then to extract the holy relics; weeping as I did so with happiness and contentment to be in such a place . . .[9]

The manner in which the relics of S. Dominica, together with those of S. Bonifacio,[10] were treated may stand as representative of what happened to so many of the others.[11] They, along with three other Sardinian martyrs, had been brought from the island—via Genoa—in a single wooden box by two Piacentine Capuchin missionaries who were on their way back from North Africa. On arrival, the relics were laid before the Episcopal Vicar, who recognized them as being genuine on 20 December 1647. In doing so, the latter was merely confirming the official recognition which already had taken place in Cagliari, as symbolized by five attached archiepiscopal seals. Some two weeks later, on 3 January 1647, the Episcopal Vicar transferred the relics by hand into lead caskets, which

<hr />

[9] *Dell'historia ecclesiastica*, 3, p. 209, cols 1–2.
[10] Campi had given this martyr to the Confraternity of the Most Holy Trinity in Piacenza for their chapel.
[11] For the following account see Campi, *Dell'historia ecclesiastica*, 3, p. 210, cols. 1–2. Marginal printed notes to Campi's text indicate several occasions on which acts were officially registered by the episcopal notary, Marco Antonio Parma, but extensive research in the relevant section of the Archivio notarile in the Archivio di Stato di Piacenza has failed to turn up any of the texts. Unfortunately the current state of the archive of the Curia Vescovile di Piacenza prevents my following up the matter there.

he then had nailed shut in his presence before letting two priests transport a casket each to Campi's private chapel.

Here the saints' bodies were revered with lighted candles and in the prayers of frequent visitors until their translation—respectively, to the Church of the Annunziata and to the Chapel of the Confraternity of the Most Holy Trinity—which took place on 23 June the same year. That day the generosity of the confraternity ensured for both martyrs a triumphal progress through the streets of Piacenza, conducted to the sound of music, trumpets, and bells and attended by a great number of people. In the case of S. Domenica, her arrival outside the Church of the Annunziata was greeted with applause by the nuns who, singing, processed the body into their church. She was then placed in the high altar, except for her head, which was reserved for a special reliquary displayed on top of the altar, together with the relics of thirteen other Sardinian martyrs, which had also been donated by Campi, who concluded his account, however, with a candidly disarming admission of his ignorance about the precise origins of these sacred treasures:

> Concerning the life of this saint (Domenica) and how she was martyred, we can know nothing with precision, nor even about the most glorious triumphs [in death] of so many other of the heroes who have come to us from Sardinia.[12]

Elsewhere, at the end of his comprehensive list of all the martyrs whose relics had recently been sent to Piacenza, Campi noted that the reader must not wonder at the fact that none of the names were listed in church saints' calendars and martyrologies, for their relics had only just been rediscovered after centuries of neglect precipitated by the Vandal and Saracen invasions of Sardinia.[13] He thus concluded:

> Our present ignorance concerning the lives and particular deeds of Saints Bonifacio, Bartolomeo and Domenica and others, must not, however, decrease in any way the duty that we have in honouring these saints in the appropriate manner as one should, for it is enough for us to know that they are true saints and glorious martyrs of Christ and as such approved and revered by the Church.[14]

---

[12] *Dell'historia ecclesiastica*, 3, p. 210, col. 2.
[13] *Dell'historia ecclesiastica*, 1, p. 183, col. 1. Cf. a letter to the same effect by de'Baccarini of 3 Nov. 1645, ibid., 3, p. 211, col. 1.
[14] *Dell'historia ecclesiastica*, 3, p. 212, col. 1.

The public processing of relics was, of course, not new. It had been an important means of reasserting local identity at times of adversity since at least the late fourth century.[15] However, the sheer number of translations, combined with the care taken to ensure the relics' proper authentication and treatment, was novel and should be seen in terms of the Catholic reaction to the Protestant critique of the cult of the saints and their relics mentioned right at the beginning of this paper. The institution which oversaw the Catholic counter-attack in respect of saints' relics and their cults—the Sacred Congregation of Rites and Ceremonies—was founded in 1588, the very year that also witnessed the publication of the first volume of Cesare Baronio's *Annales ecclesiastici*. At Baronio's death, in 1607, this work offered some 14,000 folio-size columns in demonstration of a two-word thesis: *semper eadem*—ever the same—that argued for the complete consonance between the early apostolic Church and its sixteenth-century Roman Catholic successor. In this context there could be no more concrete or expressive symbol of the continuity of Catholic devotion and ecclesiastical practice than the honouring of relics of the Early Christian martyrs. Thus, the century after the closing of the Council of Trent in 1563 saw an astonishing explosion of devotion to these *vestigia* from the most heroic epoch of the Church's history. Central to this movement was the revival of interest in the Roman catacombs, popularized so effectively by St Philip Neri in his all-night vigils, and integrated into the processions he led between the seven principal basilicas of the city.[16] But just as the consciousness of the earliest Christian centuries was becoming more intense—and, indeed, as far as Carlo Borromeo was concerned, it was the duty of each bishop to 'collect together the names, character and pastoral actions of his predecessors'[17]—the local churches found that the legitimacy of their oldest traditions came under serious question: not from the Protestant heretics, but from Rome itself.

This was due to the Tridentine standardization of the liturgy which began with the publication of the revised Roman Breviary in 1568. As

[15] See P. Brown, *The Cult of the Saints: its Rise and Function in Latin Christianity* (London, 1981), *passim*.
[16] A. Gallonio, *Vita B. Philippi Neri Florentini . . . in annos digesta* (Rome, 1600), pp. 76–9; G. Incisa della Rocchetta and N. Vian, *Il primo processo per S. Filippo Neri*, 4 vols (Città del Vaticano, 1957–63), 2, p. 323; 3, pp. 262, 386. Cf. G. Wataghin Cantino, 'Roma sotterranea. Appunti sulle origine dell'archeologia cristiana', *Ricerche di Storia dell'arte*, 10 (1980), pp. 5–14.
[17] This was in order to demonstrate the continuity of the episcopal office with its institution in apostolic times. See the relevant passage from his 3rd Provincial Council of 1573: 'Episcopus, id quod vel . . . in illa ecclesia bene gerenda', in *Acta ecclesiae Mediolanensis* (Milan, 1582), fol. 46v.

with the series of revised standard texts which succeeded it—such as the Missal of 1570, the Martyrology of 1584, and the so-called Clementine Vulgate of 1592—this new edition was a major innovation in that it was intended to be of *universal* application, any exceptions having to fulfil the strictest of criteria. It was as a direct consequence of this policy that Pietro Maria Campi's first official commission from his bishop was to produce a new edition of the *Proper Offices of Saints for the Use of the Piacentine Church*, which was finally published, after over a decade's haggling with the Congregation of Rites, in 1610.[18] Conflict here centred on the short passages summarizing local saints' lives, which were to be read out during the second nocturn of mattins, and which Campi was forced to rewrite in the light of more strictly historical criteria. Almost as if to compensate for the harsh judgements of the Congregation of Rites, Campi then went on to write individual lives of Piacentine saints, four of which were published separately in his lifetime, and in which he could accommodate circumstantial details which were unacceptable to Rome in the context of the liturgy. The *Dell'historia ecclesiastica di Piacenza* integrated all this work into the yet broader canvas of a heavily annotated episcopal calendar whose three published volumes included the texts, *in extenso*, of no less than 400 privileges and other documents.

In this context, the arrival of a host of relics of previously unknown saints from outside the existing hagiographical picture (whose co-ordinates had been substantially set out in Baronio's annotated edition of the *Roman Martyrology*, first published in 1587[19]), must have appeared as a particularly welcome 'extra' with which to supplement his account of Piacenza's earliest Christian centuries. In an important sense, therefore, Campi's history should be seen more accurately as a collection of extended annotations to the Piacentine Breviary in the way in which it sought to legitimate contemporary local devotional practice in the Tridentine terms of continuity with the distant past. Here Campi merely stands as a single, if representative, example of the numerous local Baronio-figures from provincial centres who sought to account for and

[18] The earliest complete edition that I have managed to track down is that of 1619 (BCPc, libri pallastrelli 661), which was reprinted in 1624. For a full account of the complex details of this office book's revision see my unpublished Ph.D. thesis: 'Hagiography and Ecclesiastical historiography in late 16th- and early 17th-century Italy: Pietro Maria Campi of Piacenza (1569–1649)' (University of London, Warburg Institute, 1991), pp. 120–32.

[19] Baronio's work was later supplemented by F. Ferrari in two works: *Catalogus sanctorum Italiae in menses duodecim distributo* (Milan, 1613) and *Catalogus generalis sanctorum qui in Martyrologio Rom[ano] non sunt ex variis martyrologiis, kalendariis [et] tabulis collecta* (Venice, 1625).

justify their local cults and devotions by drawing on an unprecedented range of sources during the century after the Council of Trent.

Perhaps the most conspicuous addition to the armoury of erudition deployed by such historians was provided by archaeology and the related field of epigraphy, so it is appropriate that the source of Piacenza's unexpected sacred riches should be the direct result of a spectacular archaeological discovery: namely, that of the Christian catacombs in and around Cagliari made between 1614 and 1650.

In common with so many other local churches, Cagliari had had to put its own liturgical house in order as a consequence of the introduction of the Tridentine service books (only local breviaries which had been in uninterruped use for over two centuries were to be permitted). Accordingly, we find a request made to Cardinal Sirleto for the approval of her local saints' offices even before the Congregation of Rites was set up.[20] But such detailed contestation of long-held traditions positively paled in comparison with the battle for the ecclesiastical primacy of Sardinia which then raged between the archdioceses of Cagliari and Sássari.[21] A new dimension to this two-century long struggle was added by the discovery in June 1614 of the bodies of Saints Gavino, Proto, and Gianuario, martyred under Diocletian, beneath the Basilica of S. Gavino in Porto Tórres, near Sássari. This excavation was the personal initiative of the Archbishop of Sássari, Gavino Manca de Cedrelles, who seems to have had their local cult approved already by 27 October the same year and lost no time publicizing the event in a printed account published in 1615.[22]

His opposite number in Cagliari, Francisco de Esquivel, was not slow in responding to such a dramatic assertion of Sássari's early Christian credentials. On 6 November 1614, soon after a particularly splendid celebration of the feast day of S. Saturno (or S. Saturnino, as he was referred to then), he started excavating under the eponymous Palaeochristian basilica just outside the city walls. Almost immediately, in the presence of a notary and many leading members of the local community, an inscription was uncovered whose few remaining letters were inter-

---

[20] Città del Vaticano, Biblioteca apostolica vaticana [hereafter BAV], MS Vat. Lat. 6416, fol. 355.

[21] For a full account of this rivalry which dated from 1409, see P. Martini, *Storia ecclesiastica di Sardegna*, 3 vols (Cagliari, 1839–41), 2, pp. 321ff.

[22] *Relacion de los cuerpos de los santos Martires San Gavino, San Proto y San Ianuario, patrones de la Yglesia metropolitana Turritana de Sacer en Sardena y de otros muchos que se hallaron en el año de 1614* (Madrid, 1615).

preted as an abbreviation of the phrase: 'SANCTI INNUMERABILES'.[23] Encouraged by this sign, the excavators pressed on, uncovering as they did so a sequence of burial-chambers, containing umpteen bodies and many identifying inscriptions. Each subsequent discovery was scrupulously recorded by a notary in attendance and witnessed by those present. In the early years substantial crowds flocked to see the excavations in an atmosphere of highly-charged expectation engendered by the prophecies of the Jesuit Francisco Ortolan (1544–1623), who claimed to have had revealed to him in dreams the precise location, name, age, and date of martyrdom of some 266 martyrs![24] The notarial acts (still preserved in the Archivio Arcivescovile di Cagliari), when cross-referenced with the contemporary works of Bonfant and Stefano Esquirro, enable us to list the date and place of discovery of over 300 of the 338-body total; a fact which in itself speaks eloquently for the new Tridentine spirit of regulation.[25]

Archbishop d'Esquivel early on sought wider recognition of this spectacular confirmation of Cagliari's primacy, sending to both King Philip III of Spain and Pope Paul V a detailed report of the first three years' excavations that was published in 1617.[26] On 11 November the following year d'Esquivel consecrated a sanctuary directly below the high altar of his cathedral to house the relics of the recently-discovered martyrs. Carved directly out of the rock on which the church had been built, and richly decorated with marble intarsia and an elaborate ceiling of rosette coffering, this three-chamber sanctuary constituted a potent physical symbol of the archdiocese's early Christian origins.[27]

It was undoubtedly in the hope of gaining wider recognition of this

[23] The letters were: S INNU or SINUM. Their discovery is mentioned in all the contemporary accounts of the excavations, beginning with F. d'Esquivel, *Relacion de la invencion de los cuerpos santos que en los annos 1614, 1615, 1616 fueron hallados en varias yglesias de la ciudad de Caller y su Arzobispado* (Naples, 1617), pp. 33–4. For much of what follows I am indebted to D. Mureddu, D. Salvi, and G. Stefani, *'Sancti innumerabiles'. Scavi nella Cagliari del Seicento: testimonianze e verifiche* (Oristano, 1988). An excellent survey of the contemporary sources is given on pp. 23–8.

[24] *Historiae Societatis Iesu pars sexta . . . auctore Julio Cordara* (Rome, 1750), bk viii, pp. 444–6. Cf. P. Martini, *Storia ecclesiastica di Sardegna*, 2, pp. 350–1.

[25] *Actas originales sobre la inbencion de las reliquias de santos que se hallaron en la Basilica de S. Sadorro, y otras iglesias y lugares de la ciudad de Caller y su diocesis*, Cagliari, Archivio Arcivescovile, MS 13. Cf. S. Esquirro, *Santuario de Caller, y verdadera historia de la invencion de los cuerpos santos hallados en la dicha ciudad y su Arcobispado* (Cagliari, 1624). A table of concordances between all these sources is given in Mureddu, Salvi, and Stefani, *'Sancti innumerabiles'*, pp. 109–20.

[26] See above, n. 23.

[27] For the most detailed contemporary description see bk v of Esquirro's *Santuario de Caller*; cf. that in F. Sulis, *Culto religioso dei Santi Martiri Cagliaritani provato con documenti* (Rome, 1883), p. 49, n. 1.

fact that d'Esquivel promoted the dispersal of many of the newly-discovered relics. The arrival of a significant number in Piacenza between 1643 and 1647 has already been noted,[28] but as early as 1624 the first relics of some eighty-six Cagliari martyrs arrived in Alassio, Liguria,[29] while we know for certain that others were sent to Catalonia[30] and Naples.[31]

D'Esquivel then commissioned the Capuchin Stefano Esquirro to write a fuller treatment of the new discoveries, which was a *tour de force* of Christian antiquarianism to which twentieth-century archaeologists are still indebted. For each tomb he gave the dating of its discovery; its precise location; the depth at which it was found; a description of its type and dimensions; together with its state of conservation and the transcription of any inscriptions present.[32] A companion volume was planned, but Esquirro's death intervened, and the task fell to Dionigio Bonfant, who went to work with gusto, producing in *Triumpho de los Santos del Reyno de Cerdenna* an account which sought to add the flesh and blood of the martyrs' deeds to the dry bones so exhaustively catalogued by his predecessor. The result was a book which has been dogged by controversy since 1635, when it was published only on the authority of the secular magistracy and in the face of opposition from the Inquisition.[33] Though its title referred to the whole of Sardinia, Bonfant in fact devoted his entire attention to the early history of Christian Cagliari as reflected in its martyrs. By means of a creative reading of the archaeological evidence—principally inscriptions which usually gave only the buried person's name, age, and day of death—which was then wedded to a continuous chronological framework of Baronian inspiration, Bonfant sought to write a comprehensive account of Cagliari's heroic suffering in the earliest Christian centuries, complete with the deeds, in outline, of several of its martyrs.

---

[28] A notarial act held at Piacenza, Archivio Capitolino di S. Antonino, MS, C. 37, dated 20 Dec. 1633, which records the donation to the chapter by the Capuchin Feliciano da Piacenza of a reliquary containing the relics of some fourteen martyrs including 'S. Catarina mart. Calaritana' indicates that the relics which arrived in 1643 were not the first.

[29] The only account known to me of this event is described in the celebratory booklet published on the occasion of the tercentenary of their arrival: *Solenni Feste per il terzo centenario della Traslazione dei Corpi Santi (1624–1924—Alassio—11–12–13 luglio 1924)* (n. d., n. p.), which I consulted at the BAV, R. G. Storia IV 11012 (int. 15).

[30] G. Lilliu, 'Reliquie sarde in terra di Spagna', *Quotidiano sardo*, anno 3, no. 47, 22 Feb. 1949.

[31] This is known to us because of the attack made on their authenticity by Geronimo Bruno in a manuscript held at Cagliari, Biblioteca universitaria: *De reliquis Sardiniae anno domini 1614, 1615 et 1616 inventis Hieronimi Bruni opinio.*

[32] Esquirro, *Santuario de Caller*, bks ii–iv. Cf. D. Mureddu and G. Stefani, 'Scavi "archeologici" nella cultura del Seicento in Sardegna', in T. K. Kirova, ed., *Arte e Cultura del '600 e del '700 in Sardegna* (Naples, 1984), pp. 397–406, at pp. 398–9.

[33] Martini, *Storia ecclesiastica di Sardegna*, 2, p. 563.

The execration which has since been heaped upon Bonfant by such authoritative scholars as Bolland, Muratori, and Mommsen has perhaps been as excessive as it is anachronistic.[34] A recent scholar of the epigraphical data turned up by the seventeenth-century excavations in Cagliari, Marcella Bonello Lai, has argued in particular that Mommsen's total scepticism is unjustified. Entirely ignoring the existence of the notarial depositions, he had even gone so far as to argue that there had been an organized workshop in Cagliari which had turned out a whole host of fake inscriptions.[35] Bonello Lai has shown, on the one hand, that many of the apparently non-Palaeochristian features of the inscriptions most probably derive from their likely restoration in the Middle Ages after Saracen depredations; and, on the other, that Bonfant's interpretation of the initials 'B. M.' as evidence of martyr status is not so far-fetched as at first thought. For it appears that 'B. M.' was a formula particular to North Africa (whence many martyrs' relics had come subsequent to the Vandal invasions) and Gaul (along with Sardinia a favoured destination of the refugees) in the late fourth and fifth centuries.[36]

Aside from Esquirro and Bonfant, the other principal protagonist in the fight for wider recognition of Cagliari's heroic Christian origins was Ambrogio Machin, who succeeded d'Esquivel as Archbishop in 1624. Whereas papal recognition of the martyrs' cults at anything but a local diocesan level was consistently denied by Rome,[37] Machin's crusade for the official acceptance of Cagliari's ecclesiastical primacy within Sardinia was more successful, resulting in a series of decisions by the Roman Rota in the years 1637 to 1640 that firmly rebuffed Sassarese pretensions to the title.[38] The Archbishop's struggle became linked with that to clear the name of one of his early predecessors, S. Lucifero, whose relics had been recovered in 1621. No less an authority than Baronio had accused Lucifero of schismatic behaviour at the Council of Milan in 355, where he had

---

[34] ActaSS Feb., 1, pp. xx–xxi; L. Muratori, Antiquitates Italicae, 5 (Milan, 1741), dissertatio LVIII, col. 18; Corpus inscriptionum latinarum, 10 (Berlin, 1883), pp. 779–81. According to Daniel Papenbroch (Acta SS, May, 5, p. 219) Bolland was influenced in his decision not to include the Cagliari martyrs in his collection by Cardinal Francesco Barberini, who advised him to wait for their official recognition by Rome.

[35] Corpus inscriptionem latinarum, 10, p. 57.

[36] M. Bonello Lai, 'Le raccolte epigraphiche del '600 in Sardegna', in Kirova, ed., Arte e Cultura, pp. 379–95; at pp. 385, 392.

[37] The Congregation of Rites' decision of 18 June 1689 confirmed that their cult could be observed throughout Sardinia only if the diocesan office was adhered to. See P. Martini, Storia ecclesiastica di Sardegna, 2, pp. 365–6, n. 1, for the text of the decision.

[38] These were dated 27 Nov. 1637, 14 June 1638, 10 Dec. 1638, and 27 Apr. 1640. For their texts see A. Machin, Defensionis primatus Archiepiscopi Calaritani (Cagliari, 1639), pp. 227ff.

refused to sign the condemnation of Athanasius, going on to compose polemical works against the Emperor whilst in exile.

Machin's reply drew on every resource of erudition available to his age in order to prove, firstly, that Baronio had mistaken Lucifero of Cagliari for his namesake from Smyrna; secondly, that the former had led a life of unimpeachable virtue; and, finally, that the relics discovered were genuinely his. To this end, Machin deployed the skills of textual criticism, numismatics, and epigraphy, as well as archaeology, where he made, for his time, sophisticated use of drawings to illustrate the church where his body had been found in cross-section, aerial, and façade elevations.[39] The reservations expressed later in the century by the Bollandist Daniel Papenbroch—which centre on the degree to which the rivalry between Cagliari and Sássari had led to forced readings of the evidence—merely serve to underline a point which I hope has become increasingly clear during the course of this paper: the importance of polemic as a generator of erudition.[40] Urban VIII's decree of 20 June 1641 forbidding further discussion of S. Lucifero's cult should not be interpreted as a condemnation of Machin's case, but rather illustrative of the Pope's concern that this controversy was bringing the concept of sanctity in general into disrepute.[41]

I think that most of us here would agree with Arnaldo Momigliano when he said that the two distinguishing characteristics of recognizably 'modern' historical method were, firstly, the distinction made between primary and secondary sources; and, secondly, the employment of non-literary evidence, such as coins, inscriptions, and other archaeological remains. In a seminal article published over forty years ago,[42] Momigliano applied these criteria to the works of seventeenth- and eighteenth-century antiquarians interested in the classical past, and thereby rescued for serious study a substantial genre of historiographical literature which had previously languished unread, being denied serious consideration by modern scholars for its failure to match its undoubted erudition with a correspondingly acute critical spirit.

It has been my central contention in this paper that the works of

[39] A. Machin, *Defensio Sanctitatis Beati Luciferi* (Cagliari, 1639). See pp. 110–11 for his deployment of numismatic evidence, and pp. 189–94 for his use of notarial documents when describing the discovery of S. Lucifero's body. Six illustrations appear between pp. 96–7.

[40] *Acta SS*, May, 5, pp. 197–225.

[41] See Benedict XIV, *De servorum Dei beatificatione et beatorum canonizatione*, 4 vols (Bologna, 1734–8); 1, bk i, ch. 40.

[42] Arnaldo Momigliano, 'Ancient history and the antiquarian', *Journal of the Warburg and Courtauld Institutes*, 13, 1950, pp. 285–315.

ecclesiastical erudition of a slightly earlier period pass the 'Momigliano-test'. They were written, as has been seen, to vindicate or justify local cults and devotions that were threatened by the standardizing liturgy of the Tridentine Church, which permitted local variation only if it fulfilled rigorous criteria. I chose to look at the case of Cagliari and its *sancti innumerabiles* because it is precisely in devotion to the martyrs of the Early Church that this tension exhibited itself so clearly. For here historical argument was particularly relevant if a local church was to rescue its cherished cults from the 'curial positivism' of the Roman Sacred Congregation of Rites. Even where the interpretation of the distant past was in dispute between two local churches, the criteria each had to satisfy were still those set by Tridentine Rome. It is in this sense that I intend to make my claim for the martyrological origins of the historical revolution.[43]

University of York

[43] This theme is developed in my forthcoming book-length study: *Historia Sacra: the Reform of Liturgy, Hagiography and Ecclesiastical Historiography in Tridentine Italy.*

THE VENERATION OF THE MARTYRS OF IKITSUKI (1609-1645) BY THE JAPANESE 'HIDDEN CHRISTIANS'*

by STEPHEN TURNBULL

CHRISTIANITY came to Japan in 1549 in the person of the 'Apostle to the Indies', St Francis Xavier, yet in spite of initial progress both in making converts and in becoming part of the Japanese religious milieu, within a century it had virtually disappeared, harried to its demise by savage persecutions from a government convinced that Christianity was a threat to its survival.[1] The suppression of Christianity produced many martyrs, of whom the best known are the 'Twenty-Six Martyrs of Nagasaki', crucified in 1597 and canonized in 1862.[2] Of the thousands[3] of others who perished, many are known neither by name nor date of martyrdom, but in one unique case the martyrs of a particular island are remembered and honoured by one of the world's most secretive Christian groups, the *Kakure Kirishitan*, or 'Hidden Christians' of Japan.[4]

The original *Kakure Kirishitan* communities came about as a direct result of the persecution which produced the martyrs described in this paper. By about 1645 Christianity had completely disappeared as an overt religion, and was maintained only by groups of Christians who managed to preserve their faith as an underground church throughout two and a

* Research for this paper was supported by a grant from the Great Britain-Sasakawa Foundation, which is gratefully acknowledged.

[1] For the history of Japan's 'Christian Century', see C. R. Boxer, *The Christian Century in Japan*, 2nd edn (Berkeley, 1967); George Elison, *Deus Destroyed: the Image of Christianity in Early Modern Japan* (Harvard, 1973).

[2] See the short work by Yakichi Kataoka, *Nagasaki no Junkyōsha* (The Martyrs of Nagasaki) (Tokyo, 1957), where the Ikitsuki martyrs are discussed on pp. 29–39; and his more comprehensive *Nihon Kirishitan Junkyōshi* (A History of Japanese Christian Martyrdom) (Tokyo, 1979), pp. 289–98.

[3] Johannes Laures, in his 'Die Zahl der Christen und Martyrer im alten Japan', *Monumenta Nipponica*, 7 (1951), pp. 84–101, estimates the number of martyrs as 4,045. The sources of numerical information are discussed in J. F. Schütte, S.J., *Introductio ad Historiam Societatis Jesu in Japonia 1549–1650* (Rome, 1968), pp. 435–46.

[4] The communities also refer to themselves as *Kyū Kirishitan*, or 'Old Christians'. Kōyō Tagita (see below, n. 8) preferred the term *Sempuku Kirishitan* or 'secret Christians'. Most foreign commentators have tended to refer to them as 'Crypto-Christians' or 'Crypto-Catholics', e.g., Johannes Laures, *The Catholic Church in Japan: a Short History* (Rutland, Vt., 1954); Schütte, *Introductio*, p. 426.

half centuries of prohibition, having no contact whatsoever with the rest of the Christian world, which hardly suspected their survival. So self-sufficient and independent did they become, that when Catholic missionaries finally returned, in 1859,[5] many groups of them chose to remain as a separate Christian denomination,[6] and are now found mainly in the area of Sotome (to the north-west of Nagasaki), on the Gotō island chain, and on the two islands of Hirado and Ikitsuki. In this paper we will be concerned with the last-mentioned island of Ikitsuki, where, unlike the other areas, the *kakure* faith appears to be active and flourishing, though it too is suffering from the results of emigration by the young, and the exposure to modern means of mass-communication, which have caused problems for other groups.[7]

All modern study of the *Kakure Kirishitan* derives from the pioneering work of Kōya Tagita, who spent twenty years gaining the confidence of the various *kakure* groups,[8] including Ikitsuki, and all subsequent studies[9] acknowledge their debt to him. The community on Ikitsuki is now much more open to outsiders than it was in Tagita's time, and in April 1992 I carried out research there during the period of their Easter festivities, and observed them expressing their Christian faith in ways conditioned by the years of isolation. *Kakure* worship is centred around an elaborate calendar of festivals, which are celebrated largely in private houses. Much eating and drinking is involved, a direct echo of the most convenient camouflage for such gatherings during the time of persecution. Altars, deliberately designed to appear similar to the ordinary Buddhist altars found in any Japanese home, are decorated with the precious *nandogami*, a word that literally means 'closet-gods', which include, among other sacred objects, holy water and pictorial depictions of saints and martyrs called *gozensama*. These are either bronze medals brought by the early missionaries, or

[5] O. Cary, *Christianity in Japan, a History of Roman Catholic, Protestant and Orthodox Missions* (Rutland, Vt., 1976), p. 281.

[6] The best account of the finding of the Hidden Christians is J. Marnas, *La Religion de Jésus, Iaso Ja-kyō ressuscité au Japan dans la seconde moitié du XIXᵉ siècle* (Paris, 1896), pp. 487–91.

[7] During my visit to Ikitsuki I was told that in one of the areas on the island, Ichibu, there has been a decline in numbers of 25 *Kakure* households in Ichibu between 1974 and 1988.

[8] Kōya Tagita, *Shōwa jidai no Sempuku Kirishitan* (The Secret Christians of the Shōwa Period, i.e., of the present day) (Tokyo, 1954).

[9] The best subsequent works are Kiyoto Furuno, *Kakure Kirishitan* (Tokyo, 1959); and Yakichi Kataoka's two works, *Kakure Kirishitan* (Tokyo, 1967), and *Kinsei no chika shinkō* (Underground beliefs of the present day) (Tokyo, 1974). For works dealing specifically with Ikitsuki, there is a detailed history by a former Mayor of the island, Gizaemon Kondō, *Ikitsuki Shikō* (Ikitsuki Chronicles) (Sasebo, 1977), which incorporates his short illustrated book, *Ikitsuki no Kakure Kirishitan* (Ikitsuki, 1973).

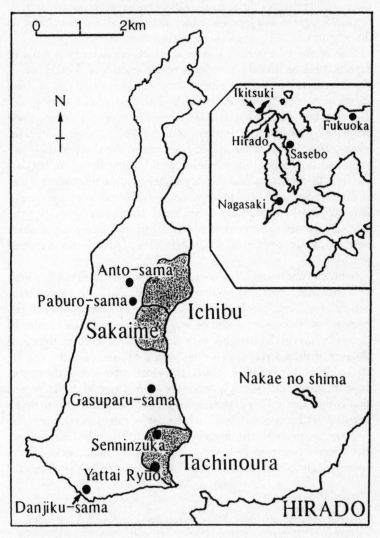

Map showing the island of Ikitsuki, and the locations of the sites of martyrdom described in the text.

painted hanging scrolls, most of which have been repeatedly copied over the years.[10] In front of the altars the *Kakure* recite prayers in a mixture of Latin, Portuguese, and Japanese, which have been shown to be based on the original Catholic prayers taught to their ancestors.[11]

One of the most important ways in which the secret faith could be expressed has been in the veneration of the martyrs of Ikitsuki, whose deaths occurred between the years 1609 and 1645. Very few of them appear in martyrologies, and, unlike the Twenty-Six Saints of Nagasaki, the places of their suffering are marked only by simple monuments, still cared for by the Hidden Christians of today. Yet, in common with the whole *kakure* tradition, the sites of martyrdom have acquired their own unique identity within the Christian world. Being forced to live outwardly as Buddhists, and unavoidably immersed in the religious traditions of Shintō, which associated local protective deities with any sites regarded as holy,[12] it is not surprising to see many features of native Japanese religion expressed in the martyrs' sites and their traditions, some of which were no doubt developed deliberately as camouflage for Christian worship.

In his study of Ikitsuki, Tagita took a great interest in the martyrs' sites, and it was with his map[13] in hand that I was able to make my own observations in 1992, conducted in the form of the traditional Japanese pilgrimage, which consists of visiting and praying at each of a number of shrines in turn.[14] The first link with Shintō to be noticed by the casual observer of the martyrs' sites is their setting. In most cases the sites are marked by a grove of trees, which look most impressive in the case of those set upon a hill. Worship originally centred around one large tree, usually a pine, as it was a practice among the Hidden Christians to bury a sacred object beneath the roots, and use the location as a place of secret meetings and prayer. Unfortunately all the central trees died in the plague that affected pine trees in Kyūshū during the late 1940s, caused by an insect brought in on imported timber.[15] It is almost certain that during the

[10] Tagita, *Shōwa*, pp. 264–9.

[11] Ibid., pp. 360–490.

[12] Shintō is the indigenous religion of Japan, and consists of the worship of numerous deities known as *kami*, many of whom are associated with particular places, such as high mountains or ancient trees, a mode of religious expression perfectly suited to the *Kakure Kirishitan*. See Ian Reader, *Religion in Contemporary Japan* (London, 1991).

[13] Tagita, *Shōwa*, p. 281.

[14] The best modern account of the place of the pilgrimage in Japanese religious life is Reader, *Religion*, pp. 134–67. The classic account of a Japanese pilgrimage is Oliver Statler, *Japanese Pilgrimage* (London, 1984).

[15] Kondō, *Ikitsuki*, p. 353.

time of persecution there was no identifying mark except for the trees, but every site now contains a stone shrine, most of which are comparatively new. The shrine itself is usually a simple affair of natural stone, arranged to make the shape of an open-fronted box, before which incense can be burned, and offerings made of *sake* and food. Some are the more elaborate versions made from carved stone called *hokora*, the small 'shrine within a shrine' often found in Shintō shrine buildings.[16] There may even be a *torii*, the traditional Shintō gateway in the shape of the Greek letter *pi*, but what distinguishes the site totally from a Shintō shrine is the presence of graves in the Christian sites.[17] We will describe the sites in roughly chronological order, beginning with two figures whose dates are unknown.

PABURO–SAMA

Kōshiro no Paburo-sama, or 'Saint Paul of Kōshiro', is the most puzzling of all the Ikitsuki sites. It is firmly established within local tradition as being associated with a martyr, but opinions differ greatly as to who it is that is honoured. Tagita suggests[18] that it may simply be the Apostle Paul, but notes a local tradition that links the site with a Christian named Paul who lived in the latter quarter of the sixteenth century.[19] Whatever his origin, Paburo-sama is one of only three Ikitsuki martyrs to be commemorated pictorially among the *nandogami*. Both in the scroll illustrated by Tagita,[20] and in the bronze medal I examined while it was on display during the *Osejo-matsuri* festival of Sakaime, Paburo-sama appears as a Dutch sea-captain holding a bow and arrow (see plate 1).[21] Tagita suggests that this may simply be Christian camouflage, but none of the *Kakure* I interviewed was able to tell me anything about Paburo-sama beyond his name. The site is again a clump of trees, with a rough stone shrine in a small clearing where there was formerly a large pine tree. It is traditional to wear new straw sandals when visiting, and a further tradition states that anyone who cuts down the grove will fall ill.[22]

---

[16] A typical *hokora* is about 1 metre high and 60 cm in cross section. It has a curved or sloping roof, and may well have doors, also of stone.

[17] A strong aversion to the pollution associated with death is one of the chief characteristics of Shintō, expressed most commonly in Japan by the universal use of Buddhist rites for funerals: Reader, *Religion*, pp. 77–106.

[18] Tagita, *Shōwa*, p. 267.

[19] The term '-sama' is an honorific form of address.

[20] Tagita, *Shōwa*, p. 283.

[21] The *Osejo-matsuri* is held every two years during the Easter period.

[22] Kondō, *Ikitsuki*, p. 354; Kataoka, *Kakure*, p. 266.

Plate 1   The bronze medal depicting 'Paburo-sama', venerated by the Hidden Christians of the Sakaime district. The actual identity of the person represented is very uncertain, but a firm local tradition identifies him as a martyr, though no details are known. He is shown as a Dutch sea captain, holding a Japanese bow and arrow. Photo: author.

ANTO-SAMA

This is the grave of the martyr Anthony Shōhei (see plate 2), of whom no other details are known. The shrine consists of a few stone slabs, and is within a grove of camellia trees on private land owned by a *Kakure* family. A bronze medal supposed to represent Anto-sama is one of the three medals (the others being of the Virgin Mary and Paburo-sama) which constitute the *gozensama* of Sakaime.[23]

GASUPARU-SAMA

We are on much firmer historical ground with the martyr Caspar Nishi, whose Christian name becomes 'Gasuparu' when written in Japanese. He was the first recorded Christian martyr of Ikitsuki, and died in 1609.[24] Caspar Nishi was *karō* (chief retainer) of Jerome Koteda, and ruled the Yamada and Tachinoura areas of Ikitsuki on Koteda's behalf. But when Koteda was exiled to Nagasaki by the *daimyō* Matsuura Shigenobu (1549–1614) he was deprived of office and his administration divided between two non-Christian officials, who were father and son. Inoue Ubasuke, the son, who received Yamada, was, in fact, married to Caspar's daughter Mary, and had allowed her to practise her faith with no interference. His father, however, set in motion a fierce persecution, and ordered the arrest of the Nishi family. Ubasuke tried to protect them, but Caspar Nishi was delivered for execution on 14 November 1609. The sword stroke was delivered by his son-in-law, as an act of honour from one member of the samurai class to another. Caspar's wife, Ursula,[25] and their elder son, John, were also put to death. Their fellow Christians were allowed to bury their bodies, and the graveyard of the family is now the shrine of Gasuparu-sama. Only the stump remains of the tree that dominated the site, but the rough stone graves are still well cared for.[26]

[23] The *nandogami* of Sakaime, which include the *gozensama*, are displayed on the altar for the New Year Festival and other events during the year such as the *Osejo-matsuri* (see above, n. 21).

[24] The most complete account of the martyrdom of the Nishi family is Hubert Cieslik, 'Junkyōsha ichizoku: Ikitsuki no Nishi-ke' (A family of martyrs: the Nishi family of Ikitsuki), *Kirishitan Kenkyū*, 21 (1982), pp. 89–184, and his short booklet, *Ikitsuki no Junkyōsha: Gasuparu Nishi Genka* (A Martyr of Ikitsuki: Caspar Nishi Genka) (Tokyo, 1988). Along with the martyrs of Nakae no shima, the Nishi family receive a full account in Leon Pagés, *Histoire Chrétienne du Japon depuis 1598 jusqu'à 1651*, 1 (Charles Douniol, Paris, 1869–7), pp. 178–80. Pagés's work, which was based on original Japanese documents, is regarded as being so authoritative that many Japanese works on the Christian martyrs cite references from him. The Nishi family are also covered in Kondō, *Ikitsuki*, pp. 207–11, 356; Kondō, *Kakure*, pp. 49–50; Kataoka, *Nihon*, p. 289; Kataoka, *Kakure*, p. 261.

[25] Ursula was the mother of martyrs. She had been a widow, and had a son by her late husband, who took the name of Caspar Nishi Toi and became a Jesuit. He died in 1612, and is noted in Schütte, *Introductio*, p. 236. Thomas, the second son spared in 1609, became a Dominican Father, and was martyred in 1634, the same year that a grandson of Caspar and Ursula was martyred. See the family tree in Cieslik, 'Junkyōsha ichizoku', p. 121.

[26] Wood from the tree of Gasuparu-sama was used to make a crucifix on display in the Museum of the Twenty-Six Martyrs of Nagasaki.

Plate 2   A member of the present-day Hidden Christian community of Ikitsuki kneels in prayer before the grave of the martyr Anthony Shōhei, who was beheaded at Matsuzaki, a site that has since disappeared under the extensive sea defences of the near-by harbour area. Photo: author.

The Martyrs of Ikitsuki

NAKAE NO SHIMA

Thirteen years went by before Ikitsuki was to suffer any more martyrdoms, but by 1622 the persecution under the *Shōgun* Tokugawa Hidetada was at its height, and foreign priests were being hunted down. The activity reached Ikitsuki with the arrest of a certain Father Camillo Costanzo, who was accompanied by a number of Christians from Ikitsuki: the catechist Caspar Koteda, John Sakamoto (Fr. Camillo's host), Damian Deguchi, Paul Tsukamoto, John Matsuzaki (also known as John Itō), and Augustin Ōta, from Hirado. On the island of Uku a Christian woman, hoping to convert her husband, told him of the presence of the priest, whereupon the husband informed the authorities, and Father Camillo was arrested.[27] He and his companions were taken back to Ikitsuki, from where he, Augustin Ōta, and Caspar Koteda were sent on to Hirado, leaving the men of Ikitsuki prisoners on their native island.

John Sakamoto was held in prison in Tachinoura for thirty-four days, and on 27 May he and Damian Deguchi were taken by boat to the island of Nakae no shima, a tiny outcrop of almost bare rock in the middle of the bay between Ikitsuki and Hirado. John Sakamoto was half-throttled by a cord round his neck and then beheaded. Damian Deguchi took the head and kissed it, then bowed his own head for an identical fate. Their remains were thrown into the sea to prevent any other Christians claiming them as relics.[28] A few days later, on 8 June, John Yukinoura, a well-respected Christian of Ikitsuki, aged 47, and the leader of the local Rosary Fraternity, was taken there and decapitated. His dying words are said to have been, 'From here it is not far to the Kingdom of Heaven', as he gazed around the bare rocks. His remains, too, were thrown into the sea.[29]

As Nakae no shima (its name simply means 'the island in the middle of the bay') is a prominent landmark visible from all parts of the populated eastern coast of Ikitsuki (see plate 3), the fourteen martyrdoms which took place there in 1622 and 1624 have made it into a place of great holiness, and the memories of the martyrs are commemorated in several ways. The most important is the association of Nakae no shima with baptism. When the priests were expelled, baptism was one of the few sacraments the secret community was able to maintain, and it has long been a tradition among the *Kakure* of Ikitsuki that the holy water used for

---

[27] Kondō, *Ikitsuki*, p. 214; Tagita, *Shōwa*, p. 347. In Pagés, *Histoire*, 1, p. 492, there is some confusion over the names of his companions.

[28] Pagés, *Histoire*, p. 493; Kondō, *Kakure*, p. 16.

[29] Pagés, *Histoire*, p. 494; Tagita, *Shōwa*, p. 348; Kondō, *Ikitsuki*, pp. 217–20.

Plate 3   The approach to the martyrs' island of Nakae no shima, located in the bay between Ikitsuki and Hirado. This is the most important martyrs' site of Ikitsuki; and a freshwater spring on the island is the source of the baptismal water used by the Hidden Christians. Photo: author.

baptism and other purposes is obtained only from Nakae no shima.[30] The actual spot is a cleft in the rocky cliff opposite the small *hokora* dedicated to 'San Juan-sama', or 'Saint John'. This name is also given to the holy water, which is regarded, like the holy pictures, as one of the *Kakure nandogami*, and the island itself is sometimes also referred to as San Juan-sama. The explanation is surely that of an association between St John the Baptist and an unexpected supply of fresh water on a holy island in the sea which was the scene of the martyrdom of two men called John. According to the boatman who took Tagita to Nakae no shima in 1931,[31] the water is supposed to flow from the spring when the prayers said in front of it are heard in Rome.

The martyrs are also remembered in a song called 'The song of San Juan-sama', sung by the Hidden Christians of Yamada at the time of their *Dōyonakayori* festival,[32] the three verses of which translate as follows:

> Before us the spring
> Behind the tall rocks
> Around us only the waters of the sea.
>
> This springtime the cherry blossoms will fall
> The flowers will bloom
> And spring will come again.
>
> Let us go and pray
> Let us go and pray at the temple of Paradise
> The temple is large,
> But, great or small, it is within your heart.

The first verse describes the view from the site of martyrdom on Nakae no shima. The second makes the classic Japanese allusion between the transience of human life and the brief flowering of cherry blossom, while the third echoes the words of the martyr John Yukinoura. He and his companions are also remembered by three statuettes erected almost certainly in recent years, as Tagita does not describe them. They are of painted stone, and kept within a shrine visible from the Ikitsuki shore, and much larger than the original one next to the spring, as described above. The central figure bears the inscription 'San Juan', and depicts a man dispensing the holy water from the flask held in his left hand. On his right

[30] Tagita, *Shōwa*, pp. 349–52; Kondō, *Kakure*, p. 16.
[31] Tagita, *Shōwa*, p. 350.
[32] My translation from Tagita, *Shōwa*, p. 346.

is another standing figure, also labelled 'San Juan', but for some reason the third figure bears the name 'San Migiru' or St Michael.[33]

The former companions of John Sakamoto and Damian Deguchi met their deaths within the next few months, and two years later the executions began again, when thirty-eight Christians from Hirado and Ikitsuki were put to death. The entire family of Gabriel Ichinose of Hirado, who had been executed in 1622 after sheltering Father Camillo, including two servants born in Ikitsuki, was killed in March 1624, and a family called Mori, originally from Ikitsuki, was martyred in Ōsaka during the following few days.[34] At the same time Nakae no shima once again became an execution ground. On 5 March the family of the martyr Damian Deguchi followed him to death on Nakae no shima. The victims were his mother Isabel, aged 69, his wife Beatrice, and their four children.[35] The youngest, a daughter aged 7, was thrown on to the dead body of her mother and killed by three sword strokes.[36] They were accompanied in death by the surviving family of John Sakamoto: his widow Mary and their four children. The children were tied in straw sacks and flung into the sea. They were the last to die on Nakae no shima, but Catherine, the widow of the other 1622 Nakae no shima martyr John Yukinoura, who was from Ichibu on Ikitsuki, was exposed naked on a tree, and finally decapitated elsewhere on the island.[37]

SENNINZUKA

Twenty years passed before persecution resumed again on Ikitsuki, and three martyrs' memorials commemorate those who perished around the year 1645. Senninzuka, 'the mound of a thousand people', is said to be the mass grave of the victims.[38] A large pine tree once grew here, and was replaced by one planted by Tagita in 1953, which is still thriving. There is a *hokora* in the centre of the compound, and of all the shrines on Ikitsuki this one looks most like a Shintō shrine, largely because of the stone *torii* at

---

[33] From my own observations in April 1992.
[34] Pagés, *Histoire*, p. 590; Kondō, *Kakure*, p. 52.
[35] As recorded by Pagés, *Histoire*, pp. 590–1; Kondō, *Kakure*, pp. 53–4; Tagita, *Shōwa*, p. 348. There is, however, some confusion within our sources over the two families. Elsewhere Kondō, *Kakure*, p. 16, has the names of the families of John and Damian interchanged, which is in accordance with Kataoka's works: *Nagasaki*, p. 30; *Kakure*, p. 259, and *Nihon*, p. 294.
[36] Pagés, *Histoire*, p. 591.
[37] Ibid., p. 592.
[38] Kondō, *Ikitsuki*, p. 353; Kondō, *Kakure*, p. 45, adds the observation that the graves are of children. Kataoka, *Nihon*, p. 298, notes that the date of martyrdom is unknown.

the entrance. It is associated with the near-by Shintō Hime no miya *jinja* (shrine). Tagita reports[39] a tradition among the Christians of Tachinoura identifying the 'princess' Hime no Miya with the Virgin Mary.

YATTAI RYŪO

Not far from Senninzuka is the tiny Yattai Ryūo, once on an open sand-hill, but now surrounded by buildings, which commemorates a group of eight Christian parents and children executed here, probably during the 1645 persecutions. The actual year is not known, but the anniversary is said to be the twelfth day of the third lunar month. One of the victims was a pregnant woman, who pleaded for the life of her child on the grounds that an unborn baby could not be executed for being a Christian. Her pleas fell on deaf ears, and both perished.[40] The shrine consists of a small *hokora*.

DANJIKU-SAMA

The final martyrs' site on Ikitsuki displays many of the elements of the Ikitsuki martyrs' tradition we have noted above; as it is honoured by non-Christians as well as the *kakure*, it has acquired an association with prayers for good fortune, and, as with Anto-sama and Paburo-sama, the martyrs of Danjiku-sama are commemorated pictorially as a *gozensama*. With the possible exception of Nakae no shima, its setting, beside a beach and among camellia trees and bamboo at the foot of steep cliffs, is also the most moving. *Danjiku* is Ikitsuki dialect for silken bamboo,[41] and it was within a grove of silken bamboo that the family of a certain Yaichibei, his wife, Mary, and their infant son, John, concealed themselves. As their hut was difficult to reach overland the officials approached the area by boat, and a lookout scanned the shore for signs of life. Tagita adds the poignant detail that the child John began to cry, and the sound gave them away.[42] Once discovered, they were immediately put to death. According to Kondō,[43] many families fled to the Gotō after this incident.

Danjiku-sama is particularly revered by the non-Christian fishermen of nearby Tachinoura, on Ikitsuki, who will visit Danjiku-sama before undertaking a long voyage, and offer petitions at the small *hokora*

---

[39] Tagita, *Shōwa*, p. 341.
[40] Kondō, *Ikitsuki*, p. 356; Kondō, *Kakure*, pp. 47-8; Tagita, *Shōwa*, p. 340.
[41] Tagita, *Shōwa*, p. 267.
[42] Tagita, *Shōwa*, pp. 267, 343-5.
[43] Kondō, *Ikitsuki*, p. 236.

established there (see plate 4). According to Tagita,[44] they believe that if they fail to make an offering at Danjiku-sama there will be rough weather on their voyage. The prayers are written on red or white banners, which are attached to tree branches at the shrine, and are left there until they naturally decay. Danjiku-sama is regarded as a suitable place at which to pray for a safe delivery in childbirth, or for protection from wounds in battle, an illustration of how the *kami* (deities) associated with a place in Shintō traditions may have a Christian origin. There is a further tradition, still firmly kept, that Danjiku-sama is never approached by sea, in memory of the way in which the family was discovered. Shrine visiting is always done overland, now an easier prospect since the construction of the new coast road in 1991.

The *gozensama* featuring the family is illustrated by Tagita,[45] who notes that the unusual Christian name credited to the husband, Jigoku (which means 'Hell' in Japanese), is probably a corruption of Diego. There is also a song, similar to the song of San Juan-sama, sung on the feast day, which is the sixteenth day of the first lunar month:

> Shibatayama now is a vale of tears
> But in the time to come there will be a way out.[46]

From 1645 onwards there were no more persecutions in Ikitsuki, the authorities believing that by the blood that had been shed the Christian religion had been stamped out. Instead, the Christians of Ikitsuki became *kakure*, and developed their faith as an underground church for two centuries. Of all the ways of expressing their faith available to them, honouring the sites of the martyrs became very important, partly because it was one of the easiest to conceal, as the sites came to be associated with powerful *kami*, whose worship was indistinguishable from that of Shintō deities. But there was one further factor involved. Every year from 1626 onwards the villagers of former Christian areas were subjected to the ritual of the *fumi-e*,[47] whereby they were required to show their rejection of Christianity by trampling on a Christian image similar to the ones they venerated in secret. The *Kakure Kirishitan* thereby made themselves technically apostates, and with no priest available to hear their confessions and grant them absolution, they remained in a state of sin, made worse by

[44] Kataoka, *Nagasaki*, p. 39; Kondō, *Ikitsuki*, pp. 236, 354; Kondō, *Kakure*, pp. 46–7.
[45] Tagita, *Shōwa*, p. 252.
[46] The reference is obscure, because there is no mountain called Shibatayama anywhere on Ikitsuki.
[47] For the *fumi-e* see Yakichi Kataoka, *Fumi-e* (Tokyo, 1969).

Plate 4   The martyrs' site of Danjiku-sama, beside the beach, near to the southern tip of Ikitsuki. In the centre of the picture is the small shrine known as a *hokora*. The flags have inscribed upon them prayers left by fishermen before setting out on long voyages. Photo: author.

the painful guilt which arose from a comparison between themselves and the noble martyrs, who had not denied their faith when challenged, and had paid for it with their lives. It may well have been an act of contrition that for two centuries the martyrs' sites were honoured so well. We have noted some loss of detail over names and dates, but in view of the conditions in which these memories were preserved, this is hardly surprising. As the years went by, the legends and traditions grew, until the memories of the Christian martyrs blended with the surrounding values of native Japanese religion in a way that was later to be identified with many other facets of the Hidden Christian life.[48]

Department of Theology and Religious Studies
University of Leeds

---

[48] For discussion of the degree of acculturation of Christianity as represented by the *Kakure Kirishitan* see Kōya Tagita, *Study of Acculturation among the Secret Christians of Japan* (privately printed, n.p., n.d.) and Ann M. Harrington's two works, 'Japan's Kakure Kirishitan' (Claremont College Ph.D. thesis, 1978) and 'The Kakure Kirishitan and their place in Japan's religious tradition', *Japanese Journal of Religious Studies*, 7 (1980), pp. 318–36.

IS MARTYRDOM MANDATORY? THE CASE OF GOTTFRIED ARNOLD

by W. R. WARD

NINETEENTH-CENTURY critics were entirely mistaken in supposing that political economy was the dismal science; it is in fact ecclesiastical history. Members of this society understand this better than any, exchanging, as they do, views and information mainly in print, and devoting their twice-yearly gatherings principally to encouraging the cheerfulness both of nature and of grace. Goethe had a word for it:

> Es ist die ganze Kirchengeschichte
> Mischmasch von Irrtum und Gewalt.[1]

But then Goethe had drunk deep at an impressionable age of Gottfried Arnold's celebrated *Unparteiische Kirchen- und Ketzerhistorie* (1699), which he discovered in his father's bookcase, and to no man was ecclesiastical history more dismal than the Arnold of the *Ketzerhistorie*. On this occasion when we are celebrating the ingrained lovelessness of organized Christianity, it is worth inquiring briefly what Arnold's views in this great work, probably the last large work of church history to have a substantial impact on the educated general public, were, and how it came about that he quickly moved beyond them, married, and took church office. Had martyrdom ceased to be mandatory? Had cheerfulness broken in? Was it, as some vocal admirers assumed, the triumph of the world's slow stain? Or was some other factor at work?

Gottfried Arnold (1666–1714) was bred in the strictest school of Lutheran Orthodoxy at Wittenberg, but by the age of thirty, while not breaking with the Church, had set himself in opposition to most of what Orthodoxy stood for, and especially its use of church history to reinforce the claims of confessional dogmatics.[2] His development, like that of so

---

[1] J. W. von Goethe, *Zahme Xenien, Gedenkausgabe der Werke*, 2, p. 402; *The Autobiography of J. W. von Goethe*, ed. K. J. Weintraub (Chicago, 1974), 1, pp. 379–80.

[2] The most useful of the older works on Arnold are Franz Dibelius, *Gottfried Arnold. Sein Leben und seine Bedeutung für Kirche und Theologie* (Berlin, 1873); Max Goebel, *Geschichte des christlichen Lebens in der rheinisch-westphalischen evangelischen Kirche* (Coblenz, 1849–52), 2, pp. 698–735. The most useful modern works are Erich Seeberg, *Gottfried Arnold, die Wissenschaft und die Mystik seiner Zeit* (Meerane, 1923); Hermann Dörries, *Geist und Geschichte bei Gottfried Arnold* (Göttingen, 1963); Ernst Benz, *Die protestantische Thebais* (Mainz and Wiesbaden, 1963); Jürgen

many theologians of his day, was influenced on one side by politics, and on the other by intellectual forces of a very international kind. Arnold's first two appointments were obtained for him by Spener; they were domestic tutorships, and the second of them was in Quedlinburg, a town and abbey not far from Halberstadt.[3] After much conflict, not only between the town and abbey, but between Saxony and Brandenburg, the territory was finally taken by the latter from the former in 1698. Almost predictably this struggle had also been fought by the churchmen in the town, the Orthodox preachers supporting Saxony, while the Hofdiakon Sprögel, a Pietist sympathetic to the awakened and the separatists locally, was inclined to Brandenburg. He was also a friend of Arnold, who without disloyalty to the Church held house-meetings open to separatists, and became a sharp critic of the Orthodox (or Saxon) party.[4] He corresponded with Jane Leade and the English Philadelphians, but more importantly was impressed by the English patristic scholar William Cave, whose *Primitive Christianity* (1673) appeared in German dress at Leipzig in 1694.[5] Arnold was not much impressed by Cave's belief that the English Church was in principle the model of the Church of primitive antiquity, but, like Wesley later, he was impressed by his picture of the 'divine and holy Precepts of the Christian Religion drawn down into action ... breathing in the hearts and lives of these good old Christians', at any rate for the first three or four centuries.[6] The early Enlightenment left its mark in Thomasius. Arnold wrote for his journal, the *Historie der Weisheit und*

Büchsel, *Gottfried Arnold. Sein Verständnis von Kirche und Wiedergeburt* (Witten, 1970); J. F. G. Goeters, 'Gottfried Arnolds Anschauung von der Kirchengeschichte in ihrem Werdegang', in B. Jaspert and R. Mohr, eds, *Traditio-Krisis-Renovatio aus theologischer Sicht. Festschrift Winfried Zeller* (Marburg, 1976), pp. 241–57; F. W. Kantzenbach, 'Gottfried Arnold', in M. Greschat, ed., *Gestalten der Kirchengeschichte*, 7, *Orthodoxie und Pietismus* (Stuttgart, 1982), pp. 261–75; T. Stählin, *Gottfried Arnolds geistliche Dichtung, Glaube und Mystik* (Göttingen, 1966). See also Klaus Wetzel, *Theologische Kirchengeschichtsschreibung im deutschen Protestantismus, 1660–1760* (Giessen and Basle, 1983); J. Büchsel and D. Blaufuss, 'Gottfried Arnolds Briefwechsel', in D. Meyer, ed., *Pietismus-Herrnhutertum-Erweckungsbewegung. Festschrift für Erich Beyreuther* (Cologne, 1982), pp. 71–107.

[3] On Quedlinburg, see J. B. Neveux, *Vie spirituelle et vie sociale entre Rhin et Baltique au XVIIme siècle* (Paris, 1967), p. 12, and *passim*.

[4] There are a few details about this in Martin Schmidt, 'Gottfried Arnold—seine Eigenart, seine Bedeutung, seine Beziehung zu Quedlinburg', in his *Wiedergeburt und neuer Mensch* (Witten, 1969), pp. 331–41. Sprögel officiated at the wedding of August Hermann Francke in 1694. See also Dibelius, *Gottfried Arnold*, pp. 55–67.

[5] W. Cave, *Erstes Christentum oder Gottesdienst der alten Christen in den ersten Zeiten des Evangelii*, tr. J. C. Frauendorf (Leipzig, 1694).

[6] Eamon Duffy, 'Primitive Christianity revived; religious renewal in Augustan England', *SCH*, 14 (1977), pp. 287–300.

Torheit, and took over in return his willingness to use German in scholarly discourse, his demand for toleration, his sharp separation between philosophy and theology, his venomous opposition to Aristotelianism in the latter, his notion that true church history was wisdom, while *historia philosophica* was foolishness. In these years Arnold lived the life of a scholarly recluse, intensively studying and translating the Fathers (one of his translations being the homilies of Macarius the Egyptian, which had an astonishing impact in the Pietist world and helped launch Wesley on his ill-fated expedition to Georgia).[7] But the organizing principle of all this learning was derived from the Netherlands. Witsius, the Utrecht Coccejan, added to the Dutch translation of Cave the disclaimer that the authority of Scripture and that of the Fathers must be strictly distinguished; this went into the German translation and was taken over by Arnold. Friedrich Spanheim the younger, who secured the triumph of the Voetian party in Leiden, taught him that the fall of the Church took place at the beginning of the fourth century. And this for Arnold was the mirror of his own day, when the Church relied on alliance with the State rather than its inner spiritual resources.[8]

Thus in his works of the mid-nineties, which secured his call to a chair at Giessen in 1697, Arnold had reached many of the positions which, after his resignation to escape the world in 1698, he took up in the *Ketzerhistorie*. As with Cave, the Early Church was an example to all, but that church was not Cave's. It was a community of the regenerate, and among the fruits of regeneration were *Unparteilichkeit* and inwardness. 'Impartiality' in Arnold's sense was a correlate of inwardness; not only did church history issue in no normative constitution, to boast of one, such as the apostolic succession, was already to surrender inwardness of faith to outward forms. The fall of the Church indeed occurred in the fourth century, when it accepted outward favour and props, and persecution ceased; but the rot had begun to set in at the end of the apostolic age, and the task of history was to unravel the interweaving of true and false. Of course, persecution never did cease for heretics, and got worse after the Church had made its bargain with the State; there was no question but that suffering was one of the marks of the True Church, and that the True Church must expect to suffer from the non-Christian Church as it had from the non-Christian State. Arnold was perfectly aware that dissent was not an *opus operatum*, and that there were generally some dissenters about,

---

[7] On this see Benz, *Die protestantische Thebais*; H. D. Rack, *Reasonable Enthusiast. John Wesley and the Rise of Methodism* (London, 1989), pp. 102, 347.

[8] Goeters, 'Gottfried Arnolds Anschauung', pp. 247, 249.

anxious to go to the stake for a nostrum; what was at fault on both sides in such cases was the disastrous desire to formulate the faith in non-scriptural terms. A heretic in the Early Church had been simply a man who denied God from heathen blindness, or denied Christ by unholy living. But, in general, church history was the intrusion of compulsion upon a voluntary society, a process intimately associated with institutionalization and the growth of hierarchy.[9]

All these ideas are recognizable in the *Ketzerhistorie*, by which Arnold is chiefly remembered, but more was to come. His early works had done well among Dutch separatists, and especially in the circle of Friedrich Breckling, a Schleswiger who had separated from the Lutheran churches, and now spread his ideas by a constant stream of letters and publications from Amsterdam. He now put down his own plans to write a church history, and pressed Arnold to set forth the issue between true and corrupt Christianity on a big scale. At the same time Arnold became subject to Behmenist influences, which led him to produce a study of the *Signs of the Times*,[10] and took up with that Cinderella of objects of Christian devotion, the heavenly Sophia, the divine wisdom.[11] The signs of the times were partly the incessant warfare of the 1690s, but more especially the false security of Christians, and, in particular, of the Lutheran Church of Saxony, blind to the fate of the Huguenots, and branding as heretics the prophets and witnesses sent to warn it. This also left its mark on the *Ketzerhistorie*, three-quarters of the vast bulk of which were devoted to the last two centuries.

The central concept of the *Ketzerhistorie*, as of the earlier works, is *Unparteilichkeit*, and Arnold makes it clear at the very beginning[12] that this did not mean mere weighing in the scale of historical scholarship, but 'true obedience to God and his eternal truths'; it meant illumination by the Holy Spirit. But there is no division of truth into secular and theological, and no division of history into profane and church history. Those enlightened by the Holy Spirit stand on God's side, but not on the

---

[9] Büchsel, *Gottfried Arnold*, pp. 32–75.

[10] *Die Zeichen dieser Zeit, bei dem Anfang der instehenden Trubsalen erwogen von einem der damit gute Absichten hat* (Aschersleben, 1698). Cf. Goeters, 'Gottfried Arnolds Anschauung', p. 252 and n. 44.

[11] On this cult see Ernst Benz, *Die Vision. Erfahrungsformen und Bildwelt* (Stuttgart, 1969), pp. 575–86. An English example of Sophiolatry, with its characteristic ambivalence as to the gender of the object of the cult, is Charles Wesley's hymn, 'Happy the man that finds the grace', no. 674 in the current British Methodist hymnbook, *Hymns and Psalms*.

[12] Gottfried Arnold, *Unpartheyische Kirchen- und Ketzerhistorie* (Frankfurt, 1729) [hereafter *KKH*] Vorrede (unpaginated), sections 1, 3, 5, 35.

side of any particular church, since God is not bound to any human institution. Arnold was here moving towards a difficulty. From the standpoint of the plain historian, the history of the institutional Church may be dismal, but it can at least be written out of the sources in the usual way; the history of the invisible Church can hardly be written from invisible sources. Arnold was feeling this difficulty before the end of the *Ketzerhistorie*, and proceeded to supply some of the illumination he had derived from the spirit in three more works, a *Vitae Patrum* (1700), *Das Leben der Glaübigen* (1701), covering the true saints of the last two centuries, and his *Historia et descriptio theologiae mysticae* (1702, German edition, 1703).

In the *Ketzerhistorie* the exemplary picture of the Early Church is tightened up. The early Christians went in not for empty opinions but for 'active Christianity',[13] and the way to distinguish teachers from heretics was in practice by their works, by their pressure for freedom of conscience and suffering. There was no infallible measure for distinguishing the two, but the pairs of opposites, freedom–compulsion, works–empty doctrine, suffering–power, gave a good practical guide to who was who. As soon as the teachers in the Church gained the power to throw their weight about with impunity Arnold christened them opprobriously *Clerisey*, a term which in English has strangely come back into favour. At any rate church history is a history of decay, especially after Constantine, when external persecution was succeeded by internal rancour. After the fifth century Arnold scarcely speaks of *Gemeinde*, congregation or community.

It is notable that Arnold speaks of Lutheran churches, but not Lutheran *Gemeinden*, indeed, the Reformation was not much to his taste. Luther indubitably began well, 'seeking to awaken in all the true fruit of the gospel, namely repentance and renewal',[14] and gave a great impulse to preaching, preaching from a full heart; but the end product was speedily clerical control and moral impotence.[15] The best that could be said was that there were some witnesses of the truth left, who pilloried the decline in Lutheranism.[16] Nor were the Protestant sects any better; there was no essential difference between the churches and sects[17]—both pushed their own authority instead of establishing Christ in the heart.[18] Arnold was now much more radical than he had been. It had once been the historian's

13 *KKH*, I, p. 202a.
14 *KKH*, I, p. 509a.
15 *KKH*, I, pp. 574–5, 578.
16 *KKH*, I, p. 927.
17 *KKH*, I, p. 20.
18 *KKH*, I, p. 1201, section 5.

task to separate the true from the false in the Church's record; now it was impossible to associate the two. 'Because the kingdom of God is always inward ... the true church of Christ among all parties, peoples and tongues is for good and all invisible and hidden.'[19] There was indeed no church or sect to which the true seeker after God could commit himself without anxiety. What had begun as the primitive Christian community had been so eaten out by its faithlessness as to leave no option to the faithful but total separation, at whatever the cost. The one hope was the eschatological hope that the time was drawing near when sects and names and parties would indeed fall, and God would be all in all.[20]

The *Ketzerhistorie* was first published in 1699 and 1700; yet in 1701 Arnold was married, and in 1702 he was back in church office, thus accepting two of the main institutions of society. How had yesterday's radical accommodated himself to what yesterday had been the sinful world?

The key to this apparent revolution has already been noted. There had been considerable development in Arnold not only between his youth and the mid-nineties, and between the mid-nineties and the *Ketzerhistorie*, but also within the latter work itself. And this development continued. In one respect this was surprising, for after resigning his chair Arnold went back to Quedlinburg, where religious disputes were as bitter as ever, were only inflamed by his intervention, and caused the Elector of Brandenburg to interfere by commission.[21] But Arnold's resignation of his chair owed something to the discovery that it did not offer an independent base from which to operate upon a church which had lost its way. Another period of inwardness followed; a period of influence by the English Behmenists, a remarkable personal vision of the heavenly Sophia,[22] an outpouring of lyric verse.[23] Even in the conclusion to the last part of the *Ketzerhistorie* he had begun slightly to soften his total rejection of institutional outwardness and to reveal the first signs of a possible connection between inwardness and the world.[24] Soon came the admission that even a community making its pilgrimage to Christ would contain the imperfect and the weak, and might even contain teachers, though they were in apostolic

---

[19] *KKH*, 2, p. 1178, section 13: 1, p. 1200, section 2.
[20] *KKH*, 2, p. 1202, section 9.
[21] Dibelius, *Arnold*, pp. 107, 131–47.
[22] On this see Seeberg, *Arnold*, pp. 22–9.
[23] K. C. E. Ehmann, ed., *Gottfried Arnolds sämmtliche Lieder mit einer reichen Auswahl aus den freieren Dichtungen* ... (Stuttgart, 1856).
[24] Büchsel, *Arnold*, p. 112; *KKH*, p. 1179, section 17.

style to bring people to Christ, not exercise force over them.[25] The next admission was that separatism as well as conformity might be due to self-will rather than the will of God, and that it was no prophylactic against temptation and danger. In any case, something was due to those who had no choice but to live under a fallen church. Arnold's return to church office was justified by love of his neighbour.[26] Paradoxically the very force of his inward mystical experience increased the assurance with which he could handle imperfect outward institutions.[27] Thundering against the abomination of desolation in the *Ketzerhistorie* had after all done no good, and at the end of 1700 he even referred to it in a private letter as 'an alien work'.[28] This did not mean that he was repudiating the book, but it clearly marked a major shift in personal attitude. The biographical collections to which reference was made above were bound to witness to the inter-mingling of good and evil in the Church as in the world, and the *History of Mystical Theology* on which Tersteegen built so splendidly two generations later was avowedly 'the immemorial theology of the truly wise ... main-tained and propagated alongside the doctrine of the schools'.[29]

Marriage required more than a shift of emphasis, required indeed another treatise, to justify.[30] Arnold did not surrender the notion that Adam before the fall had been androgynous, but had then lost his immortal paradise-body for a mortal frame akin to the beasts. But instead of pursuing the mystical assertion that the saint wed to the heavenly Sophia recovered the ground lost in Eden, Arnold came round to the view that marriage was created by God not as a requirement, but as a possibility for post-Adamic man, and not for his temporal comfort, but for his spiritual well-being. Marriage, in short, was rooted in the love of God, and that was why in Ephesians 5 it could be used as an image of the union of Christ with his congregation. Arnold, at least, was prepared to try it.

How comfortably Arnold settled into matrimony and church office in the last dozen years of his life is sufficiently indicated by the paucity of his references to either.[31] Martyrdom was no longer mandatory, and this, not

---

[25] Büchsel, *Arnold*, p. 115.
[26] Ibid., pp. 116–17; Gottfried Arnold, *Die geistliche Gestalt eines evangelischen Lehrers* (Halle, 1704), pp. 579–80, 615.
[27] Jo. Christoph Coler, *Historia Gothofredi Arnold . . .* (Wittenberg, 1718), p. 237.
[28] Ibid., p. 231.
[29] Gottfried Arnold, *Historia et descriptio theologiae mysticae* (Frankfurt, 1702), p. 22.
[30] *Das eheliche und unverehlichte Leben der ersten Christen* (Frankfurt, 1702).
[31] On the later Arnold see, besides the biographies quoted, Walter Delius, 'Gottfried Arnold in Perleburg (1707–1714)', *Jahrbuch für Berlin-Brandenburgische Kirchengeschichte*, 43 (1968), pp. 155–60.

because a great breach with the Old Adam of Arnold's early middle age had taken place, but because of a steady development powered by a basic conviction which did not change at all, that faith and life were inseparably connected, and that an active faith was the hallmark of the true Christian. Sophia had warned him to be at peace. Another unchanging conviction was that suffering was the lot of the true Christian. But whereas the radical Arnold had sought its origin in the fall of both world and church, it now seemed to be an aspect of the relation of imperfect man to God, and not to be remedied by such otherwise desirable achievements as religious toleration. Seen in this light, even Lutheran Orthodoxy appeared to have something to be said for it. For the suffering of the Christian had given Arnold to doubt whether assurance of salvation could be had from mystical union with God. Assurance was available only through the sufferings of Christ, appropriated through the promise of God that they were for us. If, therefore, neither resignation nor rejection of the world were a necessary part of preparation for union with God, it was possible to live simultaneously in grace and in the flesh, and even to stomach the institutional Church.[32] Martyrdom was no longer needed. But there is a sting in the tail. Let no ecclesiastical historian be made complacent by the story of the taming of Gottfried Arnold; for Arnold's principal vehicle of future influence,[33] that greater and better man, Gerhard Tersteegen,[34] was inspired by the radical of the *Ketzerhistorie*, the heavenly Sophia, and the *Mystical Theology*, not by the relatively painless Arnold *simul justus und peccator*.

Petersfield

---

[32] Büchsel, *Arnold*, p. 201.

[33] It is of interest to English readers to note that a proposal, perhaps occasioned by the publication of the enlarged edition of the *KKH* at Schaffhausen (1740–2), to produce an English translation in weekly instalments of three sheets, though commended by a quotation from Bayle's *Dictionary*, seems to have failed for lack of subscribers (*Certain queries with their respective answers; by way of introduction to the Rev. Mr. Godfrey Arnold's Impartial History of the Church and Hereticks* (London, 1744) [BL T. 1794 (6)]). I have not discovered the source of the proposal.

[34] See my forthcoming paper on 'Mysticism and Revival: the case of Gerhard Tersteegen' in the *Festschrift* for Dr J. D. Walsh.

MARTYRDOM IN EARLY VICTORIAN SCOTLAND: DISRUPTION FATHERS AND THE MAKING OF THE FREE CHURCH

by STEWART J. BROWN

'WHERE is the Church of Scotland to be found?' asked the leading Evangelical R. S. Candlish on 20 May 1843 at the first General Assembly of the Free Church of Scotland. 'She will not be found basking under the smiles of the great, but she is to be recognised once more, as in days of old, by her sufferings and her tears.'[1] In 1843 the Disruption of the Church of Scotland brought the birth of a new church, the Free Church of Scotland, as nearly a third of the ministers and nearly half the lay membership left the national Church of Scotland. They went out in part over a long-standing dispute concerning church patronage, but, more fundamentally, they left in protest against what they perceived as the refusal of the State to recognize the Church's independence in spiritual matters. The new Free Church claimed to be not merely a secession or schism, but rather the true national Church of Scotland, a claim its adherents based on their willingness to suffer for the principle of the headship of Christ in the Church. They were the Church of the martyrs of the Scottish Reformation and of the Covenants, willing to lay down their fortunes, even their lives, for 'the Crown rights of the Redeemer'. The true Church of Scotland, asserted the Free Church minister James Mackenzie, in 1859, 'began in 1843, when the old Church, the Church of Knox, of Melville, of Henderson, and of the martyrs, left its connexion with the State, and stood out before the world *free*, bearing the banner which our brave fathers bore.'[2]

Martyrdom played a vital role in defining the identity of the Free Church of Scotland. Martyrdom imagery appeared frequently in the pamphlets, poems, stories, and prints which celebrated the events of the Disruption and which inspired later generations of Free Church adherents. In portraying the sufferings of their martyrs, Free Church apologists drew on themes from the Romantic movement in Scottish literature—including celebrations of the beauty of Scottish scenery, the

[1] William Wilson and Robert Rainy, *Memorials of Robert Smith Candlish* (Edinburgh, 1880), p. 302.
[2] [J. Mackenzie], *Our Banner and its Battles* (Edinburgh, 1859), p. 55.

319

loyalty and courage of the Scottish Highlanders, and especially the historic drama of the later Covenanting period, as portrayed in the novels of Walter Scott, James Hogg, and John Galt. The stories of Free Church sacrifice challenged the view of Scotland as the land of rational self-interest, 'Scotch philosophy', and political economy. Free Church martyrs were prepared to sacrifice their worldly interests, even their lives, for the independence of the Church. This essay will explore the use of martyrdom imagery by the Free Church Fathers during the 1840s, and consider the role of martyrdom in making and consolidating the new Church.

I

The Disruption of 1843 had its origins in the long-standing controversy within the Church of Scotland concerning patronage, or the right of a patron to present a licensed candidate to a parish living within his gift.[3] Viewed by many as incompatible with the spiritual independence of the Church, patronage had been abolished with the re-establishment of Presbyterianism in the Church of Scotland in 1690. The law of patronage, however, was reimposed by Parliament in 1712, despite strong opposition from the courts of the Church of Scotland. For the governing elites in Scotland, patronage was a means of exercising control over the national Church and strengthening local political influence. Virtually every parish church in Scotland had a patron, and of the Scottish patronage, about a third were the property of the Crown, and nearly two-thirds were owned by the landed gentry and aristocracy. The enforcement of patronage resulted in major secessions from the national Church in 1733 and 1761. Although supported by the Moderate party, which came to dominate the Church courts after 1766, patronage was opposed by probably the majority in the Church, and especially by Evangelicals.

The Evangelical Revival of the late eighteenth and early nineteenth centuries brought the emergence within the Church of a well-organized Evangelical party, committed to increasing the Church's social influence. In 1834 this Evangelical party gained a working majority within the General Assembly of the Church. They used their new power to begin a Church extension campaign, aimed at restoring the authority of the national Church over moral discipline, education, and poor relief.

[3] For the Ten Years' Conflict and Disruption, see especially, Hugh Watt, *Thomas Chalmers and the Disruption* (Edinburgh, 1943), pp. 155–314; G. I. T. Machin, *Politics and the Churches in Great Britain 1832 to 1868* (Oxford, 1977), pp. 112–47; Stewart J. Brown, *Thomas Chalmers and the Godly Commonwealth* (Oxford, 1982), pp. 211–349.

Further, as part of their effort to popularize the Church, the Evangelical majority in the General Assembly passed the Veto Act, which gave a majority of male heads of family in a parish the right to veto an objectionable presentation and require the patron to present another candidate. Reviving the ideal of the seventeenth-century Covenanters, the Evangelicals sought to transform Scotland into a godly commonwealth.

Their campaign, however, was soon thwarted. Organized Dissent in Scotland vigorously opposed the efforts to revive the social authority of the Established Church. In 1838, under pressure from Dissenters, the Government announced that it would not provide funds for the endowment of additional parish churches and schools, thereby undermining the Church Extension campaign. In that same year, the Court of Session, the supreme civil court of Scotland, struck another blow at Evangelical hopes when it declared the Veto Act to be an illegal encroachment on the property rights of patrons—a decision confirmed by the House of Lords in March 1839. Presbyteries were now instructed to disregard the Veto Act, and proceed to the examination and ordination of patrons' candidates, regardless of the will of the parishioners.

For the Evangelical majority in the General Assembly, however, the ordination of candidates for the ministry was a spiritual act, which was beyond the authority of the civil courts. Refusing to compromise on the issue of spiritual independence, the Evangelical-dominated General Assembly instructed presbyteries to proceed according to the Church's Veto Act and resist 'intrusions' of unwanted candidates into parish churches. The Moderate party in the Assembly, on the other hand, opposed the high-handed stand of the Evangelical non-intrusionists. For Moderates, an Established Church was not above the civil law, and it must recognize the superior authority of the civil courts to interpret the civil law of patronage.

It was during the controversy surrounding the settlement at Marnoch that the conflicting parties—the Evangelical non-intrusionists and the Moderates—began to embrace the language of martyrdom. In 1837 the patron's candidate for the parish of Marnoch, in Aberdeenshire, John Edwards, was vetoed by an overwhelming majority. Edwards, however, appealed to the Court of Session, which in June 1839 instructed the presbytery of Strathbogie to proceed to his trials and ordination. The General Assembly, on the other hand, instructed the Strathbogie presbytery to take no action, while an appeal was made to Parliament for legislative redress. Seven Moderate ministers of the presbytery defied the General Assembly, obeyed the Court of Session, and took Edwards on trials. For this act of ecclesiastical insubordination, the Assembly suspended the seven from the ministry, and appointed other ministers to conduct worship in their parishes. The Court of Session responded with two interdicts, the first forbidding any ministers to enter the churches of the seven Moderates to announce the suspensions, and the second, extended interdict, forbidding non-intrusionist ministers to conduct worship anywhere within the seven Strathbogie parishes.

The extended interdict recalled for many the persecution of the Covenanters of the later seventeenth century, when congregations had worshipped in hiding from government soldiers on hillsides and in remote glens. Non-intrusionist ministers hurried to Strathbogie to break the interdict and preach in open fields, courting arrest and imprisonment.[4] The non-intrusionist publicist Hugh Miller claimed these ministers were following the example of the Covenanters and 'the other saints and martyrs of our Church' who had struggled 'on the people's behalf' against 'a grasping and selfish aristocracy'.[5] The bicentenary of the signing of the National Covenant had been celebrated in 1838, and appeals to the Covenanters struck a responsive chord among the Presbyterian public.

In January 1841 the seven suspended ministers of the presbytery of Strathbogie ordained Edwards to the parish church of Marnoch, in defiance of the instructions of the General Assembly and in obedience to the commands of the Court of Session. The congregation gathered in Marnoch Church before the ordination began—then read out a protest, collected their family Bibles from pews, and departed from the church to worship in a snow-covered open field. The Evangelical non-intrusionist press made much of the vision of sturdy peasants being driven out of the church of their fathers—reminiscent of persecuted Covenanters worshipping on snow-covered hills. Protest meetings were held throughout the country, and local non-intrusionist associations were formed.[6] In May 1841 the General Assembly solemnly deposed the seven Strathbogie ministers for their continued defiance of the Assembly's ecclesiastical authority.

The deposing of the seven for obeying the civil law now provided the Moderate minority with their own 'martyrs'. A Moderate League was formed, which refused to recognize the deposing of the seven Strathbogie

---

[4] *The Journal of Henry Cockburn*, 2 vols (Edinburgh, 1874), 1, p. 253.

[5] *Witness*, 25 March 1840.

[6] Robert Buchanan, *The Ten Years' Conflict*, 2 vols (Glasgow, 1852), 2, pp. 192–206; *Witness*, 27 Jan. 1841; *Scottish Guardian*, 26 Jan., 2 Feb. 1841.

ministers, and travelled to Strathbogie to assist them in worship.[7] Meetings were held in Edinburgh and other cities to show support for the 'martyrs for law'.[8] The 'reel of Bogie', as the Strathbogie affair became known, was caricatured in a series of prints, which poked fun at the aspirations of 'the Modern Martyrs'.[9] Yet the language of martyrdom and persecution, the appeals to memories of the Covenanters, aroused fears that each side was committed to the destruction of its opponents. Both parties now had their victims, witnesses to vital principles, who cried out for justice. This acted against compromise and did much to ensure that the patronage conflict would end in the break-up of the national Church.

II

On 18 May 1843, after failing to secure parliamentary recognition of the principle of the Church's spiritual independence, the Evangelical non-intrusionists withdrew from the General Assembly of the Established Church, marched in procession to Tanfield Hall, and constituted themselves as the first General Assembly of the Free Church of Scotland. In all, 474 ministers, about a third of the total, signed the Deed of Demission and joined the Free Church. It was an impressive act of sacrifice for the principle of the spiritual independence of the Church. The outgoing ministers surrendered incomes worth approximately £100,000 per annum, and gave up churches, manses, and status for an uncertain future. Perhaps half the lay membership of the Establishment also withdrew to join the Free Church, accepting the responsibility for building churches and supporting ministers through voluntary giving alone. While drawing adherents from throughout the country, the Free Church had special areas of strength in the urban areas, among the commercial and industrial middle class, and in the Scottish Highlands, where whole communities often left the Establishment.[10] The new Free Church ministers in the urban centres could be assured of fairly substantial incomes through the voluntary contributions of largely middle-class congregations. The prospects for rural ministers, however, were highly precarious. None the less, observers were impressed with the courage and faith with which even the outgoing rural ministers accepted their sacrifices. 'The truth is',

---

[7] *Journal of Henry Cockburn*, 1, p. 296.

[8] *Scottish Guardian*, 4, 11 June 1841.

[9] Edinburgh, New College Library, Album of Disruption Cartoons.

[10] A. Allan MacLaren, *Religion and Social Class: the Disruption Years in Aberdeen* (London, 1974), pp. 29–30.

observed the Court of Session judge, Lord Cockburn, in his journal on 8 June 1843, 'that these men would all have gone to the scaffold with the same serenity.'[11] Perhaps the major problem facing the new Church was how to ensure that wealthy urban congregations would help support the largely impoverished Highland churches.

Free Church leaders claimed that they were the true Church of Scotland, which was now freed from the bonds of an erastian State and restored to its sixteenth- and seventeenth-century purity. They were not simply another Presbyterian sect, of which there were already a disconcerting number in Scotland. Rather, through their willingness to sacrifice for the 'Crown Rights of the Redeemer' they showed themselves to be in direct succession to the martyred Reformers and Covenanters. 'We take our stand on the tombs of our martyred forefathers', wrote the Free Church minister and journalist George Lewis in 1843, 'on principles that are blazoned in Scottish history, and associated with the romantic scenery of her mountains, and floods, and rocky dells.'[12] Writing in November 1843 the Ulster Presbyterian minister William Gibson asserted that the outgoing ministers 'will go down to posterity with immortal honour, and be enrolled in that bright page which records the daring and the deed of patriots and martyrs.'[13] Just as the martyred Covenanters in the later seventeenth century had prepared the way for the re-establishment of Presbyterianism in the Church of Scotland in 1690, so, Gibson argued, the sacrifices of the outgoing ministers would again restore the glory of Scotland's national Church.[14]

Artistic representations of the Disruption combined references to the martyrs of the Covenant with visions of Scotland's romantic landscapes, of mist-covered moors and hills. One such poetic appeal to martyrdom and romance appeared in the non-intrusionist *Witness* newspaper of Edinburgh on 27 May, nine days after the Disruption:

A voice on the hills of Scotland!
A voice on the barren heath!
A stirring of the martyr dust.
That lieth underneath
The good old cause is owned again,
As in the days of yore,

[11] *Journal of Henry Cockburn*, 2, p. 32.
[12] George Lewis, *Church Principles, Illustrated by Scottish Church History* (Dundee, 1843), p. 24.
[13] William Gibson, *The Flock in the Wilderness* (Belfast, 1843), p. 24.
[14] Ibid., pp. 18–19.

And the Banner of the Covenant,
Streams on the storm once more![15]

'Scotland is Free' by the American poet Mrs Dana, which appeared in both
the Edinburgh *Witness* and the Glasgow *Scottish Guardian* in early
September 1843, reflected the romantic vision of Scotland that was being
popularized in the United States.[16] For Mrs Dana, the Disruption became
a blood sacrifice not only for the spiritual independence of the Scottish
Church, but also for the freedom of the Scottish nation.

> Oh, beautiful Scotland! thy glorious hills,
> Immortal in song—and thy lakes and thy rills
> Bore witness of yore to the faith of thy sons,
> When prayers of thy martyrs were mingled with groans;
> When thy hills and thy valleys were moistened with blood,
> Which gave its red stain to each river and flood;
> But sound the glad tidings o'er mountain and sea,
> Thy chains have been broken, and Scotland is free![17]

In August 1843, James G. Small, a Free Church probationary minister,
published a volume entitled, *The Highlands, the Scottish Martyrs and Other
Poems*, which combined a celebration of the Covenanters and the majestic
beauty of the Highlands—relating both to the heroism of the outgoing
ministers and congregations.[18] The same theme informs Francis Harper's
The Kirk of Scotland, a long narrative poem, published in January 1844, and
dedicated to the new Free Church—'the Noble, Suffering, and Illustrious
Martyrs who, for Christ and Conscience Sake, chose to resign their earthy
all, and worldly comforts, and to cast themselves upon the Unerring
Bounty of Providence.'[19]

Among those who remained within the Established Church of Scotland, the claims of the new Free Church aroused considerable resentment.
On 2 June 1843 the young Evangelical minister Norman Macleod wrote
in his journal of the forebearance required from those remaining in the
Established Church, 'while "the persecuted martyrs of the covenant" met
amid the huzzas and applauses of the multitude, with thousands of
pounds daily pouring in upon them.' The real sacrifice and self-denial,
Macleod believed, lay with those who remained at their posts in the old

[15] *Witness*, 27 May 1843.
[16] Andrew Hook, *Scotland and America 1750–1835* (Glasgow, 1975), pp. 116–73.
[17] *Scottish Guardian*, 1 Sept. 1843; *Witness*, 2 Sept. 1843.
[18] James G. Small, *The Highlands, the Scottish Martyrs and Other Poems* (Edinburgh, 1843).
[19] Francis Harper, *The Kirk of Scotland: a Poem* (London, 1844).

Kirk.[20] In *The Merry Martyrs*, Alexander Adams of the Church of Scotland protested against the claims of 'the counterfeit martyrs' of the Free Church, whose portraits were being 'hawked about the streets' or which 'graced the windows of the bookshops, and adorned the parlours of the professors of the new faith.' 'It is certainly a new reading of all of our former notions of martyrdom', he maintained, 'to associate them with the vagaries of the roystering gentry who now assume the title of martyrs.'[21] Most urban Free Church ministers, Adams asserted, were receiving as much, if not more, than before the Disruption. The only real sacrifices were made 'by simple-minded men in the rural and pastoral districts', who had been duped by the ambitious urban clerics.[22]

Despite such criticism, the Free Church claims to be the Church of the 'martyrs of the Covenant' proved effective in marshalling support both in Scotland and abroad. For its supporters, the Free Church was not a schism or sect, not a branch destined to wither. On the contrary, it was the true Church of Scotland, fighting again the heroic battles of the Church's past. Unity with the martyred Covenanters became a mark of the national Church. Money poured in, as supporters in Scotland and abroad responded to the sacrifices of the outgoing ministers. In July 1843 the attempt of Parliament to draw seceders back into the Establishment by passing Lord Aberdeen's act to limit patronage was largely ineffective. At the same time, however, the success of the new Free Church in attracting contributions and popular acclaim was stirring bitter resentments.[23] By the late summer of 1843, reports began reaching Edinburgh and Glasgow of real hardship among Free Church ministers and adherents in the rural areas, caused in part by the poverty of the congregations, but more by the efforts of certain Scottish landowners to suppress the movement.[24]

III

'The people must stand firm', maintained the Edinburgh Free Church *Witness* on 3 June 1843, at the close of the first Free Church General Assembly. 'Their ministers have stood the trial nobly; it is *they* [the people] who are on trial now.'[25] In the years immediately following the Disrup-

---

[20] Donald Macleod, *Memoir of Norman Macleod*, 2 vols (London, 1876), p. 202.
[21] [A. M. Adams], *The Merry Martyrs: or Cursory Observations on the Kirk Question* (Edinburgh, 1844), pp. 16, 19, 29, 30.
[22] Ibid., p. 28.
[23] *Journal of Henry Cockburn*, 2, p. 78.
[24] *Scottish Guardian*, 25 Aug. 1843.
[25] *Witness*, 3 June 1843.

tion, the Free Church membership contributed impressive amounts to support ministers and school teachers, the building of churches, manses, and schools, and overseas missions. In urban areas the Free Church attracted prosperous middle-class congregations and rapidly gained respectability and influence. In more remote rural districts, however, particularly in the Highlands and the Southern Uplands, Free Church adherents frequently encountered opposition from landowners who viewed the Free Church as a subversive force, threatening the social hierarchy and political order. Believing that pressure would persuade the tenants and labourers on their lands to give up the Free Church and return to the fold of the Establishment, some proprietors resorted to dismissals of Free Church servants and evictions of Free Church tenants. Further, they denied sites for Free Church churches, forcing congregations to worship in the open air, on waste ground or beyond the tide-line on sea shores. The result was widespread suffering and some deaths, and the years from 1843 to 1848 became the 'time of trial' for the new Free Church.

The cases of eviction and dismissal for Free Church adherence were difficult to prove, but they were apparently numerous. In December 1843, in the Ross-shire parish of Logie Easter, Ross of Cromarty dismissed twenty-two Free Church labourers from his employment, forcing many to leave the parish.[26] In the parish of Snizort, in Skye, about forty-five Free Church families were evicted from their crofts on Lord MacDonald's estate in 1846–7—for having collected money for the local Free Church congregation.[27] On North Uist in 1845–6, Lord MacDonald evicted nine small tenants and fined another thirteen—because they had helped to build a meeting house for Free Church worship on common land.[28] Across the country, nearly four hundred school teachers were dismissed for their Free Church adherence.[29] In some parishes, paupers adhering to the Free Church were denied parish relief; this was particularly the case with paupers discovered to have contributed small sums to the support of the Free Church.[30]

The refusal of many landed proprietors to provide sites for Free Church churches and manses created severe hardships, especially where a single landowner possessed vast tracts of land. In the mining village of

---

[26] Edinburgh, New College Library, *Chalmers Papers*, CHA 4.314.53., H. Macleod to T. Chalmers, 2 Jan. 1844.

[27] *Third Report of the Select Committee of the House of Commons on Sites*, Parliamentary Papers, 1847 (237) xiii, p. 36, q. 4724–49.

[28] Ibid., p. 24, q. 4438–59.

[29] Brown, *Annals of the Disruption*, pp. 312–13.

[30] Ibid., pp. 363–5; *Witness*, 25 May 1844.

Wanlockhead, elevation 1,500 feet, the Duke of Buccleuch refused a site for a church, forcing the congregation to worship unsheltered in a ravine through six winters. The congregation was convinced that at least two members had died as a direct result of repeated exposure to rain and snow.[31] In Canonbie, in Dumfriesshire, the Duke of Buccleuch owned all the surrounding land and refused to allow the local congregation to worship anywhere on his estate—forcing the congregation of 500–600 to worship through the winter of 1844 exposed to the elements on the side of a public highway, until July 1844, when the Duke allowed them to erect a tent in a disused gravel-pit.[32] Some landowners sought to deny Free Church ministers any place of residence near their congregations, threatening tenants with eviction if they provided shelter or hospitality.[33] Free Church ministers frequently had to live separated from their families in inadequate housing—sometimes to the permanent injury of their health. Four ministers were apparently driven to early deaths. Andrew Baird, Free Church minister of Cockburnspath, died in June 1845 of illness evidently brought on by living in a damp and drafty bothy. In the summer of 1845 the Free Church ministers Hugh McKay Mackenzie and William Mackenzie, father and son, died of illness in a room in a shepherd's cottage in Tongue, after declining to leave the congregation, which was refused a church site by the Duke of Sutherland, for translation to a comfortable living with church and manse. George Innes, the young Free Church minister of Canonbie, succumbed to illness in November 1847, his death evidently hastened by the strains of preaching in a tent and the exhaustion and exposure of continuous travel between his parish and his place of residence some miles away.[34]

Probably the most forceful memorialist of the suffering and deaths was Thomas Guthrie, an Edinburgh minister and convener of the Free Church committee charged with collecting funds for building manses. 'I say that man lies in a martyr's grave', Guthrie asserted of the recently deceased Baird of Cockburnspath at a public meeting in Glasgow in July 1845. 'His persecutors have sent him there—God forgive them for it.'[35] At a special meeting of the Free Church General Assembly, held at Inverness in August 1845, Guthrie paid tribute to the two Mackenzies of Tongue

[31] Brown, *Annals of the Disruption*, pp. 436–46; *Second Report of the Select Committee on Sites*, p. 10, q. 1543–61.
[32] Brown, *Annals of the Disruption*, pp. 430–6; *First Report of the Select Committee on Sites*, pp. 39–53, q. 544–756; pp. 86–92, q. 1273–1346.
[33] Alexander Mackenzie, *History of the Highland Clearances* (Inverness, 1883), pp. 187–8.
[34] Brown, *Annals of the Disruption*, pp. 179–84, 447.
[35] Thomas Guthrie, *Manse Fund of the Free Church* (Glasgow, 1845), pp. 9–10.

who had died 'martyrs for those great principles for which we abandoned our earthly all.'[36] Within a few days of Guthrie's speech, over £70 had been raised for a monument to the two martyrs.[37] Speaking before the Presbytery of Edinburgh in December 1847, another Free Church leader, R. S. Candlish, paid eloquent tribute to 'the martyr of Canonbie', George Innes, who had 'fallen a victim to the persecution which the congregation at Canonbie have had to bear.'[38] 'The Covenanters fell on moor and mountain', Guthrie later recalled, 'while such of our ministers as sank beneath their trials, died calmly in their beds; leaving what our ears heard, their dying testimony to the cause, and expressions of devout thankfulness to God that their pillow was not that of the recreant or apostate.'[39]

For some Free Churchmen the persecution of their communities was closely related to the Highland Clearances—especially in Sutherland, where the Duke of Sutherland was notorious both for clearing his estates of tenants and denying sites to the Free Church. The Free Church publicist Hugh Miller argued that the denial of sites was in fact part of the Duke's plan to depopulate his lands. In the Highlands, whole communities, transformed by the Evangelical Revival, had joined the Free Church. Without sites for churches, these communities would wither and be easily swept away. Further, the Duke had strong reasons for wanting to drive off the Free Church ministers, who would otherwise stand forth as English-speaking witnesses to the suffering the Clearances brought to Gaelic-speaking communities.[40] In one of the only contemporary novels to deal with the Disruption—*Passages in the Life of an English Heiress*, published anonymously in 1847 by Hugh Miller's wife, Lydia—a Highland community faced the combined trial of Clearances and site refusal with the quiet fortitude of martyrs. The same qualities of courage and loyalty celebrated in romantic accounts of Highland Jacobitism were now revealed in the Highlanders' adherence to the Free Church.[41] Indeed, through their emphasis on martyred Highland communities, the Free Church publicists managed effectively to appeal to both major traditions in the romantic vision of Scottish history—the Presbyterian-Covenanting and the Highland-Jacobite tradition: through their suffering, the Free

---

[36] *Proceedings of the General Assembly of the Free Church of Scotland*, Inverness (August 1845), pp. 82–3.
[37] *Witness*, 30 Aug. 1845.
[38] Wilson and Rainy, *Memorials of R. S. Candlish*, p. 411; *Witness*, 1, 4 Dec. 1847.
[39] Thomas Guthrie, *The Principles of the Free Church* (Edinburgh, 1859), p. 18.
[40] *Witness*, 6 Sept; see also, *Scottish Guardian*, 25 Aug. 1843.
[41] [Lydia Miller], *Passages in the Life of an English Heiress; or, Recollections of Disruption Times in Scotland* (London, 1847).

Church Highlanders now became heirs to the Lowland Covenanters, uniting the two major strands of the nation.

Opponents responded to Free Church claims of persecution by pointing to the violent language frequently used by Free Church leaders in reference to the Established Church and the landed classes.[42] The Free Church, its enemies maintained, was a subversive force, encouraging rebellion against constituted authority—as demonstrated by the riots in Ross-shire in late September and early October 1843, when Free Church supporters sought to block the settlement of a new minister in the parish church of Resolis. The Riot Act was read, shots were fired by the constables, and several arrests were made. For opponents, the riots were the inevitable result of the violent and extravagant language employed by Free Church leaders.[43] More powerful ammunition against the Free Church language of martyrdom was offered by the controversy surrounding the Free Church decision to invite contributions from churches in the slave-holding states of the American South. How, their opponents asked, could Free Churchmen appeal for sympathy for the suffering of their members at the hands of Scottish landlords, while they accepted 'blood money'—wealth derived from suffering and oppression—from American slave-owners? The 'Send Back the Money' campaign of 1844–6 proved a serious blow to Free Church claims to moral superiority through its sufferings. It may also have helped persuade Free Church leaders to moderate their claims.[44]

In 1845 the Free Church General Assembly took the significant step of petitioning Parliament for redress from the grievance of site refusals. The decision to appeal to Parliament was an admission that, unlike the Covenanters, the Free Church was not being persecuted by the State, but was rather suffering at the hands of a minority of misguided landowners. A Select Committee of the House of Commons was appointed to inquire into the sites question.[45] The report, published in July 1847, supported many of the Free Church allegations against the site refusers. Although no legislation followed, most remaining site refusers decided to give in to the discomfort aroused by the Committee's revelations, even among Free

---

[42] For example, *First Report of the Select Committee on Sites*, p. 22, q. 343–4; *Third Report*, pp. 137–40, q. 6446–54; Brown, *Annals of the Disruption*, pp. 429–30.

[43] *Edinburgh Advertiser*, 26 Sept., 3, 10 Oct. 1843; *Scotsman*, 7 Oct. 1843; *Morning Herald* (London), 29 Sept., 10 Oct. 1843.

[44] George Shepperson, 'The Free Church and American Slavery', *ScHR*, 30 (1951), pp. 126–73; C. Duncan Rice, *The Scots Abolitionists 1833–1861* (Baton Rouge, Louisiana, 1981), pp. 124–46.

[45] William Hanna, *Memoirs of Thomas Chalmers*, 4 vols (Edinburgh, 1849–52), 4, p. 497.

Church opponents. By 1848 the time of trial for the Free Church was largely over. The easing of tensions with the landowners also reflected a change in the position of the Free Church, which by 1847 had largely relinquished its claim to be the one true national Church of Scotland. In their evidence before the Select Committee on Sites, such Free Church leaders as Thomas Guthrie and Robert Gordon rested their claims to sites on the argument that toleration should be extended to every religious denomination in a free society.[46] After 1846 Free Church leaders increasingly portrayed themselves not as the national Church of Scotland, but as a gathered Church of believers, which asked only toleration and equality before the law for all denominations in a liberal State.

The suffering and deaths experienced by rural Free Church congregations between 1843 and 1848 played a major role in consolidating the new Free Church. Observers suggested that the behaviour of the site refusers proved a boon to the Free Church, bringing it public sympathy and financial support.[47] The accounts of persecution and martyrdom indeed helped ensure that the Free Church membership would not be drawn back to the Established Church, but would rather continue to shoulder the heavy burden of Free Church finance.[48] The Free Church was not simply what the Marquis of Lorne had described as a 'great measure of [Presbyterian] Church Extension', an addition of some 800 new churches and schools in loose connection with the Established Church. Rather, through its martyrs for the principle of the Church's spiritual independence, it had established a separate identity.[49] Martyrdom became an integral part of Free Church tradition, with memoirs of the years of trial preserved in such works as Thomas Brown's *Annals of the Disruption* of 1884. Such stories also helped to ensure that Free Church attention and resources would be directed to rural congregations, especially in the Highlands, where there was insufficient wealth in the congregation to support the church and school through voluntary means. For the Free Church, the language of martyrdom played much the same role as the Ecclesiastical Commission did for the Church of England—helping to direct resources from the wealthier to the poorer parts of the Church, and ensuring a national territorial ministry. The building of the Free Church was one of the great achievements of the nineteenth century. Equally impressive was the ability of the Free Church to inspire continued giving

---

[46] *First Report of the Select Committee on Sites*, p. 64, q. 964–6; pp. 85–6, q. 1259–66.
[47] 'Canonbie', *Witness*, 24 July 1844.
[48] W. G. Blaikie, *After Fifty Years* (London, 1893), p. 51.
[49] *Scottish Guardian*, 12 Sept. 1843.

for the support of churches, ministers, schools, colleges, and overseas missions long after the Disruption fires had cooled. 'You will hear unthinking people say', wrote the Free Church minister James Mackenzie in a children's history of the Scottish Church in 1859, 'that there is little difference between the Free Church and the Establishment. If that be true, the martyrs died for a small matter, and shed their blood in mistake.'[50]

University of Edinburgh

[50] [Mackenzie], *Our Banner and its Battles*, p. 55.

THE MAKING OF AN ANGLICAN MARTYR: BISHOP JOHN COLERIDGE PATTESON OF MELANESIA

by DAVID HILLIARD

SINCE the beginning of Anglican missionary activity in the south-west Pacific in the mid-nineteenth century, fifteen European missionaries and at least seven Pacific Islanders have died violently in the course of their work. In that same region, comprising island Melanesia and New Guinea, Roman Catholics, Presbyterians, Methodists, and the London Missionary Society [L.M.S.] have each had their honour roll of martyrs. Three of these have achieved a measure of fame outside the Pacific and their own denomination: John Williams of the L.M.S., killed at Erromanga in Vanuatu (formerly the New Hebrides) in 1839; James Chalmers, also of the L.M.S., killed in New Guinea in 1901; and John Coleridge Patteson, Missionary Bishop of Melanesia and head of the Melanesian Mission, killed in 1871. Patteson has been the subject of more than fifteen biographies (several of them in German and Dutch), in addition to essays in collections on English missionary heroes, scholarly articles, and pamphlets for popular consumption.[1] In Anglican churches in England, Australia, New Zealand, the United States, and elsewhere he is commemorated as missionary hero in memorial tablets and stained-glass windows.

Bishop Patteson was killed at Nukapu in the Santa Cruz group, south-east of the Solomon Islands, on 20 September 1871. The events of that day were often recounted and became part of the folklore of the Melanesian Mission. Nukapu was a small, flat, bush-covered island, inhabited by about one hundred people of Polynesian culture, quite distinct from the Melanesian peoples of the much larger adjacent island of Santa Cruz. The mission schooner *Southern Cross* had called at Nukapu on at least three

---

[1] The standard biographies are by Charlotte Mary Yonge, *Life of John Coleridge Patteson, Missionary Bishop of the Melanesian Islands*, 2 vols (London, 1874), and (Sir) John Gutch, *Martyr of the Islands: the Life and Death of John Coleridge Patteson* (London, 1971). See also David Hilliard, 'John Coleridge Patteson: missionary bishop of Melanesia', in J. W. Davidson and Deryck Scarr, eds, *Pacific Islands Portraits* (Canberra, 1970), pp. 177–200; E. S. Armstrong, *The History of the Melanesian Mission* (London, 1900), parts 1–3; and C. E. Fox, *Lord of the Southern Isles: Being the Story of the Anglican Mission in Melanesia, 1849–1949* (London, 1958), ch. 2. For a listing of the major works in English, see the bibliography of David Hilliard, *God's Gentlemen: a History of the Melanesian Mission, 1849–1942* (St Lucia, Qld, 1978).

previous occasions: in 1856, 1857, and 1870, and perhaps also in 1866 and 1867. Patteson had landed for the first time in 1857, when he was impressed, he recorded, by the 'very gentle orderly manners' of the Nukapu islanders and their 'evident desire to do anything that was in their power to please their strange visitors'. Their language was similar to Maori, so it was 'easy to converse with them sufficiently for our present purpose'.[2]

About noon on 20 September 1871 the *Southern Cross* lay off the island, the ship's boat was lowered, and the Bishop was rowed towards the shore. With him was a New Zealand-born missionary clergyman, Joseph Atkin, Stephen Taroaniara, described as a 'native teacher', from San Cristobal, in the Solomon Islands, and two youths from the island of Mota. Several canoes were seen lying off-shore, but they kept at a distance. Near the reef which surrounded Nukapu, Patteson boarded one of these canoes, on which he recognized two men from his visit the previous year. Four canoes stayed near the waiting ship's boat, which remained outside the reef, intending to enter the lagoon when the tide rose. It had been arranged that when the Bishop was ready to return he would wave a handkerchief.

The exact sequence of events ashore is unclear. It appears that on landing Patteson entered a palm hut at the centre of the small village and, as he had done on the previous year, lay down on 'a good mat', kept for the use of honoured guests. While resting he was struck at the side of the head with a heavy wooden mallet by a man named Teadule (or Tetuli). Afterwards women of the village washed and prepared the body for burial in a hastily excavated grave, wrapping it in the mat on which the visitor had rested. About three-quarters of an hour after the Bishop had gone ashore the men in the waiting canoes fired repeated volleys of arrows at the ship's boat, which returned immediately to the *Southern Cross*. Three of the four on board were seriously injured; Taroaniara was pierced in the shoulder and back with six arrows. The boat, carrying the captain and mate of the *Southern Cross*, then returned to the reef. As they waited they saw two canoes leave the shore, one of them being set adrift. Late in the afternoon, the tide having risen, they crossed into the lagoon, and in the drifting canoe found the Bishop's body, naked except for his shoes, wrapped in native matting, with a palm leaf tied into five knots on his chest. The right side of his skull was completely shattered, and there were cuts and arrow

---

[2] Melanesian Mission, *Papers relating to the Melanesian Mission with a Statement of Accounts* (Auckland, 1857).

wounds on other parts of his body. The body was brought back to the *Southern Cross* and buried at sea the following day. Atkin and Taroaniara died in agony of tetanus on 27 and 28 September and were buried together at sea. The Melanesian Mission had lost its leader and two of its most promising workers.

* * *

The news was carried to New Zealand by the *Southern Cross*, which sailed into Auckland harbour on the last day of October 1871. Little was known of Atkin (son of an Auckland settler) and Taroaniara, and in newspaper reports they remained in the background; it was only Bishop Patteson who was described as a martyr. For members of the Auckland diocesan synod, then in session, his death was felt, reported a local newspaper, to be 'the greatest calamity which has befallen not only missionary enterprise, but the cause of religion itself throughout the whole of the Southern Hemisphere.'[3] The synod adjourned for a week, and the bell of the wooden pro-cathedral toiled throughout the day. From Auckland the news was transmitted around New Zealand by telegraph. On the following Sunday throughout the country the altars and pulpits of Anglican churches were draped in black, and preachers referred to the sad events at Nakapu, a place of which they had never heard. Congregations in towns and suburbs were reported to be large, and some sermons were 'eloquent to such a degree as to affect many persons to tears'.[4] In Auckland the Revd Benjamin Dudley, who had worked with Patteson in Melanesia ten years earlier, spoke of 'the sad, sad story of the Martyr of Santa Cruz, slain treacherously at a place he was visiting on an errand of love and mercy', and wondered whether 'any event of equal moral significance [had] taken place in this generation? Will it ever be forgotten? When has any servant of the household of faith been so honoured?'[5]

The news of the violent death of Bishop Patteson and his companions arrived in Sydney on 4 November, brought by a trading vessel from New Caledonia. A brief report reached England by telegraph at the end of the month, but details were not known until late December. 'At last it has come', announced the *Guardian*, '—that call for which he was never

---

[3] *New Zealand Herald*, 1 Nov. 1871.
[4] *Wellington Independent*, 6 Nov. 1871.
[5] [B. T. Dudley], *The Martyrs of Santa Cruz: a Sermon preached in Auckland, 5th November, 1871* (Auckland, 1871), pp. 13–14.

unprepared. The patient, thoughtful, simple-hearted Missionary has found, to our great loss, to his infinite gain, the martyr's crown.'[6]

* * *

At the time of his death Patteson was head of the Melanesian Mission, which had been founded in 1849 by Bishop George Augustus Selwyn, first Bishop of New Zealand.[7] Selwyn had an expansionist vision. He saw Melanesia—which to Europeans in the 1840s was an unknown and hostile region—as designated by God to be the mission field of the infant Church of England in New Zealand. In the hope of reaching all the islands from New Caledonia to New Guinea in one fell swoop, he devised an unusual method of operation which critics dismissed as 'visionary and impracticable'. Instead of attempting to station a European missionary on each major island, as was the custom in the South Pacific of the L.M.S., the Wesleyans, the Presbyterians, and the Roman Catholics, Selwyn sought to take selected young Melanesians every year to a central boarding-school at Auckland, where they would be taught Christianity and the English language, then returned to their homes to pass on what they had learnt. In theory, this required little more than a mission vessel—'a floating mission house'—and a small band of European teachers.

Patteson, an Old Etonian, a fellow of Merton College, Oxford, and member of a family closely connected with the Selwyns, had been recruited by Selwyn during his visit to England in 1854 to be his missionary chaplain. He took to the work with enthusiasm and showed a remarkable ability to learn Melanesian languages. Almost every year from 1856 he made two or three island voyages on the *Southern Cross*, and in 1861 he was consecrated as Missionary Bishop for the 'Western Islands of the South Pacific Ocean'. As he gained experience and confidence, he made changes to the mission's methods of work, while retaining the main features laid down by Selwyn: a central school and the dream of evangelizing Melanesia through a Melanesian agency. In 1867 he moved his headquarters from Auckland to Norfolk Island.

Patteson left Norfolk Island on his last voyage in April 1871. At forty-

[6] *Guardian* (London), 29 Nov. 1871, p. 1412.
[7] David Hilliard, 'Bishop G. A. Selwyn and the Melanesian Mission', *New Zealand Journal of History*, 4 (1970), pp. 120–37; R. M. Ross, 'Evolution of the Melanesian bishopric', *New Zealand Journal of History*, 16 (1982), pp. 122–45, and *Melanesians at Mission Bay: a History of the Melanesian Mission in Auckland* (Wellington, 1983); Hugh Laracy, 'Selwyn in Pacific perspective', in Warren E. Limbrick, ed., *Bishop Selwyn in New Zealand, 1841–68* (Palmerston North, 1983), pp. 121–35.

four, mentally and physically he was exhausted. The strains of leadership, the long and uncomfortable voyages on the *Southern Cross*, and his habit of living on Melanesian islands for months at a time almost entirely on a native diet had affected his health. In 1867 he privately admitted that he did not expect to last 'overlong' at his strenuous work.[8] Although often pressed to take a wife, he had never been attracted to marriage, and he rejected suggestions from his sisters and the New Zealand bishops that he should return to England for a complete break. There was, he claimed, too much to do in Melanesia, and having been away so long he would be 'thoroughly out of my element in England'.[9] In 1870, when after a severe illness he visited New Zealand for medical treatment, his friends in Auckland were shocked by his haggard appearance. In relation to his missionary colleagues he became taciturn and moody. The Bishop's death, one of them recalled, 'became a possibility close at hand, instead of an improbability never occurring to our minds'.[10]

The Melanesian Mission was the only Christian mission in northern Vanuatu and the Solomon Islands. Its religious influence on the people of the region was small. At the end of 1870, after twenty years' work, there were 145 scholars resident at the Norfolk Island school, which by this time was a permanent institution, but fewer than half of these were baptized, and only 17 had been confirmed. Patteson himself, looking for success in the distant future, was not disappointed. He had an upper class English distaste for the dramatizing of conversion stories to drum up popular support. He wanted to lay foundations that would be lasting. During his last voyage in 1871 the first large-scale movement towards Christianity occurred in the islands. Almost three hundred adults and infants were baptized at Mota, in the Banks group of northern Vanuatu, an island which the mission had first contacted twelve years earlier.

Meanwhile the Melanesian Mission was encountering a rival European influence. Since the late 1860s recruiting vessels seeking Melanesian labourers for the cotton and sugar plantations of Fiji and Queensland had entered northern Vanuatu and the Solomon Islands.[11] It was rough work. Melanesian contract labour was virtually unregulated until an Act of the

---

[8] J. C. Patteson to his sisters, 23 Nov. 1867, Patteson Papers, U.S.P.G. Archives, Oxford, Rhodes House.

[9] J. C. Patteson to his sister Joanna, 9 Dec. 1869, Patteson Papers.

[10] C. H. Brooke, 'The finished course, being recollections of Bishop Patteson on the anniversary of his death', *Mission Life*, ns 4 (1873), p. 120.

[11] For the labour trade, see O. W. Parnaby, *Britain and the Labor Trade in the Southwest Pacific* (Durham, NC, 1964), and Peter Corris, *Passage, Port and Plantation: a History of Solomon Islands Labour Migration, 1870–1914* (Melbourne, 1973).

Queensland colonial parliament in 1868, but this did not cover recruitment in the islands. In the period of initial contact, before the emergence of 'pidgin English', when the islanders had no understanding of wage labour or terms of engagement, there were many reports of force and deceit, as recruiters sought to fill their ships as quickly and profitably as possible. At places where former mission scholars understood a few words of English there were reports that islanders had been told by unscrupulous recruiters that 'The bishop is ill—has broken his leg getting into his boat—is at Sydney—and has sent us to bring you to him.'[12] Since the beginning of the labour trade the Presbyterian missionaries of southern Vanuatu had loudly condemned it as a new form of slavery, but Patteson was more cautious. He regretted what he believed to be the damaging effects of recruiting on island communities, and he discouraged it when he could, but he did not regard the trade as wrong in principle. He knew from experience that some young Melanesians were eager to travel abroad when opportunity offered—drawn by curiosity, the spirit of adventure, and the desire to obtain more of the white man's trade goods. Patteson wanted recruiting to be undertaken only by licensed vessels and controlled by imperial legislation. In 1871 he expounded his views in a memorandum for the General Synod of the New Zealand Church. But at the same time he was worried by reports of recruiting abuses, and incidents of retaliation by islanders for 'outrages':

> In many islands where we were already on most intimate terms with the people, we are now obliged to be very cautious . . . It is the white man's fault . . . The contact of many of these traders arouses all the worst suspicions and passions of the wild untaught man.[13]

It was this idea which was to dominate the interpretation of the events at Nukapu. The missionaries on the *Southern Cross* and at Norfolk Island were convinced from the first that the killing of Patteson and his companions was attributable to the labour trade. The Bishop had been well received at Nukapu in 1870; therefore, it was inferred, the violent attacks in 1871 *must have been* an act of blind retaliation by the islanders for the misdeeds of a visiting labour recruiter in the intervening period. So wrote the Revd R. H. Codrington, headmaster of the mission school, to the Bishop of Tasmania on the day the news reached Norfolk Island:

[12] Bishop Patteson to Canon Vidal, in *Colonial Church Chronicle*, 24 (1870), p. 123.
[13] J. C. Patteson, Memorandum to the General Synod of New Zealand, 11 Jan. 1871, Great Britain, *Parliamentary Papers* [hereafter GBPP], 1872, 43 [C.496], pp. 107–9.

There is very little doubt but that the slave trade which is desolating these islands was the cause of this attack. People will call it treachery, because these same people were so friendly last year; but there is almost no doubt but that the slavers had been there and kidnapped some people, for whom revenge was sought . . . Bishop Patteson was known throughout the islands as a friend, and now even he is killed to revenge the outrages of his countrymen. The guilt surely does not lie upon the savages who executed, but on the traders who provoked the deed.[14]

In the Australasian colonies the same interpretation was almost universally accepted: the atrocity had occurred as a direct result of the cruelties of the unsupervised labour trade. 'The poor savages obeyed only the law of their race . . . when, they thought, they executed judgement in satisfaction for the wrongs done to them', pronounced the editor of the *New Zealand Herald*.[15] For those opposed to the labour trade, the killing of 'the noble-minded self-denying Bishop of Melanesia' became the decisive proof of the evil results of unregulated recruiting by British vessels, a disgrace which should not be allowed to continue. For Patteson was not an ordinary or insignificant figure. The *Sydney Morning Herald* described him as 'a man of education, holding a chief office in the largest Church of the Empire, and consecrated to his work by its most eminent prelates. His prudence and quiet energy have been long known to the colonies and to the religious world.'[16]

In New Zealand and in Australia the news of Patteson's death was said to have produced a 'profound sensation', stirred up by lengthy news reports, angry editorials, and emotional sermons.[17] In Sydney and Auckland memorial funds were established to assist the work of the Melanesian Mission. In Auckland, Melbourne, Sydney, and Hobart large public meetings were held—1,800 people in the Melbourne Town Hall—with prominent citizens and religious leaders on the platform, to express sorrow and to demonstrate opposition to the labour trade. Anglican diocesan synods, representative gatherings of Presbyterians and Wesleyans, and

---

[14] R. H. Codrington to Bishop Bromby, 16 Oct. 1871, in *Mercury* (Hobart), 18 Nov. 1871.

[15] *New Zealand Herald*, 30 Nov. 1871.

[16] *Sydney Morning Herald*, 7 Nov. 1871.

[17] For reactions in New Zealand, see Angus Ross, *New Zealand Aspirations in the Pacific in the Nineteenth Century* (Oxford, 1964), pp. 80–4, and P. J. Stewart, 'New Zealand and the Pacific labor traffic, 1870–1874', *Pacific Historical Review*, 30 (1961), pp. 50–3. Editorials from the major colonial newspapers, reports of public meetings, resolutions, and memorials are in GBPP, 1872, 43 [C.496], and 1873, 50 (244).

many other bodies passed resolutions of sympathy, coupled with demands that the British Government should suppress or regulate the recruitment of labour by its subjects in the South Pacific. In November 1871 both houses of the New Zealand Parliament adopted addresses for presentation to the Queen, deploring the deaths at Nukapu, and urging the imperial government to act without delay to stop 'this infamous traffic', which was 'a reproach and scandal to the British name'.[18]

In England the reaction to the news was muted. Scarcely anything was known of Melanesia, on the opposite side of the world. Moreover, it was sixteen years since Patteson had gone to New Zealand, and outside a small band of relatives and personal friends he was no more than a name. But he had influential connections. His mentor Bishop Selwyn since 1868 had been Bishop of Lichfield, his cousin Sir John Duke Coleridge was Attorney-General in Gladstone's first cabinet, and Lord Kimberley, the Secretary of State for the Colonies, had been a fellow pupil at Eton. For more than ten years the Colonial Office had been considering imperial legislation to regulate the recruiting of 'native labour' in the South Pacific, and a bill had been drafted, but the Treasury was worried about the legal expense, and during 1871 the Australasian colonies were asked if they would take financial responsibility for prosecutions in their courts. Then came the telegraph report of the deaths of Patteson and Atkin: massacred by a Melanesian native 'in revenge for kidnapping outrages by slavers'.[19] The news led to articles in the religious press calling for intervention to suppress 'kidnapping' in the South Pacific, a public meeting in London organized by the Aborigines' Protection Society, and a memorial to Parliament from the Society for the Propagation of the Gospel [S.P.G.].[20] Legislation could be delayed no longer. In February 1872, even before the news of the agitation in New Zealand and Australia reached London, the long-considered draft bill was introduced into the new session of Parliament. It had a rapid passage through both Houses and in June became law as the Pacific Islanders Protection Act.[21] Since then, in church circles, the idea

---

[18] GBPP, 1872, 43 [C.496], pp. 106–7.

[19] Edwin Palmer, *Bishop Patteson: Missionary Bishop and Martyr* (London, 1872), p. 3.

[20] Aborigines' Protection Society, *The Polynesian Labour Traffic and the Murder of Bishop Patteson: the Proceedings of a Public Meeting held in London, on the 13th December, 1871* . . . (London, 1872); *Church Times*, 8 Dec. 1871, p. 539; *Literary Churchman*, 9 Dec. 1871, p. 512; *Guardian*, 3 Jan. 1872, p. 96; *Mission Field*, 17 (1872), pp. 62–3; *Colonial Church Chronicle*, 26 (1872), pp. 81–7, 132–7.

[21] 35 and 36 Vict., c. 19.

has become well entrenched that the death of Patteson 'directly brought an end to the Melanesian slave trade to Fiji and Australia'.[22]

Was the killing of Patteson and his companions an act of revenge for the misdeeds of unscrupulous labour recruiters? It is not an unreasonable theory. In 1871 there had been incidents of indiscriminate shooting and smashing of canoes by Fiji recruiters in the Solomon Islands, a recruiting ship *Emma Bell* had been in the Santa Cruz region only a few days before the *Southern Cross*, and the story that four, five, or six young men had been abducted from Nukapu and taken to a plantation in Fiji (from which several of them later escaped and returned home in a stolen boat) was supported by oral testimony collected by English missionaries in subsequent years. However, their questioning always assumed the truth of the retaliation theory and was conducted through interpreters. The people of Nukapu had good reason to be wary of Europeans, for in November 1871, in a naval investigation into the killing of Patteson, they had been bombarded by HMS *Rosario*.[23] It was not until 1884 that a white missionary again went ashore at Nukapu, and a mission teacher was not placed there until 1897.

Not all attacks by Melanesians on Europeans were reprisals, yet no one thought of investigating alternative explanations. Like John Williams, killed at Erromanga in 1839, it is possible that Patteson had unintentionally offended the islanders. Such an explanation was suggested in 1894 by Acteaon Forrest, a lay missionary who had lived for eight years in the Santa Cruz group and spoke a local language. He told Sir John Thurston, then High Commissioner for the Western Pacific, that Patteson had been killed not by the Nukapu people, but by people from the Santa Cruz mainland. The motive was said to be 'jealousy and anger, because the Bishop gave a present to the Nukapu chief and either a smaller one or none at all to the Santa Cruz man who conceived himself the more important personage.'[24] Thurston, who, sailing on a Fiji-based labour-recruiting ship, had met Patteson at Mota only a few months before his death, found Forrest's explanation convincing. 'I have for many years heard something of this nature', he wrote in his diary, 'and for years have felt assured that the old story of kidnapping for Fiji was a mere surmise.'[25]

[22] E.g., 'Bishop's death woke consciences of men', *Melanesian Mission* (Christchurch), 18 (Aug. 1970).
[23] Albert Hastings Markham, *The Cruise of the 'Rosario' amongst the New Hebrides and Santa Cruz Islands* . . . (London, 1873), pp. 145–56.
[24] J. C. Thurston, Diary, entry 4 Nov. 1894, Thurston Papers, Canberra, National Library of Australia.
[25] Ibid.

Forrest's version was immediately discounted by his fellow missionaries and was forgotten after he left the mission in disgrace two years later. Its weakness is that it does not explain the attack on the waiting ship's boat and has no other corroboration. Every other version of the event collected by missionaries or, in more recent years, by anthropologists, has confirmed and added further details to what has become the standard account.[26]

Through his violent death Patteson achieved fame, whereas his two companions were almost forgotten. This was because Patteson was an English bishop with friends in high places, and because his killing was attributed to the labour trade at a time when British consciences were uneasy. In the Church of England those who had a high view of the office of a bishop were the most moved. During the nineteenth century Bishop Mackenzie in Central Africa and other Anglican missionary bishops had died of sickness, but none had met death by violence. Patteson filled a gap. As a missionary bishop he embodied the qualities which the followers of the Oxford Movement admired: scholarship, austerity, self-effacement, quiet devotion to duty, a high view of the office of bishop, a concern to lay the foundations for a Melanesian church founded on Catholic principles.[27] His violent death was hailed as a demonstration of the apostolic nature of the Anglican episcopate: Anglican bishops could be heroes. It was, minuted the S.P.G., with pride, 'an honour reflected for the first time in this age on the office of a Bishop of our Church'.[28] The novelist Charlotte Yonge, who was the Bishop's cousin and a disciple of John Keble, when invited by the Patteson family to write the official 'life and letters', found the prospect 'very awful, for it is embalming the Saint for the Church.'[29]

The dead Bishop's family, his university friends, and High Church admirers raised money for memorials. There was a wall tablet in the chapel of Merton College, Oxford, where Patteson had been a fellow, and a wayside cross of brick and marble, designed by William Butterfield, near the Patteson family home at Feniton, in Devon. At Exeter Cathedral, where he had been ordained, he was commemorated in a richly decorated 'martyrs pulpit', designed by Sir Gilbert Scott. In Sydney a life-size effigy,

---

[26] E.g., William Davenport, 'Notes on Santa Cruz voyaging', *Journal of the Polynesian Society*, 73 (1964), pp. 141–2.

[27] For a recent assessment, see Geoffrey Rowell, *The Vision Glorious: Themes and Personalities of the Catholic Revival in Anglicanism* (Oxford, 1983), pp. 175–80.

[28] S.P.G., Journal, 19 Jan. 1871, U.S.P.G. Archives, Oxford, Rhodes House.

[29] C. A. E. Moberly, *Dulce Domum: George Moberly . . . his Family and Friends* (London, 1911), p. 245.

originally intended for St Andrew's Cathedral, was placed in the city church of Christ Church St Laurence. At Nukapu an iron memorial cross, twelve feet high, which had been brought out from England, was erected in 1884. At the mission headquarters at Norfolk Island a memorial chapel was consecrated in 1880, having been five years in the building. Its rich Victorian interior reflected Patteson's associations and preferences: collegiate seating, decorated with inlaid pearl shell, a pipe organ, a font and pavement of Devonshire marble, and stained-glass windows designed by Burne-Jones.[30]

The sequence of events at Nukapu caught the imagination of the mission-supporting public, including many outside the Church of England. On an isolated tropical island had been killed a zealous missionary who had given up 'brilliant prospects' and gone to the other side of the globe 'at the simple call of duty'.[31] Before he went ashore, Patteson had preached to his Melanesian pupils on the death of St Stephen. And there was the poignant image of a drifting canoe on the lagoon containing the Bishop's mutilated body, with a calm smile on his lips and a palm leaf on his chest, which was the illustration on the dust jacket of a biography of Patteson published for the centenary of his death in 1971. The knotted palm leaf became the chief visual symbol of the martyrdom. The five knots in the fronds were thought to represent the number of young men abducted from Nukapu by labour recruiters, though it is more likely that the Nukapu people knotted the palm leaf as a charm to prevent the white man's spirit coming back to haunt them. Many attempts were made to capture the religious significance of the event in verse:

> Martyr so calm and majestic,
> Floating alone on the deep,
> In spite of the wounds on thy forehead
> Smiling as if in thy sleep:
> Martyr! thy wounds are thy glory,
> Deep-hearted ocean thy rest:
> Float by thine own beloved islands!
> Float with the palm on thy breast![32]

---

[30] H. N. Drummond, *John Coleridge Patteson: an Account of his Death at Nukapu, and Description of S. Barnabas Chapel, Norfolk Island, Dedicated to his Memory* (Parkstone, 1930); (Sir) John Gutch and John Pinder, eds, *Patteson Memorial Chapel, Norfolk Island* (Watford, 1980).

[31] E.g., *Guardian*, 13 March 1872, p. 346.

[32] *Bishop Patteson, by 'A Lady'* (n.p., 1872).

In the official histories of the Melanesian Mission by E. S. Armstrong (1900) and the veteran missionary C. E. Fox (1958), the parallels with the death of Jesus Christ became more explicit. The stabbings on Patteson's body became five sacred wounds, his body was prepared for burial by women who loved him, and it was claimed by Fox that the Bishop's death was followed by a 'great darkness' over the eastern Solomon Islands, probably caused by the active volcano of Tinakula.[33]

Patteson was killed, contemporaries agreed, because he was a white man in the wrong place at the wrong time, not in defence of the Christian faith. However, he was regarded as a martyr in the broader sense of the word because he had been killed 'in the simple performance of his duty' as a Christian missionary. In February 1872 Bishop Samuel Wilberforce told the Upper House of the Convocation of Canterbury that Patteson's devoted life and martyrdom 'ought to raise the tone' of the whole church at home, as 'an example rising out of its midst'.[34] The S.P.G. seized the opportunity. In April 1872, at the suggestion of G. H. Wilkinson, vicar of St Peter's, Eaton Square, London, it requested the Archbishop of Canterbury to approve a day of united intercessory prayer for missions, especially for 'additional labourers' for the mission field. The first Day of Intercession for Missions on 20 December 1872 was so successful that it became an annual observance, later held near St Andrew's Day. It was one of the signs of growing popular support for missions in the late nineteenth-century Church of England.[35]

At Norfolk Island, the headquarters of the Melanesian Mission until 1919, Patteson was a living presence for many years after his death. In his rooms, his furniture and books were left as they were when he set out on his last voyage. His name, 'familiar to the smallest catechumen', was 'never uttered but in reverent love'.[36] The day of his martyrdom came to be observed every year at mission stations with a special service and sermon. After the deaths of his two sisters the mat in which his body had been wrapped was given to the Melanesian Mission, while the palm leaf

[33] Armstrong, *Melanesian Mission*, pp. 124–5; Fox, *Southern Isles*, p. 26.
[34] Samuel Wilberforce, 'Upon the death of Bishop Patteson', in *Speeches on Missions, by the Right Reverend Samuel Wilberforce, D.D.* (London, 1874), pp. 325–6
[35] S.P.G., Standing Committee, minutes, 11 and 18 April 1872, 30 May 1872; S.P.G., Journal, 19 April 1872, 19 July 1872, U.S.P.G. Archives, Oxford, Rhodes House; *Times*, 21 Dec. 1872; C. F. Pascoe, *Two Hundred Years of the S.P.G.*, 2 vols (London, 1901), 2, p. 821; Arthur James Mason, *Memoir of George Howard Wilkinson*, 2 vols (London, 1909), 1, ch. 5; Eugene Stock, 'Thirty years' work in the non-Christian world: a brief survey of Protestant missions, 1872 to 1902', *The East and the West*, 1 (1903), pp. 438–62.
[36] Alfred Penny, *Ten Years in Melanesia* (London, 1887), p. 11; *Southern Cross Log* (Sydney), Nov. 1906, p. 62.

was kept in a wooden chest in the chapel of the S.P.G. in London. This relic remained there until 1971, when it was sent to the Solomon Islands, to be placed with the mat at a shrine in the new cathedral at Honiara. Meanwhile, in the 1920s, the liturgical observance in Melanesia had become more elaborate, with the addition of a special introit and collect, and Bishop Patteson's Day was observed everywhere in the diocese as a holy day. At a mission girls' school, for instance, the headmistress gave a talk in church each year on the Bishop's life and death, and the pupils made a thank-offering of shells, woven mats, and baskets for mission funds.[37] In recent years the commemoration in Melanesia has been extended to include Joseph Atkin, Stephen Taroaniara, and eight other mission workers for their 'good lives, strong faith and holy deaths',[38] but in the church calendar 20 September is still known as Bishop Patteson's Day. A mission boat, a theological college, and other institutions have been named in his memory. Although the Solomon Islands and Vanuatu are now independent nations and the Melanesian Mission has become the autonomous Church of Melanesia, the story of the martyrdom of an Old Etonian missionary bishop remains central in the traditions of Melanesian Anglicanism.

The Flinders University of South Australia

[37] Edith Safstrom, Diary, entries 20 Sept. 1928, 20 Sept. 1930, 20 Sept. 1931, 20 Sept. 1933, in possession of Diana Smith, Adelaide, South Australia.
[38] *A Book of Common Prayer in Modern English*, 3rd edn (Honiara, 1971), p. 41.

THE FIRST PROTESTANT MARTYR OF THE TWENTIETH CENTURY: THE LIFE AND SIGNIFICANCE OF JOHN KENSIT (1853–1902)

by MARTIN WELLINGS

O N Thursday 25 September 1902 Liverpool's endemic sectarian violence claimed perhaps its most notorious victim. John Kensit, founder of the Protestant Truth Society and instigator of the Kensit Crusade against ritualism in the Church of England, was attacked by a Roman Catholic crowd on his way from Birkenhead to Liverpool. An iron file was thrown, injuring the Protestant orator, and Kensit was taken to Liverpool Royal Infirmary. Although he began to recover, early in October septic pneumonia and meningitis developed, and on Wednesday 8 October, in the words of Kensit's biographer, 'his purified spirit, washed in the precious blood of the immaculate Lamb, was released from its earthly prison.'[1]

Historians have paid little attention to the life and death of John Kensit. He appears occasionally in the biographies of the Anglo-Catholics, whose services he disrupted, and in the letters of the bishops, whose patience he exercised by those missives signed 'yours for the Truth' and penned for publication by the self-styled leader of the New Reformation Movement.[2] Kensit is easy to ridicule and to dismiss: at St Cuthbert's, Philbeach Gardens, the scene of one of his best-known protests against ritualism, Kensit was immortalized in the form of a misericord of 'The Brawler', complete with ass's ears, while to Compton Mackenzie, who witnessed the uproar at St Cuthbert's, he was 'a patch of scum from some foul pond of fanaticism'.[3] It should be noted, however, that Kensit the Brawler merited an obituary in *The Times* and an article in the *Dictionary of National Biography*, while his death was widely reported in the London and

---

[1] J. C. Wilcox, *John Kensit, Reformer and Martyr. A Popular Life* (London, 1903), pp. 67–77; *The Times*, 26 Sept. 1902, p. 4; 9 Oct. 1902, pp. 7, 9.

[2] M. LaTrobe-Bateman, *Memories Grave and Gay of William Fairbairn LaTrobe-Bateman* (London, 1927), pp. 79–81; H. R. T. Brandreth, *Dr Lee of Lambeth* (London, 1951), p. 66; L. Creighton, *Life and Letters of Mandell Creighton* (London, 1904), 2, pp. 288–315; *Churchman's Magazine* [hereafter *CM*] (London), Sept. 1898, p. 257. The distinctive signature 'Yours for the Truth' first appeared in *CM* in Sept. 1893, p. 259.

[3] A. Hughes, *The Rivers of the Flood* (London, 1961), plate opposite p. 30; C. Mackenzie, *My Life and Times* (London, 1963), 2, p. 219.

provincial press.[4] A funeral service in Liverpool was attended by religious and civic leaders, and a crowd of 20,000 people lined the streets as the body was taken to the station for its journey to London, where a second service took place in the presence of another massive congregation.[5] In life and in death John Kensit made an impact on his contemporaries which has not been reflected in histories of the period.

To a considerable extent the timing and the manner of Kensit's death increased its contemporary significance. A murder charge was brought against an Irish labourer, John McKeever, and although he was acquitted, the conviction that Kensit came to an untimely end due to foul play persisted.[6] The event occurred, moreover, at a time of intense conflict between Protestants and Catholics, both within and beyond the pale of the Established Church. An anti-ritualist campaign was being energetically waged in Parliament, in the press, and through petitions, public meetings, and direct action against Anglo-Catholic practices.[7] John Kensit was a leading protagonist in this so-called 'crisis in the Church': indeed, contemporaries as distinguished as Randall Davidson and G. W. E. Russell attributed the crisis to Kensit's agency.[8]

In this context, the violent death of a leading Protestant spokesman inevitably produced strong reactions. Lord Halifax, President of the English Church Union and epitome of the churchmanship which Kensit opposed, wrote, 'The less said about him the better . . . He was an enemy of the truth, and I find it difficult to think an honest enemy . . .',[9] but the Protestant press responded in a very different vein, with black-edged pages devoted to the death of 'this martyr for the truth'. The Protestant Truth Society's monthly *Churchman's Magazine* made its entire November issue a 'Special Memorial Number' to 'John Kensit: The faithful and valiant servant of God, and first Protestant martyr of the Twentieth Century'.[10]

---

[4] *DNB Supplement*, pp. 389–90; London, Kensit Memorial Bible College, scrapbook of cuttings.
[5] *English Churchman* [hereafter *EC*] (London), 16 Oct. 1902, pp. 682–3; *The Times*, 13 Oct. 1902, p. 14.
[6] Ibid., 9–12 Dec. 1902; J. Campbell, *F. E. Smith, First Earl of Birkenhead* (London, 1983), pp. 107–8.
[7] G. I. T. Machin, 'The last Victorian anti-ritualist campaign, 1895–1906', *Victorian Studies*, 25 (1982), pp. 277–302; M. Wellings, 'Some aspects of late nineteenth century Anglican Evangelicalism' (Oxford D.Phil. thesis, 1989), chs 2, 3, and 7.
[8] *Report of the Royal Commission on Ecclesiastical Discipline* (London, 1906), 2, p. 364; G. W. E. Russell, *The Household of Faith* (London, 1902), p. 402.
[9] J. G. Lockhart, *Charles Lindley, Viscount Halifax* (London, 1936), 2, pp. 136–7. Lockhart misdates this letter 9 Feb. 1902, i.e., eight months before Kensit's death.
[10] *Rock* (London), 10 and 17 Oct. 1902; *EC*, 9 and 16 Oct. 1902; *CM*, Nov. 1902.

In the autumn of 1902 the language of martyrdom was consistently used by Protestants in relation to the death of John Kensit. The *English Churchman*'s leading article on 9 October began, 'Another witness is slain. Another martyr is added to the noble army of the past', while the following week's edition advertised sermons on 'The Martyrdom of John Kensit'. The *Churchman's Magazine* published poetic tributes which spoke movingly, albeit inaccurately, of

> Another martyr stretched upon the bier—
> Another Cranmer burnt upon the stake.[11]

This theme of martyrdom was exploited to the full in the funeral and memorial services. In Liverpool, Canon Woodward offered 'a powerful tribute to the dead martyr', while the London congregation heard F. S. Webster, Rector of All Souls', Langham Place, speak of Kensit as 'one who suffered and died in the defence of our Protestant faith.' A phalanx of 200 Orangemen escorted the cortège to Hampstead cemetery, where the body was interred after J. C. Wilcox, chaplain to the Kensit Crusade, had taken Kensit's Bible from its resting-place on the coffin and presented it to the martyr's son, with a solemn charge to continue his good work.[12]

Steps were soon taken, moreover, to preserve the memory of Kensit's martyrdom. The London Council of the United Protestant Societies, a co-ordinating body representing fifty-one organizations, issued an appeal for funds in order to erect a granite obelisk in Hampstead cemetery and a memorial drinking-fountain on the spot where the fatal blow had been struck. Plans were also laid to establish a Kensit Memorial Training Home to prepare a new generation of Wickliffe [*sic*] Preachers. The Home was duly opened as the Kensit Memorial College in October 1905.[13] In the meantime, J. C. Wilcox produced *John Kensit, Reformer and Martyr. A Popular Life*, which was published in the winter of 1902–3.

As may be imagined, Wilcox's martyrology was a blend of pious biography, shrill polemic, and apologetic, presenting Kensit as a faithful Christian, driven by a sense of duty to engage in controversies which were distasteful to him. As has already been seen, other contemporaries were less sympathetic, condemning the 'first Protestant martyr of the twentieth century' as a fanatic or a charlatan. The purpose of the present work is to set John Kensit and his 'martyrdom' in context and to consider them against the background of Victorian popular Protestantism. An attempt

[11] *EC*, 9 Oct. 1902, p. 661; 16 Oct. 1902, pp. 680, 684; *CM*, Nov. 1902, pp. 328, 330.
[12] J. C. Wilcox, *Contending for the Faith* (London, 1989), pp. 68, 70.
[13] *Rock*, 28 Nov. 1902, p. 1; *Record* [hereafter *R*] (London), 13 Oct. 1905, p. 951.

may then be made to assess Kensit's significance in the ritual controversies which bulked so large in the Victorian Church.

John Kensit was born in Bishopsgate on 12 February 1853, leaving school to become a draper's assistant in the City of London.[14] Although his biographer sought to give him a good Protestant pedigree, Kensit was briefly a choirboy at the ritualist church of St Lawrence Jewry,[15] but he soon reacted against this type of churchmanship, receiving a grounding in Protestantism from two noted Evangelicals, Josiah Pratt and Robert Maguire.[16] Kensit began addressing open air evangelistic meetings in Hackney, and in the early 1870s he took up Sunday School work. About the same time he left the drapery business and opened a stationer's shop and sub-post office in Hoxton, partly in order to supply 'pure' literature to the young people in his Sunday School.

During the 1870s and 1880s Kensit's business expanded, as did his involvement in militant Protestantism. He established a Hoxton branch of the Islington Protestant Institute and was a member of the local auxiliary of the Church Association. In 1883 Kensit wrote to the Bishop of London concerning ritualism at St Mary's, Hoxton.[17] In May 1885 the City Protestant Book Depot was opened at 18 Paternoster Row, thus uniting Kensit's professional and Protestant interests, and from 1886 he was a regular attender at the annual Church Congress.

Kensit's publishing activities brought him notoriety in 1889, when two Protestant works were censured by *Truth* as 'religious obscenity'.[18] In the same year he acquired the *Churchman's Magazine*, giving this periodical a stronger polemical tone, and also founded the Protestant Truth Society, whose object was 'the extensive circulation of Protestant literature'.[19] For several years the P.T.S. concentrated on supplying tracts and distributing literature, but gradually it began to venture into ritualist parishes, holding public meetings and services on unsympathetic territory. In August 1893 the Protestant Defence Brigade was formed to protect these meetings against disruption. Kensit's campaign against ritualism led him to stand

[14] Brief accounts of Kensit's life may be found in *DNB Supplement*, pp. 389–90, *CM*, Dec. 1892, pp. 353–6 and Sept. 1898, pp. 257–8, *EC*, 9 Oct. 1902, p. 672, and P. J. Waller, *Democracy and Sectarianism. A Political and Social History of Liverpool, 1868–1939* (Liverpool, 1981), pp. 191–3.
[15] The incumbent of St Lawrence Jewry was Benjamin Morgan Cowie, later Dean of Manchester: *DNB*, 22, pp. 498–9.
[16] Josiah Pratt the younger, son of a prominent Evangelical (*DNB*, 16, pp. 293–4), published an edition of Foxe in the mid-nineteenth century. Maguire was a prolific writer and controversialist: *DNB*, 12, p. 776.
[17] *Church Association Monthly Intelligencer* (London), July 1883, pp. 180–2.
[18] *Truth* (London), 29 Aug. 1889, p. 381.
[19] *CM*, Jan. 1890, p. vii.

for election to the London School Board in 1894. His candidature was unsuccessful, but the P.T.S. continued dauntlessly with its 'Active Protestant Work'.[20]

A new phase of activity began in 1897, when Kensit took the opportunity afforded by the confirmation of Mandell Creighton's election to the see of London to make a formal public statement against ritualism. In the course of the ceremony, objections were invited, and Kensit protested that, as Bishop of Peterborough, Creighton had worn a mitre and had given preferment to ritualists. It was a short step from this use of the confirmation procedure to the disruption of Anglo-Catholic services. In March 1897 a worshipper at St James's, Holloway, denounced Creighton's pectoral cross as idolatrous, and was given into custody. Although Kensit declared that 'he was wrong in publicly interrupting the service', he bailed the protester out of gaol, and within four months had made his own first public protest about the use of the 'Hail Mary' at All Saints', Lambeth. More public protests followed, as trepidation and restraint were increasingly cast aside.[21]

In the winter of 1897–8 Kensit returned to the parish of his birth, St Ethelburga's, Bishopsgate. This was a small parish with a non-resident incumbent, served by an Anglo-Catholic curate-in-charge, who had made the main Sunday service High Mass without communicants. Kensit rented rooms in the parish to qualify as a parishioner and then gave formal notice of his intention to take Communion. Creighton's advice to seek a more congenial church was disregarded, and considerable disruption ensued. Eventually the Bishop's chaplain was sent to give Kensit Communion, the curate-in-charge resigned, and W. F. Cobb, Assistant Secretary of the English Church Union, took his place. The controversy continued through the spring of 1898, with Kensitite protests during services, and with the institution of a lawsuit in the Consistory Court for the removal of a tabernacle and crucifixes from the church.[22]

The St Ethelburga's case was overshadowed, however, by a series of public protests during Holy Week 1898. These culminated in the

[20] Ibid., Aug. 1893; *R*, 30 Nov. 1894, p. 1181; *CM*, April 1894.
[21] Kensit's protest may have been inspired by S. D. Brownjohn's protest at Temple's confirmation in Dec. 1896. See *R*, 1 Jan. 1897, pp. 1, 20; 22 Jan. 1897, pp. 77, 89; *CM*, April 1897, pp. 107–8; Aug. 1897, p. 232; Brandreth, *Dr Lee of Lambeth*, p. 66; Wilcox, *Kensit*, pp. 33–6.
[22] The controversy is described in detail in *CM*. See also Creighton, *Mandell Creighton*, 2, pp. 288–91; Alan T. L. Wilson, 'The authority of church and party among London Anglo-Catholics, 1880–1914, with special reference to the Church crisis of 1898–1904' (Oxford D.Phil. thesis, 1988), pp. 50–1; *R*, 21 Jan. 1898, pp. 55–6; 28 Jan. 1898, pp. 79, 89; 4 Feb. 1898, p. 115; 18 Feb. 1898, pp. 149, 153; 26 May 1899, p. 530.

disruption of the veneration of the Cross at St Cuthbert's, Philbeach Gardens, on Good Friday, when Kensit reportedly seized the crucifix and said, 'In the name of God I denounce this idolatry in the Church of England; God help me.' Kensit was removed from the church by the sidesmen, arrested, and fined £3 for brawling.[23]

The spring and early summer of 1898 brought a series of similar protests carried out by the Kensitites and their imitators. In May, Kensit agreed to suspend the protests in return for Creighton's promise to present a petition to Canterbury convocation. While waiting for the bishops to take action against ritualism under threat of simultaneous protests in 1,000 churches, Kensit organized bands of Wickliffe Preachers to proclaim the Protestant message throughout England.[24] For the next four years Kensit sustained his crusade against ritualism, disrupting services, protesting at the ordination of Anglo-Catholic priests, opposing the election of Bishops Winnington-Ingram and Gore, addressing Protestant rallies, and denouncing the bishops in the press and even from the platform of the Church Congress. In the General Election of 1900 Kensit stood as the Protestant candidate in Brighton and polled 4,693 votes.[25] By the time of his death John Kensit had made a considerable impact on the political and ecclesiastical scene. His was not the sole Protestant voice of the period—the Church crisis owed much to the journalistic flair of Walter Walsh's *Secret History of the Oxford Movement* (1897) and to the intervention of the Liberal leader Sir William Harcourt—but Kensit was the most effective spokesman of popular Protestantism. Significantly, when the organizers of a 'Great United Protestant Demonstration' at the Albert Hall in January 1899 omitted Kensit from their list of speakers, the audience interrupted the set speeches with cries of 'Kensit', until the Protestant bookseller came forward to appeal for order.[26] Arguably Kensit came to symbolize traditional British anti-Catholicism, and attention may now be turned to that tradition and to his place within it.

Space precludes a detailed discussion of the ideology of Victorian anti-Catholicism. It may be noted, however, that the anti-Catholic world-view

[23] Mackenzie, *Life and Times*, 2, p. 219; *R*, 22 April 1898, p. 368; Wilson, 'Church and party', p. 61.

[24] See, e.g., *The Times*, 25 July 1898, p. 12; 26 July 1898, p. 10; 4 Aug. 1898, p. 12; *CM*, Aug. 1898, pp. 242–3; *Chronicle of Convocation* (London), 14 Vict. 1898, sess. 38, pp. 206–29.

[25] Wilcox, *Kensit, passim*; *R*, 19 April 1901, p. 387; 24 Jan. 1902, p. 79; Machin, 'Anti-ritualist campaign', p. 296.

[26] *R*, 3 Feb. 1899, pp. 131–3; *CM*, March 1899, pp. 68–71. The minutes of the Church Association council imply that attempts were being made to control Kensit.

wove together theological, political, and moral convictions. Protestants rejected Roman Catholic teaching as doctrinal falsehood and spiritual poison. They held that Romanism was incompatible with democracy and free speech, associating it with despotism, censorship, and anarchism. The Roman system was also thought to be morally corrupt, involving the suppression of truth, the iniquities of conventual institutions, and the dubious practice of auricular confession. Rome was simultaneously a false religion, a political organization seeking world domination, and the Antichrist of the biblical prophecies. These beliefs, based on centuries of theological and historical polemics, were nourished by contemporary events, especially by the debates over Irish Home Rule.[27]

During the nineteenth century, traditional anti-Catholicism extended its antipathy from Roman Catholicism proper to the Anglo-Catholic school in the Church of England, a development made possible by the rise of ritualism. Anglican ritualism had many sources, including the theology of the Oxford Movement, the eucharistic doctrine of second generation Tractarians, like R. I. Wilberforce and R. F. Littledale, the ecclesiological research of the Cambridge Camden Society, and the demands of parochial ministry in urban slums. By the 1860s doctrines and especially liturgical practices which had formerly been regarded as the preserve of Roman Catholics were becoming increasingly apparent in Anglican churches, and this trend continued for the rest of the century.[28]

Ritualist practice and Anglo-Catholic doctrine looked and sounded Roman, and therefore drew the fire of Protestant controversialists. To the traditional hostility towards Romanism, moreover, was added the accusation that the ritualists were treacherously conspiring to Romanize a Protestant church. This was the burden of Walsh's *Secret History*, and many who did not subscribe to every detail of the conspiracy theory felt that ritualism was fundamentally dishonest.[29] For those raised in the Protestant tradition, the discovery of the Mass and the confessional within the Church of England came as a profound shock, and it aroused bitter antagonism. Thus the ideology, rhetoric, and methods of the Protestant

[27] G. F. A. Best, 'Popular Protestantism in Victorian Britain', in R. Robson, ed., *Ideas and Institutions of Victorian Britain* (London, 1967), pp. 115–42; John Wolffe, *The Protestant Crusade in Great Britain, 1829–60* (Oxford, 1991), chs 1 and 4; W. L. Arnstein, *Protestant versus Catholic in Mid-Victorian England. Mr Newdegate and the Nuns* (Columbia, Missouri, 1982).

[28] G. Rowell, *The Vision Glorious. Themes and Personalities of the Catholic Revival in Anglicanism* (Oxford, 1983), chs 5 and 6; James Bentley, *Ritualism and Politics in Victorian Britain. The Attempt to Legislate for Belief* (Oxford, 1978), ch. 2.

[29] M. Wellings, 'Some aspects', ch. 2, and 'Anglo-Catholicism, the "crisis in the Church" and the Cavalier case of 1899', *JEH*, 42 (1991), p. 251.

crusade were deployed against the ritualists, and John Kensit, in many ways a typical Protestant campaigner, found his main target in Anglo-Catholicism and not the Church of Rome.

The ideology of anti-Catholicism found expression in a variety of activities, co-ordinated by a plethora of competing Protestant societies.[30] Education was high on the agenda of most of these groups, so lectures and public meetings were organized to instruct Protestants in aspects of the Roman controversy, and a considerable volume of polemical literature was produced, ranging from erudite, controversial works and editions of classics like Foxe's *Book of Martyrs* to penny and twopenny pamphlets. There was a ready market for Protestant literature, and John Kensit was not the only bookseller to specialize in this branch of the trade.[31]

Apart from their didactic and publishing activities, the Protestant societies also operated as political pressure-groups. During the 1890s the Church Association promoted a campaign of 'Protestantism before party politics', advocating a church discipline bill which would deprive ritualists of their benefices, without creating martyrs by sending them to prison. In the meantime, petitions, deputations, open letters, and stern resolutions were sent to the bishops, urging them to use their powers to suppress 'lawlessness in the National Church'.[32]

John Kensit, while copying the activities of the mainstream Protestant societies, demonstrated a flair for publicity and a disregard for respectability which ensured that he made a greater impact than most of his rivals. In 1896, for example, the shop window of 18 Paternoster Row was filled with a display of scourges and other 'instruments of torture' reputedly used by ritualists, and this attracted considerable public attention. The protests of 1898 were widely reported in the London press, and stimulated a series of articles on ritualist churches. In 1900 the P.T.S. mounted a raid on the church at Womersley, in Yorkshire, attached labels inscribed 'Kensit and Co. Removers of Illegal Ornaments' to various items, and headed for Bishopthorpe, pursued by the churchwardens and the police.[33] Kensit's gift for self-advertisement, his refusal to compromise, and his unvarnished language made him the despair of the

[30] Wolffe, *Protestant Crusade*, *passim*.
[31] *R*, 27 Aug. 1897, p. 866.
[32] Bentley, *Ritualism and Politics*, chs 4 and 5, describes the drawbacks of the Public Worship Regulation Act. On 'Protestantism before party politics', see G. I. T. Machin, *Politics and the Churches in Great Britain, 1869–1921* (Oxford, 1987), pp. 243–73, 293–5. The phrase 'lawlessness in the National Church' was used by Sir William Harcourt in his letters to *The Times*.
[33] W. Walsh, *Secret History of the Oxford Movement*, pop. edn (London, 1899), p. 27; *R*, 16 March 1900, p. 243, *CM*, April 1900, p. 109.

episcopate, a frequent embarrassment to respectable Evangelicals, and the champion of popular Protestant opinion.

Victorian anti-Catholicism had a questionable or ambiguous side, and this was also apparent in the career of John Kensit. There was, first, an overlap between Protestant polemic and pornography. Tales of convent life in the tradition of Maria Monk's *Awful Disclosures* (1836) or salacious extracts from works of moral theology like *The Confessional Unmasked* (1865) appealed to prurience as well as to Protestantism. Kensit's clash with *Truth* in 1889 began when the newspaper condemned his pamphlet *The High Church Confessional* as 'the most loathsome indecency and obscenity'. A couple of weeks later another P.T.S. publication, J. D. Fulton's *Why Priests Should Wed*, also received a vigorous censure from *Truth*. Obscene publications were a matter for public debate in 1889, because the National Vigilance Association had just successfully prosecuted the publisher Henry Vizetelly for selling English translations of the novels of Zola. *Truth* had no sympathy for the N.V.A., and was therefore delighted to discover that the wholesale agent for its *Vigilance Record* was none other than John Kensit. Kensit lost the agency, and the allegation that he had been prosecuted for publishing indecent literature remained with him until the end of his life.[34]

The second ambiguous feature of anti-Catholicism was summed up in the phrase 'the Protestantism that pays'. The movement offered scope to the dishonest and the unscrupulous to take advantage of the zeal of wealthy but gullible Protestants. In the middle of the century the Roman Catholic James Mathison was paid to provide tame Catholics for 'conversion' by Protestant debaters, while Edward Harper founded several bogus Protestant societies and pocketed the subscriptions. Following up its criticisms of Kensit's wares in October 1889, *Truth* suggested that his motive 'is as much commercial as religious'. Three years later, the newspaper launched an investigation into the finances of the P.T.S., concluding that the Society was 'merely a disguise in which Kensit appeals for money for the purchase and circulation of his own publications.' *Truth* returned to the attack in February 1895, commenting on the use of P.T.S. funds to underwrite Kensit's candidature in the London School Board election of the previous autumn.[35]

Like the obscenity accusation, the charge of profiteering remained with John Kensit until his death; indeed, Wilcox was at pains to refute the claim that the Protestant martyr only took up the cause when it became lucrative.[36] Kensit's association with militant ideology and activity pre-dated his career as a publisher, but while *Truth*'s dismissal of his religious motivation as 'sickening cant' was too sweeping, it remains the case that his gifts for organization and self-advertisement were commercially advantageous. There was, moreover, some disquiet within Protestant circles at Kensit's financial accountability, reflected in the Church Association's recommendation that P.T.S. funds should be managed by a properly constituted board of trustees.[37] As Kensit's stock as a Protestant champion rose, the fortunes of the P.T.S. and its Secretary steadily improved. A testimonial fund in 1900 raised £408 (£13,500 at 1990 prices), and Kensit's estate was valued at £2,196 gross, £1,070 net (£72,500 and £35,300 today). It may be added that martyrdom itself was marketable: the memorial edition of the *Churchman's Magazine* advertised photographs of the martyred Reformer at one shilling each, and by mid-October 1902, J. A. Kensit had launched a 'Great Extension Scheme' as 'A fitting memorial to the work of my beloved and martyred father'. The sum of £6,500 (£214,500) was eventually subscribed to pay for the Kensit Memorial College, and in the decade before the First World War the income of the P.T.S. consistently outstripped its rivals.[38]

The third area of popular Protestantism which aroused disquiet concerned the methods employed by the militants. The Church Association's policy of prosecuting ritualists aroused bitter controversy within the Evangelical school in this period,[39] and John Kensit's aggressive Protestantism was still more offensive to some. It was by no means un-precedented: William Murphy's lecture-tours provoked full-scale riots in the late 1860s, while the violence stirred up by George Wise in Liverpool thirty years later created the conditions for Kensit's 'martyrdom'.[40]

John Kensit justified his methods as regrettable, but necessary, and he poured scorn on those 'poor, timid, half-hearted souls' who advocated a

[36] Wilcox, *Kensit*, pp. 24–7.
[37] *Truth*, 5 Dec. 1889, p. 1040; London, Lambeth Palace Library, Church Society MSS, Church Association council minutes, vol. 11, pp. 198 (20 Oct. 1898) and 228 (5 Jan. 1899).
[38] *R*, 21 Dec. 1900, p. 1223; 28 Nov. 1902, p. 1143; *CM*, Nov. 1902, p. 344; *EC*, 23 Oct. 1902, p. 696; *R*, 13 Oct. 1905, p. 951; Wellings, 'Some aspects', p. 128.
[39] A. Bentley, 'The transformation of the Evangelical party in the Church of England in the later nineteenth century' (Durham Ph.D. thesis, 1971), ch. 3; Wellings, 'Some aspects', pp. 163–8.
[40] Arnstein, *Protestant versus Catholic*, pp. 88–107; Waller, *Democracy and Sectarianism*, pp. 166–206.

less aggressive approach.[41] Wilcox took the same line, emphasizing the duty of controversy, and stressing that militant Protestantism was not injurious to healthy spirituality. The ultra-Protestants of the Church Association and the *English Churchman* endorsed this position,[42] but many Evangelicals remained unconvinced. Samuel Garratt, a very staunch Evangelical Protestant, who firmly opposed any compromise with ritualism, wrote to *The Times* in August 1898 deprecating Kensit's methods as counter-productive and dishonouring to God. The *Record* attacked 'the most injudicious methods and the repulsively rude language of Mr KENSIT and his friends', while Canon Henry Lewis called the Kensitites 'fanatics' who had injured the Evangelical cause. Within two months of Kensit's death, the Revd G. S. Streetfield was describing the ritual controversy as 'little more than the flogging of a dead horse'.[43]

The success and effectiveness of the Kensit crusade may be assessed on several different levels. Wilcox devoted one chapter of his martyrology to 'In a nutshell—his life aim', quoting a letter of July 1901 in which Kensit foresaw the creation of 'a strong public opinion that shall either end or mend the disgraceful and disloyal practices now being carried on by so many of our clergy.'[44] That aim was not achieved. Far from being extirpated or even checked, Anglo-Catholicism continued to grow in influence in the Church of England, reaching its heyday between the two world wars.[45] Arguably, the Protestant agitation of the 1890s and early 1900s encouraged extremism, hindering the bishops in their attempts to negotiate a settlement, and forcing moderate High Churchmen to rally behind defiant ritualists in the face of apparent persecution. Kensit's appeal to the country could not muster sufficient support to secure legislative changes: Protestantism could not defeat party politics and had to rest content with the Royal Commission on Ecclesiastical Discipline of 1904–6, which set the Church of England on the path of Prayer Book revision. Instead of being the morning star of a new Reformation, Kensit marked one phase in the waning of popular Protestantism.[46]

Although he failed to defeat ritualism, however, John Kensit's

---

[41] *CM*, 1897, editor's introduction to the annual volume.

[42] *EC*, 9 Oct. 1902, p. 661; Wilcox, *Kensit*, pp. 59–60; Church Assocn council minutes, vol. 11, p. 132 (18 Apr. 1898).

[43] *The Times*, 2 Aug. 1898, p. 12; *R*, 28 Jan. 1898, p. 89; 12 Dec. 1902, p. 1180; H. Lewis, 'The present condition of the Evangelicals', *Nineteenth Century and After*, 19–20 (1907), p. 232.

[44] Wilcox, *Kensit*, p. 62.

[45] W. S. F. Pickering, *Anglo-Catholicsm: A Study in Religious Ambiguity* (London, 1989), ch. 2.

[46] Wellings, 'Cavalier case', pp. 256–7; 'Some aspects', pp. 193–4; Waller, *Democracy and Sectarianism*, pp. 333, 347, 349.

achievements were far from negligible. He played an important part in stirring up the last Victorian anti-ritualist campaign, in company with Walter Walsh and Sir William Harcourt. If Walsh was the movement's propagandist and Harcourt its parliamentary spokesman, Kensit was its popular champion. He was an able platform orator, adept at expressing the religious convictions of the Protestant working class and lower middle class. He was astute at self-advertisement and fertile in organization, ensuring that the various activities of the Kensit crusade fed and supported one another. He maintained a position of uncompromising militancy, and he duly reaped his reward in the loyal support of the ultra-Protestants and the undisguised loathing of Roman and Anglo-Catholics.[47]

John Kensit's Protestant Truth Society is still active, and the college continues to exist as the Kensit Memorial Bible College.[48] Wilcox's biography was reprinted as recently as 1989 under the title *Contending for the Faith*, being 'the authentic history of the life and martyrdom of John Kensit and the work that he founded'. The ritual controversies of the nineteenth century are over, and the 'Protestant underworld' has dwindled,[49] but the memory of John Kensit, 'the first Protestant martyr of the twentieth century', lives on.

Buckingham, Bicester, and Brackley Methodist Circuit

---

[47] *EC*, 9 Oct. 1902, p. 672.
[48] Since 1977 the Kensit Memorial Bible College has housed the London Theological Seminary, founded by Martyn Lloyd-Jones. The ship's boiler file which brought about Kensit's death was retained after the McKeever trial by F. E. Smith, presented to the P.T.S. by the Dowager Countess of Birkenhead, and is now kept in a glass case in the college library.
[49] The phrase is Hensley Henson's: *Retrospect of an Unimportant Life* (London, 1943), 2, p. 147.

RECLAIMING A MARTYR: FRENCH CATHOLICS AND THE CULT OF JOAN OF ARC, 1890-1920

by JAMES F. McMILLAN

JOAN OF ARC died at the stake in Rouen in 1431. She became a canonized saint of the Catholic Church only in 1920. It is well known that the wheels of the Vatican grind slowly, but 500 years is a long period to wait for sanctity, even by Roman standards. Obviously, in a short communication such as this, there is no time to explore the rich afterlife which Joan enjoyed between her death and her canonization.[1] Rather, the more modest purpose of this paper is to show how her achievement of canonical status was preceded by a well-orchestrated campaign conducted by French Catholics during the late nineteenth and early twentieth centuries. If Joan was finally reclaimed as a Catholic saint and martyr, it was primarily because she was successfully represented as the very epitome of a heady blend of religion and nationalism that was one of the more distinctive and powerful forces of the era of the *belle époque* and the First World War.

Catholics were obliged to 'reclaim' Joan at this time largely because her cult, for most of the nineteenth century, had been appropriated by the Left. Left-wing historians, for the most part republicans and anticlericals, had done much to 'rediscover' Joan since the 1820s. As Gerd Krumeich has shown, the lead was taken by romantic historians, such as Augustin Thierry and Sismondi, who began to portray Joan as a 'martyr of the people', a simple peasant girl who acted in accord with her intuitive genius, but was eventually betrayed by her social superiors. Joan and her followers, in this view, embodied the 'national will', which Charles VII and his courtiers, like later monarchs, succeeded only in thwarting. Popularized by Michelet and others (notably by Henri Martin), the leftist version of Joan's story struck chords with the Republican politicians who became the political masters of France in the years after 1870. None was more enthusiastic than the deputy Joseph Fabre, who in 1884 sponsored a bill in the Chamber, signed by 254 parliamentarians, which called for the

---

[1] The best guide is now Gerd Krumeich, *Jeanne d'Arc in der Geschichte: Historiographie, Politik, Kultur* (Sigmaringen, 1989). See also, with caution, Marina Warner, *Joan of Arc: the Image of Female Heroism* (London, 1981).

institution of a national holiday to honour the memory of the Maid of Orléans. The bill failed to become law, but, as Krumeich has observed, by the mid 1880s, 'Joan was definitely the sister of Marianne.'[2]

The resurgence of interest in the cause of Joan did not leave the French Church indifferent. Catholics had not been totally neglectful of her in the centuries following her execution: indeed, her cult was preserved at Orléans from the fifteenth century onwards. Every year on her feast day a panegyric was pronounced at the Church of Sainte-Clothilde. In Catholic and royalist circles, long-standing tradition represented her primarily as a witness that God was on the side of France in general, and of the French monarchy in particular.[3] From around the middle of the nineteenth century, however, a number of clerics, headed by Bishop Dupanloup of Orléans, began to appreciate the advantages to the Church if Joan could be projected in a more populist mode, as a saint rather than as a champion of monarchy. At a time when the French Church was already showing signs of promoting more ultramontane forms of piety—pilgrimages, cults of local saints, devotion to the Sacred Heart and the Virgin Mary, and the like—Joan appeared as a figure with strong potential to appeal to the peasant masses whom clergymen hoped to rechristianize.[4] Galvanized also by a renewed Catholic historiography, which readily incorporated elements of the *populaire*, left-wing, view of Joan, Dupanloup took the initiative in calling for her canonization in the late 1860s.

The tribulations of the terrible Franco-Prussian War, and the consequent humiliation of France through defeat, occupation, and the loss of Alsace-Lorraine, all served as a powerful stimulant to the emergence of a new, more populist, Catholic cult of Joan. At Domrémy, in Lorraine, at the house said to be that in which the Maid had been reared, the number of pilgrims who came to visit steadily increased. In 1870, the *livre d'or* was signed by 2,000 pilgrims, in 1878 by 4,500—quite impressive figures, given the relative inaccessibility of the place. In the eyes of many pilgrims Joan was already a saint, and along with prayers for her eventual canonization one finds imprecations for her celestial intervention, especially to smite the enemies of France—notably the Prussians, readily identified as

---

[2] This paragraph is based on Gerd Krumeich, 'Joan of Arc between right and left', in R. Tombs, ed., *Nationhood and Nationalism in France: from Boulangism to the Great War 1889–1918* (London, 1991).

[3] Ibid.

[4] On the diffusion of ultramontane piety, see G. Cholvy and Y.-M. Hilaire, *Histoire religieuse de la France contemporaine*, 3 vols (Toulouse, 1985–8), 1; Ralph Gibson, *A Social History of French Catholicism 1789–1914* (London, 1989).

latter-day equivalents of the English, who had been Joan's enemies in the fifteenth century.[5]

The political and ideological conflicts of the early Third Republic, epitomized by the struggles surrounding the passage of the 'laic laws' enacted between 1879 and 1889, further boosted Joan's standing among Catholics. A harbinger of things to come was the row which broke out in 1878 over Republican plans to commemorate the centenary of the death of Voltaire. Already repugnant to royalists and Catholics as the symbol of free thought and anti-clericalism, Voltaire was all the more anathema to the devotees of Joan on the grounds that he had written a poem entitled *La Pucelle d'Orléans*, which had had the temerity to poke fun at the story of the Maid, claiming that her greatest achievement was to have succeeded in preserving her virginity against the designs not only of her male comrades-in-arms, but also of an ass.[6] To add to the heightening of tensions, Voltaire happened to have died on the same day of the month—30 May—as Joan, which made the project of giving that day over to the *philosophe*'s memory still more reprehensible in the eyes of Joan's Catholic followers. Their protests were led by Mgr de Briey, Bishop of Saint Dié, in whose diocese Domrémy was situated, and who organized, with royalist backing, what his successor later described as 'a large demonstration that was at one and the same time patriotic and religious' involving about 20,000 people.[7] Immediately afterwards, the Bishop started a campaign to establish a national basilica at Domrémy, located at the Bois Chesnu, allegedly the place where the d'Arc family had themselves set up a chapel to Joan's memory. This project ground to a halt in 1882, on the death of the Bishop, but throughout the 1880s and into the 1890s there were plenty of other Catholic initiatives to foster the Maid's cult, as we shall shortly see.

By 1890, therefore, the scene was set for a fierce struggle over Joan's inheritance. On the one hand, her cult was well established among Republicans and anti-clericals, so that in various places—for example, Nancy and Chinon—there were local committees set up to erect statues and monuments to commemorate her. In 1894 Joseph Fabre, translated to the Senate, relaunched his campaign for a national Joan of Arc day. On the other hand, Catholic leaders increasingly sought to reclaim Joan as one of their own, in part to reinforce the drive to rechristianize France through

[5] Warner, *Joan of Arc*, pp. 258–9.
[6] Ibid.
[7] Archives Nationales [hereafter AN] F7 5636: Lettre de Mgr Sonnois, Evêque de Saint-Dié à tous les évêques de France, 8 Dec. 1890.

the spread of the cult of an exemplary saint and martyr who personified the notion of France as the eldest daughter of the Church, in part to give the lie to those anti-clerical Republicans who, like Gambetta, alleged that it was impossible for practising Catholics to be patriots. In February 1890 the Bishop of Verdun, Mgr Pagis, embarked on a veritable crusade for the glorification of Joan, centred on the erection of a national monument at Vaucouleurs. In an impressive service at the Church of the Madeleine, in Paris, on 16 February 1890, in the presence of the Cardinal Archbishop of Paris and other bishops, along with a goodly gathering of royalist notabilities, Pagis spoke of the need to reclaim Joan for the Church.[8] There were two ideas behind the project of a monument at Vaucouleurs, he said. One was civic and patriotic, for the virgin of Vaucouleurs would be able 'to appease our civil discords and return France to the first rank among the nations'. The second idea was religious. In the Bishop's view, it was appropriate that the initiative for the glorification of Joan should be undertaken by a bishop, 'since, although Joan of Arc belongs to the whole of France, she cannot be laicized: she belongs above all to the clergy.' True, he noted, there were those who insulted the Church and denied it this right by recalling that Joan had been condemned to the flames by a bishop. His answer was that the Church had torn up the judgement made against the Maid by the unworthy bishop of Beauvais, who was the creature of the English, and who ended up being chased from his diocese by the faithful. His memory, like his remains, should be eradicated.

The Bishop of Verdun's crusade met with widespread approval in the Catholic press. *L'Univers* observed: 'This religious and patriotic impulse will not come to a stop: funds will be found and the monument at Vaucouleurs, like the Sacré-Coeur at Montmartre, will be a new and dazzling witness to the faith of Catholic France.'[9] The paper gave extensive coverage to the fund-raising activities of Pagis, particularly when they were accompanied by speeches which stressed how Joan had to be reclaimed for the Church. For example, before an audience of Catholic students in Paris, the Bishop received a strong endorsement from the right-wing deputy for the Morbihan, Lamarzelle, who explained that the enemies of Christianity wanted to seize Joan from the Church because she troubled them. But whatever they might do, he declared, they would not succeed in separating Joan from the Church:

[8] *L'Univers*, 18 Feb. 1890.
[9] *L'Univers*, 25 Feb. 1890.

She lived as a believer, practising with zeal everything which the Church ordered her to practice. The ardent piety which she had in her humble home she transported to the military camps. Let us not forget that it is the faith of Joan which saved France and that the valiant heroine died carrying in her arms the cross of Christ.[10]

Fired by the words of the orator, the youth present on this occasion voted to send off a letter to Pope Leo XIII, requesting him to bless the work of the Bishop of Verdun for the glorification of Joan, a work that was 'so eminently Christian and French'.[11]

Mgr Pagis was by no means a lone crusader for Joan's canonization. The new Bishop of Saint-Dié, Mgr Sonnois, was also keen to resuscitate the project of a basilica at Domrémy which had been languishing since 1882.[12] On Ascension Day 1890 (15 May), he announced from the pulpit at Domrémy that a second popular demonstration would be held on 22 July. This duly took place, attracting some 25,000 pilgrims, who heard a speech from the Bishop of Nancy, Mgr Turinaz, which insisted on the need for a national monument that was 'essentially religious',[13] a quality lacking in many of the monuments to be found in other towns and provinces. Domrémy was to be a national monument and therefore, the prelate maintained, it had to recall to this century and to future centuries the origin and divine purpose of Joan's mission. Work on the Domrémy project was restarted, not without some protest from Catholics who preferred to support the campaign for Vaucouleurs: a letter to the editor of *L'Univers*, signed by the chapter of the cathedral of Saint-Dié, spoke of 'an attempt at usurpation'.[14] The ensuing rivalry allowed the anti-clerical press some opportunities to mock the motives of the various clerical initiatives: according to *La Lanterne*, financial gain was the main driving force behind the Catholic impulse to honour Joan:

> These people have only one aim, to fill their money boxes. They would issue shares in God himself if they could find subscribers.
>
> If they had a shred of patriotism, they would not speculate on the memory left by Joan of Arc. They should have the modesty not to try to make money out of our national glories and remember that it was the bishops who lit the stake at which the Maid of Orleans died.[15]

[10] *L'Univers*, 23 Feb. 1890.
[11] Ibid.
[12] AN F7 5636: lettre de Mgr Sonnois.
[13] *Le Monde*, 24 July 1890.
[14] *Le Monde*, 2 March 1890.
[15] *La Lanterne*, 30 Aug. 1891. Cf. *Le Voltaire*, 20 March 1890.

The Catholic press, on the other hand, though clearly embarrassed by the unedifying competition between Domrémy and Vaucouleurs, affirmed that there was room for all the religious initiatives undertaken on Joan's behalf. The more the better, claimed *Le Monde*:

> That Vaucouleurs raise its triumphal monument over the frontier: that Domrémy open wide the doors of its basilica to the faithful of Joan of Arc: that Orléans, the place of the decisive victory, that Compiègne, the first stage on the road to martyrdom, that Rouen, where martyrdom was achieved, that Mont Saint-Michel, dedicated to the archangel protector of France and inspirer of Joan of Arc, consecrate their recollections in bronze and marble, and celebrate the memory of the liberator sent by God, so much the better! So much the better![16]

Thus *Le Monde*, like *L'Univers*, was a strong supporter of all other Catholic projects to honour Joan: at Rouen, Orléans, Beaurevoir, Chinon, Nancy, and elsewhere. Typically, at Rouen, it was the Archbishop who took the lead in calling for a monument to Joan that would be worthy of her and who, in an explicit reference to the anti-clerical attacks from which the Church had suffered under the Third Republic, wrote in a circular letter to his suffragan bishops:

> Why defer any longer a religious homage which is obligatory for all Christian and French hearts? She who saved our country at one of the critical hours in its history can teach us how to merit new miracles of mercy in the perils of the present time.[17]

The erection of monuments was not the only means by which Catholics sought to reclaim Joan. Literature and hagiography had their place in the campaign to make Joan a saint. Hence the welcome to publications such as *La vraie Jeanne d'Arc* by Father Ayrolles, hailed by the Bishop of Rodez, Mgr Bourret, as the definitive dossier on Joan, refuting all attempts 'to laicize her and to make her into a lay saint'.[18] Likewise the Cardinal Archbishop of Toulouse, Mgr Despez, praised the book for recovering Joan from the rationalists and free thinkers and revealing 'the virgin divinely sent to France to preserve her from ruin, and to conserve

---

[16] *Le Monde*, 28 Feb. 1890.
[17] *L'Univers*, 18 Feb. 1890.
[18] *L'Univers*, 20 July 1890.

for the defence of the faith the nation so justly called the eldest daughter of the Church.'[19]

Nor was the campaign to glorify Joan a purely clerical phenomenon, though priests like the demagogic abbé Garnier, who was an enthusiast for a Joan of Arc feast day, continued to be active on the Maid's behalf throughout the 1890s. There were also lay initiatives, many of which involved Catholic women. Ultramontane piety generally seems to have had a particular appeal to women,[20] and Catholic leaders were sensitive to the part which women might play in spreading Joan's cult. Thus when asked to support a newspaper to be called *La Jeanne d'Arc, Journal des Françaises*, Mgr Pagis readily gave his support on the grounds that:

> A newspaper destined for women and which will constantly set before their eyes the ideal type of the French woman who is both a patriot and a Catholic is guaranteed to succeed. The French woman is incomparable: her soul is open to all generous ideas: her heart is made of patriotism and faith. That is why she loves Joan of Arc so much. . . . I count on the French woman for the success of the work which I have undertaken. She will collect money for Joan with love, with spirit, and when she says with all her heart: it's for Joan and for France! . . . what Frenchman will be able to resist her?[21]

The abbé Le Nordez, canon of Verdun (later a controversial bishop), was another to target women in an appeal which he launched in 1894,[22] as did a weekly newspaper called *Le Cri de France*, which described itself as 'the official organ of the *Maison de Jeanne d'Arc, à Paris*'. In 1899 an article apostrophized its female readers thus: 'Women of France, remake the work of Joan of Arc, like her be soldiers of the *Patrie*, and at the price of every devotion and every sacrifice, remake the French soul in the transfiguration of courage and honour.'[23] As the Great Exhibition of 1900 approached, the same paper claimed that the time was right to strike against those who were contemplating the most horrible of crimes, namely 'the suppression of this great, holy, and august thing which is called the *patrie*'. The women of France should lead the fight 'against those who want to break the alliance, cemented by God in the heart of man, between patriotism and the faith, and against those who would also take

---

[19] *L'Univers*, 6 Sept. 1890.
[20] Cf. Gibson, *Social History*; Cholvy and Hilaire, *Histoire religieuse*, 1.
[21] *L'Univers*, 9 Feb. 1890.
[22] *Le Figaro*, 3 May 1894.
[23] *Le Cri de France*, 17 Dec. 1899.

away from patriotism the strength of everything that derived from God.'[24] Catholic women petitioned Parliament to support the Fabre bill to create a national Joan of Arc day,[25] and in the period before the First World War, the largest Catholic organization of French women, the *Ligue Patriotique des Françaises*, founded in 1902, placed itself under the banner of Joan and campaigned constantly for her beatification and canonization.[26]

The massive Catholic effort to reappropriate Joan of Arc produced outraged comment in the Republican and anti-clerical press. *L'Estafette* dismissed the campaign as a clerical and royalist manœuvre and observed that 'in truth, it needed a certain audacity to attempt to confiscate for the profit of the partisans of throne and altar the poor girl who was abandoned by the king and martyred by the Church'. 'The most subtle doctor', it went on, 'could not deny that Joan was martyred and burned in the interests of Catholic doctrines.'[27] At Chinon, a local Republican politician objected to any special place for the Church in the ceremonies to inaugurate a statue of Joan, since in 1431 the Catholic clergy 'for the needs of its cause, burned Joan as a heretic and relapsed heretic'; and in 1890, 'still for the needs of its cause and to add another string to its bow proposes to canonize her.'[28] In 1891 *L'Estafette* insisted that if M. Carnot, the President of the Republic, were to go to Orléans to assist at the feast of Joan of Arc planned for 7 May, it would only be to take part in the *fête militaire*, not in the *fête religieuse*, adding:

> Joan of Arc is ours. She belongs to everyone. She belongs to France. The Church weeps for her as one of the victims of its cunning and fanatical policies. France honours in Joan the noble heroine whom neither the vile calumnies of the Church nor the insults of a detestable poem have dishonoured.[29]

Le Radical took exception to Mgr Pagis' attempt to monopolize the site of Vaucouleurs. His was 'the work of a faction', whereas Joan should help to unite all French people.[30] Likewise, *Le Temps* objected to Catholic

---

[24] Ibid.
[25] *La Vérité*, 29 Jan. 1898.
[26] James F. McMillan, 'Women, Religion and Politics: the Case of the *Ligue Patriotique des Françaises*', in W. Roosen, ed., *Proceedings of the Annual Meeting of the Western Society for French History*, 15 (Flagstaff, Arizona, 1988), pp. 355–64.
[27] *L'Estafette*, 19 March 1890.
[28] Mayor of Bléré, quoted in *L'Univers*, 28 Nov. 1890.
[29] *L'Estafette*, 20 March 1891.
[30] *Le Radical*, 20 Sept. 1892.

attempts to take Joan away from the Republic, simply bcause they had discovered that she was popular. It was for this reason, claimed the paper, that canonization, left to hang fire for such a long time, had suddenly made huge strides forward.[31] (The case for beatification was formally introduced in Rome in December 1893, and on 27 January 1894 the Sacred Congregation of Rites declared her Venerable.) When in January 1904 Pope Pius X promulgated a decree which established the heroism of the virtues of Joan of Arc, *La Lanterne* waxed indignant over the Church's 'insensitive audacity' in prospect of the beatification and eventual canonization of someone whom it had condemned as a heretic and burned as a witch.[32]

Such attitudes on the part of Republican supporters of Joan merely encouraged Catholic devotees to even greater intransigence and stiffened their resolve to keep her for themselves. As the Bishop of Soissons put it, the essential fact about Joan was that she was a Catholic martyr: 'Martyrdom! That is the right word for the drama in which Joan gave testimony to a faith which did not die and to the motherland which, without her, could have died.'[33] Expressing his reservations about the civic festivities projected for a ceremony to inaugurate an equestrian statue of Joan in Nancy in June 1890, the Bishop of Nancy wrote to his clergy and faithful to remind them that if Joan belonged to Lorraine and to France, she belonged also to the Church, and that she was inspired and sent by God to save the country. There ought therefore to be a religious dimension to any festivities in her honour.[34] In the event, the inauguration of the statue was marked by controversy, because, in the presence of the Bishop, the anti-clerical academic Debidour pronounced a panegyric which developed the theme that Joan should be recognized as a lay saint.[35] Thus provoked, the Bishop made a strong reply. The ecclesiastical tribunal which condemned Joan, he affirmed, was 'the miserable and bought instrument of the government of the Duke of Bedford supported by the Anglo–Burgundian political faction'. It represented neither the universal Church nor even the Church of France. He went on:

> The condemnation pronounced by Cauchon against Joan of Arc is no more the doing of the Church than the judgements given in 1793 and

[31] *Le Temps*, 4 May 1894.
[32] *La Lanterne*, 8 Jan. 1904.
[33] *L'Univers*, 2 Apr. 1890.
[34] *L'Univers*, 20 June 1890.
[35] *L'Univers*, 1 July 1890.

1794, on the requisitions of Fouquier-Tinville and under the inspiration of Robespierre, were the doing of a France enslaved under the yoke of the Commune of Paris.[36]

On the whole, Catholics wanted nothing to do with Republican projects to honour the Maid. At Domrémy they accused Méline, deputy for the Vosges and future Prime Minister, of spurning their support by making intolerance and atheism inseparable from the idea of the *patrie*.[37] According to an article in *L'Univers*, the civic project at Domrémy was inspired by a desire 'to heap abuse on ecclesiastical judges and to impute to the whole Church the crime committed by a few of its priests'.[38] Similarly at Chinon, Catholics and conservatives were suspicious of the committee set up by the municipality to erect a statue to Joan. For them, it was important not to separate 'the patriot, the believer and the martyr'.[39] Even Joseph Fabre's proposal in the Senate in 1894 for a national holiday, which obtained a majority with conservative support, did not produce any real reconciliation.[40] The right-wing press chose to represent the vote as a triumph for Christian and monarchical ideas. In *L'Autorité*, Paul de Cassagnac had no time for 'that idiot Joseph Fabre, nicknamed "Joseph d'Arc"', or for any Republican connotations that might attach to the feast day. In his view, the proposed holiday on 8 May would be a consolation for the Bastille celebrations of 14 July, of 'sinister and bloody origin'.[41] *La Lanterne* warned the Right not to crow too soon about the victory produced in the Senate by 'little combinations of clericals' and predicted—correctly, as it turned out—that the Chamber would be less susceptible to their machinations.[42] The Left objected to the proposition because, as Jaurès put it, if socialists were as patriotic as other Frenchmen, they had no desire to see their patriotism 'represented under an archaic form'.[43]

Even at the height of the *Ralliement*, therefore, it was impossible for Republicans and Catholics to unite around the memory of Joan of Arc. The development of the Dreyfus Affair and its aftermath served only to deepen the divisions between the two camps. When, despite the urging of

[36] *Le Monde*, 7 July 1890.
[37] *L'Univers*, 1 May 1890.
[38] Ibid.
[39] *Le Temps*, 2 Oct. 1890.
[40] On the Senate debate, see Rosemonde Sanson, 'La fête de Jeanne d'Arc en 1894: controverse et célébration', *Revue d'histoire moderne et contemporaine*, 20 (1973), pp. 444–63.
[41] *L'Autorité*, 11 June 1894.
[42] *La Lanterne*, 11 June 1894.
[43] *L'Eclair*, 20 June 1894.

royalist and Catholic women, the Fabre bill was not given priority in the Chamber, *L'Autorité* claimed it had no regrets, since the memory of Joan was thereby preserved from 'all profane contact with the atheist Republic'.[44] It insisted:

> The inspired and Christian Joan, whom the French venerate, has nothing in common with the dechristianized Joan which some people want to impose on us.
>
> The cult of the immodest Marianne must not be allied with the cult of Joan the Saint.[45]

That was also the view of even more strident voices on the radical Right, for whom Marianne was *la gueuse*, the slut. Incarnated in Charles Maurras and his followers in the *Action Française*, the radical Right sought to develop an alternative political idiom in which Joan of Arc became the symbol not of republicanism, but of 'integral nationalism'—a nationalism that was racist, xenophobic, and anti-democratic. In the years before 1914 *Action Française* organized its own annual *fête* for Joan, which involved a public parade through the streets of Paris, and tried to exploit her as a figure who foreshadowed their own rightful rebellion against an illegitimate government and in favour of a restoration of the monarchical regime.[46] The cause of the *Action Française* was not identical with that of the Church (as Maurras was to discover in 1926, when the movement was censored by Rome), but particularly in the years following the separation of Church and State in 1905, when Pius X appointed many sympathizers with *Action Française* to the French episcopate, Catholics both joined the league and profited from its cult of Joan to boost their own propaganda efforts on her behalf. The combination of Catholic and Right-wing pressure persuaded Pius X to beatify Joan in 1909.

The timing of Joan's canonization was determined less by the length of the debate at Rome as to whether her heroic virtue could be interpreted as being more divine than human in origin—though that was a matter which considerably exercised the theologians[47]—than by the effects of the First World War on the relations between Paris and the Holy See. In the first place, the war provided a practical opportunity for Catholics to demonstrate the depths of their patriotism. There were no firmer supporters of

[44] *L'Autorité*, 24 March 1898.

[45] Ibid.

[46] Martha Hanna, 'Iconology and ideology: images of Joan of Arc in the idiom of the Action Française, 1908–1931', *French Historical Studies*, 14 (1985), pp. 215–39.

[47] Warner, *Joan of Arc*, p. 264.

the 'Sacred Union' called for by President Poincaré (unless it was the *Action Française*), and more than 30,000 priests served in the armed forces, not merely as chaplains and medical auxiliaries, but also as fighting men. Leading clergymen, such as Cardinal Baudrillart of the Institut Catholique, were only too eager to contribute to the war effort. Despite serious misunderstandings with Rome on account of the *rumeur infâme*—the rumour put about by French anti-clericals that Pope Benedict XV, under the guise of neutrality, was in reality on the side of the Central Powers—the French government was convinced that the clergy were ready for conciliation, in marked contrast to their attitude to the pre-war period.[48] What Catholic spokesmen most wanted to see was a restoration of diplomatic relations with the Vatican, broken off since 1904, and, when the end of the war was followed by an overwhelming victory for the Right in the elections of 1919, the way was open for the initiation of negotiations with Rome. In March 1920 Prime Minister Millerand dispatched an emissary to begin talks with Cardinal Gasparri, the Pope's Secretary of State. It was in this context of religious pacification (which still awaits a full scholarly study) that Joan not only finally received the national holiday in her honour which Joseph Fabre and others had so ardently campaigned for, by a law of 10 July 1920, but also at the same time attained sainthood, with the celebrations for her canonization fixed for 16 May 1920. Gabriel Hanotaux, appointed ambassador extraordinary of the French government, headed an impressive French delegation to Rome, which included eighty parliamentarians, and was accompanied by all the French higher clergy. Though the canonization decree did not officially designate Joan as a martyr, she had been successfully reclaimed by the Church as a saint who, in a unique way and to a supernatural degree, combined the virtues of Catholic Christianity and French patriotism.

University of Strathclyde

[48] AN F7 13213: dossier *le mouvement catholique*, 1916.

DOM BEDE CAMM (1864-1942), MONASTIC MARTYROLOGIST

by DOMINIC AIDAN BELLENGER

One of the soldiers asked him what religion he was of. He readily answered, 'I am a Catholic.' 'What!' said the other, 'a Roman Catholic?' 'How do you mean a Roman?' said Father Bell, 'I am an Englishman. There is but one Catholic Church, and of that I am a member.'[1]

THESE words of a Franciscan priest, Arthur Bell, executed at Tyburn in 1643, could have been taken as his own by Dom Bede Camm, the Benedictine martyrologist, who was one of the great propagandists of those English and Welsh Catholic martyrs who died in the period from the reign of Elizabeth to the Popish Plot. The lives of the martyrs were familiar to English Catholics through the writings of Richard Challoner (1691–1781), whose *Memoirs of Missionary Priests* had been available in various forms since its publication, as a kind of Catholic reply to Foxe's *Book of Martyrs*, in two volumes in 1741–2, but in the late nineteenth century, as the English Catholics, reinforced by many converts from the Church of England, grew more combative in controversy following the relative calm of the Georgian period, the martyrs came more to the forefront. The church authorities sought recognition of the English martyrs' heroic virtue. In 1874 Cardinal Manning had put under way an 'ordinary process', a preliminary judicial inquiry, to collect evidence to elevate the 'venerable' martyrs to the status of 'beati'. In 1895, and again in 1929, large batches of English martyrs were declared blessed. In 1935 Thomas More and John Fisher were canonized. It was not until 1970 that forty of the later martyrs, a representative group, were officially declared saints.

In the research work which made these beatifications and canonizations possible the English Province of the Society of Jesus played a crucial part. Father Charles Newdigate (1863–1942) was the Vice-Postulator, the person responsible for collecting and presenting evidence in England, for those martyrs beatified in 1929. Father John Hungerford Pollen (1858–1925) had already published his *Acts of the English Martyrs* (1896) and his

---

[1] Quoted in Bede Camm, *A Birthday Book of the English Martyrs* (London, 1908), 11 Dec. (unpaginated).

Documents Relative to the English Martyrs (1908).[2] If the Jesuits played perhaps the central role in promoting the cause of the English martyrs it was the Benedictine Camm who made the English martyrs both an apostolate and a life's work. He was in a great tradition. The refounders of the English Benedictine Congregation in the seventeenth century were much concerned with their historical pedigree, and Augustine Baker (1575–1641) and Serenus Cressy (1605–74) in particular were antiquarian scholars of distinction.[3] They were contemporaries of the martyrs and proud of their brethen's heroism. Many of the scholarly English Benedictines of both the seventeenth and eighteenth century were converts from Anglicanism and shared antiquarian and genealogical interests. Their approach was annalistic, and their greatest exemplar was Benet Weldon (1674–1713), who produced the first documentary history of the revived English Benedictine Congregation.[4] Here the Benedictine martyrs get their fair share of attention, but the principal concern, from both a historical and polemical point of view, is to emphasize the antiquity of Benedictinism. Martyrology was peripheral to the central theme. English Catholic martyrology in the recusant period was often chiefly concerned with demonstrating the predominance of one particular order or other in the catalogue of the dead. It was not until Bede Camm, albeit working in a similar atmosphere of antiquarianism and rejected Anglicanism, that the Benedictines fostered an English martyrologist whose principal and passionate concern was the English martyrs.

Camm died as a member of the English Benedictine Congregation, and his first major work, *A Benedictine Martyr in England* (London, 1897), was a life of John Roberts, one of the founders of the Congregation and a martyr from Wales.[5] This book was to establish his reputation as a writer. When it was published, however, Camm, although already a Benedictine monk, was a member of a German rather than the English Congregation. Not that his background was anything other than impeccably British. Reginald Camm was born at Sunbury Park, Middlesex, on 26 December 1864, the son of John Brooke Maher Camm, sometime of the Twelfth Lancers, and his wife, Caroline. As a schoolboy at Westminster School he became a devoted ritualist and attended the services at 'his favourite

[2] Francis Edwards, *The Jesuits in England* (London, 1985), p. 239.
[3] See David Lunn, *The English Benedictines 1540–1688* (London, 1980), pp. 121–45.
[4] See Geoffrey Scott, *Gothic Rage Undone. English Monks in the Age of Enlightenment* (Bath, 1992), pp. 145–70.
[5] Bede Camm, *A Benedictine Martyr in England* (London, 1897). Translated into French by the nuns of Ste-Croix of Poitiers and published as *Le Bienheureux John Roberts* (Paris and Maredsous, 1930).

church', St Mary Magdalene, Paddington.[6] He matriculated at Keble College, Oxford, where he graduated with second class honours in theology in 1887. It was during his time at Oxford that he was shipwrecked in the Bay of Biscay, an experience which filled him, he tells us, 'with a consuming desire to consecrate to God the life which he had thus wonderfully given back to me'.[7] He then proceeded to Cuddesdon to complete his studies for the Anglican ministry, and served as curate of the Church of St Agnes, Kennington Park, until 1890, in which year he was received into the Catholic Church. He made his submission to Rome at the Benedictine Abbey of Maredsous, in Belgium, which had been founded in 1872 as a daughter house of Beuron, in Germany. The Beuronese Congregation was in the vanguard of monastic revival and liturgical reform, and Maredsous was one of its most flourishing communities. Maredsous had an imposing if somewhat ponderous church in the Gothic-revival style. Both the Anglo-Catholic churches with which he was associated were 'noble piles'. Grandeur seems to be what he was continually looking for. The English Benedictines at the time of his conversion could not provide that. The 1890s was a period of soul-searching and crisis among the English Benedictines, who were transforming themselves from being a predominantly missionary body to a more conventual congregation. The appeal of such a house as Maredsous would have been great to a man with a background like Camm's, especially as it had established an English foundation at Erdington, on the outskirts of Birmingham, in 1876.

Soon after his conversion, Camm entered the Maredsous community, taking Bede (whose *Ecclesiastical History* he had studied at Oxford) as his religious name. He made his simple profession on 8 December 1891 and was ordained priest on 9 March 1895, while completing his theological studies at St Anselmo, the recently-established international Benedictine college in Rome. He went to Erdington (elevated to abbatial status in 1896) after his ordination, and he was to remain there until 1912. He then went back briefly to Maredsous, before (in 1913) preparing the Anglican monks of Caldey Island and the nuns of St Bride's, Milford Haven, for their reception into the Roman Communion. With the shadows of war gathering, and increasing anti-German feeling, the Erdington community was becoming less viable, and Camm became affiliated to the Downside Abbey community on 21 September 1913. It was said of Dom

---

[6] Bede Camm, *Anglican Memories* (London, 1935), p. 6.
[7] Ibid., p. 17.

Bede, harshly but perhaps truly, that the title of one of his books, *A Day in the Cloister* (London, 1900), rather summed up his own monastic life, which turned out to be a long series of travels and excursions. In 1913–14 he toured England, lecturing and preaching to raise funds for Caldey and for the convent at Tyburn, in London, of which more later. With the outbreak of war he enlisted as a military chaplain, serving first as a hospital chaplain in Glasgow and then (from 1915 to 1919) in Egypt. In the Michaelmas term of 1919 he was sent to Cambridge as Master of Benet House, the Downside house of studies. Among the students who passed through the house during his years there was Dom David Knowles (1896–1974), the monastic historian and future Regius Professor. Camm remained at Cambridge until 1931. He proceeded to the degree of Master of Arts, and in 1922 was elected a Fellow of the Society of Antiquaries. He returned to Downside in 1931, and died at a nursing home at Clifton, on 8 September 1942, and was buried at Downside. Camm's personality was not an easy one, and his books, many of them written for popular consumption, reveal little of a sense of humour. When humour does break through it is unintentional. A typical Camm 'joke' (preserved in the oral community tradition at Downside) would be his reflection on the new abbey church, about which he said: 'It will made a good ruin.' 'There was a very deep kindliness and indeed simplicity, in the best sense, about Dom Bede, though this was sometimes obscured by a certain brusqueness, even perhaps tactlessness, of manner which those who know him slightly did not always understand.'[8]

Camm's interest in the English Catholic martyrs may have begun as early as his time at Cuddesdon, because in a commonplace book, among his papers at Downside, there are notes on them, although it may be that these are actually later jottings occupying some empty pages.[9] It is clear, however, that soon after his conversion he began to accumulate material on the martyrs and began to publish articles, sermons, and books. His earlier works, including *A Benedictine Martyr in England*, *In the Brave Days of Old*, and *Blessed Sebastian Newdigate* (both London, 1900), were intended to present in clear, modern English the life and message of these martyrs to the English public and especially to the English Catholics. They were a successful attempt at popularization. They were soon supplemented by his two-volume *Lives of the English Martyrs Declared Blessed by Pope Leo XIII in*

[8] Obituary of Dom Bede Camm, *Downside Review*, 60 (1942), p. 333.
[9] For a checklist of Camm's Papers, see D. A. Bellenger, 'Two antiquarian monks: the papers of Dom Bede Camm and Dom Ethelbert Horne at Downside', *Catholic Archives*, 6 (1986), pp. 11–14.

1886 and 1895 (London, 1904), which was a continuation and completion of a late Victorian project, conducted by Jesuits and Oratorians, to catalogue the lives of the martyrs. *A Birthday Book of the English Martyrs* (London, 1908), splendidly produced by Washbourne and Company, completed the first round of his work.

Forgotten Shrines, published in 1910, is perhaps Camm's most memorable and influential book. It is a handsome volume, published by Macdonald and Evans, of some four hundred pages, lavishly illustrated with photographs, mainly by Camm himself, and with drawings by Joseph Pike. It places the martyrs and their surviving relics in their context in an England which was still there to be discovered, but was under threat. The book records several of the most notable Catholic strongholds and has a decided preference for the decayed, moated manor house which has seen better days. 'The air of mystery and romance which seems to exhale from the crumbling walls of these old houses, irresistibly moves those who come across them to curiosity if not to reverence. And this is an attempt to satisfy such legitimate curiosity.'[10] Harvington Hall, near Chaddesley Corbett, in Worcestershire, not far from the sprawling mass of Birmingham, a complex and ramshackle pile of obvious and great antiquity, crowded with 'priests' holes' and Catholic memorabilia, is the ideal Camm house, and one of his photographs of the place forms the frontispiece of the book. Another of his photographs (from 1915) is reproduced here (see plate 1). The Birmingham Archaeology Society had been told in 1903 that the Hall was 'hastening to decay and before many years will be a heap of ruins',[11] and Camm was perhaps the first of its admirers to realize that the survival of so much at Harvington (which still stands, its future assured, in 1993) is due to 'two centuries of neglect and suspended animation', during which, as Christopher Hussey put it, 'Time stood still within the charmed circle of Harvington's moat.'[12]

Forgotten Shrines may have owed something to the writings of Fletcher Moss, whose *Pilgrimage to Old Houses* appeared, privately printed, between 1903 and 1906. Moss, whose observations are acute and often amusing, visited several of the houses Camm used in *Forgotten Shrines*, including Harvington, which he described as 'the ghostly home of bats'.[13] Moss, who was accompanied by his photographer, described throughout as 'X' (and identified as James Watt by Camm, whose copy of the book is in the

---

[10] Bede Camm, *Forgotten Shrines* (London, 1910), p. vii.
[11] Michael Hodgetts, *Harvington Hall* (Birmingham, 1991), p. 7.
[12] Ibid.
[13] Fletcher Moss, *Pilgrimages to Old Houses*, 4 vols (privately printed, Didsbury, 1906), 4, p. 211.

Plate 1   A Forgotten Shrine—Harvington Hall, Worcestershire, June 1915.
Photo: Downside Abbey.

Downside library), hoped 'to put on record with pen and picture' houses 'slowly perishing by time, unknown to the world, and lucky to be unknown, or their beauty and their charm would soon be gone.'[14] Camm makes an appearance himself at Baddesley Clinton, one of the most romantic of the Catholic houses, in Moss's volume, where he is described as 'a Benedictine Dom in the cowled black habit of his order. He is versed in the learning of Oxford and the Church, with a fair knowledge of the

[14] Ibid., 1, pp. vii–viii.

outer world.'[15] Baddesley Clinton, 'where Victorian chivalry' was 'carried to what some may consider absurd limits',[15] had been described with great attention to detail by Henry Norris in a book published in 1907, which again may have influenced Camm.[17] A more immediate influence or parallel are the studies by Dom Odo Blundell (1868–1943)—a Benedictine from Fort Augustus Abbey, a monastery which until 1911 was, like Erdington, part of the Beuronese Congregation—on Scotland's Catholic heritage, opening with *Ancient Catholic Homes of Scotland* (London, 1907) and continuing with two volumes on the *Catholic Highlands of Scotland* (London, 1909 and 1917). He later turned his attention to Lancashire, but this was after the publication of *Forgotten Shrines*. Blundell's interests were less martyrological than Camm's. Thomas Garner (1839–1906), a friend of Camm, a convert to Catholicism in 1896, and the architect of the choir of Downside Abbey Church (completed in 1905), was the compiler of a sumptuous book on country houses, published after his death by Batsford.[18] He may have owned something, too—especially in his telling of the story of 'The Skull of Wardley Hall'—to M. R. James (1862–1936), whose first collection of *Ghost Stories of an Antiquary*, with its combination of scholarly erudition and imagination reconstruction, both features of Camm's work also, was published in 1904.

At one level *Forgotten Shrines* is an exercise in Edwardian nostalgia. The years from 1890 until the First World War were the great period of the rediscovery of the English country house. In 1895 the National Trust was established, and in 1897 the magazine *Country Life* was founded. Camm provided his own Catholic slant to what was a much wider movement. In a changing if very prosperous world, *Forgotten Shrines* provides the reassurance that one particular group of people and places remained 'ever loyal to the ancient faith' and retained something of that character which had been lost 'ever since England broke with her merry past and with the Holy See'.[19] It celebrates the picturesque qualities of the English country house at a period when the 'genre' was being recreated by architects like Lutyens. It could be seen as an escape from encroaching suburbia, Harvington, like some recusant *Howard's End*, a flight from Sunbury-on-Thames and Bournemouth to a *Homes and Gardens* Catholicism, safe from

[15] Ibid., 4, p. 256.
[16] Mark Girouard, *The Return to Camelot* (London, 1981), p. 202.
[17] Henry Norris, *Baddesley Clinton* (London and Leamington, 1907).
[18] Thomas Garner and Arthur Stratton, *Domestic Architecture of England during the Tudor Period*, 2 vols (London, 1911).
[19] *Forgotten Shrines*, p. 1.

the harsh realities of the urban life of so much of the English Catholic life of the period.

> Mawdesley [in Lancashire] is in the very heart of that blessed land where the Faith still flourishes, where farmer, labourer and squire are united in one holy bond, and where the large plain Catholic chapels have extensive stabling attached to them for the sake of the faithful who drive or ride, sometimes from long distances, to Holy Mass.[20]

At another level, however, *Forgotten Shrines* ushers in a new angle on English Catholicism which came to be closely associated in literary and intellectual circles with an identification of things English and things Catholic, which probably had its culmination in Evelyn Waugh's *Brideshead Revisited*, published in 1945. Perhaps Camm's reverence for the country house was a convert's attempt to find a substitute for the national institutions like the ancient universities where Catholicism existed only on sufferance. Camm removed the English martyrs from the wider life of the Church and placed them fairly and squarely at the centre of English life. He was a martyrologist with a profound sense of the *genius loci*.

Forgotten Shrines was an expensive book, but its impact on more popular literature was immediate. Robert Hugh Benson (1871–1914), one of the talented and eccentric sons of Archbishop Benson of Canterbury, and a notable Catholic convert and polemicist, used material from *Forgotten Shrines* in his novel, one of several he penned on the theme of the English martyrs, *Come Rack, Come Rope*. This was published in 1912 and was in its ninth edition by 1915. It carries the message that 'far better the rack, the gallows, the disembowelled body, still horribly alive, with the poor soul still cognisant in its limbs and brain, better the fire and the cauldron than the disregarding of one syllable, even, of the imperial call of Christ.'[21] Benson's historical works are little read today, but at the time they were best-sellers, and Camm was delighted that his work was having an impact.

> Dr Barry in this week's *Tablet* [he wrote in his diary for 13 November 1912] has an article on Mgr Benson's 'Come Rack! Come Rope!' which he calls 'The Epic of the English Martyrs' and in which he urges people to visit their 'Forgotten Shrines'—He speaks of 'Forgotten Shrines' in two places. Benson's preface expresses his 'extreme indebtedness to Dom Bede Camm's erudite book—"Forgotten

---

[20] Ibid., p. 312.
[21] C. C. Martindale, *The Life of Monsignor Robert Hugh Benson*, 2 vols (London, 1916), 2, pp. 179–80.

Shrines"—from which I have taken immense quantities of information' *Deo gratias*—This will really make the martyrs known![22]

'Making the martyrs known' was at the centre of Camm's apostolate,
and all the genealogical and heraldic information, all the documentation of relics, all the 'Bede Cammery' was there to publicize and celebrate
their lives and deaths. For him, a convert to Roman Catholicism, 'making
the martyrs known' was a work of an 'important apologetic value'.[23] The
martyrs for Camm were the most solid refutation of Anglican claims. To
him there was 'nothing which refutes so simply and irresistibly the
sophisms of modern Anglican theories of "continuity" and the like, as the
simple, unvarnished history of those who died in England for the Pope
and for the Mass.'[24] Martyrology for Camm was not merely a matter of
biography or hagiography, but a wider presentation of the English
Catholic martyrs' place in English history, the 'whole subject of martyrdom and the historical events which led to the immolation of so many
gallant Englishmen for their faith'.[25]

Forgotten Shrines is not so much a travel book as an invitation to prayer,
not about a 'vulgar excursion' but 'a pilgrimage'.[26] One of Camm's
favourite schemes was to establish a pilgrimage centre for the English
martyrs as near as possible to Tyburn, the execution spot near the present
Marble Arch, in London, where many of the martyrs met their death. The
late Victorian period witnessed, with easy railway traffic, a great age of
revived interest in pilgrimages, no more clearly seen than in the development of the Marian shrine at Lourdes. He had been discussing the
possibility of a Tyburn shrine with Dudley Baxter, a like-minded convert
(he had been received into the Catholic Church in 1896), at Erdington in
1901.[27] He was involved, in 1903, with the foundation and opening of the
Tyburn convent under its French superior, Mother Mary of St Peter (née
Adèle Garnier), which rapidly became a centre for martyr devotion.[28] In
the same year the first pilgrimage to Tyburn was organized, and in 1910[29]

[22] Bede Camm, MS diary, 1912 (Downside Abbey Archives, 3004).
[23] Bede Camm, Preface to E. M. Wilmot-Buxton, *A Book of English Martyrs* (London, 1915), p. vii.
[24] Ibid., p. vi.
[25] Bede Camm, ed., *The English Martyrs* (Cambridge, 1929), p. vi.
[26] *Forgotten Shrines*, p. 254.
[27] Bede Camm, *The Foundress of Tyburn Convent, Mother Mary of St Peter (Adèle Garnier)* (London, 1934), p. 89.
[28] Ibid., p. 97.
[29] Ibid., p. 101.

the first annual walk from Newgate to Tyburn took place.[30] The Tyburn nuns were exiles in England from the anti-clerical legislation of the French Third Republic, and they were especially appropriate as the guardians of the martyrs' shrine. The show-piece of the Tyburn convent was the Martyrs' Chapel, with its specially designed altar, which owed its inspiration to Camm himself.

> I have a brilliant idea for decorating the Oratory of the Martyrs at Tyburn [he wrote in his diary]. The new altar will be put within a model of the Tyburn tree, which will form a sort of baldacchino for it. I sketched out my idea and took it to Dom Sebastian, who is very pleased with it and will work it out.[31]

This plan was carried out and remains at Tyburn, along with a formidable array of martyrs' relics. Camm collected relics with gusto and had a collection (now at Downside) which would have graced the *sainte-chapelle* of any medieval prince or pontiff. The contemplative community of Benedictine nuns at Tyburn owe their foundation to several individuals and historical circumstances, but Bede Camm was an important influence, and the continuing devotion to the English martyrs which goes on there would have pleased him. After *Forgotten Shrines* (which was to have a sequel which did not appear and which does not survive in manuscript)[32] Camm returned to a full-scale study of one group of the martyrs, the Benedictine ones, which he published as *Nine Martyr Monks* in 1931.[33]

Camm's corpus of published work was considerable. He did not have a brilliant literary style and he cannot be accused of impartiality. Few martyrologists could. He looked back to a golden age of underground Catholicism from the vantage-point of the twentieth century. He was not a hater of the modern. He loved travelling by car (the faster the better) to remote historical sites. He was a skilled photographer and an inveterate collector of postcards. He was, however, very much a Victorian. He is not the model of a modern clergyman or monk, and the Catholicism he

---

[30] Ibid., p. 116.

[31] Bede Camm, MS diary, 26 June 1912 (Downside Abbey Archives, 3004).

[32] Dom Bede Camm, *Pilgrim Paths in Latin Lands* (London, 1923) is a continental version of *Forgotten Shrines*. 'I have tried to gather together here my memories of a few of these pilgrimages in the hope that my description of them may prove as attractive as did that of the English shrines. But of course I am fully conscious that I am here treading, for the most part on well-trodden ground; and that there are many who have long frequented the shrines of Italy and France, though they know nothing or little of their own land' (p. viii).

[33] Bede Camm, *Nine Martyr Monks. The Lives of the English Benedictine Martyrs Beatified in 1929* (London, 1931).

represents is not of the type favoured in the world after Vatican II. He had a triumphalist vision of the Catholic Church which would make England truly English again. The English Catholics, according to Camm, should be the leaven in the lump.

> The English people, so long separated from the truth and ignorant almost of its first principles, turn naturally to those who have been faithful to it or whom God's mercy has led back to it, to see what it is and what it does for its professors. What they see us to be, that they judge the Church to be. If we are fervent, charitable, devout, full of good works, mortified, self-sacrificing—in a word true children of the martyrs—they will be attracted irresistibly towards the faith which we profess.[34]

Camm represents an important strand of English Catholic thought and life, and the great devotion felt by many English Catholics today to the English martyrs, given a boost in 1987 by the beatification of a further eighty-five martyrs, owes much to him. Tyburn Convent continues its work. The forgotten shrines are no longer quite so forgotten, and many of them, either privately maintained or in the care of the National Trust, attract thousands of visitors every year. The debt they owe to Bede Camm, Benedictine martyrologist, is a great one.

Downside School

[34] Bede Camm, *Tyburn and the English Martyrs* (London, 1904), p. 102.

THE MARTYR CULT OF THE
FIRST WORLD WAR

by GAVIN WHITE

'IT is certain that the unrest of Europe of the past twenty years will be
dispelled. It is even likely that our whole civilisation will be advanced.'
So wrote A. E. Lawrie, Rector of Old St Paul's Episcopal Church in
Edinburgh, in October of 1914. He was spending a three-month leave of
absence as chaplain to an army hospital behind the lines in France. He
added that the death of a particular soldier 'spoke so loudly of Another
Cruel Death, that one could not but link the two together—the spirit of
self-indulgence will be trodden underfoot and exchanged for the spirit of
self-discipline.'[1]

Lawrie's expectation that the war would be over in three months
proved mistaken, and by June 1915 he was an official chaplain to a brigade
of English troops. And yet he was optimistic, for the troops were returning
to religion. 'I'm afraid all the dreams of the Utopia of human progress and
universal brotherhood with which the wonderful opening years of this
twentieth century have been full are destined to meet with the same old
awakening', he wrote, while 'such courage and self-forgetfulness as
dignifies the Race must surely purify the nation.'[2] As 1916 wore on he
asked if it were not possible to return to 'Primitive Christianity', even
while he grieved at the bodies laid out 'like so many dead rats' at the side of
the road. But after the first two days of the Somme 'only about a fifth part
of those to whom I had ministered for the last year were left', and Lawrie
was never the same man again.[3]

But he still believed that some of the nobility of the trenches would be
carried over into church life by disbanded soldiers. 'It is to the organised
Church at Home that the men will turn for guidance ...' on social
progress, and he asked, 'Why should the church not give that lead?' To his
congregation he wrote in 1918, 'It will be very difficult for you to see how
great the impending social changes are.' And at the end of 1919 he wrote,
'We are in the dawn of a new departure for the human race.'[4] But though
he kept telling his people that he was going to reorder worship and

[1] A. E. Lawrie, in *Old St Paul's Magazine* (Edinburgh, Oct. 1914).
[2] Ibid. (March 1916).
[3] Ibid. (Aug. 1916).
[4] Ibid. (Nov.–Dec. 1919).

everything else to suit the disbanded soldiers, in fact, he made no changes. He went on as before, the Church went on as before, the country went on as before.

The martyr cult of the First World War was not widespread, but it was there. More widespread was a vague idea that if killing had to take place there must be some reason for it, and some benefit for those who had been left behind. This would make losses easier to bear, but it differed from the demand that blood should be deliberately shed to benefit the race. But there were varying degrees of acceptance of this ideal. Sir Alan Lascelles, a royal secretary in later life and a cavalryman in the war, wrote rather vaguely of martyrdom in a number of letters, most notably, 'God has a habit of giving Seydlitz powders to distempered nations from time to time—they always come so appositely. Only this time he's given it to a hemisphere. I think the world would have been intolerable without the war . . .'.[5] Yet he admitted that war had not brought spiritual blessings to him,

> In the long-drawn torture of an all-night trek; during the weary vigil at some rain-swept cross-roads, where rations were due at midnight and arrived at dawn—in all our squalid Gethsemanes, was our vision the Holy Ghost? Not mine. Mine was a crudely physical one, always the same—a white bed in a cloistered room without a clock. I thought a lot about God during the war; but it was in back-billets and clean linen.[6]

In one of the *Anne of Green Gables* books, there is a minister who greets the outbreak of war in 1914 with the words, 'Without shedding of blood there is no *anything*', and goes on to say, 'Our race has marked every step of its painful ascent with blood. And now torrents of it must flow again . . . it is the price humanity must pay for some blessing—some advance great enough to be worth the price . . .'.[7] But if these words come from popular prose, most references to the blood sacrifice came from poets.

'Life springs from death, and from the graves of patriot men and women spring nations',[8] orated Patrick Pearse at the grave of O'Donovan Rossa, and by 1915 he was applying these thoughts to the rest of Europe.

---

[5] Duff Hart-Davis, ed., *End of an Era—Letters and Journals of Sir Alan Lascelles: from 1887 to 1920* (London, 1986), p. 190.

[6] Ibid., p. 267.

[7] L. M. Montgomery, *Rilla of Ingleside* (London, 1983), p. 63.

[8] Séan Farrell Moran, 'Patrick Pearse and the Politics of Redemption; the Mind of the Easter Rising 1916' (The American University, Ph.D. thesis, 1989), p. 194.

'The old heart of the earth needed to be warmed by the red wine of the battlefields. Such august homage was never being offered to God as this, the homage of millions of lives given gladly for love of country.'[9] As one observer put it, Pearse demanded a 'blood sacrifice in every generation',[10] but in this he was not alone. Rupert Brooke never committed himself to the idea of the blood sacrifice, but he did write of the 'red sweet wine of youth', and, 'Now God be thanked who has matched us with His Hour, And caught our youth, and wakened us from sleeping.' At the very least this does bring in blood, and it holds that to die for one's country is not an unhappy duty, but, in his words, 'great fun',[11] and life would have been empty without it. Charles Péguy was another who avoided the blood image, but his battlefield death in 1914 was almost suicidal, and be constantly wrote of 'another age' to come, though to him the end of the world 'meant primarily that France and French culture would cease to exist.'[12] Yet that other age was to be won by sacrifice, and he was forever asking for regeneration through suffering. Of these three, Pearse, Brooke, and Péguy, it has been noted by Séan Farrell Moran that they all wrote in the early days of the war, and did not know the horrors of the trenches. Had they done so, they might have moderated their views, as did A. E. Lawrie.

Yet of these three, Pearse is the only one clearly teaching rebirth through the shedding of blood, and we must ask whether the apparently useless sacrifice of the Easter Rising would have been really useless had it not occurred in Ireland. Padraig O'Malley has argued that, 'Central to the myth on which the Irish state is built and to the prehistoric gestations of the Celtic ethos is the idea of heroic sacrifice.'[13] This is probably true, but Ireland is not unique in this, and O'Malley has also noted that in the decade leading to Bobby Sands's death by sacrifice in a hunger strike, there were over two hundred hunger strikes in fifty-two countries, with twenty-three deaths spread across ten countries.[14] It was the era, not the country, that mattered most. As for Ireland, it may be that the cult of martyrdom was not particularly Irish, but Irish affairs came to a head just when the cult of martyrdom was widespread throughout the world. Use

[9] Ibid., p. 201.
[10] Ibid., p. 211.
[11] M. R. Brooke, *The Collected Poems of Rupert Brooke, with a Memoir* (London, 1927), pp. 5, 7.
[12] Marjorie Villiers, *Charles Péguy—a Study in Integrity* (London, 1965), p. 197.
[13] Padraig O'Malley, *Biting at the Grave: The Irish Hunger Strikes and the Politics of Despair* (Belfast, 1990), p. 138.
[14] Ibid., p. 25.

of this cult in reference to the war in France may have prepared the Irish people, or enough of them, to apply it to the Easter Rising.

That cult of martyrdom was a spindly thing, restricted to young men of good family and poetic ambition. It could be said of all of them as it was of German devotees, 'They were willing to sacrifice their lives because they believed that through fighting, killing, and dying they were contributing to the moral elevation of their country and the progress of humanity.'[15] This was linked to a legend of 'a mutation of species'[16] in that generation, and a legend arose in Britain that, 'Once upon a time, before the Great War, there lived a generation of young men of unusual abilities. Strong, brave, and beautiful, they combined great athletic prowess with deep classical learning.'[17] Only such a generation could offer a worthy sacrifice, and only such a generation could be called upon to do so. The blood of ordinary people was not worth much. These chosen ones were wanderers between two worlds, 'one dead, the other powerless to be born', as T. S. Eliot put it.[18]

Yet this cult could hardly survive the filth and horrors of the trenches, where the dead lay unburied for years. And it did not survive; what did survive was the idea that the returning servicemen, having learned to work for the common good in war, would do the same in peace. In this way the world would be a better place, not through those who died, but through those who survived. And instead of a literary elite of the strong and beautiful, there was the 'extraordinarily strong new feeling in the Army—the result of the comradeship bred by the life of hardship and horror in the trenches. It was a feeling that ignored all barriers of class, position or rank.'[19] When it was all over, the dead were buried beneath identical headstones, and a new and equal society was to be born at home. 'I can see a million visions that are dancing overhead, Of the glory that is dawning where the sky is burning red, Of the Britain to be builded for the honour of the dead, For the army's marching home.' So wrote Woodbine Willie, who was on more solid ground here than when he wrote of 'Christ's fools', 'Who grinned in their agony sharing, The glorious madness of God.'[20]

[15] Robert Wohl, *The Generation of 1914* (Cambridge, Mass., 1979), p. 51.
[16] Ibid., p. 7.
[17] Ibid., p. 85.
[18] Ibid., p. 229.
[19] Philip Longworth, *The Unending Vigil: a History of the Commonwealth War Graves Commission 1917–1967* (London, 1967), p. 14.
[20] G. A. Studdart-Kennedy, *The Unutterable Beauty* (London, 1983), pp. 113, 11.

But there are two major questions raised by all this. The first is how Christians, and all those quoted would have wished to be called such, could demand a blood sacrifice for the future of their people. Was the sacrifice of Christ on the Cross inadequate? Did its effect only last for so long? There is a troublesome verse in Colossians about making up what is lacking in Christ's sufferings, and if that can be explained away, the whole idea of following Christ in his sacrifice cannot. If his supreme work was sacrifice, and that was sufficient for all, why should his followers follow him? He had done it. But if this is one of those paradoxes which lie at the heart of all religion, it is normally met by keeping the two opposites in tension. On the one hand, accepting the benefits of Christ's sacrifice, and, on the other, following the moral example which he gave. These two approaches are, crudely put, the atonement theories of Anselm and Abelard. But in an age, and the beginning of this century was such an age, in which moral example was everything and benefits of sacrifice were almost nothing, sacrifice would not be highly regarded. It would then be natural for sacrifice to seep back into the system, and to do so in terms of a martyr cult in which Christ was followed by making a sacrifice which was as effective in its own realm as was his in heaven. Séan Farrell Moran has compared the Republican tradition in Ireland, in which violence is prescriptive, with Donatism, and even with the Taborites, in demanding more sacrifice than Christ gave.[21] And it is probably true that any martyr cult is rooted in a theological inconsistency.

But this leaves the second question, and that is of blood. For us this is merely a useful fluid which carries nutrients around the body and disposes of waste. For our ancestors blood was special. It was the life-force of the body, and, in Antiquity, it was believed that human seed was a distillation of blood.[22] Only in this way can Tertullian's remark about the blood of the martyrs being the seed of the Church make sense. Furthermore, the blood of the martyrs was shed on the soil, and this is close to Irenaeus' teaching of the first man being formed from the virgin earth. But it also reminds us, and would have more forcefully reminded those who lived at the start of the century, of blood and soil. Bringing those together was the act which led to new life.

How much of this lay in the minds of those young men who were supposedly endued with deep classical learning we may doubt. But something may have taken root in their minds. And there was another aspect of

---

[21] Moran, 'Patrick Pearse', p. 265.
[22] Aline Rousselle, *Porneia—On Desire and the Body in Antiquity* (Oxford, 1989), p. 13.

blood which was part of their lives; bleeding the sick to induce health. If this was done routinely for patients, and the use of leeches lingered on in British hospitals through the 1930s, could it not have been done for nations?

Yet behind all this hazy theory there were real people, such as A. E. Lawrie, who had returned to his Church, no longer expecting that a sacrifice would bring an automatic reward, and gradually realizing that in the hopes of a better life after the war, there would be no part for the Church to play. And, even more sadly, those hopes of a better life came to nothing. The blood was shed, but there was no new life.

University of Glasgow

REFLECTIONS ON MODERN RUSSIAN MARTYRDOM

by SIMON DIXON

The Lord has given glory to those who preached Christ in the arena and who did not fear the threats of the ungodly. With fortitude they suffered and so cast down the pride of the transgressors.[1]

RETURNING from his visit to Catherine the Great in 1773-4, chastened by a winter of ill health and frustration, which served finally to disillusion him of the prospects to be expected of an enlightened monarch, Diderot consoled himself by writing, during a sojourn at The Hague, an acerbic critique of the *Instruction* (*Nakaz*) in which his benefactress had outlined her political principles to the Legislative Commission of 1767.[2] Most of Diderot's *Observations sur le Nakaz* concentrated on refuting particular propositions advanced by the Empress. But he began with three general statements of principle, the last of which concerns the proper place of religion and the priesthood in the State. In setting out his objections to the fact that Catherine, like her mentor, Montesquieu, had opened her treatise with reference to God, Diderot is at his most splenetically anti-clerical. Priests, he believed, were contemptible. Their 'system' was 'a tissue of absurdities'; their true social position, 'roughly, was above or below that of an actor'. By contrast, the *philosophe* is said to be preferable on every significant count. 'The *philosophes* do not promise paradise, nor threaten hell.' Fanatically rational though they may be, at least 'their fanaticism does not have a sacred character.' Above all, 'The *philosophe* has never killed priests, and the priest has killed many *philosophes*.'[3]

As Isabel de Madariaga poignantly observes, this statement is no longer

---

[1] Sessional hymn to the martyrs, in Mother Mary and Archimandrite Kallistos Ware, tr., *The Lenten Triodion* (London, 1977), p. 691.

[2] On Diderot's unfulfilled expectations, Anthony Strugnell, *Diderot's Politics: a Study of the Evolution of Diderot's Political Thought after the Encyclopédie* (The Hague, 1973); on his single journey outside France, A. M. Wilson, 'Diderot in Russia, 1773-1774', in J. G. Garrard, ed., *The Eighteenth Century in Russia* (Oxford, 1973), pp. 166-97.

[3] 'Observations sur le Nakaz', in J. H. Mason and R. Wokler, eds and trs, *Denis Diderot: Political Writings* (Cambridge, 1992), pp. 82-5. On the complex genesis of the text, see Georges Dulac, 'Pour reconsidérer l'histoire des *Observations sur le Nakaz* (à partir des réflexions de 1775 sur la physiocratie)', *Studies on Voltaire and the Eighteenth Century*, 254 (1988), pp. 467-514.

true.[4] So sanguinary was the fate suffered by some Russian churchmen in the early years of Bolshevik rule that when Father Alexander Schmemann came to that turbulent period on his journey along 'the historical road of Eastern Orthodoxy', the way seemed 'cut off': 'a new chapter in the history of the Orthodox Church' had begun 'in persecution and the blood of martyrs'.[5] Persecution of religion in the Soviet Union was unremitting, though it varied in intensity and evolved 'from its earlier and bloodier manifestations into "dissuasion", from juridical sanctions into "education", from open war into contemptuous compromise'.[6] Thus, although successive Soviet constitutions from 1918 to 1977 upheld the principle of freedom of conscience, the practice of religion was persistently frustrated by both legislative and psychological means.[7]

The Bolsheviks began by formally separating Church from State in January 1918, a move which deprived the Church of its property, its right to teach, and its rights to be considered as a juridical person.[8] Between then and the end of the Russian Civil War in 1920, the years which will form the principal focus of this paper, numerous clergy and countless laymen met a violent death. But that was only the beginning of the suffering. During the famine of 1922, the Soviets skilfully exploited arguments about the Church's wealth to exacerbate long-standing ecclesiastical divisions and drive a wedge between the reformist Living Church, on which the State conferred recognition in reward for its co-operation in the sale of the Church's valuables (nominally in aid of famine relief), and those who remained loyal to the usurped Patriarch Tikhon in an attempt to prevent widespread desecration.[9] When, on 1 June 1922, British church leaders protested against persecution of the Russian Church in the person of the Patriarch, who had been placed under house arrest on 6 May, Trotsky drafted a reply stressing that Tikhon's supporters constituted only

[4] Isabel de Madariaga, 'Catherine II and Montesquieu: between Prince M. M. Shcherbatov and Denis Diderot', in *L'Età dei Lumi, Studi storici sul settecento europeo in onore de Franco Venturi*, 2 vols (Naples, 1985), 2, p. 650.

[5] Alexander Schmemann, *The Historical Road of Eastern Orthodoxy* (London, 1963), p. 340.

[6] Pierre Pascal, *The Religion of the Russian People* (London, 1976), p. 91. The definitive history of this 'evolution' remains to be written. For the fullest extant account, see Dimitry V. Pospielovsky, *A History of Soviet Atheism in Theory and Practice, and the Believer*, 3 vols (London, 1987–8).

[7] Aryeh L. Unger, *Constitutional Development in the USSR: a Guide to Soviet Constitutions* (London, 1981), pp. 28, 156, 244.

[8] M. M. Persitz, *Otdelenie tserkvi ot gosudarstva i shkoly ot tserkvi v. S.S.S.R.* (Moscow, 1958). P. V. Gidulianov, *Otdeleni tserkvi ot gosudarstva v S.S.S.R.* (Moscow, 1926; repr. Farnborough, 1971), collects subsequent legislation.

[9] Dimitry Pospielovsky, *The Russian Church under the Soviet Regime, 1917–1982*, 2 vols (New York, 1984), 1, pp. 43–92.

'the most privileged and debauched by their connection with the Tsarist aristocracy and with capital'.[10] Once the fractious renovationists were in turn abandoned by Stalin, the Patriarchal Church, weakened by their apostasy, was itself forced to compromise with the regime, thus attracting condemnation for showing precisely the same 'sycophancy towards the state which had been the renovationists' own worst feature'.[11]

Deprived of effective institutional protection, and with much of their religious activity driven underground, millions of resilient Orthodox believers were subjected to a barrage of atheist propaganda and persecution. The only brief respite came when Stalin sought to mobilize the Church as a focus of patriotic sentiment during the Second World War. Repression was revived in a particularly brutal way under Khrushchev between 1959 and 1964.[12] Indeed, by the early 1960s, belief in God was deemed not only abnormal but a pathological condition, dangerous to society, and though they were no longer liable to be executed, religious dissenters risked incarceration in special psychiatric hospitals.[13] If we recall those persecuted for their faith under the Soviet regime, the claim that the sixty years after 1917 saw 'thousands of times more saints than during the rest of the history of the Russian Church' no longer sounds like hyperbole.[14]

All this may seem far removed from Diderot and the *philosophes*. Diderot knew little enough about the Russia of his own times.[15] Indeed, he exemplifies a remark made of the young Charles de Gaulle—'No one is more blindly contemptuous than an inexperienced traveller.'[16] Since Diderot wrote about eighteenth-century Russia with more than half an eye on *ancien-régime* France, it would be absurd to reprove him for having failed to prophesy the Soviet future. Nevertheless, his remarks serve as a convenient point of departure for the following reflections on the complex and highly sensitive question of martyrdom in modern Russia,

[10] Jan M. Meijer, ed., *The Trotsky Papers, 1917–1922*, 2 vols (The Hague, 1964–71), 2, p. 743.
[11] Geoffrey Hosking, *A History of the Soviet Union* (London, 1985), p. 234.
[12] William C. Fletcher, *The Russian Orthodox Church Underground, 1917–1970* (Oxford, 1971); Pospielovsky, *A History of Soviet Atheism*, 1, *A History of Marxist-Leninist Atheism and Soviet Antireligious Policies* (London, 1987), pp. 69–97, and 2, *Soviet Antireligious Campaigns and Persecutions* (London, 1988), pp. 91–144.
[13] Sidney Bloch and Peter Reddaway, *Russia's Political Hospitals* (London, 1978), pp. 158–70, 269–70.
[14] Pospielovsky, *Russian Church*, 2, p. 459, quoting a sermon at the Russian Orthodox Cathedral in London, 1978.
[15] Isabel de Madariaga, 'Catherine and the *Philosophes*', in A. G. Cross, ed., *Russia and the West in the Eighteenth Century* (Newtonville, Mass., 1983), pp. 30–52.
[16] Jean Lacouture, *De Gaulle: the Rebel, 1890–1944* (London, 1990), p. 57.

because the first two themes he mentions—paradise and fanaticism—may help to illuminate the different ways in which the Russian Church and the Russian intelligentsia interpreted and experienced martyrdom in the pre-revolutionary period.

Had Diderot only known it, paradise was already a key theme in Russian secular literature at the time of his visit. Towards 1800 the myth came under attack: increasingly, it seemed, 'the earthly paradise—and, indeed, any long-term happiness—was an illusion.'[17] Yet not even a century of bitter failure could persuade later revolutionary thinkers of this fact: paradise was precisely what they continued to preach. Whereas many eighteenth-century writers had associated paradise with the tsars and their service, the later intelligentsia sought it in their overthrow. The Populists believed that revolutionary regicide would redeem the suffering caused by tsarist injustice and spontaneously give birth to a just, harmonious society. That same 'vast apocalyptic assumption', rooted 'deep in the religious imagination of mankind', continued to exert a tenacious grip on Russian minds.[18] In different keys, and with varying degrees of sophistication, it permeates a wide range of cultural phenomena in the immediate post-revolutionary years, ranging from the complex symbolism of Belyi's 'Christ is Risen' (1918)—in which Russia's revolutionary ordeal is compared to Calvary, the martyrdom of the Cross being followed by the Resurrection—to the bathos of the primitive 'Paradise' signs which sprang up at peasant communes across the country.[19]

So kaleidoscopic was the variety of paradisaical fantasies thrown up by the explosion of cultural creativity following the October Revolution that the atheist Marxist Evgenii Zamiatin, himself the son of a priest, was moved to sound a note of warning in a celebrated, anti-Utopian work of science fiction. So far from being a commentary on Russia as he knew it, the indictment of the monolithic, mechanical happiness of the Single State in Zamiatin's *We* (*My*), written in Petrograd during the Civil War, was a startling prophecy of a Russia yet to come.[20] Until 1917, however, the problem for the intelligentsia had not been to restrain Utopia, but to

[17] Stephen Lessing Baehr, *The Paradise Myth in Eighteenth-Century Russia: Utopian Patterns in Early Secular Russian Literature and Culture* (Stanford, 1991), p. 149.
[18] Isaiah Berlin, *Russian Thinkers* (Harmondsworth, 1979), p. 217.
[19] Max Hayward, *Writers in Russia, 1917–1978* (London, 1983), p. 87; Richard Stites, *Revolutionary Dreams: Utopian Vision and Experimental Life in the Russian Revolution* (Oxford, 1989), p. 211.
[20] Christopher Collins, *Evgenij Zamjatin: an Interpretive Study* (The Hague, 1973), pp. 39–43; Richard Freeborn, *The Russian Revolutionary Novel: Turgenev to Pasternak* (Cambridge, 1982), pp. 123–8.

reach it. Chekhov captured their dilemma with gentle but character-istically penetrating irony in *The Cherry Orchard* (1904). Haunted by visions of future happiness, the eternal student Trofimov knows that he may never see it because the majority of Russian *intelligenty* are paralysed by inactivity. They can neither think nor study, nor act: 'In fact they don't do anything at all.'[21]

It was in order to overcome this damaging inertia that P. L. Lavrov called at the end of the 1860s for revolutionary 'martyrs' whose 'legend' could 'far outgrow their true worth and actual service' by inspiring others 'with the energy needed for the fight'.[22] In fact, the execution of the five leading Decembrists in 1825 had already generated a tradition of revolutionary martyrdom which still inspired their successors in the 1880s. Thus the young noble poet P. F. Iakubovich, descended from the Decembrist Aleksandr Iakubovich, was mesmerized by 'the thunder of heroic facts, stunning the mind and fantasy with the brilliance of sacrifice, the brilliance of struggle, and the power of our faith in the justice of our cause.'[23] If, as Tibor Szamuely declares, 'Martyrdom was the Decembrists' essential contribution to the revolutionary cause', the sacrifice made by those wives who accompanied the surviving Decembrists into exile in Siberia was no less influential in inspiring future female terrorists.[24] Vera Zasulich, would-be assassin of Governor-General Trepov in 1878, spent her childhood reading Scriptures, in which she found ample 'material for elaborate fantasies of heroism and martyr-dom'.[25] So did Vera Figner, prominent in the plot to blow up Alexander II on 1 March 1881. Figner, describing the Bible as 'the most authoritative source' she knew, concluded from Jesus' example that 'Self-sacrifice is the most supreme act of which man is capable.'[26]

In the event, both Zasulich (1849–1919) and Figner (1852–1942) lived to tell the tale. But many of their fellow Populists had indeed sacrificed themselves in the vain attempt to ignite what they believed was the innate revolutionary potential of the Russian peasantry by 'going to the people' in the summer of 1874. Whilst Stepniak-Kravchinskii looked back on 'going to the people' as 'a kind of Crusade: infectious and all-absorbing,

---

[21] A. P. Chekhov, *The Cherry Orchard*, Act II.
[22] Peter Lavrov, *Historical Letters* (Berkeley, 1967), p. 172.
[23] Richard Wortman, *The Crisis of Russian Populism* (Cambridge, 1967), pp. 181–7, quoted at p. 187.
[24] Tibor Szamuely, *The Russian Tradition* (London, 1988), p. 248.
[25] Barbara Alpern Engel, *Mothers and Daughters: Women of the Intelligentsia in Nineteenth-Century Russia* (Cambridge, 1983), p. 94.
[26] Ibid., p. 141.

exactly like any religious movement', many of the participants saw themselves in the image of the early Christians.[27] There were even Russian Socialists, like Plehve's assassin, Egor Sazonov, who believed that they were 'continuing the cause of Christ, who preached brotherly love among people and died for the people as a common criminal.'[28]

Even when the opportunity arose it was natural that such exemplary sacrifices should be commemorated by a fitting burial. A tradition of martyrs' funerals was established in 1905 by the obsequies for Nikolai Bauman, a 32-year old Bolshevik who, having been released from prison in the amnesty accompanying the October Manifesto, was shot and beaten to death by a worker sympathetic to the extreme-right Black Hundreds. Since October 1905 marked the zenith of co-operation between Revolutionary Socialists and Constitutional Liberals, a group of influential lawyers persuaded the Moscow authorities to turn a blind eye to Bauman's funeral. On 20 October a crowd (variously estimated at between 30,000 and 150,000), carrying banners emblazoned with openly seditious slogans, traipsed for eight hours behind Bauman's red-draped coffin to hear his widow make an open plea for revenge. P. A. Garvi, a Menshevik who was present, was impressed by the quasi-religious fervour that gripped them: 'It was if this were not a corpse but a symbol of revolution, a sacred object carried forward in a procession surrounded by a chain of people who had resolved to die rather than forsake the sacred object.'[29]

Among subsequent ceremonies for the revolutionary martyrs, none was more magnificent than the first Bolshevik state funeral, held in September 1918 for M. S. Uritskii, the chief of the Petrograd Cheka, murdered by Leonid Kannegiser, a fellow Jew but a more moderate Socialist. Uritskii's funeral featured not only a procession of armoured cars, but an early fly-past.[30] However, even this extravagant ritual was to be surpassed by the obsequies accorded to the man who became the ultimate martyr in the revolutionary canon, Lenin himself.[31] Lenin's

[27] Szamuely, *Russian Tradition*, p. 379; Franco Venturi, *Roots of Revolution: a History of the Populist and Socialist Movements in Nineteenth-Century Russia* (Chicago, 1960), pp. 469–506.
[28] Quoted by Nina Tumarkin, *Lenin Lives! The Lenin Cult in Soviet Russia* (Cambridge, Mass., 1983), p. 17.
[29] Laura Engelstein, *Moscow 1905: Working-Class Organization and Political Conflict* (Stanford, 1982), pp. 140–2; Abraham Ascher, *The Revolution of 1905: Russia in Disarray* (Stanford, 1988), pp. 262–5, quoted at p. 264.
[30] Stites, *Revolutionary Dreams*, p. 113. As George Leggett comments, the irony is that had Uritskii survived Lenin, whom he frequently opposed, 'he would undoubtedly have been consigned, along with his patron Trotsky, to that refuse heap of history to which Trotsky had contemptuously consigned Martov': *The Cheka: Lenin's Political Police* (Oxford, 1981), p. 269.
[31] Tumarkin, *Lenin Lives!* pp. 160–4.

immortality was to be assured by the granite shrine on Red Square, opened in November 1930.[32] But the Lenin cult dated from 30 August 1918, the day that Uritskii was killed in Petrograd, when the Socialist Revolutionary Fannie Kaplan fired three times at him as he emerged from the Mikhelson factory in Moscow. Lenin's apparently miraculous recovery from this unsuccessful attempt on his life, which wounded him in the neck and left a bullet in his body until April 1922, inspired a clutch of poems depicting him in Christlike terms. One such offering ran thus:

> You came to us, to ease
> Our excruciating torment,
> You came to us as a leader, to destroy
> The enemies of the workers' movement . . .
> We will not forget your suffering,
> That you, our leader, endured for us.
> You stood a martyr.[33]

When, six years later, Lenin died prematurely of a brain haemorrhage, the medical reports, including one from the doctor who had treated him after the shooting in 1918, emphasized his status as a martyr by claiming that Vladimir Il'ich had sacrificed himself by his unstinting labours in 'the interests of the working people'.[34]

Since the Bolsheviks' fanaticism was distinguished by precisely that 'sacred character' which Diderot so heartily despised, it is easy to understand why their conflict with the Orthodox Church should commonly have been described in terms of religious rivalry. As Peter Kenez puts it, 'The Bolsheviks fought against religion with great determination because their God was a jealous God; it tolerated no other.'[35] The violent impact of 1917 makes it tempting to jump to the conclusion that the Bolsheviks were the first recalcitrant opponents that the Orthodox had encountered. But this would be misleading. Deprived of their pastoral function since 1917, Russian Orthodox churchmen have come to seem unworldly by virtue of their concentration on the mystical contemplation for which they are principally known in the West.[36] However, it is easily forgotten

---

[32] Ibid., ch. 6; Nina Tumarkin, 'Religion, Bolshevism, and the Origins of the Lenin Cult', *Russian Review*, 40 (1981), pp. 35–46.

[33] Tumarkin, *Lenin Lives!* pp. 84, 115.

[34] Ibid., pp. 172–3.

[35] Peter Kenez, *The Birth of the Propaganda State: Soviet Methods of Mass Mobilization, 1917–1929* (Cambridge, 1985), p. 185.

[36] Among the most influential contributors to this image has been Vladimir Lossky, *The Mystical Theology of the Eastern Church* (London, 1957).

that in the nineteenth century, their position in what was effectively the
Established Church of a multi-national empire brought them not only
into contact, but into competition, with German Protestants, Polish
Catholics, Tartar Muslims, Siberian Buddhists, Jews, heathens, and
sectarians of all kinds. The Orthodox response to these multifarious
challenges, though partly intellectual, also encompassed the development
of active missionary and pastoral methods, the one to strive for conversions, the other to prevent apostasy. The success of these methods was
limited.[37] But even though many senior churchmen began to fear, from
the late 1860s, that their rivals were gaining the upper hand and that the
State was an inadequate temporal support, they were never in danger of
persecution. Indeed, in view of the legislative protection the tsars offered
to their 'pre-eminent and predominant' Church, at least until the
Toleration Edict of 17 April 1905, it seems an understatement for Bishop
Ware to remark that at many periods in Orthodox history the prospect of
death for Christ's sake has been 'fairly remote'.[38]

From the mid-seventeenth century the idea of a church founded on
blood passed instead to the persecuted schismatic rivals of the Orthodox
Church. In the mid-1660s militant disciples of the hermit Kapiton openly
sought martyrdom by burning themselves alive. Other Old Believers,
apparently unconnected with him, soon followed their example. Thus
began the thirst for mass self-immolation, reputedly in groups of up to
2,700, which was quenched only by Catherine II's toleration in the second
half of the eighteenth century.[39] Self-immolation was always controversial among the Old Believer leadership.[40] It was open to attack on the
grounds that mass self-immolation was scarcely the best way to secure the
long-term survival of Old Believer communities. More significantly from
our point of view, its critics distinguished between martyrdom and
deliberate suicide, which the Church had always condemned. The proper
Christian response to persecution, claimed the elder Evfrosin in 1691, was
flight: submission to torture and martyrdom were permissible only *in*

---

[37] I am currently writing an account of late nineteenth-century Orthodoxy which explores the
implications of this imperial perspective. For preparatory comments, see my essay, 'The
Church's Social Role in St Petersburg, 1880–1914', in Geoffrey A. Hosking, ed., *Church,
Nation and State in Russia and Ukraine* (London, 1991), pp. 167–92.
[38] *Svod zakonov Rossiiskoi imperii* (St Petersburg, 1906), I, pt I, art. 62; Timothy Ware, *The
Orthodox Church* (Harmondsworth, 1963), p. 23.
[39] D I. Sapozhnikov, *Samosozhzhenie v russkom raskole (so vtoroi poloviny XVII veka do kontsa
XVIII): istoricheskii ocherk po arkhivnym dannym* (Moscow, 1891; repr. Farnborough, 1971),
passim.
[40] Robert O. Crummey, *The Old Believers and the World of Antichrist: The Vyg Community and the
Russian State, 1694–1855* (Madison, 1970), pp. 44–5, 55–6, 102–3.

extremis. Yet, even after the triumph of moderate counsel and the arrange-
ment of a workable accommodation with the State, the thirst for martyrdom continued to inspire individuals such as brother Markel, who finally
provoked a reluctant Holy Synod into beheading him for denouncing
them as apostates. Semen Denisov's tale of the 1722 Tara Revolt shows
that those who died as 'soldiers of Christ' in armed combat against the
Antichrist were recognized as 'martyrs no less than those who suffered
torture and execution'. Indeed, the historian of the Vyg Community,
Robert Crummey, believes that 'If a single image dominates the narrative
texts of Vyg, it is that of martyrdom.'[41]

The most significant conclusion to be drawn so far is that all the
Orthodox Church's principal rivals, including the secular intelligentsia,
entered the revolutionary maelstrom armed with a highly articulate conception of martyrdom, finely tuned by decades of persecution and, at least
in the case of the intelligentsia, sharpened by contemporary experience.
By contrast, the Russian Church, despite its profound hagiographical
tradition, had been relieved for centuries of the need to think about
martyrdom in a contemporary context. For the revolutionaries, therefore,
the martyrological tradition was actual; for the Church it was purely
liturgical.

To an Orthodox the distinction may seem artificial. Bishop Ware has
emphasized the 'dramatic realism' of the Lenten offices, in which regular
hymns to the martyrs of the Early Church are sung on all weekdays. To
'*relive*' the last year of Christ's earthly ministry in the liturgy is a spiritual
experience that allows the participant to transpose 'remembrance into
reality'.[42] Though few Russians can have attended services with the
regularity and sensitivity required to experience this transposition, the
lives of the saints were so deeply embedded in their culture that we can be
sure that the majority of Orthodox did not receive their introduction to
the notion of martyrdom in the October Revolution.[43] Yet since 1917
plainly was a watershed for the Russian Church, and Orthodox themselves refer frequently to the 'new martyrs' of the twentieth century, it
seems pertinent to ask how their liturgical martyrological tradition was
converted into an actual one after 1917 by a church hitherto widely

[41] Robert O. Crummey, 'The Spirituality of the Vyg Fathers', in Hosking, ed., *Church, Nation and State*, pp. 23–37, quoted at pp. 25–6.
[42] Kallistos Ware, 'The Meaning of the Great Fast', in *The Lenton Triodion*, p. 57, emphasis in the original.
[43] Though statistical information is sparse, it is probable that in the last years of the Empire, most Orthodox confessed and communicated no more often than their annual legal obligation.

perceived by outsiders to have been more persecutor than persecuted. That is the question to which we shall offer some preliminary answers in the final part of this paper. But since we ought, first, to consider previous perspectives on modern Russian martyrdom, it is to these that we now turn.

*   *   *

Though martyrdom has not been the subject of specialist study, three mutually contradictory approaches to it may be distinguished within the more general literature on the period. The first comes from within the Orthodox tradition. Bearing in mind the labyrinthine politics into which the Orthodox lapsed following the institutional fragmentation of the Russian Church under the impact of persecution in the 1920s, it may seem rash to bracket them together in this way. We certainly need to remain conscious of their mutual suspicions. Thus, though respectful of his factual accuracy. Pospielovsky is wary of the sympathies shown by Father Pol'skii, compiler of the best-known dossier on the twentieth-century martyrs, for the monarchist *émigré* bishops based at Karlovci from 1921.[44] Anatoly Levitin—like Pospielovsky, loyal to the Patriarchal Church—stresses that Lev Regel'son's history of persecution in the 1920s and 1930s is written from the perspective of the underground catacomb church.[45]

More than mere nuances, these are profound differences of emphasis which cannot be ignored. Yet it is surely legitimate, in the context of a study of martyrdom, to speak of a single Orthodox historiographical tradition, since Orthodox scholars have been united in seeking to establish the fate of individual victims of persecution in preparation for the compilation of a martyrology. The need for such a work, urgent enough from the beginning, came to seem all the more pressing to believers under Brezhnev. By 1975, the fiftieth anniversary of the death of Patriarch Tikhon (Bellavin), only a few brave priests, including Father Gleb Yakunin and Father Dmitrii Dudko, dared publicly to recall the fate of the early victims of the Soviet State, and the fear grew within the Church that their memory would simply disappear.[46] Both within and beyond the

---

[44] Pospielovsky, *Russian Church*, I, p. 105, n. 16.

[45] Anatoly Levitin, 'The Russian Orthodox Renovationist Movement and its Russian historiography during the Soviet period', in Sabrina Petra Ramet, ed., *Religious Policy in the Soviet Union* (Cambridge, 1993), p. 290.

[46] Jane Ellis, *The Russian Orthodox Church: a Contemporary History* (London, 1986), pp. 352–5, 401; Vladimir Stepanov (Rusak), *Svidetel'stvo obvineniia* (Jordanville, NY, 1987), p. 189.

Soviet Union, a determined effort was made to prevent this from happening. Thus, whilst Pospielovsky dedicated his work to 'the remembrance and reverence of the countless new martyrs for their faith in Russia and in other lands dominated by regimes of militant atheism', Father John Meyendorff characterizes Regel'son's *The Tragedy of the Russian Church, 1917–1945* as 'not simply a work of history but also a highly contemporary manifesto of devotion to everything that is honest, pure and holy in the life of the church', and a necessary preliminary to 'the revival of the memory and cult of the martyrs'.[47]

Two things strike the reader of Orthodox work on the 'new martyrs'. The first is the difficulty of establishing precisely what happened to individual churchmen in such a stormy period as the Russian Civil War. Even before the mass mobilization of the peasantry began in the autumn of 1918, there was a mass migration from the cities to the countryside. Over a million people left Petrograd in the first six months of 1918.[48] Once the war began in earnest, Nadezhda Mandelstam's retrospective vision was of 'a great herd of cattle stampeding over a field of ripe corn and trampling it underfoot in vast swaths'.[49] Looking back from his radically different perspective, Trotsky recalled exactly the same chaos in 1918: 'Provisions were not at hand. There was no army. The state apparatus was being put together. Conspiracies were festering everywhere.'[50]

Few can have been more susceptible to conspiracy theory than the newly-formed secret police. Though Dzerzhinskii attempted to discipline his subordinates in the Cheka, setting them absurdly high standards of personal conduct, it must have been all but impossible for even the best-intentioned Chekist to remain incorruptible, given the arbitrary powers at his disposal. The Cheka, however, was not composed solely of the best-intentioned men. Its lesser ranks—those who came in closest contact with the people—included depraved individuals who sought and found, under cover of the struggle against counter-revolution, a barely regulated opportunity for perversion.

Translated extracts from Deacon Rusak's emotional work, initially issued in *samizdat*, appear in Sergei Pushkarev, Vladimir Rusak, and Gleb Yakunin, *Christianity and Government in Russia and the Soviet Union: Reflections on the Millennium* (Boulder, 1989): see p. 79.

[47] Pospielovsky, *Russian Church*, 1, p. 5; Lev Regel'son, *Tragediia russkoi tserkvi, 1917–1945* (Paris, 1977), pp. 613–14.
[48] S. A. Smith, *Red Petrograd: Revolution in the Factories, 1917–18* (Cambridge, 1983), p. 243.
[49] Nadezhda Mandelstam, *Hope Abandoned* (Harmondsworth, 1976), pp. 26–35, at p. 26.
[50] Leon Trotsky, *Lenin* (London, 1925), p. 152.

The Red Terror was formally unleashed on 5 September 1918, in response to the assassination of Uritskii and Kaplan's attempt on Lenin's life.[51] 'For the blood of Lenin and Uritskii', demanded the Red Army newspaper, *Krasnaia gazeta*, '... let there be floods of blood of the bourgeois—more blood, as much as possible.'[52] The worst atrocities were committed in the provinces, where the Cheka became a byword for torture. The clergy were not immune (though there is little evidence for the claim that they were the principal target) and had already been subject to torment earlier in 1918. The new authorities took pleasure in humiliating them. Priests in Kursk were forced to clean the streets in full clerical dress; monks in Khar'kov were ordered to swill out the Red Army barracks; and the aged Archbishop of Novocherkassk, Mitrofan (Simashkevich), was paraded by the insolent sailors who arrested him so that he could be taunted by the crowd. Others suffered a still more terrible fate. In Kharkov', the monk Amvrosii was beaten with rifle butts before being shot, and a priest was stripped and mutilated. Elsewhere priests were 'crowned' with barbed wire, whilst the Poltava and Kremenchug Chekas impaled eighteen monks on a single day.[53]

Gruesome, institutionalized violence combined with a transient population to produce circumstances ripe for the spread of rumour. Many of those who were arrested disappeared and were assumed to have been horribly murdered. Yet though the Bolsheviks chose to publish details of some executions, and the ecclesiastical press furnished stories of others, the illustrated *Black Book* (*Chernaia kniga*), compiled from the press and oral testimony by A. A. Valentinov, and published by the *émigré* National Union of Russian Students in 1924, is necessarily episodic in its account of persecution.[54] As one might expect, we know most about the fate of the hierarchy, thanks principally to the magnificent multi-volume bio-bibliography originally compiled as a *samizdat* manuscript by Metropolitan Manuil (Lemeshevskii), and subsequently published in West

[51] For contrasting interpretations of the Bolsheviks' use of terror, cf. Mary McAuley, *Bread and Justice: State and Society in Petrograd, 1917–1922* (Oxford, 1991), ch. 18, emphasizing bureaucracy and 'relatively mild social intimidation', with Richard Pipes, *The Russian Revolution, 1899–1919* (London, 1990), ch. 18, where it is claimed that 'terror was not a defensive weapon but an instrument of governance.'

[52] Quoted in Leggett, *Cheka*, p. 108.

[53] Ibid., pp. 186–203; *Chernaia kniga* ("*shturm nebes*") (Paris, 1925), pp. 33–9, 43–8.

[54] English and German versions of the *Chernaia kniga* (see above n. 53) appeared in 1924. I have seen only the Russian edition, though there are English extracts in Pospielovsky, *Russian Church*, 2, pp. 477–81. Further extracts from the Press appear in Regel'son's documentary appendix, *Tragediia*, pp. 201–521.

Germany.[55] The episcopate are also prominent in Pol'skii's two volumes, published in America by the Russian Church in Exile.[56]

More certain knowledge of the fate of others ironically awaited the creation of a more stable 'archipelago' of prison camps, whose inmates transmitted stories which eventually appeared in fragmentary form in *émigré* journals. Pierre Pascal quotes one such case, dating from Solovki in 1929. A medically-qualified prisoner was called upon to examine a group of nuns who had declined, in the face of severe physical and psychological maltreatment, either to answer questions or to work. The prison health officer regarded the nuns as 'masochistic psychopaths' who were 'looking for martyrdom', but he was prepared to ignore their obstinacy, provided that the doctor passed them unfit for work. Once the official withdrew, the nuns declared themselves perfectly healthy, but adamantly refused to work for Antichrist. They remained unmoved when told that other clerical prisoners (including the suffragan bishop of Viatka, then serving as a book-keeper in the rope workshop) were prepared to labour during the week in order to secure time for contemplation and prayer on Sunday. The doctor later discovered that the nuns had finally agreed to work on condition that they could sing psalms as they sewed. However, it transpired that they came into contact with a priest who had formerly been their confessor. He, having again prohibited them from all work, was shot. The nuns were separated and transported elsewhere. Their fate is unknown.[57]

The unusual degree of detail here—impossible in cases where the circumstances of death are obscure or disputed—points up, by contrast, the second distinguishing feature of the Orthodox historiography on martyrdom, its generally uncritical approach. Orthodox make little attempt to distinguish between those who voluntarily seek death as martyrs and those to whom it comes uninvited. Strictly speaking, the first saints to be canonized in Kievan Rus', Boris and Gleb, were, as George Fedotov has written, 'not martyrs for faith' at all. Not without anachronism, Fedotov calls them 'victims of a political crime', an appellation which might more appropriately apply to the twentieth-century

[55] Metropolit Manuil (Lemeševskij), *Die Russischen-Orthodoxen Bischöfe von 1893 bis 1965*, 5 vols (Erlangen, 1979–87).

[56] Protopresviter M. Pol'skii, ed., *Novye mucheniki rossiiskie*, 2 vols (Jordanville, NY, 1949–57). The second volume prints illustrations and corrections to the first.

[57] Pascal, *Religion of the Russian People*, pp. 105–9. Viktor (Ostrovidov), suffragan bishop of Viatka, had been sent to Solovki following his protest against Metropolitan Sergii's declaration of loyalty to the Soviet State in 1927: see Manuil, *Russischen Bischöfe*, 2, pp. 167–72; Pol'skii, *Novye mucheniki*, 2, pp. 70–7.

SIMON DIXON

martyrs. If the Kievan Church 'did not discriminate between death for faith in Christ and death in following Christ, and even held the latter in special veneration', it bequeathed a lasting notion of the primacy of suffering and meekness in martyrdom.[58] Indeed, the Russian word for martyr—*múchenik*—is derived from the word for torture—*muchénie*—rather than witness, and martyrs are sometimes referred to as passion-sufferers (*strastotérptsy*).[59] The emphasis on suffering rather than death can even allow the notion of *living* saints, again a resonant phrase in the Soviet context.[60] Thus it seemed to Edgar MacNaughten, a Western sympathizer with Orthodoxy, visiting the Soviet Union in 1927, that even 'to be a priest today means being a martyr.'[61]

Rather than dwell on individual motivation, therefore, Orthodox sources tend to move directly from an account of a martyr's fate to an attempt to calculate total numbers. Early in 1919 the Tobol'sk diocesan journal calculated that in the eight months between June 1918 and January 1919 alone, one metropolitan (Vladimir of Kiev), 18 bishops, 102 priests, 154 deacons, and 94 monks and nuns had already been killed, and a further 4 bishops and 211 members of both black and white clergy had been imprisoned.[62] These initial figures were plainly exceeded later. Though the total number of churchmen arrested or assassinated during the Civil War is commonly reckoned in the thousands, it seems unlikely that precision will ever be possible.[63] The highest estimates are those of Pospielovsky, who repeats a claim made in the contemporary *émigré* press that 'several thousand clergy and monastics and at least 12,000 lay activists' died as witnesses for their faith between 1918 and 1920.[64] The renovationist bishop Nikolai (Solovei) is his ultimate source for saying that a further 2,691 priests, 1,962 nuns, and an unknown number of

[58] George P. Fedotov, *The Russian Religious Mind (I): Kievan Christianity, the Tenth to the Thirteenth Centuries* (Belmont, Mass., 1975), pp. 94–110, quoted at pp. 95, 105; Regel'son,*Tragediia*, p. 49. See also now R. M. Price, 'Boris and Gleb: princely martyrs and martyrology in Kievan Russia', above, pp. 105–15.
[59] Remarkably, John Bowker, *Problems of Suffering in Religions of the World* (Cambridge, 1970), omits discussion of Eastern Christianity 'for reasons of space', but finds room for a chapter on Marxism: p. 98, n. 1, pp. 137–92.
[60] Father Borovoi used the expression in his 1978 sermon, quoted above, n. 14.
[61] E. MacNaughten, 'Informal Report of religious situation in Russia', 3 Oct. 1927, quoted by Pospielovsky, *Soviet Antireligious Campaigns*, p. 47.
[62] Regel'son, *Tragediia*, p. 255.
[63] Philip Walters, 'A survey of Soviet religious policy', in Ramet, ed., *Religious Policy*, p.6; Hosking, *Soviet Union*, p. 228.
[64] Dimitry V. Pospielovsky, 'The Survival of the Russian Orthodox Church in her Millennial Century: Faith as *Martyria* in an Atheistic State', in Hosking, ed., *Church, Nation and State*, p. 274; Matthew Spinka, *The Church in Soviet Russia* (New York, 1956), p. 21.

laymen were 'physically liquidated' between 1921 and 1923.[65] Access to newly opened Russian archives will almost certainly deepen our understanding of individual incidents and reveal some more about which we currently know nothing. But archives cannot tell us everything. According to the *Black Book*, the files of the Perm' Cheka betray details of only ten out of more than 550 executions over an eight-month period.[66] Even if these figures are imprecise, the general point is plausible: not all the misdeeds of the Civil War were recorded for posterity. So only an unregenerate positivist could be confident of totally overcoming our ignorance of what a Soviet dissident writing in the mid-1970s called 'those recent and innumerable martyrs whose hagiographies have not yet been written and who are remembered by only a few surviving witnesses.'[67]

One might think that, even if it were possible to calculate them more accurately, statistics are not the most important consideration in a study of martyrdom. An Schmemann remarks, 'If the truth of an idea could be established by the number of its victims, every religion could present adequate proofs.'[68] Yet it has been important to dwell on numbers, because they matter greatly to the second group of historians we need now to consider—Western historians of the early Soviet period.

Despite their professed interest in 'history from below', most recent scholars have been less concerned with the fate of the individual than with the interaction of social groups in the period of Bolshevik state-building.[69] Though they have made no attempt to diminish the scale of destruction of ecclesiastical property, those few who have discussed personal suffering have been markedly cooler than Orthodox scholars in their assessments. Whereas the aim of Orthodox scholarship, taking the individual as its starting-point, is to show that a number of casualties in the thousands must be 'very large', this conclusion has seemed less obvious to historians accustomed to dealing in aggregates.[70] Indeed, they have stressed the opposite. The national census of December 1926 recorded 60,000 'professional practitioners of religious faiths' by primary occupation. Of

[65] Pospielovsky, *Russian Church*, 1, p. 99.

[66] *Chernaia kniga*, p. 50.

[67] Evgeny Barabanov, 'The Schism Between the Church and the World', in Alexander Solzhenitsyn, ed., *From Under the Rubble* (London, 1975), p. 175.

[68] Schmemann, *Historical Road*, p. 37.

[69] A representative selection of current concerns appears in Diane P. Koenker, William G. Rosenberg, and Ronald Grigor Suny, eds, *Party, State, and Society in the Russian Civil War: Explorations in Social History* (Bloomington, 1989), though the most original contribution is Orlando Figes, 'The Red Army and Mass Mobilization during the Russian Civil War, 1918–1920', *PaP*, 129 (1990), pp. 168–211.

[70] Ware, *Orthodox Church*, p. 156.

these 51,600 were Orthodox, and so were 16,400 of the 27,000 whose secondary occupation was the practice of religion.[71] By comparison, in 1914, the last pre-revolutionary year for which reliable information is available, the Synodal Over-Procurator reported 50,105 members of the secular (white) clergy, 21,330 members of the regular (black) monastic clergy, and 73,299 nuns.[72] With the notable exception of the monastics, who are sadly under-researched but were almost certainly subject to greater persecution than the clergy, these figures are open to interpretation as evidence of relative restraint on the part of the Soviet authorities.

The fact that things might have been much worse for the Church is precisely the point emphasized by many secular historians in the West. Evan Mawdsley, describing the assassination of the Metropolitan of Kiev in January 1918 as 'exceptional', writes that the Bolsheviks' 'early attacks' were not only 'concentrated on the hierarchy', but 'mainly verbal'.[73] According to J. S. Curtiss, the new Soviet authorities, preoccupied with more pressing matters, 'executed a relatively small number of clergy, and these only in cases where they believed that the conduct of the ecclesiastics was not only hostile but dangerous.'[74] Curtiss's influential views are echoed by Kenez in his history of Bolshevik propaganda. It was because Lenin's government 'understood that a frontal attack would backfire' that it 'counselled patience and tact': indeed, 'There was no other institution that the Bolsheviks treated as patiently as they treated the church' in the early years of Soviet rule.[75]

Lenin's antipathy to the Church and to religion is not in doubt. He had, after all, written in 1913 that 'Every idea of God, even flirting with the idea of God, is unutterable vileness . . . of the most dangerous kind.'[76] Yet few leaders have been more sensitive than Lenin to the politics of power. And the clear implication of recent Western historiography is that the creation of martyrs capable of inspiring and unifying the forces of counter-revolution was the last thing that Lenin and his government wanted to risk in the early months of Bolshevik rule. As we have seen, they

[71] V. P. Danilov, *Rural Russia under the New Regime* (London, 1988), p. 77.

[72] John Shelton Curtiss, *The Russian Church and the Soviet State, 1917–1950* (Boston, 1953), p. 10.

[73] Evan Mawdsley, *The Russian Civil War* (London, 1987), p. 10. As we have seen, taunts were common.

[74] Curtiss, *The Russian Church*, p. 89. Curtiss is criticized by Pascal for showing 'extreme indulgence toward the Soviet authorities': *Religion of the Russian People*, p. 98.

[75] Kenez, *Propaganda State*, pp. 183, 68.

[76] Letter to Maxim Gorky, Nov. 1913, quoted in Robert Conquest, *The Harvest of Sorrow: Soviet Collectivization and the Terror-Famine* (London, 1986), p. 199.

were themselves all too conscious of martyrdom's political potency. Even had they chosen to make a concerted onslaught, they lacked the political infrastructure to impose their will—not only on the peasantry, but even on members of their own party. Outside the major cities, the Bolsheviks, so far from matching the highly disciplined model set out by Lenin in *What is to be done?* (1902), had yet to establish a stable power-base.[77] Even in Petrograd, they struggled in vain 'to resolve their differences, and to create an organization that would simultaneously be an effective ruler and retain the support of the factory floor.'[78] From this perspective, it would seem that what persecution churchmen did suffer at the hands of the Bolsheviks was meted out not by order of the Kremlin, but by 'local radicals who disregarded the policies set forth by Moscow'.[79]

It is worth noting that this conclusion is diametrically opposed to that drawn by Philip Walters, who argues that, though what Kenez says may have been true of persecution of believers of other denominations, 'The campaign against the Orthodox was centrally co-ordinated.'[80] Such discrepancies rather undermine Marc Raeff's superficially unexceptionable remark that 'The militantly atheistic and anticlerical position of the Soviet government needs no elaboration or comment.'[81]

However, one need only sample a fraction of the modern Soviet historiography—our third and final approach to the study of martyrdom—to see what lies behind Raeff's judgement. In Communism's penultimate years, Western scholars were often tempted to comment on the inadequacy of Soviet work, hampered by a somnolent academic establishment. Sometimes these criticisms were exaggerated. However, although there is a spectrum of Soviet writing on ecclesiastical history, as on most other subjects, it was all but impossible for a Soviet historian to write a balanced account of the fate of Orthodoxy in the revolution and Civil War. One might not expect much subtlety in works aimed at a popular readership.[82] But superficially more scrupulous books are

---

[77] Robert Service, *The Bolshevik Party in Revolution: a Study in Organisational Change, 1917–1923* (London, 1979); Orlando Figes, *Peasant Russia, Civil War: the Volga Countryside in Revolution, 1917–1921* (Oxford, 1989), ch. 5.

[78] McAuley, *Bread and Justice*, p. 412.

[79] Peter Kenez, 'The Bolsheviks and the Intelligentsia', in Koenker *et al.*, eds, *Party, State and Society*, p. 242.

[80] Walters, 'A survey', p. 6.

[81] Marc Raeff, *Russia Abroad: a Cultural History of the Russian Emigration, 1919–1939* (Oxford, 1990), p. 121.

[82] For representative examples, see M. S. Korzun, *Russkaia pravoslavnaia tserkov' 1917–1945 gody* (Minsk, 1987); R. Iu. Plaksin, *Tikhonovshchina i ee krakh: Positsiia pravoslavnoi tserkvi v period Velikoi Oktiabr'skoi sotsialisticheskoi revoliutsii i grazhdanskoi voiny* (Leningrad, 1987).

couched in no more moderate language. A. A. Shishkov blames the 'bloody excesses' that resulted from struggles between Red Guards and members of Orthodox icon processions squarely on episcopal militancy.[83] So do two more recent authors, according to whom the Church leadership indulged in 'sabotage' and 'provocation', inciting 'violent acts' that were 'precisely what the clergy and their leaders needed', in order to manufacture 'victims that could be passed off for martyrs who have suffered for their faith, and thus used for fanning religious fanaticism and for anti-Soviet propaganda.'[84]

Were there nothing more to Soviet accounts than judgements like this, one might wonder why they deserve to be mentioned here at all. It is certainly not difficult to see why Orthodox historians should have dismissed them either as 'half-truths' or as 'agitation . . . of no scholarly interest'.[85] And yet, even if we regard Soviet interpretations as vulgar, we can scarcely deny the legitimacy of questions about the conduct of the hierarchy during a period of persecution. If Lenin and his government did not set out to create martyrs, is there any evidence that the Church did? Was not the hierarchy's bravery and resistance *ipso facto* an act of provocation? After all, as Professor Lampe has written, 'The martyr is, as the word "martyr" denotes, a witness, and as a witness he is, as it were, on the offensive against the persecuting power.'[86] And is not 'provocation cast in the face of the powers of evil' a prominent feature of 'the passions of ancient martyrs'?[87] Does not Anatolii Levitin, indeed, see in 'struggle' the whole foundation of the Church: 'struggle with evil and injustice, struggle for the salvation of people, for the Kingdom of God'?[88]

The historian B. V. Titlinov had no doubt that the Church declared counter-revolutionary 'ecclesiastical war' on the Soviet regime.[89] It surely cannot be simply because Titlinov was a renovationist that subsequent Orthodox scholars have been so anxious to deny any militancy on the part of their leadership. Part of the answer, of course, lies in the fact that the

[83] A. A. Shishkin, *Sushchnost' i kriticheskaia otsenka 'obnovlencheskogo' raskola russkoi pravoslavnoi tserkvi* (Kazan', 1970), p. 33.

[84] N. S. Gordienko and M. P. Novikov, 'The Church in the Years of the Socialist Revolution and Civil War', in Alexander Preobrazhensky, ed., *The Russian Orthodox Church: Tenth to Twentieth Centuries* (Moscow, 1988), pp. 267, 270.

[85] Pospielovsky, *Marxist-Leninist Atheism*, p. 129, on Gordienko; Levitin, 'Renovationist Movement', in Ramet, ed., *Religious Policy*, p. 290, on Shishkin.

[86] G. W. H. Lampe, 'Martyrdom and inspiration', in William Horbury and Brian McNeil, eds, *Suffering and Martyrdom in the New Testament* (Cambridge, 1981), p. 118.

[87] Fedotov, *Russian Religious Mind*, p. 99.

[88] Levitin and Shavrov, *Ocherki*, 1, p. 37.

[89] B. V. Titlinov, *Tserkov' vo vremia revoliutsii* (Petrograd, 1924), p. 125.

question of martyrdom soon became inextricably linked to ideological judgements about the legitimacy and morality of the Soviet regime, as a whole, and so to the question of blame for the fate of the Church.[90] But the question of blame leads in turn to a still more fundamental issue. As we have seen, resignation and passivity in the face of suffering are commonly portrayed as distinctively Russian virtues: deprived of the opportunity of death for Christ's sake, Orthodox sought martyrdom in acts of extreme asceticism instead. But, particularly in the Soviet period, the characteristics of meekness and withdrawal gave rise to the charge that the Russian people is innately fatalistic and submissive. Recent events have done much to confirm the approach of Hosking's history of the Soviet Union, which explicitly sought to dispel the myth of a 'grey, anonymous, and rather supine' mass.[91] But in earlier years, when there seemed less reason for optimism, Orthodox thinkers themselves came to doubt the wisdom of ascetic withdrawal which might corrupt into unthinking 'obedience and humble submission to the external authorities'. Indeed, in the 1970s, it seemed to Evgeny Barabanov that 'at times . . . we Christians deliberately do not wish to understand our historical failure or to admit our historical sins. We shift the blame onto anyone we can find—the state, atheism, secularization—but ourselves always remain only innocent victims.'[92]

In this context one might recall Nadezhda Mandelstam's memoirs, which several times associate pride and arrogance not with protest but with silence. The following is perhaps the most powerful passage:

> Later I often wondered whether it is right to scream when you are being beaten and trampled underfoot. Isn't it better to face one's tormentors in a stance of satanic pride, answering them with contemptuous silence? I decided that it is better to scream. This pitiful sound . . . is a concentrated expression of the last vestige of human dignity. It is a man's way of leaving a trace, of telling people how he lived and died. By his screams he asserts his right to live, sends a message to the outside world demanding help and calling for

[90] Pospielovsky, for example, sees it as part of his function to 'help to remove the onus of blame for the persecutions from the Church, as laid upon her by Professor Curtiss, and to return it to where it belongs: to Marxism-Leninism and its first state': *Russian Church*, 1, p. 143.

[91] Hosking, *History of the Soviet Union*, p. 11.

[92] Barabanov, 'The Schism', p. 185. As Ellis has shown, Barabanov echoes an earlier essay by Michael Meerson-Aksenov, 'The People of God and the Pastors', in Michael Meerson-Aksenov and Boris Shragin, eds, *The Political, Social and Religious Thought of Russian 'Samizdat'—an Anthology* (Belmont, Mass., 1977), pp. 511–41. See Ellis, *Orthodox Church*, pp. 332–6.

resistance. If nothing else is left, one must scream. Silence is the real crime against humanity![93]

That last remark ought, perhaps, to be remembered as we turn finally to examine how the Orthodox Church reacted to its renewed experience of martyrdom after the October Revolution, bearing in mind also the crucial issues raised by the three historiographical approaches we have just reviewed.

* * *

In October 1917, the issue of martyrdom was undoubtedly brought into much clearer focus than would otherwise have been the case by the fact that the Revolution occurred whilst the long-awaited Church Council (*sobor*) was in session. Long-standing attempts to call such a council had come to a head in 1905, but had been rejected by the tsar as inopportune.[94] When it finally met in Moscow, from its convocation by the Provisional Government in August 1917 to September 1918, the council brought together 564 delegates, of whom 314 were laymen (including three elected from each diocese) and 250 were clergy (including two elected from each diocese). The kernel of the most important debate, on the restoration of the Patriarchate, shifted, by force of circumstance, from questions of dogma and church government to a question of crisis management. In the event, the proponents of firm patriarchal leadership prevailed without difficulty, and Patriarch Tikhon was installed on 21 November 1917. However, as an excellent recent study has emphasized, by demanding absolute harmony of Church and State and refusing to tolerate any antagonistic power, the final conciliar formula 'made coexistence with the new government impossible by definition'.[95]

The matter of defining the Church's view on martyrdom was made particularly urgent by the assassination of Metropolitan Vladimir of Kiev, taken from his quarters at the Monastery of the Caves (*Pecherskaia lavra*) on 25 January 1918. His corpse was found some distance away, having been stabbed, shot, and robbed of all valuables.[96] This event raises

---

[93] Nadezhda Mandelstam, *Hope Against Hope: a Memoir* (London, 1971), pp. 42–3.

[94] John Meyendorff, 'The Russian Bishops and Church Reform', in Robert L. Nichols and Theophanis George Stavrou, eds, *Russian Orthodoxy under the Old Regime* (Minneapolis, 1978), pp. 170–82.

[95] Catherine Evtuhov, 'The Church in the Russian Revolution: Arguments for and against restoring the Patriarchate at the Church Council of 1917–1918', *Slavic Review*, 50 (1991), pp. 510–11.

[96] *Chernaia kniga*, p. 35.

important questions about the victim's motivations, about Bolshevik intentions, and about ecclesiastical responses.

Vladimir (Bogoiavlenskii) was one of those relatively few Russian bishops who had earlier served as a parish priest.[97] After the death of his wife, he was tonsured in February 1886, and in 1898, following a rapid rise through the episcopal ranks and characteristically brief spells as Bishop of Samara and Exarch of Georgia, he was translated to Moscow, where he consolidated his reputation as an avowed reactionary. Vladimir achieved particular notoriety in October 1905, when he ordered his clergy to deliver a rabidly anti-revolutionary sermon composed by his suffragan bishop, Nikon (Rozhdestvenskii), in collaboration with V. A. Gringmut, founder of the Monarchist Party and editor of *Moskovskiia vedomosti*, which published the text, 'What must we do in these troubled days?' Its publication in the same month as the conciliatory October Manifesto was unfortunate: seventy-six members of the Moscow clergy complained in the press, and a group of lawyers, condemning the sermon as 'slanderous', petitioned the municipal duma for the metropolitan's removal. Vladimir was summoned to St Petersburg and threatened with dismissal. But he refused to recant. It was he who inspired the appointment of Vostorgov as Moscow's diocesan missionary, and he maintained a high public profile by accepting office as honorary president of the Union of the Russian People, 'the most numerous, noisy, intransigent and extremist of the Russian right-wing parties'.[98]

In 1912, Vladimir succeeded that most mild-mannered of Russian bishops, Antonii (Vadkovskii), as Metropolitan of St Petersburg. Antonii had been prepared to tolerate a wide range of opinon both among his clergy and among charismatic laymen, such as Ivan Churikov, whom many denounced as sectarian. But the Metropolitan's moderation had attracted fierce criticism from the right-wing press, and his health was undermined. His successor imposed a much tougher regime. However, Vladimir's reign in the capital was brief and ended in humiliation once he had fallen foul of Rasputin. Rasputin's power over the Church is easily exaggerated. Those who lean towards the view that he controlled it miss the point: the Orthodox Church was not an effectively co-ordinated body in the last years of the tsarist regime.[99] But in the last two years of his life it

---

[97] The following draws on Manuil, *Russischen Bischöfe*, 2, pp. 197–209; 5, pp. 250–61; J. H. M. Geekie, 'The Church and Politics in Russia, 1905–1917' (University of East Anglia, Ph.D. thesis, 1976), pp. 95–8, 121, 263–4; and Curtiss, *The Russian Church*, pp. 10, 12, 28.

[98] Hans Rogger, *Jewish Policies and Right-Wing Politics in Imperial Russia* (London, 1986), p. 213.

[99] Cf. Joseph T. Fuhrmann, *Rasputin: a Life* (New York, 1990), p. 148 and *passim*.

seems clear that Rasputin did at least exercise a commanding influence over episcopal appointments that mattered, and the death of Metropolitan Flavian of Kiev in 1915 presented him with the chance to be rid of his opponent in St Petersburg. Vladimir's translation to the Ukraine, and his replacement by the relatively junior Pitirim (Oknov), was an unprecedented demotion for so senior a hierarch. Yet his smouldering resentment against Rasputin did nothing to diminish Vladimir's ardent monarchism, which he continued to make public under the Provisional Government.

On one reading, therefore, Vladimir was precisely the sort of prominent reactionary cleric whom militant Bolsheviks might have been expected to target during their assault on Kiev, which they captured on 26 January 1918. This impression is strengthened by the realization that the commander of the Bolshevik troops, resident in the *lavra*, was Lieutenant-Colonel M. A. Murav'ev, a former tsarist officer sympathetic to the Left SR's, described by Richard Pipes as 'an unbalanced, sadistic megalomaniac'.[100] The basis of Murav'ev's unsavoury reputation lies in the bloodthirsty remarks he is alleged to have made to his superior, V. A. Antonov-Ovseenko, who records that Murav'ev issued orders 'to annihilate without mercy all officers and junkers, haidamaks, monarchists and all the enemies of the revolution found in Kiev'. In the light of this testimony, it is particularly striking that the fullest account of the assassination of the Metropolitan in an *émigré* ecclesiastical source, Metropolitan Evlogii (Georgievskii)'s memoir, paints a different picture.

According to Evlogii, Murav'ev gave instructions that he was to be called if anyone tried to interfere with the Metropolitan. The fact that Murav'ev was not alerted when a detachment of soldiers abducted Vladimir, having searched the monastery on the pretext of looking for machine-guns, Evlogii attributes to the malice of the monks in the *lavra*.[101] Even if we accept the plausibility of this explanation, and it cannot be dismissed out of hand, we must still account for the apparently Jekyll-and-Hyde performance of Murav'ev. How could he have been so conciliatory one day and so bloodthirsty the next? It may be that on the night of Vladimir's murder, Murav'ev, a canny commander, yet to capture Kiev, was anxious to do nothing that might incite the monks to revolt or make the monastery a focus of counter-revolution. If so, he might well have favoured restraint on the 25th, whereas, following his

[100] Richard Pipes, *The Formation of the Soviet Union*, rev. edn (New York, 1980), pp. 124–6.
[101] *Put' moei zhizni: Vospominaniia Mitropolita Evlogiia* (Paris, 1947), p. 310.

victory, it would no longer have seemed necessary. Nothing is certain, but there may be grounds for suggesting, in the case of the assassination of Vladimir, that it was indeed the work of mavericks.

Indirect support for this hypothesis is given by an earlier incident, believed by some to have hurried Lenin into his decree separating Church from State. It took place in Petrograd, and its key actor was Aleksandra Kollontai, Commissar for Health. Kollontai had already declared her intention of confiscating all monastery property to the All-Russian Central Executive Committee of Soviets on 29 December 1917:

> A beginning has been made on this in Moscow, where contact has been established with junior employees in the monasteries, who have formed a soviet. This is collecting information on behalf of the Council of People's Commissars [*Sovnarkom*] about all the monasteries' treasures, which must be enormous.[102]

Kollontai promised to submit a draft decree abolishing monastic property and turning it over to the State. But before she could do so, she took matters into her own hands by signing, in mid-January 1918, a unilateral decree authorizing the take-over of first all and later part of the Alexander Nevskii monastery in Petrograd for use as a hospital for the war-wounded.

On the face of it, there was nothing extraordinary about such a proposition. During the First World War many churches and monasteries had been converted for precisely this purpose.[103] But in the changed circumstances of post-revolutionary Petrograd—a city in which both economy and society had collapsed—churchmen suspected the worst. Their fears were exacerbated in the period between the decree's issue and 19 January, when a detachment of Red Guards and sailors was sent to put it into effect. Accounts of precisely what happened differ in detail, though it is clear that a priest, Father Petr Skipetrov, was fatally wounded after becoming embroiled in an argument with the Red Guards. The crowd that had gathered to defend the monastery then attacked the soldiers, further troops were called, and at least two others in the monastery were injured in the ensuing violence. The incident prompted leaders of the Protestant, Armenian, Jewish, and Islamic churches in the capital to issue

---

[102] Tr. and ed. John L. H. Keep, *The Debate on Soviet Power: Minutes of the All-Russian Central Executive Committee of Soviets, Second Convocation October 1917–January 1918* (Oxford, 1979), p. 256.

[103] S. G. Runkevich, *Velikaia otechestvennaia voina i tserkovnaia zhizn'. Kn. 1: Rasporiazheniia i deistviia sviateishago sinoda v 1914–1915gg.* (Petrograd, 1916).

a public statement of sympathy for the Orthodox Church.[104] No less significantly, it prompted Lenin to lecture Kollontai on the need for strict discipline in policy-making. Shortly afterwards the party's Central Committee took the opportunity to send her abroad as its representative in a delegation seeking closer ties with the Left in Western Europe.[105]

Notes for a sermon found among the posthumous papers of Andronik (Nikol'skii), formerly a missionary in Japan, and Archbishop of Perm' from 1915 until his disappearance in June 1918, show that by the first half of that year the prospect of martyrdom was prominent in the mind of at least one leading churchman:

(1) I rejoice to be put on trial in the name of Christ and for the Church . . .

(2) Counter-revolution, politics—this is none of my business . . .

(3) But the cause of the Church is sacred to me . . .

. . .

(5) Only over my dead body will you defile the sacred. This is my duty, wherefore I appeal to Christians to stand unto death.[106]

But it will be plain from the account given above that Metropolitan Vladimir did not die in such a fashion. There is no known evidence of his having contemplated martyrdom, and the circumstances of his death do not suggest that he went to it willingly. Neither did he die consciously defending his church. He was abducted. He was the victim of what Fedotov would have called 'a political crime'. Father Skipetrov, on the other hand, might certainly be said to have attempted to prevent the defilement of the sacred, and it is possible, though we cannot know, that he contemplated martyrdom in the tense days between the issue of Kollontai's decree and the arrival of the guards, though it seems equally probable that his death was the accidental result of an unpremeditated scuffle.

Distinctions of this sort made no impact on the increasingly embattled church leadership in Moscow. As if to stress their uncompromising stance, the former missionary, Father Ioann Vostorgov, a man of ultra-reactionary views from whom even Metropolitan Vladimir had eventually felt obliged to distance himself, and who was in turn to be executed

---

[104] Regel'son, *Tragediia*, pp. 226–7.

[105] Beatrice Farnsworth, *Aleksandra Kollontai: Socialism, Feminism, and the Bolshevik Revolution* (Stanford, 1980), pp. 100–1, 116.

[106] Pospielovsky, *Soviet Antireligious Campaigns*, pp. 6, 229, n. 11, drawing on Regel'son, *Tragediia*, p. 243; Manuil, *Russischen Bischöfe*, 1, pp. 256–8.

on 23 August 1918, preached an emotional sermon on 'The Struggle for Faith and the Church' on 21 January: 'Let them shoot us, shoot innocent children and women. Let us go with crosses, icons, unarmed, with prayers and hymns—let Cain and Judas kill us! The time has come to go to martyrdom and suffering!'[107] The decree separating Church from State prompted the council to issue a declaration 'To the Orthodox People', calling on them to unite against sacrilege and desecration: 'Better to shed one's blood and gain the martyr's crown than to turn the Orthodox faith over to its enemies.'[108] In the council's session on 15 February, Patriarch Tikhon declared his deep conviction that Vladimir's martyrdom would purge 'the sins of Great Mother-Russia'.[109] The council subsequently issued a further proclamation, establishing prayers 'for those persecuted now for their Orthodox Church and for those who died as martyrs' and 'an annual prayer of remembrance on January 25 . . . for all confessors and martyrs who have died in these evil times of persecution.' Furthermore, it required that 'all the parishes where confessors and martyrs lived' should 'hold, on the second day of the second week of Easter, processions with the cross and church banners to the places of their burial, and offices for the dead glorifying their memory.'[110]

All these statements served to consolidate in Bolshevik minds the image of a counter-revolutionary church. That imaged crystallized after the shooting of the imperial family in Ekaterinburg.[111] In mid-1918 the clergy were lumped together with monarchists as the subjects of one of the three investigation sections of the Cheka's Department for Combating Counter-Revolution (though by 1921, thanks to the constantly fluid administrative structure of the Secret Police, they were granted the dubious honour of being monitored by a special section of its successor, the Secret Department).[112]

How far was this counter-revolutionary image accurate? Though there were a few Bolshevik activists among the post-revolutionary clergy, the revolutions of 1917 almost certainly served to steer the majority firmly to the right. Some made their opinions plain. In 1918 the Sebezhsk Cheka shot a priest for 'holding a service for Nikolai Romanov', whilst leaflets

[107] Curtiss, *The Russian Church*, p. 50. Cf. Pospielovsky, *Soviet Antireligious Campaigns*, pp. 3–4, with Geekie, 'Church and Politics', e.g., pp. 120, 132–4.
[108] Curtiss, *The Russian Church*, p. 53 (translation amended).
[109] Regel'son, *Tragediia*, p. 42.
[110] Translated in Preobrazhensky, ed., *Russian Orthodox Church*, pp. 270–1, where the significance of the date is scrupulously not mentioned.
[111] These events are still disputed. The best guide is Pipes, *Russian Revolution*, pp. 745–88.
[112] Leggett, *Cheka*, p. 40.

SIMON DIXON

were distributed in Penza 'about the great new martyr, Nicholas' and 'the sons of Satan—the Bolsheviks'.[113] The extremist monarchist conference at Bad Reichenhall (29 May–6 June 1921) called for the primacy of the Orthodox Church and declared dignitaries of the Orthodox Church in Exile honorary members of the Supreme Monarchist Council.[114] When the twentieth-century martyrs were finally canonized by the Russian Orthodox Church in Exile on 1 November 1981 they included the imperial family.[115]

But that canonization was made only in circumstances of some controversy. And, for all the council's proclamations, it may be doubted that national politics, of whatever hue, were really uppermost in the minds of most rural clergy in the Russian Civil War. It would not be surprising to discover evidence of priests who counselled their flock on the way to respond to the tragic onslaught of Civil War. But the majority probably spent more time ensuring survival than contemplating martyrdom, and a priest's survival depended on his relationship with the peasants in his village. Of course, it always had. The Soviet scholar L. I. Emeliakh tried hard to show that the pre-revolutionary countryside was a hotbed of anti-clericalism.[116] But she relied heavily on formulaic diocesan reports. The richer testament of local sources, from what fragmentary information we have, suggests a more complex, and more convincing, picture, showing marked local variations. For if the revolution turned the Church to the right, it also 'accentuated the "peasant" nature of the parish priest', who was now forced to support himself through agricultural labour.[117] We badly need more local studies to set in perspective the propaganda produced in the later years by extremist advocates of 'priest-eating' (popoedstvo), who sought the obliteration of religion from 1923, and published in their journal, Bezbozhnik u stanka, lurid illustrations by the poster artist Dmitrii Moor, showing peasants feeding off Christ's innards and combing priestly vermin out of their hair.[118] Only then will it be possible to write convincing ecclesiastical history rather than history that is primarily ideologically charged.

In the meanwhile, as I have sought to show, those who have written

---

[113] Ibid., p. 112; Curtiss, *The Russian Church*, p. 68.
[114] Jane Burbank, *Intelligentsia and Revolution: Russian Views of Bolshevism, 1917–1922* (Oxford, 1986), pp. 184–5.
[115] Ellis, *Orthodox Church*, pp. 353–4, 401–2, 423–4.
[116] L. I. Emeliakh, *Antiklerikal'noe dvizhenie krest'ian v period pervoi russkoi revoliutsii* (Moscow and Leningrad, 1965); and *Krest'iane i tserkov' nakanune oktiabria* (Leningrad, 1976), pp. 62–151.
[117] See, e.g., Figes, *Peasant Russia, Civil War*, pp. 147–50, quoted at p. 147.
[118] Stites, *Revolutionary Dreams*, p. 106.

about modern Russian martyrdom have understandably tended to elide their conclusions with more general judgements about the Soviet State. Following the fall of the Communist regime, it may now be possible to approach the subject afresh. Yet it is scarcely to be supposed, and perhaps not to be hoped, that its history will ever be written dispassionately. For surely no historian who reflects on modern Russian martyrdom will fail to recognize that he is faced with precisely the kind of questions which, as Professor Lash declared, contemplating the form that Christian 'witness' might properly take in the late twentieth century, 'will continue, often in darkness, strenuously to engage all those resources of integrity and discernment without which patterns of human action are not responsibly undertaken or pursued.'[119]

University of Glasgow

[119] Nicholas Lash, 'What might martyrdom mean?', in Horbury and McNeil, eds, *Suffering and Martyrdom*, p. 198.

MARTYRS FOR THE TRUTH: FUNDAMENTALISTS IN BRITAIN

by D. W. BEBBINGTON

THE systematic study of religious Fundamentalism is now well under way. The first of six promised volumes under the auspices of the Fundamentalism Project of the University of Chicago, making a global examination of such movements in many religions, was published in 1991.[1] Collections of papers evaluating specific aspects of Fundamentalism have been issued,[2] and the theological method of the contemporary British movement has been scrutinized.[3] Its American equivalent is the subject of one of the most illuminating of post-war works on the history of Christianity in the United States.[4] Yet the history of the British movement has been allowed to remain in obscurity.[5] Although, as will be seen, there are understandable reasons for the neglect, the growth of interest in world-wide Fundamentalism makes study of its British expression timely. More certainly than some of the other forms of defensively-minded traditional religion elsewhere that are now being labelled 'Fundamentalist', the British movement is entitled to the name invented by its counterpart in America. It arose at the same time, looking to some of the same men for leadership, and displayed similar traits. So an attempt is made here to present an overview of the Fundamentalists in Britain.

Particular attention is given to the movement's self-image. How the

---

[1] Martin E. Marty and R. Scott Appleby, eds, *Fundamentalisms Observed* (Chicago, 1991).

[2] Lionel Caplan, ed., *Studies in Religious Fundamentalism* (London 1987); Norman J. Cohen, ed., *The Fundamentalist Phenomenon* (Grand Rapids, Mich., 1990); George M. Marsden, *Understanding Fundamentalism and Evangelicalism* (Grand Rapids, Mich., 1991); Hans Küng and Jürgen Moltmann, eds, *Fundamentalism as an Ecumenical Challenge* (*Concilium* 1992/93) (London, 1992).

[3] James Barr, *Fundamentalism* (London, 1977).

[4] George M. Marsden, *Fundamentalism and American Culture: the Shaping of Twentieth Century Evangelicalism, 1870–1925* (New York, 1980).

[5] Perhaps the most thorough case-study is Bryan R. Wilson's history of Elim Pentecostalism in *Sects and Society: a Sociological Study of Three Religious Groups in Britain* (London, 1961), ch. 2. The Pentecostalists, however, were not regarded as true Fundamentalists by others bearing the name. See also D. W. Bebbington, 'The Persecution of George Jackson', in W. J. Sheils, ed., *Persecution and Toleration, SCH*, 21 (1984), pp. 421–33; 'Baptists and Fundamentalism in Inter-War Britain', in Keith Robbins, ed., *Protestant Evangelicalism: Britain, Ireland, Germany and America, c.1750–c.1950: Essays in Honour of W. R. Ward, SCH.S*, 7 (1990), pp. 297–326; and *Evangelicalism in Modern Britain: a History from the 1730s to the 1980s* (London, 1989), ch. 6.

x

participants perceived themselves is crucial if they are to be understood. It is all too easy for us, like their critics at the time, to dismiss Fundamentalists as wild and narrow-minded fanatics, as 'intolerable cranks' pursuing a 'hectic propaganda in the name of orthodoxy'.[6] In their own minds, however, they were very different. They were simple Bible believers, loyal servants of Jesus Christ, who had no choice but to take a firm stand for their most cherished convictions. 'We cannot be too yielding as regards our own things', wrote one of them in 1926, 'but the Truth is not ours to yield.'[7] They would resist the onslaught of Modernism at whatever cost to themselves. Even if all others deserted their Lord, they would remain loyal, sharing the road to Calvary. It is no wonder that American Fundamentalists expressing such views during the Second World War attracted censure from their more moderate Evangelical allies for cultivating a 'martyr complex'. 'Some', even according to these sympathetic critics, 'have appeared to go out of their way to seek opposition in order that when opposition is aroused they may burn gloriously at the stake in the view of a great national gallery.'[8] A very similar phenomenon was evident in Britain. Harold Morton, one of the two leading lights among organized Fundamentalists in Methodism, was the editor of *The Journal of the Wesley Bible Union*, a magazine that in August 1927 changed its title to *The Fundamentalist*. Two years earlier, at the time when America was agog with the antics of the 'monkey trial' at Dayton, Tennessee, Morton dismissed the more restrained Evangelical view that controversy against Modernism could be laid aside. Quoting the text from Revelation chapter 12, about those who overcame the Devil by the blood of the Lamb and the word of their testimony, he underlined its conclusion that they loved not their lives unto the death. 'God calls us, if necessary', he warned, 'to lay down our lives in this conflict.'[9] Fundamentalists saw themselves as potential martyrs for the sake of the Gospel.

An essential preliminary to investigation of the theme of martyrdom must be the question of definition. It is often assumed that Fundamentalism can be equated with Evangelicalism as a whole, or at least that Fundamentalist theological premises have been characteristic of Evangelicals.

[6] T. Cynon Jones to C. E. Wilson, 21 Apr. 1923, in Oxford, Regent's Park College, Angus Library, Baptist Missionary Society Archives, Box H62 [hereafter 'B.M.S. Archives, H62']. *The Baptist Times*, 20 Apr. 1923, p. 271.
[7] *Bible League Quarterly* [hereafter *BLQ*], Oct.–Dec. 1926, p. 182 (H. D. Woolley).
[8] *Evangelical Action!* (Boston, Mass., 1942), p. vi, in Joel A. Carpenter, ed., *A New Evangelical Coalition: Early Documents of the National Association of Evangelicals* (New York, 1988).
[9] Elizabeth Morton and Douglas Dewar, *A Voice Crying in the Wilderness: a Memoir of Harold Christopherson Morton* (London, 1937), p. 131.

Thus in his book on Whiggish historians in Victorian England, John Burrows refers to Lord Macaulay's 'early education in Biblical fundamentalism', and in his study of Evangelical social theory in the nineteenth century Boyd Hilton writes of the sympathy between Gladstone and Non-conformity resting on 'their common acceptance of a fundamentalist theology'.[10] For much of its course, however, the Evangelical tradition was not associated with Fundamentalist attitudes to the Bible. Much more flexible notions of inspiration and its effects were generally typical of the movement, so that it was not universal or even prevalent to claim that the Bible, as the revelation of a God of truth, must necessarily be free from error. The notion of inerrancy, which has been called 'the *articulus fundamentalissimus* of all the fundamentals',[11] gradually grew in popularity within the Evangelical movement from the 1820s onwards, but it did not sway the young Macaulay, the mature Gladstone, or even (in the main) late nineteenth-century Nonconformists.[12] Likewise it was rare among British Evangelical writers in the twentieth century until, in 1958, J. I. Packer drew on American sources to popularize the idea in his *'Fundamentalism' and the Word of God*.[13] If the theological principle of the assertion of biblical inerrancy is used as a criterion of Fundamentalism, then Evangelicalism has been Fundamentalist only to a limited extent and only at certain times over the last two and a half centuries.

Nor can Fundamentalism be identified as the hallmark of those Evangelicals who in the twentieth century added 'conservative' to the label of their churchmanship. On the contrary, conservative Evangelicals were often eager to distinguish themselves from Fundamentalists. The two groups, they admitted, were substantially at one in the doctrines they wished to defend, but the conservative Evangelicals, as one of their number put it in 1931, would not 'contend for truth *at the expense of charity*'. The writer greatly annoyed true Fundamentalists. He was wrong, according to Harold Morton, because he was unwilling to enter the lists of controversy. Contending earnestly for the faith was a duty demanded by the times.[14] The disagreement was essentially about method: conservative

---

[10] J. W. Burrow, *A Liberal Descent: Victorian Historians and the English Past* (Cambridge, 1981), p. 86; Boyd Hilton, *The Age of Atonement: the Influence of Evangelicalism on Social and Economic Thought, 1795–1865* (Oxford, 1988), p. 358.

[11] Jaroslav Pelikan, 'Fundamentalism and/or Orthodoxy? Toward an Understanding of the Fundamentalist Phenomenon', in Cohen, ed., *Fundamentalist Phenomenon*, p. 6.

[12] Bebbington, *Evangelicalism*, pp. 86–91.

[13] D. F. Wright, 'Soundings in the doctrine of Scripture in British Evangelicalism in the first half of the twentieth century', *Tyndale Bulletin*, 31 (1980), pp. 87–106.

[14] Morton and Dewar, *Voice*, pp. 109–10 (Dr Graham Scroggie).

Evangelicals wished to avoid *ad hominem* denunciations; Fundamentalists were eager to engage in vigorous polemic. 'A Fundamentalist', according to the American historian George Marsden, 'is an Evangelical who is angry about something.'[15] The vitriolic tone so characteristic of Fundamentalist movements throughout the world has not been normal among twentieth-century Evangelicals in Britain, even among those of a conservative stamp. There was, admittedly, no sharp boundary between Fundamentalists and less militant Evangelicals: they could attend the same churches, they could co-operate in the same organizations, and individuals could move from one party to the other. Yet, as will appear, the difference in style was real and significant. To the theological criterion for identifying Fundamentalism should be added the social criterion of the degree of militancy. Conservative Evangelicals believed exclusively in pacific methods for spreading the Gospel; Fundamentalists were contentious by conviction and often by temperament. They formed the extremist fringe of the Evangelical movement.

The period when Fundamentalism took its rise was long thought to be the immediate aftermath of the First World War. In 1970, however, Ernest Sandeen argued that the phenomenon began not with the controversies of the 1920s but with the emergence in Britain of a premillennialist movement a century earlier.[16] Although Sandeen was right, as will be shown, to connect a sterner defence of the Bible with prophetic views, the premillennialists for most of the nineteenth century were not yet self-conscious as a distinct movement. They were generally inerrantists, and sometimes they were roused to militancy against impugners of the Bible—against the authors of *Essays and Reviews*, for instance, or Bishop Colenso. But they did not possess separate organizations and lacked the sense of isolation of their twentieth-century successors. They still felt themselves to be part of the religious government rather than of an excluded opposition.[17] There was a greater sense of having been swept aside by the tides of history about the frenetic prosecutions of ritualists by the Church Association and its allies in the later nineteenth century, but their intense hostility to sacerdotalist teaching, though in due course contributing to the rise of Fundamentalism, was not

---

[15] Marsden, *Understanding Fundamentalism*, p. 1.

[16] E. R. Sandeen, *The Roots of Fundamentalism: British and American Millenarianism, 1800–1930* (Chicago, 1970).

[17] They may be classified as Fundamentalists by a broad definition, but not by a narrow definition designed to identify the twentieth-century movement. Cf. George M. Marsden, 'Defining American Fundamentalism', in Cohen, ed., *Fundamentalist Phenomenon*, pp. 26–8.

at its core.[18] Even the closest approximations to Fundamentalist controversies during the nineteenth century, the Robertson Smith affair in the Free Church of Scotland and the Down Grade imbroglio provoked by C. H. Spurgeon among the Baptists, were not the equivalent of what was to follow in the twentieth century, because the advocates of more traditional views of the Bible were not yet persecuted victims. Robertson Smith, the innovating critical scholar, was eventually dismissed in 1881, and Spurgeon, the champion of older orthodoxies, left the Baptist Union in 1888 of his own free will.[19] During the next five years, however, the higher criticism made its full impact on Evangelical Nonconformity, percolating down for the first time from the scholars to the general religious public.[20] Although there was no sensational outburst of protest, in 1892 an undenominational evangelist named Henry Varley published *The Infallible Word*, a book marked, even according to a sympathetic reviewer, by a 'heat of spirit and use of expletives, which weaken and do not strengthen the influence of his book'.[21] On 3 May 1892 a Bible League was formed in the Exeter Hall to resist what its members saw as attacks on the Word of God.[22] Organized Fundamentalism had been born.

There were ominous rumblings over the next few years. In 1898 the Wesleyans of Brixton Hill laid a complaint before Conference against a visiting connexional professor who had admitted in his sermon that the Bible contains mistakes.[23] Twelve years later John Urquhart, the redoubtable Glasgow author of *The Inspiration and Accuracy of Holy Scripture* (1895), censured the belief of his fellow Baptist F. C. Spurr that Genesis was a compilation from various sources.[24] More serious was the schism that in 1910 divided the Cambridge Inter-Collegiate Christian Union (C.I.C.C.U.) from the Student Christian Movement (S.C.M.) because the Cambridge body insisted that Holy Scripture was an 'inerrant guide'.[25] It was a volcanic explosion that permanently altered the British religious landscape, and further eruptions were to be expected. Over the next five years a series of twelve pamphlets written by theologically conservative

---

[18] James Bentley, *Ritualism and Politics in Victorian Britain: the Attempt to Legislate for Belief* (Oxford, 1978).

[19] A. C. Cheyne, *The Transforming of the Kirk: Victorian Scotland's Religious Revolution* (Edinburgh, 1983), pp. 44–52; E. A. Payne, *The Baptist Union: a Short History* (London, 1959), ch. 7.

[20] W. B. Glover, *Evangelical Nonconformists and Higher Criticism in the Nineteenth Century* (London, 1954), p. 286.

[21] *The Christian* [hereafter *C*], 14 July 1892, p. 8 (James Douglas).

[22] Ibid., 12 May 1892, p. 7. The date is given on later headed notepaper of the League.

[23] *The Journal of the Wesley Bible Union* [hereafter *JWBU*], Dec. 1916, pp. 265–6.

[24] James Mountain, *Rev. F. C. Spurr and Keswick* (n.p., n.d.), p. 3.

[25] J. C. Pollock, *A Cambridge Movement* (London, 1953), p. 178.

Evangelicals and financed by Californian oil magnates was despatched to ministers and Christian workers throughout the English-speaking world, in due course giving its title, *The Fundamentals*, to the rising movement.[26] The first major Fundamentalist controversy in a British denomination took place in 1913, when Wesleyan dissentients tried unsuccessfully to prevent the confirmation of George Jackson, who had voiced higher critical opinions, in a chair at a connexional college.[27] Likewise Evangelical Anglicans were sharply divided between 1917 and 1922 over permissible views of the Scriptures in the Church Missionary Society, from which some of the conservatives eventually seceded to form the Bible Churchmen's Missionary Society (B.C.M.S.).[28] The Baptists underwent similar anguish in 1923 about the election of the Cambridge classical scholar and S.C.M. speaker T. R. Glover to the vice-presidency of the Baptist Union and about the fidelity to the Scriptures of the Baptist Missionary Society (B.M.S.).[29] There were also acrimonious disputes during the 1920s in the Keswick Convention, in the Churches of Christ, among the Calvinistic Methodists of Wales, and (it may be added) among the Presbyterians of Ireland.[30] Baptists suffered two further controversies, in the early 1930s, when in England, Glover's teaching was again called into question and in the mid-1940s, when in Scotland, the denominational college was assailed for spreading Modernism.[31] In all these cases, though the implicated doctrinal questions varied, a central nub was the reliability of the Bible. Not all the conservatives were plain Fundamentalists: the leading creator of the B.C.M.S., D. H. C. Bartlett, for example, declared, to the consternation of a more rigid colleague, his willingness to interpret Genesis chapter 1 differently from Genesis chapter 12.[32] But it is clear that the rancour of the American Fundamentalist controversies was also evident in Britain during the first half of the twentieth century, and

---

[26] Helen C. A. Dixon, *A. C. Dixon: a Romance of Preaching* (New York, 1931), pp. 181-4.

[27] Bebbington, 'Persecution of George Jackson'.

[28] Gordon Hewitt, *The Problems of Success: a History of the Church Misisonary Society, 1910-1942* (London, 1971), 1, pp. 461-73.

[29] Bebbington, 'Baptists and Fundamentalism'.

[30] Bebbington, *Evangelicalism*, pp. 218-19; D. M. Thompson, *Let Sects and Parties Fall: a Short History of the Association of Churches of Christ in Great Britain and Ireland* (Birmingham, 1980), pp. 131-3; K. O. Morgan, *Rebirth of a Nation: Wales, 1880-1980* (Oxford, 1981), pp. 199-200; Austin Fulton, *J. Ernest Davey* (Belfast, 1970), ch. 3.

[31] K. W. Clements, *Lovers of Discord: Twentieth-century Theological Controversies in England* (London, 1988), pp. 107-29; I. L. S. Balfour, 'The Twentieth Century since 1914', in D. W. Bebbington, ed., *The Baptists in Scotland: a History* (Glasgow, 1988), p. 74.

[32] *The Record* [hereafter *R*], 23 March 1922, p. 192. Cf. G. W. Bromiley, *Daniel Henry Charles Bartlett, M.A., D.D.: a Memoir* (Burnham-on-Sea, Somerset, 1959), p. 40.

especially in the 1920s. How did the British Fundamentalists see themselves during this phase of intermittent conflict?

In the first place, they believed themselves to be witnesses standing, and if necessary suffering, for the true faith. As much as the martyrs of the Early Church, their primary role was to bear testimony. 'Our Lord depends on His followers as witnesses', declared Benjamin I. Greenwood, a retired Baptist businessman from Shoreham-by-Sea, in 1925, 'and it is required of witnesses that they declare the truth, the whole truth, and nothing but the truth.'[33] It has been pointed out that truth has been the overriding value for Christian Fundamentalists in the United States,[34] and something of the outrage shown by their British counterparts stemmed from their belief that the truth was being surrendered. 'Many today', wrote the alarmed missionary secretary of a Baptist chapel near Brecon to the B.M.S. in 1922, 'unfortunately feel called to deliver a message which is not God given, but the outcome of their own natural minds, and in many cases a direct contradiction of Gods [sic] own word.'[35] The immediate task was to restate the Gospel again and again. The leading journal of the Brethren (the so-called Plymouth Brethren), which consistently lent its aid to Fundamentalist positions, was entitled *The Witness*. So was the magazine of Trinity Road Baptist Chapel, Upper Tooting, and it was used by its minister in 1923 as a vehicle for what he called 'witness-bearing' against 'the progress of modernism'. He appreciated receiving a note from Tunbridge Wells, expressing admiration of 'the way you are standing up for the Truth as we have received it'.[36] Bearing witness could also be a corporate activity. One of the most ingenious ploys of the Fundamentalists was the invitation sent out in 1922 by the Bible League to each Evangelical religious society, inviting it to declare its 'whole-hearted and unreserved allegiance to the veracity and Divine authority of the whole Bible'.[37] A range of minor bodies readily complied, but the long-established denominational missionary societies saw no reason why they should be subjected to a fresh religious test by an upstart organization. Greenwood found this attitude incomprehensible in the B.M.S. 'I not only believe in Christ and in the Holy Scripture', he wrote privately to its

[33] *BLQ*, Jan.–Mar. 1925, p. 5.
[34] Clark H. Pinnock, 'Defining American Fundamentalism: a response', in Cohen, ed., *Fundamentalist Phenomenon*, pp. 47–8.
[35] Mrs H. James, Hebron, Brynmawr, Brecon, to W. Y. Fullerton, 19 Jan. 1922, B.M.S. Archives, H62. The archives contain a collection of correspondence that helps illuminate the attitudes of chapel folk during the B.M.S. controversy.
[36] *The Witness* [Upper Tooting], Feb. 1923, pp. 9, 13, B.M.S. Archives, H62.
[37] *Appeal* by Bible League (London, 1923), B.M.S. Archives, H62.

secretary, himself a conservative Evangelical, 'but may God forgive me if I ever fail to identify myself with either or both, *whenever I may be invited to do so*, by any man, or any society of men, godly or ungodly.'[38] A gulf had opened between Fundamentalists, for whom public testimony was paramount, and the more moderate Evangelicals, for whom other considerations also came into play. Fundamentalists such as Greenwood had no doubt that witnessing was what religion was all about.

The target of testimony was error. The aim, according to *The Journal of the Wesley Bible Union* in 1915, was 'to stay the progress of those "destructive heresies" which Peter says will bring "swift destruction" upon their victims (2 Pet. ii.1)'.[39] Heresy-hunting, a charge often thrown at them, was a taunt Fundamentalists normally repudiated, often on the ground that false teaching was so obtrusive as to need no seeking,[40] but they undoubtedly enjoyed sniffing out fresh cases of doctrinal declension. Leaders of the Wesley Bible Union (W.B.U.) scanned every statement of connexional professors and officials in order to publicize instances of heterodoxy that would vindicate their earlier allegations. They deplored the declaration of W. B. Selbie in 1925 that Congregationalists had no fixed creed, but applauded the firmness of the Salvation Army in enforcing adherence to its articles of war.[41] Earlier the proposal of federation for the Free Churches at the end of the First World War had stimulated the creation of a Baptist Bible Union (B.B.U.) for fear of the inadequacy of the new body's statement of faith.[42] The B.M.S. likewise was urged by R. B. Jones, a leading Welsh Fundamentalist, to ensure its committee and missionary candidates were sound in their view of the Bible: 'something more explicit and frank than vague generalisations', he told the society's secretary, 'are [sic] urgently demanded'.[43] In formulating their own creeds, Fundamentalists tended to be brief but to begin with the Bible. When Brethren in Glasgow examined 'The Fundamentals' in 1914, they considered nine topics: inspiration, incarnation, the deity of Christ, the Atonement, the Holy Spirit, the Resurrection, the priesthood of Christ and of all believers, the coming of the Lord, and future punishment.[44] Six years later F. B. Meyer, the veteran Baptist minister,

[38] Benjamin I. Greenwood to W. Y. Fullerton, 20 July 1922, B.M.S. Archives, H62.
[39] *JWBU*, Jan. 1915, p. 4.
[40] Ibid., June 1916, p. 122.
[41] Ibid., Nov. 1925, p. 550; Apr. 1927, p. 93.
[42] Ibid., July 1918, pp. 174–6.
[43] R. B. Jones to W. Y. Fullerton, 24 June 1922, B.M.S. Archives, H62.
[44] *The Witness* [London] [hereafter *W*], June 1914, p. 89. I am grateful to Mr N. T. R. Dickson for several references, including this one.

listed five doctrines particularly upheld by the Advent Testimony Movement he led:

> That all Scripture is inspired, i.e., inbreathed by the Spirit of God; that the Lord Jesus was born of the Virgin, that He is the only Begotten of the Father[;] that He died to make reconciliation for the sin of the world, whereby God can be just and the justifier of the ungodly[;] that He rose from the Dead on the third day and afterwards ascended to the Father[;] and that He will come, first for His people, and ultimately to judge the world—these are among the Fundamentals of the Faith, held by the Church of the Apostles, the Martyrs, the Fathers, and transmitted to our keeping.[45]

The list, with its crotchety inclusion of distinctive premillennial teaching, is similar to the 'five points of Fundamentalism' asserted by many Americans during the 1920s.[46] To be willing to make confession of the faith, however idiosyncratically, was a Christian duty, since, as it was remarked in the *Bible League Quarterly*, the 'Holy Spirit did not descend at Pentecost to form a think-as-you-please fellowship.'[47] Fundamentalists were doctrinal people.

Hence, as the writer in the *Bible League Quarterly* continued, there must be no 'shilly-shallying ... in the name of charity'.[48] Critics of the Fundamentalists found their downgrading of courtesy distasteful. Although he was theologically conservative himself, explained one correspondent of the B.M.S. in 1922, 'the tactics of the clique of the "orthodox" party have disgusted me with them, and I fear they have forgotten Paul's lesson on Charity.'[49] But Fundamentalists, though sometimes professing love or moderation,[50] were equally likely to dismiss a charitable temper as Laodiceanism.[51] Taking sides, they argued, was essential.[52] In the Early Church, explained Basil Atkinson, the mentor of the C.I.C.C.U. on the staff of Cambridge University Library, 'Christians

---

[45] *The Monthly Bulletin of the Advent Preparation Prayer Union* [hereafter *MBAPPU*], June 1920, p. 97.

[46] Marsden, *Fundamentalism and American Culture*, p. 117 and n. 30. It is, however, significant for the contrast between the two sides of the Atlantic that in America the first point took the stronger form of affirming biblical inerrancy.

[47] *BLQ*, Oct.–Dec. 1926, p. 180 (H. D. Woolley).

[48] Ibid.

[49] C. Hanmer Jenkins to W. Y. Fullerton, 16 Sept. 1922. B.M.S. Archives, H62.

[50] *The Bible Call* [hereafter *BC*], Jan. 1926, pp. 12–13 (Benjamin I. Greenwood); Feb. 1926, p. 32 (James Mountain).

[51] *BC*, Jan. 1923, p. 12.

[52] *The Fundamentalist* [hereafter *F*], May 1935, p. 96.

preferred death and torture to compromise and contamination.'[53] This inflexible attitude was identical to the political policy of Evangelical Nonconformists that had so irritated more worldly-wise Liberal Party managers in the previous century: there could be no parleying with opponents who defended any great social evil.[54] Many an issue, whether in secular politics or ecclesiastical debate, seemed to the militant Evangelical mind a matter of black and white, all or nothing. Thus Basil Atkinson roundly condemned those Evangelicals who clung to churches where, as he put it, ministers had abandoned the preaching of the Word. The second book of Timothy chapter 3 commanded that Christians should turn away from such.[55] Similarly, Benjamin Greenwood denounced those who suppressed 'their obligatory testimony or witness', preferring 'a comfortable silence (miscalled charity)'.[56] It is hardly surprising that many conservatives who were initially attracted to the Fundamentalist stand-point in the years round 1920 soon drew back as they realized what others supposed witness to entail. F. B. Meyer, the formulator of the British Fundamentalist credo, himself moved away from Fundamentalism as the 1920s progressed.[57] Yet those who remained saw no grounds for compromise. Like J. Gresham Machen, the intellectual leader of American Fundamentalism, they believed it was ruled out by the extent of Modernist apostasy. 'Modernism', declared one of them in 1923, 'is *not* Christianity.'[58] A new religion had been plucked from the air of modern thought, sharing only some of the outward trappings of the Christian faith but not its inward reality. Loyal believers could have no truck with it.

The practical expression of witnessing to the faith was protest. In a succession of incidents during the 1920s, Fundamentalists made their views known. When R. T. Howard, Principal of St Aidan's College, Birkenhead, expressed views at the 1920 Keswick Convention that verged on pantheism, a gentleman rose indignantly in his place. 'Mr. Chairman', he called out, 'I beg to ask a question. Is this address in accordance with the Word of God and the teaching of the Keswick Convention? I contend that it is not, and here and now make a solemn protest against it.'[59] Although the chairman did nothing, others walked out, and the offending

---

[53] B. F. C. Atkinson, *"Valiant in Fight": a Review of the Christian Conflict* (London, 1937), p. 18.

[54] D. A. Hamer, *The Politics of Electoral Pressure: a Study in the History of Victorian Reform Agitations* (Hassocks, Sussex, 1977), pp. 36–7.

[55] *BLQ*, July 1926, p. 130.

[56] Ibid., Jan.–Mar. 1925, p. 4.

[57] Bebbington, 'Baptists and Fundamentalism', p. 323.

[58] *BLQ*, Oct.–Dec. 1925, p. 146 (W. M. Robertson).

[59] *JWBU*, Oct. 1920, p. 223.

address did not appear in the published version of the convention's proceedings. In the following year, when the biblical critic George Jackson preached at a Methodist chapel, he explained Uzzah's death after touching the Ark as being not a supernatural penalty for infringing the divine law, but a result of excitement and a weak heart. One of his hearers declared that he was sorry to have seen the day when one who called himself a servant of the Most High God should stand in God's house and controvert his message. The protester left the chapel and did not return.[60] Another Methodist preacher, this time a young minister fresh from college, stated in 1922 that belief in the second advent was mistaken and (reportedly) that science had ruled out the books of Daniel and Revelation. A society leader interrupted the sermon and, when asked for an undertaking not to repeat the protest, he preferred to resign his post.[61] Two ladies took issue with another young preacher who told their congregation that *Gulliver's Travels* was more suitable than the Bible for the instruction of children;[62] and a camp leader visiting a strange church was appalled by the Modernist teaching, rose, affirmed his faith, and shepherded his twenty-one boys out of the service.[63] It may be suspected that each of these protesters was made of stern stuff: Jackson's critic, for instance, had already left an Anglican congregation on account of the ritualism practised there.[64] Yet confronting traducers of the truth was seen as an unpalatable duty, a symbolic gesture of defiance. It was not usually calculated to have any effect, but instead was a cleansing of the conscience from responsibility for error. It was an act worthwhile in itself.

The basic theological error confronting Fundamentalists seemed to be a ruling out of any divine intervention that infringed the scientific laws of the natural world. Some Modern Churchmen, they complained, 'strive their utmost to eliminate the purely Supernatural from the Biblical record'.[65] Modernism was therefore reductionist, having too little place for miracle, but it was also credulous, discerning too confidently divine traces in the ordinary operations of nature. Fundamentalists claimed that much of its speculation, like the Keswick address they disliked, was pantheistic in tendency.[66] They were not far off the mark, for the main

[60] Ibid., Apr. 1921, p. 93.
[61] *BC*, Mar. 1922, p. 19.
[62] Ibid., Apr. 1922, p. 27.
[63] *BLQ*, Oct.–Dec. 1926, p. 183.
[64] *JWBU*, Apr. 1921, p. 93.
[65] *BLQ*, Apr.–June 1925, p. 67 (A. H. Finn).
[66] Ibid., Oct.–Dec. 1925, p. 144 (W. M. Robertson).

trend of liberal theology in Britain over the previous century had displayed a romantic eagerness to endow mountains, flowers, and the intimations of the heart with numinous energy. Samuel Taylor Coleridge, F. D. Maurice, and James Baldwin Brown had all pointed in this direction, and, in the first decade of the twentieth century, R. J. Campbell seemed to have brought the process to a culmination in his New Theology, which went so far as to identify the divine with the human.[67] Evangelical ministers, especially in sections of the Church of England and Congregationalism, seemed to be hastening after Campbell. Fundamentalists were troubled that students for the ministry should neglect sterner topics such as sin, the Devil, and hell.[68] They were also dismayed by instances of apparent doctrinal equivocation, as when George Jackson pointed out that the New Testament fails to insist that the Holy Spirit is God.[69] But most of all they were alarmed by assaults on the citadel of faith, the person and work of Christ. The Modernists, they argued, offered a 'non-miraculous Christ more ignorant than ourselves'.[70] Fundamentalists objected to the fashionable doctrine of kenosis, expressed, for instance, in Jackson's contention that the incarnate Christ possessed only limited knowledge.[71] And they insisted, notably against the young Donald Soper in 1935, that the virgin birth was an essential article of faith.[72] To them, furthermore, it was imperative that the sacrificial death of the Lamb of God should be proclaimed. Paradoxically, they clamoured against the teaching of W. R. Maltby, the most influential Methodist divine of the 1920s, that the Atonement was no more than an inspiring case of 'martyrdom for the truth'.[73] Likewise they had no time for the opinion expressed by Leslie Weatherhead near the opening of his ministry that the Cross was not the will of God.[74] In all these instances Fundamentalists cast themselves as the champions of a tottering orthodoxy.

If orthodoxy was to be re-established, however, it was essential to appeal to authority. The Scriptures, the divine revelation of the truth, formed the appropriate medicine for the ailments of the contemporary

---

[67] R. J. Campbell, *The New Theology* (London, 1907), p. 74. Cf. Albert Close, *The Hand of God and Satan in Modern History: a Study Historic and Prophetic of Revelation, Chapter XVI* (London, 1912), p. 106.
[68] *JWBU*, Jan. 1915, p. 8.
[69] Ibid., Aug. 1922, p. 8.
[70] *BLQ*, July–Sept. 1925, p. 89 (A. H. Finn).
[71] *JWBU*, June 1915, p. 139 (Charles W. Prest).
[72] *F*, Sept. 1935, p. 250.
[73] *JWBU*, Jan. 1921, p. 8.
[74] Ibid., May 1927, p. 104.

Church. The Bible, Fundamentalists repeatedly asserted, did not merely contain the Word of God, but was the Word of God.[75] Only if the Bible was acknowledged in this way, they believed, could they refute the higher critics' claim to set aside certain passages as inferior, superseded, or otherwise lacking in authority. Underpinning their attitude to the Bible, as much as in America, there was an unsophisticated set of assumptions, stemming ultimately from Bacon, Locke, and the common-sense philosophy of the eighteenth century.[76] Unlike the more liberal churchmen whom they attacked, Fundamentalists remained largely attached to the legacy of the Enlightenment. They contrasted the 'man-invented theories and speculations' of the higher critics with the solid evidence for their own viewpoint. 'There are no ascertained *facts*', a leader of the W.B.U. confidently told a Methodist committee of enquiry in 1917, 'which tend to discredit the Bible.'[77] The facts in the Bible itself came direct from the Almighty. Morton, for one, repudiated the belief that inspiration was a matter of mechanical dictation,[78] and yet the notion was undoubtedly abroad. A lay Fundamentalist commentator on Revelation remarked that 'John wrote it just as it was revealed and dictated to him.'[79] Although, again, Morton was careful to distance himself from the idea of verbal inspiration,[80] many other Fundamentalists held it to be axiomatic.[81] But the guarantee of the reliability of the Bible that bound all Fundamentalists together was the belief that it contained no errors. When the prominent Bible teacher G. Campbell Morgan aligned himself with those willing to question 'the literal inerrancy of Scripture', the stance put him in the conservative Evangelical rather than the Fundamentalist camp.[82] The same dividing-line was again apparent between the Keswick leaders, who believed that critical study would establish the Bible as the Word of God, and true Fundamentalists, such as the circle in south Wales round R. B. Jones, who held that no reader could understand the Bible unless he assumed in advance that it was wholly infallible—which for Jones meant inerrant.[83] It was a matter of *a priori* reasoning that the Scriptures,

[75] *BC*, Oct.–Dec. 1919, p. 4; July 1923, p. 103. *BLQ*, Oct.–Dec. 1925, p. 150.
[76] Marsden, *Fundamentalism and American Culture*, pp. 55–6.
[77] *JWBU*, Nov. 1917, p. 243 (G. Armstrong Bennetts).
[78] Morton and Dewar, *Voice*, p. 211.
[79] Close, *Hand of God*, pp. 12–13.
[80] *JWBU*, Oct. 1921, p. 227; Apr. 1924, p. 80. *F*, Jan. 1929, p. 10.
[81] *The Advent Witness* [hereafter *AW*], Apr. 1924, p. 40 (A. H. Burton). *R*, 22 Dec. 1921, p. 855 (E. L. Langston); 19 June 1931, p. 407 (B. C. F. Atkinson). *F*, May–June 1949, p. 61 (H. K. Bentley).
[82] *F*, Aug. 1928, p. 180.
[83] B. P. Jones, *The King's Champions* (n.p., 1968), p. 136.

expressing the mind of God, could not possibly err. Fundamentalists were convinced that the Bible was 'inspired, authoritative and inerrant'.[84]

Accordingly, their fiercest condemnations were reserved for those who betrayed the Bible. The great feature of the times, Basil Atkinson told the Bible League in 1926, was an attack on the Word of God, not by infidels from outside but by scholars from inside the Christian Church.[85] Fundamentalists turned on biblical critics in the ranks of their own denominations with all the vehemence of the partisan against the traitor. The critics were *traditores*, leaders who were willing to hand over the sacred book to the enemies of the Church. They were 'Guess-Critics' who, by teaching that much of the Bible is folk-lore, legend, and myth, pitted their vaunted intellect against the wisdom of the Almighty.[86] A. S. Peake, the Primitive Methodist biblical scholar, was the target for much of this abuse. The verdict of Graham Scroggie, minister of Charlotte Baptist Chapel, Edinburgh, and normally moderate in his views, that Peake's commentary was 'sodden with infidelity' was long bandied about among Fundamentalists.[87] Any contributor to the commentary, or even any preacher who recommended it, attracted guilt by association.[88] Likewise T. R. Glover, the Cambridge classical scholar, was persistently assailed both before and after his election to the vice-presidency of the Baptist Union. His *Jesus in the Experience of Men* (1920) was dismissed in the journal of the B.B.U. as 'a long elaboration of the conventional fallacies and falsehoods of modern scepticism'.[89] Glover was a 'certain notorious Modernist' whose popular weekly religious column in the *Daily News* did the work of the Devil.[90] Glover, who was deeply hurt by the barrage of insults and who never suffered fools gladly, turned his fire on the Fundamentalists, and so perpetuated his standing as the man they loved to hate.[91] Their acerbic approach may be unappealing, but it is at least comprehensible when it is put in the context of the Fundamentalist mind-set about bearing witness. The times threatened to extinguish the Gospel; only by resolute testimony

[84] Atkinson, *"Valiant in Fight"*, p. 23.

[85] BLQ, July 1926, pp. 128–9.

[86] Morton and Dewar, *Voice*, p. 124.

[87] *Llanelly Mercury*, 31 May 1923, p. 3, B.M.S. Archives, H62 (J. I. Macdonald). F. W. Pitt, ed., *Windows on the World: a Record of the Life of Alfred H. Burton, B.A., M.D.* (London, [1937]), p. 139.

[88] W. M. Robertson to W. Y. Fullerton, 29 Oct. 1921, B.M.S. Archives, H62 (on Wheeler Robinson and Herbert Wood). James Mountain, *The Keswick Convention and the Dangers which threaten it* (n.p., 1920), p. 5 (on Charles Brown).

[89] BC, Mar.–Apr. 1921, p. 4.

[90] BLQ, Oct.–Dec. 1925, p. 144 (W. M. Robertson); Jan.–Mar. 1925, p. 21 (A. C. Dixon).

[91] Ibid., Apr.–June 1926, p. 55.

to Scripture could the truth be established; but Peake, Glover, and their kind were treacherously destroying belief in the Bible. They were deserters from the noble army of martyrs.

A second dimension of martyrdom which Fundamentalists appropriated was the role of victim. Basil Atkinson selected as the epigraph for his Fundamentalist version of church history the passage from Hebrews chapter 9 about heroes of faith who were 'destitute, afflicted, tormented'.[92] Members of the movement were conscious of suffering oppression. It could command overwhelming support in a few small denominations—the Brethren, the Strict Baptists, the Free Presbyterians of Scotland—but in general it constituted a small minority whose efforts were constantly resisted by the ecclesiastical authorities. In the wider society it was even more marginal. British Fundamentalism, unlike its American counterpart, failed to attract the attention of the secular media during the first half of the twentieth century. Only in the mid-1950s, with the advent of Billy Graham, did a newspaper controversy erupt around the phenomenon, and at that point the more conservative contributors to the discussion were eager to deny that either they or (with less justice) the visiting American evangelist could properly be called Fundamentalist.[93] There was a sense in which British Fundamentalism was victimized by neglect, and so much of the awareness of oppression was drawn from the past. Anglicans could think of the Protestant martyrs (of whom more will need to be said), or else, as did Basil Atkinson, appropriate the Scottish Covenanters as exemplars of heroic suffering.[94] Nonconformists could identify with the experience of John Bunyan in Bedford gaol, for the enduring hold of *Pilgrim's Progress* over their imaginations made the outlines of his biography familiar.[95] 'Our leaders', wrote a Fundamentalist Baptist minister in 1922, 'must take the trouble to remember that they sometimes address men whose forefathers were not frightened by prison, or stake, or gallows.'[96] He and his fellows were only too willing to dramatize themselves as the innocent prey of overbearing predators.

Methodists were most likely to cast themselves in this role, primarily

---

[92] Atkinson, *"Valiant in Fight"*, p. iv. Although the epigraph begins with verse 34 ('waxed valiant in fight') and so also has a combative message, it culminates with verse 38.

[93] *Fundamentalism: a Religious Problem: Letters to the Editor of The Times and a Leading Article* (London, 1955).

[94] Atkinson, *"Valiant in Fight"*, p. 194.

[95] Even when growing up in the United States A. C. Dixon had read *Pilgrim's Progress* 'and had the imagery of Bunyan pretty clear in my boyish mind'. Dixon, *Dixon*, p. 30.

[96] *The Witness* [Upper Tooting], Aug. 1922, p. 63, B.M.S. Archives, H62 (Henry Oakley).

because their connexional structure had long possessed authoritarian tendencies. Wesleyan Fundamentalists recalled having been 'terrorized' at the 1913 Conference when they had wanted to press charges against Jackson, and by 1927 they were noting, perhaps rather ingenuously, that candidates for the ministry were being rejected simply because of their orthodoxy.[97] When they persistently tried to raise questions of discipline at Conference they were shouted down, formally condemned as trouble-makers, or not called by the president in the first place. 'I know', wrote Harold Morton, 'just what Paul meant by "fighting with beasts at Ephesus".' For nearly twenty years there had been 'a reign of terror in Methodism'. 'Anyone', he went on, 'who dared to fight the fight of the Faith, according to the constitutional procedures of Wesleyan Methodism, has been the butt of ceaseless attacks and abuse and persecution and ostracism, so that very few have dared to open their mouths.'[98] They did not even have scope for redress through the denominational press, for their letters were not given space.[99] The B.B.U. likewise found it impossible to obtain publicity in the denominational newspaper.[100] Among the Baptists, despite their low degree of central control, there was in 1930 an episode of apparent discrimination against a probationer minister for professing Fundamentalist views. W. E. Dalling, an angular personality, was directed to read higher critical works in order to qualify for ministerial recognition and so felt bound to resign from the probationers' list, seeing to it that the case received maximum publicity.[101] At a lower level the two ladies who protested about *Gulliver's Travels* found themselves arraigned before their church meeting for causing a disturbance in public worship.[102] Evangelical Anglicans had grown accustomed over the years to exclusion from preferment, and, though in 1918 it was noted by Ronald Knox that liberal Evangelicals were beginning to enjoy the fruits of patronage, no conservative Evangelical, let alone Fundamentalist, reached the episcopal bench in the inter-war years.[103] Fundamentalists felt themselves to be the objects of discrimination.

Secular authorities were normally more remote and so less of a

---

[97] *JWBU*, Feb. 1927, p. 27; Apr. 1927, p. 83.
[98] Morton and Dewar, *Voice*, p. 62.
[99] *JWBU*, Mar. 1924, p. 65; Apr. 1922, p. 79.
[100] *BC*, Oct.–Dec. 1919, p. 6.
[101] *F*, Aug. 1930, pp. 176–7; May 1931, pp. 104–7.
[102] *BC*, Apr. 1922, p. 27.
[103] *R*, 25 July 1918, p. 471. Randle Manwaring, *From Controversy to Co-existence: Evangelicals in the Church of England, 1914–1980* (Cambridge, 1985), p. 43.

problem. *The Bible Call* of the B.B.U. reported that Lowestoft Council was trying to stop the work of the Salvation Army on the promenade, and that Weston-super-Mare had passed a by-law against the distribution of Gospel tracts. The editor might see in these measures 'an indication of the mobilization of the forces of Anti-Christ', but in fact they were directed against intrusive evangelism (the Salvation Army band was said to be an 'infernal nuisance') rather than against Fundamentalists as such.[104] Musing on martyrdom in the Early Church, Basil Atkinson suggested that the equivalent in their own day would be 'burning alive in the market place' for leaders of Christian Unions. 'Would a man', he asked, 'allow himself under such circumstances to be elected president of the C.I.C.C.U.?'[105] The question was not as fanciful as might be supposed, coming as it did in 1937, when Hitler was persecuting the Confessing Church, and Stalin was raging against religion in all its forms. But in Britain the chief practical problem was with the media. Radio and the press were closed to Evangelicals, Atkinson declared, by 'a sort of conspiracy'.[106] There had been earlier efforts to bring the B.B.C. to heel. Benjamin Greenwood protested in 1926 about a broadcast sermon by W. R. Matthews in which he spoke of the God presented on many pages of the Bible as not being worthy of his allegiance.[107] Harold Morton elicited an emollient reply from Sir John Reith when he objected to space on the air-waves being allocated to Julian Huxley for a talk on religion in the light of science.[108] The Evolution Protest Movement kept up the barrage into the 1940s.[109] Fundamentalists were right in supposing that they themselves were being kept off the air because they were not mainstream.[110] It was another instance of discrimination, and a significant one in the modern world.

The burdensome sense of being treated shabbily was given added weight by the apocalyptic dimension of Fundamentalist thought. As in America, the chief ideological stimulus of the Fundamentalist movement was premillennialism.[111] Students of prophecy, as they often called themselves, believed that before the coming millennium Jesus Christ would return in person to the earth. This ancient expectation had enjoyed a

---

[104] *BC*, June 1922, p. 42.
[105] Atkinson, *"Valiant in Fight"*, p. 21.
[106] Ibid., p. 209.
[107] *BLQ*, Oct.–Dec. 1926, p. 197.
[108] Morton and Dewar, *Voice*, pp. 160–5.
[109] *F*, Mar. 1943, p. 24; Sept. 1945, p. 73.
[110] Kenneth M. Wolfe, *The Churches and the British Broadcasting Corporation, 1922–1956* (London, 1984), pp. 111–12.
[111] Marsden, *Fundamentalism and American Culture*, chs 4–7, 16.

revival in the early nineteenth century, had gathered force in the Victorian period, especially among Anglican Evangelicals and Brethren, and by the first years of the twentieth century had an extensive following of conservative Evangelicals. The crisis of the First World War drew fresh attention to the advent hope. In particular, the fall of Jerusalem to British troops in 1917 seemed to presage important new events in the prophetic calendar, and immediately afterwards an Advent Testimony Movement was launched under the leadership of the venerable F. B. Meyer.[112] Its central beliefs were set out in a letter read to its opening meeting from the American Baptist minister A. C. Dixon. The Lord, he declared, would come again in his Resurrection body at a time known only to God, but suddenly, unexpectedly, and gloriously. The unbelieving world would be engaged in pleasure-seeking, business, and sin, but Christ's own people would be caught up to meet him in the air, and then, after a time during which certain great world events would take place, he would come with his people to establish his millennial reign. Believers ought to be full of expectation, but, far from being mystical dreamers, they should be faithful servants, feeling a constraint to maintain purity of life.[113] The alluring vision of the Second Coming was based partly on Old Testament passages that were coldly dissected by higher critics, and so fired its adherents with zeal for the defence of the Scriptures. 'We are here this morning', Prebendary H. W. Webb-Peploe told the inaugural meeting of Advent Testimony, '. . . to affirm that we accept this blessed Book as the Word of God, from Gen. i to Rev. xxii.'[114] By 1923 the council of the movement was insisting that every speaker acknowledged 'the Divine inspiration, authority, and absolute accuracy and inerrancy in every part (including, of necessity, the historical parts) of all the canonical books of the Bible'.[115] Advent Testimony was fertile soil for the growth of Fundamentalist attitudes.

The adventist movement, however, was divided into two main schools of thought that cultivated significantly different outlooks. The dominant tradition in the nineteenth century, especially in the Church of England, had been the historicist school of interpretation, whose most popular statement was Henry Grattan Guinness's *The Approaching End of the Age*

---

[112] D. W. Bebbington, 'The Advent Hope in British Evangelicalism since 1800', *The Scottish Journal of Religious Studies*, 9 (1988), pp. 103–14.

[113] *Advent Testimony Addresses delivered at the Meetings at Queen's Hall, London, W.C., December 13th, 1917* (London, 1918), pp. 53–4.

[114] Ibid., p. 9.

[115] *AW*, May 1923, p. 59.

(1878). The Book of Revelation, according to the historicists, should be read as a blueprint of the history of Christendom down the ages. Its exegesis was an intricate exercise in matching texts to world events that could prove a fascinating if time-consuming process. During 1939–40, for instance, John Kensit junior, of the Protestant Truth Society (P.T.S.), spent every Sunday morning over twelve months expounding successive passages from Revelation.[116] This mode of thinking spawned some extraordinary effusions from undisciplined minds. There was, for instance, *The Divine Programme of the World's History*, published in 1916 by Albert Close. Its section headings included 'The German Submarine Blockade of A.D. 1915', 'The Coming Great World Revolution', 'How Jesuits acquire Business Firms' Secrets', 'Voltaire, the Father of German Rationalism', 'What an English Physician saw in Paris, 1871 A.D.', and 'Converts who disappear in Ireland To-Day'.[117] Rather more disciplined was a historicist exposition of Revelation called *The War with Satan*, written by Basil Atkinson as Europe slid into the Second World War, but its opinions were very similar to those expressed in another book by Close. They coincided, for instance, in holding that the campaigns of Napoleon were divine vengeance for the seventeenth-century persecutions of Waldensians in the same general area.[118] Both writers loved to dwell on martyrdom as the lot of faithful Christians down the ages. Close wrote of the Marian martyrs and the Spanish Inquisition along with the Waldensians as instances of the persecutions that prevailed between 1200 and 1871, Atkinson of the early Christian persecutions, the Reformation martyrs, and the Roman Inquisition.[119] Although neither suggested that steadfast believers were being persecuted in their own day for their loyalty to the Scriptures, the whole atmosphere of their books is charged with awareness of the powerful forces arrayed against the true Church. Historicist interpretation of the Bible undoubtedly contributed to the expectation that the faithful were destined to suffer.

The alternative method of prophetic interpretation, the futurist approach, denied that the events described in the Book of Revelation referred at all to the past. They were still to take place, in the 'last days' at the end of the age. Most futurists upheld the dispensationalist teaching of the early Brethren leader John Nelson Darby that divided history into

---

[116] *The Protestant Truth Society: Annual Report, 1939–40* (London, 1940), p. 12.
[117] Albert Close, *The Divine Programme of World History* (London, [1916]), pp. viii–x.
[118] Close, *Hand of God*, p. 23; Basil C. F. Atkinson, *The War with Satan: an Explanation of the Book of Revelation* (London, [1940]), p. 137.
[119] Close, *Hand of God*, ch. 3. Atkinson, *War with Satan*, pp. 67–8, 125–6.

different epochs, or dispensations. They contended that the present dispensation, the church age, was about to end with the rapture of the saints, the catching up of the faithful to meet Christ in the air. 'We believe', declared the editor of *The Advent Witness* in 1927, 'that there is nothing to hinder the immediate return of the Lord to remove the Church.'[120] Such views had become the settled orthodoxy of the Brethren[121] and gradually gained ground among Fundamentalists of other denominations during the first half of the twentieth century. Although at first Advent Testimony was neutral between the schools of prophetic exposition, by 1950 the dispensationalist version of futurism was dominant.[122] Premillennial teaching had consistently been associated with the literal interpretation of the Bible, but dispensationalism was particularly insistent on the principle. Thus E. L. Langston, the most articulate of Anglican dispensationalists, argued that the promises of the Old Testament were to be 'literally fulfilled'.[123] Biblical literalism naturally fostered Fundamentalism. Dispensational teaching had a further effect on its adherents. Whereas Close, as a historicist, professed to be neither optimistic nor pessimistic about the course of world history,[124] dispensationalists were uniformly gloomy. A. H. Burton, the Brethren editor of the Advent Testimony journal, decried optimism as 'silly', remarked that 'the tendency of things human is generally retro-grade', and declared that 'sorrows will go on increasing until the great tribulation takes place.'[125] The secret rapture was the only hope for the saints; the rest of humanity was doomed. Dispensationalists were confident that their testimony would be vindicated by God, but they fully expected that it would be spurned by an unheeding world.[126] Their outlook was tinged with despair.

Consequently it is not surprising that the Fundamentalists affected by the rising prophetic views—a considerable majority—saw international politics as leading towards a climactic struggle. The Balfour Declaration, the migration of Jews to the promised land, and supremely the creation of the State of Israel all seemed to confirm their conviction that the end of

---

[120] *AW*, Aug. 1927, p. 128.
[121] *W*, May 1919, p. 78; June 1919, p. 95.
[122] *AW*, Sept. 1950, p. 164 (V. C. Oltrogge); Oct. 1950, p. 183.
[123] E. L. Langston, *How God is Working to a Plan* (London, [1933]), p. 22.
[124] Close, *Hand of God*, p. ix.
[125] Pitt, ed., *Windows on the World*, pp. 148, 100, 136.
[126] On the dispensationalist world-view, see T. P. Weber, *Living in the Shadow of the Second Coming: American Premillennialism, 1875–1925* (New York, 1979). I am grateful to Dr David Elliott for discussion of this point.

the current dispensation was at hand.[127] The Antichrist would make war on the Jewish people, and then, as Burton put it, 'the blood of the martyrs will flow.'[128] The period of suffering, the so-called 'great tribulation', would not, however, fall on the Church, which would already have been translated to the skies. Only faithful Jews would have to endure the persecution. But the course of events was moving towards this eschatological crisis before the rapture took place. The pieces on the divine chessboard were already being moved into threatening positions. Thus the League of Nations, seen by liberal Protestants as the great hope for peace, was viewed by dispensationalists in a very different light. According to Burton, it was an anticipation of the league of ten kings predicted in Revelation chapter 17, whose aim would be to make war with Christ.[129] There would be a reconstitution of the Roman Empire, a political confederacy under the thumb of the Roman Catholic Church, which would 'persecute to death all who refuse to bow to its unholy allurements'.[130] Already in the 1920s there was an ominous enhancement in the power of Italy under Mussolini.[131] Rome might well turn to a policy of oppression in the last days, just as it had in the first Christian centuries. Long before the Treaty of Rome, which was to arouse similar fears in the same quarters, European developments seemed to augur no good to the true Church. For all its abstruseness, prophetic teaching powerfully reinforced the self-image of Fundamentalists as victims.

In the third place, members of the movement saw themselves as soldiers. The early martyr was praised as a *miles Christi*, doing battle with the enemies of his Lord and eventually with the last enemy itself. In a comparable way martial imagery surrounded the Fundamentalist endeavour. 'Sound the alarm'; prepare for 'the coming conflict'; join the 'warfare against religious error'; 'rally under the Banner of Truth.'[132] Such sentiments were pervasive, especially during the mobilization phase of the early 1920s. No scriptural text was more frequently quoted in the movement's literature than Jude 3, the exhortation that 'Ye should earnestly

---

[127] E. L. Langston, *The Second Coming of Our Lord Jesus Christ in Relation to the Jew* (London, 1926). *AW*, Apr. 1933, p. 54; Mar.–Apr. 1949, p. 410.

[128] *AW*, Mar. 1928, p. 41. I am grateful to the Revd Ian Randall for several references, including this one.

[129] *AW*, Nov. 1923, p. 123.

[130] Pitt, ed., *Windows on the World*, p. 31.

[131] Ibid., p. 77.

[132] *W*, Nov. 1919, p. 170 (Alex Marshall). *BC*, Feb. 1924, p. 17 (Harry Tydeman Chilvers). *BLQ*, Jan.–Mar. 1925, p. 2 (Benjamin Greenwood). *Llanelly Mercury*, 31 May 1923, p. 3, B.M.S. Archives, H62 (J. I. Macdonald).

contend for the faith.' It formed the motto of the Baptist Bible Union and of the Wycliffe Preachers sent out by the Protestant Truth Society. Under the heading 'Contending for the Faith', A. H. Burton, of Advent Testimony, wrote that, 'We are up against a tremendous fight, and neutrality is out of the question. . . . The enemy of souls and of Christ's glory is on the warpath, and there is a call to every living Christian to be on the alert.'[133] There was praise for heroic virtues. It was right, declared James Mountain, to take 'the manly course'; we need, wrote an indignant correspondent of the B.M.S., 'men of gut and backbone'.[134] 'If our own generation of compromise', reflected Basil Atkinson ruefully in his church history, 'were only to realise what it owes to the stand taken by the early saints and martyrs, it might have a chance of gaining a little backbone.'[135] Fundamentalists were expected to quit themselves like men and be strong. Fighting has been identified by The Fundamentalism Project as the most salient feature held in common by the movements that it has examined world-wide.[136] They planned, the president, John Thomas, told the annual meeting of the B.B.U. in 1920, 'to organise the Army of the Lord Jesus for the coming great battle'.[137] That was the ambition of all Fundamentalists.

The militaristic note came readily to Evangelicals because it had been consecrated by their tradition. During the Indian Mutiny, General Havelock, the Baptist hero of the relief of Lucknow who died of disease shortly afterwards, had been canonized by the Evangelical public, and in later years General Gordon, the victim of the Mahdi at Khartoum, had created the ideal of a God-fearing soldier.[138] Sankey's hymns, extremely popular in the revivalist milieu that was most susceptible to Fundamentalism, were studded with military metaphors: 'Hold the Fort, for I am coming' is perhaps the best known.[139] The moment of conversion could be described as enlisting as a common soldier.[140] In the year of the Oxford Union 'King and Country' debate, Harold Morton remarked that 'As a general thing you will never find an evangelical pacifist.' Although he

[133] Pitt, ed., *Windows on the World*, pp. 138–9.
[134] *BC*, Mar. 1922, p. 19. Miss Margaret E. Lofthouse to W. Y. Fullerton, 29 Nov. 1923, B.M.S. Archives, H62.
[135] Atkinson, *"Valiant in Fight"*, p. 18.
[136] Marty and Appleby, ed., *Fundamentalism Observed*, pp. ix–x.
[137] *BC*, Jan.–Feb. 1921, p. 10.
[138] Olive Anderson, 'The growth of Christian militarism in mid-Victorian Britain', *EHR*, 86 (1971), pp. 46–72.
[139] John Kent, *Holding the Fort: Studies in Victorian Revivalism* (London, 1978), p. 218.
[140] Clyde Binfield, *So Down to Prayers: Studies in English Nonconformity, 1780–1920* (London, 1977), p. 233.

exaggerated, the principle applied more accurately to the Fundamentalist hard core. Appealing to the Old and New Testaments, Morton argued that 'Force must and ought to be used on the side of goodness and of justice.'[141] Fundamentalists who could accept the slaughter of the Amalekites recorded in II Samuel 15 as the will of God would have few qualms about taking up arms in a less literal fashion. Furthermore, officers of the armed forces were prominent in Fundamentalism. In 1921 Colonel D. F. Douglas-Jones, a stalwart of the Soldiers' Christian Association and later a member of the B.C.M.S. committee, headed an attack on the chairman of the Keswick Convention for protecting a user of biblical criticism.[142] Admiral Sir George King-Hall asserted the infallibility of the Word of God at a 1926 meeting 'in outspoken seamanlike fashion'.[143] Lieutenant-Colonel L. Merson-Davies stood up to protest against Modernism in an inaugural lecture at New College, Edinburgh, in 1949.[144] Fundamentalist officials had often held commissions in the armed forces. The secretary of the Bible League in the mid-1920s was Captain James A. Campbell,[145] and of the president and sixteen vice-presidents of the P.T.S. in 1940, eight were high-ranking officers.[146] At a mass level, of the first 1,103 recruits to Advent Testimony two decades previously, eighteen were naval or military men.[147] It came naturally to such figures to fall into rank behind leaders such as A. C. Dixon when he lectured on 'The Battle-Lines between Christianity and Modernism'.[148] Fundamentalists were predisposed to belligerence.

The anti-Catholic dimension of their tradition in particular en-couraged a truculent tone. Evangelicals had grown more hostile to the Roman Catholic Church in the mid-nineteenth century, the progress of Anglican ritualism had outraged them, and the proposal of Irish Home Rule, which many equated with Rome Rule, had provoked them further.[149] At the turn of the century there was a sustained but fruitless Protestant campaign to eliminate 'popish' innovations in the Church of

141 *F*, June 1933, p. 128.
142 *R*, 13 Jan. 1921, p. 32.
143 Ibid., 16 Dec. 1926, p. 890.
144 *F*, Jan.–Feb. 1949, pp. 15–16.
145 *BLQ*, Jan.–Mar. 1925, p. 1.
146 *Protestant Truth Society: Annual Report 1939–40*, p. 1.
147 *MBAPPU*, Sept. 1919, p. 32.
148 *BLQ*, Jan.–Mar. 1925, pp. 23–9.
149 John Wolffe, *The Protestant Crusade in Great Britain, 1829–1860* (Oxford, 1991); Bentley, *Ritualism and Politics*; D. W. Bebbington, *The Nonconformist Conscience: Chapel and Politics, 1870–1914* (London, 1982), ch. 5.

England.[150] Its most dramatic episode was the felling of John Kensit, the founder of the P.T.S. a few years before, by a two-foot iron file and his subsequent death in hospital during sectarian disturbances on Merseyside in 1902.[151] This instance of martyrdom brought his son, John Kensit junior, who was languishing at the time in Walton gaol for refusing to abstain from holding anti-ritualist meetings, to the fore in popular Protestant activities. For the next half-century the P.T.S. under his leadership was the lynch-pin of organized anti-Catholic effort in England.[152] Its members felt an automatic affinity for the rising Fundamentalist bodies, with which there was much coming and going. John Kensit junior was a speaker at the first summer conference of the W.B.U. in 1923 and was still a vice-president of its sucessor, the British Bible Union, in 1946.[153] Harold Morton of the W.B.U. and F. Martyn Cundy of the Fellowship of Evangelical Churchmen, which co-ordinated the work of Fundamentalist and other conservative Evangelical Anglicans, addressed a P.T.S. demonstration in 1924. They were under a threefold attack, Cundy told the meeting, from Romanism, criticism of the Bible, and evolutionists.[154] In the years round 1930 Cundy and Kensit acted together as secretaries of a movement holding meetings up and down the country called Britons Back to the Bible.[155] *The English Churchman*, a journal sponsored by the P.T.S., was classified in 1932 as the only fighting Fundamentalist weekly.[156] Other Protestant organizations, of which there were legion, gravitated in the same direction. Thus Captain J. W. D. Barron, secretary of the Church Association, dealt 'very forcibly' with the Modernists in an address to the National Protestant League in 1922.[157] The causes of Protestantism and Fundamentalism became interwoven at a popular level.

Consequently the Fundamentalists took over the anti-Catholic martyrology that had grown up over the centuries. In 1928 Albert Close compiled a catalogue of the Protestant martyrs of the British Isles for

[150] G. I. T. Machin, 'The last Victorian anti-ritualist campaign, 1895–1906', *Victorian Studies*, 25 (1981–2), pp. 277–302.
[151] Frank Neal, *Sectarian Violence: the Liverpool Experience, 1819–1914* (Manchester, 1988), ch. 8. See also now, Martin Wellings, 'The first Protestant martyr of the twentieth century: the life and significance of John Kensit (1853–1902)', above, pp. 347–58.
[152] There were vigorous separate campaigns in Scotland: Tom Gallagher, *Edinburgh Divided: John Cormack and No Popery in the 1930s* (Edinburgh, 1987), and *Glasgow: the Uneasy Peace: Religious Tension in Modern Scotland* (Manchester, 1987).
[153] *JWBU*, July 1923, p. 148. *F*, Jan.–Feb. 1946, p. ii.
[154] *R*, 9 Oct. 1924, p. 658.
[155] Ibid., 28 Mar. 1930, p. 203.
[156] *F*, Dec. 1932, p. 270.
[157] *R*, 23 Mar. 1922, p. 204.

publication in the magazine of the Protestant Alliance, another of the minor anti-Catholic organizations. It was more complete, he claimed, than any previously issued.[158] But most people preferred to turn to John Foxe, who was still being quoted extensively in an account of Protestant martyrs under Mary Tudor by the P.T.S. in 1957.[159] The booklet also surveyed their monuments, which remained surprisingly numerous, and which were still being erected or restored in the twentieth century. At the rededication in 1924 of the memorial to the eighteen Essex martyrs at Stratford, in east London, a Protestant Alliance representative prayed that 'if the necessity arose there would again be an army of men and women prepared in Christ's name and for His sake to die for the truth.'[160] The organization tried to maintain what it saw as a public Reformation witness by holding open-air lectures, especially in the metropolitan area. A Wimbledon speaker had the window of his home broken; at Finsbury Park the Romanists (it was said) 'fiercely rave at the lecturer with clenched fists and gnashing of teeth'; speakers were maltreated by 'Romish ruffians' at Forest Gate; and in Hyde Park a Protestant Alliance orator ingenuously described how when he called the confessional system immoral, Catholics in the crowd responded 'by calling me filthy, knocking me off the platform and smashing up the same, instead of doing as any reasonable logical-minded people would do, viz., give up the nasty system.'[161] Ignoring all the deliberate provocation involved, readers of such accounts learned the lesson that standing for the truth remained a hazardous enterprise.

Contemporary events served to reinforce the same message. The heightened atmosphere of the First World War made militancy in a righteous cause seem natural, even overdue, and so it is not surprising that most of the Fundamentalist crises came to a head shortly after it. The circumstance that higher criticism originated in Germany seemed particularly sinister. German thought, commented Morton in 1917, was worse than German armies.[162] Two years later Woodbrooke Hall, one of the Selly Oak Colleges, was described by James Mountain as an 'Augean stable of Germanized Rationalism'.[163] 'The rank and file of Biblical

---

[158] *Protestant Alliance Magazine* [hereafter *PAM*], Mar. 1928, p. 21; Apr. 1928, p. 30 (and subsequent issues to Oct.).

[159] *Protestant Martyrs under Mary Tudor: their Lives and their Memorials* (London, [1957]).

[160] *PAM*, Nov. 1924, p. 86 (J. Marchant).

[161] Ibid., Apr. 1924, p. 31; July 1924, p. 54; Sept. 1924, p. 69; Jan. 1925, pp. 5–6.

[162] *JWBU*, Jan. 1917, p. 10.

[163] *BC*, Oct.–Dec. 1919, p. 11.

Christians', he wrote in the following year, 'are nearing a public revolt against the Germanical Theologians in our midst.'[164] The Russian Revolution and its aftermath conjured up almost as much of a spectre. 'Anarchists, Bolshevists, and fanatics of every shade', declared A. H. Burton in 1922, 'have been, and are, busy murdering all against whom they have a grudge.'[165] The Russian Misionary Society, a tiny organization, but one that gave accommodation to the B.B.U. in London and to many Fundamentalist conferences at 'Slavanka' on the coast at Bournemouth, helped to keep the increasingly parlous state of Evangelical Christianity in the Soviet Union before the public.[166] By 1930 *The Advent Witness* was reporting, not without reason, that many Christians in Russia were suffering indescribable tortures for their faith.[167] In Fundamentalist eyes there was a connection between Communism in the Soviet Union and theological liberalism in Britain. 'The Modernist movement', according to Mountain, 'is the religious wing of anarchy, revolution and Bolshevism. Lawlessness and rebellion against authority is [sic] a characteristic of the last days.'[168] Anti-Communism was to become as settled a Fundamentalist trait as anti-Catholicism itself, surviving the Second World War to flourish in the climate of the beginnings of the Cold War. In times of crisis, threatened groups tend to flex their muscles, especially if they have apocalyptic tendencies. War and revolution helped mobilize the Fundamentalist army.

Adherents of the movement were acutely aware of the powerful forces leagued against them. In the first place, there was 'The Menace of Modernism',[169] but behind that they discerned Antichrist and apostasy, and behind them, in turn, the Devil himself. They were engaged in a 'stern conflict with the powers of darkness'.[170] Their world was one of stark antitheses: light and darkness were forever grappling in almost Manichaean struggle. Hence Fundamentalists saw connections where others would not suspect them, as their perception of Hollywood illustrates.

[164] Mountain, *Keswick Convention*, p. 10.
[165] *AW*, Aug. 1922, p. 87.
[166] *BC*, Nov.–Dec. 1921, p. 15; June 1925, p. 81. Cf. Archibald McCaig, *Grace Astounding in Bolshevik Russia* (London, n.d.).
[167] *AW*, Sept. 1930, p. 134.
[168] *BC*, June 1922, p. 41.
[169] *R*, 3 Nov. 1927, p. 777.
[170] *JWBU*, Jan. 1927, p. 2.

It is very freely asserted [wrote Morton in 1926] that the film industry of America, in which such millions of money have been sunk, is in the hands of the Jews, and that the flooding of the Picture Palaces with sex vulgarities and ostentatious and imbecile and criminal 'luxury pictures' is their intentional doing. The 'American Standard' affirms that the Jesuit is also behind the scenes.[171]

Entertainments, capitalism, Jews, pornography—these might possibly be linked, as they were by others at the time: but the addition of the skulking Jesuit, to whom in reality all these elements were highly suspect, is a touch of what Richard Hofstadter has called 'the paranoid style'.[172] In a dualist world, if anyone is not for us he is against us. Thus (according to a letter to *The Fundamentalist* in 1935) Jesuits and Ashkenazi Jews, both out for world domination, both anti-Christian and anti–British, must be secret agents of revolutionary movements.[173] It followed that Fundamentalists were sometimes prey to the other alarmist ideologies of the times. Anti-Semitic voices were heard quite often in the inter-war years, but they were normally drowned by protests from organizations evangelizing the Jews or else by writers pointing to prophecies of eventual Jewish triumph in the purposes of God.[174] Likewise the national variety of Fascism, though it had British Bible Union members in its ranks, was repudiated by Morton as the editor of its journal on the grounds that it was a threat to democracy.[175] Yet even if for most Fundamentalists the tendency to resort to conspiracy theories had its limits, the inclination was ever present. 'Protestant Christian soldiers'[176] inhabited a land full of enemies, and there were likely to be casualties in the war.

The fourth and final aspect of martyrdom embraced by the Fundamentalist was sacrifice. The first martyrs gave up homes, friends, families, even their very lives, and when actual death was no longer possible, as in the thought of Origen and the practice of the early Desert Fathers, the ideal of marytrdom was translated into asceticism.[177] Likewise Fundamentalists often voluntarily surrendered what they valued for the sake of the sacred cause. Morton used to muse on the cost of his path of discipleship, taking comfort from the text that 'He that saveth his life shall lose it.'

---

[171] Ibid., Feb. 1926, p. 12.
[172] Richard Hofstadter, *The Paranoid Style in American Politics and Other Essays* (New York, 1963).
[173] *F*, Mar. 1935, pp. 66–7 (H. James, Yarmouth).
[174] *The Life of Faith*, 30 June 1926, p. 691. *F*, July 1938, p. 158.
[175] Ibid., Sept. 1933, pp. 211–12 (G. H. Woods); Nov. 1933, pp. 246–7.
[176] Close, *Hand of God*, p. iv (Alexander Robertson).
[177] Henry Chadwick, *The Early Church* (Harmondsworth, 1967), p. 177.

His stern refusal to lead the life of an ordinary Methodist minister meant that invitations to take special services and occupy other pulpits ceased, that friends shunned him at Conference, and that his sons had to be removed from a Methodist school because of the taunts they suffered. Overwork in the service of the W.B.U., if his wife is to be believed, also ruined his health.[178] Unlike in America, as Morton ruefully observed, money was never plentiful in Fundamentalist organizations,[179] and the consequence for the small knot of leaders was unremitting effort in fund-raising. But the most frequently quoted penalty of professing Funda-mentalist views was mockery. 'We are despised', a visiting speaker told a meeting in south Wales; 'treated with contempt.'[180] They suffered 'a campaign of spiteful personal defamation and disparagement'.[181] They might 'alienate valued and valuable friends. We might be thought singular and narrow-minded. Or one might be accused of setting him up to be better than others—perhaps ruin his prospects, or find himself ostracised and outside the church circle so long loved.'[182] W. M. Robert-son, a Baptist pastor in Liverpool, accused the B.M.S. secretary of not wanting to lose 'the esteem of the high & mighty in the religious world' by joining the Fundamentalist ranks, but praised the Bible League for not heeding the cost. 'Maligned, misrepresented and misjudged', he declared, 'it pursues its way through evil report and good.'[183] The reproach was gladly, even triumphantly, borne, a sign of the righteousness of the cause. The early Christians, wrote Basil Atkinson, could be understood 'by their spiritual descendants, the Evangelicals of to-day. We all know the mis-understanding and the sneers that sometimes arise.'[184] By taking up their cross, they were aligning themselves with true confessors in every age.

One feature of their position that readily drew contempt was their lack of support. Most conservative Evangelical organizations—the Church Pastoral Aid Society, the Fellowship of Evangelical Churchmen, the B.C.M.S., the Fraternal Union for Bible Testimony, even Advent Testimony and the Protestant societies—drew in more moderate people alongside Fundamentalists. Only the Bible League, the W.B.U., and B.B.U., the three organizations that combined to present an All-Day

[178] Morton and Dewar, *Voice*, pp. 46, 20, 53–4.
[179] *JWBU*, Apr. 1926, p. 82.
[180] *Llanelly Mercury*, 31 May 1923, p. 3, B.M.S. Archives H62 (J. I. Macdonald).
[181] *BC*, Feb. 1922, p. 13 (John Thomas).
[182] *BLQ*, Oct.–Dec. 1926, p. 183 (H. D. Woolley).
[183] W. M. Robertson to W. Y. Fullerton, 31 Aug. 1920 [sc. 1922], B.M.S. Archives, H62, *BLQ*, Oct.–Dec. 1925, p. 147.
[184] Atkinson, *"Valiant in Fight"*, p. 18.

Bible Demonstration at the Metropolitan Tabernacle in 1922, perhaps together with the tiny Sovereign Grace Advent Testimony,[185] were more or less uniformly Fundamentalist in membership. They failed to issue membership statistics, but the B.B.U., which merged with the W.B.U. in 1928, was never large, and the W.B.U. itself enjoyed only a small annual income.[186] Although the attitudes they expressed were undoubtedly more widespread among the supporters of faith missions, such as the China Inland Mission, and youth agencies, such as the National Young Life Campaign,[187] organized Fundamentalism in Britain was never a large-scale affair. The membership, furthermore, tended to be elderly. James Mountain founded the B.B.U. when he was already in his seventies, the weightiest layman of the W.B.U. in its early years, W. Shepherd Allen, was in his eighties, and the chairman of Sovereign Grace Advent Testimony, John Hunt Allen, died in 1940 in his nineties.[188] Hence the strength of Fundamentalism lay partly in retirement areas. Advent Testimony, though not wholly Fundamentalist, published a helpful list of its first 1,103 members. A majority lived in London and the Home Counties, and of these a significant number had homes in quiet spots such as Tunbridge Wells. A high proportion lived along the south coast, the largest number in a single town being the thirty-eight in Bournemouth.[189] The other concentrations of Fundamentalists were in remoter parts of Britain. Cornwall was particularly responsive to the message of the W.B.U., and though the main Scottish Presbyterian bodies knew virtually nothing of Fundamentalism during the period, Welsh speakers from the south of the principality were disproportionately represented in the B.B.U.[190] Altogether the Fundamentalist movement seemed a marginal affair, a throw-back to the past. To identify at all with the cause was a sacrifice.

Fundamentalists shunned much of the modern world. Although Morton resisted pressures to campaign against the wireless, the cinema, which by 1938 sold nearly a thousand million tickets a year, was closed to

[185] *BC*, Mar. 1922, p. 18. *F*, Aug. 1933, p. 177.
[186] Bebbington, 'Baptists and Fundamentalism', pp. 320–1; and 'Persecution of George Jackson', p. 428.
[187] Phyllis Thompson, *D. E. Hoste: "A Prince with God"* (London, 1947); Frederick P. Wood, *Youth Advancing* (London, 1961).
[188] *BC*, Aug. 1923, p. 128. *JWBU*, Mar. 1915, p. 60. *AW*, Feb. 1941, p. 15.
[189] *MBAPPU*, Sept. 1919, p. 32; Mar. 1920, p. 88; May 1920, p. 96.
[190] *JWBU*, July 1921, p. 161; Aug. 1924, p. 198; July 1927, p. 154. *Life and Work*, June 1924, p. 122 (J. N. Ogilvie); June 1936, pp. 255–6 (G. S. Hendry). Bebbington, 'Baptists and Fundamentalism', pp. 306–7.

the committed Fundamentalist.[191] Football, which reached the peak of its popularity as a spectator sport in inter-war Britain, was viewed with jealous suspicion. Instead of starting football teams for their teenagers, Brethren were advised, their young people should take 'heathful exercise' by organizing groups for tract distribution.[192] Fundamentalists were aware that, with the multiplication of alternative leisure facilities, the social climate was growing less hospitable to single-minded religious activity. Their remedy for falling church attendance, however, was the precise opposite of what was generally canvassed in the early twentieth century, the sponsorship of recreation by religious bodies. This approach was condemned as 'the entertainments curse', a calamity that was secularizing the Church rather than converting the world—and their diagnosis contained more than an element of truth.[193] Noting that a London vicar was trying by such techniques to attract people to church, A. H. Burton in *The Advent Witness* contrasted the antics of smoking, drinking, dancing, and theatricals on church premises with the right method, the 'faithful preaching of the Word'.[194] Socials, concerts, and clubs were no doubt good in themselves, admitted Morton more generously, but because they diverted people from prayer meetings and Bible studies, believers should recognize 'the mark of the cloven hoof on these "good plans"'.[195] Even innocent recreation must be eschewed because the good could so easily turn out to be the enemy of the best. Fundamentalists were fertile in inventing taboos.

Apart from contemporary social pressures, a further explanation of their eagerness to avoid any hint of worldliness lay in the holiness movement. The spirituality associated with the Keswick Convention, though by no means confined to the more conservative Evangelicals, had by 1914 become widespread in their ranks, especially in the Church of England. The way in which it fostered a species of self-denial may be illustrated from an address on the unwise association of the godly King Jehoshaphat with the wicked King Ahab given by H. Earnshaw Smith at the 1930 convention. 'God was calling them', he told his audience, 'to an utter separation from everything that was questionable. Spiritual powerlessness was the result of conformity with the world and with the flesh. Was not

[191] *F*, Apr. 1929, p. 89. Stephen Constantine, *Social Conditions in Britain, 1918–1939* (London, 1983), p. 16. *BC*, July/Aug. 1920, p. 3.
[192] *W*, July 1920, p. 304.
[193] *JWBU*, Dec. 1916, p. 274. Jeffrey Cox, *The English Churches in a Secular Society: Lambeth, 1870–1930* (New York, 1982), pp. 218–20.
[194] *AW*, May 1922, p. 51.
[195] *JWBU*, July 1921, p. 160.

that the position of the church to-day?'[196] Convention-goers knew that sacrifice was expected of them. Admittedly it is true that, since the Keswick message discouraged militancy, it is one of the chief explanations for the weakness of the Fundamentalist tendency in comparison with the milder strand within conservative Evangelicalism.[197] Yet it had shaped many of the Fundamentalist leaders, including A. C. Dixon and James Mountain,[198] and its ethos was the normative devotional temper of the movement. On the fringe of Keswick were Bible teachers with even more uncompromising views. Jessie Penn-Lewis, the promoter of the Over-comer League, called believers to an experience of being identified with Christ in his death as 'the secret of rest and power'.[199] With Evan Roberts, the mercurial spirit who had kindled the Welsh Revival of 1904–5, Mrs Penn-Lewis published *War on the Saints*, a widely circulated book full of warnings against the supernatural snares laid for the Christian by the powers of darkness.[200] Less enigmatically, but no less powerfully, the Methodist tradition of entire sanctification was a major rationale in the W.B.U. for resisting the unhallowed influences of the day.[201] Holiness teaching goes a long way towards explaining the ascetic element in Fundamentalism.

The desire to flee the taints of the world reinforced the sectarian inclinations within the movement. A Sunday school superintendent who claimed to be resisting the destructive criticism of those with prayerless lives said he had nevertheless assembled 'a faithful band', and the minister of Upper Tooting Baptist Chapel was aware of being part of 'a protesting remnant'.[202] A perplexing question was whether the remnant could maintain its existing variety of ecclesiastical allegiances without undue compromise. By 1929 Morton was expecting that eventually secessions from the denominations would lead to the establishment of a single Evangelical Church.[203] There was the example of Spurgeon's withdrawal from the Baptist Union to invoke,[204] and for a long time Brethren had been contending that real Christians must abandon their man-made

---

[196] *R*, 18 July 1930, p. 474.
[197] Bebbington, 'Baptists and Fundamentalism', p. 323.
[198] Dixon, *Dixon*, pp. 161, 206. *R*, 21 July 1933, p. 423.
[199] Mary N. Garrard, *Mrs. Penn-Lewis: a Memoir* (London, 1930), p. 199.
[200] Jessie Penn-Lewis and Evan Roberts, *War on the Saints* (Leicester, 1912).
[201] *JWBU*, Feb. 1915, p. 47; May 1915, p. 105; July 1915, p. 148; Mar. 1917, pp. 53–60; Oct. 1925, p. 527. Cf. Bebbington, *Evangelicalism*, pp. 153–5, 171–4.
[202] *BLQ*, Oct.–Dec. 1925, p. 150. *Witness* [Upper Tooting], Feb. 1923, p. 9, B.M.S. Archives, H62.
[203] *F*, Mar. 1929, p. 53.
[204] Ibid., Nov. 1931, p. 260.

churches to join their own body, the only pure one in existence. 'Wherever saint and sinner, saved and unsaved, are federated', said their magazine in 1920, 'there is the clarion call "COME OUT".'[205] Although some hard-line Fundamentalists such as R. B. Jones resisted the temptation to leave their denominations, there existed from 1922 a Fellowship of Independent Evangelical Churches, waiting to gather up dissident congregations.[206] Ecclesiastical separatism, though much weaker than in the United States, did make some headway in Britain. It was more generally agreed among Fundamentalists that there should be withdrawal from public affairs and avoidance of social questions. At the 1929 general election a faint echo of the Nonconformist conscience was still heard in the call of *The Fundamentalist* to vote against the Sunday opening of theatres and increased public funding for Roman Catholic schools,[207] but any broader version of social policy was avoided. To many of the Fundamentalists, often Conservative by politics as well as conservative by disposition, any attempt to promote the welfare of the people by the State stood self-condemned as flirting with Socialism.[208] Former keen Liberals began to associate political reconstruction with Modernism during the First World War,[209] and thereafter it was standard for Fundamentalists to reject the social gospel as a replacement for the true one. 'Social gospel' might well be spelt with a little 'g', wrote Mountain in 1922, 'for it is not the Gospel of Christ.'[210] There was a retreat from the issues of society as well as from the affairs of the denominations. In varying degrees Fundamentalists had the withdrawal instinct of the sectarian.

They were also willing to make sacrifices in the realm of the intellect. Nowhere was the gulf between the Fundamentalist world-view and the contemporary consensus clearer than over the principle of evolution. Morton, who specialized in assaulting evolutionary doctrine, dismissed it as a theory unsupported by any facts about the transmutation of species.[211] According to T. B. Bishop, the author of *Evolution Criticised* (1918), it was clear from scientific research that life could be produced only by life. Hence there was a gap between the inanimate world and living creatures that could have been filled only, as Genesis records, by the interposition of

[205] *W*, Jan. 1920, p. 210.
[206] Jones, *King's Champions*, pp. 205–6. D. G. Fountain, *E. J. Poole-Connor (1872–1962): Contender for the Faith* (Worthing, 1966), pp. 121–8.
[207] *F*, May 1929, p. 109.
[208] Close, *Hand of God*, p. vii.
[209] *JWBU*, July 1917, pp. 159–61.
[210] *BC*, June 1922, p. 42.
[211] Morton and Dewar, *Voice*, p. 233.

the Almighty.[212] Fundamentalists did cling to scientific respectability by reading papers to each other at the Victoria Institute, a scholarly body that had fallen into their hands, and by parading the support of Sir Ambrose Fleming, the retired professor of engineering at University College, London,[213] but in general their stance on evolution gave them an ante-diluvian air. Their attitude to learning on a broader front was ambivalent. They lamented that ministers worshipped scholarship, and liked to point out that the faith was delivered to the saints rather than to professors, doctors of divinity, or compilers of commentaries.[214] Yet the *Bible League Quarterly* published learned refutations of Old Testament source criticism, and Morton went out of his way to acquire an M.A. from the Intercollegiate University of Britain and America and, highly sus-piciously, a Ph.D. from the same organization less than six months later.[215] They were not simply anti-intellectual, even if on occasion they could be unsparing about academic institutions. 'If the Colleges were burned down', wrote 'a devoted Christian worker' in 1920, 'it would be so much the better for Christianity.'[216] What they objected to was any academic body that propagated error. Consequently they established several colleges of their own: the transient Bible Institute of the Bible League, the All Nations Missionary College, promising to ground its students in the 'fundamentals', John Thomas's Bible College of Wales for graduates, and R. B. Jones's South Wales Bible Training Institute, with a library 'almost entirely free from radical books or commentaries showing higher-critical positions'.[217] Although such institutions were few and small in com-parison with their American counterparts, they helped transmit the Fundamentalist temper to a fresh generation.

So, too, did the Christian Unions associated with the Inter-Varsity Fellowship. During the 1920s the student bodies that aligned themselves with C.I.C.C.U. against the S.C.M. were rooted in the Fundamentalist sub-culture. Representatives of the London Inter-Faculty Christian Union (L.I.F.C.U.) assured readers of the *Protestant Alliance Magazine* that they upheld 'the fundamental truths of the Christian faith', Morton addressed both L.I.F.C.U. and C.I.C.C.U. on the perils of evolution, and Basil

---

[212] *R*, 30 Sept. 1920, p. 754. Cf. *T.B.B. of the C.S.S.M.* (London, 1923), ch. 11.
[213] *C*, 31 Jan. 1935, p. 6.
[214] Close, *Hand of God*, p. iv; Pitt, ed., *Windows on the World*, p. 138.
[215] E.g. F. R. Montgomery Hitchcock, 'Ezekiel and the Pentateuch', *BLQ*, Jan.–Mar. 1925, pp. 6–18. *JWBU*, Nov. 1923, p. 248; Mar. 1924, p. 59.
[216] Morton and Dewar, *Voice*, p. 121.
[217] *JWBU*, Dec. 1919, p. 286. *C*, 10 Nov. 1921, p. 7. Jones, *King's Champions*, pp. 215, 219.

Atkinson successfully canvassed for funds among members of the Bible League in order to establish for C.I.C.C.U. a 'small lending library of books setting forth God's Truth and exposing Modernism'.[218] The ethos of the Christian Unions was keen, intense, introverted, with its own hearty jargon. The president of L.I.F.C.U., when making a point in a talk to the Bible League, drew attention to 'some priceless lines in the C.S.S.M. chorus book which sum this up rippingly'.[219] In 1926 the approximately 800 members of the Inter-Varsity bodies were conscious of being a small minority among the roughly 50,000 undergraduates of the day.[220] They were overshadowed by the 'spiritual hulk' of the S.C.M.,[221] which wanted to swallow them up, and their views were held up to derision. Cambridge, according to the president of C.I.C.C.U., was a 'hot-bed of criticism'; young men from sound homes 'succumbed to Modernism when at the University'; a medical student was 'mercilessly assailed by a sceptical professing Christian'.[222] Atkinson wrote of 'the severe difficulties under which university students are placed in their stand against Modernism'.[223] They experienced something akin to intellectual martyrdom. 'They thought us fools', recalled Norman Anderson, president of C.I.C.C.U. in 1930 and subsequently a chairman of the House of Laity of the General Synod.[224] Yet from their ranks came many who, like Anderson, rendered distinguished service to British Christianity in the later twentieth century. Some, like Hugh Gough, who as Bishop of Barking was to champion Billy Graham's first crusade in Britain, were to remain, if not Fundamentalists, then conservative Evangelicals.[225] Others, such as Donald Coggan, were to mellow further but to continue within the Evangelical camp.[226] Yet others, including the present Archbishop of York and Professor James Barr, the arch-critic of Fundamentalism, were to disavow their early partisanship. Nevertheless, perhaps the chief long-term significance of the Fundamentalists was that they injected their resolve, but not their rancour, into a younger set of Christian leaders. The sacrifice they made at university steeled the members of the new generation for their later

---

[218] *PAM*, Sept. 1924, p. 74. *JWBU*, Apr. 1925, p. 281. *F*, Jan. 1933, p. 17. *BLQ*, July–Sept. 1925, p. 116.
[219] *BLQ*, July 1926, p. 143 (Howard Guinness).
[220] Ibid., Oct.–Dec. 1926, p. 185 (Douglas Johnson).
[221] Ibid., p. 186.
[222] Ibid., July 1926, p. 127 (Hugh Gough); Oct.–Dec. 1925, p. 150.
[223] Ibid., July–Sept. 1925, p. 106.
[224] Margaret Pawley, *Donald Coggan: Servant of Christ* (London, 1987), p. 28.
[225] John Pollock, *Billy Graham* (London, 1967 edn), p. 145.
[226] Pawley, *Coggan*.

duties. In one sense, at least, the blood of the Fundamentalist martyrs was the seed of the Church.

One of the aims of The Fundamentalism Project is to explore how far movements bearing the label vary among themselves. If Fundamentalism in the United States is taken as the bench-mark for assessment, to what extent did its British counterpart differ? Certainly several traits clustering around the theme of martyrdom that were present in America have been documented here for Britain. On both sides of the Atlantic Fundamentalists saw themselves as bearing witness, being victimized, fighting as soldiers, and making sacrifices for the cause. In substance the movements were identical. Yet there were contrasts too. In particular, the scale of the movement and the tendency to ecclesiastical separatism were weaker in Britain than in America, factors which were crucial for subsequent developments. In the years after 1950, British Fundamentalism, unlike its American equivalent, was largely reabsorbed into conservative Evangelicalism. Fundamentalism was neither big enough nor distinct enough to assert an independent presence in the public arena. Perhaps surprisingly, a scholarly version of biblical inerrancy tended to grow under the influence of J. I. Packer, but militancy, the other defining quality of the Fundamentalists, fell out of favour. From the 1950s onwards conservative Evangelicals, including some with leanings towards inerrancy, were more inclined to carefully planned evangelism than to truculent denunciation of opponents.[227] *The Fundamentalist* had ceased publication in 1950, and by 1956 John Stott was treating Fundamentalism as an exclusively American phenomenon whose 'extravagances' were happily absent from Britain.[228] Hence there was insufficient ground swell for the emergence of any equivalent of Jerry Falwell's Moral Majority during the 1970s and 1980s.[229] The heyday of British Fundamentalism came in an earlier era. For about half a century a section of the Evangelical world had maintained a vigorous defence of a narrow orthodoxy. 'Truth has prevailed', declared W. M. Robertson of Liverpool in 1925, 'when men have been willing to suffer and die for it.'[230] The spirit of martyrdom lived on among the Fundamentalists of early twentieth-century Britain.

University of Stirling

[227] *Church of England Newspaper*, 21 June 1957, p. 7 (J. Stafford Wright).
[228] J. R. W. Stott, *Fundamentalism and Evangelism* (London, 1956), ch. 1.
[229] Cf. D. W. Bebbington, 'Evangelicalism in its Settings: a comparison of the British and American movements since 1940', in Mark A. Noll *et al.*, eds, *Transatlantic Evangelicalism* (forthcoming).
[230] *BLQ*, Oct.–Dec. 1925, p. 146.

VIVIAN REDLICH, 1905–1942: A MARTYR IN THE TRADITION

by RACHEL MORIARTY

I N early August 1942 an English Anglican missionary priest named Vivian Redlich met his death at the hands of the Japanese in Papua, then in the Anglican diocese of New Guinea. Redlich is one of a group of Papua New Guinea martyrs commemorated by the Anglican Church. I first heard his story when I joined the staff of his former theological college at Chichester, where he is remembered every year with a Eucharist at which an account of his martyrdom is liturgically read, and where he stands as a model of priestly dedication and sacrifice for those approaching ordination. I have prepared this paper to remember him on this fiftieth anniversary of his death, and in particular to set his story in the context of the earliest tradition of martyrology.

Our liturgical 'martyrology' is based on Redlich's obituary by the Principal, Canon C. S. Gillett, in the College's magazine, *The Cicestrian*, for Trinity 1945, and includes quotations from a first-hand account of his last hours. It begins with an introduction to Redlich, who joined an Australian Bush Brotherhood in 1935 or 1936, after serving his first curacy in Yorkshire, and later moved to the New Guinea Mission. His health was poor, and, as the story begins, on 23 July 1942, he is returning after a period of illness to his station at Sangara, in Papua, while the Japanese are shelling Buna beach nearby. The account continues:

> He could easily have gone back in the boat to safety, but told his flock that he would stay with them. A Roman Catholic Doctor, writing from Australia, takes up the story:
>
> > 'Shortly after dawn he woke me up, saying, "There is a big number of people here. I am going down to say Mass." He began to vest, and was nearly finished when a native boy rushed to us, crying out, "Father! Doctor! Go, do not wait! During the night Embogi [a local Papuan] came and had a look at where you are, and he has just gone to tell the Japanese, because he wants them to come and kill you."
> >
> > There was dead silence. I looked at Fr Vivian. He bowed his head in prayer for a few moments, and then said to the people, "Today is Sunday. It is God's Day. I shall say Mass. We shall worship God" . . .
> >
> > I do not think I have ever witnessed a more devout congregation.

The fervour expressed in those faces would have equalled that of the early Christians assisting at Mass in some hidden catacomb. . . .

The dense silence of the jungle was broken only by the sound of the priest's voice praying for his people. Then came the rustle of movement as those bare brown feet moved near the altar at the time of Communion. He, who was about to go down to his own bitter Gethsemane and Passion, offered up for the last time before the throne of God for his people the saving sacrifice of Christ. . . .

After the Mass the people quietly dispersed. Fr. Vivian and I moved on. The following day it became necessary for us to part. . . . The decision he made cost him his life. He died by enemy hands on Buna beach. As his head was struck from his body and the white sand of the beach crimsoned with his blood there died a missionary whom we in Papua shall never forget. He died because he remained true to his trust. When he might have fled he did not flee. He remained because he considered it his duty to remain, and because he remained he died. To us who knew him, his memory will never die, and ever shall we think of him as a brave man, "strong in faith".'

Eight other missionaries, including Fr Redlich's fiancée, were also killed by the Japanese.[1]

This moving account tells its story in two layers: at one level it is a tribute to the courage of a friend in the context of the Second World War, but with the author's comments and in the liturgical context it shares a style and form recognizable from the earliest martyrologies, themselves often based on the Passion. The whole account belongs to an ancient genre which has embraced a modern one.

Any 'martyrdom', used liturgically, involves the interplay of three parties, the martyr who dies in faith, the chronicler who points to the elements of faith and sacrifice which make his death martyrdom, and the believer who gains edification and example from it; the whole genre depends on the informed piety shared by all three, who can include it within a common tradition. This account is also a war story told within a different context of shared understanding; and there are echoes of other strands of writing, including the literature of the missionary tradition, which in recounting the spreading of the Gospel relives the experience of

---

[1] This is part of the account read at the Thanksgiving Eucharist in Chichester Cathedral, 5 June 1992, for the fiftieth anniversary of Redlich's death. It is printed by kind permission of the Principal, the Revd Canon P. G. Atkinson.

the Early Church, and has its own literary shape and origins. To understand the Redlich martyrdom we should take account of them all.

We must begin, as with any such account, with its historical context
and its source, so as to identify and evaluate martyr and chronicler. For
this I am grateful to Chris Luxton of the Papua New Guinea Church
Partnership, who made available a great deal of wisdom and material.[2]
The background to the story is the Japanese occupation of what is now
Papua New Guinea from July 1942 to January 1943, in which many
expatriate Europeans and Australians died, some of them English
missionaries. Eight victims were executed with Vivian Redlich at Buna
beach, and others perished elsewhere. Twelve Anglican martyrs are
named, and tribute is paid to '15 Lutheran, 24 Methodist and 188 Roman
Catholic missionaries and church workers [who] died for their faith in
Papua New Guinea and the Solomon Islands during World War II'.[3]

The stories of these 'New Guinea martyrs' are well documented; there
were eyewitness accounts at the time, letters sent out from the martyrs
themselves and others fleeing from the Japanese invaders, and reports by
the Australian Board of Missions and the world Press. As early as 1944, the
Society for the Propagation of the Gospel (S.P.G.) published a collection of
documents on the Martyrs entitled 'South Sea Epic', assembled by Ruth
Henrich, its Assistant Editorial Secretary;[4] and after the war survivors
were contacted and their recollections published in several books. These
are generally compiled from the missionaries' standpoint, and combine
original accounts into continuous narrative within a firm editorial framework, so that small individual sources are not apparent, but where longer
material exists it is often quoted verbatim.[5]

Our story of Vivian Redlich is one of these; the 'Roman Catholic
Doctor' of the liturgical account quoted was a European medical assistant
in the Papuan government named Harry Bitmead,[6] who was with Redlich

---

[2] The Papua New Guinea Church Partnership [hereafter P.N.G.C.P.] is at Partnership House, Waterloo Road, London SE1 8XA: the New Guinea Mission changed its name to this when the Anglican Province of Papua New Guinea was inaugurated in 1977.
[3] From material issued by P.N.G.C.P. for the Jubilee Eucharist for the New Guinea Martyrs, held on 5 September 1992.
[4] Ruth Henrich, ed., *South Sea Epic: War and the Church in New Guinea 1939–43* (London, 1944) [hereafter *SSE*].
[5] Dorothy Tomkins and Brian Hughes, *The Road from Gona* (Sydney, 1969) [hereafter *RG*], includes continuous narrative based on several manuscripts and the reports of eyewitnesses. In his foreword, Frank W. Coaldrake, Chairman of the Australian Board of Missions, writes that the compiler sometimes 'recast their stories to fit the over-all perspective which the ABM asked him to adopt'.
[6] See David Wetherell, ed., *The New Guinea Diaries of Philip Strong 1936–1945* (Melbourne, 1981) [hereafter *NGDPS*], p. 113, and n. 2; the Diaries are important material on this subject, as is

at the time and wrote of his experiences after the war. In a longer and slightly different form (which I shall call 'the longer account'), it appears as a chapter in a little book called *Heroes of the Church Today: Stories from the Far East*, compiled again by Ruth Henrich and published in 1948.[7] This is a collection of edited eyewitness narratives of 'the heroism of Christian men and women of many races in the Far East'; the pieces were originally prepared for parish magazines, and intended to recount Christians' sufferings and to show that Christ lives still in his Church.[8]

We can supplement our story a little from the extra material. In February 1942, when a Japanese attack seemed imminent, Bishop Philip Strong, Anglican Bishop of New Guinea, broadcast to the missionaries in his province, strongly urging them to remain at their posts with the Papuan Christians they had nurtured. 'We cannot leave. We must not leave. We shall stand by our trust. We shall stand by our vocation.'[9] In July the north coast of New Guinea was invaded. As we have seen, Redlich remained at the mission in spite of threats of attack, and openly celebrated the Eucharist with a large congregation. Information about the Mission reached the Japanese from a powerful local leader named Embogi, who had political and personal reasons for helping the Japanese and disliking missionaries.[10] The expected attack did not come, and after the Eucharist Redlich and Bitmead set off to join other missionaries and expatriates. The group soon divided and sought safety by different routes. Bitmead and his companions reached the coast and got away, carrying a letter from Redlich to his father; the missionaries remained for a time, but became convinced that it was in the interests of the Papuan people that they, too, should leave, and with others finally set out to cross the mountains to the south. They found the local people increasingly reluctant to help them, and eventually were handed over to the Japanese, who executed them on Buna beach. Japanese war diaries are said to be the source of the details that their executioner volunteered for the task, and that another Japanese

D. Wetherell's *Reluctant Mission: the Anglican Church in Papua New Guinea 1891–1942* (St Lucia, Queensland, 1977).

[7] Ruth Henrich, ed., *Heroes of the Church Today: Stories from the Far East* (London, 1948) [hereafter *HCT*], pp. 5–9.

[8] Selections from Bitmead's story are often quoted in material on Redlich produced in this country and Australia, but I have not managed to discover the immediate context of its writing.

[9] Quoted in, e.g., *RG*, pp. 27–9.

[10] In Christopher Garland, *A Centenary History of the Diocese of Popondota* [*sic*, sometimes 'Popondetta'], p. 9. No publisher is named; an extract was given me by P.N.G.C.P.

soldier turned away, sickened by the sight.[11] Elsewhere in the island other missionaries, including Redlich's fiancée, May Hayman, also fled, and most died with their own stories of heroism.[12]

When Harry Bitmead reached safety he sent on Redlich's letter to his father. He had written, 'I'm going to stick it out whatever happens. If I don't come out of it just rest content that I've tried to do my job faithfully.' That letter is now displayed in St Paul's Cathedral, in London. After the war, we are told that Embogi was converted to Christianity while awaiting execution for murder, and implored his followers to embrace his new faith.[13]

The whole story as it emerges in these accounts invites some interesting questions—about the extent of Japanese opposition to Christians as such, and the relationships of different groups of Papuans to one another and to foreigners, whether the Japanese invaders or the English missionaries and other resident expatriates; there is matter for reflection, too, on issues surrounding the whole Western colonial missionary endeavour. These questions lie beyond my present scope; but before we can examine the account as a martyrdom we must, I think, look at three questions about its historical context, to illuminate the framework of shared understanding in action here, and the way the chronicler uses it.

First, does it give an exaggerated picture of the scale of Redlich's decision and demonstration of faith? Was not his capture and death really only a matter of time, or chance? After the war Bishop Strong was criticized, especially by the families of the 'martyrs', for putting his missionaries and others at risk. It was argued that they could have survived by going into hiding in the interior of the island before the invasion, and lived to continue their work after it was over; but once the invasion had begun it is not certain that their deaths could have been easily avoided in any case.[14] In the longer account, after the Mass, Bitmead says, 'My own duty bade me escape. The decision he made cost him his life.'[15] Certainly Bitmead did reach safety, and Redlich might have accompanied him; but others who fled at once did not survive.

Second, does it go beyond the evidence in suggesting that he was martyred *because* he was a Christian priest? Again, the picture is

[11] See *RG*, p. 62.
[12] For these stories, see all the books quoted, esp. *SSE*, where their letters are quoted.
[13] J. W. S. Tomlin, *Awakening. A History of the New Guinea Mission* (London, 1951), p. 192.
[14] I am grateful to Dr David Hilliard, of The Flinders University, Adelaide, South Australia, for details of this; and see Paul Richardson, in the *Weekly Times of Papua New Guinea*, 23 Apr. 1992, p. 16.
[15] *HCT*, p. 8.

heightened in some of the other accounts; Bishop Strong notes Redlich's words, reported by Bitmead, as 'I am going first to celebrate Mass, and will not move from here till I have done as I am a priest and must feed my people, and will not run away from them.'[16] The Japanese were, perhaps, more concerned with seeking out enemy nationals than Christians as such; the group killed with Redlich included the manager of a local plantation, and others with no particular connection with the Mission, and apparently not later counted as martyrs. Redlich and the missionaries were certainly working in Papua 'for their faith', and accepted the risks that carried; but it may not have been their faith which in an immediate sense caused their deaths.

Third, is Embogi's role, in reality part of a complex political and national picture, fairly presented? In the longer account, Redlich, says, 'Why has Embogi done this? We have never harmed him'; and the people reply, 'Embogi is not a Christian.'[17] The position of local people, pulled between internal and external pressures, has perhaps been distorted in the interests of a simplistic perception of Christian good and heathen evil.

There are many pitfalls in the objective analysis of such stories as Bitmead's of Redlich, with its sensitive mix, to modern minds, of religious conviction, colonialism, war, and brutality. But, on its own terms, Bitmead's story here seems to stand up quite well to historical scrutiny, in spite of some selective editing in both versions. Bitmead does not use the word 'martyr' of Redlich in either account. What he says about his faith and actions is what he observed, and while he shared the faith, he clearly did not always approve the actions. He saw that Redlich deliberately rejected opportunities to improve his chance of safety; that he showed courage and faith in celebrating the Sunday Eucharist when he knew it might draw attention to him and provoke an attack; that without reproach he experienced betrayal, by a Papuan he knew, to the invading power from whom he could expect neither sympathy nor clemency. In the event, perhaps, neither the decision, nor the Eucharist, nor Embogi's information was decisive; but Redlich's courage, dedication, and death for his Christian ideals are evident enough. But Bitmead does expect from his readers a shared understanding of faith and sacrifice; and, because this is a war story, of loyalty and patriotism as well.

Bitmead's account is not presented in either version as a full historical analysis, but as a tribute by one Christian to another to an act of bravery

---

[16] *NGDPS*, p. 179.
[17] *HCT*, pp. 7–8.

and commitment; it contains reflection which relates that act to Christ's Passion and death, and to the Church's own traditions. Its status as a 'martyrdom' comes from this and the surrounding comments, especially in the liturgical context. It is here that the links with early martyrdoms become significant.

So we turn to this early literature of martyrdom. This account is strikingly in the same model as the earliest accounts, such as those of Polycarp in Smyrna, Perpetua and Felicitas in Carthage, and the Martyrs of Lyons, described in *The Acts of the Christian Martyrs*.[18] Redlich's death echoes these both in its account of the individual's deliberate sacrifice and in the links clearly drawn with the Gospel Passion narratives. In these accounts the martyrs all died for their faith, more or less judicially, in the Roman arena, and their chroniclers draw precise lessons from them. In 167 or 168 (the most likely date), Polycarp the Bishop, we are told, was dragged to the arena in response to demands from the audience, after refusing to flee; he died with eucharistic parallels clearly drawn. Perpetua, a wealthy Roman woman, with her slave Felicitas and others, died in about 203 after resisting considerable pressure from her family to renounce her faith and save her life; their witness would convince others of the Spirit's continued presence. The Martyrs of Lyons died in about 177, after an anti-Christian uprising, and their deaths were reported by letter to their original home, far away in modern Turkey.

The ancient historian explains the form of this early source material in terms of the conventions of history, biography, rhetoric, and Christian apologetic of the time. Within this context, early narrative martyrdoms form a distinctive genre, which owes much to rhetorical models and so to non-Christian classical roots. V. Saxer, writing in *The Encyclopaedia of the Early Church*, says, 'From the start the account of martyrdom is structured as a demonstration and presented as a circular.'[19] The martyrdom of Polycarp is in the form of a letter from the church in Smyrna to the church in Philomelium and beyond;[20] he died to show 'witness in accordance with the Gospel—"$\tau\grave{o}$ $\kappa\alpha\tau\grave{a}$ $\tau\grave{o}$ $\epsilon\vartheta\alpha\gamma\gamma\acute{\epsilon}\lambda\iota\text{o}\nu$ $\mu\alpha\rho\tau\acute{\nu}\rho\iota\text{o}\nu$"'.[21] The story of the Martyrs of Lyons is sent from Lyons to its parent community in 'Asia' (modern Turkey);[22] and Perpetua and Felicitas'

---

[18] H. Musurillo, ed., *The Acts of the Christian Martyrs* (Oxford, 1972) [hereafter *ACM*]. Cf. on Perpetua and Felicitas, Stuart G. Hall, 'Women among the early martyrs', above, pp. 1–21.

[19] Angelo di Bernardino, ed., and Adrian Walford, tr., *Encyclopaedia of the Early Church*, 2 vols (Cambridge, 1991), 2, p. 533, under Martyr III.

[20] *ACM*, pp. 16–17 (*Polycarp*, 20).

[21] Ibid., pp. 2–3 (*Polycarp*, 1,1).

[22] Ibid., pp. 62–3 (*Martyrs of Lyons*, 1,1).

deaths are told in a broader way, 'to render honour to God and comfort to humanity—"ut ... et Deus honoretur et homo confortetur"',[23] and include first-hand and eyewitness accounts within an outer framework of eulogy.

The Redlich martyrdom is of exactly this kind, the account, apologetic itself, given within a more precisely apologetic framework; in the longer version it was received by the editor at SPG in London, and circulated by that body to the faithful via parish magazines. It, too, was structured as a demonstration and presented as a circular. The account itself follows the same pattern: there is the fateful decision to persist when prudence suggests flight, the defiant proclamation, in words and action, of the supremacy of Christ, the inevitable consequence borne with fortitude. The martyr's words are noted: as Polycarp answers the Romans,[24] and Perpetua her father, 'I am a Christian',[25] so Redlich says, 'It is God's day. I shall say Mass.'

The match is not total. Redlich has no trial, indeed, he has no exchange with his persecutors at all; and there is no account of his death. But, as in the early accounts, the parallels with the Gospels and the martyrs are explicitly drawn. Polycarp shares Christ's cup in sacrifice and resurrection;[26] the Martyrs of Lyons are 'eager to emulate Christ—"ζηλωταὶ καὶ μιμηταὶ Χριστοῦ ἐγένοντο"'.[27] Redlich, too, is seen as directly facing his own Gethsemane. In the same way, there is an explicit reference to the early martyrs in the mention of the silent Mass in the catacombs; it is not, perhaps, within the modern scholarly view of catacombs, but its purpose is plain enough. Especially interesting is the parallel of the Double Enemy. In the Passion narratives, as in some of the Early Church martyrdoms, two levels of persecution are present, that of the ruling Power, Rome, which has the power to put to death, and the subject people, the Jews (or the local people), whose support of either side is at best unpredictable. This, to Christians, was aptly echoed in Papua. The Japanese neatly fitted the role of Romans, as the hostile and effective power. The Papuans, like the Jews, had little actual power, but could sway the fates of individuals in particular cases. So the 'villain' Embogi falls easily into the role of Judas, or even of the Evil One in some early martyrdoms, and is readily, if unconsciously, seen as the betrayer.

[23] Ibid., pp. 106–7 (Perpetua, 1,1).
[24] Ibid., pp. 10–11 (Polycarp, 10,1).
[25] Ibid., pp. 108–9 (Perpetua, 3,2).
[26] Ibid., pp. 12–13 (Polycarp, 14,2).
[27] Ibid., pp. 82–3 (Martyrs of Lyons, 2,2).

Again, like the early accounts, Redlich's martyrdom is explicitly confessional. We hear of a man 'strong in faith', 'true to his trust', one whom 'we in Papua shall never forget', and this is clearly there to evoke admiration, if not emulation. The liturgical or narrative packaging directs attention to Redlich's status as a martyr; the longer version is prefaced by the words, 'Christ lives as truly in the members of his Mystical Body today as in any former period of the Church's life.'[28] So Perpetua's biographer, opposing those who restrict God's favour to the past, asks, 'Should not more recent examples be set down' that glorify God and encourage human beings—'nova documenta aeque utrique causae convenientia'?[29] Thus, as well as echoing the early accounts in structure and imagery, Redlich's martyrdom exhibits the quality of shared piety; to understand it fully one must know something of the tradition into which it fits.

But am I really suggesting that Bitmead and his editors modelled their tribute on some second-century Greek and Latin martyrologies which they, and we, may never have heard of? Not precisely; but I suggest that they tap a living tradition led by these early martyrs' deaths. Redlich is lined up with the Noble Army of Martyrs in imitating Christ to the death. As an informed Roman Catholic, Bitmead must, surely, have encountered stories of martyrdoms from his Christian education, and used their form, consciously or unconsciously, as a model for his own story. Those who edited it shared the same models.

The genre of martyrology surfaces regularly in Church History, and is much cherished, especially, it seems, at times when there is a conscious looking back to the Early Church and to classical languages, as at the Reformation and in the nineteenth and twentieth centuries. But in this twentieth-century example I should like to point to two more models for literature of heroism, familiar from childhood to people of Redlich and Bitmead's age. They are to be found in missionary stories and among the heroes of the Ancient World.

As an example of the missionary model, I refer to a book called *Heroic Deeds on the Mission Field*, by Annie S. Strachan.[30] My copy was originally awarded as a prize for Regular and Punctual Attendance at Crimsworth Wesleyan Sunday School in 1912; Redlich was born in 1905. Among its tales of devotion and courage are some set in the South Sea Islands; a chapter on missionary martyrs ends as follows: 'The Gospel can work many miracles, but none can be greater than the change wrought in these

[28] *HCT*, foreword.
[29] *ACM*, pp. 106–7 (*Perpetua*, 1,1).
[30] Annie S. Strachan, *Heroic Deeds on the Mission Field* (London, n.d., but before 1912, see text).

formerly cruel, dishonest and treacherous people, who caused the death of the white men who had come to help them to know and love Christ and who received for their reward nothing on earth, but in heaven the martyr's crown.' It is, of course, a far cry from the Wesleyan Sunday School to the Roman Catholic Bitmead; but as a type of improving story such children's books were widely read and taken as exemplary. In this kind of book, perhaps, the ancient genre lived on, and was influential as a literary model for some of Redlich's contemporaries (and even, in a rather more modern form, for my own wartime generation).

For my second model, of classical heroes, I turn to Macaulay. His story of Horatius includes the lines:

> For how can man die better
> Than facing fearful odds,
> For the ashes of his fathers
> And the temples of his Gods?[31]

The early Romans were great models of heroism, and not only to the classically educated; many early twentieth-century children grew up with the exploits of Horatius and his friends ringing in their ears and stamped in their memories, as they were good for learning by heart. This model informed attitudes to patriotism and heroism very widely in Britain and the Empire at the time, and again lingered into my own childhood. It probably made its contribution to the missionary tales and certainly shared their market; someone who quotes the catacombs is very likely to know how Horatius kept the bridge. Although there is some ambiguity about its relationship to Christian models, the two models of self-sacrifice existed side by side, and they are evident in some First World War poetry.[32] These stories were cherished by those who looked to Greek and Roman literature and civilization to inspire their British Imperial successors, including missionaries, in their Christian context: but the stories originally come from Roman authors like Livy (first century BC), who are themselves among the literary ancestors of the genre of early Christian martyrdoms. Livy's contemporary Horace wrote, 'Dulce et decorum est pro patria mori';[33] for the Christian, heaven is that native

---

[31] Macaulay, *Lays of Ancient Rome*, Horatius, xxvii; in, for example, Macaulay, *Lays of Ancient Rome, Essays and Poems* (London, 1963).

[32] For instance, though disparagingly, in Wilfred Owen's *Dulce et decorum est* in his *Collected Poems* (London, 1963).

[33] Horace, *Odes* III, ii, 13: discussed in G. Williams, *The Third Book of Horace's Odes* (Oxford, 1979), pp. 32–7.

land to be died for. To complete the circle, Augustine, like most educated early Christians, was classically trained to admire the same heroism, for his classical education was very similar to that of many devout classicists in Redlich's generation.[34]

I suggest, therefore, that the correspondence between the account of Redlich's heroic death and the second-century Christian martyrdoms are real and significant; that they are the result of a continuous tradition of writing which survives to our own time, and is kept alive in liturgy; and that because of its familiarity Bitmead adopted it, perhaps unconsciously, as a suitable vehicle for his own story of a comparable heroism. The combination of history, structure, and example is powerful still, but requires some understanding of its context to deliver its message.

But nothing in the scholarly discussion of such material reduces the very real courage and commitment of Vivian Redlich and his companions; and half a century on, they stand as models of Christian dedication. May they rest in peace.

Chichester Theological College

---

[34] For Augustine, see, for example, his treatment of the story of Regulus in *De civitate Dei*, I, xv, accessible in English in Augustine, *City of God*, tr. H. Bettenson (London, 1972).

'TO SUFFER GRIEF IN ALL KINDS OF TRIALS': PERSECUTION AND MARTYRDOM IN THE AFRICAN CHURCH IN THE TWENTIETH CENTURY

by DAVID KILLINGRAY

THERE is a good case for regarding the twentieth century as the century of Christian persecution and martyrdom. Both individual Christians, as well as the Church as a whole, have suffered severely at the hands of authoritarian regimes in Europe and Asia and also from institutional and state hostility in all but a few areas of the world. The Church has invariably been divided and split in its reactions to these pressures. This paper focuses upon the experience of Christians in sub-Saharan Africa where the Church has grown very rapidly in size and significance this century, most notably since the 1940s.

Since the mid-nineteenth century the Church in many African countries has suffered persecution for its actual or supposed threat to social and political order. In the infant Church in pre-colonial Africa converts, some of whom were boldly if not foolishly confrontational, faced opposition as their new faith brought them into conflict with indigenous beliefs and rituals which challenged centres of established political power. They also encountered the opposition of relatives who feared the consequences of offending traditional spiritual powers.[1] The most savage persecution was in Madagascar from 1837 to 1857 and Buganda in 1886, which produced a crop of Roman Catholic and Protestant martyrs,[2] but there are also many instances throughout Africa of Christians who faced persecution and death, and where the record of their suffering is buried in mission accounts or only preserved in oral form.[3] By contrast, and if we discount the effects of disease, there were

---

[1] In Chinua Achebe's now classic novel, *Things Fall Apart* (London, 1958), ch. 22, Enoch, son of the snake priest and 'over-zealous convert', unmasks an *egwugwu* in public, an act of desecration which 'touched off the great conflict between church and clan in Umuofia'.

[2] John Iliffe, 'Persecution and toleration in pre-colonial Africa: Nineteenth-century Yorubaland', in W. J. Sheils, ed., *Persecution and Toleration, SCH*, 21 (1984), pp. 357–78. There is a substantial literature on the Baganda martyrs, most recently Ronald Kassimir, 'Complex Martyrs: Symbols and Catholic Church formation and political differentiation in Uganda', *African Affairs*, 90, 360 (1991), pp. 357–82.

[3] Elizabeth Isichei, 'Christians and Martyrs in Bonny, Owa and Lokoja (ca.1874–ca.1902)', in Isichei, ed., *Varieties of Christian Experience in Nigeria* (London, 1982), pp. 62–78.

relatively few foreign missionary martyrs in nineteenth-century Africa. However, it is in the twentieth century that Africa has seen a much greater level of persecution of Christians and Christian-derived movements in both the colonial period and since independence.

This paper addresses three main areas. First of all, there is an attempt to clear the hagiographical undergrowth and more closely to define persecution and martyrdom in the African context. Secondly, to look at why the Church in this century has been persecuted, particularly by secular authorities, and the extent and impact of that persecution on the role of the Church and ordinary Christian believers. And, finally, the pattern of persecution of the Christian Church and Christian-derived movements under colonial rule and in the post-independence period since about 1960 is discussed.

CHURCH GROWTH IN TWENTIETH-CENTURY AFRICA

Church growth in twentieth-century sub-Saharan Africa has been rapid and particularly dynamic since the 1940s.[4] Foreign missionary-run churches certainly had an influence out of all proportion to their size, number of personnel, and finance, but the most important means of spreading Christianity has been African agencies, often outside mission control. Christianity in its various forms has been largely planted, nurtured, and directed by ordinary Africans. And where opposition and persecution have occurred they appear to have had a result contrary to the destruction intended. In accounting for African Church growth, some Christian apologists have claimed Tertullian's equation. This may be true, but it is difficult to test, let alone prove. A much more likely reason for Church growth, much of which has occurred in areas where there has not been persecution, is that economic and social change and instability, and the movement of people, tend to fracture traditional institutions and call into question indigenous beliefs, while providing a climate for the reception of new ideas, including new religious beliefs and values.

The European missionary churches in Africa, many with roots in the nineteenth century, were both aided and compromised by the colonial presence. In certain colonies, notably the Portuguese, Belgian, and Spanish territories, the Roman Catholic Church enjoyed a privileged position. Foreign-directed mission churches did not wane or decline

---

[4] David B. Barrett, *World Christian Encyclopaedia* (Oxford, 1982), p. 796, suggests that of Africa's population in 1900 a mere 9% were Christian, by 1970 this had risen to 143 million (40%), and by 1980 to 203 million (44%), who formed the majority in 26 states.

following independence. Indeed, the opposite happened, and both Roman Catholic and Protestant churches have seen steady, and sometimes spectacular, increase. The old missionary churches have remained, although now largely indigenized and led by African clergy and lay people. Since the 1970s, Evangelical revival and accelerated church growth has turned Kenya, Ghana, and southern Nigeria into new Protestant heartlands.

Some of the most remarkable church growth, sometimes in the face of great adversity, has been by African independent churches. Established in reaction to mission control or to emphasize African spiritual and cultural values and beliefs, independent churches of all shapes and sizes have proliferated, especially throughout southern, central, and eastern Africa. Many of these Zionist or Ethiopian churches are syncretic and have had a millennial focus. Today the majority would stress prophetism and thaumaturgical healing. It is of great significance that these churches and movements are and always have been under indigenous leaders. As a result, they were often resented and opposed by foreign mission churches and viewed by colonial rulers as a potential threat to political and social order. At the same time it is worth noting that not all independency was syncretic or secessionist from the mission churches.

Rapid church growth in twentieth-century Africa has promoted Christian ideas and expressions. Under colonial rule Christian churches and church leaders often had a prominent position. Since the transfer of political power in the late 1950s and 60s that position in many sub-Saharan states has been strengthened, based on substantial nationwide or regional constituencies, while at the same time that very prominence has placed churches and church leaders in a vulnerable position *vis-à-vis* the rulers of the state and their political ambitions. Unlike the privatized religion of Europe in Africa, religious belief is publicly proclaimed and gossiped about. It is not altogether surprising, then, that serious Church–State conflict has developed; or that more recently in a good number of states, once the churches had abandoned their passivity and regained their prophetic voice, they should become, with other dissidents, leaders of the 'legal' opposition, demanding democratization and an end to the single-party state system.

PERSECUTION AND MARTYRDOM

Persecution and even martyrdom in recent African history are not always what they are proclaimed to be. This is not to minimize individual suffering, denigrate causes, or engage in semantic hair-splitting. Martyrdom in particular perhaps needs to be more carefully defined. Established typologies of martyrdom do not appear to be helpful in analysing the spectrum of trials and griefs experienced by adherents of the wide variety of churches and movements in sub-Saharan Africa, while David Barrett's numerical scale provides only a general indication of Church–State relations in the 1970s.[5] The modern history of Christian Africa is patchy,[6] and the full record suffers not only from the lack of documentation, but also the loss or destruction of records, particularly in those areas where the Church has suffered most. Brutal or anarchic regimes (for example, Uganda under Amin, and then Obote, 1971–85) operated with little reference to the due processes of law, and arbitrary acts of punishment and injustice have gone unrecorded. Rats, ants, tropical damp, and plain neglect can also take some blame for the loss of records.

Recent church history has also become blurred by confessional and denominational claims, especially where suffering has occurred; it is certainly true, as Ronald Kassimir has recently reminded us, that 'Martyrs are made not simply by their belief and actions but by those who witnessed them, remembered them, and told their story.'[7] Missionary organizations, and especially mission literature directed at the metropolitan faithful, may not have 'invented' martyrs, but they have been eager to claim them. A good case in point is Hilda Stumpf, a missionary of the African Inland Mission who was murdered in Kenya in 1930.[8]

The idea of persecution as an expected response, indeed, as a litmus test, of faithful witness and work is well established in Christian doctrine and tradition. This 'martyr thesis' has also been taken up, maybe exaggerated, by independent churches and movements such as the Jehovah's Witnesses. For example, the Musamo Disco Christo Church in Ghana sees its history as made up of persecutions and trials of a small band of followers journeying to the Holy City, modern-day Israelites fleeing to

[5] Barrett, World Christian Encyclopaedia, p. 777, and Global table 16 and map 4, p. 866.
[6] Two masterly surveys of the history of Christianity in Africa are Richard Gray, 'Christianity', ch. 3, in A. D. Roberts, ed., The Cambridge History of Africa, 7, From 1905 to 1940 (Cambridge, 1986), pp. 140–90, and Adrian Hastings, A History of African Christianity 1950–1975 (Cambridge, 1979). See also the essays in Edward Fasholé-Luke, Richard Gray, Adrian Hastings, and Godwin Tasie, eds, Christianity in Independent Africa (London, 1978).
[7] Kassimir, 'Complex Martyrs', p. 362.
[8] Virginia Blakeslee, Behind the Kikuyu Curtain (London, 1956); David Anderson, 'Missions, Maidens and Morality: the female circumcision "crisis" in colonial Kenya' (unpublished paper given to the African History Seminar, School of Oriental and African Studies, University of London, 4 December 1991).

Canaan from Egypt.[9] And, like the very early Church, millennialist ideas may inspire ambitions to sacrifice life.

Many Christians, both European and African, who suffered ill-treatment or were killed, did not necessarily die as witnesses to their faith. In anti-colonial revolts Christian missions, Europeans, and African converts were obvious targets because they were identified with alien rule. For example, during the Maji Maji revolt in southern Tanzania, from 1905 to 1906, Christians suffered and were killed, not because they were necessarily Christian, but in what Iliffe calls 'an explosion of hatred of European rule'.[10] Samuel Otu, Ghana's sole martyr, was executed by the Asante during the rising of 1900, but he appears to have been put to death for a political offence rather than for being a Christian.[11] Similarly, the death of that extraordinary ascetic monk Charles de Foucauld, taken from his Saharan mud fort and shot one December evening in 1916, probably owed more to politics and accident than to religion.[12]

In the mid-twentieth century, Christian missionaries, and a host of ordinary African Christians, have died as a result of ethnic and political rivalries and violence, the victims of revolt and war rather than of specific assaults on Christian disciples. More than a hundred European missionaries died in the anarchic violence in the Congo during the early 1960s, and, as Max Warren, the Anglican missionary statesman, puts it: 'Very understandably they are considered to be martyrs. They were, however, not killed because they were Christians. They were killed because they were white. It was their colour not their creed which led to their deaths.'[13] Something similar can be said of the more than thirty foreign and indigenous missionaries and clergy killed by one side or the other (there is considerable dispute as to responsibility) during the Zimbabwe war of independence in the 1970s. And cardinals and bishops in secular cloth who attempt to manipulate political affairs, or clergy who organize rebellion, are not exempt from prison, the death sentence, or the assassin's

---

[9] Kofi A. Opuku, 'Changes within Christianity and the case of the Musama Disco Christo Church', in Fasholé-Luke, *Christianity in Independent Africa*, pp. 111–21.

[10] John Iliffe, *A Modern History of Tanganyika* (Cambridge, 1979), p. 168. For a biography of an African martyr killed in the 1896 rising in Southern Rhodesia, see Jean Farrant, *Mashonaland Martyr: Bernard Mizeki and the Pioneer Church* (Cape Town, 1966).

[11] I owe this information to Dr Hans W. Debrunner, Riehen, Switzerland.

[12] See Douglas Porch, *The Conquest of the Sahara* (London, 1985), ch. 18.

[13] Max Warren, 'Martyrdom', in Stephen Neill, Gerald H. Andrews, John Goodwin, eds, *Concise Dictionary of the Christian World Mission* (London, 1973), p. 373. Cf. Homer E. Dowdy, *Out of the Jaws of the Lion* (New York, 1965). James C. Hefley and Marti Hefley, *By Their Blood: Christian Martyrs of the Twentieth Century* (Grand Rapids, 1979), provides accounts of martyrdoms in thirty African states.

bullet, and it may be seriously doubted whether they qualify for a martyr's crown.[14] Even the attribute of martyr for the saintly Janani Luwum, Archbishop of Uganda, has been questioned by those who argue that his death at Idi Amin's hands—Amin is reported to have shot him personally—was due more to his Acholi origin and to ethnic politics than to his Christian condemnation of a brutal dictatorship.

Whatever the reason for Luwum's murder, the significance of his death for the Ugandan Church was profound, while the circumstances of his funeral offered a rich spiritual symbolism. On the day of the funeral, Sunday 20 February 1977, Namirembe Cathedral, in Kampala, was packed with mourners; the grave was dug, but there was no body, as the regime had refused to release it and ordered burial in Luwum's village far away. A participant at the service records:

> As the service came to its end, the unusually long procession slowly moved out, followed by the congregation. No one dispersed. Everyone stood as if they were waiting for something to happen, for someone to say something. Then suddenly voices began to sing, over and over again the hymn sung by the first Ugandan martyrs: 'Daily, daily sing the praises ...' Thus Janani, our beloved archbishop, was proclaimed the first martyr of the second century of the Church of Uganda, following the steps of those earlier martyrs who had died so soon after its birth. ... Then our eyes fell on the empty grave, a gaping hole in the earth. The words of the angel to the two women seeking Jesus's body flashed into our minds. 'Why do you seek the living among the dead?' Namirembe hill resounded with the sound that the Bakolole have taken as their own, *Tukutendereza Yesu* ... We came away from the service praising, healed by the revelation of the empty grave. We greeted each other, using the words of the old Easter greeting: 'Christ is risen'—'He is risen indeed!'[15]

The definition of Christian persecution and particularly martyrdom, that is, suffering for religious belief and witness, is often complex. In Uganda's recent history the nineteenth-century Baganda martyrs have been used as political symbol and recast as myth for contemporary

---

[14] I have in mind here that admittedly often narrow line between Christian protest and militant action, e.g., Father Saturnino, a Roman Catholic priest and a leader of the Anya Nya in the southern Sudan, for whom a requiem Mass was announced in the Catholic cathedral, Khartoum, following his death in Uganda in 1967.

[15] Margaret Ford, *Janani: The Making of a Martyr* (London, 1978), pp. 91–3; John Mbiti, *Bible and Theology in African Christianity* (Nairobi, 1986), pp. 103–11.

populist purposes. This paper does not address African political martyrs. It is a fruitful topic, but not the concern here. Let it merely be said that most African nationalist parties, eager for a legitimate historical legacy, lay claim to martyrs fallen in the struggle for freedom—and they embrace an ill-assembled motley of kings, chiefs, brigands, idealists, self-serving elite politicians, ex-servicemen, religious and labour leaders. Christian metaphor has often been enlisted to clothe their martyr reputations. This is no more apparent than in South African history, which offers a litany of political martyrs—the victims of Slagter's Neck, Abraham Esau, the women and children of the concentration camps, to Steve Biko. In Rhodesia many Whites used Christian language to describe European settlers killed in the 1896 rising, while the picture of the fated Shangani patrol, surrounded by Ndebele warriors and entitled 'Wilson's last stand', hung in many class-rooms to remind white children of the sacrifice made on behalf of their inheritance.

This paper is concerned solely with Christian martyrs, whom I define as those who died because of their Christian faith, or whose death was directly attributable to an action that they could have avoided, and which was motivated solely by Christian duty and love. This is similar to the position adopted by the Roman Catholic Church in defining martyrs.[16] From a Protestant perspective, Joe Church asks the blunt question of Yona Kanamuzeyi, the Tutsi Anglican pastor shot by soldiers in Rwanda in January 1964:

> Are we right in comparing Yona with Stephen, the martyr? Many other Tutsi were put to death at the same time. . . . Without question it was for Christ's sake that Yona . . . left the safety of Burundi to serve Him at Nyamata. It was for Christ's sake that he stayed on there when, time and time again, he was warned of his danger and could have easily and justifiably escaped. It was for Christ's sake . . . that he chose to wear the garments of the Word of God and His love and compassion.[17]

For the African theologian John Mbiti, persecution and martyrdom is firmly grounded not just in belief in God but 'faith in and through Jesus Christ'. Christians 'suffer and die for their conviction out of a living relationship with Jesus Christ.'[18] And the examples that he provides from Uganda demonstrate a quality of faith, endurance, and gracious

---

[16] T. Gilby, 'Martyrdom', in *New Catholic Encyclopaedia*, 9 (Washington, DC, 1967).
[17] J. E. Church, *Forgive Them. The Story of an African Martyr* (London, 1966), p. 120.
[18] Mbiti, *Bible and Theology*, p. 106.

generosity far removed from the realms of politics. Bishop Festo Kivengere, forced to flee for his life, wrote a brief book with the title, perhaps surprising to those unversed in Christian theology, *I Love Idi Amin*. Of course, Christian witness may take political form, and Christians may suffer for political actions motivated by their faith. There are examples of this from all over Africa, perhaps best illustrated by opposition to apartheid in South Africa. However, many people have suffered and been killed for political reasons, and although at times the distinction may be rather fine to draw, this is not quite the same thing as Christian persecution and martyrdom.

For the rest of the paper I want to look in more detail at the pattern of persecution and martyrdom in sub-Saharan Africa throughout the twentieth century. The approach will be essentially chronological.

COLONIAL RULE

In the nineteenth and the early twentieth centuries Christian missionaries, white and black, presented a serious challenge to indigenous belief systems and also local state power. The response by African societies varied greatly, the very small number of martyred missionaries speaking much for the benign curiosity or tolerance of Africans. Buganda, rent by foreign pressures and internal dissension, offered a fruitful ground for Christianity, whereas Asante political and cultural cohesion easily resisted such new ideas. Predictably, Islamic states proved to be both resistant to a Christian missionary presence and hostile to any local converts. Christian converts, drawn not exclusively from the poorest and most despised sections of society, were often marked by considerable boldness, not only in witness to their new faith, but in denouncing indigenous beliefs and practices.

Popular hostility and persecution were inevitable. Some Christian converts, to escape opposition, but also believing that they should be separate, established new villages, such as the Salems on Akwapim ridge, in southern Ghana, or the villages with biblical names atop the Usambura hills of north-eastern Tanzania.[19] In other cases Christians were ostracized, their property was pilfered, they were forcibly driven from the community or killed. The history of this persecution and martyrdom and its extent is relatively unknown, either unrecorded or confined to local

[19] David L. Brokensha, *Social Change at Larteh, Ghana* (Oxford, 1966), ch. 2; Iliffe, *Modern History of Tanganyika*, p. 231.

church registers and oral accounts.[20] Such conflict between church and indigenous beliefs and practices continues to the present day. For example, in Wassa, south-western Ghana, early in 1992 chiefs and elders suspended the activities of the local Church of Pentecost and fined its members for violating the traditional beliefs of the people in the area.[21]

The privileged position often enjoyed by Christian missions under colonial rule had advantages and disadvantages. In the eyes of many Africans the Church and its work was compromised by its close identity with the alien masters. At the same time the colonial State needed the services of the Church, and specially its provision of schools and hospitals. In the Portuguese and Spanish colonies the Roman Catholic Church held a special and at times exclusive position. Protestant missionaries were excluded from Spanish Guinea and also from areas of southern Angola, and the few local adherents were harried by the authorities. Many French colonial officials were anti-clerical, for example, Victor Augagneur, Governor-General of Madagascar, 1905–10, who closed many mission schools and banned open-air religious meetings. The Italian Fascist conquerors of Ethiopia promoted Islam as a counter to the influence of the Orthodox Church, whose power they attempted to break by execution and mass murder, especially after the attempt on Graziani's life in February 1937.[22]

Colonial administrative wisdom excluded or limited the role of Christian missionaries in strong Islamic areas, unwilling to see the tenuous control of the colonial State rocked by unnecessary religious tensions. As a result the Christian presence in regions such as northern Nigeria and northern Sudan was severely limited and curtailed. Where Christian communities existed they were often viewed with considerable hostility by Muslims. Christian missions, when they gained access, invariably found such areas harsh and largely unfruitful soil for their endeavours. The same was largely true of North Africa. As a result, Christian missionary activity was concentrated in the non-Muslim areas of colonies, for example, the southern Sudan, thus creating the conditions for future territorial religious strife in the post-independence period.

Christian missions, both Roman Catholic and Protestant, were

---

[20] Isichei, 'Christians and Martyrs in Bonny', pp. 73–4; Isichei, ed., *Varieties of Religious Experience in Nigeria*, p. 124.

[21] Reported in *West Africa*, 10–16 Feb. 1992, p. 255.

[22] Alberto Sbacchi, *Ethiopia under Mussolini. Fascism and the Colonial Experience* (London, 1985), pp. 182, 194ff. The Orthodox Church and the Ethiopian State harried converts to Evangelical churches from the 1920s; see Peter Cotterell, *Born at Midnight* (Chicago, 1973), pp. 148–56.

invariably hostile to African independent churches and movements. They were seen as purveyors of syncretic falsehood, atavistic, given to ecstatic excess, and, moreover, liable to poach church members. When the colonial State acted against independency, the mission-controlled churches either endorsed the action or remained passive and sometimes satisfied bystanders. Even movements within an *ecclesia* that refused to secede, such as the revivalist Roman Catholic and Afrocentric Jamaa in Zaire in the 1960s, which was largely free from clerical control, met with official opposition and was virtually driven underground.[23] Similar opposition met the *Balokole* revival—a holiness movement—in the Anglican community in East Africa in the early 1940s,[24] while Cardinal Milongo's popular charismatic and healing ministry in Zambia in the 1980s was viewed by the Roman Catholic Church as treading close to syncreticism, so that he was removed to Rome.[25]

Independent churches often acted as counter-centres of authority to mission-controlled churches and also to the colonial State. Large or vociferous movements posed challenges to the power of the State. In West Africa in 1913–16 visionary prophets such as William Wade Harris and Garrick Braide gained mass followings in a relatively short time.[26] Preaching simple messages of conversion they denounced ancestral shrines and alcohol, thus threatening traditional social order and government revenues. Harris was expelled by the French from the Ivory Coast, and Braide briefly imprisoned by the Nigerian authorities.

The most serious and sustained threat perceived by colonial rulers came from independent millennialist-minded movements in east and central Africa during and immediately following the First World War. These perceptions were fuelled by the Chilembwe rising in Nyasaland in 1915,[27] and by the growth and spread of independent churches, many

[23] Willy De Craemer, *The Jamaa and the Church. A Bantu Catholic Movement in Zaire* (Oxford, 1977), ch. 8.

[24] C. Robins, 'Tukutendereza. A study of social change and sectarian withdrawal in the Balokole revival of Uganda' (Northwestern University, Ph.D. thesis 1975), ch. 4ff.

[25] Gerrie ter Haar, *Spirit of Africa. Healing Ministry of Archbishop Milingo of Zambia* (London, 1992); Adrian Hastings, *African Catholicism. Essays in Discovery* (London, 1989), ch. 8, 'Emmanuel Milingo as Christian healer'.

[26] Sheila S. Walker, *The Religious Revolution in the Ivory Coast. The Prophet Harris and the Harrist Church* (Chapel Hill, 1983); O. U. Kalu, 'Waves from the Rivers: the spread of the Garrick Braide movement in Igboland 1914–1934', *Journal of the Historical Society of Nigeria*, 8 (1977), pp. 95–110; G. O. M. Tasie, 'The prophetic calling: Garrick Sokari Braide of Bakana', in Isichei, ed., *Varieties of Christian Experience in Nigeria*, pp. 99–115.

[27] George Shepperson and Thomas Price, *Independent African. John Chilembwe and the Origins, Setting and Significance of the Nyasaland native rising of 1915* (Edinburgh, 1958).

proclaiming a millennialist message, throughout the areas so seriously affected by the War and the influenza pandemic of 1918.[28] An external influence was the literature and the missionaries of the New York-based Unitarian Jehovah's Witnesses, or Watch-tower movement (Kitawala, as it is widely known in central Africa), which not only preached an eschatological message, but seditiously denounced racialism and proclaimed the colonial State the work of Satan. The small-scale restrictions imposed on Watch-tower activities by colonial rulers before 1914 predictably were increased in the inter-war years.

One outcome of the attempts by the British, French, and Belgian colonial authorities in central Africa to ban and restrict independent churches was to drive the movements underground and provide martyrs. An outstanding example is Simon Kimbangu, who was hailed as prophet and healer in the Lower Congo in 1921. His movement attracted followers and also the attention of the Belgian authorities, fearful that it was anti-white and a threat to European rule. Kimbangu was arrested, tried by a military court, and sentenced to death for treason in October 1921. Reprieved, he spent the rest of his life in prison, dying in 1951.[29] In the lived-out theology of the Kimbanguists the prophet Simon is portrayed as sharing the sufferings of Jesus Christ in the Stations of the Cross. The *Eglise* also has its temple and shrine, at N'Kamba, a Zairian Jerusalem, where Simon received his Pentecost in 1921. Kimbanguism was repeatedly prohibited in the Belgian Congo, as were similar prophet movements, apostolic churches (Nawezi Petro, the first Zairian convert to the Maranke, or Vapostori, church was arrested sixteen times in connection with church activities between 1956 and 1966),[30] and also pentecostal churches, such as that founded by the Angolan evangelist Simao Toco in 1949.[31] Toco was deported to Angola, where the Portuguese authorities, having failed to suppress the movement, then attempted to neutralize it. Persecution did not destroy these movements, and the Kimbanguist *Eglise* grew in its clandestine years, to resurface in the late 1950s as a strong indigenous church, claiming over one million members, and with a heritage of a martyred leader and a persecuted body.

---

[28] Karen E. Fields, *Revival and Rebellion in Colonial Central Africa* (Princeton, 1985).

[29] Marie-Louise Martin, *Kimbangu. An African Prophet and his Church* (Oxford, 1975).

[30] Bennetta Jules-Rosette, 'Prophecy and leadership in the Maranke Church. A case study of continuity and change', in George Bond and Sheila S. Walker, eds, *African Christianity. Patterns of Religious Continuity* (New York, 1979), pp. 109–36.

[31] Alfredo Margarido, 'The Tokoist Church and Portuguese Colonialism in Angola', in R. H. Chilcote, ed., *Protest and Resistance in Angola and Brazil: Comparative Studies* (Berkeley, 1972), pp. 29–52.

If independent churches were often regarded with suspicion by the European rulers, then throughout the colonial period African members of mission-controlled churches might be denounced for their opposition to African cultural practices and also become targets of anti-colonial insurgents. In Kenya, from the 1920s on, Gikuyu Christians became involved in the bitter dispute over female circumcision and were persecuted for their opposition to this traditional practice. However, across the continent during the colonial period relatively few African Christians suffered solely for their supposed identification as agents of European rule, although European-run missions might be the focus of assault; this was especially the case in territories where the missions were closely identified with the colonial State or with racial segregation. When this did occur the lines distinguishing opponents and issues were invariably blurred, and Christians, like other people, were caught in the rival cross-fire.

During the Gikuyu peasant war in Kenya (1952–60), the anti-settler Mau Mau movement was often openly hostile to the missionary-run churches and to African, particularly Gikuyu, Christians. Gikuyu Revival Christians strongly opposed oath-taking and other traditional 'pagan' practices. At the same time many *Balokole* were also opposed to the racialist policies of the colonial government. As vocal opponents of Mau Mau, and also as 'Loyalist' home guards and oath cleansers, many Gikuyu Christians put themselves in the front line.[32] In the ensuing violence Mau Mau killed Christians, but not necessarily because they were Christians. At the same time the harsh, repressive policies of the security forces killed some Christians and rounded up many others into the mass detention camps. An example of that confusion is John Kamau, who in 1957, newly released from detention, became assistant editor of a new Christian news-paper, *Rock*.[33]

Protestant missions in Angola and Mocambique were long regarded with suspicion as seditious by the Portuguese authorities. Educated church members were subject to surveillance by the security police, the PIDE, and became victims of state violence following the abortive revolt in northern Angola in early 1961. During the revolt, Roman Catholic missions, identified with Portuguese rule, were attacked, while Protestant

[32] E. N. Wanyoike, *An African Pastor* (Nairobi, 1974), ch. 7; E. M. Wiseman, *Kikuyu Martyrs* (London, 1958); T. F. C. Bewes, *Kikuyu Conflict. Mau Mau and the Christian Witness* (London, 1953); Donald L. Barnett and Karari Njama, *Mau Mau from Within. Autobiography and Analysis of Kenya's Peasant Revolt* (London, 1966), p. 201.
[33] W. B. Anderson, *The Church in East Africa 1840–1974* (Nairobi, 1977), p. 131.

missions were not molested. In the aftermath almost all Protestant missionaries were expelled from the country, their property destroyed or closed, and eight African Methodist pastors killed by either white civilians or soldiers.[34] The authorities also arrested a handful of Roman Catholic clergy. In Mocambique the Concordat similarly gave the Roman Catholic hierarchy a close identification with the Portuguese regime. However, as the FRELIMO-led war for independence grew more fierce in the early 1970s, Catholic missionaries and some members of the hierarchy condemned Portuguese excesses, and for their outspokenness were expelled or arrested.[35]

The Church was also divided, often bitterly so, and exposed during the confusing politics that characterized the war for independence in Zimbabwe. Pietist and quietist Christians generally eschewed politics although, as in Uganda, brutal assaults on Christians of their own kind might force them into belated action. The firmest opponents of the Rhodesian settler regime and its racist policies came from those sections of the Church that had attempted to implement non-racist policies, Clutton-Brock, at St Faith's Farm, the Methodist Episcopal Church, the St Francis Community, where Father Basil Nyabadza was murdered by government soldiers in April 1970, and increasingly from a radicalized Roman Catholic Church. When Bishop Donal Lamont denounced the regime's brutalities and racialism in mid-1974 he was stripped of his citizenship and deported.[36] As in South Africa and Namibia, a white regime which argued for the defence of 'Christian civilization' became a persecutor of its Christian opponents, not necessarily for their political actions, but all too often for the uncomfortable shape that their Christian witness took.

---

[34] W. Sidney Gilchrist, 'A Suffering Church', in Robert T. Parsons, ed., *Windows on Africa: a Symposium* (Leiden, 1971), pp. 190–7; Clifford Parsons, 'The Makings of a Revolt', in *Angola: a Symposium. Views of a Revolt* (Oxford, 1962), pp. 58–79; Len Addicott, *Cry Angola* (London, 1962), chs 7ff.

[35] Hastings, *History of African Christianity*, pp. 211–12; Adrian Hastings, *Wiriyamu. Massacre in Mocambique* (London, 1974).

[36] Donal Lamont, *Speech from the Dock* (Leigh-on-Sea, 1977). The difficulties faced by the Church are described in Carl Hallencreutz and Ambrose Moyo, eds, *Church and State in Zimbabwe* (Gweru, 1988), pt 1. See also Ian Linden, *The Catholic Church and the Struggle for Zimbabwe* (London, 1980), and Terence Ranger, 'Holy Men and rural communities in Zimbabwe, 1970–1980', in W. J. Sheils, ed., *The Church and War, SCH*, 20 (1983), pp. 443–61.

DAVID KILLINGRAY

The transfer of power in Africa increased opportunities for Church–State conflict. New political institutions and plans for nation building accentuated old and new rivalries, ethnic, communal, religious, and ideological, while some churches offered a rival focus of loyalty and authority to that of the State. In certain states the last thirty years for the Church has been a dark period, although the tradition of religious tolerance has been strongly upheld in a number of countries. The new rulers were often products of mission schools and claimed adherence to one part of the Church or another, but potential for conflict existed between Church and State, for example, over control of schools or loyalty to a single party system of government. In certain states religion and politics had already become tightly interwoven. Ethnic and religious factionalism lay at the centre of Buganda's politics, while in Cameroon the Roman Catholic Church had strongly opposed the Union de Populations du Cameroun, so that in the sporadic guerrilla war of 1957–62 its missions became targets.[37]

Military regimes and doctrinaire single-party states, in a variety of guises, heightened Church–State confrontation. Church response was divided and uncertain; the quietists, mainly Evangelical, but also some Roman Catholic hierarchies, eschewed politics, although roused to protest when the State usurped the person of Christ or became increasingly brutal to its own constituency. The earliest direct challenge to the single-party State came from, or was perceived to be offered by, other-worldly, independent churches that provided an alternative focus for loyalty and authority. In Zambia in the early 1960s Alice Lenshina's millennialist Lumpa Church, congregated in segregated villages, opposed both the ruling United National Independence Party as well as civil authority, a dissidence which in government eyes spoke of treason.[38] Action by the authorities in July 1964 was met by 'a terrifyingly uncompromising commitment within the Lumpa villages, perhaps even a thirsting for martyrdom'.[39] In the ensuing suppression, over 700 of Lenshina's followers died. The benign attitude of Jehovah's Witnesses towards the State and politics—mainly over

[37] J. Mfoulou, 'The Catholic Church and Camerounian nationalism', in Fasholé-Luke, *Christianity in Independent Africa*, pp. 212–22.
[38] A. D. Roberts, 'The Lumpa Church of Alice Lenshina', in R. O. Rotberg and Ali A. Mazrui, eds, *Protest and Power in Black Africa* (New York, 1970), pp. 513–68; George C. Bond, 'A Prophecy that Failed. The Lumpa Church of Uyombe, Zambia', in Bond and Walker, *African Christianity*, ch. 5.
[39] Hastings, *History of African Christianity*, p. 157.

schooling, political party membership, and refusal to acknowledge national emblems or bear arms—and its persistent proselytization, resulted in the theocratic organization being banned and savagely persecuted in Malawi. Several other countries banned and persecuted the Jehovah's Witnesses for similar reasons.[40]

Programmes of *authenticité*, of radical decolonization, most notably in Zaire and Chad in the 1970s, sought to make the churches more subject to the State. In Zaire action was directed largely at Roman Catholic organizations and media, but also at Protestants and even the indigenous Kimbanguists;[41] in Chad it was more violent, and 130 Protestant pastors alone were killed in the period November 1973 to November 1974.[42] Ethnic and religious rivalries underlay the persecution of Christians in Chad. This was also the case in the southern Sudan, where opposition to the centralizing and Islamic policies of the Khartoum government sucked the churches into an intermittent complex political-religious civil war for seccession which has raged over the last thirty years. Christians have been killed, clergy and foreign missionaries expelled, churches razed to the ground, and thousands of refugees forced into the bush or neighbouring countries.[43]

African Marxist regimes also attempted to curb the influence of the churches. Where a church could be readily identified with a former regime, for example, the Orthodox Church in Ethiopia, persecution and oppression was particularly savage. Following the coup of 1975 Bishop Hosana was deposed and murdered, and later the ruling Derg arrested Patriarch Abuna Teweflos, who died in detention, and several bishops. Church lands were confiscated, and churches and properties closed. Other Christian churches, particularly Evangelicals and Pentecostalists, also suffered from the atheist policies of the Marxist-Leninist regime.[44] In

[40] Tony Hodges, *Jehovah's Witnesses in Africa* = The Minority Rights Group Report, 29, rev. edn (London, 1985); Bryan Wilson, 'Jehovah's Witnesses in Kenya', *Journal of Religion in Africa*, 5 (1973), pp. 128–49; Sholto Cross, 'Independent Churches and independent state: Jehovah's Witnesses in East and Central Africa', in Fasholé-Luke, *Christianity in Independent Africa*, pp. 304–15.

[41] Nginda Mashete, 'Authenticity and Christianity in Zaire', in Fasholé-Luke, *Christianity in Independent Africa*, pp. 228–41.

[42] *Keesing's Contemporary Archives* (London, 1974), p. 27073.

[43] Lillian Passmore and G. N. Sanderson, *Education, Religion and Politics in the Southern Sudan 1899–1964* (London, 1981); William B. Anderson, 'The Role of Religion in the Sudan's Search for Unity', in David B. Barrett, ed., *African Initiatives in Religion* (Nairobi, 1971), pp. 73–90.

[44] John Brown, 'Religion and revolution in Ethiopia', *Religion in Communist Lands*, 9 (1981), pp. 50–5; Mikail Doulos, 'Christians in Marxist Ethiopia', *Religion in Communist Lands*, 14

DAVID KILLINGRAY

Mocambique the campaign against the churches intensified in early 1979, as they were increasingly identified as the main opponents of the policies of 'scientific socialism'.[45]

The Church suffered most grievously in three states during the 1970s, Burundi governed by the Tutsi ethnic minority, and Uganda and Equatorial Guinea both under particularly brutal and paranoic dictators. The full history of persecution and martyrdom in those states has yet to be written; indeed, can it ever be fully written, when the killing was so extensive and the destruction so widespread?

In Burundi in 1972 the Hutu majority staged a poorly organized rising against their Tutsi rulers. Many Hutu Christians who refused to join the revolt were killed. Tutsi repression was savage, and in May to June as many as 150,000 Hutu were killed in what has been labelled 'selective genocide', while a similar number was driven into exile.[46] Although it was essentially an ethnic conflict, further government policies in the 1970s and 1980s were directed at curbing the powers and influence of the churches. Uganda's years of sorrow under Idi Amin and Milton Obote are well known, if not yet fully documented;[47] the case of Equatorial Guinea under Macias Nguema, where the Church was banned and all clergy killed, imprisoned, or in exile, has received less attention.[48] The list of those persecuted and martyred for their witness to Christ is long and moving; it includes senior figures in hierarchies, such as Archbishop Luwum of Uganda, and many ordinary members of churches.

The Church in South Africa for many years has been divided by race and politics, and yet Christianity and politics have been closely inter-twined. The Dutch Reformed Church legitimized apartheid while most Anglicans and Roman Catholics kept quiet; even when the latter two issued statements denouncing racialism they were slow to put their own houses in order. There were notable exceptions, prophetic voices which

---

(1986), pp. 134–47; Haile Larebo, 'The Orthodox Church and the State in the Ethiopian Revolution, 1978–84', *Religion in Communist Lands*, 14 (1986), pp. 148–58.

[45] Piero Gheddo, 'Mocambique: a new church is born under persecution', *Religion in Communist Lands*, 10 (1982), pp. 156–67.

[46] Reginald Kay, *Burundi Since the Genocide* = The Minority Rights Group Report, 20, rev. edn (London, 1987).

[47] M. Louise Pirouet, 'Religion in Uganda under Amin', *Journal of Religion in Africa*, 11 (1980), pp. 13–29; Dan Wooding and Ray Barnett, *Uganda Holocaust* (Grand Rapids, 1980); Anne Coomes, *Festo Kivengere. A Biography* (Eastbourne, 1990), chs 15–20; Edward Muhima Bakaitwako, 'The fellowship of suffering: a theological interpretation of Christian suffering under Idi Amin' (Northwestern University, Ph.D. thesis 1981).

[48] Randall Negley, *Equatorial Guinea. An African Tragedy* (New York, 1989), ch. 3.

became well known—Scott, Huddleston, Reeves, Desmond, ffrench-Beytagh, and Naudé—who faced deportation, banning, and dismissal, but where prominence, colour, or a foreign passport protected them from the long years of detention and repeated torture experienced by black Christian protestors such as Frank Chikane and Sinangaliso Mkhatshwa.[49] For much of this century an oppressive structure was maintained by state power, endorsed by a selfish white indifference which claimed a Christian intent. The remarkable contrast is in the degree of graciousness shown by black people in the face of appalling sustained discrimination, which one might suggest is a profound testimony to the power of the Christian Gospel in South Africa.

CONCLUSION

The last thirty years have been a harsh time for Christians in many parts of Africa; those who died for their faith are not, in Origen's phrase 'easily numbered'. It is reasonable to assume that many deaths did not occur in public. To die for faith in a dark corner, the sacrifice unrecognized as an example to others or as a contribution to the tradition of the Church, calls for great boldness of faith and purpose. And yet, despite the torment, the African Church has grown in size and significance. With the increase in membership the churches emerged by the late 1980s to lead the 'legal opposition' in demanding democratization, and they have continued to suffer for that stand.[50] Another area of conflict, with a very real potential for increase, is between Christian and Muslim Fundamentalism. Aggressive confrontation, avid proselytization, and economic disparities have resulted in serious outbreaks of religious and communal violence in

[49] Desmond Tutu, 'Persecution of Christians under Apartheid', in J. B. Metz and E. Schillebeeckx, eds, *Martyrdom Today* (Edinburgh, 1983), pp. 63–9; John W. de Gruchy, *The Church Struggle in South Africa* (Grand Rapids, 1979); Frank Chikane, *No Life of My Own* (London, 1988), pp. 53–7; *Transformation: An International Dialogue on Evangelical Social Ethics*, 3, 2 (April/June 1986), special issue on South Africa; Peter Walshe, 'South Africa: Prophetic Christianity and the liberation movement', *Journal of Modern African Studies*, 29 (1991), pp. 27–60.

[50] David M. Gitari, 'The Church's Witness to the Living God: Seeking just political, social and economic structures in contemporary Africa', *Transformation*, 5 (1988), pp. 13–20; Gitari, 'Church and Politics in Kenya', *Transformation*, 8 (1991), pp. 7–17; Tony Lane, 'Kenya's turbulent priest', *Christianity and History Newsletter*, 8 (1991), pp. 22–35. On Zaire see Paul Gifford, 'Endgame for Mobutu', *The Tablet*, 14 Sept. 1991, pp. 1110–11, and 'Massacre of church goers', *Amnesty Journal* (June/July 1992), p. 1, reporting troops shooting nineteen people in a peaceful religious demonstration in Kinshasa, Zaire, on 16 February 1992.

northern Nigeria in the late 1980s,[51] and further martyrs claimed by both Christians and Muslims.[52]

As historians we are meant to learn from what we study, and possibly this has greater pertinence when it is contemporary history. Reading about the suffering of Christians in modern Africa has been for me a humbling experience. This is not to ignore the complexities of Africa's political situation, or to gloss over the waywardness of some of those who experienced persecution and death. But it does raise the as yet untested question for me as a Christian: in the face of similar challenges, would I have sufficient faith in Jesus Christ 'to suffer grief in all kinds of trials'?

Goldsmiths' College, University of London

[51] Jibrin Ibrahim, 'Religion and turbulence in Nigeria', *Journal of Modern African Studies*, 29 (1991), pp. 115–36.

[52] For example, G. J. O. Moshay, *Who is this Allah?* (Ibadan, 1990), 'dedicated to the memory of all the christians who were slaughtered in Northern Nigeria by the servants of Allah in March 1987 . . . and particularly to the memory of Elder Kaduzu Shebuka of the ECWA Church, Tundun Wada, Kaduna, who during one of the crises, was "doused with petrol and set ablaze", burning to death in front of his church.'

INDEX

Note: page references in italics indicate illustrations.

Khrushchev, Nikita, 391
Kierkegaard, Søren, 209
Kiev, princely martyrs, 105–15, 401–2
Killingray, David, 465–82
Kimbangu, Simon, 475
King-Hall, Sir George, 439
kings
    as innocent martyrs, 81–92
    as martyr saints, 57–66, 105–15
Kivengere, Festo, 472
Klawiter, Frederick C., 9, 14
Knowles, Dom David, 374
Knox, John, 236–9, 259–60, 264, 269
Knox, Ronald, 432
Kolb, Robert, 209 n. 3, 218–19
Kollontai, Aleksandra, 411–12
Kondō, Gizaemon, 306 n. 38, 307
Krumeich, Gerd, 359–60
Krusch, B., 68 n. 7
Lactantius, 33
laments, in martyrologies, 112–14
Lamont, Donal, 477
Lampe, G. W. H., 406
Langmuir, Gavin, 164
Langston, E. L., 436
Langton, Stephen, 129–31, 134–9
lapsed, reconciliation, 2, 9, 11–15
Lascelles, Sir Alan, 384
Lash, Nicholas, 415
Latimer, Hugh, xv, xvi, xvii, 231
Laures, Johannes, 295 n. 3
Lavrov, P. L., 393
law, Roman, and women, 23–34
Lawrie, A. E., 383–5, 388
Leggett, George, 394 n. 30
Leland, John, 125
Lenin, V. I.
    and persecution of the Church, 400,
      404–6, 411–12
    as revolutionary martyr, 394–5
Lennard, Samson, 202
Lenshina, Alice, 478
Leo IX, Pope, 97, 100, 103
Leonides, father of Origen, 36–7
*Lesson about the Life and Murder of the Blessed
    Passion-sufferers Boris and Gleb*, 106,
    110–12
Levitin, Anatoly, 398, 406

Lewis, George, 324
Lewis, Henry, 357
Licinius, persecution, 47
Life of Alexis, 113 n. 26
Life of St Eustace, 112–13
Life of Seinte Juliana, 156
literalism, biblical, 436
liturgy, and martyrdom, 155, 287–9, 294,
    344–5, 397, 453–4, 463
Loades, David, 80 n. 62, 231–44
Lollards, 177–8, 190–1, 193–4, 202, 206
Longworth, Philip, 386
Lothar, I, 68–9, 71
Loud, G. A., 141–52
Louis I, the Pious, Emperor, 68–9, 76–7
Löwe, H., 78 n. 53
Lucius, martyr, 17–18
Ludwig, U., 79 n. 58
Luke of Prague, 199, 200
Lumpa Church, 478
Luther, Martin, 257, 315
    and heretics, 185–8, 199
    and martyrdom, 209–19
Lutherans, Saxony, 236, 311–12, 314–15,
    318
Luwum, Janani, 470, 480
Luxton, Chris, 455
Lydgate, John, 165–7
Lyons, Council of
    1245, 141
    1274, 161
Lyons, martyrs, 10–11, 14, 459–60

Machen, J. Gresham, 426
Machin, Ambrogio, 292–3
Mackenzie, Compton, 347
Mackenzie, Hugh McKay, 328–9
Mackenzie, James, 319, 332
Mackenzie, William, 328–9
Macleod, Norman, 325–6
MacNaughten, Edgar, 402
Madariaga, Isabel de, 389–90
Magnus of Orkney, 108–10
Maltby, W. R., 428
Mancio, 75
Mandelstam, Nadezhda, 399, 407–8
Manning, Henry Edward, 371